I saw that island _____ *ng. The moon was to the* ı _____ *the east, and right amid ships of the dawn, which was all pink, the daystar sparkled like a diamond. The land breeze blew in our faces, and smelt strong of lime and vanilla. . . . Here was a fresh experience . . . and the look of those woods and mountains, and the rare smell of them, renewed my blood.*

—ROBERT LOUIS STEVENSON
ISLAND NIGHTS

TONGA~ SAMOA HANDBOOK

TONGA~SAMOA
HANDBOOK

FIRST EDITION

DAVID STANLEY

MOON
TRAVEL
HANDBOOKS

TONGA-SAMOA HANDBOOK
FIRST EDITION

Published by
 Moon Publications, Inc.
 5855 Beaudry St.
 Emeryville, CA 94608, USA

Printed by
 Colorcraft Ltd.

Please send all comments,
corrections, additions,
amendments, and critiques to:

**DAVID STANLEY
MOON TRAVEL HANDBOOKS
5855 BEAUDRY ST.
EMERYVILLE, CA 94608, USA
e-mail: travel@moon.com
www.moon.com**

Printing History
1st edition—1999
 5 4 3 2 1 0

ISBN: 1-56691-174-5
Library of Congress Cataloging-in-Publication-Data has been applied for.

Editor: Asha Johnson
Production & Design: Carey Wilson
Cartography: Mark Stroud, Moon Street Cartography
Index: Deana Shields

Front cover photo: © Richard Eastwood

All photos by David Stanley unless otherwise noted.
All illustrations by Bob Race unless otherwise noted.

Distributed in the United States and Canada by Publishers Group West

Printed in China

CONTENTS

INTRODUCTION

SAMOA

TONGA

NIUE

ABBREVIATIONS

A$—Australian dollars
a/c—air-conditioned
ATM—automated teller machine
C—Centigrade
C$—Canadian dollars
CDW—collision damage waiver
EEZ—Exclusive Economic Zone
E.U.—European Union
4WD—four-wheel drive
km—kilometer

kph—kilometers per hour
LDS—Latter-day Saints (Mormons)
LMS—London Missionary Society
MV—motor vessel
No.—number
N.Z.—New Zealand
NZ$—New Zealand dollars
pp—per person
P.W.D.—Public Works Department

S$—Samoan *tala*
SDA—Seventh-Day Adventist
SPF—South Pacific Forum
STD—sexually transmitted disease
tel.—telephone
T$—Tongan *pa'anga*
U.S.—United States
US$—U.S. dollars
WW II—World War Two

ACCOMMODATIONS PRICE RANGES

Throughout this book, accommodations are generally grouped in the price categories which follow. Of course, currency fluctuations and inflation can lead to slight variations.

Shoestring	under US$15 double
Budget	US$15-35 double
Inexpensive	US$35-60 double
Moderate	US$60-85 double
Expensive	US$85-110 double
Premium	US$110-150 double
Luxury	over US$150 double

EXCHANGE RATES

(approximate figures as of 1999, for orientation only)

US$1 = NZ$1.94 (New Zealand dollars)
US$1 = A$1.65 (Australian dollars)
US$1 = T$1.65 (Tongan *pa'anga*)
US$1 = S$3.01 (Samoan *tala*)

MAPS

MAP SYMBOLS

══════ Primary Road	⊛ Capital City	▲ Mountain
─────── Secondary Road	○ City	🖎 Waterfall
┝━┿━┿━ Railroad	○ Town	Mangrove
············· Ferry	• Accommodation	Reef
─ ─ ─ ─ ─ Trail	▪ Sight	Water
✗ Airfield/Airstrip	♫ Golf Course	

HANDBOOK DIVISIONS

SAVAI'I

OPULU

S A M O A

THE MANU'A GROUP

TUTUILA

AMERICAN SAMOA

THE NIUAS

T O N G A

NIUE

THE VAVA'U GROUP

THE HA'APAI GROUP

NIUE

TANGATAPU

EUA ISLAND

© DAVID STANLEY

ACKNOWLEDGMENTS

The nationalities of those listed below are identified by the following signs that follow their names: as (American Samoa), at (Austria), au (Australia), ca (Canada), ch (Switzerland), dk (Denmark), gb (Great Britain), nl (Netherlands), nu (Niue), nz (New Zealand), pt (Portugal), to (Tonga), us (United States), ws (Samoa), and za (South Africa).

The antique engravings by M.G.L. Domeny de Rienzi are from the classic three-volume work *Oceanie ou Cinquième Partie du Monde* (Paris: Firmin Didot Frères, 1836).

Special thanks to Armand Kuris (us) for correcting the section on coral reefs, to David Fanshawe (gb) and Ad Linkels (nl) for information on Pacific music, to Antonio Trindade (pt) for surfing tips, to Stafford Guest (nu) for providing useful materials about Niue, to Garry Hawkins (gb) for a detailed report on almost all the areas covered in this book, to Gabriel Teoman (at) for his priceless insights, and to my wife Ria de Vos for her continuing assistance, suggestions, and support.

Although this is the first edition of *Tonga-Samoa Handbook,* all the areas included herein have been covered in the author's *South Pacific Handbook* since 1979, and here's a list of readers who took the trouble to send us feedback about the Samoas, Tonga, and Niue:

Prof. Nan van der Bergh (za), Claire Brenn (ch), John Connell (au), Paul A. Cote (nz), Patrick Cuff (us), Louie DeNolfo (nz), Richard Eastwood (au), Mary Graham (us), Linda Greenman (us), Pauline M. Grocki (us), Daniel Haenggi (ch), Lisanne Bruno Hansen (dk), Louie the Fish (as), John Maidment (gb), Philip R. Marshall (us), Doug and Kristine Moser (us), Leroy Lefty Pfistener (us), Juan Rabasa (us), Barbara Schniter (ch), Bernhard Sengstschmid (at), Eugene L. Sly (us), Keoki Stender (us), Brent Webb (us), J.R. Williams (us), and Arthur and Jane Zeeuw (nl).

All their comments have been incorporated into the volume you're now holding. To have your own name included here next edition, write: David Stanley, c/o Moon Publications, Inc., 5855 Beaudry St., Emeryville, CA 94608, U.S.A. (e-mail: travel@moon.com)

Attention Hotel Keepers, Tour Operators, and Divemasters

The best way to keep your listing in Tonga-Samoa Handbook up to date is to send us current information about your business. If you don't agree with what we've written, please tell us why—there's never any charge or obligation for a listing. Thanks to the following island tourism workers and government officials who did write in:

Ford Aho (to), James Atherton (ws), Jon Beauchamp (to), Gerry Bourke (to), Ned Brown (us), Peter Davidson (us), Chande L. Drabble (as), Kathleen Dunlap (us), James Faasolo (to), Alise Faulalo-Stunnenberg (ws), Kevin Fawcett (nu), John Harrison (as), Claus Hermansen (ws), Christine Hipa (nu), Losaline Kaho (to), Mats Loefkvist (ws), Ron Loni (to), 'Okusitino Mahina (to), Pat McKee (to), Francis Mortimer (nz), Joanna Oberloskamp (to), Helene Pascal (us), John J. Pereira (as), Sven Quick (to), Lofa Rex (nu), Barry Rose (us), Carl Sanft (to), Mary Saunders (nu), Viliami Sisifa (to), Doug Spence (ca), Vosa Telefoni (to), Virginia Tuatagaloa (ws), and Rainer Urtel (to).

A Final Note

While out researching my books I find it cheaper to pay my own way, and you can rest assured that nothing in this book is designed to repay freebies from hotels, restaurants, tour operators, or airlines. I prefer to arrive unexpected and uninvited, and to experience things as they really are. On the road I seldom identify myself to anyone. Unlike many other travel writers, I don't allow myself to be chaperoned by local tourist offices or omit necessary criticism just to boost book sales. The essential difference between this handbook and the myriad travel brochures free for the taking in airports and tourist offices all across the region is that this book represents you, the traveler, while the brochures represent the travel industry. The companies and organizations included herein are there for information purposes only, and a mention in no way implies an endorsement.

YOU WILL HAVE THE LAST WORD

Travel writing is among the least passive forms of journalism, and every time you use this book you become a participant. I've done my best to provide the sort of information I think will help make your trip a success, and now I'm asking for your help. If I led you astray or inconvenienced you, I want to know, and if you feel I've been unfair somewhere, don't hesitate to say. If you thought I sounded naive, starry-eyed, co-opted, servile, or unable to separate the good from the bad, tell me that too. Some things are bound to have changed by the time you get there, and if you write and tell me I'll correct the new edition, which is probably already in preparation even as you read this book.

Unlike many travel writers, this author doesn't accept "freebies" from tourism businesses or obtain VIP treatment by announcing who he is to one and all. At times that makes it difficult to audit the expensive or isolated resorts, thus I especially welcome comments from readers who stayed at the upmarket places, particularly when the facilities didn't match the rates. If you feel you've been badly treated by a hotel, restaurant, car rental agency, airline, tour company, dive shop, or whomever, please let me know, and if it concurs with other information on hand, your complaint certainly will have an impact. Of course, we also want to hear about the things you thought were great. Reader's letters are examined during the concluding stages of editing the book, so you really will have the final say.

When writing, please be as precise and accurate as you can. Notes made on the scene are far better than later recollections. Write comments in your copy of *Tonga-Samoa Handbook* as you go along, then send me a summary when you get home. If this book helped you, please help me make it even better. Address your feedback to:

> David Stanley
> c/o Moon Publications Inc.
> 5855 Beaudry St.
> Emeryville, CA 94608, U.S.A.
> e-mail: travel@moon.com

INTRODUCTION

Samoa, American Samoa, Tonga, Niue

THE ENTICING TROPICAL ISLES *of Tonga, Samoa, and Niue lie astride the international date line in the heart of the South Pacific. Together they comprise Western or "old" Polynesia, settled by Austronesian migrants over three thousand years ago. Only much later did the canoes set forth once again to colonize Eastern or "new" Polynesia, a cultural region that embraces the Society, Marquesas, and Cook Islands, Hawaii, and New Zealand. Fiji, to the west, is in Melanesia.*

Western Polynesia is bedrock of tradition where the indigenous Polynesian chiefs (called nobles in Tonga) still wield decisive political power. Of the four countries and territories covered in this book, Tonga and Samoa are fully independent states, while American Samoa is a U.S. dependency and Niue is associated with New Zealand. Most are only semi-democracies: in Tonga the king and nobles remain firmly in control, in Samoa only chiefs may be elected to parliament, and in American Samoa the elected government operates by the grace of federal officials in Washington.

The timeworn traditions of Polynesia are better preserved here than anywhere else in the South Pacific: traditional dancing is actively practiced and quality handicrafts are made. Most people still make a living from fishing or gardening, and only in American Samoa has consumerism really caught on. Superimposed on this hierarchical society is an austere 19th-century brand of Christianity in which the old Polynesian taboos have been superimposed on narrow Protestant piety. Tonga and Samoa form the core of the South Pacific Bible Belt.

Until recently Tonga and Samoa were well off the beaten track of South Pacific tourism, involving an expensive side trip from Fiji or New Zealand. Now with regular flights linking the islands directly to Auckland, Honolulu, and each other, travelers can easily include them in a longer Pacific routing or make Western Polynesia a whole trip in itself. It's a fascinating area to visit, full of diversity and surprises. Far fewer tourists visit this region than go to Fiji, Tahiti, or Hawaii, so you'll be in for something special.

M.G.L. DOMENY DE RIENZI

INTRODUCTION
THE LAND

Plate Tectonics

Much of the western Pacific is shaken by the clash of tectonic plates (a phenomenon once referred to as continental drift), when one section of earth's drifting surface collides head-on with another. The northern and central Pacific rest on the Pacific Plate, while New Guinea, Australia, Fiji, New Caledonia, and part of New Zealand sit on the Indo-Australian Plate. The west edge of the Pacific Plate runs northeast from New Zealand up the eastern side of Tonga to Samoa, where it swings west and continues up the southwestern side of Vanuatu and the Solomons to New Britain.

The dividing line between the Pacific Plate and the plates to the west is known as the Andesite Line, part of the circumpacific "Ring of Fire." In the South Pacific much of the land west of this line remains from the submerged Australasian continent of 100 million B.C. East of the line, only volcanic and coraline islands exist. Three-quarters of the world's active volcanoes occur around the edge of the Pacific Plate, accounting for 85% of the world's annual release of seismic energy. As the thinner Pacific Plate pushes under the thicker Indo-Australian Plate at the Tonga Trench it melts; under tremendous pressure, some of the molten material escapes upward through fissures, causing volcanoes to erupt and atolls to tilt.

Coral atolls can be uplifted by adjacent volcanoes. The upper crust of earth is an elastic envelope enclosing an incompressible fluid. When this envelope is stretched taut, the tremendous weight of a volcano is spread over a great area, deforming the seabed. In Tonga, Vava'u and Tongatapu were uplifted by the weight of Kao and Tofua. Niue is an elevated atoll pushed up by some trauma of nature to become a platform of coral rock rising 20 meters above sea

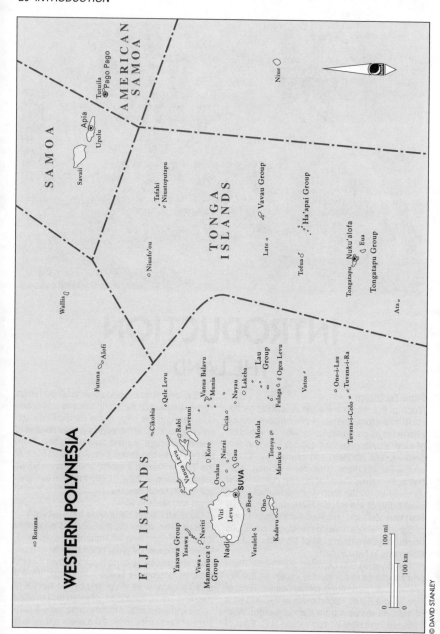

WESTERN POLYNESIA

FIJI ISLANDS

SAMOA

AMERICAN SAMOA

TONGA ISLANDS

Rotuma

Wallis

Futuna

Alofi

Niuafo'ou

Savaii

Apia
Upolu

Tutuila
Pago Pago

AMERICAN
SAMOA

Niue

Tafahi
Niuatoputapu

Vavau Group

Ha'apai Group

Late

Tofua

Tongatapu
Tongatapu Group

Nuku'alofa
Eua

Ata

Yasawa Group
Yasawa

Viwa
Mamanuca
Group

Naviti

Nadi

Vatulele

Viti
Levu

SUVA

Beqa

Ono

Kadavu

Vanua Levu

Rabi

Taveuni

Koro

Ovalau

Nairai

Gau

Cikobia

Qele Levu

Vanua Balavu
Munia

Navau

Cicia

Lakeba

Lau
Group

Ogea Levu

Fulaga

Moala

Totoya

Matuku

Vatoa

Ono-i-Lau

Tuvana-i-Colo

Tuvana-i-Ra

0   100 mi

0   100 km

© DAVID STANLEY

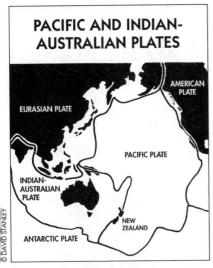

PACIFIC AND INDIAN-AUSTRALIAN PLATES

AMERICAN PLATE

EURASIAN PLATE

PACIFIC PLATE

INDIAN-AUSTRALIAN PLATE

NEW ZEALAND

ANTARCTIC PLATE

© DAVID STANLEY

level. It's known for its huge sea caves and steep oceanside cliffs. The whole evolution of islands from youth to old age can be followed in Samoa, beginning with Savai'i, which erupted this century, to older and more weathered Upolu, Tutuila, and the Manu'as, and finally ancient Rose Atoll, where coral built up as the original volcano sank.

CORAL REEFS

To understand how a basalt volcano becomes a limestone atoll, it's necessary to know a little about the growth of coral. Coral reefs cover some 200,000 square km worldwide, between 35 degrees north and 32 degrees south latitude. A reef is created by the accumulation of millions of calcareous skeletons left by myriad generations of tiny coral polyps, some no bigger than a pinhead. Though the skeleton is usually white, the living polyps are many different colors. The individual polyps on the surface often live a long time, continuously secreting layers to the skeletal mass beneath the tiny layer of flesh.

They thrive in clear salty water where the temperature never drops below 18° C. They must also have a base not over 50 meters below the water's surface on which to form. The coral colony grows slowly upward on the consolidated

skeletons of its ancestors until it reaches the low-tide mark, after which development extends outward on the edges of the reef. Sunlight is critical for coral growth. Colonies grow quickly on the ocean side due to clearer water and a greater abundance of food. A strong, healthy reef can grow four to five centimeters a year. Fresh or cloudy water inhibits coral growth, which is why villages and ports all across the Pacific are located at the reef-free mouths of rivers. Hurricanes can kill coral by covering the reef with sand, preventing light and nutrients from getting through. Erosion caused by logging or urban development can have the same effect.

Polyps extract calcium carbonate from the water and deposit it in their skeletons. All limy reef-building corals also contain microscopic algae within their cells. The algae, like all green plants, obtain energy from the sun and contribute this energy to the growth of the reef's skeleton. As a result, corals behave (and look) more like plants than animals, competing for sunlight just as terrestrial plants do. Many polyps are also carnivorous; with minute stinging tentacles they supplement their energy by capturing tiny planktonic animals and organic particles at night. A small piece of coral is a colony composed of large numbers of polyps.

Coral Types
Corals belong to a broad group of stinging creatures, which includes polyps, soft corals, stony corals, sea anemones, sea fans, and jellyfish. Only those types with hard skeletons and a single hollow cavity within the body are considered true corals. Stony corals such as brain, table, staghorn, and mushroom corals have external skeletons and are important reef builders. Soft corals, black corals, and sea fans have internal skeletons. The fire corals are recognized by their smooth, velvety surface and yellowish brown color. The stinging toxins of this last group can easily penetrate human skin and cause swelling and painful burning that can last up to an hour. The many varieties of soft, colorful anemones gently waving in the current might seem inviting to touch, but beware: many are also poisonous.

The corals, like most other forms of life in the Pacific, colonized the ocean from the fertile seas of Southeast Asia. Thus the number of species declines as you move east. Over 600 species of

acropora

staghorn fire coral
(Millepora accicornis)

CORALS OF THE PACIFIC

table coral

mushroom coral
(Fungia fungites)

elkhorn fire coral
(Millepora platyphylla)

brain coral
(Meandrina)

honeycomb coral (Favia matthaii)

DIANA LASICH HARPER

coral make their home in the Pacific, compared to only 48 in the Caribbean. The diversity of coral colors and forms is endlessly amazing. This is our most unspoiled environment, a world of almost indescribable beauty.

Exploring a Reef

Until you've explored a good coral reef, you haven't experienced one of the greatest joys of nature. While one cannot walk through pristine forests due to the lack of paths, it's quite possible to swim over untouched reefs. Coral reefs are the most densely populated living space on earth—the rainforests of the sea! It's wise to bring along a high quality mask you've checked thoroughly beforehand as there's nothing more disheartening than a leaky, ill-fitting mask. Otherwise dive shops throughout the region rent or sell snorkeling gear, so do get into the clear, warm waters around you.

Conservation

Coral reefs are one of the most fragile and complex ecosystems on earth, providing food and shelter for countless species of fish, crustaceans (shrimps, crabs, and lobsters), mollusks (shells), and other animals. The coral reefs of the South Pacific protect shorelines during storms, supply sand to maintain the islands, furnish food for the local population, form a living laboratory for science, and are major tourist attractions. Without coral, the South Pacific would be immeasurably poorer.

DIANA LASICH HARPER

The crown-of-thorns starfish (Acanthaster planci) *feeds on living coral.*

Hard corals grow only about 10 to 25 millimeters a year and it can take 7,000 to 10,000 years for a coral reef to form. Though corals look solid they're easily broken; by standing on them, breaking off pieces, or carelessly dropping anchor you can destroy in a few minutes what took so long to form. Once a piece of coral breaks off it dies, and it may be years before the coral reestablishes itself and even longer before the broken piece is replaced. The "wound" may become infected by algae, which can multiply and kill the entire coral colony. When this happens over a wide area, the diversity of marinelife declines dramatically.

Swim beside or well above the coral. Avoid bumping the coral with your fins, gauges, or other equipment and don't dive during rough sea conditions. Proper buoyancy control is preferable to excessive weight belts. Snorkelers should check into taking along a float-coat, which will allow equipment adjustments without standing on coral.

We recommend that you not remove seashells, coral, plantlife, or marine animals from the sea. Doing so upsets the delicate balance of nature, and coral is much more beautiful underwater anyway! This is a particular problem along shorelines frequented by large numbers of tourists, who can completely strip a reef in very little time. If you'd like a souvenir, content yourself with what you find on the beach (although even a seemingly empty shell may be inhabited by a hermit crab). Also think twice about purchasing jewelry or souvenirs made from coral or seashells. Genuine traditional handicrafts that incorporate shells are one thing, but by purchasing unmounted seashells or mass-produced coral curios you are contributing to the destruction of the marine environment. The triton shell, for example, keeps in check the reef-destroying crown-of-thorns starfish.

The anchors and anchor chains of private yachts can do serious damage to coral reefs. Pronged anchors are more environmentally friendly than larger, heavier anchors, and plastic tubing over the end of the anchor chain helps minimize the damage. If at all possible, anchor in sand. A longer anchor chain makes this easier, and a good windlass is essential for larger boats. A recording depth sounder will help locate sandy areas when none are available in shallow water.

If you don't have a depth sounder and can't see the bottom, lower the anchor until it just touches the bottom and feel the anchor line as the boat drifts. If it "grumbles" lift it up, drift a little, and try again. Later, if you notice your chain grumbling, motor over the anchor, lift it out of the coral and move. Not only do sand and mud hold better, but your anchor will be less likely to become fouled. Try to arrive before 1500 to be able to see clearly where you're anchoring—Polaroid sunglasses make it easier to distinguish corals. If you scuba dive with an operator who anchors incorrectly, let your concerns be known.

There's an urgent need for stricter government regulation of the marine environment, and in some places coral reefs are already protected.

THE GREENHOUSE EFFECT

The gravest danger facing the atolls of Oceania is the greenhouse effect, a gradual warming of earth's environment due to fossil fuel combustion and the widespread clearing of forests. By the year 2030 the concentration of carbon dioxide in the atmosphere will have doubled from preindustrial levels. As infrared radiation from the sun is absorbed by the gas, the trapped heat melts mountain glaciers and the polar ice caps. In addition, seawater expands as it warms up, so water levels could rise almost a meter by the year 2100, destroying shorelines created 5,000 years ago.

A 1982 study demonstrated that sea levels had already risen 12 centimeters in the previous century; in 1995 2,500 scientists from 70 countries involved in an Intergovernmental Panel on Climate Change commissioned by the United Nations completed a two-year study with the warning that over the next century air temperatures may rise as much as 5° Celsius and sea levels could go up 95 centimeters. Not only will this reduce the growing area for food crops, but rising sea levels will mean salt water intrusion into groundwater supplies—a horrifying prospect if accompanied by the droughts that have been predicted. Coastal erosion will force governments to spend vast sums on road repairs and coastline stabilization.

Increasing temperatures may already be contributing to the dramatic jump in the number of hurricanes in the South Pacific. For example, Fiji experienced only 12 tropical hurricanes from 1941 to 1980 but 10 from 1981 to 1989. After a series of devastating hurricanes in Samoa, insurance companies announced in 1992 that they were withdrawing coverage from the country. In 1997 and 1998 the El Niño phenomenon brought with it another round of devastating hurricanes, many hitting Cook Islands and Tahiti-Polynesia, which are usually missed by such storms. The usual hurricane season is November to April but in June 1997 Hurricane Keli struck Tuvalu becoming the first hurricane ever recorded in the South Pacific that month. The 1998 drought wiped out two-thirds of Fiji's sugar crop and half of Tonga's squash, both key export crops.

Coral bleaching occurs when an organism's symbiotic algae are expelled in response to environmental stresses, such as changes in water temperature, and widespread instances of bleaching and reefs being killed by rising sea temperatures have been confirmed in Tahiti-Polynesia and Cook Islands. To make matters worse, the coral-crunching crown-of-thorns starfish is again on the rise throughout the South Pacific (probably due to sewage and fertilizer runoff that nurture the starfish larvae). Reef destruction will reduce coastal fish stocks and impact tourism.

As storm waves wash across the low-lying atolls, eating away the precious land, the entire populations of archipelagos such as Tokelau and Tuvalu may be forced to evacuate long before they're actually flooded. The construction of seawalls to keep out the rising seas would be prohibitively expensive and may even do more harm than good by interfering with natural water flows.

Unfortunately, those most responsible for the problem, the industrialized countries led by the United States (and including Australia) have strongly resisted taking any action to significantly cut greenhouse gas emissions, and new industrial polluters like India and China are sure to make matters much worse. And as if that weren't bad enough, the hydrofluorocarbons (HFCs) presently being developed by corporate giants like Du Pont to replace the ozone-destructive chlorofluorocarbons (CFCs) used in cooling systems are far more potent greenhouse gases than carbon dioxide. This is only one of many similar consumption-related problems, and it seems as if one section of humanity is hurtling down a suicidal slope, unable to resist the momentum, as the rest of our race watches the catastrophe approach in helpless horror. It will cost a lot to rewrite our collective ticket but there may not be any choice.

Appeals such as the one above have only limited impact—legislators must write stricter laws and impose fines. Unfortunately fishing with the help of dynamite, scuba gear, and poisons are all too common, almost entirely practiced by local residents. If you witness dumping or any other marine-related activity you think might be illegal, don't become directly involved but take a few notes and calmly report the incident to the local authorities or police at the first opportunity. You'll learn something about their approach to these matters and make them aware of your concerns.

Resort developers can minimize damage to their valuable reefs by providing public mooring buoys so yachts don't have to drop anchor and pontoons so snorkelers aren't tempted to stand on coral. Licensing authorities can make such amenities mandatory whenever appropriate, and in extreme cases, endangered coral gardens should be declared off limits to private boats. As consumerism spreads, once-remote areas become subject to the problems of pollution and overexploitation: the garbage is visibly piling up on many shores. As a visitor, don't hesitate to practice your conservationist attitudes.

CLIMATE

The Pacific Ocean has a greater impact on the world's climate than any other geographical feature on earth. By taking heat away from the equator and toward the poles, it stretches the bounds of the area in which life can exist. Broad circular ocean currents flow from east to west across the tropical Pacific, clockwise in the North Pacific, counterclockwise in the South Pacific. North and south of the "horse latitudes" just outside the tropics the currents cool and swing east. The prevailing winds move the same way: the southeast tradewinds south of the equator, the northeast tradewinds north of the equator, and the low-pressure "doldrums" in between. Westerlies blow east above the cool currents north and south of the tropics. This natural air-conditioning system brings warm water to Australia and Japan, cooler water to Peru and California.

The climate of the high islands is closely related to these winds. As air is heated near the equator it rises and flows at high altitudes toward the poles. By the time it reaches about 30 degrees south latitude it will have cooled enough to cause it to fall and flow back toward the equator near sea level. In the southern hemisphere the rotation of the earth deflects the winds to the left to become the southeast trades. When these cool moist tradewinds hit a high island, they are warmed by the sun and forced up. Above 500 meters elevation they begin to cool again and their moisture condenses into clouds. At night the winds do not capture much warmth and are more likely to discharge their moisture as rain. The windward slopes of the high islands catch the trades head-on and are usually wet, while those on the leeward side may be dry.

Rain falls abundantly and frequently in the islands during the southern summer months (Nov.-April). This is also the hurricane season south of the equator, a dangerous time for cruising yachts. However, New Zealand and southern Australia, outside the tropics, get their finest weather at this time; many boats head south to sit it out. The southeast tradewinds sweep the South Pacific May-Oct., the cruising season. Cooler and drier, these are the ideal months for travel in insular Oceania, though the rainy season is only a slight inconvenience and the season shouldn't be a pivotal factor in deciding when to go.

Over the past few years climatic changes have turned weather patterns upside down, so don't be surprised if you get prolonged periods of rain and wind during the official "dry season" and drought when there should be rain. A recent analysis of data shows that in 1977 the belt of storms and winds abruptly shifted eastward, making Tonga drier and Tahiti wetter. Hurricanes are also striking farther east and El Niño is expected to recur more frequently.

Temperatures range from warm to hot year-round; however, the ever-present sea moderates the humidity by bringing continual cooling breezes. Countries nearer the equator (Samoa) are hotter than those farther south (Tonga). There's almost no twilight in the tropics, which makes Pacific sunsets brief. When the sun begins to go down, you have less than half an hour before darkness.

When to Go

Compared to parts of North America and Europe, the seasonal climatic variations in the South Pacific are not extreme. There is a hotter,

TROPICAL HURRICANES

The official hurricane (or cyclone) season south of the equator is Nov.-April, although hurricanes have also occurred in May and October. Since the ocean provides the energy, these low pressure systems can only form over water with a surface temperature above 27° C; during years when water temperatures are high (such as during the recent El Niño) their frequency increases. The rotation of the earth must give the storm its initial spin, and this occurs mostly between latitudes five and 20 on either side of the equator.

As rainfall increases and the seas rise, the winds are drawn into a spiral that reaches its maximum speed in a ring around the center. In the South Pacific a cyclone develops as these circular winds, rotating clockwise around a center, increase in velocity: force eight to nine winds blowing at 34 to 47 knots are called a gale, force 10 to 11 at 48 to 63 knots is a storm, force 12 winds revolving at 64 knots or more is a hurricane. Wind speeds can go as high as 100 knots with gusts to 140 on the left side of the storm's path in the direction it's moving.

The eye of the hurricane can be 10 to 30 kilometers wide and surprising clear and calm, although at sea contradictory wave patterns continue to wreak havoc. In the South Pacific most hurricanes move south at speeds of 5-20 knots. As water is sucked into the low-pressure eye of the hurricane and waves reach 14 meters in height, coastlines can receive a surge of up to four meters of water, especially if the storm enters a narrowing bay or occurs at high tide.

M.G.L. DOMENY DE RIENZI

a waterspout during a tropical cyclone or hurricane

more humid season Nov.-April and a cooler, drier time May-October. These contrasts are more pronounced in countries closer to the equator such as Samoa and less noticeable in Tonga. Hurricanes can also come during the "rainy" season but they only last a few days a year. The sun sets around 1800 year-round and there aren't periods when the days are shorter or longer.

Seasonal differences in airfares are covered in the Getting There section that follows and these should be more influential in deciding when to go. On Air New Zealand flights from North America to Tonga and Samoa the low season is mid-April to August, the prime time in those countries. Be aware the both Australians and New Zealanders flock to the islands in July and August to escape winter weather in their home countries. Christmas is also busy with islanders returning home. In February and March many hotels stand half empty and special discounted rates are on offer.

In short, there isn't really any one season which is the "best" time to come. Go whenever you can, but book your airline seat well in advance as many flights from the U.S. run 90% full.

FLORA AND FAUNA

FLORA

The flora and fauna of Oceania originated in the Malaysian region; in the two regions, ecological niches are filled by similar plants. Yet one sees a steady decline in the variety of genera as one moves east: even in distant Hawaii very few native plants have an American origin. New Guinea has over 5,000 vegetal species, New Caledonia 3,250, and Tahiti-Polynesia only 1,000. Some species such as casuarinas and coconuts were spread by floating seeds or fruit, and wind and birds were also effective in colonization. The microscopic spores of ferns can be carried vast distances by the wind. Yet how creatures like Tonga's banded iguana or the flightless megapode bird of Niuafo'ou reached the Pacific islands remains a mystery. Later, humans became the vehicle: the Polynesians introduced taro, yams, breadfruit, plantains, coconuts, sugarcane, kava, paper mulberry, and much more to the islands.

The high islands of the South Pacific support a great variety of plantlife, while the low islands are restricted to a few hardy, drought-resistant species such as coconuts and pandanus. Rainforests fill the valleys and damp windward slopes of the high islands, while brush and thickets grow in more exposed locations. Hillsides in the drier areas are covered with coarse grasses. Yet even large islands such as Savai'i have an extremely limited variety of plantlife compared to Indonesia.

BREADFRUIT

The breadfruit *(uru)* is the plant most often associated with the South Pacific. The theme of a man turning himself into such a tree to save his family during famine often recurs in Polynesian legends. Ancient voyagers brought breadfruit shoots or seeds from Southeast Asia. When baked in an underground oven or roasted over flames, the now-seedless Polynesian variety resembles bread. Joseph Banks, botanist on Captain Cook's first voyage, wrote:

If a man should in the course of his lifetime plant 10 trees, which if well done might take the labor of an hour or thereabouts, he would completely fulfill his duty to his own as well as future generations.

The French naturalist Sonnerat transplanted breadfruit to Reunion in the Indian Ocean as early as 1772, but it's Captain William Bligh who shall always be remembered when the plant is mentioned. In 1787 Bligh set out to collect young shoots in Tahiti for transfer to the West Indies, where they were to be planted to feed slaves. On the way back, his crew mutinied in Tongan waters and cast off both breadfruit and Bligh. The indomitable captain managed to reach Dutch Timor in a rowboat and in 1792 returned to Tahiti with another ship to complete his task.

The breadfruit *(Artocarpus altilis),* a tall tree with broad green leaves, provides shade as well as food. A well-watered tree can produce as many as 1,000 pale green breadfruits a year. Robert Lee Eskridge described a breadfruit thus:

Its outer rind or skin, very hard, is covered with a golf-ball-like surface of small irregular pits or tiny hollows. An inner rind about a half-inch thick surrounds the fruit itself, which when baked tastes not unlike a doughy potato. Perhaps fresh bread, rolled up until it becomes a semifirm mass, best describes the breadfruit when cooked.

The starchy, easily digested fruit is rich in vitamin B. When consumed with a protein such as fish or meat it serves as an energy food. The Polynesians learned to preserve breadfruit by pounding it into a paste, which was kept in leaf-lined pits to ferment. Like the coconut, the breadfruit tree itself had many uses, including the provision of wood for outrigger canoes.

The absence of leaf-eating animals allowed the vegetation to develop largely without the protective spines and thorns found elsewhere.

Distance, drought, and poor soil have made atoll vegetation among the most unvaried on earth. Though a tropical atoll might seem "lush," no more than 15 native species may be present! On the atolls, taro, a root vegetable with broad heart-shaped leaves, must be cultivated in deep organic pits. The vegetation of a raised atoll is apt to be far denser, with many more species, yet it's likely that less than half are native.

Mangroves can occasionally be found along some high island coastal lagoons. The cable roots of the saltwater-tolerant red mangrove anchor in the shallow upper layer of oxygenated mud, avoiding the layers of hydrogen sulfide below. The tree provides shade for tiny organisms dwelling in the tidal mudflats—a place for birds to nest and for fish or shellfish to feed and spawn. The mangroves also perform the same task as land-building coral colonies along the reefs. As sediments are trapped between the roots, the trees extend farther into the lagoon, creating a unique natural environment. The past decade has seen widespread destruction of the mangroves.

In our day man has greatly altered the original vegetation by cutting the primary forests and introducing exotic species. For example, most of the plants now seen in the coastal areas of the main islands are introduced. The virgin rainforests of the world continue to disappear at the rate of 40 hectares a minute, causing erosion, silting, flooding, drought, climatic changes, and the extinction of countless life forms. Samoa has been hard hit by commercial logging.

Because the flying fox or fruit bat (Pteropus tonganus) is tapu in Tonga, this is the only place in the Pacific where the animal may be easily seen.

FAUNA

As with the flora, the variety of animal and bird species encountered in Oceania declines as you move away from the Asian mainland. The Wallace Line between Indonesia's Bali and Lombok was once believed to separate the terrestrial fauna of Southeast Asia from that of Australia. Although it's now apparent that there's no such clear-cut division, it still provides a frame of reference. The fauna to the east of New Guinea is much sparser, with flying foxes and insect-eating bats the only mammals that spread to all of Oceania (except Eastern Polynesia) without the aid of man.

Birds

Island birdlife is far more abundant than land-based fauna but still reflects the decline in variety from west to east. Birdwatching is a highly recommended pursuit for the serious Pacific traveler; you'll find it opens unexpected doors. Good field guides are few (ask at local bookstores, museums, and cultural centers), but a determined interest will bring you into contact with fascinating people and lead to great adventures. The best time to observe forest birds is in the very early morning—they move around a lot less in the heat of the day.

Introduced Fauna

Ancient Polynesian navigators introduced pigs, dogs, and chickens; they also brought along rats. Captain Cook contributed cattle, horses, and goats; Captain Wallis left behind cats. Giant African snails (Achatina fulica) were brought to the islands by the Japanese as a wartime emergency food. The snails have gradually spread to many islands, and they now crawl wild across Samoa, destroying the vegetation.

Perhaps the most unfortunate newcomer of all is the hopping Indian mynah bird (Acridotheres tristis), introduced to many islands from Indonesia at the turn of the century to control insects, which were damaging the citrus and coconut plantations. The mynahs multiplied profusely and have become major pests, inflicting

GIANT AFRICAN SNAIL

In 1993 the giant African snail (Achatina fulica) arrived at Apia in a container of hurricane relief supplies from American Samoa. The snails may first have arrived in the Pacific during WW II, when the Japanese introduced them to Micronesia as an emergency wartime food supply. They're now well established in all the French colonies of the South Pacific, plus Vanuatu and Tutuila, and now Samoa has been infested. The nocturnal mollusks thrive in humid conditions and can grow up to 20 centimeters long. A hermaphrodite, the great African snail lays hundreds of eggs at a time and eats all types of green plantlife, ravaging vegetable gardens and plantations. This gastropod uses a broad muscular organ to crawl, and unfortunately is too tough to eat, otherwise the Samoans would make short work of them. The giant African snail is also a possible carrier of meningitis unless boiled for 15 minutes. An initial spraying campaign when the snails first arrived was unsuccessful as some landowners refused to cooperate. Then a bounty program was started, but this collapsed when it was reported that Samoans had begun farming the snails to collect the rewards. The snails are still confined to the area around Apia and inspectors at Mulifanua wharf and the airports are attempting to keep them from spreading to Savai'i, although this is probably only a matter of time. Japan has offered to support a massive eradication program using herbicides and pesticides, itself a serious threat to the environment. Experiments with biological control using cannibalistic snail species have thus far been unsuccessful.

maining on our globe are swimming in this great ocean. Coral pinnacles on the lagoon floor provide a safe haven for angelfish, butterfly fish, damselfish, groupers, soldierfish, surgeonfish, triggerfish, trumpet fish, and countless more. These fish seldom venture more than a few meters away from the protective coral, but larger fish such as barracuda, jackfish, parrot fish, pike, stingrays, and small sharks range across lagoon waters that are seldom deeper than 30 meters. The external side of the reef is also home to many of the above, but the open ocean is reserved for bonito, mahimahi, swordfish, tuna, wrasses, and the larger sharks. Passes between ocean and lagoon can be crowded with fish in transit, offering a favorite hunting ground for predators.

In the open sea the food chain begins with phytoplankton, which flourish wherever ocean upwellings bring nutrients such as nitrates and phosphates to the surface. In the western Pacific this occurs near the equator, where massive currents draw water away toward Japan and Australia. Large schools of fast-moving tuna ply these waters feeding on smaller fish, which consume tiny phytoplankton drifting near the sunlit surface. The phytoplankton also exist in tropical lagoons where mangrove leaves, sea grasses, and other plant material are consumed by far more varied populations of reef fish, mollusks, and crustaceans.

It's believed that most Pacific marine organisms evolved in the triangular area bounded by New Guinea, the Philippines, and the Malay Peninsula. This "Cradle of Indo-Pacific Marinelife" includes a wide variety of habitats and has remained stable through several geological ages. From this cradle the rest of the Pacific was colonized.

great harm on the very trees they were brought in to protect. Worse still, many indigenous birds are forced out of their habitat by these noisy, aggressive birds with yellow beaks and feet. This and rapid deforestation by man have made the South Pacific the region with the highest proportion of endangered endemic bird species on earth.

Fish
The South Pacific's richest store of life is found in the silent underwater world of the pelagic and lagoon fishes. It's estimated that half the fish re-

Marine Mammals
While most people use the terms dolphin and porpoise interchangeably, a porpoise lacks the dolphin's beak (although many dolphins are also beakless). There are 62 species of dolphins, and only six species of porpoises. Dolphins leap from the water and many legends tell of their saving humans, especially children, from drowning (the most famous concerns Telemachus, son of Odysseus). Dolphins often try to race in front of ferries and large ships.

Whales generally visit the tropical South Pacific between July and October. Humpbacks arrive in Tonga about this time to give birth in the warm waters off Vava'u. Whales are also commonly seen off Niue. As the weather grows warmer they return to the summer feeding areas around Antarctica. (Sadly, Japanese whalers continue to hunt the animals in Antarctica for "scientific purposes," and endangered fin and humpback whales are hidden among the 400 minke whale kills reported each year. Whale meat is openly available at Tokyo restaurants.)

Sharks

The danger from sharks has been greatly exaggerated. Of some 300 different species, only 28 are known to have attacked humans. Most dangerous are the white, tiger, and blue sharks. Fortunately, all of these inhabit deep water far from the coasts. An average of only 50 shark attacks a year occur worldwide, so considering the number of people who swim in the sea, your chances of being involved are about one in ten million. In the South Pacific shark attacks on snorkelers or scuba divers are extremely rare and the tiny mosquito is a far more dangerous predator.

Sharks are not aggressive where food is abundant, but they can be very nasty far offshore. You're always safer if you keep your head underwater (with a mask and snorkel), and don't panic if you see a shark—you might attract it. Even if you do, they're usually only curious, so keep your eye on the shark and slowly back off. The swimming techniques of humans must seem very clumsy to fish, so it's not surprising if they want a closer look.

Sharks are attracted by shiny objects (a knife or jewelry), bright colors (especially yellow and red), urine, blood, spearfishing, and splashing (divers should ease themselves into the water). Sharks normally stay outside the reef, but get local advice. White beaches are safer than dark, and clear water safer than murky. Avoid swimming in places where sewage or edible wastes enter the water, or where fish have just been cleaned. You should also exercise care in places

The zebra or lionfish is among the most toxic in the Pacific. Its striking red coloration and long spines may be nature's warning.

LOUISE FOOTE

where local residents have been fishing with spears or even hook and line that day.

Never swim alone if you suspect the presence of sharks. If you see one, even a supposedly harmless nurse shark lying on the bottom, get out of the water calmly and quickly, and go elsewhere. Studies indicate that sharks, like most other creatures, have a "personal space" around them that they will defend. Thus an attack could be a shark's way of warning someone to keep his distance, and it's a fact that over half the victims of these incidents are not eaten but merely bitten. Sharks are much less of a problem in the South Pacific than in colder waters because small marine mammals (commonly hunted by sharks) are rare here, so you won't be mistaken for a seal or an otter.

Let common sense be your guide, not irrational fear or carelessness.

Sea Urchins

Sea urchins (living pincushions) are common in tropical waters. The black variety is the most dangerous: their long, sharp quills can go right through a snorkeler's fins. Even the small ones, which you can easily pick up in your hand, can pinch you if you're careless. They're found on rocky shores and reefs, never on clear, sandy beaches where the surf rolls in.

Most sea urchins are not poisonous, though quill punctures are painful and can become infected if not treated. The pain is caused by an injected protein, which you can eliminate by holding the injured area in a pail of very hot water for about 15 minutes. This will coagulate the protein, eliminating the pain for good. If you can't heat water, soak the area in vinegar or urine for a quarter hour. Remove the quills if possible, but being made of calcium, they'll decompose in a couple of weeks anyway—not much of a consolation as you limp along in the meantime. In some places sea urchins are considered a delicacy: the orange or yellow urchin gonads are delicious with lemon and salt.

Other Hazardous Sea Creatures

Although jellyfish, stonefish, crown-of-thorns starfish, cone shells, eels, and poisonous sea snakes are dangerous, injuries resulting from any of these are rare. Gently apply methylated spirit, alcohol, or urine (but not water, kerosene, or gasoline) to areas stung by jellyfish. Stonefish rest on the bottom and are hard to see due to camouflaging; if you happen to step on one, its dorsal fins inject a painful poison, which burns like fire in the blood. Fortunately, stonefish are not common.

It's worth knowing that the venom produced by most marine animals is destroyed by heat, so your first move should be to soak the injured part in very hot water for 30 minutes. (Also hold an opposite foot or hand in the same water to prevent scalding due to numbness.) Other authorities claim the best first aid is to squeeze blood from a sea cucumber scraped raw on coral directly onto the wound. If a hospital or clinic is nearby, go there immediately.

Never pick up a live cone shell; some varieties have a deadly stinger dart coming out from the pointed end. The tiny blue-ring octopus is only five centimeters long but packs a poison that can kill a human. Eels hide in reef crevices by day; most are harmful only if you inadvertently poke your hand or foot in at them. Of course, never tempt fate by approaching them.

Reptiles and Insects

Very few land snakes live in Oceania and the more common sea snakes are shy and inoffensive. This, and the relative absence of leeches, poisonous plants, thorns, and dangerous wild animals, makes the South Pacific a paradise for hikers. One creature to watch out for is the centipede, which often hides under stones or anything else lying around. It's a long, flat, fast-moving insect not to be confused with the round, slow, and harmless millipede. The centipede's bite, though painful, is not lethal to a normal adult.

Geckos and skinks are small lizards often seen on the islands. The skink hunts insects by day; its tail breaks off if you catch it, but a new one quickly grows. The gecko (*mo'o* in Samoan) is nocturnal and has no eyelids. Adhesive toe pads enable it to pass along vertical surfaces, and it changes color to avoid detection. Unlike the skink, which avoids humans, geckos often live in people's homes, where they eat insects attracted by electric lights. Its loud clicking call may be a territorial warning to other geckos. Two species of geckos are asexual: in these, males do not exist and the unfertilized eggs hatch into females identical to the mother. Geckos are the highest members of the animal world where this phenomenon takes place. During the 1970s a sexual species of house gecko was introduced to Samoa, and these larger, more aggressive geckos have drastically reduced the population of the endemic asexual species.

Six of the seven species of sea turtles are present in the South Pacific (the flatback, green, hawksbill, leatherback, loggerhead, and olive ridley turtles). These magnificent creatures are sometimes erroneously referred to as "tortoises," which are land turtles. All species of sea turtles now face extinction due to ruthless hunting, egg harvesting, and beach destruction. Sea turtles come ashore Nov.-Feb. to lay their eggs on the beach from which they themselves originally hatched, but female turtles don't commence this activity until they are twenty years old. Thus a drop in numbers today has irreversible consequences a generation later, and it's estimated that breeding females already number in the hundreds or low thousands. Turtles are often choked by floating plastic bags they mistake for food, or they drown in fishing nets. Importing any sea turtle product is prohibited in most developed countries, but protection is often inadequate in the South Pacific countries themselves.

HISTORY

THE ERA OF DISCOVERY AND SETTLEMENT

Prehistory

Oceania is the site of many "lasts." It was the last area on earth to be settled by humans, the last to be discovered by Europeans, and the last to be both colonized and decolonized. Sometime around 1600 B.C., broad-nosed, light-skinned Austronesians entered the South Pacific from Indonesia or the Philippines. They settled in enclaves along the coast of New Guinea and gradually populated the islands of Melanesia as far east as Fiji. The Austronesians introduced pottery to the Papuan peoples already in Melanesia and had more advanced outrigger canoes.

Distinctive *lapita* pottery, decorated in horizontal geometric bands and dated from 1500 to 500 B.C., has been found at sites ranging from New Britain to New Caledonia, Tonga, and Samoa. *Lapita* pottery has allowed archaeologists to trace the migrations of an Austronesian-speaking race, the Polynesians, with some precision. These *Lapita* people were great traders: obsidian from New Britain Island in Papua New Guinea was exported to Santa Cruz in the Solomons—some 1,700 km away. By A.D. 300 at the latest the Polynesians had ceased to make pottery. Recent comparisons of DNA samples have confirmed that the Polynesians traveled from Taiwan to the Philippines, Indonesia, New Guinea, Fiji, and Samoa.

The colorful theory that Oceania was colonized from the Americas is no longer seriously entertained. The Austronesian languages are today spoken from Madagascar through Indonesia all the way to Easter Island and Hawaii, half the circumference of the world! All of the introduced plants of old Polynesia, except the sweet potato, originated in Southeast Asia. The endemic diseases of Oceania, leprosy and the filaria parasite (elephantiasis), were unknown in the Americas. The amazing continuity of Polynesian culture is illustrated by motifs in contemporary tattooing and tapa, which are very similar to those on ancient *lapita* pottery.

The Colonization of Polynesia

Three thousand five hundred years ago the early Polynesians set out from Southeast Asia on a migratory trek that would lead them to make the "many islands" of Polynesia their home. Great voyagers, they sailed their huge double-hulled canoes far and wide, steering with huge paddles and pandanus sails. To navigate they read the sun, stars, currents, swells, winds, clouds, and birds. Sailing purposefully, against the prevailing winds and currents, the *Lapita* peoples reached the Bismarck Archipelago by 1500 B.C., Tonga (via Fiji) by 1300 B.C., and Samoa by 1000 B.C. Around the time of Christ they pushed out from this primeval area, remembered as Havaiki, into the eastern half of the Pacific.

Perhaps due to overpopulation in Samoa, some Polynesians had pressed on to the Society Islands and the Marquesas by A.D. 300. Easter Island (A.D. 400), Hawaii (A.D. 500), and Mangareva (A.D. 900) were all reached by Polynesians from the Marquesas. Migrants to the Tuamotus (A.D. 900), the Cook Islands (A.D. 900), and New Zealand (A.D. 1100) were from the Society Islands. These were not chance landfalls but planned voyages of colonization: the Polynesians could (and often did) return the way they came. The stone food pounders, carved figures, and tanged adzes of Eastern Polynesia are not found in Samoa and Tonga (Western Polynesia), indicating that they were later, local developments of Polynesian culture.

The Polynesians were the real discoverers of the Pacific, completing all their major voyages long before Europeans even dreamed this ocean existed. In double canoes lashed together to form rafts, carrying their plants and animals with them, they penetrated as close to Antarctica as the South Island of New Zealand, as far north as Hawaii, and as far east as Easter Island—a full 13,000 km from where it's presumed they first entered the Pacific!

Neolithic Society

The Polynesians kept gardens and a few domestic animals including chickens and pigs. Taro was cultivated on ingenious terraces or in or-

DISCOVERY AND SETTLEMENT OF THE PACIFIC

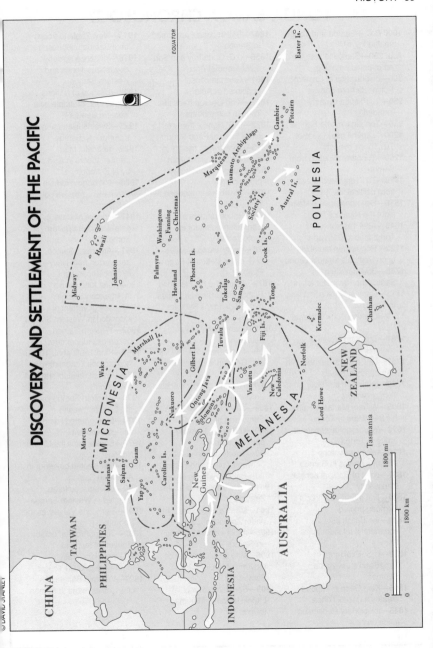

© DAVID STANLEY

TONGA-SAMOA CHRONOLOGY

1000 B.C.—Samoa and Tonga settled

A.D. 200—Samoans lose the art of pottery making

300—colonization of Eastern Polynesia from Samoa

950—Tu'i Tonga dynasty founded

950—Tongans invade Samoa

1200—Lapaha made seat of Tu'i Tonga dynasty

1250—Tongans expelled from Samoa

1470—Tu'i Tonga withdrawns from political life

1616—Schouten and Le Maire sight the Niuas of Tonga

1643—Abel Tasman visits Tongatapu and Ha'apai

1722—Roggeveen stumbles upon Samoa's Manu'a Group

1768—Bougainville calls Samoa the Navigator Islands

1773—Captain Cook's first visit to Tonga

1774—Captain Cook contacts Niue

1781—Spaniard Mourelle contacts Vava'u

1787—La Pérouse clashes with Samoans on Tutuila

1789—mutiny on the *Bounty* in Tongan waters

1806—William Mariner begins his four years in Tonga

1822—Wesleyan missionaries arrive in Tonga

1830—missionary John Williams arrives in Samoa

1831—chief of Ha'apai accepts Christianity

1834—first missionary tracts in Samoan printed

1838—the British establish commercial relations with Samoa

1839—U.S. Exploring Expedition surveys the Samoas

1845—King George Tupou I creates a united Tonga

1846—missionary Peniamina lands on Niue

1847—British consul appointed to Samoa

1856—J.C. Godeffroy and Son established at Apia

1861—German consul appointed at Apia

1862—King George frees the Tongan commoners

1872—U.S. signs a treaty for naval base at Pago Pago

1873—Steinberger assists in creation of a constitution

1875—Tongan Constitution proclaimed

1876—Steinberger deported to Fiji by British

1877—Britain refuses a Samoan request for a protectorate

1878—treaty allows creation of U.S. naval station at Pago Pago

1879—Deutsche Handels-und Plantagen-Gesellshaft takes over Godeffroy's Samoan interests

1879—municipality of Apia established

1889—hurricane sinks six U.S. and German warships at Apia

1890—Robert Louis Stevenson arrives in Samoa

1894—death of Robert Louis Stevenson at Vailima

1899—U.S. and Germany partition Samoa

1900—Treaty of Friendship between Tonga and Britain

1900—Britain annexes Niue

1901—Niue transferred to New Zealand

1904—Manu'a Group brought under American rule

1905—major volcanic eruption on Savai'i

1908—Mau a Pule resistance movement to Germans in Samoa

1909—Samoan orator chief Lauaki exiled to Mariana Islands

1914—New Zealand troops take Samoa unopposed

1918—influenza epidemic devastates Tonga and western Samoa

1920—League of Nations grants N.Z. mandate over western Samoa

1925—Swains Island annexed to American Samoa

1929—peaceful Mau demonstrators in Apia shot by N.Z. troops

1936—Labor government reverses repressive policies in Samoa

1947—council of state established in Western Samoa

1951—American Samoa transferred from Navy to Interior Department

1954—first tuna cannery opens in American Samoa

1957—self-government extended in Western Samoa

1962—Western Samoa becomes independent

1967—King Taufa'ahau Tupou IV assumes Tongan throne

1970—Tonga reestablishes full sovereignty

1970—Western Samoa joins the Commonwealth

1974—Niue granted internal self-government

1976—Samoa joins the United Nations

1977—first elected governor in American Samoa

1990—universal suffrage adopted in Western Samoa

1991—Hurricane Val lashes the Samoas

1992—Tonga Pro-democracy Movement founded

1996—pro-democracy journalists jailed in Tonga

1997—Western Samoa changes its name to Samoa

ganic pits; breadfruit was preserved by fermentation through burial (still a rare delicacy). Stone fishponds and fish traps were built in the lagoons. Pandanus and coconut fronds were woven into handicrafts. On the larger Polynesian islands these practices produced a surplus, which allowed the emergence of a powerful ruling class. The common people lived in fear of their gods and chiefs.

The Polynesians were cannibals, although the intensity of the practice varied from group to group. Early European explorers were occasionally met by natives who would kneel beside them on the shore, squeezing their legs and pinching their posteriors to ascertain how tasty and substantial these white people would be to eat. It was believed that the mana or spiritual power of an enemy would be transferred to the consumer; to eat the body of one who was greatly despised was the ultimate revenge.

Jean-Jacques Rousseau and the 18th-century French rationalists created the romantic image of the "noble savage." Their vision of an ideal state of existence in harmony with nature disregarded the inequalities, cannibalism, and warfare that were a central part of island life, just as much of today's travel literature ignores the poverty and political/economic exploitation many Pacific peoples now face. Still, the legend of the South Pacific maintains its magic hold.

EUROPEAN CONTACT

Terra Australis Incognita

The systematic European exploration of the South Pacific was actually a search for *terra australis incognita,* a great southern continent believed to balance the continents of the north. There were many daring voyages during this period. The 17th century was the age of the Dutch explorations in search of new markets and trade routes. The first Dutch ships followed the routes pioneered by the 16th century Spanish and made few discoveries of significance. However, Anthony van Diemen, the Dutch governor-general of Batavia (present-day Jakarta) and a man of vision and great purpose, provided the backing for Abel Tasman's noteworthy voyage of 1642, which entered the Pacific from the west, rather than the east.

Tasman was instructed to find "the remaining unknown part of the terrestrial globe"—your basic Herculean task. Because of his meticulous and painstaking daily journals, Tasman is known as the historian of Pacific explorers. His observations proved invaluable to geography, adding Tasmania, New Zealand, Tonga, and parts of Fiji to Western knowledge. Tasman was the first to sail right around Australia. Jacob Roggeveen's voyage in 1722 also failed to discover the unknown continent, but he narrowed down the area of conjecture considerably.

The exploratory success of the 18th-century English was due to this 17th-century scientific labor. Although using 17th-century equipment, William Dampier explored with an 18th-century attitude. In 1745, the British Parliament passed an act promising £20,000 to the first British subject who could, in a British ship, discover and sail through a strait between Hudson's Bay and the South Seas. Thus many explorers were spurred to investigate the region. This route would have proven infinitely shorter than the one around Cape Horn, where the weather was often foul and the ships in perpetual danger; on Samuel Wallis's voyage of 1766-67, his two ships took four months to round the chaotic Straits of Magellan.

Captain Cook

The extraordinary achievements of James Cook (1728-1779) on his three voyages in the ships *Endeavor, Resolution, Adventure,* and *Discovery* left his successors with little to do but marvel over them. A product of the Age of Enlightenment, Cook was a mathematician, astronomer, practical physician, and master navigator. Son of a Yorkshire laborer, he learned seamanship on small coastal traders plying England's east coast. He joined the British Navy in 1755 and soon made a name for himself in Canada where he surveyed the St. Lawrence River, greatly contributing to the capture of Quebec City in 1759. Later he charted the coast of Newfoundland. Chosen to command the *Endeavor* in 1768 though only a warrant officer, Cook

Captain James Cook

M.G.L. DOMENY DE RIENZI

Captain Cook and his crew witnessed female boxing matches during their 1777 visit.

was the first captain to eliminate scurvy from his crew (with sauerkraut).

The scientists of his time needed accurate observations of the transit of Venus, for if the passage of Venus across the face of the sun were measured from points on opposite sides of the earth, then the size of the solar system could be determined for the first time. In turn, this would make possible accurate predictions of the movements of the planets, vital for navigation at sea. Thus Cook was dispatched to Tahiti, and Father Hell (a Viennese astronomer of Hungarian origin) to Vardo, Norway.

So as not to alarm the French and Spanish, the British admiralty claimed Cook's first voyage (1768-71) was primarily to take these measurements. His real purpose, however, was to further explore the region, in particular to find *terra australis incognita*. After three months on Tahiti, he sailed west and spent six months exploring and mapping New Zealand and the whole east coast of Australia, nearly tearing the bottom off his ship, the *Endeavor,* on the Great Barrier Reef in the process.

Nine months after returning to England, Cook embarked on his second expedition (1772-75), resolving to settle the matter of *terra australis incognita* conclusively. In the *Resolution* and *Adventure,* he sailed entirely around the bottom of the world, becoming the first to cross the Antarctic Circle and return to tell about it. On this voyage Cook visited Tonga for the first time and became the first European to see Niue.

In 1776 Cook set forth from England for a third voyage to find a Northwest Passage from the Pacific to the Atlantic. He rounded the Cape of Good Hope and headed east to New Zealand, Tonga, and Tahiti. Then he headed due north, discovering Kauai in what we know as the Hawaiian Islands on 18 January 1778. After two weeks in Hawaii, Cook continued north via the west coast of North America but was forced back by ice in the Bering Strait. With winter coming, he returned to Hawaiian waters and located the two biggest islands of the group, Maui and Hawaii. On 14 February 1779, in a short, unexpected, petty skirmish with the Hawaiians, Cook was killed. Today he remains the giant of Pacific exoloration. He'd dispelled the compelling, centuries-old hypothesis of an unknown continent, and his explorations ushered in the British era in the South Seas.

CONVERSION, COLONIALISM, AND DECOLONIZATION

Conversion

The systematic explorations of the 18th century were stimulated by the need for raw materials and markets as the Industrial Revolution took hold in Europe. After the American Revolution, much of Britain's colonizing energy was deflected toward Africa, India, and the Pacific. This gave them an early lead, but France, Germany, and the U.S. weren't far behind.

As trade with China developed in the late 18th and early 19th centuries, Europeans combed the Pacific for products to sell to the Chinese. Ruffian whalers, sealers, and individual beachcombers flooded in. Most were unsavory characters who acted as mercenaries or advisers to local chiefs, but one of them, William Mariner, left a valuable account of early Tonga.

After the easily exploited resources were depleted, white traders and planters arrived to establish posts and to create copra and cotton plantations on the finest land. Missionaries came to "civilize" the natives by teaching that all their customs—cannibalism, warring with their neighbors, having more than one wife, wearing leaves instead of clothes, dancing, drinking kava, chewing betel nut, etc.—were wrong. They taught hard work, shame, thrift, abstention, and obedience. Tribes now had to wear sweaty, rain-soaked, germ-carrying garments of European design. Men dressed in singlets and trousers, and the women in Mother Hubbards or *mu'umu'u*, one-piece smocks trailing along the ground. To clothe themselves and build churches required money, obtained only by working as laborers on European plantations or producing a surplus of goods to sell to European traders. In many instances this austere, harsh Christianity was grafted onto the numerous taboo systems of the Pacific.

Members of the London Missionary Society arrived at Tahiti in 1797, though it was not until 1815 that they succeeded in converting the Tahitians. One famous LMS missionary, Rev. John Williams, spread Protestantism to the Cook Islands (1823) and Samoa (1830). Methodists were active in Tonga (1822) and Fiji (1835). The children of some of the European missionaries who "came to do good, stayed to do well" as merchants. Later, many islanders themselves became missionaries: some 1,200 of them left their homes to carry the word of God to other islands.

After the 1840s, islanders were kidnapped by "blackbirders," who sold them as slaves to planters in Fiji and Queensland. Worst were the Peruvians, who took 3,634 islanders to Peru in 1862 and 1863, of whom only 148 were returned.

Colonialism

The first European colonies in Oceania were Australia (1788) and New Zealand (1840). Soon after, the French seized Tahiti-Polynesia (1842) and New Caledonia (1853). Not wishing to be burdened with the expense of administering insignificant, far-flung colonies, Britain at first resisted pressure to officially annex other scattered South Pacific island groups, though Fiji was reluctantly taken in 1874 to establish law and order. In 1877 the Western Pacific High Commission was set up to protect British interests in the unclaimed islands.

Then the emergence of imperialist Germany and construction of the Panama Canal led to a sudden rush of annexations by Britain, France, Germany, and the U.S. between 1884 and 1900. In 1899 Samoa was partitioned between Germany and the U.S., with Tonga and the Solomon Islands added to the British sphere of influence as compensation. Around the time of WW I Britain transferred responsibility for many island groups to Australia and New Zealand; for example, Niue was given to New Zealand. The struggle for hegemony in imperialist Europe in 1914-18 prompted Germany's South Pacific colonies, New Guinea and Samoa, to be taken by Australia and New Zealand.

By the late 19th century, the colonies' tropical produce (copra, sugar, vanilla, cacao, and fruits) had become more valuable and accessible. Total control of these resources passed to large European trading companies, which owned the plantations, ships, and retail stores. This colonial economy led to a drop in the indigenous populations in general by a third, not to mention the destruction of their cultures.

Decolonization

In 1960 the United Nations issued a Declaration of Granting of Independence to Colonial Countries and Peoples, which encouraged the trend toward self-government, yet it was not until the independence of Samoa from New Zealand in 1962 that a worldwide wave of decolonization reached the region. During the 1960s and 1970s seven South Pacific countries (Fiji, Papua New Guinea, Solomon Islands, Tonga, Tuvalu, Vanuatu, and Samoa) became independent as Britain, Australia, and New Zealand dismantled their colonial systems. Niue has achieved de facto independence in association with New Zealand. American Samoa remains firmly tied to Washington by the subsidies it receives.

The postwar period also witnessed the growth of regionalism. In 1947 the South Pacific Commission (now called the Secretariat of the Pacific Community) was established by Australia, Britain, France, the Netherlands, New Zealand, and the U.S. to maintain the status quo through coordination among the colonial powers, yet conferences organized by the SPC brought the islanders together for the first time. In 1971 the newly independent states formed the South Pacific Forum, a more vigorous regional body able to tackle political as well as social problems.

The South Pacific Regional Environment Program (Box 240, Apia, Samoa; tel. 685/21-929, fax 685/20-231, www.sprep.org.ws, e-mail: sprep@sprep.org.ws), established in 1982 by the SPC, the SPF, and the United Nations, became an autonomous regional organization with 26 member countries in 1993. With a budget of US$7 million and a staff of over 50, SPREP promotes sustainable development by creating programs in fields such as environmental management, global change, species conservation, nature reserves, and pollution management, and through education and international coordination.

DIANA LASICH HARPER

ECONOMY

Trade

Australia and New Zealand have huge trade surpluses with the Pacific islands. Ten South Pacific countries participate in the Pacific Forum Line, a shipping company set up by the South Pacific Forum to facilitate trade with Australia and New Zealand, but in practice, the Line's large container ships run full northbound and empty southbound. The trade deficits make the industrialized, exporting nations the main beneficiaries of the island economies. For Australia and New Zealand, the South Pacific market is not very important, but for every island nation this trade is vital to their interests.

Products such as bananas, cacao, coconut oil, copra, taro, and vanilla are subject to price fluctuations over which local governments have no control, plus low demand and strong competition from other third-world producers. Most are processed and marketed outside the islands by transnationals. Even worse, efforts to increase the output of commodities such as these reduces local food production, leading to expensive imports of processed food. In recent years Tonga has exported large quantities of squash (pumpkin) to Japan. New Zealand meat exporters routinely ship low-quality "Pacific cuts" of fatty, frozen mutton flaps unsalable on world markets to countries like Tonga and Samoa. American companies dump junk foods such as "turkey tails" in the islands, and tinned mystery meats arrive from afar.

Aid, investment, remittances, and tourism help offset the trade imbalances, but this also fosters dependence. Trade between the various South Pacific countries is limited by a basic similarity of their products and shipping tariffs that encourage bulk trade with Australia and New Zealand rather than local interisland trade. Tonga and Fiji do have a limited free-trade agreement and steps are being taken toward creating a larger regional free-trade area.

Trade Agreements

The current trend toward "globalization" is not to the islands' advantage. Free trade forces Pacific countries to compete with low-wage producers in Asia and Latin America where human rights and the environment are of scant concern. The World Bank and other international banks aggressively market "project loans" to facilitate the production of goods for sale on world markets. The initial beneficiaries of these projects are the contractors, while the ability of transnational corporations to exploit the region's natural resources is enhanced. Subsistence food production is reduced and the recipient state is left with a debt burden it can only service through exports.

Should commodity exports fail, the International Monetary Fund steps in with emergency loans to make sure the foreign banks don't lose their money. Local governments are forced to accept "structural adjustment programs" dictated from Washington, and well-paid Western bankers dictate that social spending be cut. Another favorite trick is persuade governments to shift the tax burden from rich to poor by replacing income and company taxes with a value-added tax. Tottering administrations are forced to clearcut their rainforests and sell their soil to meet financial obligations. This kind of chicanery has caused untold misery in Africa, Asia, and Latin America, often with the connivance of corrupt local officials.

Since 1980 New Zealand and Australia have tried to help the island countries balance their trade deficits by allowing most of the products of the South Pacific Forum countries unrestricted duty-free entry on a nonreciprocal basis, provided they have 50% local content. The only exceptions are sugar, steel, motor vehicles, and clothing, which are subject to quotas in Australia. The **South Pacific Regional Trade and Economic Cooperation Agreement** (SPARTECA) has allowed Tonga, Samoa, and others to set up Small Industries Centers producing manufactured goods for export south. A large Japanese-owned factory in Samoa exports automotive electrical parts to Australia. Women make up the vast majority of the workforce, earning less than a tenth as much as their counterparts in Australia and New Zealand, where working conditions are far better.

Critics of SPARTECA say the 50% local content rule discourages companies from operating efficiently by reducing local costs, and relegates them to the bottom end of the market since the raw materials required for quality products are not available in the islands. Now with universal trade barriers falling in the wake of the 1994 signing of the GATT, the value of selective trade agreements such as SPARTECA is decreasing, and in the future it will be much more difficult for Pacific island industries to compete with cheap-labor areas in Asia. The 1994 Bogor Declaration reduces tariffs between the 19 members of the Asia Pacific Economic Cooperation (APEC) to 25% by 2000 and to zero by 2010, thereby eliminating the competitive advantage of SPARTECA by granting Asian producers similar access to Australia and New Zealand.

Other Income

Since the late 1980s, Tonga, Samoa, and Niue have offered offshore banking facilities to foreign corporations attempting to avoid taxation in their home countries. Hundreds of dummy corporations and brass-plate banks now operate in these countries with little or no staff, fixed assets, or capital. In 1990 Australia plugged the loopholes, thus saving millions of dollars a year in lost taxation, and most of the clients of the "financial centers" are now companies based in Asia.

Tonga sells its sovereignty to foreigners in the form of dummy Tongan passports intended to be used to slip into third countries. A sizable Chinese transient population is in Nuku'alofa awaiting the chance to move on to greener pastures. Niue has leased its international telephone circuits to the operators of sex-by-phone hot lines.

One of the largest sources of income for Tonga and Samoa is remittances sent home by emigrants living in New Zealand and Australia. The Diaspora also provides the bulk of visitors to these countries.

New Zealand is the main source of visitors to Niue, Tonga, and Samoa, and it's the number-one industry in those countries. Yet tourism is very low key: overcrowded Hawaii gets 10 times as many annual visitors as the entire South Pacific region combined, and places like Tonga, Samoa, and Niue get only a fraction as many arrivals as Fiji and Tahiti. Yet increasing numbers of European and North American visitors to the South Pacific can be expected if airfares remain low and the region's many advantages over competing Mediterranean and Caribbean destinations can be effectively marketed. Only the "tyranny of distance" has thus far prevented the islands from being spoiled.

THE PEOPLE

Population

The high birth rate and rapid urbanization can tax the best efforts of governments with limited resources. The most densely populated Pacific countries are the Polynesian islands of American Samoa, Tokelau, Tonga, and Tuvalu. American Samoa is highly urbanized with around half the population town dwellers. Samoa is the opposite with about 85% still living in villages. The rapid growth of cities like Apia, Nuku'alofa, and Fagatogo has led to high levels of unemployment and social problems such as alcoholism, petty crime, and domestic violence.

Emigration relieves the pressure a little and provides income in the form of remittances sent back. However, absenteeism also creates the problem of idled land and abandoned homes. Niueans, Tongans, and Samoans emigrate to New Zealand, and American Samoans to the U.S. In American Samoa and Niue, more islanders now live off their home islands than on them. In 1987 New Zealand withdrew visa-free entry facilities for Tongans and Samoans to limit the flow.

Many Pacific countries conduct a census only once every 10 years, and the population statistics provided in the "At a Glance" charts in the chapter introductions of this book were the most up-to-date available at the time we went to press. Rather than publish estimates or projections, we've tried to provide hard facts. Actual population growth rates are about zero in Niue and Tonga where people are constantly emigrating.

Pacific Women

Traditionally Pacific women were confined to the home, while the men would handle most matters outside the immediate family. The clear-cut roles of the woman as homemaker and the man as defender and decision-maker gave stability to village life. Western education has caused many Pacific women to question their subordinate position, and the changing lifestyle has made the old relationship between the sexes outmoded. As paid employment expands and—thanks to family planning—women are able to hold onto their jobs, they demand equal treatment from society. Polynesian women are more emancipated than their sisters in Melanesia, though men continue to dominate public life throughout the region. Tradition is often manipulated to deny women the right to express themselves publicly on community matters

There are cultural barriers hindering women's access to education and employment, and the proportion of girls in school falls rapidly as the grade level increases. Female students are nudged into low-paying fields such as nursing or secretarial services; in Samoa and elsewhere, export-oriented factories exploit women workers with low wages and poor conditions. Levels of domestic violence vary greatly, but those little signs on buses reading "real men don't hit women" suggest the problem. Travelers should take an interest in women's issues.

Traditional Customs

Although the South Pacific is a region of great variety, there are a number of rituals and ceremonies that many islands have in common. The most important of these is the kava ceremony found in Fiji, Samoa, Tonga, and Vanuatu. Kava is a drink made from the crushed root of the pepper plant. The powder or pulp is strained or mixed with water in a large wooden bowl and drunk from a coconut-shell cup. Elaborate protocols accompany formal kava ceremonies although kava is also a social drink consumed by ordinary people when they get together to relax and chat. Recently German pharmaceutical firms have discovered kava's usefulness in the manufacture of nonaddictive painkillers and antidepressants.

Another widespread feature of Pacific culture is the making of bark cloth called tapa used for clothing or decoration. This felt-like cloth with stenciled or printed designs is described under Arts and Crafts in this introduction. Other unique customs include the use of an earth oven called an *umu* and tattooing. These traditions are a thread uniting the diverse peoples of the Pacific.

THE POLYNESIANS

The Polynesians, whom Robert Louis Stevenson called "God's best, at least God's sweetest work," are a tall, golden-skinned people with straight or wavy, but rarely fuzzy, hair. They have fine features, almost intimidating physiques, and a soft, flowing language. One theory holds that the Polynesians evolved their great bodily stature through a selective process on their long ocean voyages, as the larger individuals with more body fat were better able to resist the chill of evaporating sea spray on their bodies (polar animals are generally larger than equatorial ani-

M.G.L. DOMENY DE RIENZI

an 18th-century kava ceremony on Tongatapu

mals of the same species for the same reason). Other authorities ascribe their huge body size to a high-carbohydrate vegetable diet.

The ancient Polynesians developed a rigid social system with hereditary chiefs; descent was usually through the father. In most of Polynesia there were only two classes, chiefs and commoners, but in Hawaii, Tahiti, and Tonga an intermediate class existed. People lived in scattered dwellings rather than villages, although there were groupings around the major temples and chiefs' residences.

They lived from fishing and agriculture, using tools made from stone, bone, shell, and wood. The men were responsible for planting, harvesting, fishing, cooking, house and canoe building; the women tended the fields and animals, gathered food and fuel, prepared food, and made clothes and household items. Both males and females worked together in family or community groups, not as individuals.

The Polynesians lost the art of pottery making during their long stay in Havaiki and had to cook their food in underground ovens *(umu)*. Breadfruit, taro, yams, sweet potatoes, bananas, and coconuts were cultivated (the Polynesians had no cereals). Pigs, chickens, and dogs were also kept for food, but the surrounding sea yielded the most important source of protein.

Numerous taboos regulated Polynesian life, such as prohibitions against taking certain plants or fish that were reserved for exploitation by the chiefs. Land was collectively owned by families and tribes, and there were nobles and commoners. Though the land was worked collectively by commoners, the chiefly families controlled and distributed its produce by well-defined customs. Large numbers of people could be mobilized for public works or war.

Two related forces governed Polynesian life: mana and *tapu*. Mana was a spiritual power of which the gods and high chiefs had the most and the commoners the least. In this rigid hierarchical system, marriage or even physical contact between persons of unequal mana was forbidden, and children resulting from sexual relations between the classes were killed. Our word "taboo" originated from the Polynesian *tapu*. Early missionaries would often publicly violate the taboos and smash the images of the gods to show that their mana had vanished.

Gods

The Polynesians worshipped a pantheon of gods, who had more mana than any human. The most important were Tangaroa (the creator and god of the oceans), and Oro, or Tu (the god of war), who demanded human sacrifices. The most fascinating figure in Polynesian mythology was Maui, a Krishna- or Prometheus-like figure who caught the sun with a cord to give its fire to the world. He lifted the firmament to prevent it from crushing mankind, fished the islands out of the ocean with a hook, and was killed trying to gain the prize of immortality for humanity. Also worth noting is Hina, the heroine who fled to the moon to avoid incest with her brother, and so the sound of her tapa beater wouldn't bother anyone. Tane (the god of light) and Rongo (the god of agriculture and peace) were other important gods.

The old Polynesian religions of Western Polynesia were low-key, with few priests or cult images. No temples have been found in Tonga and very few in Samoa. There was an undercurrent of ancestor worship, but this was nowhere as strong as in Melanesia. The ancestors were more important as a source of descent for social ranking, and genealogies were carefully preserved. Surviving elements of the old religion are the still-widespread belief in spirits, the continuing use of traditional medicine, and the influence of myth. More than 150 years after conversion by early missionaries, most Polynesians maintain their early Christian piety and fervid devotion.

RELIGION

Religion plays an important role in the lives of the Polynesians, holding communities together and defending moral values. No other non-European region of the world is as solidly Christian as the South Pacific, and unfortunately it sometimes seems to be one of the most uncritical, obedient, narrow-minded, and hypocritical strains of Christianity extant on the planet. The first missionaries to arrive were Protestants, and Catholic missionaries landed much later. The established Protestant denominations are the Methodists of Tonga and the Congregationalists of Samoa and Niue. The South Pacific is one of the few areas of the world with a large surplus of ministers of religion.

Since the 1960s, the old rivalry between Protestant and Catholic has been largely replaced by an avalanche of well-financed American fundamentalist missionary groups that divide families and spread confusion in an area already strongly Christian. While the indigenous churches have long been localized, the new evangelical sects are dominated by foreign personnel, ideas, and money. American televangelists proselytize from TV screens clear across the South Pacific Bible Belt and the ultraconservative outlook of the new religious imperialists continues the tradition of allying Christianity with colonialism or neocolonialism.

The fundamentalists tend to portray God as a white man and discourage self-sufficiency by telling the islanders to await their reward in heaven. They stress passages in the Bible calling for obedience to authority and resignation, often providing the ideological justification for the repression of dissent. "Liberation theologists," on the other hand, whether Catholic or Protestant, try to apply the spirit of the Bible to everyday life by discussing social problems and protecting the human rights of all. The late Roman Catholic Bishop of Tonga, Patelisio Finau, was a good example of a church leader with the courage to identify social injustices and take an active role in correcting them.

Of course, the optimum way to experience religion in the South Pacific is to go to church on Sunday. Just be aware that the services can last one and a half hours and will often be in the local language. If you decide to go, don't get up and walk out in the middle—see it through. You'll be rewarded by the joyous singing and fellowship, and you'll encounter the islanders on a different level. After church, people gather for a family meal or picnic and spend the rest of the day relaxing and socializing. If you're a guest in an island home you'll be invited to accompany them to church.

The Mormons

Mormon missionaries arrived on Tubuai in the Austral Islands as early as 1844, and today "Mormonia" covers much of the South Pacific. You don't have to travel far in the South Pacific to find the assembly-line Mormon chapels, schools, and sporting facilities, paid for by church members who are expected to tithe 10% of their incomes. The Mormon church spends over US$500 million a year on foreign missions and sends out almost 50,000 missionaries, more than any other American church by far. Like Thor Heyerdahl, Mormons believe that Polynesia was settled by American Indians, who were themselves descendants of the 10 lost tribes of Israel, and that they must be reconverted to hasten the second coming of Christ. So the present church is willing to spend a lot of time and money spreading the word.

The Mormons are especially successful in countries like Tonga and Samoa, which are too poor to provide public education for all. Mormon fascination with genealogy parallels the importance of descent in Polynesian society where it often determines land rights. There's a strong link to Hawaii's Brigham Young University (www.byuh.edu), and many island students help pay for their schooling by representing their home country at the Mormon-owned Polynesian Cultural Center on Oahu. The pairs of clean-cut young Mormon "elders" seen in the islands—each in shirt and tie, riding a bicycle or driving a minibus—are sent down from the States for two-year stays.

LANGUAGE

Some 1,200 languages, a third of the world's total, are spoken in the Pacific islands, though most have very few speakers. The Austronesian language family includes over 900 distinct languages spoken in an area stretching from Madagascar to Easter Island. Of all the Oceanic languages, only the Papuan languages spoken in New Guinea and the Solomons do not belong to this group. English is the predominant language of business and government.

Polynesian

The Polynesians speak about 21 closely related languages with local variations and consonantal changes. They're mutually unintelligible to those who haven't learned them, although they have many words in common. For instance, the word for land varies between *whenua, fenua, fanua, fonua, honua, vanua,* and *henua.* In the Polynesian languages the words are softened by the removal of certain consonants. Thus the

Tagalog word for coconut, *niog,* became *niu, ni,* or *nu.* They're musical languages whose accent lies mostly on the vowels. Polynesian is rhetorical and poetical but not scientific, and to adapt to modern life many words have been borrowed from European languages; these too are infused with vowels to make them more melodious to the Polynesian ear. Special vocabularies used to refer to or address royalty or the aristocracy also exist.

CONDUCT AND CUSTOMS

Foreign travel is an exceptional experience enjoyed by a privileged few. Too often, tourists try to transfer their lifestyles to tropical islands, thereby missing out on what is unique to the region. Travel can be a learning experience if approached openly and with a positive attitude, so read up on the local culture before you arrive and become aware of the social and environmental problems of the area. A wise traveler soon graduates from hearing and seeing to listening and observing. Speaking is good for the ego and listening is good for the soul.

The path is primed with packaged pleasures, but pierce the bubble of tourism and you'll encounter something far from the schedules and organized efficiency: a time to learn how other people live. Walk gently, for human qualities are as fragile and responsive to abuse as the brilliant reefs. The islanders are by nature softspoken and reserved. Often they won't show open disapproval if their social codes are broken, but don't underestimate them: they understand far more than you think. Consider that you're only one of thousands of visitors to their country, so don't expect to be treated better than anyone else. Respect is one of the most important things in life and humility is also greatly appreciated.

Don't try for a bargain if it means someone will be exploited. What enriches you may violate others. Be sensitive to the feelings of those you wish to "shoot" with your camera and ask their permission first. Don't promise things you can't or won't deliver. Keep your time values to yourself; the islanders lead an unstressful lifestyle and assume you are there to share it.

If you're alone you're lucky, for the single traveler is everyone's friend. Get away from other tourists and meet the people. There aren't many places on earth where you can still do this meaningfully, but the South Pacific is one. If you do meet people with similar interests, keep in touch by writing. This is no tourist's paradise, though,

and local residents are not exhibits or paid performers. They have just as many problems as you, and if you see them as real people you're less likely to be viewed as a stereotypical tourist. You may have come to escape civilization, but keep in mind that you're just a guest.

Most important of all, try to see things their way. Take an interest in local customs, values, languages, challenges, and successes. If things work differently than they do back home, give thanks—that's why you've come. Reflect on what you've experienced and you'll return home with a better understanding of how much we all have in common, outwardly different as we may seem. Do that and your trip won't have been wasted.

The Pacific Way

A smile costs nothing but is priceless. Islanders smile at one another; tourists look the other way. In Western societies wealth is based on the accumulation of goods; in Pacific societies it's based on how much you can give away. Obligations define an individual's position in society, while sharing provides the security that holds a community together. If people are hospitable, look for some way of repaying their kindness and never exploit their goodwill. It's an island custom that a gift must be reciprocated, which is why tipping has never caught on.

Questions

The islanders are eager to please, so phrase your questions carefully. They'll answer yes or no according to what they think you want to hear—don't suggest the answer in your question. Test this by asking your informant to confirm something you know to be incorrect. Also don't ask negative questions, such as "you're not going to Apia, are you?" Invariably the answer will be "yes," meaning "yes, I'm not going to Apia." It also could work like this: "Don't you have anything cheaper?" "Yes." "What do you have that is cheaper?" "Nothing." Yes, he doesn't have anything cheaper. If you want to be sure of something, ask several people the same question in different ways.

Dress

It's important to know that the dress code in the islands is strict. Short shorts, halter tops, and bathing costumes in public are considered offensive: a *lavalava* wrapped around you solves this one. Women should wear dresses that adequately cover their legs while seated. Nothing will mark you so quickly as a tourist, and—if you're a woman—send the wrong signal to the local men, than scanty dress. Of course, there *is* a place for it: on the beach in front of a resort hotel. In a society where even bathing suits are considered extremely risqué for local women, public nudity is unthinkable.

Women

In many traditional island cultures a woman seen wandering aimlessly along a remote beach or country road was thought to be in search of male companionship, and "no" meant "yes." Single women hiking, camping, sunbathing, and simply traveling alone may be seen in the same light, an impression strongly reinforced by the type of videos available in the islands. In some cultures local women rarely travel without men, and some day-hikes and interisland ship journeys mentioned in this book may be uncomfortable or even dangerous for women. Two women together will have little to worry about in most cases, especially if they're well covered and look purposeful. But the danger of sexual assault does exist.

Women traveling alone should avoid staying in isolated tourist bungalows or *fales* by themselves—it's wise to team up with other travelers before heading to the beach. In many Polynesian cultures there's a custom known as "sleep crawling" in which a boy silently enters a girl's home at night and lies beside her to prove his bravery, and visiting women sometimes become objects of this type of unwanted attention.

Annette Nyberg of Sweden sent us this:

The South Pacific is an easy place for a single woman, as long as she's not stupid. I'm talking about shorts, minitops, bikinis, etc., which place an unnecessary barrier between you and the local women. In the handbook a lot of traditional ceremonies are described, and I think it's important to point out that some of them (such as a traditional kava party) are open to men only. On the other hand, as a woman I could sit down with the local women when they were weaving, cooking, etc. and get plenty of contact, something a man couldn't do. There's nothing like weaving a mat to make a Tongan woman more talkative! I've had "complicated" discussions I believe wouldn't have taken place if both of us hadn't been so occupied with those pandanus leaves! Don't attempt to be an "independent modern woman" trying to get a close look at every aspect of village life, but take advantage of those opportunities which come naturally from your being a woman.

Women planning a trip on their own can obtain useful general information on what to expect by visiting www.journeywoman.com.

Children

Karen Addison of Sussex, England, sent us the following:

Traveling with children can have its ups and downs, but in the Pacific it's definitely an up. Pacific islanders are warm, friendly people, but with children you see them at their best. Your children are automatically accepted, and you, as an extension of them, are as well. As the majority of the islands are free of any deadly bugs or diseases, acclimatizing to the water, food, and climate would be your paramount concern. Self-contained units, where you can do your own cooking, are easy to find and cheap; having set meals every day gives children a sense of security. Not having television as a distraction, I've attempted to teach my son the rudiments of reading and writing. As a single mother with a little boy, traveling with him opened my eyes to things I'd normally overlook and has been an education to us both.

18th-century Tongan men preparing an umu (earth oven)

M.G.L. DOMENY DE RIENZI

ON THE ROAD
SPORTS AND RECREATION

Scuba Diving

Scuba diving is offered in resort areas throughout the region, with certification courses usually available. The waters are warm, varying less than one degree centigrade between the surface and 100 meters, so a wetsuit is not essential (although it will protect you from coral cuts). Lagoon diving is recommended for beginners; those with some experience will find the most beautiful coral along reef dropoffs and the most fish around passes into the lagoon.

Commercial scuba operators know their waters and will be able to show you the most amazing things in perfect safety. Dive centers at all the main resorts operate year-round, with marinelife most profuse July to November. Before strapping on a tank and fins you'll have to show your scuba certification card, and occasionally divers are also asked to show a medical report from their doctor indicating that they are in good physical condition. A one-tank dive with equipment will cost about US$55. Most dive shops tack on an extra US$10 or more for "equipment rental" (regulator, buoyancy compensator, and gauges) and frequent divers will save a lot by bringing their own. Precise information on scuba diving is provided throughout this handbook, immediately after the sightseeing sections.

Many of the scuba operators listed in this book offer introductory "resort courses" for those who only want a taste of scuba diving, and full NAUI or PADI open-water certification courses for those wishing to dive more than once or twice. Scuba training will enhance your understanding and enjoyment of the sea.

Snorkeling

Scuba diving can become expensive if you get addicted, but snorkeling is free—all you need is a mask and pipe. Be careful, however, and know

10 SAFETY RULES OF DIVING

1. The most important rule in scuba diving is to BREATHE CONTINUOUSLY. If you establish this rule, you won't forget and hold your breath, and overexpansion will never occur.

2. COME UP AT A RATE OF 18 METERS PER MINUTE OR LESS. This allows the gas dissolved in you body under pressure to come out of solution safely and also prevents vertigo from fast ascents. Always make a precautionary decompression stop at a depth of five meters.

3. NEVER ESCAPE TO THE SURFACE. Panic is the diver's worst enemy.

4. STOP, THINK, THEN ACT. Always maintain control.

5. PACE YOURSELF. KNOW YOUR LIMITATIONS. A DIVER SHOULD ALWAYS BE ABLE TO REST AND RELAX IN THE WATER. Proper use of the buoyancy vest will allow you to rest on the surface and maintain control under water. A diver who becomes fatigued in the water is a danger to himself and his buddy.

6. NEVER DIVE WITH A COLD. Avoid alcoholic beverages but drink plenty of water. Get a good night's sleep and refrain from strenuous physical activities on the day you dive. Dive conservatively if you are overweight or more than 45 years of age. Make fewer dives the last two days before flying and no dives at all during the final 24 hours.

7. PLAN YOUR DIVE. Know your starting point, your diving area, and your exit areas. DIVE YOUR PLAN.

8. NEVER EXCEED THE SAFE SPORT DIVING LIMIT OF 30 METERS. Make your first dive the deepest of the day.

9. All equipment must be equipped with QUICK RELEASES.

10. WEAR ADEQUATE PROTECTIVE CLOTHING AGAINST SUN AND CORAL.

the dangers. Practice snorkeling over a shallow sandy bottom and don't head into deep water or swim over coral until you're sure you've got the hang of it. Breathe easily; don't hyperventilate. When snorkeling on a fringing reef, beware of deadly currents and undertows in channels that drain tidal flows. Before going into the water, ask a local to point the channels out to you, and observe the direction the water is flowing before you swim into it. If you feel yourself being dragged out to sea through a reef passage, try swimming across the current rather than against it. If you can't resist the pull at all, it may be better to let yourself be carried out. Wait till the current diminishes, then swim along the outer reef face until you find somewhere to come back in. Or use your energy to attract the attention of someone onshore.

Snorkeling on the outer edge or drop-off of a reef is thrilling for the variety of fish and corals, but attempt it only on a very calm day. Even then it's wise to have someone stand onshore or paddle behind you in a canoe to watch for occasional big waves, which can take you by surprise and smash you into the rocks. Also, beware of unperceived currents outside the reef—you may not get a second chance. Many scuba operators will take snorkelers out on their regular trips for a third to a quarter the cost of diving. This is an easy way to reach some good snorkeling spots, just don't expect to be chaperoned for that price.

A far better idea is to limit your snorkeling to the protected inner reef and leave the open waters to the scuba diver. Yet while scuba diving quickly absorbs large amounts of money, snorkeling is free and you can do it as often as you like. You'll encounter the brightest colors in shallow waters anyway as beneath six meters the colors blue out as short wavelengths are lost. By diving with a tank you trade off the chance to observe shallow water species in order to gain access to the often larger deep water species. The best solution is to do a bit of both. In any case, avoid touching the reef or any of its creatures as the contact can be very harmful to both you and the reef. Take only pictures and leave only bubbles.

Ocean Kayaking
This is a viable sport best practiced in sheltered lagoons, such as the one at Vava'u (Tonga).

You can rent kayaks in some places, but it's better to bring your own folding kayak. See **Getting Around,** later in this chapter, for more information on kayaking.

Yachting
Cruising the South Pacific by yacht is also covered in Getting Around, and for those with less time there are several established yacht charter operations based at Vava'u. Turn to **Getting There,** which follows, and check the **Vava'u** section of this book.

Hiking
This is an excellent, inexpensive way to see the islands. Two outstanding treks covered in this handbook are Lake Lanoto'o on Upolu and Mt. Matafao on Tutuila, and there are many others, especially in Samoa.

Surfing
The region's most renowned surfing camps are the Ha'atafu Beach Resort on Tongatapu and the Salani Surf Resort on Upolu. Other famous Samoan surfing spots include Lauli'i and Sololo on Upolu, and Salailua and Lano on Savai'i. The top surfing season is generally July-Sept. when the tradewinds push the Antarctic swells north. During the hurricane season Jan.-March tropical storms can generate some spectacular waves. Pago Pago Harbor would be the windsurfing locale par excellence if the quality of the water weren't so poor.

Hunting and Fishing
There isn't much to hunt in the islands, and the wretches who shoot flying foxes and birds are worthy only of contempt. Sportfishing is also a questionable activity—especially spearfishing, which is sort of like shooting a cow with a handgun. An islander who spearfishes to feed his family is one thing, but the tourist who does it for fun is perhaps worthy of the attention of sharks. Deep-sea game fishing from gas-guzzling powerboats isn't much better, and it's painful to see noble fish slaughtered and strung up just to inflate someone's ego. That said, one has to admit that taking fish from the sea one by one for sport is never going to endanger the stocks the way net fishing by huge trawlers does. It's a viable sport and we cover it throughout this book. On most big-game boats, the captain keeps the catch.

Golf
One benign vestige of colonialism is the abundance of golf courses throughout the South Pacific, and virtually all are open to visitors. Greens fees are reasonable: Tonga Golf Club, US$4; Tutuila's 'Ili'ili Golf Course, US$7; Apia's Royal Samoa Country Club, US$7. Club and cart rentals are usually available for a bit less than the greens fees and most of the courses have clubhouses with pleasant colonial-style bars.

Package tours incorporating the activities just mentioned are described under **Getting There** in this introduction. For information on bicycling, see **Getting There,** which follows.

ENTERTAINMENT

Considering the large expatriate presence and the temperature, it's not surprising that the South Seas has its fair share of colorful bars where canned or bottled beer is consumed cold in amazing quantities. These are good places to meet local characters at happy hour around 1700, and many bars become discos after 2200. Respectably attired visitors are welcome at the ex-colonial "clubs," where the beer prices are generally lower and the clientele more sedate. Barefoot (or flip-flop-shod) beachcombers in T-shirts and shorts may be refused entry, and you should take off your hat as you come in. Don't overlook the resort bars, where the swank surroundings cost only slightly more.

A small glass of draft beer at a normal bar will cost just over US$1 in Samoa, under US$2.50 in Tonga, and US$3 or more in American Samoa. Needless to say, Apia is a beer drinkers paradise. Don't worry about the quality as it's excellent everywhere, in fact, despite the price, Samoa's Vailima beer may be the best.

Many tourist hotels run "island nights" or fia fia, feasts at which you get to taste the local food and see traditional dancing. If you don't wish to splurge on the meal, it's always possible to witness the spectacle for a cover charge and the price of a drink. These events are held weekly on certain days, so ask. On most islands Friday night is the time to let it all hang out; on Saturday many people are preparing for a family get-together or church on Sunday. Everything grinds to a halt Saturday at midnight and Sunday is very quiet—a good day to go hiking or to the beach.

It's cheap to go to the movies, though romance, horror, and adventure are standard fare, and as everywhere, good psychological films are the exception. Video fever is an island craze, and you often see throngs of locals crowded into someone's living room watching a violent and/or sexy tape rented from one of the ubiquitous video rental shops. Some guesthouses have video too, so make sure your room is well away from it.

Music and Dance

Traditional music and dance is alive and well in the South Pacific. British ethnomusicologist David Fanshawe (see **Resources**) has suggested that the sitting dances common in Tonga and elsewhere may be related to the movements of the upper part of the body while paddling a canoe. The graceful *siva* of Samoa is unforgettable.

The slit-log gong beaten with a wooden stick is a common instrument throughout Polynesia. Nose flutes were once used in Tonga and the 'Atenisi Institute has tried to revive the art. In the early 19th century, missionaries replaced the old chants of Polynesia with the harmonious gospel singing heard in the islands today, yet even the hymns were transformed into an original Oceanic medium. Contemporary Pacific music includes brass bands and localized Anglo-American pop. String bands have made European instruments such as the guitar and ukulele an integral part of Pacific music.

HOLIDAYS AND FESTIVALS

The special events, holidays, and festivals of each island group are described in the respective chapters. Their dates of observance often vary from year to year, so it's good to contact the local tourist information office soon after your arrival to learn just what will be happening during your stay. The most important annual festivals are the following:

April: Flag Day in American Samoa
May: Vava'u Festival, Tonga
May: Tourism Week in American Samoa
June: Ha'apai Festival, Tonga

June: Independence Celebrations in Apia, Samoa
July: Heilala Festival at Nuku'alofa, Tonga
September: Teuila Tourism Festival in Apia, Samoa
October: White Sunday in both Samoas
October: Moso'oi Tourism Festival in American Samoa
October: Constitution Celebrations on Niue

Catch as many of these as you can and try to participate in what's happening, rather than merely watching like a tourist.

ARTS AND CRAFTS

Tonga and Samoa are good countries in which to purchase handicrafts. Not surprisingly, the traditional handicrafts that have survived best are the practical arts done by women (weaving, basketmaking, tapa). Polynesian men produce fine woodcarvings, especially kava bowls and war clubs. In cases where the items still perform their original function (such as the astoundingly intricate fine mats of Samoa—not for sale to tourists), they remain as vital as ever.

A tourist will purchase whatever corresponds to his image of the producing community and is small enough to be accepted as airline luggage. Thus a visitor to Samoa may be looking for masks, figures with large penises, or carvings of pigs, even though none of these has any place in Samoan tradition. The mock-Hawaiian "tikis" of Tonga also have no precedents in traditional Tongan art. Traditionally, the Polynesians used no masks and few colors, usually leaving their works unpainted.

Whenever possible buy handicrafts from local women's committee shops, church groups, local markets, or from the craftspeople themselves, but avoid objects made from turtle shell/leather, clam shell, or marine mammal ivory, which are prohibited entry into many countries under endangered species acts. Failure to declare such items to customs officers can lead to heavy fines. Also resist the temptation to purchase jewelry or other items made from seashells and coral, the collection of which damages the reefs. Souvenirs made from straw or seeds may be held for fumigation or confiscated upon arrival.

Weaving

Woven articles are the most widespread handicrafts, with examples in almost every South Seas country. Pandanus fiber is the most common, but coconut leaf and husk, vine tendril, banana stem, and tree and shrub bark are all used. On some islands the fibers are passed through a fire, boiled, then bleached in the sun. Vegetable dyes of very lovely mellow tones are sometimes used, but gaudier store dyes are much more prevalent. Shells are occasionally utilized to cut, curl, or make the fibers pliable. Polynesian woven arts are characterized by colorful, skillful patterns.

Tapa

To make tapa (*siapo* in Samoan), the white inner bark of the tall, thin paper mulberry tree *(Broussonetia papyrifera)* is stripped and scraped with shells, rolled into a ball, and soaked in water. The sodden strips are then pounded with wooden mallets until they reach four or five times their original length and width. Next, several pieces are placed one on top of another, pressed and pounded, and joined together with a manioc juice paste. Sheets of tapa feel like felt when finished.

In Tonga, tapa (*ngatu*) is decorated by stitching coconut fiber designs onto a woven pandanus base that is placed under the tapa, and the stain is rubbed on in the same manner one makes temple rubbings from a stone inscription. The artisan then fills in the patterns freehand. Sunlight deepens and sets the copper brown colors.

Each island group has its characteristic colors and patterns, ranging from plantlike paintings to geometric designs. On some islands tapa is still used for clothing, bedding, and room dividers, and as ceremonial red carpets. Tablecloths, bedcovers, place mats, and wall hangings of tapa make handsome souvenirs.

an antique Tongan coconut fiber bag adorned with shell beads

ACCOMMODATIONS

Hotels

With *Tonga-Samoa Handbook* in hand you're guaranteed a good, inexpensive place to stay on every island. Each and every hotel in the region is included herein, not just a selection. We do this consistently to give you a solid second reference in case your travel agent or someone else recommends a certain place. To allow you the widest possible choice, all price categories are included, and we've tried to indicate which properties offer value for money. If you think we're wrong or you were badly treated, be sure to send a written complaint to the author of this handbook. Equally important, let us know when you agree with what's there or if you think a place deserves a better rave. Your letter will have an impact!

Throughout the region, double rooms with shared bath at budget guesthouses average US$20-40, dorm beds US$6-12 pp. The least expensive accommodations are found in Tonga and Samoa, but in American Samoa very few rooms are as low as US$40 double. Moving into the medium-price category, you'll be able to get a quality a/c room with all the facilities for US$75 double almost anywhere. Unlike Tahiti and Fiji, there aren't a lot of luxury hotels in these islands, although a couple of upscale resorts exist on the south side of Upolu. Even if you don't plan on staying at any of the expensive city hotels, they're still worth visiting as sightseeing attractions, watering holes, or sources of entertainment.

Dormitory, guesthouse, or backpacker accommodations are available on all the islands, with communal cooking facilities usually provided. If you're traveling alone these are excellent since they're just the place to meet other travelers. Couples can usually get a double room for a price only slightly above two dorm beds. For the most part, the dormitories are safe and congenial for those who don't mind sacrificing their privacy to save money. Needless to say, always ask the price of your accommodations before accepting them. Otherwise, hotel prices are usually fixed and bargaining isn't the normal way to go.

Be aware that some of the low-budget places included in this book are a lot more basic than what are sometimes referred to as "budget" accommodations in the States. The standards of cleanliness in the common bathrooms may be lower than you expected, the furnishings "early attic," the beds uncomfortable, linens and towels skimpy, housekeeping nonexistent, and window screens lacking, but ask yourself, where in the U.S. are you going to find a room for a similar price? Luckily, good medium-priced accommodations are usually available for those of us unwilling to put up with Spartan conditions, and we include all of them in this book too.

A new development in Samoa is the appearance of basic beach resorts run by local families who supply meals, bedding, and *fale* (hut) accommodations at set rates. See the Samoa chapter for details. This is genuine ecotourism for you, and we hope people on some of the other islands catch on and start doing the same sort of thing.

When picking a hotel, keep in mind that although a thatched bungalow is cooler and infinitely more attractive than a concrete box, it's also more likely to have insect problems. If in doubt check the window screens and carry mosquito coils and/or repellent. Hopefully there'll be a resident lizard or two to feed on the bugs. Always turn on a light before getting out of bed to use the facilities at night, as even the finest hotels in the tropics have cockroaches.

ACCOMMODATIONS PRICE RANGES

Throughout this book, accommodations are generally grouped in the price categories which follow. Of course, currency fluctuations and inflation can lead to slight variations.

Shoestring	under US$15 double
Budget	US$15-35 double
Inexpensive	US$35-60 double
Moderate	US$60-85 double
Expensive	US$85-110 double
Premium	US$110-150 double
Luxury	over US$150 double

ECOTOURISM

Recently "ecotourism" has become the thing, and with increasing concern in Western countries over the damaging impact of solar radiation, more and more people are looking for land-based activities as an alternative to lying on the beach. This trend is also fueled by the "baby boomers" who hitchhiked around Europe in the 1970s. Today they're looking for more exotic locales in which to practice "soft adventure tourism" and they've got a lot more money to spend this time around. In the South Pacific the most widespread manifestation of the ecotourism/adventure phenomenon is the current scuba diving boom, and tours by chartered yacht, ocean kayak, surfboard, bicycle, or on foot are proliferating.

This presents both a danger and an opportunity. Income from visitors wishing to experience nature gives local residents and governments an incentive for preserving the environment, although tourism can quickly degrade that environment through littering, the collection of coral and shells, and the development of roads, docks, and resorts in natural areas. Means of access created for ecotourists often end up being used by local residents whose priority is not conservation. Perhaps the strongest argument in favor of the creation of national parks and reserves in the South Pacific is the ability of such parks to attract visitors from industrialized countries while at the same time creating a framework for the preservation of nature. For in the final analysis, it is governments that must enact regulations to protect the environment—market forces usually do the opposite.

Too often what is called ecotourism is actually packaged consumer tourism with a green coating, or just an excuse for high prices. Some four-wheel-drive jeep safaris, jet boat excursions, and heli-copter trips have more to do with ecoterrorism than ecotourism. In 1997 the Tourism Council of the South Pacific conferred its highest ecotourism award on a local guide on Niue who captured endangered coconut crabs for the amusement of tourists!

A genuine ecotourism resort will be built of local materials using natural ventilation. This means no air conditioning and only limited use of fans. The buildings will fit into the natural landscape and not restrict access to customary lands or the sea. Local fish and vegetables will have preference over imported meats on tourist tables, and wastes will be minimized. The use of aggressive motorized transport will be kept to an absolute minimum. Cultural sensitivity will be enhanced by profit sharing with the landowning clans and local participation in ownership. It's worth considering all of this as a flood of phony ecotourism facilities are popping up.

Through this handbook we've tried to encourage this type of people-oriented tourism, which we feel is more directly beneficial to the islanders themselves. Whenever possible we've featured smaller, family-operated, locally owned businesses. By patronizing these you'll not only get to meet the inhabitants on a person-to-person basis, but also contribute to local development. Guesthouse tourism offers excellent employment opportunities for island women as proprietors, *and* it's exactly what most visitors want. Appropriate tourism requires little investment, there's less disruption, and full control remains with the people themselves. The luxury a/c hotels are monotonously uniform around the world—the South Pacific's the place for something different. (For a more complete discussion of this topic than can be included here, click on www2.planeta.com/mader/ecotravel/etour.html.)

A room with cooking facilities can save you a lot on restaurant meals, and some moderately priced establishments have weekly rates. If you have to choose a meal plan, take only breakfast and dinner (Modified American Plan) and have fruit for lunch. As you check into your room, note the nearest fire exits. And don't automatically take the first room offered; if you're paying good money look at several, then choose.

Reserving Ahead

Booking accommodations in advance usually works to your disadvantage as full-service travel agents will begin by trying to sell you their most expensive properties (which pay them the highest commissions) and work down from there. The quite adequate middle and budget places included in this handbook often aren't on their screens or are sold at highly inflated prices. Herein we usually provide the rates for direct local bookings, and if you book through a travel agent abroad you could end up paying considerably more as multiple commissions are tacked on. Thus we suggest you avoid making any hotel reservations at all before arriving in the South Pacific (unless you're coming for a major event).

We don't know of any island where it's to your advantage to book ahead in the medium to lower price range, but you can sometimes obtain substantial discounts at the top hotels by including them as part of a package tour. Even then, you'll almost always find medium-priced accommodations for less than the package price and your freedom of choice won't be impaired. If, however, you intend to spend most of your time at a specific first-class hotel, you'll benefit from bulk rates by taking a package tour instead of paying the higher "rack rate" the hotels charge to individuals who just walk in off the beach. Call Air New Zealand's toll-free number and ask them to mail you their *Go As You Please* brochure, which lists deluxe hotel rooms in Tonga and Samoa that can be booked on an individual basis at slightly reduced rates. Polynesian Airlines has a similar *Polypac Hotel Accommodation* brochure covering their destinations. Also call Discover Wholesale Travel and some of the other agents listed herein in **Getting There.**

Camping

Organized campgrounds exist in Tonga and Samoa. Elsewhere get permission of the landowner; you'll rarely be refused in places off the beaten track. Set a good precedent by not leaving a mess or violating cultural norms. If you pitch your tent near a village or on private property without asking permission, you're asking for problems. Otherwise, camp out in the bush well away from gardens and trails.

Make sure your tent is water- and mosquito-proof, and try to find a spot swept by the trades. Never camp under a coconut tree, as falling coconuts hurt (actually, coconuts have two eyes so they only strike the wicked). If you hear a hurricane warning, pack up your tent and take immediate cover with the locals.

FOOD AND DRINK

The traditional diet of the Pacific islanders consists of root crops and fruit, plus lagoon fish and the occasional pig. The vegetables include taro, cassava (manioc), breadfruit, and sweet potatoes. The sweet potato *(kumala)* is something of an anomaly—it's the only Pacific food plant with a South American origin. How it got to the islands is not known.

Taro is an elephant-eared plant cultivated in freshwater swamps. Papaya (pawpaw) is nourishing: a third of a cup contains as much vitamin C as 18 apples. To ripen a green papaya overnight, puncture it a few times with a knife. Don't overeat papaya—unless you *need* an effective laxative.

Raw fish or *sashimi* (called *oka* in Samoan and *ota* in Tongan) is an appetizing dish enjoyed in many Pacific countries. To prepare it, clean and skin the fish, then dice the fillet. Squeeze lemon or lime juice over it, and store in a cool place about 10 hours. When it's ready to serve, add chopped onions, garlic, green peppers, tomatoes, and coconut cream to taste. Local fishmongers know which species make the best raw fish, but know what you're doing before you join them—island stomachs are probably stronger than yours. Health experts recommend eating only well-cooked foods and peeling your own fruit, but the islanders swear by raw fish.

Lobsters have become almost an endangered species on some islands due to the high prices they fetch on restaurant tables. Countless more are airfreighted to Hawaii and Tokyo. Before asking for one of these creatures to be sacrificed for your dinner, consider that the world will be poorer for it. Coconut crabs are even more threatened and it's almost scandalous that local governments should allow them to be fed to tourists. Sea turtles and flying foxes are other delicacies to avoid, although these are seldom offered to tourists.

Never order mutton at a restaurant as the lowest quality New Zealand mutton flaps are exported to the South Pacific and you could get some very fatty pieces. Also beware of "exotic" meats like "lamb" and goat to which your stomach may not be accustomed. The turkey tails shipped in from the U.S. are solid chunks of fat. Chicken is safer provided it is freshly cooked. In general, the low-fat or diet foods popular in the States are unknown in the islands. Vegetarianism is poorly understood.

Islanders in the towns now eat mostly imported foods, just as we Westerners often opt for fast foods instead of meals made from basic ingredients. The Seventh-Day Adventists don't smoke, dance, eat pork or rabbit, or drink tea, coffee, or alcohol. If you're going to a remote area, take as many edibles with you as you can; they're always more expensive there. And keep in mind that virtually every food plant you see growing on the islands is cultivated by someone. Even sea shells washed up on a beach, or fish in the lagoon near someone's home, may be considered private property.

Restaurants

Eating out is an adventure, and first-rate restaurants are found in all the main towns, so whenever your travels start to get to you and it's time for a lift, splurge on a good meal and then see how the world looks. Nuku'alofa, Apia, and Pago Pago offer an increasing number of good inexpensive places to eat.

You should be able to get a filling meal at a restaurant serving the local population for under US$3 in Samoa and Tonga, and for under US$5 in American Samoa. At a tourist restaurant, expect to pay about US$12 throughout the region. Unlike Australia and New Zealand, it's not customary to bring your own (BYO) booze into restaurants.

Cooking

The ancient Polynesians stopped making pottery over a millennium ago and instead developed an ingenious way of cooking in an underground earth oven known as an *umu*. First a stack of dry coconut husks is burned in a pit. Once the fire is going well, coral stones are heaped on top, and when most of the husks have burnt away the food is wrapped in banana leaves and placed on the hot stones—fish and meat below, vegetables above. A whole pig may be cleaned, then stuffed with banana leaves and hot stones. This cooks the beast from inside out as well as outside in, and the leaves create steam. The food is then covered with more leaves and stones, and after about two and a half hours everything is cooked.

THE COCONUT PALM

Human life would not be possible on most of the Pacific's far-flung atolls without this all-purpose tree. It reaches maturity in eight years, then produces about 50 nuts a year for 60 years. Aside from the tree's esthetic value and usefulness in providing shade, the water of the green coconut provides a refreshing drink, and the white meat of the young nut is a delicious food. The harder meat of more mature nuts is grated and squeezed, giving rise to a coconut cream eaten alone or used in cooking. The oldest nuts are cracked open, the hard meat removed, then dried to be sold as copra. It takes about 6,000 coconuts to make a ton of copra. Copra is pressed to extract the oil, which in turn is made into candles, cosmetics, and soap. Scented with flowers, the oil nurtures the skin.

The juice or sap from the cut flower spathes of the palm provides toddy, a popular drink; the toddy is distilled into a spirit called arrack, the whiskey of the Pacific. Otherwise the sap can be boiled to make candy. Millionaire's salad is made by shredding the growth cut from the heart of the tree. For each salad, a fully mature tree must be sacrificed.

The nut's hard inner shell can be used as a cup and makes excellent firewood. Rope, cordage, brushes, and heavy matting are produced from the coir fiber of the husk. The smoke from burning husks is a most effective mosquito repellent. The leaves of the coconut tree are used to thatch the roofs of the islanders' cottages or are woven into baskets, mats, and fans. The trunk provides timber for building and furniture. Actually, these are only the common uses: there are many others as well.

RICHARD EASTWOOD

coconut palms, Fai'aai Beach, Savai'a Island

SERVICES AND INFORMATION

VISAS AND OFFICIALDOM

If you're from an English-speaking country or Western Europe you won't need a visa to visit the countries included herein. Unlike the U.S., which is very sticky about visas, American Samoa does not require a visa of most tourists (although travelers arriving at Pago Pago on the ferry from Apia have reported irregularities).

Everyone must have a passport, sufficient funds, and a ticket to leave. Your passport should be valid six months beyond your departure date. Some officials object to tourists who intend to camp or stay with friends, so write the name of a likely hotel on your arrival card (don't leave that space blank).

Immigration officials will often insist on seeing an air ticket back to your home country, no matter how much money you're able to show them. The easy way to get around this if you're on an open-ended holiday or traveling by yacht is to purchase a full-fare one-way ticket to Hawaii or Los Angeles from Air New Zealand. This will be accepted without question, and Air New Zealand offices throughout the Pacific will reissue the ticket, so you'll always have a ticket to leave from the next country on your itinerary. When you finally get home, you can turn in the unused coupons for a full refund. (See also **Getting There.**)

The easiest way to obtain a residence permit in Tonga or Samoa is to invest money in a small business. Both countries have special government departments intended to facilitate investment and the local tourist office will be able to tell you who to contact. As little as US$50,000 of capital may be required, and lots of low-tech opportunities exist in the tourist industry. Drawbacks are that you may be obliged to accept a local partner, you'll be subject to immediate deportation if get on the wrong side of any local politicians, and your residence permit will end as soon as you cease to be actively involved in the business. Unconditional permanent residence and citizenship are rarely granted to persons of ethnic origins other than those prevailing in the countries.

Customs

Agricultural regulations in most Pacific countries prohibit the import of fresh fruit, vegetables, flowers, seeds, honey, eggs, milk products, meat (including sausage), live animals and plants, as well as any old artifacts that might harbor pests. If in doubt, ask about having your souvenirs fumigated by the local agricultural authorities and a certificate issued prior to departure. Processed food or beverages, biscuits, confectionery, sugar, rice, seafood, dried flowers, mounted insects, mats, baskets, and tapa cloth are usually okay. If you've been on a farm, wash your clothes and shoes before going to the airport, and if you've been camping, make sure your tent is free of soil.

MONEY

All prices quoted herein are in the local currency unless otherwise stated. Each Monday the *Wall Street Journal* runs a "World Value of the Dollar" column that lists the current exchange rates of all Pacific currencies. If you have access to the internet you'll find most of the rates at www.oanda.com.

Both international airports in Samoa and Tongatapu airport have banks changing money at normal rates, but Pago Pago airport does not. The most convenient currencies to carry are Australian, N.Z., and U.S. dollars. If you'll be visiting American Samoa, be sure to have enough U.S. dollar traveler's checks to see you through, as foreign currencies are little known in the States and whopping commissions are charged.

The bulk of your travel funds should be in traveler's checks, preferably American Express, although that company has no representation in the region. To claim a refund for lost or stolen American Express traveler's checks, call their Sydney office collect (tel. 61-2/9886-0689). They'll also cancel lost credit cards, provided you know the numbers. The banks best represented in this part of the world are the ANZ Bank, the Bank of Hawaii, and the Westpac Bank, so if you need to have money sent, you'll want to work through one of them.

If you want to use a credit card, always ask beforehand, even if a business has a sign or brochure that says it's possible. Visa and MasterCard can be used to obtain cash advances at banks in most countries, but remember that cash advances accrue interest from the moment you receive the money—ask your bank if they have a debit card that allows charges to be deducted from your checking account automatically. The use of bank cards such as Visa and MasterCard is expensive in Samoa because thus the charge must first be converted into N.Z. dollars, then into your own currency, and you'll lose on the exchange several times. American Express is probably the best card to use as they don't go through third currencies (this could vary—ask).

When you rent a car the agency will probably ask you to sign a blank credit card charge slip as security on the vehicle. As you do so, be sure to count the number of pages in the slip, and if you later pay cash and the blank slip is returned to you, make you sure you get all the pages back. Otherwise a dishonest operator could have removed the page to be sent to the credit card company with the intention of processing the charge a second time. Another way to protect yourself is to retain the blank slip as proof that it was returned when you paid cash, but be sure to write Void across it in case it's stolen or lost. Also keep your signed cash receipt, and don't let your credit card out of sight, even for a moment. Credit card fraud is not common in the South Pacific, but cases have occurred.

Many banks now have automated teller machines (ATMs) outside their offices and these provide local currency against checking account Visa and MasterCard at good rates without commission. Occasionally the machines don't work due to problems with the software, in which case you'll almost always be able to get a cash advance at the counter inside. To avoid emergencies (such as if a machine were to "eat" your card), it's smart not to be too dependent on ATMs. Ask your bank what fee they'll charge if you use an ATM abroad and find out if you need a special personal identification number (PIN).

Cost-wise, you'll find Tonga and Samoa to be the least expensive countries. The lack of budget accommodations makes the price of a visit to American Samoa stiff. Inflation is high in Tonga and Samoa, something to keep in mind when looking at the prices in this book.

Upon departure avoid getting stuck with leftover local banknotes, as currencies such as Samoan *tala* and Tongan *pa'anga* are difficult to change and heavily discounted even in neighboring countries. Change whatever you have left over into the currency of the next country on your itinerary.

Don't show everyone how much money you have in your wallet, as this causes resentment and invites theft. Bargaining is not common: the first price you're quoted is usually it. Tipping is *not* customary in the South Pacific and often generates more embarrassment than gratitude.

POST AND TELECOMMUNICATIONS

Postal Services

Always use airmail when posting letters from the South Pacific. Airmail takes two weeks to reach North America and Europe, surface mail takes up to six months.

When writing to South Pacific individuals or businesses, include the post office box number, as mail delivery is rare. If it's a remote island or small village you're writing to, the person's name will be sufficient. Sending a picture postcard to an islander is a very nice way of saying thank you.

When collecting mail at general delivery, be sure to check under the initials of your first and second names, plus any initial that is similar. Have your correspondents print and underline your last name.

Telephone Services

Unfortunately, Tonga and Samoa still don't have card (or coin) telephones, and to place local calls you must go to a telephone center and book the call through a clerk at the desk. This situation is the result of the stranglehold inefficient state monopolies have over the local telephone systems there. Samoa's telephone system is easily the most primitive in the Pacific. Card phones for international calls do exist in Tonga and hopefully they'll made be available for domestic calls soon. American Samoa's system is adequate and local calls are only 10 cents from pay phones.

A three-minute station-to-station call to the U.S. will cost under US$7 from both Samoas and under US$8 from Tonga. Calling from the U.S. to the South Pacific is cheaper than going in the other direction, so if you want to talk to someone periodically, leave a list of your travel dates and hotel telephone numbers (provided in this book) where friends and relatives can try to get hold of you. All the main islands (except Samoa) have direct dialing via satellite.

To place a call to a Pacific island from outside the region, first dial the international access code (check your phone book), then the country code, then the number. The country codes are:

Tonga	676
Niue	683
American Samoa	684
Samoa	685

None of these countries have local area codes, but local telephone numbers have varying numbers of digits: four digits in Niue; five digits in Tonga and Samoa; and seven digits in American Samoa.

If a fax you are trying to send to the South Pacific doesn't go through smoothly on the first or second try, wait and try again at another time of day. If it doesn't work then, stop trying as the fax machine at the other end may not be able to read your signal, and your telephone company will levy a minimum charge for each attempt. Call the international operator to ask what is going wrong.

Electronic Mail

An increasing number of tourism-related businesses in the region have e-mail addresses, which makes communicating with them from abroad a lot cheaper and easier. To allow ourselves the flexibility of updating our listings more frequently, we have committed most e-mail and website addresses to this book's backmatter (some overseas addresses meant to be used prior to arrival are embedded in the introductions). If you use the web, have a look at that part of the appendix now, if you haven't already done so.

Websites and e-mail addresses based in the islands are recognizable by their country codes: American Samoa (as), Niue (nu), Samoa (ws), and Tonga (to). Some countries have made a profitable business out of selling website domain names using these codes.

When sending e-mail to the islands never include a large attached file with your message unless it has been specifically requested as the recipient may have to pay US$1 a minute in long distance telephone charges to download it. This is a serious breach of etiquette and not the best way to win friends or influence people.

TIME

The international date line generally follows 180 degrees longitude and creates a difference of 24 hours in time between the two sides. It swings east to avoid slicing Fiji in two. This can be confusing, as Tonga, which chooses to observe the same day as neighboring Fiji and New Zealand, has the same clock time as Samoa but is a day ahead! Everything in the Eastern Hemisphere west of the date line is a day later, everything in the Western Hemisphere east of the line is a day earlier (or behind). Air travelers lose a day when they fly west across the date line and gain it back when they return. Keep track of things by repeating to yourself, "If it's Sunday in Samoa, it's Monday for the monarch."

You're better off calling from North America to the South Pacific in the evening as it will be mid-afternoon in the islands (plus you'll probably benefit from off-peak telephone rates). From Europe, call very late at night. In the other direction, if you're calling from the islands to North America or Europe, do so in the early morning as it will already be afternoon in North America and evening in Europe. The local time at almost any point worldwide is available at www.isbister.com/worldtime.

In this book all clock times are rendered according to the 24-hour airline timetable system, i.e. 0100 is 1:00 a.m., 1300 is 1:00 p.m., 2330 is 11:30 p.m. The islanders operate on "coconut time"—the nut will fall when it is ripe. In the languid air of the South Seas punctuality takes on a new meaning. Appointments are approximate and service relaxed. Even the seasons are fuzzy: sometimes wetter, sometimes drier, but almost always hot. Slow down to the island pace and get in step with where you are. You may not get as much done, but you'll enjoy life a lot more. Daylight hours in the tropics run 0600-1800 with few seasonal variations.

WEIGHTS AND MEASURES

The metric system is used everywhere except in American Samoa. Study the conversion table in the back of this handbook if you're not used to thinking metric. Most distances herein are quoted in kilometers—they become easy to comprehend when you know than one km is the distance an average person walks in 10 minutes. A meter is slightly more than a yard and a liter is just over a quart.

Unless otherwise indicated, north is at the top of all maps in this handbook. When using official topographical maps you can determine the scale by taking the representative fraction (RF) and dividing by 100. This will give the number of meters represented by one centimeter. For example, a map with an RF of 1:10,000 would represent 100 meters for every centimeter on the map.

Electric Currents

If you're taking along a plug-in razor, radio, computer, electric immersion coil, or other electrical appliance, be aware that two different voltages are used in the South Pacific. American Samoa uses 110 volts AC, while the rest of the region uses 220-240 volts AC. Take care, however, as some luxury hotel rooms have 110-volt outlets as a convenience to North American visitors. A 220-volt appliance will only run too slowly in a 110-volt outlet, but a 110-volt appliance will quickly burn out and be destroyed in a 220-volt outlet.

Most appliances require a converter to change from one voltage to another. You'll also need an adapter to cope with different socket types, which vary between flat two-pronged plugs in American Samoa and three-pronged plugs with the two on top at angles almost everywhere else. Pick up both items before you leave home, as they're hard to find in the islands. Some sockets have a switch that must be turned on. Remember voltages if you buy duty-free appliances: dual voltage (110/220 V) items are best.

Videos

Commercial travel video tapes make nice souvenirs, but always keep in mind that there are three incompatible video formats loose in the world: NTSC (used in North America, American Samoa, and Tonga), PAL (used in Britain, Germany, Australia, New Zealand, Cook Islands, and Samoa), and SECAM (used in France, Tahiti-Polynesia, New Caledonia, and Russia). Don't buy prerecorded tapes abroad unless they're of the system used in your country.

MEDIA AND INFORMATION

Daily newspapers are published in American Samoa *(The Samoa News)* and Samoa *(The Samoa Observer).* The *Tonga Chronicle* appears weekly.

The leading regional news magazines are *Islands Business Pacific* and *Pacific Islands Monthly,* both published in Fiji, and *Pacific Magazine* from Honolulu. Copies of these are well worth picking up during your trip, and a subscription will help you keep in touch. Turn to Resources at the end of this book for more Pacific-oriented publications.

Radio

A great way to keep in touch with world and local affairs is to take along a small AM/FM shortwave portable radio. Your only expense will be the radio itself and batteries. Throughout this handbook we provide the names and frequencies of local stations, so set your tuning buttons to these as soon as you arrive. At least once a day the major local stations rebroadcast news reports from the BBC World Service, Radio Australia, and Radio New Zealand International, and we've tried to provide the times.

You can also try picking up the BBC World Service directly on your shortwave receiver at 5.98, 7.15, 9.66, 9.74, 11.77, 11.96, 12.08, or 15.36 MHz. (15.36 MHz generally works best). For Radio Australia try 6.08, 7.24, 9.66, 11.88, 12.08, 15.51, and 17.71 MHz. Look for Radio New Zealand International at 6.10, 6.14, 9.87, 11.69, 11.73, and 17.67 MHz. These frequencies vary according to the time of day and work best at night. (Unfortunately both RNZI and Radio Australia have recently faced cutbacks that could impact their services.)

Information Offices

All the main countries have official tourist information offices. Their main branches in the capitals open during normal business hours but the information desks at the airports only open for the arrival of international flights, if then. Always visit the local tourist office to pick up brochures and ask questions. Their overseas offices, listed in this handbook's appendix, often mail out useful information on their country and most of them have internet websites.

HEALTH

For a tropical area, the South Pacific's a healthy place. The sea and air are clear and usually pollution-free. The humidity nourishes the skin and the local fruit is brimming with vitamins. If you take a few precautions, you'll never have a sick day. The information provided below is intended to make you knowledgeable, not fearful. If you have access to the internet, check www.cdc.gov/travel/index.htm for up-to-the-minute information.

The government-run medical facilities mentioned in this book typically provide free medical treatment to local residents but have special rates for foreigners. It's usually no more expensive to visit a private doctor or clinic, and private doctors can afford to provide faster service since everyone is paying. We've tried to list local doctors and dentists throughout the handbook. In emergencies and outside clinic hours, you can always turn to the government-run facilities. Unfortunately, very few facilities are provided for travelers with disabilities.

American-made medications may by unobtainable in the islands, so along bring a supply of whatever you think you'll need. If you need to replace anything, quote the generic name at the drug store rather than the brand name. Antibiotics should only be used to treat serious wounds, and only after medical advice.

Travel Insurance

The sale of travel insurance is big business but the value of the policies themselves is often questionable. If your regular group health insurance also covers you while you're traveling abroad it's probably enough as medical costs in the South Pacific are generally low. Most travel policies only pay the amount above and beyond what your national or group health insurance will pay and are invalid if you don't have any health insurance at all. You may also be covered by your credit card company if you paid for your plane ticket with the card. Buying extra travel insurance is about the same as buying a lottery ticket: there's always the chance it will pay off, but it's usually money down the drain.

If you do opt for the security of travel insurance, make sure emergency medical evacuations are covered. Some policies are invalid if you engage in any "dangerous activities," such as scuba diving, parasailing, surfing, or even riding a motor scooter, so be sure to read the fine print. Scuba divers should be aware that no recompression chambers are available in the islands covered in this book. In case of need, you'll require an emergency medical evacuation to Fiji or New Zealand and there isn't any point buying a policy that doesn't cover it. Medical insurance especially designed for scuba divers is available from **Divers Alert Network** (6 West Colony Pl., Durham, NC 27705, U.S.A.; tel. 1-800/446-2671 or 1-919/684-2948, fax 1-919/490-6630, www.dan.ycg.org). In Australia, New Zealand, or the South Pacific, write Box 134, Carnegie, Victoria 3163, Australia (tel. 61-3/9563-1151, fax 61-3/9563-1139).

Some companies will pay your bills directly while others require you to pay and collect receipts that may be reimbursed later. Ask if travel delays, lost baggage, and theft are included. In practice, your airline probably already covers the first two adequately and claiming something extra from your insurance company could be more trouble than it's worth. Theft insurance never covers items left on the beach while you're in swimming. All this said, you should weigh the advantages and decide for yourself if you want a policy. Just don't be influenced by what your travel agent has to say as they'll only want to sell you coverage in order to earn another commission.

Acclimatizing

Don't go from winter weather into the steaming tropics without a rest before and after. Minimize jet lag by setting your watch to local time at your destination as soon as you board the flight. Westbound flights into the South Pacific from North America or Europe are less jolting since you follow the sun and your body gets a few hours extra sleep. On the way home you're moving against the sun and the hours of sleep your body loses cause jet lag. Airplane cabins have low humidity, so drink lots of juice or water instead of carbonated drinks, and don't overeat in-flight. It's also wise to forgo coffee, as it will only keep you awake, and alcohol, which will dehydrate you.

Scuba diving on departure day can give you a severe case of the bends. Before flying allow a minimum of 12 hours surface interval after a non-decompression dive and a minimum of 24 hours after a decompression dive. Factors contributing to decompression sickness include a lack of sleep and/or the excessive consumption of alcohol before diving.

If you start feeling seasick onboard a ship, stare at the horizon, which is always steady, and stop thinking about it. Anti-motion-sickness pills are useful to have along; otherwise, ginger helps alleviate seasickness. Travel stores sell acubands that find a pressure point on the wrist and create a stable flow of blood to the head, thus miraculously preventing seasickness!

Frequently the feeling of thirst is false and only due to mucous membrane dryness. Gargling or taking two or three gulps of warm water should be enough. Keep moisture in your body by having a hot drink like tea or black coffee, or any kind of slightly salted or sour drink in small quantities. Salt in fresh lime juice is remarkably refreshing.

The tap water is usually safe to drink in the main towns, but ask first elsewhere. If in doubt, boil it or use purification pills. Tap water that is uncomfortably hot to touch is usually safe. Allow it to cool in a clean container. Don't forget that if the tap water is contaminated, the local ice will be too. Avoid brushing your teeth with water unfit to drink, and wash or peel fruit and vegetables if you can. Cooked food is less subject to contamination than raw.

Sunburn

Though you may think a tan will make you look healthier and more attractive, it's actually very damaging to the skin, which becomes dry, rigid, and prematurely old and wrinkled, especially on the face. Begin with short exposures to the sun,

perhaps half an hour at a time, followed by an equal time in the shade. Drink plenty of liquids to keep your pores open and avoid the sun 1000-1500, the most dangerous time. Clouds and beach umbrellas will not protect you fully. Wear a T-shirt while snorkeling to protect your back. Sunbathing is the main cause of cataracts to the eyes, so wear sunglasses and a wide-brimmed hat, and beware of reflected sunlight.

Use a sunscreen lotion containing PABA rather than oil, and don't forget to apply it to your nose, lips, forehead, neck, hands, and feet. Sunscreens protect you from ultraviolet rays (a leading cause of cancer), while oils magnify the sun's effect. A 15-factor sunscreen provides 93% protection (a more expensive 30-factor sunscreen is only slightly better at 97% protection). Apply the lotion *before* going to the beach to avoid being burned on the way, and reapply every couple of hours to replace sunscreen washed away by perspiration. Swimming also washes away your protection. After sunbathing take a tepid shower rather than a hot one, which would wash away your natural skin oils. Stay moist and use a vitamin E evening cream to preserve the youth of your skin. Calamine ointment soothes skin already burned, as does coconut oil. Pharmacists recommend Solarcaine to soothe burned skin. Rinsing off with a vinegar solution reduces peeling, and aspirin relieves some of the pain and irritation. Vitamin A and calcium counteract overdoses of vitamin D received from the sun. The fairer your skin, the more essential it is to take care.

As earth's ozone layer is depleted due to the commercial use of chlorofluorocarbons (CFCs) and other factors, the need to protect oneself from ultraviolet radiation is becoming more urgent. In 1990 the U.S. Centers for Disease Control and Prevention in Atlanta reported that deaths from skin cancer increased 26% between 1973 and 1985. Previously the cancers didn't develop until age 50 or 60, but now much younger people are affected.

Ailments

Cuts and scratches infect easily in the tropics and take a long time to heal. Prevent infection from coral cuts by immediately washing wounds with soap and fresh water, then rubbing in vinegar or alcohol (whiskey will do)—painful but effective. Use an antiseptic like hydrogen peroxide

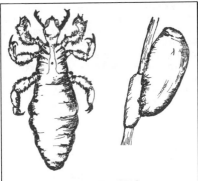

LICE FACTS

The louse *(Pediculus capitis)* is a small, wingless insect that can infest the hairy areas of all warm-blooded beasts. It's untrue that personal cleanliness prevents lice—anyone can get them, whether clean or dirty. The parasite attaches its egg securely to the side of hair shafts. By applying a solution available at any drugstore, you can zap the varmints in minutes.

and an antibacterial ointment such as neosporin, if you have them. Islanders usually dab coral cuts with lime juice. All cuts turn septic quickly in the tropics, so try to keep them clean and covered.

For bites, burns, and cuts, an antiseptic such as Solarcaine speeds healing and helps prevent infection. Pure aloe vera is good for sunburn, scratches, and even coral cuts. Bites by sandflies itch for days and can become infected if scratched. Not everyone is affected by insect bites in the same way. Some people are practically immune to insects, while traveling companions experiencing exactly the same conditions are soon covered with bites. You'll soon know which type you are.

Prickly heat, an intensely irritating rash, is caused by wearing heavy clothing that is inappropriate for the climate. When the glands are blocked and the sweat is unable to evaporate, the skin becomes soggy and small red blisters appear. Synthetic fabrics like nylon are especially bad in this regard. Take a cold shower, apply calamine lotion, dust with talcum powder, and take off those clothes! Until things improve,

avoid alcohol, tea, coffee, and any physical activity that makes you sweat. If you're sweating profusely, increase your intake of salt slightly to avoid fatigue, but not without concurrently drinking more water.

Use antidiarrheal medications such as Lomotil or Imodium sparingly. Rather than take drugs to plug yourself up, drink plenty of unsweetened liquids like green coconut or fresh fruit juice to help flush yourself out. Egg yolk mixed with nutmeg helps diarrhea, or have a rice and tea day. Avoid dairy products. Most cases of diarrhea are self-limiting and require only simple replacement of the fluids and salts lost in diarrheal stools. If the diarrhea is persistent or you experience high fever, drowsiness, or blood in the stool, stop traveling, rest, and consider seeing a doctor. For constipation eat pineapple or any peeled fruit.

If you're sleeping in villages or with the locals you may pick up head or body lice. Pharmacists and general stores usually have a remedy that will eliminate the problem in minutes (pack a bottle with you if you're uptight). You'll know you're lousy when you start to scratch: pick out the little varmints and snap them between your thumbnails for fun. The villagers pluck the creatures out of each other's hair one by one, a way of confirming friendships and showing affection. Intestinal parasites (worms) are also widespread. The hookworm bores its way through the soles of your feet, and if you go barefoot through moist gardens and plantations you may pick up something.

AIDS

In 1981 scientists in the United States and France first recognized the Acquired Immune Deficiency Syndrome (AIDS), which was later discovered to be caused by a virus called the Human Immuno-deficiency Virus (HIV). HIV breaks down the body's immunity to infections leading to AIDS. The virus can lie hidden in the body for up to 10 years without producing any obvious symptoms or before developing into the AIDS disease and in the meantime the person can unknowingly infect others.

HIV lives in white blood cells and is present in the sexual fluids of humans. It's difficult to catch and is spread mostly through sexual intercourse, by needle or syringe sharing among intravenous

Speech bubble: CONDOMAN SAYS: DON'T BE SHAME BE GAME

PROTECT YOURSELF!

drug users, in blood transfusions, and during pregnancy and birth (if the mother is infected). Using another person's razor blade or having your body pierced or tattooed are also risky, but the HIV virus cannot be transmitted by shaking hands, kissing, cuddling, fondling, sneezing, cooking food, or sharing eating or drinking utensils. One cannot be infected by saliva, sweat, tears, urine, or feces; toilet seats, telephones, swimming pools, or mosquito bites do not cause AIDS. Ostracizing a known AIDS victim is not only immoral but also absurd.

Most blood banks now screen their products for HIV, and you can protect yourself against dirty needles by only allowing an injection if you see the syringe taken out of a fresh unopened pack. The simplest safeguard during sex is the proper use of a latex condom. Unroll the condom onto the erect penis; while withdrawing after ejaculation, hold onto the condom as you come out. Never try to recycle a condom, and pack a supply with you as it's a nuisance trying to buy them locally.

HIV is spread more often through anal than vaginal sex because the lining of the rectum is much weaker than that of the vagina, and ordinary condoms sometimes tear when used in anal sex. If you have anal sex, only use extra-strong condoms and special water-based lubricants since oil, Vaseline, and cream weaken the rubber. During oral sex you must make sure you don't get any semen or menstrual blood in your mouth. A woman runs 10 times the risk of contracting AIDS from a man than the other way around, and the threat is always greater when another sexually transmitted disease (STD) is present.

The very existence of AIDS calls for a basic change in human behavior. No vaccine or drug exists that can prevent or cure AIDS, and because the virus mutates frequently, no remedy may ever be totally effective. Other STDs such as syphilis, gonorrhea, chlamydia, hepatitis B, and herpes are far more common than AIDS and can lead to serious complications such as infertility, but at least they can usually be cured

The euphoria of travel can make it easier to fall in love or have sex with a stranger, so travelers must be informed of these dangers. As a tourist you should always practice safe sex to prevent AIDS and other STDs. You never know who is infected or even if you yourself have become infected. It's important to bring the subject up *before* you start to make love. Make a joke out of it by pulling out a condom and asking your new partner, "Say, do you know what this is?" Or perhaps, "Your condom or mine?" Far from being unromantic or embarrassing, you'll both feel more relaxed with the subject off your minds and it's much better than worrying afterwards if you might have been infected. The golden rule is safe sex or no sex.

By 1999 an estimated 33 million people worldwide were HIV carriers, and millions had already died of AIDS. In the South Pacific, the number of cases is still extremely small compared to the 650,000 confirmed HIV infections in the United States. Nevertheless, it's worth noting that other STDs have already reached epidemic proportions in some urban areas, demonstrating that the type of behavior leading to the rapid spread of AIDS is present.

An HIV infection can be detected through a blood test because the antibodies created by the body to fight off the virus can be seen under a microscope. It takes at least three weeks for the antibodies to be produced and in some cases as long as six months before they can be picked up during a screening test. If you think you may have run a risk, you should discuss the appropriateness of a test with your doctor. It's always better to know if you are infected so as to be able to avoid infecting others, to obtain early treatment of symptoms, and to make realistic plans. If you know someone with AIDS you should give them all the support you can (there's no danger in such contact unless blood is present).

Toxic Fish

Over 400 species of tropical reef fish, including wrasses, snappers, groupers, jacks, moray eels, surgeonfish, shellfish, and especially barracudas are known to cause seafood poisoning (ciguatera). There's no way to tell if a fish will cause ciguatera: a species can be poisonous on one side of the island, but not on the other.

In 1976 French and Japanese scientists working in the Gambier Islands determined that a one-celled dinoflagellate or plankton called *Gambierdiscus toxicus* was the cause. Normally these microalgae are found only in the ocean depths, but when a reef ecosystem is disturbed by natural or human causes they can multiply dramatically in a lagoon. The dinoflagellates are consumed by tiny herbivorous fish and the toxin passes up through the food chain to larger fish where it becomes concentrated in the head and guts. The toxins have no effect on the fish that feed on them.

The symptoms (numbness and tingling around the mouth and extremities, reversal of hot/cold sensations, prickling, itching, nausea, vomiting, erratic heartbeat, joint and muscle pains) usually subside in a few days. Induce vomiting, take castor oil as a laxative, and avoid alcohol if you're unlucky. Symptoms can recur for up to a year, and victims may become allergic to all seafoods. In the Marshall Islands, an injected drug called Mannitel has been effective in treating ciguatera, but as yet little is known about it.

Avoid biointoxication by cleaning fish as soon as they're caught, discarding the head and organs, and taking special care with oversized fish caught in shallow water. Small fish are generally safer. Whether the fish is consumed cooked or raw has no bearing on this problem. Local residents often know from experience which species may be eaten.

Other Diseases

Infectious hepatitis A (jaundice) is a liver ailment transmitted person to person or through unboiled water, uncooked vegetables, or other foods contaminated during handling. The risk of infection is highest among those who eat village food, so if you'll be spending much time in rural areas an immune globulin shot provides six months protection. Better is a vaccine called Havrix, which provides up to 10 years protection (given in two doses two weeks apart, then a third dose six months later). If you've ever had hepatitis A in your life you are already immune. Otherwise, you'll know you've got the hep when your eyeballs and urine turn yellow. Time and rest are the only cure. Viral hepatitis B is spread through sexual or blood contact.

Typhoid fever is acquired via contaminated food or water, so avoid uncooked foods, peel your own fruit, and drink bottled drinks if you're paranoid. Tetanus (lockjaw) occurs when cuts or bites become infected. Horrible disfiguring diseases such as leprosy and elephantiasis are hard to catch, so it's extremely unlikely you'll be visited by one of these nightmares of the flesh. Malaria does not exist in the countries covered in this book and cholera outbreaks haven't occurred in living memory.

More of a problem is dengue fever, a mosquito-transmitted disease endemic in the South Pacific. In early 1998 a major outbreak in Fiji resulted in an estimated 25,000 cases and 11 deaths. Tonga, Cook Islands, and Vanuatu have also experienced dengue fever epidemics recently. Signs are headaches, sore throat, pain in the joints, fever, chills, nausea, and rash. This painful illness also known as "breakbone fever" can last anywhere from five to 15 days. Although you can relieve the symptoms somewhat, the only real cure is to stay in bed, drink lots of water, and wait it out. Avoid aspirin as this can lead to complications. No vaccine exists, so just try to avoid getting bitten (the *Aedes aegypti* mosquito bites only during the day). Dengue fever can kill infants so extra care must be taken to protect them if an outbreak is in progress.

Vaccinations

Most visitors are not required to get any vaccinations at all before coming to the South Pacific. Tetanus, diphtheria, and typhoid fever shots are not required, but they're worth considering if you're going off the beaten track. Tetanus and diphtheria shots are given together, and a booster is required every 10 years. The typhoid fever shot is every three years. Polio is believed to have been eradicated from the region.

A yellow-fever vaccination is required if you've been in an infected area within the six days prior to arrival. Yellow fever is a mosquito-borne disease that only occurs in Central Africa and northern South America (excluding Chile), places you're not likely to have been just before arriving in the South Pacific. Since the vaccination is valid 10 years, get one if you're an inveterate globe-trotter.

Immune globulin (IG) and the Havrix vaccine aren't 100% effective against hepatitis A, but they do increase your general resistance to infections. IG prophylaxis must be repeated every five months. Hepatitis B vaccination involves three doses over a six-month period (duration of protection unknown) and is recommended mostly for people planning extended stays in the region.

WHAT TO TAKE

Packing

Assemble everything you simply must take and cannot live without—then cut the pile in half. If you're still left with more than will fit into a medium-size suitcase or backpack, continue eliminating. You have to be tough on yourself and just limit what you take. Now put it all into your bag. If the total (bag and contents) weighs over 16 kg, you'll sacrifice much of your mobility. If you can keep it down to 10 kg, you're traveling *light*. Categorize, separate, and pack all your things into clear plastic bags or stuff sacks for convenience and protection from moisture. Items that might leak should be in resealable bags. In addition to your principal bag, you'll want a day pack or flight bag. When checking in for flights, carry anything that cannot be replaced in your hand luggage.

Your Luggage

A soft medium-size backpack with a lightweight internal frame is best. Big external-frame packs are fine for mountain climbing but get caught in airport conveyor belts and are very inconvenient on public transport. The best packs have a zippered compartment in back where you can tuck in the hip belt and straps before turning your pack over to an airline or bus. This type of pack has the flexibility of allowing you to simply walk when motorized transport is unavailable or unacceptable; and with the straps zipped in it looks like a regular suitcase, should you wish to go upmarket for a while.

Make sure your pack allows you to carry the weight on your hips, has a cushion for spine support, and doesn't pull backwards. The pack should strap snugly to your body but also allow ventilation to your back. It should be made of a water-resistant material such as nylon and have a Fastex buckle.

Look for a pack with double, two-way zipper compartments and pockets you can lock with miniature padlocks. They might not *stop* a thief, but they will deter the casual pilferer. A 60-cm length of lightweight chain and another padlock will allow you to fasten your pack to something. Keep valuables locked in your bag, out of sight, as even upmarket hotel rooms aren't 100% safe.

Clothing and Camping Equipment

Take loose-fitting cotton washable clothes, light in color and weight. Synthetic fabrics are hot and sticky, and most of the things you wear at home are too heavy for the tropics—be prepared for the humidity. Dress is casual, with slacks and a sports shirt okay for men even at dinner parties. Local women often wear long colorful dresses in the evening, but respectable shorts are okay in daytime. If in doubt, bring the minimum with you and buy tropical garb upon arrival. Stick to clothes you can rinse in your room sink. In midwinter (July and August) it can be cool at night in Tonga, so a light sweater or windbreaker may come in handy. (Reader Claire Brenn writes: "If you have some good but unfashionable clothes you don't want to take home, just leave them behind in your hotel room with a small thank you note. The locals will gladly have them but to offer them directly might be embarrassing.")

The *lavalava* is a bright two-meter piece of cloth both men and women wrap about themselves as an all-purpose garment. Any islander can show you how to wear it. Missionaries taught the South Sea island women to drape their attributes in long, flowing gowns, called muumuus in Hawaii. In the South Pacific, the dress is better known as a Mother Hubbard for the muumuu-attired nursery rhyme character who "went to the cupboard to fetch her poor dog a bone."

Take comfortable shoes that have been broken in. Running shoes and rubber thongs (flip-flops) are handy for day use but will bar you from nightspots with strict dress codes. Scuba divers' wetsuit booties are lightweight and perfect for both crossing rivers and lagoon walking, though an old pair of sneakers may be just as good (never use the booties to walk on breakable coral).

A small nylon tent guarantees backpackers a place to sleep every night, but it *must* be mosquito- and waterproof. Get one with a tent fly, then waterproof both tent and fly with a can of waterproofing spray. You'll seldom need a sleeping bag in the tropics, so that's one item you can easily cut. A youth hostel sleeping sheet is ideal—all HI handbooks give instructions on how to make your own or buy one at your local hostel.

You don't really need to carry a bulky foam pad, as the ground is seldom cold.

Below we've provided a few checklists to help you assemble your gear. The listed items combined weigh well over 16 kg, so eliminate what doesn't suit you:

> pack with internal frame
> day pack or airline bag
> sun hat or visor
> essential clothing only
> bathing suit
> sturdy walking shoes
> rubber thongs
> rubber booties
> nylon tent and fly
> tent-patching tape
> mosquito net
> sleeping sheet

Accessories

Bring some reading material, as good books can be hard to find in some countries. A mask and snorkel are essential equipment—you'll be missing half of the Pacific's beauty without them. Scuba divers will bring their own regulator, buoyancy compensator, and gauges to avoid rental fees and to eliminate the possibility of catching a transmissible disease from rental equipment. A lightweight 3-mm Lycra wetsuit will provide protection against marine stings and coral.

Neutral gray eyeglasses protect your eyes from the sun and give the least color distortion. Take an extra pair (if you wear them). Keep your laundry soap inside a couple of layers of plastic bags.

Also take along postcards of your hometown and snapshots of your house, family, workplace, etc; islanders love to see these. Always keep a promise to mail islanders the photos you take of them.

> portable shortwave radio
> camera and 10 rolls of film
> compass
> pocket flashlight
> extra batteries
> candle
> pocket alarm calculator
> extra pair of eyeglasses
> sunglasses

> mask and snorkel
> padlock and lightweight chain
> collapsible umbrella
> string for a clothesline
> powdered laundry soap
> universal sink plug
> minitowel
> silicon glue
> sewing kit
> miniscissors
> nail clippers
> fishing line for sewing gear
> plastic cup and plate
> can and bottle opener
> corkscrew
> penknife
> spoon
> water bottle
> matches
> tea bags

Toiletries and Medical Kit

Since everyone has his/her own medical requirements and brand names vary from country to country, there's no point going into detail here. Note, however, that even the basics (such as aspirin) are unavailable on some outer islands, so be prepared. Bring medicated powder for prickly heat rash. Charcoal tablets are useful for diarrhea and poisoning (they absorb the irritants). Bring an adequate supply of any personal medications, plus your prescriptions (in generic terminology).

High humidity causes curly hair to swell and bush, straight hair to droop. If it's curly have it cut short or keep it long in a ponytail or bun. A good cut is essential with straight hair. Water-based makeup is preferable, as the heat and humidity cause oil glands to work overtime. High-quality locally made shampoo, body oils, and insect repellent are sold on all the islands, and the bottles are conveniently smaller than those sold in Western countries. See **Health** for more ideas.

> wax earplugs
> soap in plastic container
> soft toothbrush
> toothpaste
> roll-on deodorant
> shampoo
> comb and brush

skin creams
makeup
tampons or napkins
toilet paper
vitamin/mineral supplement
insect repellent
PABA sunscreen
Chap Stick
a motion-sickness remedy
contraceptives
iodine
water-purification pills
delousing powder
a diarrhea remedy
Tiger Balm
a cold remedy
Alka-Seltzer
aspirin
antihistamine
antifungal
Calmitol ointment
antibacterial ointment
antiseptic cream
disinfectant
simple dressings
adhesive bandages (like Band-Aids)
painkiller
prescription medicines

Money and Documents

All post offices have passport applications. If you lose your passport you should report the matter to the local police at once, obtain a certificate or receipt, then proceed to your consulate (if any!) for a replacement. If you have your birth certificate with you it expedites things considerably. Don't bother getting an international driver's license as your regular license is all you need to drive here (except in Tonga where you'll be required to buy a local license).

Traveler's checks in U.S. dollars are recommended, and in the South Pacific, American Express is the most efficient company when it comes to providing refunds for lost checks. Bring along a small supply of US$1 and US$5 bills to use if you don't manage to change money immediately upon arrival or if you run out of local currency and can't get to a bank.

Carry your valuables in a money belt worn around your waist or neck under your clothing;

most camping stores have these. Make several photocopies of the information page of your passport, personal identification, driver's license, scuba certification card, credit cards, airline tickets, receipts for purchase of traveler's checks, etc.—you should be able to get them all on one page. On the side, write the phone numbers you'd need to call to report lost documents. A brief medical history with your blood type, allergies, chronic or special health problems, eyeglass and medical prescriptions, etc., might also come in handy. Put these inside plastic bags to protect them from moisture, then carry the lists in different places, and leave one at home.

How much money you'll need depends on your lifestyle, but time is also a factor. The longer you stay, the cheaper it gets. Suppose you have to lay out US$1,000 on airfare and have (for example) US$50 a day left over for expenses. If you stay 15 days, you'll average US$117 a day ($50 times 15 plus $1,000, divided by 15). If you stay 30 days, you'll average US$83 a day. If you stay 90 days, the per-day cost drops to US$61. If you stay a year it'll cost only US$53 a day.

passport
airline tickets
scuba certification card
driver's license
traveler's checks
some U.S. cash
credit card
photocopies of documents
money belt
address book
notebook
envelopes
extra ballpoints

Film and Photography

Scan the ads in photographic magazines for deals on mail-order cameras and film, or buy at a discount shop in any large city. Run a roll of film through your camera to be sure it's in good working order; clean the lens with lens-cleaning tissue and check the batteries. Remove the batteries from your camera when storing it at home for long periods. Register valuable cameras or electronic equipment with customs before you leave home so there won't be any argument over where you bought the items when you return, or at least carry a copy of the original bill of sale.

The type of camera you choose could depend on the way you travel. If you'll be staying mostly in one place, a heavy single-lens reflex (SLR) camera with spare lenses and other equipment won't trouble you. If you'll be moving around a lot for a considerable length of time, a 35-mm automatic compact camera will be better. The compacts are mostly useful for close-up shots; landscapes will seem spread out and far away. A wide-angle lens gives excellent depth of field, but hold the camera upright to avoid converging verticals. A polarizing filter prevents reflections from glass windows and water, and makes the sky bluer.

Take double the amount of film and mailers you think you'll need: film is expensive here, and you never know if it's been spoiled by an airport X-ray on the way. On a long trip mailers are essential as exposed film shouldn't be held for long periods. Choose 36-exposure film over 24-exposure to save on the number of rolls you have to carry. When purchasing film in the islands take care to check the expiration date. Specialty films like black and white or color slides is hard to find; standard color print film will be all you'll see in most places.

Films are rated by their speed and sensitivity to light, using ISO numbers from 25 to 1600. The higher the number, the greater the film's sensitivity to light. Slower films with lower ISOs (like 100-200) produce sharp images in bright sunlight. Faster films with higher ISOs (like 400) stop action and work well in low-light situations, such as in dark rainforests or at sunset. If you have a manual SLR you can avoid overexposure at midday by reducing the exposure half a stop, but *do* overexpose when photographing dark-skinned islanders. From 1000 to 1600 the light is often too bright to take good photos, and panoramas usually come out best early or late in the day.

Keep your photos simple with one main subject and an uncomplicated background. Get as close to your subjects as you can and lower or raise the camera to their level. Include people in the foreground of scenic shots to add interest and perspective. Outdoors a flash can fill in unflattering facial shadows caused by high sun or backlit conditions. Most of all, be creative. Look for interesting details and compose the photo before you push the trigger. Instead of taking a head-on photo of a group of people, step to one side and ask them to face you. The angle improves the photo. Photograph subjects coming toward you rather than passing by. Ask permission before photographing people. If you're asked for money (rare) you can always walk away—give your subjects the same choice.

When packing, protect your camera against vibration. Checked baggage is scanned by powerful airport X-ray monitors, so carry both camera and film aboard the plane in a clear plastic bag and ask security for a visual inspection. Some airports will refuse to do this, however. A good alternative is to use a lead-laminated pouch. The old high-dose X-ray units are seldom seen these days but even low-dose inspection units can ruin fast film (400 ASA and above). Beware of the cumulative effect of X-ray machines.

Keep your camera in a plastic bag during rain and while traveling in motorized canoes, etc. In the tropics the humidity can cause film to stick to itself; silica-gel crystals in the bag will protect film from humidity and mold growth. Protect camera and film from direct sunlight and load the film in the shade. When loading, check that the takeup spool revolves. Never leave camera or film in a hot place like a car floor, glove compartment, or trunk.

GETTING THERE

Preparations

First decide where and when you're going and how long you wish to stay. Some routes are more available or practical than others. The major transit points for visitors are Auckland, Honolulu, and Nadi; you'll notice how feeder flights radiate from these hubs. All North Americans and Europeans will pass through Los Angeles International Airport (code-named LAX) unless it's another routing via Honolulu.

Your plane ticket will be your biggest single expense, so spend some time considering the possibilities. Before going any further, read this entire chapter right through and check the **Transportation** sections in the various chapter introductions for more detailed information. If you're online, peruse the internet sites of the airlines that interest you, then call them up directly over their toll-free 800 numbers to get current information on fares. The following airlines have flights from the United States:

Air New Zealand (tel. 1-800/262-1234, www.airnz.co.nz, flies to Apia and Tongatapu)

Air Pacific (tel. 1-800/227-4446, www.bulafiji.com/airlines/airpac/htm, flies to Apia and Tongatapu via Nadi)

Hawaiian Airlines (tel. 1-800/367-5320, www.hawaiianair.com, flies to Pago Pago)

Polynesian Airlines (tel. 1-800/644-7659, www.polynesianairlines.co.nz, flies to Apia, Pago Pago, and Tongatapu)

Royal Tongan Airlines (tel. 1-800/486-6426, http://kalianet.candw.to/rta, flies to Apia, Niue, Vava'u, and Tongatapu)

Sometimes Canada and parts of the U.S. have different toll-free numbers, so if the number given above doesn't work, dial 800 information at 1-800/555-1212 (all 800 and 888 numbers are free). In Canada, Air New Zealand's toll-free number is tel. 1-800/663-5494.

Call all of these carriers and say you want the *lowest possible fare*. Cheapest are the excursion fares but these often have limitations and restrictions, so be sure to ask. Some have an advance-purchase deadline, which means it's wise to begin shopping early. Also check the fare seasons.

If you're not happy with the answers you get, call the number back later and try again. Many different agents take calls on these lines, and some are more knowledgeable than others. The numbers are often busy during peak business hours, so call first thing in the morning, after dinner, or on the weekend. *Be persistent.*

Cheaper Fares

Over the past few years South Pacific airfares have been deregulated and companies like Air New Zealand no longer publish set fare price lists. Their internet websites are also evasive, usually with tariff information kept secret (they might have prices for their all-inclusive package tours on the web but not air prices alone). Finding your way through this minefield can be the least enjoyable part of your pre-trip planning, but you'll definitely pay a premium if you take the easy route and accept the first or second fare you're offered. With fares in flux, the airline employees you'll get at the numbers listed above probably won't quote you the lowest fare on the market, but at least you'll have their official price to use as a benchmark.

After you've heard what they have to say, turn to a "discounter," specialist travel agencies that deal in bulk and sell seats and rooms at wholesale prices. Many airlines have more seats than they can market through normal channels, so they sell their unused long-haul capacity to "consolidators" or "bucket shops" at discounts of 40-50% off the official tariffs. The discounters buy tickets on this gray market and pass the savings along to you. Many such companies run ads in the Sunday travel sections of newspapers like the *San Francisco Examiner, New York Times,* or *Toronto Star,* or in major entertainment weeklies.

Despite their occasionally shady appearance, most discounters and consolidators are perfectly legitimate, and your ticket will probably be issued by the airline itself. Most discounted tickets look and are exactly the same as regular full-fare tickets but they're usually nonrefundable. There may also be penalties if you wish to change your routing or reservations, and other restrictions not associated with the more expensive tickets. Rates are competitive, so allow yourself time to shop around. A few hours spent on the phone, doing time on hold and asking questions, could save you hundreds of dollars.

Travel Agents

Be aware that any travel agent worth his/her commission will probably want to sell you a package tour, and it's a fact that some vacation packages actually cost less than regular roundtrip

airfare! If they'll let you extend your return date to give you some time to yourself this could be a good deal, especially with the hotel thrown in for "free." But check the restrictions.

Pick your agent carefully as many don't want to hear about discounts, cheap flights, or complicated routes, and will give wrong or misleading information in an offhand manner. They may try to sell you hotel rooms you could get locally for a fraction of the cost. Agencies belonging to the American Society of Travel Agents (ASTA), the Alliance of Canadian Travel Associations (ACTA), or the Association of British Travel Agents must conform to a strict code of ethics. Some protection is also obtained by paying by credit card.

Once you've done a deal with an agent and have your ticket in hand, call the airline again

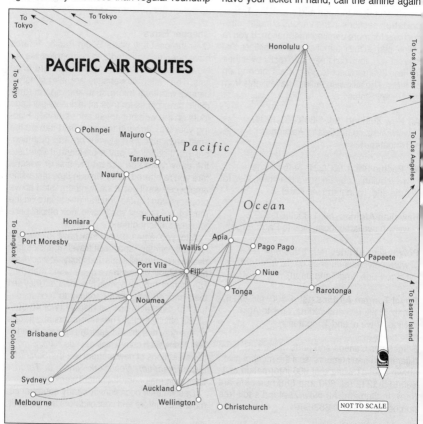

over their toll-free reservations number to check that your flight bookings and seat reservations are okay. If you got a really cheap fare, make sure the agent booked you in the same class of service as is printed on your ticket. For example, if you've got a K-coded ticket but your agent was only able to get a higher B-code booking, you could be denied boarding at the airport (in fact, few agents would risk doing something like this). A crooked agent might also tell you that you're free to change your return reservations when in fact you're not.

One of the most knowledgeable Canadian travel agents for South Pacific tickets is the **Adventure Centre** (25 Bellair St., Toronto, Ontario M5R 3L3; tel. 1-800/267-3347 or 1-416/922-7584, fax 1-416/922-8136, www.trek.ca, e-mail: info@tor.trek.ca) with offices in Calgary (tel. 1-403/283-6115), Edmonton (tel. 1-403/439-0024), and Vancouver (tel. 1-604/734-1066). Ask for their informative brochure *South Pacific Airfare Specials.*

Similar tickets are available in the U.S. from the **Adventure Center** (1311 63rd St., Suite 200, Emeryville, CA 94608, U.S.A.; tel. 1-800/227-8747 or 1-510/654-1879, fax 1-510/654-4200, e-mail: tripinfo@adventure-center.com).

Discover Wholesale Travel (2192 Dupont Dr., Suite 116, Irvine, CA 92612, U.S.A.; tel. 1-800/576-7770, 1-800/759-7330, or 1-949/833-1136, fax 1-949/833-1176, www.discovertravel.net, e-mail: disc_tvl@ix.netcom.com) sells discounted air tickets and offers rock-bottom rates on rooms at the top hotels. They sometimes have significantly lower fares for passengers booking within two weeks of departure ("distressed seats"). President Mary Anne Cook claims everyone on her staff has 10 years experience selling the South Pacific and "most importantly, we all love the area!"

Some of the cheapest return tickets to the South Pacific are sold by **Fiji Travel** (8885 Venice Blvd., Suite 202, Los Angeles, CA 90034, U.S.A.: tel. 1-800/500-3454 or 1-310/202-4220, fax 1-310/202-8233, www.fijitravel.com). They make their money through high volume, and to attract customers they keep their profit margins as low as possible. Thus you should absorb the airline's time with all your questions about fare seasons, schedules, etc., and only call companies like Fiji Travel and Discover Wholesale

Travel after you know exactly what you want and how much everybody else is charging.

One U.S. agent willing to help you work out a personalized itinerary is Rob Jenneve of **Island Adventures** (574 Mills Way, Goleta, CA 93117, U.S.A.; tel. 1-800/289-4957 or 1-805/685-9230, fax 1-805/685-0960, e-mail: motuman@aol.com). Rob can put together flight and accommodation packages that are only slightly more expensive than the cheapest return airfare, and it's often possible to extend your return date to up to 30 days on the lowest fares or up to 90 days for a bit more. This option combines the benefits of packaged and independent travel, and you could end up spending a week at a medium-priced hotel with transfers for only US$50-100 more than you'd have to spend anyway just to get to the islands! Rob also books complex circle-Pacific routes and can steer you toward deluxe resorts that offer value for money.

Student Fares

If you're a student, recent graduate, or teacher, you can sometimes benefit from lower student fares by booking through a student travel office. There are two rival organizations of this kind: Council Travel Services, with offices in college towns across the U.S. and a sister organization in Canada known as Travel Cuts; and STA Travel (Student Travel Australia) with a wholesale division known as the Student Travel Network. Both organizations require you to pay a nominal fee for an official student card, and to get the cheapest fares you have to prove you're really a student. Slightly higher fares on the same routes are available to nonstudents, so they're always worth checking.

STA Travel (www.sta-travel.com) offers special airfares for students and young people under 26 years with minimal restrictions. Their prices on roundtrip fares to single destinations are competitive but they don't sell more complicated tickets (standard routings like Los Angeles-Fiji-Auckland-Sydney-Bangkok-London-Los Angeles are their style). Call their toll-free number (tel. 1-800/777-0112) for the latest information.

Different student fares are available from **Council Travel Services,** a division of the nonprofit Council on International Educational Exchange (CIEE). Both they and **Travel Cuts** (tel. 1-800/667-2887, www.travelcuts.com) in Cana-

STUDENT TRAVEL OFFICES

STA Travel, 297 Newbury St., Boston, MA 02115, U.S.A (tel. 617/266-6014)

STA Travel, 429 S. Dearborn St., Chicago, IL 60605, U.S.A. (tel. 312/786-9050)

STA Travel, 920 Westwood Blvd., Los Angeles, CA 90024, U.S.A. (tel. 310/824-1574)

STA Travel, 10 Downing St. (6th Ave. and Bleecker), New York, NY 10014, U.S.A. (tel. 212/627-3111)

STA Travel, 3730 Walnut St., Philadelphia, PA 19104, U.S.A. (tel. 215/382-2928)

STA Travel, 51 Grant Ave., San Francisco, CA 94108, U.S.A. (tel. 415/391-8407)

STA Travel, 4341 University Way NE, Seattle, WA 98105, U.S.A. (tel. 206/633-5000)

STA Travel, 2401 Pennsylvania Ave. #G, Washington, DC 20037, U.S.A. (tel. 202/887-0912)

STA Travel, 222 Faraday St., Carlton, Melbourne 3053, Australia (tel. 61-3/9349-2411)

STA Travel, 855 George St., Sydney, NSW 2007, Australia (tel. 61-2/9212-1255)

STA Travel, 10 High St., Auckland, New Zealand (tel. 64-9/309-0458)

STA Travel, #02-17 Orchard Parade Hotel, 1 Tanglin Road, Singapore 1024 (tel. 65/737-7188)

STA Travel, Suite 1406, 33 Surawong Road, Bangkok 10500, Thailand (tel. 66-2/236-0262)

STA Travel, Bockenheimer Landstrasse 133, D-60325 Frankfurt, Germany (tel. 49-69/703-035)

STA Travel, 117 Euston Road, London NW1 2SX, United Kingdom (tel. 44-171/465-0484)

ule your vacation slightly to take advantage of a lower fare.

Air New Zealand has their low (or "basic") season on flights to Samoa and Tonga from mid-April to August, shoulder season from September to November and in March, and high (or "peak") season from December to February. They've made April to November—the top months in the South Pacific—their off-season because that's winter in Australia and New Zealand. If you're only going to the islands and can make it at that time, it certainly works to your advantage.

Current Trends

High operating costs have caused the larger airlines to switch to wide-bodied aircraft and long-haul routes with less frequent service and fewer stops. In the South Pacific this works to your disadvantage, as many islands get bypassed. Most airlines now charge extra for stopovers that once were free, or simply refuse to grant any stopovers at all on the cheapest fares.

Increasingly airlines are combining in global alliances to compete internationally. Thus Air Pacific is part of a family comprising Qantas, American Airlines, Canadian Airlines, British Airways, and Japan Airlines, while Air New

da are stricter about making sure you're a "real" student: you must first obtain the widely recognized International Student Identity Card (US$20) to get a ticket at the student rate. Some fares are limited to students and youths under 26 years of age, but part-time students and teachers also qualify. Circle-Pacific and round-the-world routings are also available from Council Travel Services and there are special connecting flights to Los Angeles from other U.S. points.

Seasons

The month of outbound travel from the U.S. determines which seasonal fare you'll pay, and inquiring far in advance could allow you to resched-

Zealand has close links to Ansett Australia, United Airlines, Lufthansa, and Singapore Airlines. This is to your advantage as within the different blocks frequent flier programs are often interchangeable, booking becomes easier, flight schedules are coordinated, and through fares exist. The different blocks have special air passes and round-the-world deals combining the networks of a variety of affiliated carriers, several of which are discussed below.

Within the South Pacific, many regional carriers have attempted to cut costs by pooling their services through "code sharing." This means that two or three different airlines will "own" seats on the same flight which they sell under their own two-letter airline code. Flights from Nadi to Tongatapu are designated both FJ (Air Pacific) and WR (Royal Tongan Airlines). The flights to/from Honolulu and Los Angeles sold by Polynesian Airlines and Royal Tongan Airlines are actually code shares operated by Air New Zealand.

Circular Tickets

If you plan a wide-ranging trip with stops on several continents, the **Global Explorer** may be the ticket for you. This fare allows six free stops selected from over 400 destinations on 28,500 miles of routes. You can use the services of any of these airlines: Air Liberté, Air Pacific, American Airlines, British Airways, Canadian Airlines, Deutsche Airlines, and Qantas. This costs US$3,089 in the U.S. or CDN$3,969 in Canada, and additional stops after the first six are US$100 each. You must purchase the pass a week in advance and it's valid one year. Date changes and the first rerouting are free (additional reroutings US$100). Ask Qantas about this ticket.

A similar fare available only in the South Pacific and Europe is the **World Navigator**, which encompasses the networks of Aircalin, Air New Zealand, Air UK, Ansett Australia, Emirates, KLM Royal Dutch Airlines, Northwest Airlines, Kenyan Airlines, and South African Airways. From London, the World Navigator costs £1,099/1,199/1,299 in the low/shoulder/peak seasons (the low season is April to June only). From Australia, it's A$2,569/2,779/2,979/3,189 according to season with the lowest season running from mid-January to February and October to mid-November.

In North America, Air New Zealand sells a **World Escapade** valid for a round-the-world journey on Air New Zealand, Ansett Australia, and Singapore Airlines. You're allowed 29,000 miles with unlimited stops at US$2,799. One transatlantic and one transpacific journey must be included, but the ticket is valid one year and backtracking is allowed.

Air New Zealand's **Pacific Escapade** allows a circle-Pacific trip on the same three airlines. With this one you get 22,000 miles at US$2,600 with all the stops you want (maximum of three each in Australia and New Zealand). You'll have to transit Singapore at least once and travel must begin in either Los Angeles or Vancouver (no add-ons). On both Escapades, should you go over the allowable mileage, 4,500 extra miles are US$300. Reservation changes are free the first time but extra after that.

COUNCIL TRAVEL OFFICES

Council Travel, 2486 Channing Way, Berkeley, CA 94704, U.S.A. (tel. 510/848-8604)

Council Travel, 273 Newbury St., Boston, MA 02115, U.S.A. (tel. 617/266-1926)

Council Travel, 1153 N. Dearborn St., 2nd Floor, Chicago, IL 60610, U.S.A. (tel. 312/951-0585)

Council Travel, 10904 Lindbrook Dr., Los Angeles, CA 90024, U.S.A. (tel. 310/208-3551)

Council Travel, One Datran Center, Suite 220, 9100 S. Dadeland Blvd., Miami, FL 33156, U.S.A. (tel. 305/670-9261)

Council Travel, 205 East 42nd St., New York, NY 10017-5706, U.S.A. (tel. 212/822-2700)

Council Travel, 1430 SW Park Ave., Portland, OR 97201, U.S.A. (tel. 503/228-1900)

Council Travel, 953 Garnet Ave., San Diego, CA 92109, U.S.A. (tel. 619/270-6401)

Council Travel, 530 Bush St., San Francisco, CA 94108, U.S.A. tel. 415/421-3473)

Council Travel, 1314 N.E. 43rd St., Suite 210, Seattle, WA 98105, U.S.A. (tel. 206/632-2448)

Travel Cuts, 187 College St., Toronto, ON M5T 1P7, Canada (tel. 416/979-2406)

Travel Cuts, 567 Seymour St., Vancouver, BC V6B 3H6, Canada (tel. 604/681-9136)

SYFS, 102/12-13 Koasan Road, Banglumpoo, Bangkok 10200, Thailand (tel. 66-2/282-0507)

HKST, 921a Star House, Tsimshatsui, Kowloon, Hong Kong (tel. 852/2730-3269)

CIEE, Cosmos Aoyama, B1, 5-53-67 Jingumae, Shibuya-ku, Tokyo, Japan (tel. 81-3/5467-5501)

Council Travel, 18 Graf Adolph Strasse, D-40212 Düsseldorf 1, Germany (tel. 49-211/363-030)

Council Travel, 22 rue des Pyramides, 75001 Paris, France (tel. 33-1/4455-5544)

Council Travel, 28A Poland St., near Oxford Circus, London W1V 3DB, United Kingdom (tel. 44-171/437-7767)

Northwest Airlines in conjunction with Air New Zealand offers a **Circle-Pacific fare** of US$2,650 from Los Angeles with add-on airfares available from other North American cities. This ticket allows four free stopovers in Asia and the South Pacific, additional stops US$50 each. To reissue the ticket also costs US$50. It's valid six months and date changes are free. You must travel in a continuous circle without any backtracking. Air Pacific also has a Circle-Pacific fare, so compare.

Alternative methods of flying around the region are explained in the **Getting Around By Air** section that follows. For example, you may be better off using a "Visit South Pacific Pass" or a "Polypass" from a gateway city such as Nadi or Honolulu, accessible on cheap flights from cities worldwide.

Onward Tickets

All of the South Pacific countries require an onward ticket as a condition for entry. Although the immigration officials don't always check it, the airlines usually do. If you're planning a long trip including locally arranged sea travel between countries, this can be a nuisance. One way to satisfy the ticket-to-leave requirement is to purchase a full-fare one-way economy ticket out of the area from Air New Zealand (valid one year). As you're about to depart for the next country on your route have the airline reissue the ticket, so it's a ticket to leave from there. Otherwise buy a full-fare ticket across the Pacific with stops in all the countries you'll visit, then use it *only* to satisfy check-in staff and immigration. When you finally complete your trip return the ticket to the issuing office for a full refund. Remember that airline tickets are often refundable only in the place of purchase and that the sort of deals and discount airfares available elsewhere are not available in the South Pacific. Have your *real* means of departure planned.

AIR SERVICES

From North America

Air New Zealand is the major carrier serving Tonga and Samoa out of Los Angeles. Polynesian Airlines and Royal Tongan Airlines own seats on these Air New Zealand flights, and it's always possible that they'll be selling them for a lower price. Air New Zealand passengers originating in Canada must change planes in Honolulu or Los Angeles.

The only U.S. airline serving Tonga or Samoa is **Hawaiian Airlines,** which offers flights to Pago Pago via its base in Honolulu with connections to/from Las Vegas, Los Angeles, San Francisco, Portland, and Seattle. To Pago Pago the 30-day advance purchase fare is US$499 (plus US$29 tax) from Honolulu or US$799 from the U.S. west coast year-round. Date changes after ticketing are US$75. A free stop in Honolulu is available. Other flights out of Honolulu include Polynesian Airlines to Apia and Royal Tongan Airlines to Tongatapu.

If flying from the U.S. to Vava'u for a yacht charter, it may be easier to fly to Nadi on Air Pacific or Air New Zealand, connecting in Fiji with the Royal Tongan Airlines flight direct to Vava'u.

Air New Zealand

In the 1950s Air New Zealand pioneered its "Coral Route" using Solent flying boats, and today the carrier has achieved a death grip over long-haul air routes into the region by allowing stopovers in Samoa, Tonga, Fiji, Cook Islands, and Tahiti-Polynesia as part of through services between North America and New Zealand. Smaller island-based carriers have difficulty competing due to Air New Zealand's lower operating costs and high capacity, and this advantage is backed up by self-serving government restrictions.

Air New Zealand's first priority is to fly people to Auckland, and it's sometimes cheaper to buy a return ticket to Auckland with a couple of free stops in the islands than a roundtrip ticket from Los Angeles only as far as Tongatapu and Apia. If you don't wish to visit New Zealand, you can transit Auckland the same day. Despite Air New Zealand's frequent services, travelers in Europe and North America often have difficulty booking stops in the islands on their way down under and it's advisable to reserve seats well ahead. Air New Zealand's near monopoly does have the advantage of allowing you to include a number of countries in a single ticket if you do some advance planning.

A return advance-purchase ticket from Los Angeles to a single island is the cheapest way to go. For example, a "No Stop Apex" from Los Angeles to either Apia or Tongatapu is US$973 Jan.-April and Aug.-Nov., or US$1,231 other months (maximum stay one month, 21-day advance purchase, 50% cancellation fee). From Honolulu the same thing is about US$200 less. Also compare Polynesian Airlines and Royal Tongan Airlines, which may be offering better deals. In the high season especially, consider Polynesian's Polypass, which offers visits to Samoa, American Samoa, Tonga, and Fiji during a 45-day period for less than $200 more than a No Stop Apex.

Cheaper tickets to multiple destinations involve a number of restrictions. Air New Zealand's "Coral Experience" allows one stop plus your destination with additional stops available at US$145 each. Thus you can fly Los Angeles-Apia-Tongatapu-Auckland-Los Angeles for US$1,343/1,593/1,843 low/shoulder/high season if you leave at the beginning of the week for a trip of six months maximum. Add US$60 if you'd like to set out on Thursday, Friday, Saturday, or Sunday. Drop either Apia or Tongatapu from your itinerary and you'll save US$145. Trips originating in Honolulu are US$200 cheaper. Remember that the "Coral Experience" must be purchased 14 days in advance and there's a US$75 penalty to change your flight dates. A 35% cancellation fee also applies after the 14-day ticket deadline.

For a more wide-ranging trip with fewer restrictions, ask for Air New Zealand's "Coral Explorer Airpass" which costs US$1,758/2,008/2,258 low/shoulder/high season. This worthwhile ticket allows you to fly Los Angeles-Tahiti-Rarotonga-Fiji-Auckland-Tongatapu-Apia-Honolulu-Los Angeles or vice versa. Extend the ticket to Australia for US$100 more; begin in Honolulu and it's US$200 less. You can stay up to one year but rerouting costs US$75 (date changes are free). There's no advance purchase requirement and you can go any day. To follow the same routing minus two stops on a six-month "Coral Experience" with all its restrictions costs US$1,633/1,883/2,133.

In Canada, Air New Zealand calls the same thing by different names: the "No Stop Apex" is the "Shotover Fare" while the "Coral Experience" is the "Bungy Fare" (the "Explorer" is still the "Explorer"). There's also a cheaper "Backpacker Downunder" fare that must be purchased 14 days in advance and does not cover hotel expenses due to flight misconnections.

On most tickets, special "add-on" fares to Los Angeles or Vancouver are available from cities right across the U.S. and Canada. Also ask about Air New Zealand's "Pacifica Airpass," which covers side trips to destinations not directly on their Coral Route (details in **Getting Around,** which follows).

Air New Zealand's cabin service is professional, and you'll like the champagne breakfasts and outstanding food with complimentary beer and wine. Another plus are the relaxing seats with adjustable head rests and lots of leg room. The *Blue Pacific* videos about their destinations are entertaining the first time you see them, but after a while you get bored. The only reading material provided is the *Pacific Wave* inflight magazine, the *Skyshop* duty free catalog, and the *Primetime* entertainment magazine. These are unlikely to hold your attention for long, so bring along a book or magazine of your own (the daily newspaper is provided only to passengers in first class).

Samoa to Tonga

Air New Zealand flies between Apia and Tongatapu as part of their weekly Los Angeles-Honolulu-Apia-Tongatapu-Auckland service, but this leg is heavily booked and should be reserved as far in advance as possible. If you wait too long and can't obtain a seat for that sector, consider leaving it open and going Apia-Pago Pago-Vava'u-Ha'apai-Tongatapu. Air tickets Pago Pago-Vava'u can only be purchased in Samoa or Tonga, but you'll have no difficulty making bookings at the Samoa Air office in Apia and boats ply regularly from Apia to Pago Pago and Vava'u to Ha'apai and Tongatapu. Your unused Apia-Tongatapu coupon will probably be non-refundable, so this sidetrip will cost extra, but you'll see a lot without having to backtrack. Further information is provided under **Transportation** in the American Samoa chapter.

From Australia

Since the Australian government sold Qantas and deregulated airfares, the cost of flying out of

Australia has dropped dramatically. Now you can often find deals much better than the published Apex fares, especially during off months. Air New Zealand is competing fiercely in the Australian market, and they offer competitive fares to many South Pacific points via Auckland. You can usually buy such tickets for a lower price than you'd pay at the airline office itself by working through an agent specializing in bargain airfares. Check the travel sections in the weekend papers and call Flight Centres International. For information on slightly reduced fares available from STA Travel, see **Student Fares,** above.

The Circle-Pacific and round-the-world fares described above are also available here. Apex (advance purchase excursion) tickets must be bought 14 days in advance and heavy cancellation penalties apply. The low season ex-Australia is generally mid-January to June, mid-July to mid-September, and mid-October to November to Apia, but this varies. A return fare from Sydney to Apia via Auckland will cost A$1,167 in the low season.

Royal Tongan Airlines flies to Tongatapu from Sydney, and **Polynesian Airlines** has direct flights to Apia from Melbourne and Sydney. The Polypass described under Polynesian Airlines in Getting Around may be your best option.

From New Zealand

Unrestricted low airfares to the South Pacific are surprisingly hard to come by in New Zealand. Some tickets have advance purchase requirements, so start shopping well ahead. Ask around at a number of different travel agencies for special unadvertised or under-the-counter fares. Agents to call include STA Travel and Flight Centres International.

Air New Zealand offers reduced excursion fares from Auckland to all the main South Pacific islands with a maximum stay of 90 days to Tonga and Samoa. Fares depend on the season with the low season to Tonga and Samoa from January to mid-April and Oct.-November. In the low/high seasons expect to pay NZ$979/1,169 to Tongatapu and NZ$1,202/1,392 to Apia. It's often cheaper to buy a package tour to the islands with airfare, accommodations, and transfers included, but these are usually limited to seven nights on one island and you're stuck in a boring touristic environment. Ask if you'll be allowed to extend your return date and still get the low inclusive tour price.

Air New Zealand flies from their Auckland gateway to Apia and Tongatapu. Other airlines with flights from Auckland include **Polynesian Airlines** to Tongatapu and Apia, and **Royal Tongan Airlines** to Tongatapu and Niue.

From Europe

Since few European carriers reach the South Pacific, you may have to use a gateway city such as Singapore, Sydney, Honolulu, or Los Angeles. Air New Zealand offers nonstop flights London-Los Angeles five times a week and Frankfurt-Los Angeles three times a week, with connections in L.A. to their Coral Route.

Air New Zealand reservations numbers around Europe are tel. 03/202-1355 (Belgium), tel. 0800/907-712 (France), tel. 01/3081-7778 (Germany), tel. 1678-76126 (Italy), tel. 08-002527 (Luxembourg), tel. 06/022-1016 (Netherlands), tel. 900/993241 (Spain), tel. 020/792-939 (Sweden), tel. 0800/557-778 (Switzerland), and tel. 44-181/741-2299 (United Kingdom). Call them up and ask about their Coral Route fares. Be aware that Air New Zealand flights from Europe are heavily booked and reservations should be made far in advance.

The British specialist in South Pacific itineraries is **Trailfinders** (44-50 Earls Court Rd., Kensington, London W8 6FT; tel. 44-171/938-3366, fax 44-171/937-9294), in business since 1970. They offer a variety of discounted round-the-world tickets through the South Pacific that are often much cheaper than the published fares. Call or write for a free copy of their magazine, *Trailfinder,* which appears in April, July, and December. **Bridge the World** (47 Chalk Farm Rd., Camden Town, London NW1 8AN; tel. 44-171/911-0900, fax 44-171/813-3350, e-mail: sales@bridge-the-world.co.uk) also has good tickets. Check the ads in the London entertainment magazines for other such companies.

In Holland **Pacific Island Travel** (Herengracht 495, 1017 BT Amsterdam, the Netherlands; tel. 31-20/626-1325, fax 31-20/623-0008, e-mail: pitnet@xs4all.nl) sells most of the air passes and long-distance tickets mentioned in this section, plus package tours. **Barron & De Keijzer Travel** (Herengracht 340, 1016 CG Amsterdam, the Netherlands; tel. 31-20/625-8600, fax 31-20/622-7559) sells Air New Zealand's Coral Route via travel via London. Also in Amsterdam, **Reisbureau Amber** (Da Costastraat 77, 1053 ZG Amsterdam, the Netherlands; tel. 31-20/685-1155, fax 31-20/689-0406) is one of the best places in Europe to pick up books on the South Pacific.

In Switzerland try **Globetrotter Travel Service** (Rennweg 35, CH-8023 Zürich, Switzerland; tel. 41-1/213-8080, fax 41-1/213-8088), with offices in Baden, Basel, Bern, Luzern, St. Gallen, Thun, Winterthur, Zug, and Zürich. Their quarterly newsletter, *Ticket-Info,* lists hundreds of cheap flights, including many through the South Pacific.

Bucket shops in Germany sell a "Pacific Airpass" on Air New Zealand from Frankfurt to the South Pacific that allows all the usual Coral Route stops and is valid six months. All flights must be booked prior to leaving Europe, and there's a charge to change the dates once the ticket has been issued. One agency selling such tickets is **Walther-Weltreisen** (Hirschberger Strasse 30, D-53119 Bonn; tel. 49-228/661-239, fax 49-228/661-181). The **Pacific Travel House** (Bayerstrasse 95, D-80335 München; tel. 49-89/530-9293) offers a variety of package tours. **Schöner Tauchen** (Hastedter Heerstr. 211, D-28207 Bremen; tel. 49-421/450-010, fax 49-421/450-080, www.schoener-tauchen.com, e-mail: info@schoener-tauchen.com) specializes in dive tours to Tonga.

Regional Airlines

Aside from the international routes described above, a number of island-based carriers fly around the region. These include the Fijian carrier **Air Pacific,** with flights from Fiji to Apia and Tongatapu. Samoa's **Polynesian Airlines** serves Auckland, Honolulu, Los Angeles, Melbourne, Nadi, Pago Pago, Sydney, Tonga, and Wellington from Apia. Pago Pago-based **Samoa Air** services only Apia and Vava'u. **Royal Tongan Airlines** has flights from Tongatapu to Auckland, Honolulu, Nadi, Niue, and Sydney, and from Vava'u to Nadi. Details of these services are included in the relevant destination chapters of this book. Keep in mind that few regional flights operate daily and quite a few are only once or twice a week.

POLYNESIAN AIRLINES

Polynesian Airlines was founded by Australian aviator Reginald Barnewall in 1959. Daily return flights from Apia to Pago Pago began in 1960, and Polynesian had a monopoly on the route until 1975. In 1964 Polynesian extended service to Fiji, Tonga, and Wallis Island. The Samoan government bought a controlling interest in the fast-growing airline in 1971, and in 1977 flights began to Niue and Rarotonga, extending to Auckland and Tahiti in 1978.

In 1981 Polynesian bought a new 737 directly from Boeing, but overly rapid expansion and cutthroat competition from other carriers soon led to a financial crisis. Thus in 1982 a five-year management contract was signed with Ansett Airlines of Australia, extended for a further 10 years in 1987. At this time Ansett was also managing Air Vanuatu, and in 1982 Polynesian and Air Vanuatu began joint flights from Sydney to Apia via Port Vila. Changes in Australian aviation laws led Ansett to abruptly terminate its contract in 1992 after it obtained authorization to fly internationally under its own colors.

Soon after, Polynesian leased two 737s to service its South Pacific routes, and in May 1993 the airline launched direct air service from Apia to Honolulu and Los Angeles using a 767 leased from Air Canada. By mid-1994 losses totaled US$40 million and only government loan guarantees saved the company from bankruptcy. In late 1994 those responsible for this reckless growth were sacked, the 767 and one 737 withdrawn, and the money-losing U.S. routes dropped. Polynesian's current Honolulu and Los Angeles routes are part of a more sensible code-sharing arrangement with Air New Zealand, and Polynesian is back in the black.

Important Note

Airfares, rules, and regulations tend to fluctuate a lot, so some of the information above may have changed. For more specific information, check the **Getting There** sections in the four chapter introductions. But this is only a guide; we've included a few fares to give you a rough idea how much things might cost. Your travel agent will know what's available at the time you're ready to travel, but if you're not satisfied with his/her advice, keep shopping around. The biggest step is deciding to go—once you're over that, the rest is easy!

PROBLEMS

When planning your trip allow a minimum two-hour stopover between connecting flights at U.S. airports, although with airport delays on the increase even this may not be enough. In the islands allow at least a day between flights. In some airports, flights are not called over the public address system, so keep your eyes open. Whenever traveling, always have a paperback or two, some toiletries, and a change of underwear in your hand luggage.

If your flight is canceled due to a mechanical problem with the aircraft, the airline will cover your hotel bill and meals. If they reschedule the flight on short notice for reasons of their own or you're bumped off an overbooked flight, they should also pay. They may not feel obligated to pay, however, if the delay is due to weather conditions, a strike by another company, national emergencies, etc., although the best airlines still pick up the tab in these cases. Just don't expect much from local, "third-level" airlines on remote islands where such difficulties are routine.

It's an established practice among airlines to provide light refreshments to passengers delayed two hours after the scheduled departure time and a meal after four hours. Don't expect to get this on an outer island, but politely request it if you're at a gateway airport. If you are unexpectedly forced to spend the night somewhere, an airline employee may hand you a form on which they offer to telephone a friend or relative to inform them of the delay. Don't trust them to do this, however. Call your party yourself if you want to be sure they get the message.

Overbooking

To compensate for no-shows, most airlines overbook their flights. To avoid being bumped, ask for your seat assignment when booking, check in early, and go to the departure area well before flight time. Of course, if you *are* bumped by a reputable international airline at a major airport you'll be regaled with free meals and lodging and sometimes even free flight vouchers (don't expect anything like this from a domestic carrier on a remote Pacific island).

Whenever you break your journey for more than 72 hours, always reconfirm your onward reservations and check your seat assignment at the same time. Get the name of the person who takes your reconfirmation so they cannot later deny it. Failure to reconfirm could result in the cancellation of your complete remaining itinerary. This could also happen if you miss a flight for any reason. If you want special vegetarian or kosher food in-flight, request it when buying your ticket, booking, and reconfirming.

When you try to reconfirm your Air New Zealand flight the agent will tell you that this formality is no longer required. Theoretically this is true, but unless you request your seat assignment in advance, either at an Air New Zealand office or over the phone, you could be "bumped" from a full flight, reservation or no reservation. Air New Zealand's ticket cover bears this surprising message:

. . . no guarantee of a seat is indicated by the terms "reservation," "booking," "O.K." status, or the times associated therewith.

They do admit in the same notice that confirmed passengers denied seats may be eligible for compensation, so if you're not in a hurry, a night or two at an upmarket hotel with all meals courtesy of Air New Zealand may not be a hardship. Your best bet if you don't want to get "bumped" is to request seat assignments for your entire itinerary before you leave home, or at least at the first Air New Zealand office you pass during your travels. Any good travel agent selling tickets on Air New Zealand should know enough to automatically request your seat assignments as they make your bookings. In the islands Air New Zealand offices will still accept a local contact telephone number from you. Check Air New Zealand's reconfirmation policy at one of their offices as it could change.

Baggage

International airlines allow economy-class passengers either 20 kilos of baggage or two pieces not over 32 kilos each (ask which applies to you). Under the piece system, neither bag must have a combined length, width, and height of

INTERNATIONAL AIRPORT CODES

AKL—Auckland	RAR—Rarotonga
APW—Apia/Faleolo	SEA—Seattle
CHC—Christchurch	SFO—San
FGI—Apia/Fagalii	Francisco
HNL—Honolulu	SUV—Suva
IUE—Niue	SYD—Sydney
LAX—Los Angeles	TBU—Tongatapu
MEL—Melbourne	TYO—Tokyo
NAN—Nadi	WLG—Wellington
OSA—Osaka	YVR—Vancouver
PPG—Pago Pago	YYZ—Toronto
PPT—Papeete	

over 158 centimeters (62 inches) and the two pieces together must not exceed 272 centimeters (107 inches). On most long-haul tickets to/from North America or Europe, the piece system should apply to all sectors, but check this with the airline. The frequent flier programs of some major airlines allow participants to carry up to 10 kilos of excess baggage free of charge.

Domestically, Royal Tongan Airlines restricts you to 10 kilos total if you book your ticket in Tonga, so it's better to pack according to the lowest common denominator. Polynesian Airlines allows only five kilograms on its domestic flights! Excess baggage charges are not excessive but your luggage may arrive on a later flight and you'll have to go back to the airport to collect it. Polynesian Airlines and Samoa Air are notorious for baggage irregularities on their Apia-Pago Pago services.

Bicycles, folding kayaks, and surfboards can usually be checked as baggage (sometimes for an additional US$50-100 charge), but windsurfers (sailboards) may have to be shipped airfreight. If you do travel with a windsurfer, be sure to call it a surfboard at check-in.

Tag your bag with name, address, and phone number inside and out. Stow anything that could conceivably be considered a weapon (scissors, penknife, toy gun, mace, etc.) in your checked luggage. One reason for lost baggage is that some people fail to remove used baggage tags after they claim their luggage. Get into the habit of tearing off old baggage tags, unless you want your luggage to travel in the opposite direction!

As you're checking in, look to see if the three-letter city codes on your baggage tag receipt and boarding pass are the same.

If your baggage is damaged or doesn't arrive at your destination, inform the airline officials *immediately* and have them fill out a written report; otherwise future claims for compensation will be compromised. Airlines usually reimburse out-of-pocket expenses if your baggage is lost or delayed over 24 hours. The amount varies from US$25 to US$50. Your chances of getting it are better if you're polite but firm. Keep receipts for any money you're forced to spend to replace missing articles.

Claims for lost luggage can take weeks to process. Keep in touch with the airline to show your concern and hang on to your baggage tag until the matter is resolved. If you feel you did not receive the attention you deserved, write the airline an objective letter outlining the case. Get the names of the employees you're dealing with so you can mention them in the letter. Of course, don't expect any pocket money or compensation on a remote outer island. Report the loss, then wait till you get back to their main office. Whatever happens, try to avoid getting angry. The people you're dealing with don't want the problem any more than you do.

BY BOAT

Even as much Pacific shipping was being sunk during WW II, airstrips were springing up on all the main islands. This hastened the inevitable replacement of the old steamships with modern aircraft, and it's now extremely rare to arrive in the South Pacific by boat (private yachts excepted). Most islands export similar products and there's little interregional trade; large container ships headed for Australia, New Zealand, and Japan don't usually accept passengers.

Those bitten by nostalgia for the slower prewar ways may like to know that a couple of passenger-carrying freighters do still call at the islands, though their fares are much higher than those charged by the airlines. A specialized agency booking such passages is **TravLtips** (Box 188, Flushing, NY 11358, U.S.A.; tel. 1-800/872-8584 or 1-718/939-2400, fax 1-718/939-2047, www.TravLtips.com, e-mail: info@travltips.com).

Also try **Freighter World Cruises** (180 South Lake Ave., Suite 335, Pasadena, CA 91101, U.S.A.; tel. 1-818/449-9200, fax 1-818/449-9573, www.gus.net/travel/fwc/fwc.html).

Nature Expeditions International (6400 E. El Dorado Circle, Suite 210, Tucson, AZ 85715, U.S.A.; tel. 1-800/869-0639 or 1-520/721-6712, fax 1-520/721-6719, www.naturexp.com, e-mail: NaturExp@aol.com) books cruises to the farthest corners of Polynesia on the expedition ship *World Discoverer*. Passengers land on remote islands from Zodiacs and there are on-board lectures by world authorities. Island-hopping voyages from Tahiti to Apia and Fiji to Rarotonga are offered.

ORGANIZED TOURS

Packaged Holidays

While packaged travel certainly isn't for everyone, reduced group airfares and hotel rates make some tours worth considering. For two people with limited time and a desire to stay at a first-class hotel, this may be the cheapest way to go. The "wholesalers" who put these packages together get their rooms at rates far lower than individuals pay. Special-interest tours are very popular among sportspeople who want to be sure they'll get to participate in the various activities they enjoy. The main drawback to the tours is that you're on a fixed itinerary in a touristic environment, out of touch with local life. Singles pay a healthy supplement. Some of the companies mentioned below do not accept consumer inquiries and require you to work through a travel agent.

Sunspots International (1918 N.E. 181st, Portland, OR 97230, U.S.A.; tel. 1-800/334-5623 or 1-503/666-3893, fax 1-503/661-7771, www.sunspotsintl.com) has an informative color brochure on Samoa, plus a good website.

Sunmakers (100 West Harrison, South Tower, Suite 350, Seattle, WA 98119, U.S.A.; tel. 1-800/359-4359 or 1-206/216-2900, fax 1-206/216-2906) also books customized itineraries in Samoa.

The **Pacific Destination Center** (18685 Main St., A622, Huntington Beach, CA 92648, U.S.A. (tel. 1-800/227-5317 or 1-714/960-4011, fax 1-714/960-4678, e-mail: pdc@deltanet.com) also specializes in Tonga and Samoa.

Travel Arrangements Ltd. (1268 Broadway, Sonoma, CA 95476, U.S.A.; tel. 1-800/392-8213 or 1-707/938-1118, fax 1-707/938-1268) has individual color brochures depicting upmarket accommodations in Tonga and in Samoa.

From Australia and New Zealand

Hideaway Holidays (Val Gavriloff, 994 Victoria Rd., West Ryde, NSW 2114, Australia; tel. 61-2/9807-4222, fax 61-2/9808-2260, www.hideawayholidays.com.au, e-mail: sales@hideawayholidays.com.au) specializes in off-the-beaten-track packages to every part of the South Pacific and can organize complicated itineraries.

Coral Seas Travel (Suite 1405, 33 Bligh St., Sydney, NSW 2000, Australia; tel. 61-2/9231-2944, fax 61-2/9231-2029, e-mail: cst@acay.com.au) offers a wide range of package tours to Samoa, Tonga, and Niue, departing Sydney. Ask for their attractive color brochures.

The **Pacific and International Travel Company** (Level 1, 91 York St., Sydney, NSW 2000, Australia; tel. 61-2/9244-1811, fax 61-2/9262-6318, e-mail: andrewc@pitc.com.au) books package tours to the South Pacific. Also check **Adventure World** (Box 480, North Sydney, NSW 2059, Australia; tel. 61-2/9223-7966, fax 61-2/9956-7707, www.adventureworld.com.au, e-mail: syd@adventureworld.com.au).

From New Zealand **ASPAC Vacations Ltd.** (Box 4330, Auckland; tel. 64-9/623-0259, fax 64-9/623-0257, e-mail: southpacific@aspac-vacations.co.nz) has packaged tours to most of the areas covered in this book including Niue. **Travel Arrangements Ltd.** (Box 297, Auckland; tel. 64-9/379-5944, fax 64-9/373-2369) offers sailing holidays and package tours throughout the region.

Scuba Tours

The South Pacific is one of the world's prime scuba locales, and most of the islands have excellent facilities for divers. Although it's not that difficult to make your own arrangements as you go, you should consider joining an organized scuba tour if you want to cram in as much diving as possible. To stay in business, the dive travel specialists mentioned below are forced to charge prices similar to what you'd pay on the beach, and the convenience of having everything prearranged is often worth it. Before booking, find out exactly where you'll be staying and ask if daily transfers and meals are provided. Of course, diver certification is mandatory.

One of the top American scuba wholesalers selling the South Pacific is **Poseidon Ventures Tours** (359 San Miguel Dr., Newport Beach, CA 92660, U.S.A.; tel. 1-800/854-9334 or 1-949/644-5344, fax 1-949/644-5392, www.poseidontours.com, e-mail: poseidon@fea.net; or 3724 FM 1960 West, Suite 114, Houston, TX 77068, U.S.A.; tel. 1-281/586-7800, fax 1-281/586-7870).

Tropical Adventures Travel (Box 4337, Seattle, WA 98104-0337, U.S.A.; tel. 1-800/247-3483 or 1-206/441-3483, fax 1-206/441-5431, www.divetropical.com, e-mail: dive@divetropical.com) is similar. Ask for Tropical's South Pacific specialist, Geoff Hynes. Over 6,000 divers a year book through this company, which has been in business since 1973.

In 1998 the noted underwater photographer and author, Carl Roessler, closed down See & Sea Travel Service, which he'd founded in 1966, and became an independent consultant providing advice on scuba facilities and sites worldwide. He makes his money out of "finder fees" paid by selected island suppliers, and his 35 years of experience leading dive tours around the Pacific costs nothing extra to you. Check out his website at www.divxprt.com/see&sea and if you like what you see get in touch with him at **Sea Images** (Box 471899, San Francisco, CA 94147, U.S.A.; tel. 1-415/922-5807, fax 1-415/922-5662, e-mail: divxprt@ix.netcom.com).

In Australia try **Dive Adventures** (Level 9, 32 York St., Sydney, NSW 2000; tel. 61-2/9299-4633, fax 61-2/9299-4644, www.diveadventures.com.au, e-mail: advnture@magna.com.au), a scuba wholesaler with packages to Tonga. Also check **Allways Dive Expeditions** (168 High St., Ashburton, Melbourne, Victoria 3147, Australia: tel. 61-3/9885-8863, fax 61-3/9885-1164, www.allwaysdive.com.au, e-mail: allways@netlink.com.au).

Dive 'N Fishing Travel (15E Vega Pl., Mairangi Bay, Auckland 10, New Zealand; tel. 64-9/479-2210, fax 64-9/479-2214, e-mail: divefish@ihug.co.nz) arranges scuba and game fishing tours to Tonga at competitive rates. They can book cruises in Tongan waters June-Oct. on humpback whalewatching expeditions, with cave, reef, and wreck diving thrown in! ("We

have always seen humpbacks but only 70-80% of the time have the whales shown interest in us and allowed us to join them.")

Alternatively, you can make your own arrangements directly with island dive shops. Information about these operators is included under **Sports and Recreation** in the respective destination chapters of this book.

Tours for Naturalists

Perhaps the most rewarding way to visit the South Seas is with **Earthwatch** (Box 9104, Watertown, MA 02272, U.S.A.; tel. 1-800/776-0188 or 1-617/926-8200, fax 1-617/926-8532, www.earthwatch.org, e-mail: info@earthwatch.org), a nonprofit organization founded in 1971 to serve as a bridge between the public and the scientific community. The programs vary from year to year, but in past they've sent teams to examine the coral reefs or save the giant clams of Tonga. These are not study tours but opportunities for amateurs to help out with serious work, a kind of short-term scientific Peace Corps. As a research volunteer, a team member's share of project costs is tax-deductible in the U.S. and some other countries. For more information contact Earthwatch at the address above, or 126 Bank St., South Melbourne, Victoria 3205, Australia (tel. 61-3/9682-6828, fax 61-3/9686-3652), or Belsyre Court, 57 Woodstock Rd., Oxford OX2 6HU, England (tel. 44-1865/311-600, fax 44-865/311-383), or Technova Inc., Imperial Tower, 13 F Uchisaiwai-Cho 1-1-1, Chiyoda-Ku, Tokyo 100-0011, Japan (tel. 81-3/3508-2280, fax 81-3/3508-7578).

Tours for Seniors

Since 1989 the **Pacific Islands Institute** (Box 1926, Kailua, HI 96734, U.S.A.; tel. 1-808/262-8942, fax 1-808/263-0178, www.pac-island.com, e-mail: info@pac-island.com) has operated educational tours to most of the South Pacific countries in cooperation with Hawaii Pacific University. Their **Elderhostel** people-to-people study programs designed for those aged 55 or over (younger spouses welcome) last two or three weeks. For example, the 24-day tour of Fiji, Tonga, and Samoa offered about 10 times a year costs US$4,400 from Los Angeles or US$4,771 from Boston including airfares, meals, double-occupancy accommodations, transfers, excursions, admissions, tips, taxes, and insurance (singles pay US$435 extra). These culturally responsible trips are highly recommended.

Kayak Tours

The **Friendly Islands Kayak Company** operates ocean kayaking tours through Tonga's Vava'u and Ha'apai groups from Vava'u's Tongan Beach Resort, at US$995/1,220 for nine/11-day packages (ground cost only). May-Dec. the Canadian managers, Doug and Sharon Spence, will be in Tonga (Private Bag, Neiafu, Vava'u, Tonga; tel./fax 676/70-173, www.fikco.com/kayaktonga, e-mail: kayaktonga@kalianet.to), but Jan.-April they should be contacted at their New Zealand address (Box 142, Waitati, Otago 9060; tel./fax 64-3/482-1202). In North America, kayaking tours to Tonga can be booked through **Ecosummer Expeditions** (5640 Hollybridge Way, No. 130, Richmond, BC V7C 4N3, Canada; tel. 1-604/214-7484, fax 1-604/214-7485, www.ecosummer.com, e-mail: trips@ecosummer.com). Call them toll-free at 1-800/465-8884 in Canada or 1-800/465-8884 in the United States. These trips are highly recommended.

Surfing Tours

The largest operator of surfing tours to the South Pacific is **The Surf Travel Company** (Box 446, Cronulla, NSW 2230, Australia; tel. 61-2/9527-4722, fax 61-2/9527-4522, www.surftravel.com.au, e-mail: surftrav@ozemail.com.au) with packages to Ha'atafu Beach (Tonga) and Upolu (Samoa). In New Zealand book through Mark Thompson (7 Danbury Dr., Torbay, Auckland; tel./fax 64-9/473-8388).

One of the largest American companies offering surfing tours to Samoa and Tonga is **Waterways Travel** (15145 Califa St., Suite 1, Van Nuys, CA 91411, U.S.A.; tel. 1-800/928-3757 or 1-818/376-0341, fax 1-818/376-0353, www.waterwaystravel.com).

Yacht Tours and Charters

If you were planning on spending a substantial amount to stay at a luxury resort, consider chartering a yacht instead! Divided up among the members of your party the per-person charter price will be about the same, but you'll experience much more of the Pacific's beauty on a boat than you would staying in a hotel room. All charterers visit remote islands accessible only by small boat and thus receive special insights into island life unspoiled by normal tourist trappings. Of course, activities such as sailing, snorkeling, and general exploring by sea and land are included in the price.

Yacht charters are available either "bareboat" (for those with the skill to sail on their own) or "crewed" (in which case charterers pay a daily fee for a skipper plus his/her provisions). On a "flotilla" charter a group of bareboats follow an experienced lead yacht.

One of the finest companies arranging such charters is **Ocean Voyages Inc.** (1709 Bridgeway, Sausalito, CA 94965, U.S.A.; tel. 1-800/299-4444 or 1-415/332-4681, fax 1-415/332-7460, www.crowleys.com/ocean.htm, e-mail: voyages@ix.netcom.com). Unlike their competitors, Ocean Voyages organizes "shareboat" charters in which singles and couples book a cabin on yachts sailing to the remotest corners of the South Pacific. Ask about shareboat yacht cruises on fixed itineraries of anywhere from one week to two months. Individuals are welcome and there are about 50 departures a year on a range of vessels. Prices average US$100-250 pp a day, and scuba diving is possible at extra cost on some boats (ask). This is perfect if you're alone or in a party of two and can't afford to charter an entire bareboat yacht. Most vessels take only four to eight passengers but the brigantine *Soren Larsen* can accommodate up to 22. For groups four or six they can help select the right charter yacht for a dream vacation.

One of the classic "tall ships" cruising the South Pacific is the two-masted brigantine *Soren Larsen,* built in 1949. May-Nov. this 42-meter square rig vessel operates 10-19 day voyages to Tonga, Fiji, Vanuatu, and New Caledonia costing NZ$2,500-3,680. The 12-member professional crew is actively assisted by 22 voyage participants. For information contact **Square Sail Pacific** (Box 310, Kumeu, Auckland 1250, New Zealand; tel. 64-9/411-8755, fax 64-9/411-8484). Ocean Voyages handles bookings in North America. In the U.K. contact **Explore Worldwide** (1 Frederick St., Aldershot, Hants GU11 1LQ, United Kingdom; tel. 44-1252/319-448, fax 44-1251/343170, www.explore.co.uk).

The Moorings (4th Floor, 19345 U.S. 19 North, Clearwater, FL 34624, U.S.A.; tel. 1-

800/535-7289, fax 1-813/530-9747, www.moorings.com, e-mail: yacht@moorings.com) offers bareboat and crewed yacht charters from their own base at Vava'u where charters are US$300-720 a day. The low season is January to mid-March at Tonga. Prices are for the entire boat, but extras are airfare, food (US$32 pp daily), skipper (US$100 daily plus food, if required), and cook (US$80 plus food, if desired). They check you out to make sure you're really capable of handling their vessels. Other obligatory extras are security insurance (US$25 a day), cancellation insurance (US$75 pp), and local tax (7.5% in Tonga). Always ask about "specials," such as nine days for the price of seven (reservations clerks often don't volunteer this information). Their New Zealand office is **The Moorings Yacht Charters** (Box 90413, Auckland, New Zealand; tel. 64-9/377-4840, fax 64-9/377-4820, e-mail: info@clubseafarer.co.nz).

Before deciding, turn to the Vava'u section of this book for information on The Mooring's competitor, **Sunsail** (www.sunsail.co.nz). A local Vava'u operation called **Sailing Safaris** is less expensive than either, catering to couples who want a small boat just to get a taste of chartering.

A few private brokers arranging bareboat or crewed yacht charters at Vava'u are **Sun Yacht Charters** (Box 737, Camden, ME 04843, U.S.A.; tel. 1-800/772-3500, fax 1-207/236-3972, www.sunyachts.com), **Charter World Pty. Ltd.** (23 Passchendaele St., Hampton, Melbourne 3188, Australia; tel. 61-3/9521-0033, fax 61-3/9521-0081), **Sail Connections Ltd.** (Box 3234, Auckland 1015, New Zealand; tel. 64-9/358-0556, fax 64-9/358-4341, e-mail: jeni@sailconnections.co.nz), **Yachting Partners International** (28-29 Richmond Pl., Brighton, Sussex, BN2 2NA, United Kingdom; tel. 44-1273/571-722, fax 44-1273/571-720, e-mail: ypi@ypi.co.uk), and **Crestar Yachts Ltd.** (125 Sloane St., London SW1X 9AU, United Kingdom; tel. 44-171/730-9962, fax 44-171/824-8691). As they don't own their own boats (as The Moorings does), they'll be more inclined to fit you to the particular boat that suits your individual needs.

GETTING AROUND

BY AIR

In 1995 the Association of South Pacific Airlines introduced a **Visit South Pacific Pass** to coincide with "Visit South Pacific Year" and the pass has been so successful that the Association decided to extend it indefinitely. This pass allows travelers to include the services of 10 regional carriers in a single ticket. The initial two-leg air pass has to be purchased in conjunction with an international ticket into the region, but additional legs up to eight maximum can be purchased after arrival. Only the first sector has to be booked ahead.

The flights are priced at three different levels. For US$175 per sector you can go Fiji-Apia/Nauru/Tongatapu/Port Vila/Vava'u/Funafuti, Apia-Tongatapu, Nouméa-Port Vila, Nauru-Pohnpei/Tarawa, Niue-Tongatapu, or Funafuti-Tarawa. For US$220 you have a choice of Honiara-Nadi/Port Vila/Port Moresby, Nouméa/Tahiti-Nadi, Funafuti-Majuro, Fiji-Tarawa, or a variety of flights from Australia and New Zealand to the islands. For US$320 there's Honiara-Auckland, Tahiti-Nouméa, Sydney-Tongatapu, and Fiji-Majuro. It's a great way of getting around the South Pacific.

Air New Zealand calls this ticket the "Pacifica Airpass" and it can only be purchased in North or South America, Europe, or Asia. One North American agent selling the Visit South Pacific Pass is **Air Promotions Systems** (5757 West Century Blvd., Suite 660, Los Angeles, CA 90045-6407, U.S.A.; tel. 1-800/677-4277 or 1-310/670-7302; fax 1-310/338-0708, www.pacificislands.com). They handle the pass for flights on Aircalin, Air Nauru, Air Vanuatu, and Solomon Airlines. For information on using the pass on Air Pacific, Polynesian Airlines, Qantas, or Royal Tongan Airlines, call the toll-free 800 numbers of those airlines provided at the beginning of **Getting There**.

Also compare the price of regular one-way tickets with stopovers as a way of island hopping around the South Pacific, linking flights together with a free stop in the home country of the airline. For example, buy Port Vila-Apia or Honiara-Nuku'alofa with a free stop in Fiji from Air Pacific, Apia-Auckland or Niue-Fiji with a free stop in Nuku'alofa from Royal Tongan Airlines, etc. You may have to buy these tickets directly from the airlines themselves as travel agents will want to add up all the sector fares, but full-fare tickets like these are valid one year and have virtually no restrictions. Compare prices and be creative.

Polynesian Airlines

Polynesian Airlines flies to Apia, Auckland, Honolulu, Los Angeles, Melbourne, Nadi, Pago Pago, Sydney, Tongatapu, and Wellington, and if you've got a month and a half to see a slice of the South Pacific, their **Polypass** may be for you. This allows 45 days unlimited travel between Nadi, Tongatapu, Apia, and Pago Pago, plus one roundtrip from Sydney, Melbourne, Auckland, or Wellington for US$999. From Honolulu the pass costs US$1,149, from Los Angeles US$1,399. Restrictions are that your itinerary must be worked out in advance and can only be changed once. Thus it's important to book all flights well ahead. A 20% penalty is charged to refund an unused ticket (no refund after one year).

Also ask about Polynesian's **Pacific Triangle Fare** (US$450), which allows one a full year to complete the Apia-Tongatapu-Nadi loop. For more information, see www.polynesianairlines.co.nz or call tel. 1-800/644-7659.

Air Pacific

Air Pacific has a **Pacific Triangle Fare,** a good way to get around and experience the region's variety of cultures: Fiji-Apia-Tonga-Fiji (F$724). It's valid for one year and can be purchased at any travel agency in Fiji or direct from the airline. It's usually only good for journeys commencing in Fiji. Flight dates can be changed at no charge. When booking this circular ticket, be aware that it's much better to go Fiji-Apia-Tonga-Fiji than vice versa, because the flights between Apia and Fiji are often fully booked while it's easy to get on between Tonga and Fiji. Also obtainable locally are Air Pacific's special 28-day roundtrip excursion fares from Fiji to Apia (F$561) and Tonga (F$469). Some of these fares have seasonal variations.

A **Pacific Air Pass** allows 30 days travel (on Air Pacific flights only) from Fiji to Apia, Tonga, and Port Vila (US$462). This pass can only be purchased from Qantas Airways offices in North America and Europe, or from Air Pacific's U.S. office, Suite 475, 841 Apollo St., El Segundo, CA 90245-4741 (tel. 1-800/227-4446 or 1-310/524-9350, fax 1-310/524-9356, www.bulafiji.com/airlines/airpac/htm).

BY SEA

Ninety-nine percent of international travel around the South Pacific is by air. With few exceptions travel by boat is a thing of the past, and about the only regular international service is Apia to Pago Pago. Local boats to the outer islands of Tonga and Samoa are readily available, however. Among the local trips you can easily do by regularly scheduled boat are Tongatapu-Vava'u, Tongatapu-'Eua, and Upolu-Savai'i. Details of these and other shipping possibilities are explored in the different destination chapters of this book.

the ferry Queen Salamasina *with* Rainmaker Mountain *in the background*

MARITIME COORDINATES

ISLAND GROUP

ISLAND	LAND AREA (SQ KM)	HIGHEST POINT (M)	POPULATION	LATITUDE	LONGITUDE
SAMOA					
Savai'i	1,709.0	1,858	45,050	13.60°S	172.45°W
Upolu	1,114.0	1,100	115,121	13.95°S	171.70°W
AMERICAN SAMOA					
Aunuu	2.0	88	400	14.29°S	170.55°W
Ofu	7.0	494	353	14.19°S	169.65°W
Olosega	5.0	639	225	14.19°S	169.62°W
Rose Atoll	1.0	5	nil	14.53°S	168.87°W
Swains	3.0	5	16	11.06°S	171.08°W
Ta'u	46.0	965	1,136	14.25°S	169.47°W
Tutuila	137.0	652	44,643	14.30°S	170.75°W
TONGA					
Ata	2.3	355	2	22.20°S	176.12°W
'Eua	87.0	312	4,924	21.20°S	174.57°W
Foa	13.4	14	1,413	19.74°S	174.30°W
Fonuafo'ou	0.0	varies	nil	20.32°S	175.42°W
Fonualei	4.3	195	nil	18.01°S	174.19°W
Ha'ano	6.6	8	581	19.67°S	174.28°W
Hunga	4.7	75	345	18.41°S	174.08°W
Hunga Ha'apai	0.7	122	nil	20.55°S	175.42°W
Hunga Tonga	0.4	149	nil	20.53°S	175.42°W
Kao	11.6	1,046	nil	19.40°S	175.01°W
Kapa	6.0	96	410	18.43°S	174.03°W
Late	17.4	519	nil	18.48°S	174.39°W
Lifuka	11.4	14	2,990	19.80°S	174.35°W
Niuafo'ou	50.3	205	735	15.35°S	175.38°W
Niuatoputapu	18.0	146	1,161	15.58°S	173.45°W
Nomuka	7.1	51	551	20.15°S	174.48°W
Noapapu	2.7	64	381	18.42°S	174.05°W
Pangaimotu	8.9	88	837	18.40°S	174.00°W
Tafahi	3.4	506	122	15.51°S	173.43°W
Tofua	55.6	505	5	19.45°S	175.05°W
Tongatapu	257.0	82	66,577	21.10°S	175.20°W
Vava'u	89.7	204	12,320	18.39°S	174.00°W
NIUE					
Niue	259.0	73	1,900	19.05°S	169.85°W

BY SAILING YACHT

Getting Aboard

Hitch rides into the Pacific on yachts from California, Panama, New Zealand, and Australia, or around the yachting triangle Papeete-Suva-Honolulu. At home, scrutinize the classified listings of yachts seeking crews, yachts to be delivered, etc., in magazines like *Yachting, Cruising World, Sail,* and *Latitude 38.* You can even advertise yourself for about US$25 (plan to have the ad appear three months before the beginning of the season). Check the bulletin boards at yacht clubs and explore the links at www.cruisingworld.com and www.seafaring.com. The **Seven Seas Cruising Association** (1525 South Andrews Ave., Suite 217, Fort Lauderdale, FL 33316, U.S.A.; tel. 1-954/463-2431, fax 1-954/463-7183, www.ssca.org, e-mail: SSCA1@ibm.net) is in touch with yachties all around the Pacific, and the classified section "Crew Exchange" in their monthly *Commodores' Bulletin* contains ads from captains in search of crew.

Cruising yachts are recognizable by their foreign flags, wind-vane steering gear, sturdy appearance, and laundry hung out to dry. Put up notices on yacht club and marine bulletin boards, and meet people in bars. When a boat is hauled out, you can find work scraping and repainting the bottom, varnishing, and doing minor repairs. It's much easier, however, to crew on yachts already in the islands. In Tahiti, for example, after a month on the open sea, some of the original crew may have flown home or onward, opening a place for you. Pago Pago, Vava'u, Suva, Musket Cove, and Port Vila are other places to look for a boat.

If you've never crewed before, it's better to try for a short passage the first time. Once at sea on the way to Tahiti, there's no way they'll turn around to take a seasick crew member back to Hawaii. Good captains evaluate crew on personality, attitude, and a willingness to learn more than experience, so don't lie. Be honest and open when interviewing with a skipper—a deception will soon become apparent.

It's also good to know what a captain's *really* like before you commit yourself to an isolated month with her/him. To determine what might happen should the electronic gadgetry break down, find out if there's a sextant aboard and whether he/she knows how to use it. A run-down-looking boat may often be mechanically unsound too. Also be concerned about a skipper who doesn't do a careful safety briefing early on, or who seems to have a hard time hanging onto crew. If the previous crew have left the boat at an unlikely place such as the Marquesas, there must have been a reason. Once you're on a boat and part of the yachtie community, things are easy. (P.S. from veteran yachtie Peter Moree: "We do need more ladies out here—adventurous types naturally.")

Time of Year

The weather and seasons play a deciding role in any South Pacific trip by sailboat and you'll have to pull out of many beautiful places, or be unable to stop there, because of bad weather. The favorite season for rides in the South Pacific is May-Oct.; sometimes you'll even have to turn one down. Around August or September start looking for a ride from the South Pacific to Hawaii or New Zealand.

Be aware of the hurricane season: Nov.-March in the South Pacific, July-Dec. in the northwest Pacific (near Guam), and June-Oct. in the area between Mexico and Hawaii. Few yachts will be cruising those areas at these times. A few yachts spend the winter at Pago Pago and Vava'u (the main "hurricane holes"), but most South Pacific cruisers will have left for hurricane-free New Zealand by October.

Also, know which way the winds are blowing; the prevailing trade winds in the tropics are from the northeast north of the equator, from the southeast south of the equator. North of the tropic of Cancer and south of the tropic of Capricorn the winds are out of the west. Due to the action of prevailing southeast tradewinds, boat trips are smoother from east to west than west to east throughout the South Pacific, so that's the way to go.

Yachting Routes

The South Pacific is good for sailing; there's not too much traffic and no piracy like you'd find in the Mediterranean or in Indonesian waters. The common yachting route or "Coconut Milk Run" across the South Pacific utilizes the northeast and southeast trades: from California to Tahiti via the Marquesas or Hawaii, then Rarotonga, Niue, Vava'u, Suva, and New Zealand. Some yachts continue west from Fiji to Port Vila. In the other direction, you'll sail on the westerlies from New Zealand to a point south of the Australs, then north on the trades to Tahiti.

Some 300 yachts leave the U.S. west coast for Tahiti every year, almost always crewed by couples or men only. Most stay in the South Seas about a year before returning to North America, while a few continue around the world. About 60-80 cross the Indian Ocean every year (look for rides from Sydney in May, Cairns or Darwin from June to August, Bali from August to October, Singapore from October to December); around 700 yachts sail from Europe to the Caribbean (from Gibraltar and Gran Canaria from October to December).

Cruising yachts average about 150 km a day, so it takes about a month to get from the U.S. west coast to Hawaii, then another month from Hawaii to Tahiti. To enjoy the finest weather conditions many yachts clear the Panama Canal or depart California in February to arrive in the Marquesas in March. From Hawaii, yachts often leave for Tahiti in April or May. Many stay on for the *Heiva i Tahiti* festival, which ends on 14 July, at which time they sail west to Vava'u, where you'll find them in July and August. In mid-September the yachting season culminates with a race by about 40 boats from Musket Cove on Fiji's Malololailai Island to Port Vila (it's very easy to hitch a ride at this time). By late October the bulk of the yachting community is sailing south via New Caledonia to New Zealand or Australia to spend the southern summer there. In April or May on alternate years (1995, 1997, etc.) there's a yacht race from Auckland and Sydney to Suva, timed to coincide with the cruisers' return after the hurricane season.

Blue Water Rallies (Peter Seymour, Windsor Cottage, Chedworth, Cheltenham, Gloucestershire GL54 4AA, United Kingdom; tel./fax 44-1285/720-904) organizes annual round-the-world yachting rallies, departing Europe each October. Inquiries from both owners and potential crew members are welcome for these 20-month circumnavigations that visit Galapagos, the Marquesas, Tahiti, Tonga, and Fiji. Blue Water's professional support services will help make that "voyage of a lifetime" a reality! Similar events are organized by Jimmy Cornell's **World Cruising** (Box 165, London WC1B 3XA, United Kingdom; tel. 44-171/405-9905, fax 44-171/831-0161), departing Fort Lauderdale, Florida, in February.

Be aware that a law enacted in New Zealand in 1995 requires foreign yachts departing New Zealand to obtain a "Certificate of Inspection" from the New Zealand Yachting Federation prior to customs clearance. This regulation has led to a 30% decline in the number of yachts visiting New Zealand, and it's wise to consider alternative summer anchorages before sailing into a situation where some clerk may force you to spend of thousands of dollars upgrading safety standards on your boat before you'll be permitted to leave.

Life Aboard

To crew on a yacht you must be willing to wash and iron clothes, cook, steer, keep watch at night, and help with engine work. Other jobs might include changing and resetting sails, cleaning the boat, scraping the bottom, pulling up the anchor, and climbing the main mast to watch for reefs. Do more than is expected of you. A safety harness must be worn in rough weather. As a guest in someone else's home you'll want to wash your dishes promptly after use and put them, and all other gear, back where you found them. Tampons must not be thrown in the toilet bowl. Smoking is usually prohibited as a safety hazard.

You'll be a lot more useful if you know how to tie knots like the clove hitch, rolling hitch, sheet bend, double sheet bend, reef knot, square knot, figure eight, and bowline. Check your local library for books on sailing or write away for the comprehensive free catalog of nautical books available from International Marine Publishing, Box 548, Black Lick, OH 43004, U.S.A. (tel. 1-800/262-4729, fax 1-614/759-3641, www.pbg.mcgraw-hill.com/im).

Anybody who wants to get on well under sail must be flexible and tolerant, both physically and emotionally. Expense-sharing crew members pay US$10 a day or more per person. After 30 days you'll be happy to hit land for a freshwater shower. Give adequate notice when you're ready to leave the boat, but *do* disembark when your journey's up. Boat people have few enough opportunities for privacy as it is. If you've had a good trip, ask the captain to write you a letter of recommendation; it'll help you hitch another ride.

Food for Thought

When you consider the big investment, depreciation, cost of maintenance, operating expenses, and considerable risk (most cruising yachts are not insured), travel by sailing yacht is quite a luxury. The huge cost can be surmised from charter fees (US$500 a day and up for a 10-meter yacht). International law makes a clear distinction between passengers and crew. Crew members paying only for their own food, cooking gas, and part of the diesel are very different from charterers who do nothing and pay full costs. The crew is there to help operate the boat, adding safety, but like passengers, they're very much under the control of the captain. Crew has no say in where the yacht will go.

The skipper is personally responsible for crew coming into foreign ports: he's entitled to hold their passports and to see that they have onward tickets and sufficient funds for further traveling. Otherwise the skipper might have to pay their hotel bills and even return airfares to the crew's country of origin. Crew may be asked to pay a share of third-party liability insurance. Possession of dope can result in seizure of the yacht. Because of such considerations, skippers often hesitate to accept crew. Crew members should remember that at no cost to themselves they can learn a bit of sailing and visit places nearly inaccessible by other means. Although not for everyone, it's *the* way to see the real South Pacific, and folks who arrive by *kalia* (sailing canoe) are treated differently than other tourists.

OTHER TRAVEL OPTIONS

By Bus

Most of the islands have highly developed bus systems serving mostly local people. In this handbook, we cover them all. Buses are also a good and inexpensive way to get around Tongatapu, Tutuila, Upolu, and Savai'i. A local bus ride will cost under US$0.25 in Tonga and both Samoas.

By Car

A rental car with unlimited mileage will generally cost around US$40 a day in Samoa and Tonga, and US$50 in American Samoa. The price of a liter of gasoline varies slightly: American Samoa US$0.37, Samoa US$0.39, and Tonga US$0.55. To determine the price of an American gallon, multiply any of these by 3.7854.

Due to the alternative means of travel available, the only places where you really need to consider renting a car is on Upolu and Savai'i in Samoa. Renting a car is an unnecessary luxury in American Samoa due to the excellent public transportation available. In Tonga one must pay a stiff fee for a local driver's license (international driver's license not recognized) and it's better to tour that country by rented bicycle anyway.

The car rental business is very competitive and it's possible to shop around for a good deal upon arrival. Although the locally operated companies may offer cheaper rates than the international franchises, it's also true that the agents of Avis, Budget, and Hertz are required to maintain recognized standards of service and they have regional offices where you can complain if anything goes seriously wrong. Always find out if insurance, mileage, and tax are included, and check for restrictions on where you'll be allowed to take the car. If in doubt, ask to see a copy of their standard rental contract before making reservations.

Driving is on the right (as in continental Europe and North America) in Samoa and American Samoa, and on the left (as in Britain, New Zealand, and Japan) in Tonga and Niue. If you do rent a car, remember those sudden tropical downpours and don't leave the windows open. Also avoid parking under coconut trees (a falling nut might break the window), and never go off and leave the keys in the ignition.

By Bicycle

Bicycling in the South Pacific? Sure, why not? It's cheap, convenient, healthy, quick, environmentally sound, safe, and above all, *fun.* You'll be able to go where and when you please, stop easily and often to meet people and take photos, save money on taxi fares—really *see* the countries. Cycling every day can be fatiguing, however, so it's smart to have bicycle-touring experience beforehand. Savai'i may be the best island for an extended trip, if you're well prepared. Most roads are flat along the coast, but be careful on coral roads, especially inclines: if you slip and fall you could hurt yourself badly. On the high islands such as Upolu, interior roads tend to be very steep. Never ride your bike through mud.

A sturdy, single-speed mountain bike with wide wheels, safety chain, and good brakes might be ideal. Thick tires and a plastic liner between tube and tire will reduce punctures. Know how to fix your own bike. Take along a good repair kit (pump, puncture kit, freewheel tool, spare spokes, cables, chain links, assorted nuts and bolts, etc.) and a repair manual; bicycle shops are poor to nonexistent in the islands. Don't try riding with a backpack: sturdy, waterproof panniers (bike bags) are required; you'll also want a good lock. Refuse to lend your bike to *anyone.*

Most international airlines will carry a bicycle as checked luggage, usually free but sometimes at the standard overweight charge or for a flat US$50 fee. The charter carriers are the more likely to charge extra, but verify the airline's policy when booking. Take off the pedals and panniers, turn the handlebars sideways and tie them down, deflate the tires, and clean off the dirt before checking in (or use a special bike-carrying bag) and arrive at the airport early. The commuter airlines usually won't accept bikes on their small planes. Interisland boats sometimes charge a token amount to carry a bike; other times it's free. If you'd just like to rent a bicycle lo-cally, you'll have the most opportunities to do so in Tonga.

By Ocean Kayak

Ocean kayaking is experiencing a boom in Hawaii, but the South Pacific is still largely virgin territory. Virtually every island has a sheltered lagoon ready-made for the excitement of kayak touring, but this effortless transportation mode hasn't yet arrived, so you can be a real independent 20th-century explorer! Many international airlines accept folding kayaks as checked baggage at no charge.

For a better introduction to ocean kayaking than is possible here, check at your local public library for sea kayaking manuals. Noted author Paul Theroux toured the entire South Pacific by kayak, and his experiences are recounted in *The Happy Isles of Oceania: Paddling the Pacific* (London: Hamish Hamilton, 1992).

By Canoe

If you get off the beaten track, it's more than likely that a local friend will offer to take you out in his outrigger canoe. Never attempt to take a dugout canoe through even light surf: you'll be swamped. Don't try to pull or lift a canoe by its outrigger—it will break. Drag the canoe by holding the solid main body. A bailer is *essential* equipment.

SAMOA

INTRODUCTION

The sultry, verdant isles of Samoa, two-thirds of the way between Hawaii and New Zealand, lie in the very heart of the South Pacific. Independent since 1962 and called Western Samoa until 1997, this is the larger portion of an archipelago split apart by colonialism in 1899. Although both Samoa and American Samoa sprang from the same roots, differing patterns of development are reflected in contrasting lifestyles—this highlights the impact of westernization on a Pacific people. Yet on both sides of the 100-km strait separating Upolu from Tutuila, Samoans have retained their ancient customs as nowhere else in Polynesia, and the *fa'a Samoa,* or Samoan way, continues to flourish.

This society has attracted poets rather than painters. Robert Louis Stevenson spent his last five years here, and Rupert Brooke was enraptured by the islands and their people:

You lie on a mat in a cool Samoan hut, and look out on the white sand under the high palms, and a gentle sea, and the black line of the reef a mile out, and moonlight over everything. . . . And then among it all are the loveliest people in the world, moving and dancing like gods and goddesses, very quietly and mysteriously, and utterly content. It is sheer beauty, so pure that it's difficult to breathe it in.

Travelers inbound from a dreary industrial world may be forgiven if they imagine they've arrived in the garden of Eden, but there's more to it. In a series of provocative novels, Samoan author Albert Wendt has portrayed the conflicting pressures of *palagi* (foreign) life on his people. The protagonist in *Sons for the Return Home* finds he can no longer accept the *fa'a*-sanctioned authority of his mother, while *Leaves of the Banyan Tree* explores the universal themes of a changing Samoan society. In *Pouliuli,* the complex social relationships of village life unravel in a drama of compelling force. Wendt's books bring us closer to the complexity of a third-world Samoa shaken by economic crises, incompetence, and corruption, and searching desperately for a formula to reconcile timeworn traditions and contemporary consumer needs. "Gauguin is dead! There is no paradise!" shouts a character in Sia Figiel's recent novel *Where We Once Belonged.*

Paradoxically, although your status as a foreigner will never be in doubt, you'll find the Samoans to be among the South Pacific's most approachable peoples. You'll sight some really striking physical types and meet a few unforgettable characters. Some visitors find it too intense, but almost everyone will leave with a story to tell about Samoa. Alongside the human element, an outstanding variety of landscapes and attractions are packed into a small area made all the more accessible because this is one of the least expensive countries in the region. Everything is vividly colorful and well-groomed, and it's still undiscovered by mass tourism. Add it up and you'll recognize Samoa as one of the world's top travel destinations and an essential stop on any South Pacific trip.

The Land

Samoa is made up of four inhabited and five uninhabited islands totaling 2,842 square km, a bit bigger than the American state of Rhode Island. Unlike most Pacific countries, which are scattered across vast areas, all of these islands are in one main cluster, which makes getting around fairly easy. Upolu is the more developed and populous, containing the capital, Apia; Savai'i is a much broader island. Together these two account for 96% of Samoa's land area and 99% of the population. Between them sit populated Apolima and Manono, while the five islets off

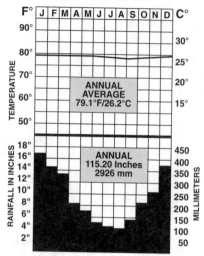

APIA'S CLIMATE

southeast Upolu shelter only seabirds. The fringing reefs around the two big islands protect soft, radiantly calm coastlines.

Samoa's lush volcanic islands increase in age from west to east. Savai'i, though dormant, spewed lava within this century; the now-extinct cones of western Upolu erupted much more recently than those farther east. Well-weathered Tutuila and Manu'a in American Samoa are older yet, while 10-million-year-old Rose Island is a classic atoll.

Savai'i is a massive shield-type island formed by fast-flowing lava building up in layers over a long period. The low coast gradually slopes upward to a broad, 1,858-meter center of several parallel chains. Upolu's elongated 1,100-meter dorsal spine of extinct shield volcanoes slopes more steeply on the south than on the north. The eastern part of the island is rough and broken, while broad plains are found in the west.

Climate

Samoa is closer to the equator than Fiji, Tonga, or Rarotonga, thus it's noticeably hotter and more humid year-round. May-Oct. (winter) the days are cooled by the southeast trades; winds vary from west to north in the rainy season, Nov.-April (summer). Practically speaking, the sea-

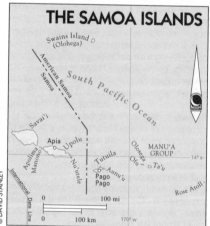

THE SAMOA ISLANDS

© DAVID STANLEY

sonal variations are not great, and long periods of sun are common even during the "rainy" months. Southern Upolu gets more rain than northern, but much of it falls at night. The rainfall feeds Samoa's many spectacular waterfalls and supports the luxuriant vegetation.

December to March is hurricane time; ships at Apia should put to sea at the first warning as the harbor is unsafe when a storm blows out of the north. In recent years, Samoa has suffered an increasing number of devastating hurricanes partially due to the greenhouse effect as the surrounding seas warm up.

Flora and Fauna

Rainforests thrive in the mountain areas, where heavy rainfall nurtures huge tree ferns and slow-growing, moss-laden hardwoods. The vegetation is sparse in the intermediate zones, where more recent lava flows fail to hold moisture or soil. The richer coastal strip is well planted in vegetable gardens and coconut plantations. The national flower is the *teuila* or red ginger *(Alpinia purpurata),* an elongated stalk with many waxy red petals.

Although Upolu is smaller than Savai'i, its rich volcanic soil supports 72% of the population of Samoa; much of Savai'i is barren due to recent lava flows and the porousness of the soil, which allows rapid runoff of moisture. The rainforests of Samoa are threatened by exploitive logging operations for short-sighted economic gain and already 80% of the lowland tropical rainforests have been replaced by plantations or logged. On a square kilometer basis, deforestation is occurring much faster than in the Amazon. Re-

planting is usually done in teak and mahogany, which native birds cannot use.

About 16 of 34 land bird species are unique to Samoa. One such species, the toothbilled pigeon or *manumea (Didunculus strigirostris),* is thought to be a living link with toothbilled birds of fossil times. Due to overhunting and habitat destruction, all native species of pigeons and doves are approaching extinction. Parliament has banned all hunting of fruit bats (flying foxes) and Pacific pigeons, but this is not enforced and the populations have not recovered from the carnage on the 1980s. From 1981 to 1986 over 30,000 flying foxes were exported from Samoa to Guam for gastronomical purposes, a trade that ended only in 1989 when the bats were added to the endangered species list. No snakes live on Upolu, although two harmless species are found on Savai'i. Attack dogs are a nuisance throughout Samoa, but unless you've actually entered someone's yard, they'll soon retreat when they see you reaching down to pick up a stone.

HISTORY AND GOVERNMENT

Prehistory

Samoa was named for the sacred *(sa)* chickens *(moa)* of Lu, son of Tagaloa, the god of creation. Samoan tradition asserts that Savai'i was Hawaiki, the legendary Polynesian homeland where the Samoans originated. Archaeologists confirm that the Polynesians had settled in Samoa by 1000 B.C. and here evolved their distinctive culture. It was a beautiful, comfortable, productive place to live. Their vegetables thrived

SAMOA AT A GLANCE

ISLAND	POPULATION (1991)	AREA (SQUARE KM)	HIGHEST POINT (METERS)
Savai'i	45,050	1,709	1,858
Apolima	63	1	168
Manono	1,064	3	107
Upolu	115,121	1,114	1,100
SAMOA (total)	161,298	2,842*	

*The uninhabited islands of Nu'usafe'e, Nu'utele, Nu'ulua, Namu'a, and Fanuatapu are included in this total.

in the rich volcanic soil, and the lagoon provided ample fish. They had found their true home; not for another millennium did small groups push farther east from this "cradle of Polynesia" to colonize Tahiti and the Marquesas.

The ancient Samoans maintained regular contact with Fiji and Tonga; Tongan invaders ruled Samoa from A.D. 950 to 1250 and the oral traditions of Samoa date back to the expulsion of the Tongans. This feat was accomplished by the first holder of what is still the highest chiefly title, Malietoa, meaning brave *(malie)* warrior *(toa)*. The legendary 15th-century queen, Salamasina, became the only Samoan ruler ever to unite the four chiefly titles into one, and for 60 years Samoa enjoyed peace. The *matai,* or chiefly system, was well developed for almost 1,000 years before Europeans arrived in the late 18th century. Religion was less developed, and the chiefs were elected from high-ranking lineages: everywhere else in Polynesia they were hereditary.

Christianity and Commercialization

Although several Dutch and French explorers had sighted Samoa during the 18th century, none had any impact until Rev. John Williams of the London Missionary Society called at Savai'i aboard the *Messenger of Peace* in 1830. The ruling chief, Malietoa Vainu'upo, welcomed Williams, and by 1840 most Samoans had been converted to Protestantism. The missionaries taught the need for clothing, and white traders were soon arriving to sell the required cotton cloth. The first copra trader in Samoa was John Williams Jr., son of the missionary, who exported six tons in 1842. In 1844 Malua College was established on Upolu by the church. In true Samoan fashion, Malietoa's rival Mata'afa Iosefo converted to Catholicism in 1845.

In 1856 the German trading firm Johann Godeffroy and Son opened a store at Apia, and within a few years over a hundred Europeans resided in the new town, which soon became one of the main trading centers of the South Pacific. The first central government was formed by a group of district chiefs at Mulinu'u in 1868. During the 1870s German businessmen purchased large tracts of family land from individual chiefs for the establishment of coconut plantations using Chinese and Melanesian labor. Germany, Britain, and the U.S. soon appointed consuls.

In 1873 an American, Col. A.B. Steinberger, assisted the Samoan chiefs in creating a constitution; two years later he had himself appointed premier. His role was not supported by the U.S., however, although he was an official State Department agent. After five months in the premiership, Steinberger was arrested and taken to Fiji by the captain of a British warship who suspected him of German sympathies. He never returned.

Instability and Intrigue

The new Samoan government fumbled on and signed treaties of friendship with the U.S. and Germany. An intermittent civil war between the

Sunday worship, Apia

chiefly orator groups Pule and Tumua over the four highest ceremonial titles dragged on through most of the late 19th century. Rival Europeans sided with the different factions, but no one was able to establish a single, stable government. In 1879 the European residents of Apia took advantage of the situation to enact a municipal convention, which put control of the town in their hands.

In 1887 the German company Deutsche Handels-und Plantagen-Gesellshaft (successor to Godeffroy), tiring of the vicissitudes of native government in an area where they controlled 80% of the business, staged an unofficial coup. The nominal king, Malietoa Laupepa, was forced to flee, and the Germans installed a puppet in his place. The German regime, supported by German naval units but not sanctioned by Berlin, soon alienated Samoans, British, and Americans.

In March 1889 an armed Samoan rebellion brought the warships of Germany, Britain, and the U.S. to Apia's port in a major international confrontation. This came to a ludicrous pass when the seven men-of-war refused to abandon Apia Harbor in the face of a hurricane, for fear of leaving the field to the opposing Great Powers. This colonial stupidity and arrogance caused the wreck of four ships; two others were beached and damaged; 92 German and 54 American lives were lost. The German ship *Adler* was thrown up onto the reef, and only the British *Calliope* escaped to the open sea. The Samoans saw it as an act of God.

After this disaster the military posturing abated, and in June 1889 a Tripartite Treaty was signed in Berlin under which the three powers agreed to the formation of a neutral government led by Malietoa Laupepa with the three consuls controlling Apia. Yet instability and open factional warfare alternated with ineffectual government until 1899 when new treaties were drawn up partitioning Samoa between Germany and the U.S. (see **American Samoa**). Britain, distracted at the time by the Boer War in South Africa, withdrew completely in exchange for German concessions in Tonga and the Solomons.

The Colonial Period

On 1 March 1900 the German flag was raised over Samoa. Under Governors Wilhelm Solf (1900-1912) and Erich Schultz (1912-1914), the Germans created the first public school system, built and staffed a hospital, and constructed the only roads that existed right up until 1942. Though both Solf and Schultz tried to work according to the principle that the Samoans could be guided but not forced, they deported Samoan resisters to the Mariana Islands in 1909. The Germans carefully studied traditional Samoan culture in order to play rival factions off against each other. From Berlin, Samoa was seen as the brightest jewel of Germany's colonial empire.

On 29 August 1914, at the beginning of WW I, the last German governor surrendered without a fight to a New Zealand Expeditionary Force. The vast German plantations seized at the time are still held by the government-owned Samoa Land Corporation. Most of the 2,000 Chinese the Germans had brought from southern China to work the plantations were repatriated.

The new N.Z. administrators were real bunglers compared to the Germans. In November 1918, they allowed the SS *Talune* to introduce influenza to the territory, and 8,000 Samoans—22% of the population—died; a stricter quarantine kept the epidemic out of American Samoa and Fiji. This awkward administration revived a strong opposition movement, the Mau, which had existed during German times. The Mau not only rejected colonial authority but turned away from Western development and culture. Boycotts of imported goods were organized. In 1929 New Zealand crushed the Mau by military force, although the movement continued to enjoy the support of most of the villages, chiefs, and part-Samoan businessmen.

Only in 1947 was there a concrete step toward independence when a legislative assembly was created with some members elected from among the *matai* (chiefs). In 1960 a constitution was adopted; a year later both constitution and independence were approved in a plebiscite by universal ballot. And finally in 1962, with a Labor government in power in N.Z., Samoa became the first Polynesian nation to reestablish its independence in the 20th century. In 1976 Samoa joined the United Nations.

Government

Samoa has a parliamentary system with a prime minister elected by Parliament from its ranks. The prime minister chooses a 12-member Cabinet, also from among Parliament. Since independence, His Highness Malietoa Tanumafili II, Paramount Chief of Samoa, has been the ceremonial head of state, a position he may hold for life. The next head of state will be chosen by Parliament for a five-year term from among the four *tama aiga* or paramount chiefs (Malietoa, Mata'afa, Tuimalealiifano, and Tupua Tamasese).

Until recently, 47 of the 49 members of parliament were elected every five years by the 20,000 registered chiefs or *matai* (most of them men) on a constituency basis, and only two by non-Samoan residents on the Individual Voters Roll. In 1990 all citizens aged 21 and over were allowed to vote in a referendum that approved universal suffrage and an extension of the term of office from three to four years. The old system of only allowing *matai* to run for the 47 Samoan seats was retained, however. An untitled person *(tautau)* can only be elected to parliament after he/she first becomes a *matai,* a situation that helps preserve traditional Samoan culture.

There are two main political parties, the Human Rights Protection Party and the Samoa National Development Party. As elsewhere in Anglophone Oceania, political parties revolve more around personalities than policies. Campaign funds are used to "buy" votes and official corruption is rampant. A traditional coalition of orators and chiefs, the Tumua, Pule, and Aiga, has staged mass demonstrations in Apia against high taxes and government financial mismanagement.

The 11 administrative districts (A'ana, Aiga-i-le-Tai, Atua, Fa'asaleleaga, Gaga'emauga, Gagaifomauga, Palauli, Satupa'itea, Tuamasaga, Va'a-o-Fonoti, and Vaisigano) are used only for the organization of government services, and district officers don't exist. Samoa has no army and very few police: those responsibilities are assumed by the *matai.* The only police station on Upolu is the one in Apia; elsewhere the authority of village law prevails.

ECONOMY

In recent years Samoa's economy has been battered by hurricanes, agricultural decline, and government mismanagement. Despite all the revenue collected from the 10% value-added tax (VAGST) imposed in 1994, the foreign debt has remained high at around S$400 million, owed mostly to international agencies such as the Asian Development Bank and the World Bank for infrastructure and agricultural loans. In 1993-94 tens of millions went down the drain to support a reckless expansion program by Polynesian Airlines, and vast sums have been squandered on flashy new office buildings and a hilltop prayer house in Apia.

In 1994 Samoa's chief auditor submitted a report alleging high-level corruption and nepotism, but this was successfully swept under the carpet and the chief auditor himself was given the boot. Many government departments keep no accurate financial records and no serious audits are carried out. Foreign business has been impacted by the incompetence: in 1998 the Samoan government inexplicably canceled the import permits of British Petroleum and handed Mobil Oil a monopoly. Tourism has been stifled by customary landowners who have demanded exhorbitant land-use fees for areas slated for resort development. When the an attempt was made to locate the resorts on government lands, the chiefs laid claim to those lands too. Major chains like Intercontinental and Marriott have withdrawn after seeing their costs spiral before they'd even turned any sod.

Samoa's per-capita gross domestic product is A$1,288 (1995) compared to A$6,660 (1985) in nearby American Samoa. Thus many Samoans migrate to Pago Pago to seek employment in the tuna canneries where the starting rate is US$3.10 an hour (in independent Samoa the private-sector statutory minimum wage is S$1.25 an hour). Tens of thousands of Samoans now live in American Samoa, the U.S., New Zealand, and Australia, and the S$100 million a year in private remittances they send home accounts for about half the country's gross domestic product.

Two-thirds of the workforce is engaged in subsistence agriculture, and fisheries and agriculture make up over a third of the gross domestic product, the highest such proportion in the Pacific excluding Solomon Islands. Since the opening of a freezer plant in Apia in 1997, longline fishing for tuna from aluminum *alia* catamaran boats has experienced a boom. Only 27% of Samoans have non-agricultural employment, the lowest such percentage of any Polynesian country. Samoans have to hustle to obtain cash money, one reason why they look leaner and meaner than American Samoans (only those who have been to Tutuila will understand this comment).

In 1988 Samoa launched an off-shore banking center similar to that of Vanuatu and Cook Islands. Foreign companies can pay a one-time registration fee that allows them to undertake tax-evasion operations for 20 years (local companies are barred from participating and face strict bureaucratic regulation). Companies in Hong Kong, South Korea, Indonesia, and Eastern Europe especially, download their profits here. In 1997 a new scam was uncovered when it was revealed that regular Samoan passports were being sold under the counter to Chinese businessmen at US$26,000 apiece. A good part of Samoa's immigration department was implicated in the scandal.

Samoa gets around 65,000 overseas tourists a year, 35% of them from American Samoa, 30% from New Zealand, and about 10% each from Australia, the U.S., and Europe. Well over half of these arrivals are expatriate Samoans visiting relatives and friends, and less than a third declare their purpose as tourism. About the only occasions on which Apia sees large numbers of tourists is during brief cruiseships dockings, and these doesn't happen very often. Recently "ecotourism" has been embraced as the way forward for Samoan tourism, and at times it seems that almost everything is eco this or that: there are even aerial ecotours by helicopter! Business interests often exploit the term to justify eco-prices, but real ecotourism is alive and well out in the villages—the way to go in Samoa.

Industry

To stimulate light industry the government has established a "small industries center" at Vaitele, on the airport highway five km west of Apia, where investing companies can obtain long-term leases at low rentals. Cheap labor and 15-year tax holidays are the main incentives to investing here. Most Samoan products have duty-free access to Australia and New Zealand under SPARTECA, to Europe under the Lomé Convention, and to the U.S., Canada, and Japan under the Generalized System of Preferences (GSP) scheme. Unfortunately these competitive advantages are declining as free trade expands worldwide.

The copra-crushing mill at Vaitele has experienced a turnaround since privatization in 1993, and it now processes all local copra into coconut oil. To full utilize the mill's capacity, additional copra is imported from Cook Islands and Tonga. The nearby government-owned Samoa Breweries has been highly successful with its excellent Vailima beer, and the Rothmans factory at Vaitele produces 50,000 cartons of cigarettes a month from raw materials imported from New Zealand.

In 1991 the Japanese corporation Yazaki transferred its automobile electrical wiring sys-

LOUISE FOOTE

*taro (*Colocasia antiquorum *or* Colocasiae sculenta*): The staple of many Pacific islanders, taro requires moist soil and matures 8-15 months after planting. When ripe, the edible portion of this thick starchy root is cut off below the stalk, and the stalk is then replanted. The tender elephant ear-like leaves are eaten as greens after thorough cooking, and the root is boiled or baked until tender, then peeled. Cooked taro can be creamed, scalloped, sliced, or fried—even made into taro chips.*

tems assembly plant from Melbourne to Vaitele, and Yazaki now exports A$75 million in automotive products to Australia each year. Since Yazaki pays low wages to its 3,000 mostly female local employees, gets the factory rent-free from the government, and pays no company taxes, its real value to the Samoan economy is less than one would expect. All of the materials used at Yazaki's Vaitele plant are imported. A garment factory is also planned for Vaitele.

Trade

Imports run seven times higher than exports; food imports alone exceed all exports. Bony junk food not sold in its place of origin is dumped in Samoa: chicken backs and turkey tails from the U.S., mutton flaps and fatty canned corned beef from New Zealand. In 1996 even McDonald's got into the act. The main export items are automotive electrical systems, fresh fish, coconut oil, coconut cream, beer, kava, and cocoa.

During the 1950s Samoa exported 1.2 million cases of bananas a year to New Zealand, but shipping problems, hurricanes, disease, and inefficiency cost them this market, which is now supplied by Ecuador. Cacao continues to decline, and taro shipments to the Polynesian community in N.Z. were halted in 1994 due to an outbreak of taro leaf blight. A blight-resistent variety is now being developed. Infestations by rhinoceros beetles and giant African snails have hurt Samoan agriculture, and some 7,000 hectares of prime real estate is held by inept government agencies.

Japan, the U.S., and New Zealand profit most from the trade imbalance—a classic case of economic neocolonialism. New Zealand exports 10 times more to Samoa than it buys, the U.S. 20 times more, Japan 2,404 times more! An exception is Australia, which buys more than it sells due to the Yazaki operation previously mentioned. Foreign aid covers about 27% of the trade imbalance with the main donors being China, the Asian Development Bank, Japan, Australia, New Zealand, the European Union, and the United Nations Development Program, in about that order of importance. Taiwan has funded the opposition in Samoa in an attempt to break this country's close relationship with mainland China. American aid is negligible.

THE PEOPLE

Samoans are the second-largest group of full-blooded Polynesians in the world, behind the Maoris. About 89% of the population is Samoan and another 10% is part-Samoan *(afakasi)* with some European or Chinese blood. Although half of Samoa's people live in the northwest corner of Upolu, from Apia to the airport, only 21% live in the capital itself. Due to large-scale emigration to New Zealand and the U.S., the population growth rate is very low, averaging only 0.5% a year. In all, 85,000 Samoans live in N.Z. and 50,000 in the U.S. (compared to around 175,000 in Samoa itself).

While almost everyone in Apia speaks good English, the same is not always true in the villages. The Samoan language has similarities to Tongan, but the k sound in Tongan is replaced in Samoan by a glottal stop (rather like the English sound oh-oh). It's among the most sweetly flowing of Polynesian languages, and an entire special vocabulary exists for formal or polite discourse among the various levels of society.

The Samoan approach to life is almost the opposite of the European: property, wealth, and success are all thought of in communal or family rather than individual terms. Eighty percent of the country's land is owned communally by family groups *(aiga)* and cannot be sold or mortgaged. The *matai* work to increase the prosperity and prestige of their *aiga*.

Samoans are very conservative and resist outside interference in village affairs. The Samoans have an almost feudal concern for protocol, rank, and etiquette. They lead a highly complex, stylized, and polished way of life. Today, however, they are being forced to reconcile the *fa'a Samoa* with the competitive demands of Western society, where private property and the individual come first. The greatest burden of adjustment is on the young; between 1982 and 1992, Samoa experienced 230 suicides plus an equal number of unsuccessful attempts, 70% of them involving males aged 15-24, the highest suicide rate in the world.

Social Structure

Since ancient times, Samoan society has been based on the *aiga,* a large extended family group with a *matai* as its head, who is elected by consensus of the clan. The *matai* is responsible for the *aiga*'s lands, assets, and distribution. He ensures that no relative is ever in need, settles disputes, sees to the clan's social obligations, and is the *aiga*'s representative on the district or village council *(fono)*. A *pulenu'u* (village mayor) appointed by the government presides over the *fono*. Around 85% of the total population lives under the direct authority *(pule)* of a *matai* (only residents of Apia are largely exempt from this). The 80% of Samoa's surface area that is customary land is under *matai* control (another 10% of the land is freehold and the government owns the balance).

The weight of traditional village law is enshrined in the Samoan constitution, and judges in the regular courts can take into account village lines or whether the offender has performed the traditional apology *(ifoga)* when passing sentence. A villager who chooses to ignore the rulings of his village *fono* faces ostracism, banishment, and worse. In exceptional cases, stoning, arson, and even murder have resulted.

Blood relationships count to a large extent in the elections of the *matai*, but even untitled persons can be elected on merit. (Foreigners can also be granted honorary *matai* titles, but these carry no social or legal weight.) In this formalized, ritualized society the only way a person can achieve place is to become a *matai*. This semidemocracy gives Samoan society its enduring strength.

A number of *aiga* comprise a village *(nu'u)* under an orator or talking chief *(tulafale)* and a titular or high chief *(ali'i)*. The high chiefs are considered too grand to speak for themselves at ceremonies, thus the need for orators. The *tulafale* conduct eloquent debates, give ceremonial speeches, and are the real sources of authority in the community. Direct conflicts are avoided through consensus decision-making. The villages are largely autonomous, and family welfare comes before individual rights—pure preindustrial socialism.

Villages

Samoans live in 362 villages near the seashore. Families share their work and food, and everyone has a place to live and a sense of belonging. It's difficult for individuals to get ahead in this communal society because as soon as anyone obtains a bit of money they're expected to spread it around among relatives and neighbors. Each immediate family has its own residence, called a *fale* (pronounced "fah-lay"), which may be round or oval. Without walls, it's the least private dwelling on earth. The only furniture may be a large trunk or dresser. A *fale* is built on a stone platform, with mats covering the pebble floor. Mats or blinds are let down to shelter and shield the *fale* from storms—a very cool, clean, fresh place to live.

Most food is grown in village gardens, and cooking is done in an earth oven *(umu)*. Families are large, eight children being "about right." The men wear a vivid wraparound skirt known as a *lavalava*. The women of the village are often seen working together in the women's committee *fale,* making traditional handicrafts. The *fono* meets in the *fale taimalo*. Also a part of each village is the cricket pitch—looking like an isolated stretch of sidewalk. Notice too the *tia,* stone burial mounds with several stepped layers under which old chiefs are buried.

Kava and Tattoos

Unlike Fiji and Tonga, the Samoan kava ceremony is an exceptional occurrence held at important gatherings of *matai*, seldom witnessed by visitors. A *taupou* prepares the drink in a traditional wooden bowl; in the old days she was the fiercely guarded virgin daughter of a village high chief, a ceremonial princess. Chanting and dancing usually accompany this serving ceremony.

Tattooing is one of the few Polynesian cultural attributes adopted by Western civilization, and although missionaries a hundred years ago predicted its demise, it's still widespread among Samoan men. The navel-to-knees tattoos are a visual badge of courage, as 16 or more highly painful sessions are required to apply a full *pe'a* using purple candlenut dyes. Once the tattooing begins it cannot end until completed, or the subject will be permanently marked with dishonor. Until recently a full body tattoo could only be applied to a talking chief as a mark of his rank, but today anyone who can stand the pain is eligible. The designs originally represented a large fruit bat, although this is only recognizable today in the lines of the upper wings above the waist. This art dates back to ancient times, and contemporary Samoan tattoo designs are strikingly

SAMOAN TATTOOING

The Samoan art of tattooing is as old as human habitation of these islands itself. Tattooing needles and combs have been discovered alongside *lapita* pottery, and the designs and incising techniques are similar whether applied to skin or clay. Traditionally, tattooing was part of a boy's initiation into manhood. Young boys between the ages of 12 and 15 would receive a full body tattoo or *pe'a* in a painful ritual that lasted up to three months. Then as now, a *pe'a* was a status symbol carried through life, and a tattoo incomplete due to the pain involved was a lifelong mark of dishonor.

The tattoo artists or *tufuga* would be paid with fine mats, and boys destined to inherit a *matai* title received a higher quality tattoo than other boys. The *tufuga* had at his disposal a variety of tattooing tools consisting of wooden mallets with combs made from human bone or pig's teeth attached to turtle-shell heads. The pigment was made by mixing water with ashes obtained from burning candlenuts.

The tattooing begins at the small of the back, then proceeds to the lower back and legs down to the knees, and finishes with the navel, the most sensitive area. The designs are ruled by tradition: a canoe appears on the lower back, and other natural or cultural objects may be depicted in an abstract manner. In Samoan, the word *pe'a* also means flying fox and the wings of the creature wrap around the person's waist. The patterns are structured in a way that vaguely resembles the interior of a Samoan *fale*.

similar to incised decorations on *lapita* pottery thousands of years old.

Religion

Ever since Rev. John Williams landed in 1830, the Samoans have taken Christianity very seriously and Samoan missionaries have gone on to convert the residents of many other island groups (Tuvalu, the Solomons, and New Guinea). Every Samoan banknote bears a radiant cross and the slogan *Fa'avae i le Atua Samoa* (Samoa is founded on God). Yet while the Samoans have embraced the rituals of Christianity, concepts such as individual sin are less accepted.

About 43% of the population belong to the Congregational Christian Church, 21% are Catholic, 17% Methodist, and 10% Mormon. The numbers of Mormons, Seventh-Day Adventists, and Assemblies of God are growing fast as the Congregational Christian Church declines. During the 19th century the main rivalry was between the British-connected Congregationals from the London Missionary Society active in Tahiti and Cook Islands and the Australian-based Methodists or Wesleyans who dominated the Tongan and Fijian missionary fields. Although the Methodists landed in Samoa first, they later withdrew until 1857 at the behest of the church authorities in England.

Today each village has one or more churches and the pastor's house is often the largest residence. Minister of religion is usually the best paying job in the village and many pastors enjoy an affluent lifestyle at the expense of their congregations (often the pastor will be the only one in the village who owns a car). There's a continuous pressure on villagers to contribute money to the church and much of it goes into outlandishly huge and luxurious churches, which is rather scandalous in such a poor country. Some villages have regulations that *require* villagers to attend church as many as three times on Sunday and choir practice weekly. Public education is neither free nor compulsory and many of the schools are church-operated.

There's a daily vespers called *sa* around 1800 for family prayers. All movement is supposed to cease at this time; some villages are rather paranoid about it and levy fines on offenders. It only lasts about 10 minutes, so sit quietly under a tree or on the beach until you hear a gong, bell, or somebody beating a pan to signal "all's clear." Even if you're in a car on the main road at vespers, some remote villages may not allow you to continue driving through the village, although most will. If you do get stopped by white-shirted morality police, just wait patiently in the car until you get an all clear signal after about 10 minutes (don't get out). Many villages also have a 2200 curfew.

CONDUCT AND CUSTOMS

Custom Fees

In many parts of Samoa it's an established village law that outsiders pay a set fee to swim at the local beach or waterhole, or to visit a cave, lava tube, waterfall, etc. Sometimes the amount is posted on a sign and collected at a regular booth, but other times it's not. It's usually S$1 to S$5 either per person or per vehicle. In a few places, such as Falealupo on Savai'i, separate fees are charged for each individual thing you wish to see or do in the village. Although it may seem to Westerners that the Samoans have no *right* to charge for these things, the way the Samoans look at it, visitors have no right to enjoy them free of charge. The best solution, if you don't wish to pay, is to just carry on quietly to some other beach or waterhole that is free or where no one's around. Complaining will get you nowhere.

Be aware, however, that a few ripoffs have become associated with this—sometimes an unauthorized person will demand payment, and you can't really tell if it's for real. We recommend that you only pay customary fees of this kind if there's a sign clearly stating the amount or someone asks for the money *beforehand,* thus giving you the choice of going in or not. Resist paying anything if someone tries to collect as you're leaving (unless there's a sign), and *never* give the money to children. If there's a dispute or you're in doubt about the authenticity of a customary fee, politely say you want to give the money directly to the *pulenu'u.* He will straighten things out quickly. Keep your cool in all of this—Samoans respect courtesy far more than anger or threats. To give you the opportunity to decide beforehand whether you feel a visit is still worth it, all customary fees we know about are listed in this book. Please let us know if we missed any.

Culture Shock

This can work two ways in Samoa, both you being intimidated by the unfamiliar surroundings and the Samoans being put off by your seeming affluence and intrusiveness. Because Samoan culture is a group culture, people can be over-friendly and unwilling to leave you alone. Of course, this doesn't apply in Apia, but in remote villages you may be viewed with suspicion, especially if you arrive in a taxi or rental car, the daily hire of which costs more than an average Samoan villager might earn in a month. You can easily smooth the situation over by smiling, waving, and saying *talofa* to those you meet. Be the first to say hello and everyone will feel a lot more comfortable.

Requests

Samoan culture is extremely manipulative, and there's a saying that you can buy anything with a *fa'amolemole* (please). Samoans are constantly asking each other for things; it's not just a game they play with foreigners. If you're staying in a village for long, somebody from another

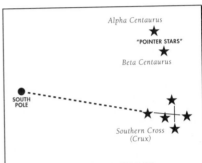

SOUTHERN CROSS STARGAZING

Look for the Southern Cross (Crux), a constellation in the Milky Way near the south celestial pole. There's a much larger false cross to the right, but the real one is brighter. The "pointer stars," Alpha and Beta Centaurus, make it easy to positively identify the Southern Cross. Follow the longer axis of the Cross to the left about five times its length to locate the South Pole. When you are near the equator this line will intersect the horizon. As you move farther south the axis will indicate a location higher in the sky until it points directly overhead when you are at the South Pole itself. Thus, Crux can be used both to find south and to determine latitude, which is 0° at the equator, 13° 50' at Apia, and 90° at the South Pole. At Apia, if you follow the axis line of the Southern Cross about five times its length to the left it will indicate a point of 13° 50' above the horizon, the latitude of Apia. Seen only from below about 20° north latitude, the Southern Cross is like a brilliant cluster of jewels in the southern sky. It appears on the national flags of Samoa, New Zealand, Australia, and Papua New Guinea.

household may eventually come and ask you for money or something you're carrying. It's important that you be firm with them. Explain that you're sharing what you have with your hosts, and you simply don't have money to give out. If you "loan" money, consider it a gift, for if you insist on being repaid you will only make an enemy without collecting anything. Samoans will often invite you home for a meal, or ask you to accompany them on an excursion, and they're usually sincere and only wish to share some time with you. Occasionally, however, it will be someone who only wants to get something out of you, to have you pay their expenses at a restaurant, bar, nightclub, or whatever. You have to form appropriate defenses in Samoa.

Theft and Violence

Nobody means any harm, and violent crime is almost unknown, but be careful: the concept of individual ownership is not entirely accepted by the Samoans. Don't leave valuables unattended. Someone might even steal your laundry off the line, so it's better to hang it up in your room. Theft from hotel rooms and even beach *fales* in remote areas is also not unusual. The banks will keep a sealed envelope containing unneeded tickets, documents, and checks in their vault for a nominal fee—a good precaution if you'll be staying long.

The wisest policy when visiting Samoa is to remain low-key. Don't put yourself in high-risk situations, and if you ever have to defend yourself, it's always better to try to run away. If confronted by a belligerent drunk (quite possible in the evening), humble yourself, apologize even if you did nothing wrong, and ease yourself out of the confrontation. If it ends in violence, you'll always lose, because the culture pressures relatives and friends to join in the attack even if their side is clearly wrong. Loyalty is priority number one, and proving that is a lifelong obligation.

Getting Stoned

Some Samoans in remote areas resent sightseers who drive through their village in a rented automobile, especially if they're thought to be going a little fast. Cases of local children shouting insults, baring their bottoms, and even stoning motorists are not unknown. Sometimes *palagi* on buses, cycling, or even walking get this reaction if they're thought to be intruding (Though the kids know how to throw stones with deadly accuracy, they seldom actually h. tourists.) Try to smile and keep your cool.

Children

At times village children can be a bit of a nuisance, calling to you and crowding around in an almost mocking way. You can forestall much of this by smiling and saying *talofa* (hello) as soon as you see them. Just keep smiling, keep going and you'll soon leave them behind. It's important not to show any anger or irritation at their behavior, as this will only delight them and make them all the more unmannered with the next visitor who happens by.

If you're resting somewhere and don't really want to move on, the only way to get rid of annoying children is to complain very politely to their parents or to a local *matai*. Beware of ordering them away yourself as tourists who thought they could do whatever they liked have been stoned by local children many times. As always, a kind smile is your best defense. Occasionally you'll be accosted by groups of children who have been given money by tourists and if they think you might do the same they'll stick to you like glue.

Love and Marriage

After a few days in the country it'll become fairly obvious to male visitors that Samoan women like to marry Western men. Age is not an important factor here: teenagers smile invitingly at middle-aged bachelors, and obesity is viewed as a sign of wealth. Samoans associate Europeans with the sort of affluence they see on television, and when a girl marries a *palagi* her economic situation, and that of her entire *aiga*, suddenly improves, or so they think.

If you're really smitten with a Samoan, you'll be expected to satisfy much more than just her needs. Be aware too that Samoan women are expert at stopping just short of lovemaking before they're married, and their brothers can be very hard on an insincere man who thinks he can play the game to his own advantage. Note too that marriage to a Samoan woman does not imply any legal right to stay in Samoa; in fact, the idea is that you take the woman *and* her family back and support them in your own home counry. Somerset Maugham's story, "The Pool," in *The Trembling of a Leaf* deals with this subject.

Fa'a Samoa

It's considered impolite to eat while walking through a village, or to talk or eat while standing in a *fale*. Sit down cross-legged on a mat, *then* talk and eat. Don't stretch out your legs when sitting: it's bad form to point your feet at anyone or prop them up, and also a discourtesy to turn your back on a *matai*. Swaying from side to side indicates anger or contempt, and gesturing with the hands is considered bad taste.

If you arrive at a house during the family prayer session, wait outside until they're finished. A sign that you are invited to enter is the laying out of mats for you to sit on. Walk around the mats, rather than over them. Shoes should be removed and left outside. Your host will give a short speech of welcome, to which you should reply by giving your impressions of the village and explaining your reason for coming, beginning with the words *susu mai* (listen). If you are offered food, try to eat a small amount even if you're not hungry.

Some villages object to the use of their beach on Sunday, and some object anytime. If someone's around, ask, or find a beach that's secluded. Public nudism is prohibited; cover up as you walk through a village. Women receive more respect when dressed in a *puletasi* (long dress) or *lavalava,* and not slacks or shorts. It's inappropriate to wear flowers or bright clothing to church.

This said, don't be intimidated by Samoan customs. Do your best to respect tradition, but rest assured that the Samoans are indulgent with foreigners who make an honest blunder. Samoans are fiercely proud of the *fa'a Samoa* and will be honored to explain it to you. It's all part of the Samoan experience, not an inconvenience at all.

In fact, the *fa'a Samoa* is open to interpretation, and even "world authorities" such as Margaret Mead and Derek Freeman can create diametrically opposed theories as to just what Samoan customs were or are. Mead's version of happy, uninhibited sexuality presented in *Coming of Age in Samoa* has been challenged by Freeman's description of a violent, competitive society that prizes virginity and forbids premarital sex (see **Resources**). Albert Wendt's 1979 novel, *Pouliuli,* is a superb analysis of that "laboratory of contradictions" that is Samoa.

SAMOA

SAMOA $2·50

Moon Festival

ON THE ROAD

Highlights

Your most long-lasting impression of Samoa may be of people living in harmony with nature, and there's no better way to experience it than by sleeping in a Samoan *fale* at any of the growing number of beach *fale* resorts around the country. The bus rides from Apia to Aleipata and Lepa are also superb introductions to this exotic environment.

Samoa's most unforgettable sights draw their beauty from their natural surroundings, from the tomb of Robert Louis Stevenson on Mt. Vaea, to the Piula Cave Pool, the waterfall and pyramid at Savai'i's Letolo Plantation, and the nearby Taga blowholes. O Le Pupu-Pu'e National Park on Upolu's south side is Samoa's largest. You also won't want to miss the Cindy Show at Margrey-Ta's Beer Garden in Apia.

Sports and Recreation

Samoa has fewer organized recreational possibilities than some other Pacific countries, but there are unlimited opportunities to do your own thing. **Hiking** trails quickly become overgrown, which often makes local guides a good idea. Experienced hikers should be able to do the Lake Lanoto'o trip on their own.

The only **scuba diving** companies are in Apia and at Coconuts Beach Resort (scuba diving is not offered on Savai'i). A reasonable **snorkeling** locale, the Palolo Deep, is right in Apia, but Savai'i's Faga Beach is better. There are fewer options elsewhere, due in part to narrow fringing reefs, deadly currents, hurricane-impacted corals, and fishing with dynamite. Samoa Marine in Apia offers deep-sea **fishing.**

Samoa is a **surfing** paradise and the top waves are off the north-facing coasts in summer, off the south-facing coasts in winter. Thus optimum conditions are encountered at Lauli'i, Faleapuna, and Lano Dec.-March, and at Aufaga, Salani, Tafatafa, and Salailua May-August.

If you bring your own **bicycle** on the flight, many wonderful opportunities to use it will present themselves here. Both main islands have excellent paved roads and there isn't much traffic except on northern Upolu. The only real hazard is sudden chases by dogs, but one must also be prepared for the heat. Allow a week or more to cycle around each island, staying at village *fale* resorts along the way. The 176-km road around Savai'i is flat, except for the stretch between Asau and Sasina, which at 229 meters elevation is still lower than the passes on Upolu. (If you stop to talk to an adult on the road, be sure to get right off your bicycle, otherwise you might be seen as speaking down at a *matai*.)

Golfers will enjoy the 18-hole course at Apia.

Public Holidays and Festivals

Public holidays include New Year's Days (1, 2 January), Head of State's Birthday (first Monday in January), Good Friday, Easter Monday (March/April), ANZAC Day (25 April), Mothers of Samoa Day (a Monday in mid-May), Independence Days (1, 2, 3 June), Labor Day (a Monday in early August), White Monday (the Monday after the second Sunday in October), Arbor Day (the first Friday in November), and Christmas Days (25, 26 December).

decorative hat, Flower Gala Week, Apia

THE RISING OF THE PALOLO

The palolo *(Eunice viridis)* is a segmented saltwater reef worm that lives below the low tide level in the crevices of shallow coral reefs. The worms seldom leave their burrows and are active mostly at night. Once or twice a year, however, great masses of the worms swarm to the ocean's surface to spawn as part of a predictable life cycle.

The palolo itself consists of two parts, a worm-like forward portion up to 10 centimeters long with eyes and a mouth, and a narrower 20-centimeter rear portion which is used for reproduction. The rear part is blue-green in the female and reddish in the male, and has a light-sensitive eyespot. When the moment to spawn arrives one night, the palolos back out of their burrows and detach their rear portions. The front parts squirm back into the reef to begin growing new appendages for the next season, while the male and female tails swarm to the surface, writhing together until dawn when they burst, releasing the eggs and sperm. The fertilized eggs become larvae that drift along until they find a place in the coral to colonize.

The numberless worms must rise simultaneously for fertilization to take place, and this mass spawning always occurs on the evening of the last quarter moon in late spring, which in Samoa is seven days after full moon in late October or early November. Swarming can occur on two or three successive nights, with the second night being the most important. A brown foamy slick on the ocean surface and a strong salty smell, usually caused by a mass spawning of corals, often signals that the palolo will spawn two days later.

This event takes place in spring because at that time the larvae have their best chance of survival. Many species of fish and shellfish have adapted their lifecycles to that of the palolo, spawning around the same time so the palolo larvae will be available as a food source for their own offspring.

Although the palolo is common throughout the South Pacific, it doesn't swarm everywhere. The phenomena is best known in Samoa and Fiji, although it also occurs in Tonga and parts of Melanesia. The islanders have long considered palolo a delicacy to be eaten raw or fried, and it has an extremely rich taste and is high in protein. Thus each year on the assigned night, locals will be waiting with hand nets to scoop up in large numbers this caviar of the Pacific.

In Samoa, the people traditionally adorn themselves in the fragrant yellow blossoms of the *moso'oi* flower for the occasion. If you happen to be in Western Polynesia or Fiji in October or early November, it's certainly worth asking when the rising of the palolo will occur. Sadly, however, environmental degradation and overharvesting have taken their toll, and you must get away from major population centers to witness this spectacle at its best.

a palolo worm

Don't expect to get any official business done during the three-week period beginning a week before Christmas and ending a week after New Year's as most government employees knock off for extended holidays around then and many offices will be closed. Even basic public facilities such as the post office shut down for a week at a time! Also beware of Independence Days since the three public holidays in a row mean that all banks, offices, and most stores will be closed for five consecutive days, at least. Easter is also a bad time to come if you have anything specific to do.

Many Western countries celebrate Mother's Day and Father's Day, but only Samoa has made Children's Day (White Monday, the day after White Sunday) a public holiday. On White Sunday, children dressed in white parade to church; after the service, they take the places of honor and eat first at family feasts.

The big event of the year is the **Independence Days** celebrations during the first week of June with dancing, feasting, speeches by *tulafale* (talking chiefs), horse races, and other sporting events. A highlight is the *fautasi* race on the Saturday closest to Independence Days, with teams of dozens of men rowing great longboat canoes. Though Samoa actually attained independence on 1 January 1962, the celebrations are held in June to avoid total paralysis around Christmas (which usually occurs anyway, however).

The **Teuila Tourism Festival** in early September is also a good time to be there. Among the many cultural activities are church choir competitions, dance and beauty contests, squash and cricket finals, *fautasi* (long-boat) races, traditional games, talent shows, etc.

Once a year the palolo reef worm *(Eunice viridis)* rises from the coral before dawn according to a lunar cycle (October on Upolu, November on Savai'i). The Samoans wait with lanterns and nets to catch this prized delicacy, the "caviar of the Pacific." This remarkable event takes place in Samoa, Fiji, and some other islands, but never in Hawaii.

Dance

The *sasa* is a synchronized group dance in which the rhythm is maintained by clapping or by beating on a rolled mat or drum. The *siva* is a graceful, flowing dance in which the individual is allowed to express him/herself as he/she sees fit The *fa'ataupati* or slap dance employs body percussion. Knife-fire dances are done solo or in small groups, and they can be dangerous to the performers. Tradition holds that only men who are afraid will be burned during the fire dance. The waving of flaming weapons was originally done in times of war, to warn a tribe of approaching enemies.

Arts and Crafts

The Samoan love of elaborate ceremony is illustrated in the fine mat *(ie toga)*. Exquisitely and tightly plaited from finely split pandanus leaves, a good example might take a woman a year of her spare time to complete. Fine mats are prized family heirlooms used as dowries, etc., and they acquire value as they're passed from

Apart from the coconut tree, the pandanus shrub, or screw pine, is one of the most widespread and useful plants in the Pacific. Among other things, the islanders use the thorny leaves for weaving mats, baskets, and fans. The seeds are strung into necklaces. The fibrous fruit makes brushes for decorating tapa cloth and can be eaten. The aerial roots can be made into fish traps.

person to person at ceremonial exchanges *(lafo)*. Mats of this kind cannot be purchased.

Samoan tapa cloth *(siapo)* is decorated by rubbing the tapa over an inked board bearing the desired pattern in relief. In Samoa the designs are usually geometric but with a symbolism based on natural objects.

Traditional woodcarving includes kava bowls, drums, orator's staffs, and war clubs. In Tonga and Fiji, kava bowls have only four circular legs, while Samoan bowls are usually circular with a dozen or more round legs. A large kava bowl is an impressive object to carry home if you have six or seven kilograms to spare in your baggage allowance. Paradoxically, although carved from endangered trees such as the *ifilele,* the local production of kava bowls actually helps protect the rainforests as it greatly increases the value of the trees in the eyes of local villagers who become far less willing to sign away their timber rights for a pittance. A tree used to make handicrafts could be worth S$2,000 while a logging company would only pay about S$30 to cut it down.

It's also interesting to note that the tikis you see here are mock Maori or Hawaiian, not Samoan—don't buy the grotesque, grimacing little devils. Also beware of imitation tapa crafts in the Tongan style imported from Pago Pago, New Guinea-style masks, and turtle-shell jewelry, which is prohibited entry into many countries. If what you see in the craft shops of Samoa seems less impressive than what you might encounter in some other Pacific countries, remember that oratory and tattooing were the maximum expressions of Samoan culture, followed by the kava ceremony itself.

ACCOMMODATIONS

The higher-priced hotels usually quote their rates in U.S. dollars to make them seem lower, but in this book we've converted all prices into *tala* to make them easier to compare. Whenever a hotel mentions dollars when you ask the price of the room, be sure to clarify how they wish to be paid. If the amount has to be converted into *tala,* whether you're paying in *tala* cash or by credit card, your bill could be inflated about 15% due to the exchange rates used. You can sometimes avoid this by paying in U.S. dollars, cash or trav-

eler's checks, otherwise ask them to quote a price in *tala* as that could work out cheaper. In all cases, a 10% value added tax is charged and you should also ask if it's included. Failure to pay attention to these details could well result in a bill 25% higher than you'd expected!

During the off season (Jan.-April) some of the upscale hotels in outlying areas slash their rates to attract business. The hotels on Savai'i often do this, but those at Apia and Siumu don't. About the only way to find out about these specials is to call and ask, although Samoa's primitive telephone system makes this hard to do. Other travelers may know about some of the deals. In Apia, plenty of rooms are available and there's no need to reserve. The only exceptions might be around Christmas and during the Independence Celebrations at the beginning of June, but even then you'll invariably find something as most of the people arriving for these events will be overseas Samoans who generally stay with friends and family. Accommodations and transfers booked from abroad are always much more expensive than what you'd pay locally.

Most of the regular hotels and guesthouses are in Apia, but an increasing number of places to stay are found on Savai'i and around Upolu. In the past few years numerous locally operated low-impact ecotourism resorts have opened on outlying beaches. These offer mattresses, blankets, and mats in Samoan *fales* right on the beach, with local meals provided at reasonable cost. Virtually all are run by the villagers themselves, and they're an excellent way to combine hiking, snorkeling, swimming, surfing, and just plain relaxing with a sampling of Samoan life. They're covered in the **Around Upolu** and **Savai'i** sections of this chapter and are highly recommended.

Staying in Villages

Staying in villages is a wonderful way to experience true Samoan culture and hospitality. The growing number of *fale* resorts makes it a simple matter to sleep on a beach adjacent to a village, such as at Saleapaga, Saluafata, Satapuala, and Sa'anapu on Upolu, and at Falealupo, Manase, and Satuiatua on Savai'i, to name only a few. It's also possible to stay right in the homes of local families themselves. Formal arrangements for this exist in villages that have organized conservation programs, such as Uafato on Upolu, and Letui, Sasina, Satoalepai, and Tafua-tai on Savai'i, but it's possible almost anywhere.

The Samoans are among the most hospitable people in the world, proud that a stranger can go to any house and request food or shelter and rarely be turned away. This admirable characteristic should not be abused, however. It's part of their culture that a gift will be reciprocated—if not now, then sometime in the future. Tourists who accept gifts (such as food and lodging) without reciprocating undermine the culture.

For this reason it's strongly recommended that, in situations where there's no fixed price, you look for a way of repaying any courtesies received. Thanks is not enough, and a casual offer of payment might be offensive in situations where you were accommodated informally. The Samoans are a very proud people, among the proudest in the Pacific, and you must phrase things carefully to avoid misunderstandings. If your attitude is wrong, they will sense it.

Upon departure, sit down with your hosts for a formal thank you. Say something like, "Hospitality is not something that can be paid for, and I don't know how to show my appreciation fully, but I would like to leave a *mea alofa* (gift)." Then tender about the same amount you would have paid at a *fale* resort, which is at least S$15 pp per night to sleep, plus S$5 pp per meal. Give more if they've been especially helpful by taking you out fishing, guiding you through the mountains, etc. If you ask them to buy something for the children the money, they'll smile and accept.

There's a Samoan proverb about guests who abuse hospitality, *ua afu le laufala* (the floor mats are sweating). Talk these matters over with your traveling companions before you set out, and don't go on a trip with one of the insensitive few. Foreigners who seem to be trying to take advantage of Samoans often become victims of theft.

Other Tips

It's a good idea to make known the approximate length of your stay as soon as a family invites you. If one of your hosts' neighbors invites you to come stay with them, politely refuse. This would bring shame on the first family. It's a Samoan custom that travelers may spend the night at the pastor's house. If you do, make an appropriate contribution to the church. The pastor's

views on religion, values, and development in general will fascinate you.

Samoans are still unfamiliar with camping and might be offended if they feel you're refusing their hospitality. A tactful explanation of your desire to be close to nature might be accepted, though Samoans are naturally suspicious of those who try to remain apart from the group. Always ask permission of a responsible adult, or camp well out of sight of all roads, trails, and villages. To do otherwise is to place yourself beyond the protection of village law.

FOOD

Try *palusami*—thick coconut cream, onions, canned corned beef *(pisupo),* and young taro leaves wrapped in a breadfruit leaf, then baked on hot stones and served on slices of baked taro—a very tasty dish when well prepared. Other traditional Samoan specialties include *taofolo* (kneaded breadfruit and sweet coconut cream wrapped in taro leaves and baked), *fa'ausi* (grated taro and coconut cream pudding), *lua'u* (taro leaves cooked in coconut cream), *suafa'i* (ripe bananas with coconut cream), *faia'ife'e* (octopus in coconut cream), *faiaipusi* (sea eel in coconut cream), and *oka* (marinated raw fish).

If you spend a night in a village or *fale* resort, notice how almost everything you eat is locally grown. Taro and breadfruit are the staples, but there's also pork, fish, chicken, *ta'amu* (a large root vegetable like taro), and bananas. If you're a strict vegetarian, mention it at the outset, although this concept is often not understood in Samoa. In the villages food is normally eaten with the hands (no cutlery). After a meal with a family linger a while; it's considered rude for a guest to get up and abruptly leave. Don't continue to occupy the table if others are awaiting their turn to eat, however. Samoans are big people. Most of us eat till we're full, but Samoans eat till they're tired.

SERVICES AND INFORMATION

Visas and Officialdom

No visa is required for a stay of up to 30 days although you must have a ticket to leave (this ticket may not be looked at by the officials upon arrival at Apia airport, but it certainly will be requested by the airline staff when you're checking in for your flight to Samoa). Samoan immigration will stamp your passport to the date of your flight out, but you can get the 30 days without a struggle.

Apia is the only port of entry for cruising yachts and arriving boats can call customs over VHF channel 16. Clearance is done at the main wharf, then yachts anchor in the harbor off Aggie Grey's Hotel. Yachts may stop at Savai'i after checking out at Apia, provided they get prior permission.

Money

The Samoan *tala* is divided into 100 *sene*. There are coins of one, two, five, 10, 20, and 50 *sene* and one *tala,* and banknotes of two, five, 10, 20, 50, and 100 *tala.* The plastic S$2 banknotes make nice souvenirs. Samoans often speak of dollars when they mean *tala,* and many tourism-related businesses add to the confusion by quoting prices in U.S. dollars. Always note the currency carefully as the difference is around three to one! For consistency, we've quoted most prices in Samoan currency (S$).

Both banks charge 50 cents stamp duty per traveler's check, but only the Pacific Commercial Bank charges S$3 commission (no commission at the ANZ Bank). Traveler's checks attract an exchange rate about four percent higher than cash, but it's always good to have some U.S. currency in small bills in case you happen to run out of *tala,* as everyone will gladly accept it (though at a low rate). If you plan to go upmarket, also have an adequate supply of U.S. dollar traveler's checks in small denominations (see below).

Upmarket facilities that quote prices in dollars are often cheaper if you pay them the exact amount in U.S. dollars, cash or traveler's checks. If you pay by credit card you risk having the charge inflated 15% because the dollar amount must be converted into *tala,* then the bank converts the *tala* into New Zealand dollars because all credit card charges are cleared through New Zealand, then the NZ$ are converted into your own home currency, all at rates unfavorable to you. This situation definitely applies to bank cards such as Visa and MasterCard, however it may be possible to be charged the exact amount in U.S. dollars if you use a private card such as American Express (ask the merchant/hotel).

Tala are heavily discounted outside Samoa, so change only what you think you'll need. If you overestimate, excess *tala* can be changed back into U.S. dollars at the airport bank without question. As you're doing so, try to pick up some Tongan or Fijian banknotes, if that's where you're headed.

Camera film is expensive here and the selection is poor, so bring a good supply. When buying drinks at a grocery store, be aware that there's a

---

VAILIMA LAGER

Samoa's Vailima beer may be the South Pacific's top beer, with more life, sparkle, and bite than any other lager you'll taste around this ocean. Since 1978 it's been brewed at Vaitele between Apia and Faleolo Airport by government-owned Samoa Breweries Ltd. under a management agreement with Haase Brauerei of Hamburg, Germany. The version of Vailima sold in Samoa is 4.9% alcohol but if you cross to American Samoa you should reduce your intake slightly as Vailima Export is 6.7%. Back in Apia, the same brewery's Eku Bavaria beer is 5.3% and excellent (brewed under license from Erste Kulmbacher Aktien-brauerei). In 1990, 1992, 1995, and 1998, Vailima was awarded the Grand Gold Medal at the Le Monde Selection in Brussels, Belgium, and as you sit in front of a cold one at the RSA Club, Peninsula Club, Otto's Reef, or any one of a dozen atmospheric Apia bars, you'll swear Samoa is paradise, and in this regard you will be right.

30-cent deposit on large beer or soft drink bottles, 10 cents on small bottles, although many stores refuse to refund the deposit. Although annual inflation averages 10%, Samoa is still a very inexpensive country. Tipping is discouraged, and avoid giving money to children as this only creates a nuisance. There's a 10% sales tax.

Post and Telecommunications
Express Mail Service (EMS) is available from Apia to Australia, Fiji, Hong Kong, New Zealand, Papua New Guinea, Vanuatu, and the U.S.A. The charge to the U.S. is S$40 for the first 500 grams, then another S$8 for each additional 500 grams up to 20 kilos maximum. Delivery is guaranteed within less than one week. Small packets under one kg benefit from a special reduced rate by regular mail.

Samoa is one of the few Pacific countries without card telephones (or any public telephones at all, for that matter). As in Tonga, the domestic telephone service is controlled by an inefficient state monopoly, which explains the appalling service. About the only easy way to make even a local call is to do so from your hotel, but you should ask how much you'll be charged beforehand. Turn to the **Apia** section for the price of calls made from the main telephone company office.

If you do manage to get access to a phone, make an operator-assisted domestic call by dialing 920. For the international operator, dial 900. If you have access to a direct-dial phone, the international access code is 0. For domestic directory assistance, dial 933; for international numbers, dial 910.

The country code for American Samoa is 684; for Samoa it's 685.

Business Hours and Time
Business hours are weekdays 0800-1200 and 1330-1630, Saturday 0800-1200, with government offices closed on Saturday. Banks open weekdays 0900-1500, the post office 0900-1630 weekdays. Expect most businesses to be closed on Sunday, although Samoa's Sunday closing laws are much more lenient than those of Tonga. Grocery stores aren't supposed to sell beer on Sunday (but some will if nobody's watching).

Both Samoas share the same hour, and since the international date line is just west of here, this is where the world's day really comes to an end. Tonga and Samoa are on the same hour but Samoa is 24 hours behind Tonga. The Samoas are three hours behind California time, 21 hours behind eastern Australian time.

Weights and Measures
In American Samoa Imperial measurements (yards, miles) are used, while in Samoa it's all metric (meters, kilometers). Unlike American Samoa, where the electric voltage is 110 volts, in Samoa it's 240 volts AC, 50 cycles. However, if you plan to plug in an appliance (such as a hair drier or electric razor) at a deluxe hotel in Samoa, check the voltage carefully as some supply 110 volts instead of the usual 240 volts.

Print Media
The main English-language newspaper is the *Samoa Observer* (Box 1572, Apia; tel. 21-099, fax 21-195), which appears daily except Monday and Saturday. Founded in 1979 by the acclaimed poet and novelist Sano Malifa, the *Observer* has faced constant government harassment and even mysterious arson attacks due its exposures of official corruption. All government advertising has been canceled, and to plug leaks, a law has been passed forcing journalists to reveal their information sources, the compulsory registration of publications and their employees has been imposed, and lawsuits against those accused of libeling government ministers are paid out of the public purse (all this, ironically, by the "Human Rights Protection Party" administration). Of course, this situation makes the *Observer* all the more worth reading (provided it's still publishing when you get there).

Newsline (Box 2441, Apia; tel. 24-216, fax 23-623), published on Wednesday and Sunday, carries general interest wire service news and a local gossip column titled "Rant Rave." **Savali** is an irregular government-run newspaper of little value.

Radio
The government-operated Broadcasting Department (Box 1868, Apia; tel. 21-420, fax 21-072) transmits over two AM radio frequencies. Radio 2AP at 540 kHz airs bilingual programs (English and Samoan) Mon.-Sat. 0600-1900. Their local news is at 0700 and 1200, the international news at 0800 and 0900 (rebroadcast from Australia or New Zealand). Radio 2AP's programming Mon.-

Sat. 1900-2300 is in Samoan only, and Sunday 1100-2200 you'll hear nonstop Samoan hymns. Sunday 0800-1600 switch to 747 kHz AM for varied music introduced in English. For over a decade, a directive from the "Human Rights Protection Party" leadership has prevented this station from airing interviews with opposition politicians.

A private commercial station, Magik 98 FM (Box 762, Apia; tel. 25-149, fax 25-147; e-mail: magic98fm@samoa.net), broadcasts over 98.1 MHz to points west of Apia and over 99.9 MHz east of Apia. They're on the air 0600-midnight weekdays and Saturday 0800-midnight. Magik 98 rebroadcasts the Radio New Zealand International news at 0700 and 0800 weekdays, and on Saturday at 0800 only. Local news comes right after the 0700 international news weekdays, then again at noon, 1700, and 1900. On Saturday there's local news at 0700 and 1200.

Health

Although no vaccinations are required (except yellow fever or cholera in the unlikely case that you're arriving directly from an infected area), is may be worthwhile to have been immunized against hepatitis A, typhoid fever, and tetanus (in case a dog bites you). Details of these are provided in the main introduction. Body lice and intestinal parasites are widespread among Samoan villagers; any pharmacy will have a remedy for the former. Check the expiration date before buying any medicines in Samoa. And take care with the tap water in Apia—boiled water or beer is safer.

In case of need, you'll receive faster attention from any of the private doctors and dentists listed in this book's **Apia** section than you would at a government hospital or clinic.

GETTING THERE

By Air

Polynesian Airlines (Box 599, Apia; tel. 685/21-261, fax 685/20-023, e-mail: enquiries@polynesianairlines.co.nz), Samoa's government-owned flag carrier, connects Apia to Auckland, Melbourne, Pago Pago, Sydney, Tongatapu, and Wellington. Their schedules to Honolulu and Los Angeles are code shares with Air New Zealand, to Nadi with Air Pacific. Their Polypass

allows 45 days unlimited travel over Polynesian's modest South Pacific network (a roundtrip to/from Australia and New Zealand included) for a flat US$999. From Honolulu/Los Angeles, the Polypass costs US$1,149/1,399. Details of this and their triangle fares are provided under **Getting Around** in the main introduction to this book. Also check their useful internet website (www.polynesianairlines.co.nz), which contains information about the Polypass. Polynesian's Los Angeles office can be reached at tel. 1-310/830-7363, fax 1-310/830-7782.

Air Pacific (tel. 22-693) has flights to Apia from Nadi and Suva (often full) with connections in Fiji to/from Japan. **Royal Tongan Airlines** (tel. 22-901) has a weekly flight to/from Tongatapu. **Air New Zealand** (tel. 20-825) arrives from Auckland, Tongatapu, and Honolulu with immediate connections in Honolulu to/from Los Angeles. See **Getting Around** in the main introduction for information on circular tickets between Fiji, Apia, and Tonga.

Both Polynesian Airlines and **Samoa Air** (tel. 22-901) operate shuttles between Pago Pago and Apia six or seven times a day. For the Pago Pago flights, check carefully which airport you'll be using as they alternate between Faleolo and Fagali'i and the ticket may only say "Apia." Both airlines charge identical fares from Apia to Pago Pago (S$120/189 one-way/roundtrip), and it's cheaper to buy your ticket in Samoa than elsewhere due to currency differences. Samoa Air also has direct flights between Pago Pago and Maota airstrip on Savai'i (S$145/244 one-way/roundtrip). Samoa Air offers through an excursion fare from Apia to Vava'u via Pago Pago that is the equivalent of the fare to Pago Pago plus US$178/365 one-way/roundtrip. American Samoan airport and customs taxes of US$8 must be added to these prices.

On both airlines, when the flight to/from Pago Pago is full all baggage may be bumped due to the limited carrying capacity of the aircraft (all passengers must be weighed and the average weight of Samoans is substantial). When the baggage does arrive on a later flight, you'll have to go back to the airport and clear it personally through customs. Don't expect compensation for any of this, and be aware that the check-in staff probably won't inform you about what's going on until they're just about to close the aircraft door. If the flight is full and you see people with mountains of excess luggage, expect this to happen. In any case, carry everything you can't afford to lose or might need during the first few days in your hand luggage.

In January 1997, a Polynesian Airlines Twin Otter aircraft arriving from Pago Pago crashed into a hillside near Upolu's Faleolo Airport in circumstances that have still not been adequately explained (pilot error and poor maintenance have been alleged). Three of the five persons on board, including the New Zealander pilot himself, were killed.

By Ship

The **Samoa Shipping Corporation** (Private Bag, Apia; tel. 20-935, fax 22-352) runs the car ferry *Queen Salamasina* from Apia to Pago Pago Wednesday at 2200 (nine hours, S$40/60 one-way/roundtrip). Buy your ticket before 1200 on Tuesday at their Vaea Street office and have your passport ready. If you wait to buy your ticket at the wharf you won't be allowed aboard until the last minute and all of the good places to sleep on deck will have been taken (it's an overnight trip). Expect basic conditions on the ship: bring a mat, take seasickness precautions, etc. During holiday periods the ship makes two trips, leaving Apia at 2200 on Tuesday and Thursday, and at these times it's often fully booked. If you'll be returning to Apia, be sure to get a roundtrip ticket, as the fare charged in Pago Pago is much higher. But if you won't be returning, change excess *tala* back into dollars at the bank the day before as there are no facilities on the wharf. Going by sea you save the S$20 airport departure tax paid by air travelers (although the US$5 American Samoan "entry declaration fee" must still be paid).

In early 1999 a new ferry, the 220-passenger *Lady Naomi*, was brought into service between Apia and Pago Pago. Unlike the *Queen Salamasina,* this ship offers berths at S$60 each way, while seats are S$40.

For information on the supply ship to the Tokelau Islands, contact the transport manager at the **Tokelau Apia Liaison Office** (Box 865, Apia; tel. 20-822, fax 21-761). There's about one a month, and a cabin would run NZ$528 roundtrip. Turn to the Tokelau chapter for more information.

The **Pacific Forum Line** (Box 655, Apia; tel. 20-345, fax 22-179), at the entrance to the main wharf, will know the departure dates of container ships to Tonga and elsewhere. Passage is sometimes possible but to arrange this you must see the captain when the ship arrives.

AIRPORTS

Faleolo International Airport

Faleolo Airport (APW), Samoa's main international airport, is 35 km west of Apia. All flights to points outside the Samoas, as well as some services to Pago Pago, depart from here. The airport bus (tel. 23-014; S$6) will take you right to your hotel, or you can wait on the highway for a public bus, which is only S$1.50, but very scarce after 1600 and on Sunday. Airport-bound, the airport bus departs Apia two hours before international flights. It picks up passengers in front on the Hotel Insel Fehmarn, then at Aggie Grey's Hotel, and finally at the Kitano Tusitala.

The airport taxi drivers often try to overcharge foreign tourists, so take the bus if you can. A taxi from the airport to Apia should cost S$30 (30 *tala*) for the car but they will often insist on being paid US$30 in American currency, so be careful. It's a bit safer taking a taxi back to the airport as they'll know you're already familiar with Samoan currency and probably won't try this trick.

The Pacific Commercial Bank (S$3 commission) and the ANZ Bank (50 cents commission) in the arrivals area open for international flights (excluding those from Pago Pago) and change traveler's checks for similar rates. For changing excess *tala* back, both banks in the departures hall at the airport are open for all international departures *except* those to Pago Pago. There's no left luggage room. In a pinch you can sleep on the floor upstairs in the terminal.

The airport post office (weekdays 0900-1530) sells philatelic stamps, a good way to unload excess *tala*. The duty-free shop in the departure lounge sells only expensive luxury goods and imported alcohol, so don't wait to do your shopping there. In general, alcohol and beer are relatively cheap in Samoa anyway.

The international departure tax is S$20 (children aged 5-9 pay S$10). You don't have to pay the tax if you stay less than 24 hours (transit), and if you'll be departing Samoa twice within any 30-day period, so keep your tax receipt if you have it as you can avoid paying the tax a second time.

Fagali'i Airport

Fagali'i Airport (FGI) is near the golf course on the east side of Apia, just five km from the center of town. All Polynesian Airlines flights to Savai'i leave from here. Some flights to Pago Pago use Fagali'i, others Faleolo, so check carefully to avoid disastrous mistakes. The local Fagali'i-uta bus should pass Fagali'i Airport Mon.-Sat. but service is irregular and not all of the Fagali'i buses come up here. However, just 200 meters west of the airport is a junction where the more frequent Vaivase or Moata'a buses pass. Taxi drivers charge US$5 from Fagali'i to Apia but only S$5 from Apia to Fagali'i. If you're unwilling to pay this arbitrary premium, try bargaining or just walk off and look for a bus. The Pacific Commercial Bank has a branch at Fagali'i Airport and there's a duty-free shop. The usual international departure tax applies.

swimming crab

UPOLU

Although much smaller than Savai'i, Upolu is Samoa's chief island with its stirring capital, international airport, industry, business, attractions, visitor facilities, and 71% of the total population. Physically, it's rather like Tahiti on a smaller scale with high verdant mountains in the background of Apia and a seaside boulevard encircling the harbor. The villages along the north coast also remind one of Tahitian villages, as do the valleys and black beaches. But Upolu is much wilder and more traditional, and less impacted by international tourism.

Although Savai'i commands a faraway mystique, Upolu is much more beautiful and varied, especially the eastern half. Roads wind around the coast and across the center of the island. Some of the South Pacific's finest beaches with facilities for budget travelers are at Lepa and Aleipata. Waterfalls cascade from the luxuriant green hillsides and there are countless places to swim. Hikers will feel rather like Tarzans and Janes cutting paths through exuberant jungles, and travelers will be enchanted by the easygoing Polynesian lifestyle. Upolu is an insular uncut jewel.

APIA AND ENVIRONS

Central Apia has been transformed in recent years, with enormous government buildings overshadowing the older churches and trading companies that still line the waterfront in the traditional South Seas movie-set manner. Yet away from the center this city of 35,000 is only a cluster of villages. In Apia Harbor, where the Vaisigano River has cut an opening in Upolu's protective reef, rock a motley assortment of interisland ferries, container ships, fishing boats, and cruising yachts. As at Papeete, you'll see teams of men paddling outrigger racing canoes around the harbor at sunset, about the only two towns in the South Pacific where this is still so. Yet the languid inertia of Apia is pervasive.

Apia makes a good base from which to explore northern Upolu, and there's lots of accommodation in all price brackets. The food and entertainment possibilities are also very good, so give yourself a break and see the city one step at a time. Get into the culture and prepare yourself for that big trip around Savai'i. Samoa is Polynesia's heart and Apia is the bright light around which the country revolves.

SIGHTS AND RECREATION

Central Apia

By the harbor side where Falealili Street meets Beach Road is the **John Williams Memorial,** dedicated to the missionary who implanted Protestantism in Samoa in 1830. Nine years later Williams was killed and eaten by cannibals on Erromango Island in the New Hebrides (presently Vanuatu). Later his remains were returned to Samoa and buried beneath the porch of the old **Congregational Christian Church** (1898) across the street.

A block west on Beach Road is the historic wooden **Courthouse** dating from German times, which served as government headquarters until 1994. On Black Saturday, 29 December 1929, Tupua Tamasese Lealofi III, leader of the Mau Movement, was shot in the back by the N.Z. Constabulary while trying to calm his people during a demonstration against the colonial regime in front of this building. Eight other Samoans were also killed and five years of severe repression followed, only ending with a change of government in New Zealand.

West again is imposing **Mulivai Catholic Cathedral** (1885-1905), formerly a landmark for ships entering the harbor, and **Matafele Methodist Church,** a fine building where marvelous singing may be heard during Sunday services. Across the street is the gigantic eight-story **Government Building,** erected in 1994 with a S$35-million interest-free loan from the People's Republic of China. It and the neighboring seven-story **Central Bank of Samoa** wouldn't be out of place in Abu Dhabi, Dubai, or Kuwait, and stand as stunning examples of third-world megalomania. Earthquakes are common at Apia and both of these massive buildings stand on unstable reclaimed land, which tends to magnify the impact of quakes, so you could be looking at ancient ruins in the making. The police band marches from their barracks near the Courthouse and plays the national anthem at the raising of the flag here at 0750 on weekday mornings.

Nearby is the **Chief Post Office** with the modern headquarters of the **ANZ Bank** opposite. A block west in the center of the traffic circle where Vaea Street meets Beach Road is a **Clock Tower** built as a WW I memorial. On opposite corners of Vaea Street and Beach Road are the former Burns Philp store, now Chan Mow Supermarket, the **National Provident Fund** building housing the agency that administers the country's pension fund, and the **Nelson Memorial Public Library,** named for Olaf Nelson (1883-1944), a leader of the Mau Movement.

Farther west facing a small harbor is the **Fish Market.** The numerous locally owned longline fishing boats here have made fish a leading export during the past few years, but safety standards are minimal and several boats and crews are lost each year. The **Flea Market** nearby was Apia's main vegetable market until 1995 when it was moved three blocks inland. You can shop for handicrafts and clothing here, and cheap food stalls are along the side closest to the harbor. One of Apia's two bus stations is also here, and just beyond is the flashy new **Women's Center,** built with another Chinese loan. The large wooden building almost across the street is the headquarters of the **Samoa Trust Estates Corporation.** These were once the premises of the German trading companies whose assets were seized when New Zealand invaded in 1914.

Mulinu'u Peninsula

Just northwest of the old market is the **Kitano Tusitala Hotel,** which is well worth entering to appreciate the great hand-tied roofs of the main *fale*-like neo-Samoan buildings erected in 1974.

Continue northwest on Mulinu'u Street, past two monuments on the left commemorating the disastrous 1889 naval debacle when the German cruiser *Adler* and several other ships sank during a hurricane. There's also a monument on the right that recalls the raising of the German flag on 1 March 1900 *(die deutsche Flagge gehisst).*

The large beehive-style building farther along on the left is the neo-Samoan **Parliament of Samoa** (1972). The smaller old Fono House nearby now houses the office of the Ombudsman. Across the field is the **Independence Memorial** (1962), which declares, "The Holy Ghost, Council of all Mankind, led Samoa to Destiny," and behind it is the **Lands and Titles Court,** which reviews village council decisions, disagreements over customary lands, and *matai* title disputes.

At the end of the Mulinu'u Peninsula is the **Apia Observatory,** founded by the Germans in 1902. After the unexpected hurricane of 1889, the Germans weren't taking any more chances. Note the many impressive **royal tombs** of former paramount chiefs both here and down the road to the left. Mulinu'u is the heartland of modern Samoan history.

Vailima

In 1889 Robert Louis Stevenson, Scottish author of the adventure classic *Treasure Island,* purchased approximately 162 hectares of bushland at the foot of Mt. Vaea, three and a half km inland from Apia and high above the sea, for US$4,000. Stevenson named the place Vailima, meaning "five waters," for the small streams that ran across the property, and here he built his home and spent the last five years of his life.

During a power struggle between rival Samoan factions, some chiefs were imprisoned at Mulinu'u. Stevenson visited them in confinement, and to show their gratitude, these chiefs built him a road up to Vailima when they were released. The Samoans called Stevenson Tusitala, or "Teller of Tales." On 3 December 1894, at

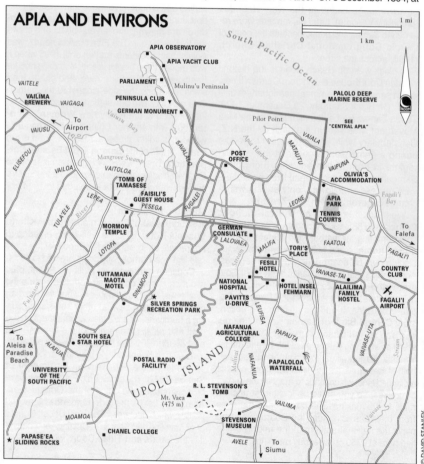

APIA AND ENVIRONS

APIA OBSERVATORY
APIA YACHT CLUB
South Pacific Ocean

VAITELE
VAILIMA BREWERY
VAIGAGA
PARLIAMENT
Mulinu'u Peninsula
PENINSULA CLUB
PALOLO DEEP MARINE RESERVE
GERMAN MONUMENT
Vaiusu Bay
To Airport
VAIUSU
Pilot Point
SEE "CENTRAL APIA"
ELISEFOU
VAILOA
Mangrove Swamp
VAITOLOA
POST OFFICE
Apia Harbor
VAIALA
MATAUTU
VAIPUNA
OLIVIA'S ACCOMMODATION
Fagali'i Bay
TOMB OF TAMASESE
LEPEA
FAISILI'S GUEST HOUSE
PESEGA
SAVALALO
FUGALEI
LEONE
APIA PARK
TENNIS COURTS
To Falefa
TULA'ELE
River
MORMON TEMPLE
LOTOPA
GERMAN CONSULATE
LALOVAEA
Stream
MALIFA
TORI'S PLACE
FAATOIA
FAGALI'I
TUITAMANA MAOTA MOTEL
SINAMOGA
FESILI HOTEL
VAIVASE-TAI
COUNTRY CLUB
SILVER SPRINGS RECREATION PARK
NATIONAL HOSPITAL
PAVITTS U-DRIVE
HOTEL INSEL FEHMANN
ALAILIMA FAMILY HOSTEL
FAGALI'I AIRPORT
Fuluasou
LEUFISA
NAFANUA AGRICULTURAL COLLEGE
PAPAUTA
VAIVASE-UTA
Stream
To Aleisa & Paradise Beach
SOUTH SEA STAR HOTEL
ALAFUA
POSTAL RADIO FACILITY
Mulivai
NAFANUA
PAPALOLOA WATERFALL
UNIVERSITY OF THE SOUTH PACIFIC
UPOLU ISLAND
MOAMOA
R. L. STEVENSON'S TOMB
Mt. Vaea (475 m)
VAILIMA
Vaivase Stream
PAPASE'EA SLIDING ROCKS
CHANEL COLLEGE
AVELE
STEVENSON MUSEUM
To Siumu

0   1 mi
0   1 km

© DAVID STANLEY

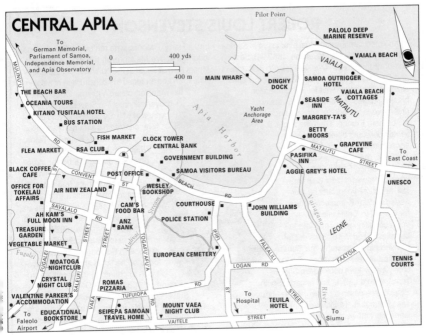

CENTRAL APIA

Pilot Point

To
German Memorial,
Parliament of Samoa,
Independence Memorial,
and Apia Observatory

PALOLO DEEP
MARINE RESERVE

VAIALA BEACH

0   400 yds

0   400 m

VAIALA

MAIN WHARF   DINGHY
DOCK

SAMOA OUTRIGGER
HOTEL

THE BEACH BAR

OCEANIA TOURS

KITANO TUSITALA HOTEL

BUS STATION

Apia Harbor

Yacht
Anchorage
Area

VAIALA BEACH
COTTAGES

SEASIDE
INN

MARGREY-TA'S

MATAUTU

BETTY
MOORS

FISH MARKET   CLOCK TOWER
CENTRAL BANK

FLEA MARKET   RSA CLUB

GOVERNMENT BUILDING

MATAUTU

GRAPEVINE
CAFE

PASIFIKA
INN

To
East Coast

STREET

BLACK COFFEE
CAFE

OFFICE FOR
TOKELAU
AFFAIRS

CONVENT

POST OFFICE

ST

SAMOA VISITORS BUREAU

AGGIE GREY'S HOTEL

UNESCO

AIR NEW ZEALAND

WESLEY
BOOKSHOP

BEACH
RD

SAVALALO

CAM'S
FOOD BAR

COURTHOUSE

JOHN WILLIAMS
BUILDING

Vaisigano

LEONE

AH KAM'S
FULL MOON INN

RD

ANZ
BANK

POLICE STATION

RIFI

FALEALILI

FAATOIA

TREASURE
GARDEN

STREET

STREET

VEGETABLE MARKET

Fugalei

Mulivai

Togafuafua

EUROPEAN CEMETERY

LOGAN   RD

River

TENNIS
COURTS

MOATOGA
NIGHTCLUB

CRYSTAL
NIGHT CLUB

FUGALEI

ROMAS
PIZZARIA

TUFUIOPA

RD

To
Hospital

TEUILA
HOTEL

VALENTINE PARKER'S
ACCOMMODATION

VAEA

SALEUFI

To
Faleolo
Airport

EDUCATIONAL
BOOKSTORE

SEIPEPA SAMOAN
TRAVEL HOME

MOUNT VAEA
NIGHT CLUB

VAITELE

ST

STREET

To
Siumu

the age of 44, Stevenson suffered a fatal brain hemorrhage while helping his wife Fanny fix dinner. He's buried just below the summit of Mt. Vaea, overlooking Vailima, as he'd requested.

The stately mansion with its beautiful tropical gardens was first sold to a retired German businessman, then bought by the German government as the official residence of their governor. Of the present complex, Stevenson had the central building erected in 1890, and in 1891-92 the east wing was added to provide proper quarters for his mother. The Germans built the westernmost wing in 1897. The N.Z. regime took it over when they assumed power in 1914, and until recently Villa Vailima was Government House, official residence of Samoa's head of state.

In early 1992, after Hurricane Val did serious damage to Vailima, Mormon businessmen from Utah and Arizona obtained a 60-year lease on the property with the intention of creating a museum. The complex was largely rebuilt, and in 1994 the **Robert Louis Stevenson Museum** (tel. 20-798) opened on the centenary of

the writer's death. You'll be led through a series of bedrooms dedicated to various members of the Stevenson family, but all of the furniture and heirlooms on display are replicas except for three chairs and a few books. Temporary exhibits are housed in a gallery upstairs in the west wing and you may visit these on your own after the tour. There's a marvelous view from the breezy upper verandah.

A bit east of the Stevenson mansion is a smaller red-roofed house once occupied by a son of the head of state but now empty. Outside this building is an old-fashioned mahogany steering wheel inscribed "Fear God and Honor the King, Samoa 1889." This is from the British ship *Calliope*, the only one to survive the naval debacle of that year. Britain donated the wheel to Samoa when the ship was broken up after WW II.

Entry to the museum grounds is free with admission to the house S$15 for adults and S$5 for children under 12. It's open Mon.-Fri. 0900-1530, Saturday 0900-1200, with the last tour commencing 30 minutes before closing.

ROBERT LOUIS STEVENSON

The most famous individual ever to live in Samoa was Robert Louis Stevenson (1850-94), Scottish author of the novels *Treasure Island, Kidnapped,* and *Dr. Jekyll and Mr. Hyde.* Always of frail constitution, Stevenson was forced to abandon his law studies at Edinburgh University and move to the gentler surroundings of southern France. There he wrote travel books and other works which soon made his name known. In 1876 he met an American divorcee named Fanny Osbourne who was 11 years older than himself, and three years later he journeyed to San Francisco where they wed. In California Stevenson's condition worsened into tuberculosis, and in 1888 his doctor advised him to travel to the South Pacific for health reasons. By this time wealthy from book sales, Stevenson chartered a yacht and began a South Seas cruise which took him to the Marquesas, Tuamotus, Tahiti, Hawaii, and the Gilbert Islands. He first visited Samoa in 1889, returning for good a year later. Here he befriended American trader Harry J. Moors, who rented the Stevensons lodgings above his store on the Apia waterfront. Moors also assisted in the purchase of land above the town and arranged the construction of a splendid mansion called Vailima. Of course, a conversationalist like Stevenson got along very well with the Samoans, who quickly recognized his stature. They called him Tusitala, or Teller of Tales. When some high chiefs were imprisoned during the power struggles of the time, Stevenson managed to have them freed, and in gratitude they built a track from Apia to Vailima so Stevenson could ride in his carriage back and forth from town. His 1892 book, *A Footnote to History: Eight Years of Trouble in Samoa,* describes the anarchy of the time, and includes eyewitness accounts of the terrible hurricane of 1889. On 3 December 1894, Stevenson suffered a cerebral hemorrhage while helping his wife mix mayonnaise for dinner on the back porch of Vailima. His grave lies on Mount Vaea overlooking Apia.

Vailima, home of
R.L. Stevenson

In 1978 a **Botanical Garden Reserve** with a loop trail was established at the bottom of the hill adjoining Vailima. Adjacent is a pool for swimming and a small waterfall (dry except during the rainy months). The hiking trail up to Stevenson's grave on Mt. Vaea begins here, and both it and the gardens are open 24 hours, admission free. A map of area is just down the road to the grave to the right of museum gate. The Avele or Vaoala buses (80 cents) will bring you directly here from the markets, otherwise a taxi should cost around S$6.

Mount Vaea

An almost obligatory pilgrimage for all visitors to Samoa is the 45-minute climb along a winding trail to the tomb of Robert Louis Stevenson, just below the 475-meter summit of Mt. Vaea. After the small bridge turn left. Five hundred meters up, the trail divides with a shorter, steeper way to the right and a much longer less-used trail to the left. A good plan is to go up by the short trail and come back down the longer way. After rains, the trail can get muddy.

The path to the top was cut by 200 sorrowful Samoans as they carried the famous writer's body up to its final resting place in 1894. From the tomb there's a sweeping panorama of the verdant valley to the east with the misty mountains of Upolu beyond, and in the distance the white line of surf breaking endlessly on the reef. The red roof of Vailima directly below is clearly visible. It's utterly still—a peaceful, poignant, lonely place. Stevenson's requiem reads:

Under the wide and starry sky,
Dig the grave and let me lie.
Glad did I live and gladly die,
And I laid me down with a will.

This be the verse you grave for me:
Here he lies where he longed to be;
Home is the sailor, home from the sea,
And the hunter home from the hill.

Stevenson's wife Fanny died in California in 1914 and a year later her ashes were brought back to Samoa and buried at the foot of her husband's grave. The bronze plaque bears her Samoan name, Aolele, and the words of Stevenson:

Teacher, tender comrade, wife,
A fellow-farer true through life
Heart-whole and soul free,
The August Father gave to me.

Side Trip East

Buses marked Falefa, Falevao, and Lufilufi depart the Apia markets every hour or so for Falefa, 29 km east (you can also pick up these buses on Matautu Street). You'll get many fine views of Upolu's north coast as you pass along Upolu's finest summer surfing beach, Lauli'i, a long right point break (beware of undertow). No barrier reef breaks the waves that crash onto these black sandy shores. Change rooms and showers (S$1 pp) are provided at **Saoluafata Beach,** but no visitors are allowed on Sunday.

A km east of Saoluafata Beach is Piula Theological College with the superb **Piula Cave Pool,** a natural freshwater pool fed by a spring directly below a large Methodist church. The water is unusually clear, despite all the carefree locals soaping up and washing clothes in it. Swim into the cave below the church. This is connected to a second cave by a small underwater opening on the left near the back. The second cave is long, dark, and deep, but can be explored with a mask and snorkel. The pool is open Mon.-Sat. 0800-1630, admission S$1, and there are changing rooms. If you leave Apia in the morning you'll have time for a swim in the pool before catching a midday bus to the beach *fales* at Lalomanu or Lepa (ask).

Falefa Falls, two km east of Piula through Falefa village, is impressive during the rainy season and it's freely visible beside the road. The Falefa bus turns around here.

Side Trip Southwest

Catch a Seesee, Siusega, or Tafaigata bus at the markets and ask the driver to drop you at the closest point to **Papase'ea Sliding Rocks.** You can also come on the Alafua bus to the university (see below), but this will add about 15 minutes to your walking time. Even from the closest bus stop you'll still have to hike uphill two km and pay S$2 admission (don't give the money to children—only to the adult at the entrance). You slide down three rocks into freshwater pools—don't forget your bathing suit. It's open daily (Sunday included!).

At Alafua, below and to the east of this area, is the 30-hectare Samoan campus of the **University of the South Pacific** (the main campus is in Fiji). In 1977 the university's School of Agriculture was established here, with assistance from New Zealand. To the left of the main gate is an agricultural training center funded by the European Union. The university's two semesters run from February to the end of June and late July to mid-November. The university library (tel. 21-671) is open weekdays 0800-1200/1300-1600.

On the way back to Apia notice the **Apia Samoa Temple** (1983) on the airport highway. The golden angel Moroni trumpets The Word from above, but only Mormons are allowed inside. The Church of Jesus Christ of Latter-day Saints established its Samoan headquarters here in 1902. Just a few minutes' walk west along the highway from the temple is the impressive four-tier **tomb of Tupua Tamasese Lealofi III,** the Mau Movement leader.

Beer lovers might like to visit the **Vailima Brewery** at Vaitele on the road to the airport. You'll only be allowed in on Thursday, and it's a good idea to call the Personnel Manager (tel. 20-200) beforehand to make sure he'll be available for a tour (no tasting). Plenty of buses run out this way (including those marked Afega, Faleula, Puipa'a, Toamua, Vaigaga, Vaiusu, or Vaitele).

Central Upolu

For a bit of heavy hiking, catch a Mulivai, Salani, Sapunaoa, Siumu, or Vaovai bus up the Cross Island Highway to an unmarked turnoff on the right for **Lake Lanoto'o,** otherwise known as "Goldfish Lake," high in the center of Upolu at 590 meters above sea level. Walk straight west on the dirt access road for just under an hour until you see the power lines end abruptly at a transformer on a pole, plus several radio towers down a road to the left. Continue straight ahead another 500 meters to a point where the access road turns left (south). Walk 400 meters south on this road until the radio towers are visible again on the left. On the right directly opposite here an overgrown trail runs due west to the lake, another one-hour walk. When you arrive at a destroyed microwave reflector on top of a hill, the lake is just below you to the left.

The unmarked way takes a bit of intuition to find and some of the locals living on the main road to the trail ask exorbitant fees such as S$40 to act as guides. There's no admission fee to the lake, so just take your time and follow the instructions provided above and you'll be okay. The route to the lake is very muddy following heavy rains, so only go after a couple of days of sunny weather. Expect fallen trees across the route and some confusion toward the end. This is a *very* strenuous hike, so be prepared.

The opaque green waters of this seldom-visited crater lake are surrounded by a mossy green bush dripping from the mist. Swimming in the lake is an eerie experience. To add to the otherworldliness of the place, Lake Lanoto'o is full of goldfish, but you'll have to wait patiently if you want to see any from shore (bread crumbs might help). This hike is ideal for seeing Upolu's high-altitude vegetation without going too far from town, but sturdy shoes and long pants are essential.

On your way back to Apia stop to visit the **Baha'i House of Worship** (1984), Mother Temple to all Baha'is in the region. The temple is at Tiapapata, eight km from Apia and a 30-minute walk down the highway from the Lanoto'o turnoff.

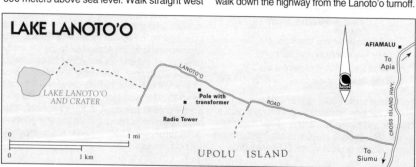

LAKE LANOTO'O

LAKE LANOTO'O AND CRATER

AFIAMALU

To Apia

LANOTO'O

Pole with transformer

ROAD

Radio Tower

CROSS ISLAND HWY.

0   1 mi
0   1 km

UPOLU ISLAND

To Siumu

© DAVID STANLEY

The monumental dome soars 30 meters above the surrounding area and has nine sides, symbolizing the unity of the nine major religions of the world. Inside, the latticework of ribs forms a nine-pointed star at the apex of the dome. The seating is arranged facing the Holy Land (Israel) because this is the final resting place of Baha 'Ullah (1817-92), Prophet-Founder of the Baha'i Faith. This majestic building, funded by Baha'is around the world, is open to all for prayer and meditation daily 0900-1700. Also visit the information center (tel. 24-192), to the left as you approach the temple. The Vaoala bus comes to within a 30-minute walk of the temple.

Palolo Deep

One of Apia's nicest attractions is the **Palolo Deep Marine Reserve** (daily 0800-1800, admission S$2), a natural reef aquarium operated by the Division of Environment and Conservation. The signposted entrance to the reserve is near the main wharf at Matautu, in fact, the Deep's main draw is its convenience to Apia. You can easily wade out to the Deep at low tide if you have something to protect your feet, and although the reef has been heavily damaged by hurricanes, much of the coral has regenerated and there are plenty of colorful fish (bring along bread to feed to them). Even if you don't intend to swim, the reserve garden is a very nice place to sit and read with lots of benches and relaxing lagoon views. This place is so peaceful it's hard to believe you're just a five-minute walk from the center of a capital city. The helpful staff do their best to serve visitors, but they also let you relax in privacy. Facilities include toilets, showers, and changing rooms. You can rent snorkeling gear (S$10) and buy cold soft drinks (no beer). The Deep is a perfect escape on Sunday—make an afternoon of it.

Scuba Diving

Sqvama Divers (Box 843, Apia; tel./fax 24-858), upstairs at Pasefika Inn, charges S$120/210 for one/two tank dives. Their open-water certification course is S$1,050. To dive at Aleipata or in the Apolima crater they require a minimum of six divers at S$390 each for two tanks including lunch.

Scuba diving is also available at the **Samoan Outrigger Hotel** (tel. 20-042) costing S$130 for a one-tank shore dive, or S$150/200 for a one/two tank boat dive at Lalomanu (two-per-

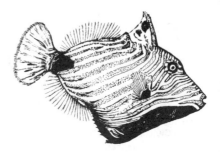

The undulate triggerfish (Balistapus undulatus) gets its name from a triggerlike mechanism controlling the dorsal fin, which the fish uses to wedge itself into coral crevices when threatened.

son minimum). The hotel's Danish dive instructor, Claus, also does open-water certification courses at S$880 for hotel guests only.

Pacific Quest Divers (Gayle and Roger Christman, Box 9390, Apia; tel. 23-914, fax 24-728, VHF channel 16 or 68), based at Coconuts Beach Club, offers scuba diving at S$150 including gear. If you just want a taste of scuba, a no-experience-required resort dive is S$135. They also do PADI certification courses at S$1,155.

Many of the reefs off Upolu's north coast have been damaged by hurricanes and local poachers who use dynamite or a type of poison to bring up fish, so the south coast is now favored for its calmer seas and variety of attractions. The reef channels teem with fish, best seen on an incoming tide. **Nu'usafe'e Island** just off Poutasi is a favorite for its coral heads, wavy coral, and variety of fishlife (including harmless sand sharks). You can hand-feed the tame fish. Five lava chutes penetrate 10-25 meters and open into clear water. If that sounds good, try going down the main lava chute at Lefaga through a strong current as the surf roars overhead, then over the edge of the reef. This is for experienced divers only.

Other good spots are the drop-offs at Nu'utele and Nu'ulua Islands in Aleipata, the western reef areas off Manono, and the edge of the barrier reef, three km offshore from Lalomalava, Savai'i.

Other Sports and Recreation

Samoa Marine (Box 4700, Apia; tel. 22-721, fax 20-087), near the Seaside Inn, offers deep sea fishing for marlin, mahimahi, wahoo, yellowfin, skipjack, and dog tooth tuna at S$1,050/2,100 a half/full day (up to five anglers, gear included). You supply the beer and they'll supply the snacks. This firm isn't there only for tourists: if nobody charters their powerboat, the *Ole Pe'a*, they'll often go out anyway in the hope of catching enough fish for sale on the local market to make it worth their while. Their guarantee is "no fish, no pay!"

The 18-hole golf course of the **Royal Samoa Country Club** (tel. 20-120) is just beyond Fagali'i Airport east of Apia (Fagali'i-uta bus). The clubhouse bar has a pleasant balcony overlooking the course and the sea—recommended for an afternoon drink. The course is open to nonmembers daily except Saturday (open to all on Sunday). Tuesday is Ladies Day with tee-off at 1330 and 1430. Greens fees are S$20. The big tournaments of the year are the Head of State Tournament in early January and the Samoa Open in June.

Saturday afternoons see exciting rugby or soccer from the grandstand at **Apia Park** (tel. 21-400). The main rugby season is February for "sevens" and July-Nov. for league rugby. You shouldn't miss a chance to see a game by the famous national team, Manu Samoa. The gymnasium at Apia Park (a gift of the People's Republic of China for the 1983 South Pacific Games) hosts basketball (Tuesday and Thursday at 1700), badminton (Wednesday and Friday at 1900), and volleyball (Saturday from May to July) in the gym.

The **tennis courts** behind Apia Park are open to the public daily (nightly until 2200; S$5 pp an hour, plus S$10 an hour for night lights). The **Apia Squash Center** (tel. 20-554) is next to the Seaside Inn.

Kirikiti (cricket) is played mostly in rural villages at 1400 on Saturday throughout the year with the competition season July-September. Other traditional sports include *igavea* (hide and seek), *lape* (handball), *sioga afi* (fire making), and *oagapopo* (coconut husking).

ACCOMMODATIONS

Shoestring
Betty Moors Accommodation (Box 18, Apia; tel. 21-085), just before the Mobil station on Matautu St., has 13 cell-like cubicles with shared bath at S$20 pp (you'll almost certainly get one to yourself). Ask about the better room behind the main building. Out of safety considerations, no cooking facilities are provided in this wooden building (also no breakfast, towels, or hot water), and on weekends loud music spills over from nearby nightclubs. If you come back on foot at night, beware of a sudden attack by dogs from the adjacent laundromat (have a few stones ready). Betty's an interesting person to chat with, and her husband was the son of trader Harry J. Moors, an adviser and close friend of Robert Louis Stevenson. She'll hold excess luggage while you're off touring Savai'i or south Upolu.

Farther along in the same direction, behind the gasoline station beyond the bank, is **Olivia's Accommodation** (Box 4089, Apia; tel./fax 23-465). There are eight three-bed rooms with shared bath in the main building at S$20 per bed in a shared room. Be sure to get a room with a fan. A large communal kitchen and lounge are provided. Peace and quiet at night depend on who your neighbors are, and Olivia's roosters and pigs will wish you a good morning. For more privacy ask for one of the two self-catering units in a three-unit block at back that cost S$44/55 double/triple. The family atmosphere is nice, but at times you may get lonely at Olivia's as not many people stay here these days (it's not in the mass-market Australian guidebooks). Olivia's is near Apia Park, which should be avoided for evening walks as there have been reports of incidents. Get to either Olivia's or Betty's on the Apia Park, Letogo, or Vailele buses from the markets.

On the other side of town, **Valentine Parker's Accommodation** (Box 395, Apia; tel. 22-158, fax 20-886) at Fugalei has nine double rooms at S$20 pp on the airy second floor of an old wooden building. Showers, toilets, and a TV room are downstairs, but no communal cooking facilities are provided. A new block next to the main street has a couple of rooms with private bath at S$60 double and some three-bed dorms at S$20 pp (rarely crowded). There's a nice lawn out back where you can sunbathe whenever the sky is clear. It's the most convenient accommodations to the vegetable market bus station.

Budget
The **Seipepa Samoan Travel Home** (Box 1465, Apia; tel./fax 25-447), off Vaitele St. near the Mount Vaea Club, is an oasis of peace just a 10-

minute walk from the city center. It's sort of like living in the middle of a village while still enjoying some privacy. There are four fan-cooled rooms with shared bath in a European-style house and a few Samoan *fales* in the garden, one of them with an upper and lower floor! The overnight charge is whatever you wish to pay (offer at least S$25 pp) and includes a large tropical breakfast served Samoan style. Singles must be prepared to share. Cooking facilities are provided and at lunchtime on Sunday a traditional *umu* feast is prepared for guests at S$10 pp (S$15 for nonguests). Run by a Swede named Mats and his Samoan wife Sia, this place is highly recommended—so good all 16 beds are often full.

The **Seaside Inn** (Box 3019, Apia; tel. 22-578, fax 22-918), near the main wharf at Matautu, has a good location near the Palolo Deep and is also convenient to town. Several of Apia's top bars are only a few minutes walk away. The three rooms with shared bath are S$45/55 single/double, or S$28 pp if rented out as three-bed dorms. The 11 rooms with private bath are S$50/60/72 single/double/triple, and there's also a larger unit with fridge in the rear garden at S$60/72/88. The rooms aren't entirely soundproof and they're sometimes rented out to couples with "night exercise" on their minds. The rates include a uniform breakfast (served 0700-0900 only), and communal cooking facilities are available (shortage of utensils). A small bar is attached and there's a nice veranda overlooking the harbor. This place is usually full of travelers and it's a good place to meet people, although the staff is often moody and the toilets could use a cleaning. Occasional water problems are another drawback, and don't leave things lying around as there have been several reports of petty theft from the rooms. Lock your door at night. Car rentals are arranged and bicycles are available at S$15/20 a day to guests/nonguests.

Almost opposite the entrance to the main wharf at Matautu is the two-story **Harbour Light Hotel** (Box 5214, Apia; tel. 21-103). Its 18 motel-style rooms with private bath are S$45/56/68 single/double/triple, a spaghetti-and-eggs breakfast included. In recent years this place has gone downhill with air conditioners that no longer work and unsavory characters hanging around. There's 24-hour service and you can always consider crashing here for one night if you arrive late on the ferry from Pago Pago. A small store is on the premises.

Facing breezy Vaiala Beach, along in the opposite direction from town, is the **Samoan Outrigger Hotel** (Box 4074, Apia; tel./fax 20-042), a six-minute walk from the main wharf. It occupies a stately old mansion built in 1894 for Jonas Coe, the American consul of the time, and since 1994 it has been one of the finest backpackers' hostels in the South Pacific (no connection with the Hawaii-based Outrigger hotel chain). Rooms are S$44/55 single/double with shared bath, S$66/88 with private bath, or S$28 pp in the dorm, breakfast and tax included. Facilities include a communal kitchen and fridge, lounge, bar, and a washing machine (S$6 a load). An outrigger canoe is for rent at S$10. The presence of resident Danish dive instructor (and manager) Claus makes the Outrigger an ideal place to stay for scuba freaks, and a variety of sightseeing tours are offered in the hotel minibus. The lagoon views from the front lounge are very nice, and you'll enjoy sitting on the steps in the evening chatting with other guests. It's clean and pleasant, or sterile and business-like, depending on your tastes. You won't get bored here. Ask for their minibus at the airport.

The **Alailima Family Hostel** (Box 4228, Apia; tel. 24-147, fax 26-905), next to a taxi stand a bit east of Heem's Fitness Center in Vaivase-tai, has eight basic rooms with shared bath in an old colonial mansion at S$40 pp. There's a huge communal kitchen and lounge downstairs often used by cultural exchange groups from American Samoa (Fagali'i Airport is just a short drive away). Better value are the two apartments in an adjacent building that go for S$500/1,200 for a one/four-bedroom per month. Fay Alailima (who wrote Aggie Grey's biography) is helpful with ecotourism or cultural contacts.

Another offbeat place is **Faisili's Guest House** (Box 6605, Pesega; tel. 22-336, fax 23-929), at Pesega on the road from the airport. The 18 fan-cooled rooms with shared bath are S$20/52/62 dorm/double/triple, while the nine a/c rooms with private bath cost S$88 single or double. Ask for a room on the back side of the building if traffic noise might bother you. There are no communal cooking facilities, but the Oriental Restaurant (closed Sunday), a bank, and a post office are right downstairs. Faisili's would be a good choice if you had business at the huge Mormon temple across the street.

Visiting academics might choose the **South Sea Star Hotel** (Box 800, Apia; tel./fax 21-667), at Alafua near the entrance to the University of the South Pacific. The 30 fan-cooled rooms with shared bath are S$30/50 single/double, plus 10% tax. The minimum stay is two nights and there are weekly and monthly discounts. This two-story building (no sign) in a garden setting is accessible on the regular Alafua bus. A free breakfast is included, but only if you request it. It's forbidden to consume alcohol in the rooms.

The **Tuitamana Maota Motel** (Box 2854, Apia; tel. 23-146, fax 22-741) at Sinamoga (Alafua bus) has six spacious rooms with bath at S$50 pp. A fridge and cooking facilities can be provided upon request, but it's far from everything and not really worth the price.

Inexpensive
Ah Kam's Full Moon Inn (Box 1299, Apia; tel. 20-782, fax 20-782), on Savalalo Rd. in downtown Apia, has 10 fan-cooled rooms with fridge at S$99/132/165 single/double/triple. An a/c room will be about S$30 more. This two-story motel has a nice little bar in the courtyard—drop in for a drink at happy hour (1630-1900) even if you're not staying there.

The **Pasefika Inn** (Box 4213, Apia; tel. 20-971, fax 23-303), on Matautu St., has 26 rooms in a three-story building above the Peace Corps office. These begin at S$122/149/176 single/double/triple, plus S$27 extra if you want a balcony. Most rooms are a/c with a fridge and access to common cooking facilities, but seven budget rooms without a/c are S$81/95 single/double. There's also an eight-bed dorm at S$41 pp. Breakfast is included in all rates, but to be frank, this place is overpriced.

Tori's Place (Box 1604, Apia; tel./fax 23-431), not far from the hospital at Moto'otua, offers 12 fan-cooled rooms at S$95/115/135 single/double/triple. Although this two-story building is clean and new, these prices are too high for accommodations with shared bath. There is a swimming pool.

Across the street from the National Hospital is the **Fesili Motel** (Box 1062, Apia; tel. 26-476, fax 22-517), a bizarre five-story building with a laundromat and chapel in the basement, a supermarket on the second floor, motel rooms on the third and fourth floors, and "Faupepe's Sky Village" on the roof. The 10 big a/c rooms with private bath, fridge, and TV are S$134/164 single/double. Like the Teuila, it caters mostly to overseas Samoans interested in showing off to local relatives without paying the bigger bucks collected at Aggie's and the Tusitala.

Moderate
The **Vaiala Beach Cottages** (Box 2025, Apia; tel. 22-202), facing the lagoon at Vaiala, offers seven pleasant, fan-cooled bungalows with cooking facilities and fridge at S$175/200/230 single/double/triple, plus 10% tax. Children 12 and under are free. Discounts are possible for long stays if you book directly, but bookings made through a travel agent or airline are 10% higher. The aggressive guard dogs of this neighborhood make it unwise to walk back here from town late at night, so take a taxi.

The two-story **Teuila Hotel** (Box 182, Apia; tel. 23-959, fax 23-000), on Vaitele St. opposite the Teachers College, has 15 exorbitant a/c rooms with fridge and private bath at S$165/195/255 single/double/triple, breakfast included.

The three-story **Hotel Insel Fehmarn** (Box 3272, Apia; tel. 23-301, fax 22-204), up Falealili St. in Moto'otua, has 54 functional rooms at S$195/225/255 single/double/triple plus 10% tax. Each a/c unit has a fridge, full cooking facilities, video/TV, balcony, and private bath. The Insel Fehmarn caters to business travelers: typing, photocopying, and fax services are available. A swimming pool, tennis courts, guest laundromat, restaurant, and bar are on the premises. Apia's top pizzeria is right across the street and there are several car rental agencies nearby offering good rates. This unpretentious, well-managed hotel is a good alternative to Aggie's and the Tusitala for those who want value for money. Ask for a room on the top floor for panoramic views.

Expensive
Apia's premier tourist hotel, **Aggie Grey's** (Box 67, Apia; tel. 22-880, fax 23-626), on the east side of the harbor, originated in March 1942 as a hamburger stand catering to U.S. servicemen stationed in the area. Aggie's son Alan has continued the tradition of catering to American tastes,

although the hotel lost much of its original South Seas atmosphere when the main waterfront building was reconstructed in mock-colonial style in 1989. The 154 rooms now begin at S$285/300/315 single/double/triple in the old section around the pool. Bungalows are about S$60 more, rooms in the main lobby wing 50% more, suites 100% more. The cheaper rooms are rather shabby and stuffy, but the expensive ones facing the harbor are quite luxurious. Children under 16 are not allowed in the new wing or suites, but a fourth person in the old wing is S$15 regardless of age. Add 10% tax to these prices, and if you pay by credit card expect to have your bill inflated slightly due to the exchange rate scam discussed previously. Meals are S$150 pp extra. Weekly events include the barbecue on Sunday night and the Samoan feast on Wednesday. Aggie's is often full of dull business guests and rather bored conference participants, but the bar is nice and there's even an island in the large swimming pool!

The Japanese-owned **Kitano Tusitala Hotel** (Box 101, Apia; tel. 21-122, fax 23-652), at the beginning of the Mulinu'u Peninsula, is a complex of two-story blocks containing 96 a/c rooms with private bath beginning at S$225/255/285 single/double/triple, plus 10% tax, with children under 12 free. The open *fale* architecture of the main buildings is pleasant, and perhaps because it's a little disorganized, the atmosphere is surprisingly relaxed. Mosquitoes permitting, the poolside bar is a pleasant place to visit in the afternoon or early evening, and the snack bar serves good food at reasonable prices. Expect the waiters to try to shortchange you or to ask for a "loan" or a free trip to America. There's more local flavor than at Aggie's, just don't expect everything to work perfectly. For example, don't count on receiving your telephone messages or having your faxes go out. Occasionally overseas Samoans throw all-night parties in the rooms and the night manager may be unwilling to try to control these regular guests just to please a one-time tourist like you.

West of Apia

Dave Parker's Silver Streams (Box 3456, Apia; tel. 71-189) is a bar in a lovely location at Tapatapao, about four km south of Tanumapua Plantation. There's a wonderful swimming hole full of shrimp in the river itself, and you can hike up a nearby hill for a view of Apia in about 15 minutes. At last report there were only three simple huts with shared bath by the river at S$30 double, but plans call for 20 more upmarket units to replace these soon, so check before you come. Meanwhile you could probably ask Liz Parker for permission to use her kitchen to prepare meals. The Aleisa bus passes a couple of km below the property (a long hot walk), so a taxi from Apia (S$15) would be better. Budget.

East of Apia

Rainforest Ecolodge (Ava and Steve Brown, Box 4609, Matautu-uta; tel. 22-144, fax 26-941), at Vailele-uta, five km east of town, caters mostly to people who book from overseas through Eco-Tour Samoa. The two guest rooms with shared bath in a modern two-story cement house are S$120 per room, including breakfast. Lunch (S$15) and dinner (S$30) can be supplied. Numerous hiking possibilities are available in the area, including a trail to a waterfall on the Letogo River. Frequent buses pass on the main road about 700 meters below the Ecolodge. Inexpensive.

Beach *Fales* East of Apia

The closest village-run beach resort to Apia is **Saoluafata Beach Fales** (Box 820, Apia; tel. 40-216) on a nice beach near the Piula Cave Pool, 26 km east of Apia. To sleep in one of the three *fales* here costs S$16 pp, plus S$10 per meal. Picnickers pay S$2 pp. It's a good choice for a taste of this lifestyle without the long trip to Aleipata. Surfers come in summer (Dec.-March) for the reef break right-hander, 90 meters off nearby Faleapuna. Shoestring.

FOOD

Budget

The food stalls at Apia's vegetable and flea markets are the cheapest places to eat (S$3-5), and it's hard to beat a breakfast of hot chocolate with buttered bread, or a large bowl of cocoa and rice. Surprisingly, there's quite a bit here for vegetarians, including *palusami* and roasted breadfruit.

Skippy's (tel. 25-050; closed Sunday), in the arcade beside the Pacific Commercial Bank on Beach Rd., has fish and chips, hamburgers, and other rather fatty local meals.

Many of Apia's cheapest eateries are near the corner of Vaea and Convent Streets, most of them open only until 1600 weekdays and 1300 Saturday. Here you'll find **Betty's Restaurant,** which dishes out huge lunches to huge Samoans, but you'll need a strong stomach to join them. **Pinati's** (tel. 26-395), next to Betty's, has no sign outside and no menu inside, but the large crowd of locals tells you it's something good. There are only a few choices, including curry, chop suey, fish, and chicken, all around S$3 a big plate. **Nana's Restaurant** (tel. 25-578), a few doors east on Convent St., is better than Betty's and the stuff in the warmer is only S$2 a scoop. Another choice is **Amani's Takeaway** (tel. 25-363), next to Retzlaff's Travel on Vaea St., with inexpensive chop suey, curries, and fish and chips.

A step up is the **Gourmet Seafood and Grill** (tel. 24-625; closed Sunday), on Convent St. a block back from the Chief Post Office, with lunch specials, sashimi, fried fish, and steaks. While the food certainly isn't "gourmet," the nautical decor is rather pleasant and their burgers are said to be the best in town (certainly more appealing than the predictable products doled out at the nearby McDonald's). You must pay a cashier first and get a number.

More Samoan-style fast food is scooped out at **Cam's Food Bar** (tel. 22-629; Mon.-Sat. 0800-2100), a block and a half behind the Chief Post Office (check the map). Cam's is great for lunch, passable at breakfast, but overpriced at dinner.

Pele Rose Mini Market (tel. 24-062), opposite the Samoa Visitors Bureau, has coffee, sandwiches, and other takeaway foods, and they're open 0500-2130 seven days a week.

Barbecues

For S$5 you can get a huge barbecue lunch at the **Maua Barbecue** (daily except Sunday until 1630) in the two-story stone building at the corner of Convent and Fugalei Streets. Watch for the smoke rising from the outdoor grill on Fugalei St. (the dining room is inside). Be sure to order chicken and not the tough, fatty mutton flaps or turkey tails.

More S$5 takeaway barbecue meals are available at the store in front of Crystal Night Club at Fugalei, south of the vegetable market. Try their *oka* (raw fish). Just down the road is **Frosty Boy** where obese passengers tumble out of taxis and order five soft-serve ice cream cones at a time.

If mystery meats are not for you, **The Steak House** (tel. 22-962; closed Monday), in the same block as the ANZ Bank Saleufi Agency on Vaea St., grills quality cuts fresh from the adjacent butcher shop at fair prices.

Pub Food

For Mexican food and cold beer it's the **Grapevine Cafe and Vineyard Bar** (tel. 25-612; open Mon.-Sat. 0800-2200, Sunday 1200-2100), on Matautu St. just east of the Mormon church. Yachties often drop in for a cold one at happy hour (weekdays 1600-1800) and the management caters to this market with a paperback exchange and free showers in the adjacent fitness center. The Grapevine has one of the few compact disc jukeboxes in Apia (S$1 for three plays), and although owner Kasimani Lautusi looks as mellow as the Buddha, be aware that he's got a black belt in karate and runs his own private security firm. This is a great place to begin a pub crawl.

Another Apia institution is **Maua's Store** (tel. 23-942), next to Margrey-Ta's Beer Garden.

THE PALM ARRIVES IN SAMOA

Tuna, a young Fijian, once fell in love with Sina, a lovely visitor from Samoa. He asked her to marry him, but she could not decide and returned home. Tuna changed himself into an eel and followed her to Savai'i, taking refuge in a pool. Sina came to visit Tuna regularly there, but alas, he forgot the chant required to change back into a man. Eventually, Sina's brothers discovered the affair and came to kill Tuna. Before Tuna died, he asked Sina to bury his head, out of which a wonderful life-giving tree would grow. The fruit would contain his eyes and mouth, and every time Sina lifted one to drink, she would be able to kiss her lost lover. That's how the coconut tree came to Samoa.

It's open on Sunday and when the beer garden's open you can consume your takeaway food in there. The *oka* (raw fish) is a great bargain at S$2.50.

Jean's Blue Marlin Restaurant & Bar (tel. 24-065), next to Sails Restaurant on Beach Rd., has hamburgers and there's sometimes live music.

Chinese

Apia insiders reckon that finest Chinese food in town is served at the **Hua Mei Restaurant** (tel. 25-598; closed Sunday), upstairs in the Lotemau Center behind Air New Zealand. The lunch specials are inexpensive and there's a good medium-priced dinner menu.

Substantial Chinese meals are served at the **Treasure Garden Restaurant** (tel. 22-586; weekdays 1100-1400/1700-2200, Saturday 1700-2200) on Fugalei St. near the vegetable market. Although the food is good the noisy TV set in the dining room is jarring and the air conditioning may give you a chill. On Sunday (0930-1200) all you can get is takeaways from the counter outside (always a good option if you've rented a car and want to carry a cheap dinner back to your hotel).

For many years **Wong Kee's Restaurant** (tel. 26-778), in a ramshackle building behind Otto's Reef, was the "in" place to eat in Apia, and despite a recent change of ownership you'll still get some very good Chinese food here. It's not a bad plan to order extra rice and share one main dish between two people. The *aiga* lunch served weekdays is much less expensive than dinner. ("The routine of a friendly Samoan waitress translating my American English into Samoan English for the benefit of the Chinese-speaking cook was Monty Pythonesque.")

The **Canton Restaurant** (tel. 22-818), on Matautu St. near Betty Moors, gets varied reports, but it's one of the few places that opens for dinner on Sunday (1730-2100). Try the saltwater crabs.

Italian

Romas Pizzeria (tel. 25-948; daily until 2200, no lunch on Tuesday and Sunday), on Vaea St. a couple of blocks south of the clock tower, serves huge American-style pizzas (the large S$29 size is enough for three normal people). You can order a beer and have your pizza here, or take it away for the same price.

Giordano's Pizzeria (tel. 25-985; closed Monday), near the Hotel Insel Fehmarn on the road connecting the National Hospital to the Cross Island Rd., has richer pizza than Romas but it's a bit more expensive and the portions are smaller. Those who know say it's the best pizza in town and the candlelit courtyard dining area is agreeable.

Fine Dining

The **Restaurant Belle Ile** (tel. 21-010; weekdays 1200-1400, Mon.-Sat. 1830-2300), on the second floor of the John Williams Building on Beach Rd., was once the place to splurge on fresh fish, lobster, octopus, and steak. The word these days is that the quality no longer justifies the price and you won't see many people in there.

Apia cognoscente now say the number-one place in town is **Sails Restaurant and Bar** (tel. 20-628), above Fale Tifaga Tauese Mini Cinemas on Beach Road. Their airy terrace provides pleasing harbor views to complement the fancy seafood, steaks, pastas, and sashimi, just count on paying at least S$20/40 pp for lunch/dinner here. Proprietors Ian and Livia Black managed top hotels in Tahiti and Fiji before settling in Apia. Thanks to Samoa's location next to the international date line, Sails can claim to be the last restaurant in the world to close every day. The wooden restaurant building itself was built by trader Harry Moors, and Robert Louis Stevenson himself stayed here before Vailima was built.

Sunday

Sunday brunch (S$22.50), either Western or Japanese style, is served 1030-1430 at the **Hotel Kitano Tusitala.**

A better bet might be the *to'onai* served around noon on Sunday at the **Pasefika Inn.** For S$30 you can eat as much *umu*-baked Samoan specialties as you wish.

For Sunday night dinner consider the poolside barbecue at **Aggie Grey's Hotel,** which offers a good selection of Samoan dishes for S$35. There's no traditional dancing but a corny hotel band is on the stage.

Cafes

The **Black Coffee Cafe** (tel. 26-528), on Convent St., opens for breakfast at 0630 Mon.-Sat., and has a choice of teas, coffees, spicy snacks, and healthy main courses all day.

Le Moana Cafe (tel. 24-828), in the Lotemau Center off Convent St. behind Air New Zealand, prepares good medium-priced meals and is also nice for a coffee. They also open for breakfast 0900-1300 on Sunday.

Gensil's Ice Cream Parlor, on the back side of the Lotemau Center off Vaea St., has real two-scoop cones for S$2.50, plus milk shakes, sundaes, and banana splits.

The **Rainforest Cafe** (tel. 25-030), next to Kava & Kavings on Beach Rd., really lives up to its name with the wood shavings on the floor and potted plants. It's run by a German couple named Barbara and Christian. They usually open weekdays only, serving breakfast and lunch 0900-1700, dinner from 1800 until late. You can also get handicrafts, postcards, and local guidebooks here.

ENTERTAINMENT

Fale Tifaga Tauese Nos. 1 & 2 mini-cinemas on Beach Rd. next to Don't Drink The Water shows the type of adventure and romance movies popular around the world.

Midcity Cinema on Vaea St. runs similar downmarket videos at 1400, 2000, and 2200 (no program Monday and Saturday nights, admission S$2.50).

Weekday mornings at 0750 the police band marches up Beach Road to the new Government Building for the flag-raising ceremony at 0800, and all traffic is stopped. Church choirs are worth a listen on Sunday morning (dress neatly and avoid bright clothing or shorts).

Nightclubs

Not to be missed is the Cindy Show Thursday at 2130 (S$7 cover) at **Margrey-Ta's Beer Garden** (tel. 25-395), near the Seaside Inn on Beach Road. It's great fun to watch the talented *fa'afafine* (female impersonators) do take offs on Tina Turner hits, and the fire dancing is spectacular. The audience will be mostly Samoan (this is definitely no tourist thing) and it's necessary to arrive half an hour early to get a good seat as the place will be packed. It's probably the number-one cabaret show in the South Pacific,

but if you're a single male, be prepared to be approached after the show by entertainers interested in drinks, meals, and more (clear out as soon as it's over if you might find this offensive). Margrey-Ta's is open Mon.-Sat. 1000-midnight—always rowdy and fun.

Evening Shades (tel. 23-906), corner of Beach Rd. and Matautu St. not far from Margrey-Ta's, is the current "in" disco where Apia's trendy youth congregate on Saturday nights (S$3 cover).

Rougher is the **Mount Vaea Nightclub** (tel. 21-627) on Vaitele St., open Mon-Sat. 1900-midnight, Apia's meet market since 1968. It's fast and loud with the best band in town, and there are lots of boys/girls. Things don't get going until late, and drunks often spin into squabbles, so stay out of the middle and be really polite to everyone. The trouble is usually between local Samoans, rarely tourists.

The **Moatoga Nightclub** (no phone), opposite the Apia vegetable market, is a large Samoan dancehall with live music nightly except Sunday from 2200 (no cover). Take the same precautions you would at the Mount Vaea.

Crystal Night Club (tel. 22-155), south on Fugalei St. from the vegetable market, opens Wed.-Sat. 1830-midnight with live music from 2000. Friday is the best night to come with happy hour drink discounts 1700-1930 and free snacks including morsels of roast pig. Ask about fundraising benefits here (the admission fee usually includes stacks of local food). Crystal offers a good mix of people, no rowdies, and no trouble.

As elsewhere in the South Pacific, places like these can be challenging for women. Many problematical situations revolve around the Samoan "nightclub custom" of asking any female to dance who is not currently dancing, whether she came with a date or not. It can be taken as an insult to say no in this situation, so a female who only wants to dance with her date must dance every dance with him or be bombarded with requests she cannot lightly refuse. Otherwise she can say that her foot hurts and forgo dancing with anyone, including her date.

After midnight the police begin making the rounds of the clubs and bars closing everything down, and by 0100 the city is dead. Everything except the hotel bars is tightly shut on Sunday and that day you're supposed to be a hotel guest to be drinking there. Persons under the age of 21 aren't supposed to be drinking at all.

Bars

Apia's favorite drinking place is the **RSA Club** (tel. 20-171; Mon.-Sat. 0900-midnight) on Beach Rd. in the center of Apia. Happy hour is 1600-2100 with free *pupu* (snacks) Friday at 1800. Whenever there's music here it's *loud*. Foreign visitors are welcome.

Otto's Reef (tel. 22-691) on Beach Rd. is a safe, casual place to drink or play pool. Check out their Samoan *oka* (spicy raw fish) served after 1600 (S$2.70). **Don't Drink the Water** (tel. 20-093), next to Kava & Kavings, is a no-smoking bar famous for its pitchers of piña colada and chocolate cake.

Apia's most atmospheric drinking place is hidden down the road beside the oil tanks directly opposite the German Flag Monument on the Mulinu'u Peninsula. The **Peninsula Club** (tel. 24-375; open Mon.-Sat. 1000-midnight), has open-air seating below three immense banyan trees and a main room with live music by Samoa's original pop band, Penina o le Tiafau, nightly except Sunday at 2000.

At the **Apia Yacht Club** (tel. 21-313), also out on the Mulinu'u Peninsula, you can get a great cheeseburger and a drink on Friday night, a barbecue on Sunday 1100-1600. All visitors are welcome *with* a member; polite, nicely dressed visitors *without* a member are usually invited in too.

Friday nights a rock band shakes **The Beach Bar** (tel. 25-956), just up the Mulinu'u Peninsula from the Kitano Tusitala. It's frequented by a congenial expatriate crowd.

Another safe Friday event is happy hour 1700-2000 at the bar of the **Insel Fehmarn Hotel** in Moto'otua with half-price drinks and free *pupu* (snacks). There's live music.

Cultural Shows for Visitors

An essential part of any visit to Samoa is attendance at a *fia fia* where the Polynesian dancing on stage comes with a buffet dinner of local foods (look over the whole spread before getting in line). There's usually a *fia fia* at **Aggie Grey's Hotel** on Wednesday and at the **Kitano Tusitala** on Thursday. The show at the Kitano Tusitala includes dances from several Pacific countries, while the "We Are Samoa" program put on by the

hotel staff at Aggie Grey's is strictly Samoan and usually includes an appearance by a female member of the Grey clan, carrying on a tradition established by the late Aggie Grey herself. Another tacky touch at Aggie's is the Robert Louis Stevenson requiem set to music and sung in English and Samoan.

At Aggie's the show is before dinner at 1830, while at the Tusitala it's after dinner at 2000 (check these times). Admission for the show and the buffet is around S$45, otherwise there's a S$11 cover charge for the show alone. Patrons wearing T-shirts or shorts are not allowed in. Don't forget the Cindy Show at Margrey-Ta's Beer Garden on Thursday, which would be preferable to the Tusitala *fia fia*.

SHOPPING

Apia's colorful **vegetable market** or *maketi fou,* three blocks inland on Fugalei or Saleufi Streets, throbs with activity 24 hours a day—families spend the night here rather than abandon their places. You'll see a marvelous array of local produce, all with prices clearly marked, plus an eating area and a great assortment of classic Polynesian types.

Go native in Samoa by changing into some colorful, eye-catching clothing. Female travelers especially will enhance their appearance and acceptance by wearing a long muumuu gown, a two-piece *puletasi,* or a simple wraparound *lavalava* available at the **Flea Market** on the waterfront. This is also a good place to shop for handicrafts.

Kava & Kaving Handicrafts (Box 853, Apia; tel. 24-145), on Beach Rd., has war clubs, kava bowls, baskets, fly whisks, tapa cloth, model canoes, slit drums, shell necklaces, and coconut shell jewelry. They carry mostly authentic traditional handicrafts at good prices. Handicrafts are also available at **Aggie's Gift Shop** (tel. 22-880), next to Aggie Grey's Hotel, **Chan Mow Supermarket** (tel. 22-615), opposite the Clock Tower, and **Perenise Handicrafts** (tel. 26-261), in the Lotemau Center behind Air New Zealand. Most shops are closed Saturday afternoon and Sunday.

The Samoa **Philatelic Bureau** (tel. 20-720) is in the Chief Post Office and at the airport—beautiful stamps at face value.

SERVICES

Money

The ANZ Bank gives cash advances on Visa credit cards, while the Pacific Commercial Bank (a joint venture of the Bank of Hawaii and the Westpac Bank) takes MasterCard. Obtaining money this way is expensive as you'll lose about 15% on the exchange, and interest is charged from the moment you collect the money.

The main branch of the ANZ Bank opposite the Chief Post Office changes traveler's checks weekdays 0900-1500, Saturday 0830-1130. Several small agencies of the ANZ Bank around Apia will also change traveler's checks at the same rate. The ANZ Bank charges 50 cents commission on traveler's checks, whereas the Pacific Commercial Bank deducts S$3.

The locally owned National Bank of Samoa in the NPF Building behind Polynesian Airlines and at the vegetable market charges 50 cents commission. Their market branch also changes traveler's checks Saturday 0830-1230.

policeman, Apia

The rate of exchange for traveler's checks is considerably better than that for cash. Changing foreign currency outside Apia can be a nuisance, so do it here. On Saturday afternoon and Sunday, Aggie Grey's Hotel will change traveler's checks for a rate a bit lower than the bank. Allow extra time in any case as anything associated with bureaucracy moves slowly in Samoa.

There is no American Express representative in Apia.

Post and Telecommunications

The Chief Post Office in central Apia is open weekdays 0900-1630. Poste restante mail is held two months at a counter in the room with the post office boxes. Branch post offices exist at Matautu, Pesega, and Faleolo Airport.

Make long-distance telephone calls from the International Telephone Bureau (daily 0700-2200), inside the Chief Post Office. Three-minute station-to-station calls are S$7.50 to American Samoa, S$9 to Australia or New Zealand, S$13.50 to North America, and S$18 to Europe. Person to person service is only S$3 extra. These prices are about the lowest in the South Pacific. If you wish to receive a fax at this office, have it sent to fax 685/25-617. Public telephones for local calls are also available here, but you must ask at the counter (no public phone booths are available anywhere in Samoa). If you arrive to find a huge crowd of people waiting on lines of benches to place telephone calls, be aware that they're probably waiting to place overseas calls *collect*. If you're willing to pay for your call, you'll get priority and can go straight to the counter without waiting.

In late 1997 Pacific Internet Services, private operator of the talofa.net, was taken over by Computer Services Limited's samoa.net (try substituting this new stem to any old talofa.net addresses you come across). They operate a cybercafe (tel. 20-926; e-mail: cafe@samoa.net) in the Lotemau Center behind Air New Zealand.

Immigration Office

For a visa extension, go to Immigration (tel. 20-291) in the Government Building (access from the parking lot at rear) with S$50, two photos, your onward ticket, sufficient funds, proof that you're staying at a hotel, and a good reason. You may also be asked to obtain a local sponsor who'll accept responsibility for you.

Embassies

The Australian High Commission (tel. 23-411; Mon.-Thurs. 0830-1600, Friday 0830-1200), next to The Rainforest Cafe on Beach Rd., issues tourist visas mandatory for everyone other than New Zealanders. Australia also represents Canada in Samoa.

Three countries have diplomatic missions in the John Williams Building on Beach Rd.: The Netherlands (tel. 24-337), 4th floor, the European Union (tel. 20-070), 4th floor, and the United States (tel. 21-631 or 22-696; weekdays 0930-1230), 5th floor. The New Zealand High Commission (tel. 21-711) is nearby on Beach Rd. opposite the John Williams Memorial (the a/c reading room here is an attraction in itself).

The British consul is Bob Barlow (tel. 21-406), a solicitor with an office on the 2nd floor of the NPF Building above Polynesian Airlines. France is represented by Norman Paul (tel. 20-469), upstairs in the Gold Star Building opposite the RSA Club.

The Swedish Consulate (tel. 20-345) is at the Pacific Forum Line at the entrance to the main wharf. The German consul (tel. 24-981) is at the Rosenberg Clinic on the road up to the National Hospital. The Chinese Embassy (tel. 22-474) is at Vailima, a bit below the Robert Louis Stevenson Museum, down the road opposite the Carmelite Monastery.

Laundromats and Public Toilets

Cleanmaid Laundrette (tel. 21-934; Mon.-Sat. 0700-1900, Sunday 0700-1630), on Matautu St. between Betty Moors and the harbor, charges S$2.50 to wash, S$4 to dry. Bring your own laundry soap. At night, beware of vicious dogs here that often attack pedestrians headed for the guesthouses down the road.

Near the vegetable market is Homestyle Laundromat (tel. 21-551; closed Saturday), hidden behind A & S Hunt Service Center on Fugalei Street. Laundrette Sil, across the street, is open on Saturday.

Public toilets are behind the clock tower in the center of town.

INFORMATION

Samoa Visitors Bureau

The government-run Samoa Visitors Bureau (Box 2272, Apia; tel. 26-500, fax 20-886, www.samoa.co.nz; weekdays 0800-1630, Saturday 0800-1200) is in a *fale* on Beach Rd. between the Government Building and the Catholic cathedral. A large part of the job training of the people behind the counter involves memorizing their own brochures, and they'll repeat information printed there even if it's out of date or incorrect.

Statistics and Maps

The Department of Statistics (Box 1151, Apia; tel. 21-371, fax 24-675), 1st floor, Government Buildings, sells the *Annual Statistical Abstract* and *Quarterly Statistical Bulletin* (S$5 each).

Get large topographical maps of Apia and Samoa for S$7 each at the Lands, Survey, and Environment Department (tel. 22-481) in the building marked "Matagaluega o Eleele, Faugafanua & Siosiomaga" next to the New Zealand High Commission on Beach Road. The *Samoa* map published by Hema Maps (S$12) is excellent and it's available both here and at Aggie's Gift Shop.

Books and Periodicals

The Wesley Bookshop (tel. 24-231) on Beach Rd. has a reasonable Samoa and Pacific section but the proprietors have long refused to sell the works of Samoa's leading novelist, Albert Wendt, which are too critical for their taste. For Wendt's novels you could try the **Educational Bookstore** (tel. 20-817), at the south end of Vaea St., although they're often out of stock.

The place to buy Australian and New Zealand newspapers and magazines is Le Moana Cafe (tel. 24-828), in the Lotemau Center off Convent St. behind Air New Zealand.

P. Ah Him Co. General Merchants (tel. 24-559), on Saleufi St. near the vegetable market, has a good selection of used paperbacks for sale at the back of the store.

The **Nelson Memorial Public Library** (Box 598, Apia; tel. 20-118; Mon.-Thurs. 0900-1630, Friday 0800-1600, Saturday 0830-1200) is opposite the Clock Tower on Beach Road. Special permission of the librarian is required to enter the Pacific Room.

Environmental Information

Samoa's environmental group, the Siosiomaga Society (Box 5774, Matautu-uta, Upolu; tel./fax 21-993), in the office building above the Educational Bookstore at the south end of Vaea St., has a large library of environmentally oriented videos, which you can view at their office weekdays 0800-1630 or rent for 50 cents a day.

The South Pacific Regional Environmental Program (Box 240, Apia; tel. 21-929, fax 20-231, www.sprep.org.ws), opposite the Yazaki Samoa plant near the Vailima Brewery at Vaitele, sells many specialized publications on the South Pacific environment. (This office is to move to a new site near the Robert Louis Stevenson Museum in late 1999—ask before making the long trip out to Vaitele.)

Travel Information

Island Hopper Vacations (Box 2271, Apia; tel. 26-940, fax 26-941), in the Lotemau Center behind Air New Zealand, is an inbound tour operator that handles bookings from overseas.

Apia's airline offices are Air New Zealand (tel. 20-825), corner of Convent and Vaea Streets, Samoa Air (tel. 22-901), next to Molesi Supermarket on Beach Rd., and Polynesian Airlines (tel. 21-261), opposite the clock tower. Polynesian represents Air Pacific (tel. 22-693) while Samoa Air is the Royal Tongan Airlines agent.

HEALTH

You can see a doctor for S$20 anytime at the National Hospital (tel. 21-212), in Moto'otua south of the center, but bring along a thick book to read while you're waiting. You can call an ambulance at tel. 996. The Moto'otua bus passes the hospital.

A good alternative to trekking out to the hospital is visiting Dr. Leota Malaki Malaki of L.M.M. Medical Clinic (tel. 26-565; weekdays 0830-1200/1300-1630, Saturday 0830-1200), in the back of the strip mall opposite Western Union on Vaea Street. Like most private doctors, he charges S$30 for a nonresident consultation.

Dr. Toga T. Potai of L.T.P. Surgery (tel. 21-652), behind the post office and opposite Gourmet Seafood, specializes in aviation and travel medicine, plus ear, nose, and throat.

One of Apia's preeminent private doctors is Dr. John Atherton of Soifue Manuia Clinic (tel. 26-113), next to UNESCO above the post office at Matautu-uta. Call ahead for an appointment, if possible.

Dr. A.P. Leavai (tel. 20-172) operates a dental surgery above Business Systems Ltd. at the south end of Vaea Street.

Samoa Pharmacy (tel. 22-595) is next to the Pacific Commercial Bank on Beach Road. Both of the chemists (pharmacies) on Beach Rd. are only open weekdays 0830-1630, Saturday 0830-1230.

TRANSPORTATION

By Bus

Local buses for Apia and vicinity, and long-distance buses for points all around Upolu, leave from the bus stations adjacent to the two Apia markets: the Flea Market on the waterfront and the vegetable market three blocks inland. The bus station at the Flea Market has separate areas marked Falelatai, Falealili, Taulaga, and Aleipata but in practice these divisions are not followed.

The police do not allow buses to stand for long periods waiting for passengers at the vegetable market, so the buses make a loop between the two markets every 10 minutes or so until they're full. Long-distance buses have been known to drive around town for an hour looking for passengers. There are no set schedules but you can find a bus to virtually anywhere if you're there by 1000 Mon.-Saturday.

There are buses to the Robert Louis Stevenson Museum (marked Avele or Vaoala), the Papase'ea Sliding Rocks (Seesee, Siusega, or Tafaigata), the University of the South Pacific (Alafua), the main wharf (Matautu-tai), Fagali'i Airport (Fagali'i-uta or Vaivase), the National Hospital (Moto'otua), Piula Cave Pool (Falefa, Falevao, or Lufilufi), O Le Pupu-Pu'e National Park (Salani, Sapunaoa, or Vaovai), Faleolo Airport and the Savai'i ferry wharf (Falelatai, Manono, Mulifanua, Samatau, or Pasi Ole Va'a), and Manono Island (Falelatai, Manono, or Samatau).

Long-distance buses run to Lalomanu, Lepa, Safata, Sataoa, Siumu, and Lefaga. Buses to the Savai'i ferry wharf at Mulifanua begin their trips at the vegetable market, whereas all of the other buses begin from the Flea Market and only visit the vegetable market to pick up additional passengers. Buses to Mulifanua leave the vegetable market two hours before the scheduled departure times of the ferries to Savai'i (if you board this particular bus at the Flea Market, you won't get a good seat).

On Friday afternoon all buses departing Apia tend to be crowded with workers headed home. Saturday morning is a good time for buses, but on Saturday afternoon, Sunday, and evenings, service is very limited. It's not possible to make a day-trip to Aleipata or Lepa from Apia by bus—you must spend the night there.

In outlying villages only bus drivers are reliable sources of information about bus departure times. Others may give misleading information, so ask three or four people. On weekdays buses to Apia often leave villages in south and east Upolu at 0500, and then again at 1130. They often set out from Apia to return to their villages at 1100 and 1600.

Most of these colorful homemade wooden buses are village-owned and trying to use them to go right around Upolu is very difficult, as they serve remote villages by different routes that don't link up. The Lalomanu bus goes via Falevao and Amaile, while the Lepa bus goes via Lotofaga to Saleapaga.

The Salani, Sapunaoa, and Vaovai buses follow the Cross Island Highway to Siumu, then run along the south coast via Poutasi toward Salani. Four buses serve this route, but they all seem to run about the same time, making three or four trips a day. The last bus back to Apia from Salani is at 1400 (important to know if you're making a day-trip to O Le Pupu-Pu'e National Park).

There are good paved roads from Mafa Pass to Amaile and Lepa. The road along the south coast is paved from Siumu to Salani, but at Salani a river blocks eastbound vehicular traffic and cars must make a loop up and around via Sopo'anga Falls (no bus service). There's very little traffic along the south coast of Upolu if you intended to hitch.

Bus service is also very limited west of Siumu on the south coast. The Lefaga and Safata buses follow the north coast west to Leulumoega, then drive south through Tanumalamala to Matautu (Paradise Beach) or Tafitoala. There's no road between Lefaga and Falelatai. The only convenient way to go right around Upolu is to rent a car.

The buses are without cushions, but they do have destination signs and their fares are the lowest in the South Pacific. Buses around Apia cost 50 *sene;* S\$1.50 to the Savai'i ferry wharf or Falefa; S\$2 to Lefaga or Mafa Pass; S\$2.50 to Siumu; S\$3 to Lalomanu or Saleapaga. The bus fare from Apia to Lalomanu is supposed to be S\$3, but some drivers ask S\$5. On local buses around Apia, you pay as you get off. On long-distance buses, tell the driver where you're going as you board. You'll make a better impression on everyone if you have small change to pay your fare. Standing isn't allowed, so once a bus is full, extra passengers must sit on the knees of existing passengers! (Half of all traffic convictions in Samoa are for overloading vehicles.) The stereo music is a bus plus.

Taxis

Taxis have license plates bearing the prefix "T." Taxis parked outside the two airports and at the upmarket hotels tend to be a rip-off, while those waiting at taxi stands used mostly by local people are usually okay. Average taxi prices from the taxi stand adjacent to the Flea Market bus station are S\$3 to the main wharf, S\$5 to Fagali'i Airport, S\$6 to the Robert Louis Stevenson Museum, S\$30 to Faleolo Airport, or S\$35 to Coconuts Beach Club.

Since the taxis don't have meters, always agree on the price before you get in and make sure you're both talking Samoan *tala,* otherwise the driver could insist on the same amount in U.S. dollars (a favorite trick). If you intend to get out and have the driver wait awhile, ask the price of that too. Failure to do so will lead to unpleasant demands for extra money at the end of the trip and ugly threats if you resist. To hire a taxi should cost S\$25 an hour around town or S\$30 into the countryside. There should be no additional charge for luggage, and tipping is unnecessary.

Beware of the taxis parked in front of Aggie Grey's Hotel, as these drivers are some of the most seasoned hustlers you'll ever meet. If you're staying at Aggie's and want a taxi, turn right as you come out the door, cross the bridge, and about a hundred meters in front you'll see a regular taxi stand. In general, taxis are abundant in Apia.

Car Rentals

The international driver's license isn't recognized in Samoa. Officially you're supposed to get a local driver's license at the licensing office (open weekdays 0930-1200/1300-1500) opposite the main police station in Apia. A temporary 30-day driving permit costs S$10 with no photos required, while a regular Samoan license valid one year is S$30 and two photos. Some car rental agencies require the Samoan driver's license, while others don't. According to the Samoa Visitors Bureau, it's actually up to the agency!

Many side roads are too rough for a car and most agencies will tell you the insurance isn't valid if you drive on them. Make reservations well ahead if you want a jeep. A few of the car rental agencies are evasive about what is and isn't covered by the optional collision insurance, and some rental cars don't carry any collision insurance at all. Even with collision insurance you're still responsible for the "excess" or minimum deductible amount. Check the car *very carefully* before you drive off, and don't under any circumstances leave your passport as security on a car rental. Be suspicious, as we get more than the usual number of complaints about car rentals at Apia (if you get the feeling that a company is unreliable, trust that impression and don't do business with them). On the positive side, car rental rates in Samoa are the lowest in the South Pacific. Despite occasional shortages, gasoline prices in Samoa and American Samoa are also the best in the region.

As in American Samoa, driving is on the right. Speed limits are 40 kph around Apia or 56 kph on the open road. Drive very slowly and avoid hitting any people or animals—it can be as bad as in Mexico. Many drivers resist using their headlights after dark, and outside Apia pedestrians dominate the roadways. You'll often see people walking along a paved highway oblivious to approaching traffic, especially in the late afternoon. If you're forced to swerve dangerously to miss them or have to stop to avoid hitting another car, they'll just laugh. If you do hit something valuable like a large pig, drive back to Apia and turn yourself in to the police (tel. 22-222). If you stop you could be stoned, and heaven help you if you hit a Samoan! One Apia car rental company has this line in their brochure: "Stopping to verify the extend (sic) of possible injuries sustained to a third party could prove fatal to yourself." If you do become involved in a roadside dispute, don't react to excited bystanders—ask to speak to the *pulenu'u* right away. Occasionally Samoan children throw stones at cars they think

are driving through their village too quickly and the rental agency may hold you responsible for the broken windshield. If you park a rental car in a village, you risk having it vandalized.

Except for two gas stations near Fasito'out out toward Faleolo Airport, fuel isn't usually available outside Apia, so plan ahead. Ask the car rental company which gas station they recommend, as some stations have tanks that let rain water leak in. If you want to take the car to Savai'i make sure it's allowed before signing the car contract (most agencies won't allow you to do this). You can reserve a car space on the ferry at the office of the Samoa Shipping Corporation (tel. 20-935) on Vaea St. in Apia. However taking a rental car from Upolu to Savai'i is always risky because if there's any problem with the car you'll be responsible for getting it back to Upolu.

Budget Rent-a-Car (tel. 20-561, fax 22-284) between Polynesian Airlines and the Pacific Commercial Bank in the center of town, has Samurai jeeps at S$110/100/90 per day for one/three/seven days all inclusive. Sidekick jeeps are S$132/120/110. The deductible insurance "excess" for which you are responsible is S$675 and you cannot take the vehicle to Savai'i.

Avis Rent-a-Car (tel. 20-486, fax 26-069), behind the taxi stand at Beach Rd. and Matautu St., charges S$175 for their cheapest car with unlimited mileage (US$500 deposit). Avis cars also cannot be taken to Savai'i.

Pacific Helicopters Ltd. (tel. 20-047), opposite Aggie Grey's Hotel, rents Suzuki jeeps at S$130 a day including tax and mileage, but there's no insurance.

G & J Transport (Box 1707, Apia; tel. 21-078, fax 21-078), next to Kava & Kavings on Beach Rd., has cars at S$110. Unlimited mileage and S$500 deductible collision insurance are included and it's okay to take the car to Savai'i.

P & K Filo Car Rentals (Box 4310, Matautu; tel. 26-797, fax 25-574), in the mall behind Air New Zealand, has cars at S$110 a day for one or two days, including tax, mileage, and insurance (S$600 deductible). If you rent for six days the seventh is free. You must leave S$100 deposit and you may take the car to Savai'i.

Apia Rentals (Box 173, Apia; tel. 24-244, fax 26-193), on Vaea St., has Samurais at S$110 a day and Sidekicks at S$132 all inclusive (S$1,000 deductible insurance, S$200 deposit).

Billie's Car Rentals (Box 1863, Apia; tel. 25-363, fax 23-038), inside Amani's Takeaways on Vaea St., has cars that may be taken to Savai'i by ferry. This company is owned by Retzlaff Travel.

Another local company with a good reputation is **Pavitt's-U-Drive** (tel. 21-766, fax 24-667), between the National Hospital and Insel Fehmarn Hotel, with Suzuki jeeps beginning at S$100 one day or S$80 a day for two or more days. Also try **Hibiscus Rentals** (tel. 24-342, fax 20-162), opposite the Hotel Insel Fehmarn, and **Le Car Rentals** (Box 3669, Apia; tel./fax 22-754) on Fugalei St. near the vegetable market.

Scooter and Bicycle Rentals

The agencies renting motorbikes and bicycles change all the time, so ask at the Visitors Bureau for current locations. With scooters the insurance is usually included, but the gas is extra. A cash deposit will be required.

Local Tours

Several companies offer organized day tours of Upolu from Apia. Prices vary according to the number of participants, whether you travel by private car or minibus, if lunch is included, etc. Don't expect much "narration" from the guide—it's mainly a way of getting around. The tours don't operate unless at least eight people sign up, so ask about that, and if it looks questionable, check elsewhere. Even if organized sightseeing isn't your usual thing, the convenience and price makes it worth considering here.

Samoa Scenic Tours (tel. 22-880, fax 23-626), next to Aggie Grey's Hotel, charges S$38 pp for an afternoon tour around town or a morning trip to the Piula Cave Pool. Full-day trips including lunch cost S$70 pp to Lefaga's Paradise Beach (Tuesday and Friday) or Aleipata (Wednesday and Saturday). Their full-day Manono Island excursion on Monday and Thursday is S$78 pp, lunch included.

Jane's Tours (Box 70, Apia; tel. 20-954, fax 22-680) on Vaea St. offers full-day trips to Aleipata on Wednesday and Saturday, and Paradise Beach on Thursday, both S$65 pp including lunch. The Manono trip on Tuesday is S$75 (half price for children under 12).

Cheaper are the minibus tours offered by **Outrigger Adventure Tours** (tel. 20-042), based at the Samoan Outrigger Hotel. The Aleipata beach tour on Sunday is S$40, the Manono Island tour on Tuesday S$60, and the Paradise and Matareva beaches/Togitogiga Waterfall tour on Wednesday S$40, a Samoan lunch included in all. A minimum of six persons is required to operate a tour and you must book by 1500 the day before.

Oceania Tours (tel. 24-443, fax 22-255), near the Kitano Tusitala Hotel, has a variety of overnight tours to Savai'i. These trips are reasonable value for those with limited time, but compare prices and book ahead.

Eco-Tour Samoa Ltd. (Steve Brown, Box 4609, Matautu-uta; tel.22-144, fax 26-941), at Vailele-uta, five km east of Apia, offers seven-day Samoan safaris, plus sea kayaking trips of two, four, and six days. They cater mostly to people who book from abroad, and prices are steep at S$450 pp per day and up all inclusive.

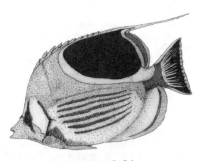

saddleback butterfly fish

DIANA LASICH HARPER

AROUND UPOLU

Like most other South Pacific "Bible Belt" towns, Apia is pretty dead on Saturday afternoon and Sunday. Luckily a number of *fale* resorts have opened on beaches around Upolu and Savai'i in recent years, giving visitors the option of evacuating Apia on Saturday morning. These are basically in two resort areas on Upolu, Aleipata/Lepa in the southeast corner of the island and Lefaga/Safata in the southwest. These also get quite a few Samoan day-trippers on the weekends, so be prepared.

There's no bus service right around Upolu, and if you want to do a circle trip without renting a car or returning to Apia, you'll need several days and a willingness to walk for long stretches. If you must choose only one destination, Saleapaga is a good bet.

SIGHTS AND RECREATION

Northeastern Upolu

The bridge above Falefa Falls previously mentioned gives access to a little-traveled seven-km road east along Upolu's north coast to **Saua-go** and **Saletele** villages, an unspoiled corner of old Samoa worth exploring if you have your own transport. After the twin village, the onward track to **Fagaloa Bay** becomes much worse and only passable in a vehicle with high clearance. Fagaloa Bay's flooded volcanic crater is more easily reached via a steep side road off the paved road to Aleipata, a bit north of Mafa Pass. A road continues along Fagaloa Bay's south side to remote **Uafato** village, 14 km east of the turnoff. At Uafato one finds waterfalls, rainforests, flying foxes, and legendary sites associated with the demigod Moso, plus village *fale* accommodations (ask for Sulia) and a daily bus to/from Apia. It's possible to hike east along the coast to Ti'avea.

Eastern Upolu

Some eight km south of Falefa Falls, the road works its way over **Mafa Pass** (276 meters), beyond which is a junction, with Aleipata to the left and Lepa to the right. If you take the left-hand highway or "Richardson Road" toward Amaile (Lalomanu bus) you'll pass alongside the **Afulilo Reservoir** where Afulilo Falls above Fagaloa Bay were harnessed in 1993 in a US$33-million, four-megawatt hydroelectric development. Over half of Upolu's electricity comes from this and other hydroelectric projects.

Aleipata and **Lepa** districts feature many excellent and unspoiled white-sand beaches with good swimming but only average snorkeling. The authentic ecotourism resorts of this area are covered below, and a stay at one of them would allow the time to explore this attractive area. Visit the beautiful offshore islands at high tide with fishermen from Lalomanu. **Nu'utele Island,** a leper colony from 1916 to 1918, is now uninhabited, and two beautiful beaches flank the steep forested slopes. Hiring a boat out to Nu'utele would run about S$50 roundtrip (ask at Ulutogia village just north of Lalomanu). A trail to the volcanic crater behind Lalomanu begins behind the hospital in Lalomanu. A large colony of flying foxes lives here and a guide would be useful.

From Lalomanu it's seven km along the south coast to Saleapaga. The Lepa bus runs from Apia to Saleapaga via Mafa Pass and Lotofaga. Five km south of the pass, deep in the interior, are **Fuipisia Falls** (S$3 admission), signposted on the west side of the road. Just a 300-meter walk inland from the road, the falls plunge 56 meters down into a fern-filled valley of which you can get a good view from on top.

Three km south of Fuipisia, the same river plummets over 53-meter-high **Sopo'aga Falls** (admission S$3 per car, S$6 per bus). The signposted viewpoint is just a few hundred meters south of the junction with the westbound road to O Le Pupu-Pu'e National Park. A trail heads down to the falls from the viewpoint.

If you don't have your own transportation, you'll probably have to walk the four km from Sopo'aga Falls to the Salani turnoff. Buses run along the south coast from Salani to the National Park and Apia, but they're infrequent, and there's next to no traffic, so you're not likely to hitch a ride. The south coast of Upolu is more tra-

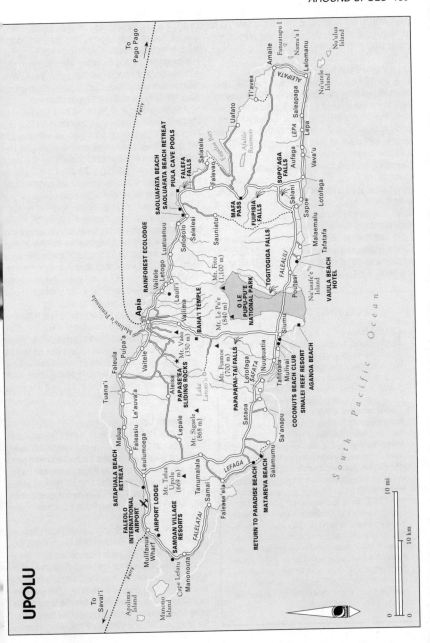

UPOLU

ditional than the north, and the people take pride in keeping their villages clean and attractively decorated with flowers.

O Le Pupu-Pu'e National Park

This 2,850-hectare national park (tel. 24-294), created in 1978, stretches along the insular divide from the summits of Mt. Le Pu'e (840 meters), the double-cratered peak east of Afiamalu, and Mt. Fito (1,100 meters), highest point on Upolu, right down to the lava fields of O Le Pupu and the south coast. The park is intended to provide a habitat for the endangered Tongan fruit bat, or flying fox *(Pteropus tonganus)*. In past these giant bats with one-and-a-half-meter wingspans would soar above the treetops at dusk, but illegal hunting has sharply reduced their numbers.

At Togitogiga, 28 km south of Apia via the Cross Island Highway, five km east of Siumu junction and just a short walk from the main road, are beautiful **Togitogiga Falls**, good for swim-ming, wading, and diving (middle pool). There are toilets, change rooms, and shelters at the falls. After heavy rains Togitogiga Falls becomes a raging torrent. It's crowded with Samoan pic nickers on weekends (admission is free). With permission of the park staff, you may camp free near the falls for two nights maximum.

An overgrown trail from the falls leads up to **Peapea Cave**, three hours roundtrip on foot. It's hard to find the way on your own, so consider hir ing a guide at the house on the right just be yond a gate a few hundred meters up the track (S$10/20 a half/full day). Beyond the cave, a trail continues north up the stream another four km to a waterfall where you could camp.

A rough four-km road begins two km west of the falls and leads across the lava fields to the black coastal cliffs in the southern section of the park. It probably isn't worthwhile to hike all the way down on foot and the road is too rough for a normal car, but you could do it in a jeep for fun. The **O Le Pupu Trail** follows the coast east from the end of the road, and the spent shotgun shells seen along the way are disheartening.

It's possible to do O Le Pupu-Pu'e National Park as a day-trip by catching a Salani, Sa-punaoa, or Vaovai bus from the markets in Apia, but you'll probably only have an hour or two at Togitogiga Falls. Ask the driver what time he'll be returning to Apia, or better, get together with other travelers from your hotel and rent a vehicle for the day.

Southwest Upolu

The Cross Island Highway runs 23 km south from Apia to Siumu. To the right near the road, three km south of the Lake Lanoto'o turnoff (and 13.5 km from Apia), are **Papapapai-tai Falls**, also known as Tiavi Falls. The unmarked view-point (free) is near a store beside the road but it's only worth stopping if you have your own trans-portation.

From Siumu the South Coast Road contin-ues west, reaching Sinalei Reef Resort and Co-conuts Beach Club after one or two km, Sala-mumu Beach after 11 km, and Return to Par-adise Beach after 13 km. Catching a bus along this way would be pure chance. One interest-ing south coast attraction is the **Sa'anapu-Sa-taoa Mangrove Forest,** accessible from either Sa'anapu or Sataoa villages. Each village has an

---

FLYING FOXES

Flying foxes are found from Madagascar to the Cook Islands with 55 species of the genus *Pteropus* living on different islands. In Western Polynesia, *Pteropus samoensis* is a daytime feeder that roosts alone or in small groups in the rainforest canopy, while the noc-turnal *Pteropus tonganus* lives in colonies of several hundred, either in the forest or in trees along roads. Its feeding flights begin just before dusk and many species of rainforest trees and plants depend on the bats for pollination and seed dispersal. Flying foxes produce only one offspring per year and it's cared for by the moth-er for six to eight months. During the 1980s tens of thousands of flying foxes were slaugh-tered in Samoa for export to Guam where they're considered a delicacy. Luckily this trade largely came to an end in 1989 when most is-land bats were listed as endangered species. Today habitat destruction is the gravest threat facing the animals in both Tonga and Samoa. On Tongatapu only one small tract of old growth rainforest still remains, although the surviving bats enjoy royal protection. In Samoa they are still hunted by villagers.

information *fale* where you can pay S$1 pp to visit the mangroves on foot (only at low tide), or S$20 pp for an outrigger canoe tour (best at high tide). You'll see two types of mangroves here, the red mangrove with stilt roots and the oriental mangrove with buttress roots of knee-like extensions. Birds include the grey duck and reef heron. Both villages have guest *fales* where you can spend the night at S$20 pp.

The paved Lefaga/Safata road follows an inland course a few km from the coast and you must pay fees to visit the beaches. **Return to Paradise Beach,** named for a 1952 Gary Cooper film based on a James Michener novel of the same name, is accessible via a rocky two-km side road (S$5 per car, S$3 per motorbike, or S$1 per pedestrian).

ACCOMMODATIONS

Beach *Fales* at Aleipata and Lepa

During the past few years over a dozen basic ecotourism resorts have sprung up at Lalomanu (Aleipata), on the golden sands facing Nu'utele Island, and on a less-frequented beach at Saleapaga (Lepa). These clusters of small two-person beach *fales* are simple, and amenities like electricity, toilets, and running water are provided at some but not at others. As well as being great shoestring places to stay, they're a wonderful introduction to Samoan culture.

For S$15-20 pp you'll get *fale* accommodation with a mat, pillow, and mosquito net but no bed. Food prices vary, costing anywhere from S$5 pp for one meal to S$26 pp for all three. Of course, these are open thatched *fales* with no walls or doors, so keep valuables well stowed at night, and if you go off during the day, it's wise to pack your bags and leave them with your hosts. Hurricanes tend to wipe these places out, but they're quickly rebuilt. There's always lots of space for visitors who show up unannounced (most don't have phones anyway).

At Saleapaga and Lalomanu the bus drops you right at the gates of the resorts, while at Lefaga in southwest Upolu you'll have a long hike down to the beach (which does enhance privacy). Picnickers pay S$2 pp or S$10 per car to use the facilities for the day (if you're just walking along the road and stop to sit down in an empty beach *fale* for a rest, someone will soon appear with a mat and the expectation of receiving the standard fee). Most day-trippers arrive on weekends, so during the week you could have the entire beach to yourself. It's lovely—the perfect antidote to Apia.

Lalomanu

As you come down from Lalomanu village and go west along the coast you'll pass Lusi and Gata's, Litia Sini's, Taufua's, Sieni & Ropert's, Romeo's, and Malo, in that order. Taufua's, Sieni and Ropert's, and Romeo's are used mostly by day-trippers and not recommended for an overnight stay.

Your best bet may be the one you reach first, **Lusi and Gata's Beach Fales,** which has a secluded beach all to itself, whereas all the other resorts share the same long beach. Lusi and Gata charge S$15 pp to sleep, plus S$5 per meal. The friendly demeanor, private beach, and low price recommend this place, but be prepared for some rather primitive toilets and showers.

Litia Sini's Beach Fales is better developed with 16 *fales* in a long row closed to the road but open to the sea (S$20 to sleep, plus S$10 a meal). **Taufua's Beach Fales** (Box 4802, Apia; tel. 20-180) has a bar you may visit but their beach is usually crowded with Samoan day-trippers and not recommended. **Sieni & Ropert's Beach Fales,** right next to Tuafua's, is also noisy and has poor security. **Romeo's** (tel. 20-878) is part of the same strip.

Half a km west of Romeo's is **Malo Beach Fales,** which is much better protected from the road and picnickers. The 15 thatched *fales* here are S$20 pp to sleep, plus S$10 a meal. Their slogan is "my home your paradise." You're paying a bit extra here for the privacy, security, and a degree of comfort. Several unnamed collections of beach *fales* between Romeo's and Malo are cheaper and more basic.

Saleapaga

Whereas Lalomanu wins in the scenery category with its spectacular views of Nu'utele, Saleapaga offers a better choice of places to stay, fewer day-trippers, and good hiking possibilities in the hills overlooking the village. You may also find it quieter, friendlier, and safer—the whole South Seas dream.

Facing the white sands of Saleapaga Beach, seven km west of Lalomanu, are Lalopapa, Boomerang Creek, Tauiai, Gogosiva, Tila's Tropical Fales, Vaotea, Le Ta'alo, Faofao, Tagiilima, Tama o Le Aufuaina, Malaefono, Niusilani, Manusina, and Saleapaga Ocean View, cited here from east to west. All of the *fale* resorts charge S$15 pp to sleep and S$5 for breakfast, but at some it's S$10 each for lunch and dinner while at others it's only S$5 per meal. No alcohol is allowed at Saleapaga village.

Lalopapa Beach Fales is nicely isolated a few hundred meters east of Boomerang Creek (meals S$5 each).

Boomerang Creek Tourist Accommodation (Box 3680, Apia; tel. 40-358) is different from all the other places in that the *fales* are up on the hillside rather than on the beach. It's run by an Australian named Steve Harrison who charges S$40 pp including all meals. The communal toilets are clean, there's a small restaurant with a mini-library, and the security is good, although it's not quite the full Samoan experience of the others. It might be a good choice if you intended to stay longer than just one or two nights.

Gogosiva Beach Fales offers five thatched *fales* right on the beach at S$15 pp, meals S$5 each. Electricity and running water are available, and the family that runs the place is very helpful. Though open to the road, Gogosiva has one of the finest views of the crashing surf, the sound of which will lull you to sleep.

Vaotea Beach Fales (tel. 41-155) is sheltered from the road by trees and flowers, and it offers a bit more space. They charge S$15 pp to sleep, plus S$5 per meal.

Le Ta'alo Beach Fales is protected from the road by bushes and a fence, as is Tapu Legalo's **Faofao Beach Fales** (Box 2272, Apia; tel. 41-067). These neighboring places are run by related families and both charge S$30 pp with breakfast and dinner. Backpackers often stay here.

Buses leave Apia for Saleapaga Mon.-Sat. at 1000, and again at 1600 weekdays and Sunday. The return trip from Saleapaga to Apia is Mon.-Sat. at 0530, and again at 1200 weekdays and Sunday. There's no need to rent a car to come to Saleapaga or Lalomanu—just catch a bus.

Aufaga

At Aufaga, a few km west of Saleapaga, are three adjacent *fale*-style resorts, but these are different in that they're at the bottom of a high cliff. The largest such resort is **Fagatele Beach Fales** with 16 *fales* facing a wide sandy beach. Nearby is **Faga Beach** (formerly called Vailaasia Beach), which has 14 *fales,* including one on a tiny island accessible by canoe and another on an isolated hill. **Sinalele Beach** is separated from Faga by a rocky headland and features 12 *fales.* The surfing is good at high tide.

In recent years these three resorts have been leased out to a Mormon organization called Paradise Cove Corporation (tel. 41-076) for the rehabilitation of delinquent teenage boys from the United States, so check with the Visitors Bureau before coming.

At last report the upscale **Vava'u Beach Fales** (tel. 20-954), a 10-minute walk west of Aufaga, was closed due to an ownership dispute. The six attractive bungalows with kitchenettes (built with European Union aid money) are still there, and the beach is as lovely as ever, but don't plan a stop unless you hear for sure that they've reopened.

Beach *Fales* at Falealili

The **Salani Surf Resort** (George Danellis, Box 6089, Pesega; tel./fax 41-069), at the end of the paved road in Salani village, is right beside the Salani River and near the beach. The 10 fan-cooled thatched *fales* have electric lighting but the toilets and showers are outside. The S$243 pp per day price is inclusive of room and board, airport transfers, surf guiding, kayaking, local tours, hammocks, and evening entertainment. No surfing is allowed on Sunday, so they usually take guests to the national park that day. It's used almost exclusively by surfers who book through Waterways Travel, 15145 Califa St., Suite 1, Van Nuys, CA 91411, U.S.A. (tel. 1-800/928-3757 or 1-818/376-0341, fax 1-818/376-0353, www.waterwaystravel.com). There's a long, solid left-hander out in the channel, and the surf is down on this side of the island they'll drive you up to the north. Other activities include canoeing in the mangroves or up the jade-green river to a waterfall, crab fishing, using the nearby village bathing pool, and exploring the south coast.

Backpackers and anyone interested in finding a quiet little hideaway are welcome at **Vaiula Beach** (Box 189, Apia; no phone), one and a half km off the main highway at Tafatafa, nine km east of the junction of the Cross Island and South Coast Highways. There are five open *fales* at S$15 pp. You can use a communal kitchen and there are shared toilets and showers. Camping is S$5 pp (in your own tent) and picnic tables, toilets, and shelters are provided. The place fills up with picnickers on Saturday and Sunday (S$5 per car) but during the week it's usually empty. The snorkeling off their beach is only mediocre, but there's the possibility of surfing the hollow, fast right-hander out on the reef (boat required). Owner David Petersen is the grandson of a Danish sea captain and a bit of a character. Vaiula Beach makes a good base from which to explore O Le Pupu-Pu'e National Park and it's an okay stop on your way around the island.

Beach *Fales* in Southwestern Upolu

Another assortment of beach *fales* is found in Lefaga district, but these are quite a hike down from the main highway if you arrive on the Lefaga or Safata buses. It's possible to camp or sleep in a *fale* for S$10 pp at famous **Return to Paradise Beach,** two km off the main road, but obtaining drinking water is sometimes a problem.

Matareva Beach Fales at Lefaga charges only S$10 per carload or group of pedestrians to camp or stay overnight in one of their beach *fales*. Day use of the beach is S$5 per car or S$2 pp for pedestrians. Although there's a small store it's better to bring your own food from Apia. The money is collected up at main road, then it's a three km hike down to the beach. The swimming here is safer than at Paradise Beach as there are no rocks and the location is nicely secluded.

More *fales* are available at **Salamumu Beach,** a few km east of Matareva, and showers are provided. Picnickers pay S$5 per car. The money is collected up at the main road, then it's five km to the beach. Beach hikes from Salamumu are possible to Matareva (30 minutes) and Nuu-o-Vasa (one hour).

Anapu Resort at Nuu-o-Vasa Beach near Sa'anapu-tai is also five km off the main road via a very rough track best covered in a pickup or by 4WD. The small *fales* stand along a lovely white beach flanked by black lava rock. A perfect

small island is easily accessible just offshore and the snorkeling is good. At last report this resort was closed.

Sa'anapu

There are three places to stay at Sa'anapu-tai between Lefaga and Siumu. The first you reach is the **Manuia Wetland Holiday Retreat** (Ray Hepehi, Box 900, Apia; tel. 26-225) with private self-catering bungalows at S$80/120/150/170 single/double/triple/quad. To sleep in an open Samoan *fale* on their white beach is S$20 pp including bedding and a mosquito net. There's a bar and lots of free parking for overnight guests. Day visitors pay S$10 per car, plus another S$10 if the group wants a *fale* for the day, S$5 to use a barbecue, and S$20 to rent an outrigger canoe. It's a good bet if you want quality without the pricing of Coconuts and Sinalei.

Lagoon Lodges (Box 1319, Apia; tel. 20-196 or 20-965, fax 22-714), also known as Sa'anapu Beach Resort, right on the same lovely white beach, has five budget cottages with private bath, fridge, and stove at S$44/88 single/double. One larger five-person unit is also S$88, and if you stay three nights the price drops to S$66 double. The resort has a bar and outside alcohol is discouraged—if you do bring your own supply be prepared to pay S$20 "corkage" per cooler. Picnickers are welcome at S$5 pp per car, but there are no Samoan beach *fales* for overnighting. For that walk a hundred meters farther west along the beach to a secluded spot where a family rents *fales* at S$10 pp a night.

Around Faleolo Airport

O Le Satapuala Beach Retreat (Box 1539, Apia; tel. 42-212, fax 42-386), on Fusive'a Beach near Satapuala village, is a 15-minute walk or a S$6 taxi ride east of the airport. Three fan-cooled bungalows with private bath and fridge cost S$65/85/100 single/double/triple, and for shoe-stringers there's an open Samoan *fale* costing S$22 pp a night. Camping is S$10 pp (own tent). Resort owner High Chief To'alepaialii Siueva or his wife Teri can arrange for you to stay in the local village, if you'd like. (Chief To'alepaialii is currently the Samoa Labor Party's only member of parliament and he's one of Samoa's most colorful figures—it's worth staying here just to have the opportunity to meet him.) The adjacent restaurant specializes in local dishes, and there's also a seaside bar with live music on Friday and Saturday nights. On Sunday an *umu* is prepared (S$25 pp). Despite the proximity to the airport, it's peaceful and there's a good view of Savai'i from the beach. Since it's right on the main road to Apia, getting around is easy, and it's also a good choice if you're only in transit through Samoa and don't want to go into Apia from the airport. A drawback is that the reef is far away and you have to swim quite a distance from shore to reach deep water. Windsurfing is a possible activity. Some 800 giant clams are being farmed offshore.

Airport Lodge (Box 498, Apia; tel. 45-583, fax 45-584), two km southwest of the Mulifanua ferry wharf or six km from the airport, opened 1997. The eight pleasant oval bungalows with fridge, fan, and private bath are S$77 single or double including breakfast. Communal cooking facilities are next to the bar and a grocery store is only a short walk away. You get a nice view of Manono, Apolima, and Savai'i from their beach *fales* and there's safe swimming for children in the shallow water just off their beach (although no fish or corals to see). It's an agreeable budget place to relax after visiting Savai'i if you don't wish to head straight back to Apia, and convenient to the ferries to Savai'i and Manono. A taxi from Mulifanua wharf will be about S$3.

Manono Island View Cottages (tel. 23-259, fax 23-287), on Cape Tulivae a bit south of Manono-uta village, has three budget cottages with bath at S$50 single or double. There's a large restaurant on the premises. If nobody's around, ask at the house by the shore a bit back towards Apia.

Expensive Beach Resorts

The **Samoa Village Resorts** (Bob Roberts, Box 3495, Apia; tel. 46-028, fax 46-098), on Cape Fatuosofia opposite Manono Island, 10 km southwest of the airport, has two superior *fales* at S$300 single or double, seven deluxe *fales* at S$375 double (plus S$50 per extra person to four maximum), and one honeymoon *fale* with its own jacuzzi at S$450, plus tax. These are the largest accommodation units on the island and each has its own bathroom, cooking facilities, veranda, and living room. From some you can even fish right off your porch. The resort features a swimming pool and restaurant/bar, and canoes and snorkeling gear are loaned free. The snorkeling here is poor, but the manager can arrange a boat hire out to the reef at around S$50. When enough guests are present there's a special torch lighting ceremony at sunset Saturday night. Somehow the Samoan Village doesn't have the atmosphere of Upolu's other two top resorts. The American ownership is evident in the uniformed security guards at the gate, the imported U.S. beef served in the restaurant, and the 120-volt electricity in the outlets. Airport transfers are S$20 for the car (four people).

Also American-operated is **Coconuts Beach Club** (Jennifer and Barry Rose, Box 3684, Apia; tel. 24-849, fax 20-071), which opened in 1992 at Maninoa on the south side of Upolu, a km west of Siumu. Coconuts offers six categories of nicely appointed accommodations from standard courtyard rooms at S$255/285 single/double to a deluxe beach villa with kitchen at S$825/975 (plus 10% tax). The spacious treehouse rooms are cleverly designed with good ventilation and large covered balconies and Tahitian-style overwater bungalows were added in 1997. Some of the cheaper rooms at the rear of the complex are rather dark, and children are not allowed in the frontside deluxe units. Rates include a full cooked breakfast and the minimum stay is three nights. Their tariff is listed in U.S. dollars and that's how they prefer to be paid (cash or traveler's checks). Otherwise use your American Express card, but avoid Visa and MasterCard, which involve exchanges at unfavorable rates. Snorkeling gear is loaned free. Gayle and Roger at the water sports hut (known variously as "Coconuts Watersports" or "Pacific Quest Divers") offer scuba diving at S$150 (snorkeling S$54), one/two-person kayak rentals at S$15/30 an hour, and a jungle boat cruise to a nearby mangrove swamp at S$50 pp (no charge for mosqui-toes). Roger is friendly but he'll often cancel a scheduled trip if fewer than six people sign up. Jeeps are for rent at S$190 a day (free if you're staying in one of their deluxe units). On Saturday night, Coconuts has a *fia fia* on the beach under the stars (free admission to nonguests who order something at the restaurant or bar). Day visitors who patronize their beachside bar and seafood restaurant are welcome to use the facilities, oth-erwise they'll be asked to leave. Day-trippers cer-tainly aren't allowed to bring their own food or drink into the resort. For picnics, the adjacent vil-lage beach is available at S$5 per car. Coconuts has a more funky personal character than the slick Sinalei Reef Resort next door, and a more in-teresting mix of guests, but it's also less exclu-sive and the sight of a throng of Samoan kids splashing in the gecko-shaped swimming pool may discourage you from using it. Past readers have commented on "a certain edgy, underlying tension" at Coconuts, although efficiency has im-proved since Ned Brown took over as manager. Airport transfers are free.

The **Sinalei Reef Resort** (Box 1510, Apia; tel. 25-191, fax 20-285), next to Coconuts at Siumu, opened in 1996. This attractive interna-tional resort owned by Apia businessman Joe Annandale and family is a good choice if price is no concern of yours. The 16 a/c bungalows begin at S$480 single or double, S$570 triple (S$90 extra for ocean view), and there are four oceanside suites at S$780 single or double, S$945 triple (plus 10% tax). The neat rectan-gular bungalows have open bathrooms for showering under the stars, and the reception, restaurant, and bar are in the traditional Samoan style. Friday nights at 1900 a fire-knife act is performed, followed by a barbecue dinner (S$40). Sunday lunch (S$33) is an *umu* affair. The swimming pool is spectacular since the water is constantly replaced by a natural spring and it's strictly for house guests only. A 70-seat meeting room, nine-hole golf course, and two tennis courts are on the premises. For scuba diving and some other activities you must go to Coconuts, and rental cars must be ordered from Apia. Airport transfers are S$54 pp each way (otherwise take the airport bus to Apia for S$6, then a taxi direct to the hotel at S$35 for the car). Luxury.

MANONO ISLAND

Three-km-square Manono Island, four km off the west end of Upolu, is sheltered within the larger island's protective reef. Four villages are on Manono (Faleu, Lepuia'i, Apai, and Salua) but cars, dogs, and hotels aren't present, which makes it a delightful place (horses and bicycles are also banned). Electricity was installed on Manono in 1995, but as yet there are only a few small village stores, which are closed most of the time.

The trail around the island can be covered on foot in a little over an hour. Near the landing at Faleu is a monument commemorating the ar-rival of the first European Methodist missionary to Samoa, Rev. Peter Turner, who landed here on 18 June 1835. A five-minute walk west of the missionary monument is the **Grave of 99 Stones** (Pa Le Soo) at Lepuia'i, with one stone for each of the wives of the chief buried here. On a hill in the center of the island is an ancient **star mound** (Mauga Fetu), but a guide will be necessary to find it. Manono has a few nice beaches, and the tour groups use one on the less-populated north-ern side of the island facing Apolima.

As yet the only place to stay is **Vaotu'ua Beach Fales** (tel. 46-077) run by Uili and Tau-vela Vaotu'ua who live in the large white house in Faleu village. They charge S$45 pp to sleep in one of their two large *fales* including three meals and an island tour, perhaps less without lunch and the tour. It's a pleasant place and the Samoan food they serve is among the best. Hopefully more places like this will soon open as Manono is a great place to hang loose.

Getting There

Village boats to Manono depart from a landing just south of the Samoa Village Resorts at the west tip of Upolu. The Falelatai, Manono, and Samatau buses from Apia will bring you to the landing, and the boat leaves soon after the bus arrives, provided there are enough passengers. The boat operators always try to charge tourists ridiculous fares like "only 10 *tala*," but arrive early and show no impatience. Once they realize you're not about to pay these prices, they'll tell everyone to get aboard and leave (have small bills ready so there's no argument over change).

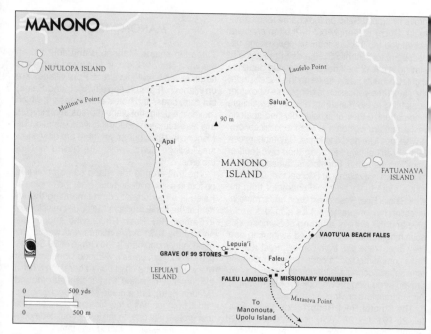

MANONO

NU'ULOPA ISLAND

Laufelo Point

Mulinu'u Point

Salua

▲ 90 m

Apai

MANONO
ISLAND

FATUANAVA
ISLAND

Lepuia'i

VAOTU'UA BEACH FALES

GRAVE OF 99 STONES

Faleu

LEPUIA'I
ISLAND

FALEU LANDING   MISSIONARY MONUMENT

Matasiva Point

To
Manonouta,
Upolu Island

0   500 yds
0   500 m

The Samoan passengers pay only S$1 each, so if you give S$2 pp you'll already be paying double.

There are two landings on Manono, at Faleu on the south side of the island and at Salua on the northeast side. Get off at the first stop they visit, and when you want to return to Upolu, go back to the landing (before 1600) and wait patiently. When the boat finally arrives just get on with the others and pay the same exact fare when you reach the other side.

Some travel agencies in Apia offer full-day tours to Manono at S$78 pp, lunch included. Rather than taking the tour, get a small group together and charter a boat to Manono from the landing at S$20 each way for the whole boat. Pack a picnic lunch as little is available on the island. You could also visit nearby Apolima Island, in the strait between Upolu and Savai'i, this way by paying S$50 return to charter a boat. It takes about two hours to hike right around Apolima but you're supposed to be invited before you go.

SAVAI'I

Savai'i is just 20 km northwest of Upolu across the Apolima Strait. Although 50% larger and higher than its neighbor, Savai'i has less than two-fifths as many people. This unspoiled big island offers ancient Polynesian ruins, waterfalls, clear freshwater pools, white beaches, vast black lava fields, massive volcanoes, innumerable churches, and traditional Samoan life. Robert Flaherty's classic, *Moana of the South Seas* (1926), was filmed on Savai'i. Most of the villages are by the seashore, strung along the fully paved circuminsular highway, and they're a pleasure to stroll through when the kids decide to leave you alone. Yet for an island, a visit to Savai'i is not sea-oriented since many of the attractions are away from the coast.

Savai'i is the largest island in Polynesia (outside of Hawaii and New Zealand). Though about the same length as Upolu, it's 50% wider with broad lava plateaus in the interior. Most of the northeast side of this high volcanic island was transformed in the great eruptions of Mt. Matavanu between 1905 and 1911, which buried much fertile land and sent refugees streaming across to Upolu. Vast tracts of virgin rainforest survive despite agricultural clearings and heavy logging, but in 1998 large areas in the west were destroyed by forest fires facilitated by the drought associated with El Niño. Coral reefs are present along the east coast from Salelologa to Pu'apu'a, on the north coast from Saleaula to Sasina, then from Asau to Vaisala, and on the south coast at Palauli. Expect to pay a custom fee of anywhere from S$2 pp to S$10 per car to a responsible adult (not a child or teenager) to use a village beach.

Orientation

Other than Salelologa, there's nothing that could be called a town on Savai'i; it's just one village after another around the coast, with large gaps on all sides. In recent years Salelologa has developed into a busy little town with a market, stores, laundromat, several small restaurants and takeaways, and a couple of places to stay. The market and bus station are less than a km north of where the Upolu ferry lands.

Actually, Salelologa is a dismal, uninteresting place best avoided by jumping directly on a bus to Lalomalava, Manase, Satuiatua, or Falealupo-tai.

Police stations are found at Asau and Fagamalo, but the main police station (tel. 53-515;

also handling immigration matters) is in the small government complex at Tuasivi, about 10 km north of Salelologa. There are post offices at Salelologa, Tuasivi, Fagamalo, Asau, and Salailua, and district hospitals at Sataua (tel. 58-086) and Tuasivi (tel. 53-510).

SIGHTS AND RECREATION

Tafua

The paved six-km side road to Tafua village begins directly opposite the access road to Maota Airport. To the left (east) of the road, two km before the village, is a grassy track around the north side of Tafua Crater (560 meters). The footpath up into the crater is 500 meters down this road: it's the second and larger trail to the right. It's worth the hike for a chance to see the crater's tooth-billed pigeons and diurnal flying foxes. In 1990 a Swedish environmental group and the Tafua villagers signed a covenant in which the villagers agreed to protect their forests from logging and other misuse for 50 years in exchange for Swedish financial aid to local health and education. Tafua village itself is just above the beach, and one can walk east along the coast to black cliffs where lava flows from the volcano entered the sea. A S$2 pp entry fee to the Tafua Rainforest Reserve is collected at Maota at the start of the Tafua road. To stay in the village ask for Ulu or Anita.

Letolo Plantation

Catch a bus from the Salelologa ferry wharf to Letolo Plantation, eight km west in Palauli District. The largest remaining prehistoric monument in Polynesia is here, as well as an idyllic waterfall and pool. The huge **Pulemelei stone pyramid** *(tia)*, on a slope about two km from the main circuminsular highway, was concealed by thick undergrowth until the 1960s. This immense stone platform on a hillside in the middle of the coconut plantation is 73 meters long, 60 meters wide, and 15 meters high, and stones used in religious ceremonies are scattered around it. The structure is similar to some of the stone temple mounds of Tahiti and is possibly their predecessor, though its origins have been completely erased from the memories of present-day Samoans.

The route to the still-overgrown pyramid can be hard to follow. About 100 meters after a bridge just west of Vailoa village, turn right onto an un-

marked farm road into Letolo Plantation. You can only drive a car 200 meters down the access road to the first river crossing. Continue on foot past a two-story concrete house on the right. About 200 meters beyond the house you'll notice an entrance through a stone wall on the right. Here a faint track heads east between the trees of a coconut grove where cows are grazing to **Afu Aau Falls** (also known as Olemoe Falls). Rather than visit the falls immediately, continue north on the main track toward the pyramid.

About 20 minutes from the main road, start watching for a small stream with a sizable concrete drainage pipe across the road (the only such pipe you'll see). The unmarked trail to the pyramid is on the left at the top of a small slope about 100 meters beyond the pipe. The pyramid is completely covered by ferns and bush but a trail runs right up and around the top.

After exploring the pyramid return to the falls for a well-deserved swim. The edge of the ravine is 400 meters straight east through the coconut plantation, and the steep path down to the pool is fairly obvious. The crystal-clear waters of Falea-

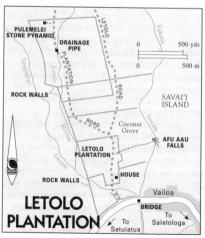

Letolo Plantation's Afu Aau Falls tumble into a pool where you can swim.

ta Stream running down the east side of the plantation plunge over a cliff into a large, deep pool into which you can dive from the sides. Brown prawns live in the pool: drop in bread crumbs and wait for them to appear.

During your visit here, keep in mind that you're on private property, courtesy of the Nelson family. Politely ask permission to proceed of any people you meet along the way. Admission should be free.

The Southwest Coast

Eight km west of Letolo Plantation at the east entrance to Gautavai village is the **Mu Pagoa Waterfall** where the Vaiola River—Samoa's largest—tumbles over black cliffs into the sea just below the highway bridge. The best view is from the west side (free).

The **Alofaaga Blowholes** are along the coast near Cape Asuisui, 16.5 km west of the Mu Pagoa bridge and 40 km from Salelologa wharf. Just a short walk from Taga village, this series of rather spectacular blowholes *(pupu)* are at their best at high tide. Throw in a coconut and watch the roaring jet propel it skyward. (If you allow a boy to perform this trick for you he'll want a substantial tip.) Avoid getting too close to the blowholes as cases have occurred of people being dragged by the surge across the sharp rocks to their deaths. A S$1 pp admission fee is collected at the turnoff.

There's good **surfing** in winter (June-Sept.) at high tide just off the point at Salailua, 13 km northwest of Taga. At Fagafau, 11.5 km northwest of Satuiatua Beach Resort, the sheer cliffs of **Lovers' Leap** drop precipitously to the sea (S$2 pp fee if you stop by the road to peer down the cliffs). The story goes that due to family problems, an elderly blind woman and her only child jumped from the cliff. The woman turned into a turtle while the child became a shark. It's said that a certain magic chant can still bring the turtle and shark back to these shores.

Matega i Si'uvao Beach (S$2 pp admission, plus S$5 for video cameras) is four km northwest of Lovers' Leap. Waves crash into the black rocky coast right next to the road, 600 meters beyond the Si'uvao Beach turnoff, and you can stop and look for free.

Falealupo

From Falealupo-uta on the circuminsular highway it's nine km down a paved road to Falealupo-tai, which stretches 1.5 km along a white sandy beach. A unique attraction of this area is the **Rain Forest Canopy Walkway,** two km up the Falealupo-tai access road. The stories of stairways ascend a Garuga floribunda tree to a suspension bridge spanning a 30-meter gap to a large banyan tree. Then the stairways climb another five stories to a large platform high above the rainforest canopy. Built in 1997 by the Seacology Foundation of Utah (www.seacology.org), it's part of a conservation project intended to provide local villagers with a financial incentive to preserve their lowland forests. At S$20 pp, ad-

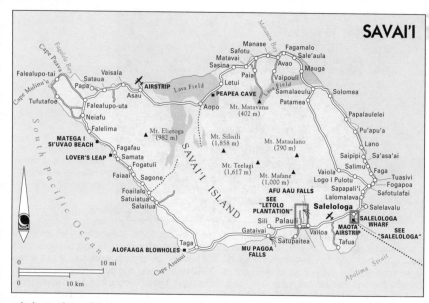

mission to the walkway may seem expensive, but the money goes to supporting conservation efforts throughout this area. It's also possible to sleep on the uppermost platform at S$50 pp including dinner and breakfast.

Four km beyond the Canopy Walkway is **Moso's Footprint,** on the right beside the road. Three meters long, it's said to have been left when the war god Moso leaped from Samoa to Fiji. You'll pay S$5 per group to stop and admire the print.

Another designated tourist attraction is the **House of Rocks,** in the bush 300 meters behind the ruined Methodist church at Falealupo-tai, three km beyond Moso's Footprint. Here your guide will point out a row of stone seats, the largest belonging to Maleatoa, in a lava tube with a hole in its roof. You'll pay either S$5 per person or per group (make sure the price is understood).

Falealupo-tai village was devastated by Hurricane Val in 1991 and the picturesque thatched *fales* of before have now been replaced by modern housing. To use the beach at Falealupo-tai is S$5 per car. If you're staying at one of the *fale* resorts of this area, a good day hike is east along

the coast to sandy Fagalele Bay and the lava cliffs of Cape Puava.

Three km southwest of Falealupo-tai is palm-covered **Cape Mulinu'u,** shaped like an arrow aimed against Asia and the spirit land of Pulotu. This lovely white beach is Samoa's westernmost tip and the place where the world's day comes to an end. Dubbed Sunset Beach for tourists, it's controlled by Tufutafoe village and entry is S$10 per car. The rough track continues past Tufutafoe, 1.5 km southeast of the cape, to Neiafu on the main highway, a couple of hours walk.

As you may have gathered by now, the Falealupo/Tufutafoe locals are quite adept at collecting multiple customary fees from foreigners and it's one of their few sources of income. If you're driving you can usually get everyone in your vehicle in for the basic amount (or just drive on), but individuals roughing it on public transport may have to pay the same fees per person (or bargain). Unless you have your own transport, getting to Falealupo is difficult—there's only one bus a day, which leaves the village for Salelologa wharf at 0500 every morning, although it's usually possible to hitch a ride in a pickup. There's no store in Falealupo-tai village.

The North Coast

The road around the island continues past **Asau,** the main supply center on the north side of Savai'i. There's good holding for yachts in the well-protected small boat harbor in Asau Bay, but the channel is subject to silting, so seek local advice before attempting to enter. Asau wharf is seldom used but there's a large sawmill belonging to Samoa Forest Products and an airstrip with direct Polynesian Airlines flights from Apia's Fagali'i Airport (see **Getting There,** below).

From Asau, the newly paved road turns inland and climbs around a lava flow dating from an eruption in 1760. Very serious hikers can ascend **Mt. Silisili** (1,858 meters), Samoa's highest peak, from Aopo, 24 km east of Asau. The trail begins on the east side of the village. The charge for the three-day trip will be S$30 pp a day without a guide (not recommended) or S$50 pp a day with a guide. A tent and warm clothing will be required. To hike to the Aopo lava tube cave from the village is S$5 pp (two hours). Accommodations in the village are easily arranged. **Peapea Cave,** a lava tube that runs under the highway five km northeast of Aopo, is S$3 pp admission. Numerous white swiftlets live in the cave.

Soon after you rejoin the coast, you reach Matavai, 9.5 km northeast of Peapea Cave. The **Matavai Pool** here is fed by a strong freshwater spring *(mata ole alelo)* and you can swim for S$1 pp or S$5 per car. A *fale* is provided for resting. Ask a local to tell you the legend of "Sina and the spirit eel" associated with the pool.

You'll find more freshwater pools *(vaisafe'e)* at **Safotu** village, three km east of Matavai. Three huge churches stand in a row in Safotu: Catholic, Congregational, and Methodist. A picturesque beach lined with small dugout fishing canoes is opposite the Catholic church.

Three km south of Safotu is **Paia** village with a lava tube *(nu'uletau),* the "short people's cave," three km farther inland. You'll need guides and kerosene lamp to visit it (S$20 fee per group, plus S$5 for a lamp). Meter-high midgets are said to live inside.

A grassy road beginning beside the Mormon church in Paia leads eight km south to the crater of **Mt. Matavanu** (402 meters), which the locals call *mata ole afi* (eye of the fire). This was the source of the 1905-11 volcanic outbreak that covered much of northeast Savai'i with black lava.

You don't really need a guide to find the crater—just look for a trail to the left where the road dips, about two and a half hours out of Paia. Beware of deep crevices and crumbling edges as you near

---

REVEREND JOHN WILLIAMS

Credit for converting the Samoans to Christianity and establishing the Congregational Church in both Samoas goes to Rev. John Williams (1796-1839) of the London Missionary Society. In 1817 the young missionary and his wife Mary arrived at Tahiti, but the next year they shifted to Raiatea in the Leeward Islands, and this served as Williams' base for many years. With the help of native teachers, Williams spread his faith to Aitutaki (1821) and Rarotonga (1823) in the Cook Islands. At Rarotonga his converts constructed a ship, the *Messenger of Peace,* which Williams sailed to Samoa in 1830, landing at Sapapali'i on Savai'i. He happened to arrive at an auspicious moment as a female prophet named Nafanua had predicted the coming of strangers bringing a new faith. The chief of Savai'i, Malietoa Vainu'upo, was receptive, and in 1832 Williams returned from Raiatea with Polynesian missionaries who stayed to teach the meaning of the new doctrine. This westward penetration of Williams' Tahiti-based London Missionary Society, or *Lotu Ta'iti,* was resented by the Tongans who looked upon Samoa as their sphere of interest, and thus best evangelized by Wesleyanism or the *Lotu Toga.* A "gentlemen's agreement" between the parent churches in England led to several Wesleyan (or Methodist) missionaries—who had first visited Samoa two years before Williams—being recalled, much to the displeasure of the King of Tonga. Williams, meanwhile, had himself returned to England where he wrote a book, raised funds for his mission, and had a new ship constructed, the *Camden.* In 1838 he was back, setting up a fresh base at Malie on northern Upolu. In 1839 he sailed west again on what was to be his last voyage, for in 1839 he was killed and eaten by cannibals as he attempted to land on Erromango Island in the New Hebrides, today Vanuatu. Local tradition holds that his bones were later collected and reburied below the porch of the Congregational Church in Apia.

the crater; they have claimed at least one life. There's no charge to come up here. If you're a really intrepid explorer you could hike northeast down the lava field from Mt. Matavanu and turn north on any road you meet, which should bring you through Vaipouli to the coast. You'll on your own if anything goes wrong and a guide would be advisable unless you're a very experienced hiker.

The main north coast tourist resorts, Stevenson's and Tanu Beach, are only four km east of the turnoff to Paia at Safotu. May-Oct. a safe, though exposed, yacht anchorage is found at Matautu Bay, two km farther east.

The Lava Field

The road south of Saleaula runs across a wide, barren lava flow. A large stone Methodist church, nearly engulfed by the lava at the beginning of the century, is on the northeast side of the road under a large tree about 100 meters off the road near the flow's northern edge. The so-called **Virgin's Grave** is about 150 meters east of the church near a mango tree. Look for a rectangular depression about two meters deep in the lava; the grave is clearly visible at the bottom.

Someone will collect S$2 pp admission at this managed tourist site signposted "Saleaula village lava ruins (1905-1911)."

As the fast-flowing *pahoehoe* lava approached the coast here in the early years of this century, it built up behind the reef and spread out in both directions. The highway now runs across it for eight km. It's intriguing to stop anywhere and go for a walk on the lava to get a feel for this awesome geological event. Maunga village, 3.5 km southeast of the Virgin's Grave, is built around a circular crater.

The East Coast

Picturesque villages and intermittent white beaches are scatteredall along the route south from Pu'apu'a to the wharf. **Lano** is a favorite surfing beach in summer (Dec.-March), and there's good snorkeling at **Faga.** In front of the large Congregational Christian Church at **Sapapali'i,** eight km north of Salelologa wharf, is a stone monument to John Williams. This marks the site where the missionary arrived in 1830 and converted the local chiefs to Christianity in a couple of days. Several hotels are found around here.

PRACTICALITIES

SALELOLOGA

Accommodations

A few minutes walk from the ferry wharf is the **Savai'i Ocean View Motel** (Tui and Maselina Retzlaff, tel. 51-258), with two self-contained rooms with fridge in a large *fale* at S$77/99 single/double. Unfortunately loud music from the adjacent Le La-Oso Nite Club erases peace and quiet here Wed.-Saturday.

Next door to the Ocean View is Manumalo Baptist Church where Rev. Seumanu Alofa operates **Rita's Accommodation** (Box 5066, Salelologa, Savai'i; tel. 51-236) with one two-room *fale* at S$15/25 single/double. Reverend Seumanu also organizes circle island tours in his car or taxi at S$150 for one or two people, S$200 for three. This place makes a good base for visiting the island thanks to the radiating bus services.

A little farther up the road from Rita's, before the market, is **Taffy's Paradise Inn** (tel. 51-544) with five rooms with shared bath in an airy European-style house overlooking the lagoon at S$33 pp. This place would be noisy if full, but it seldom is. The people in the store upstairs in the ferry terminal will know about this place (same ownership).

Food and Entertainment

The restaurant (tel. 51-354) upstairs in the ferry terminal at Salelologa serves basic meals. It's closed on Sunday but the small shop here remains open. The store opposite the Ocean View Motel at Salelologa serves a good plate lunch weekdays for about S$6. You can also get lunch at the food stalls in the market but there's nowhere to order dinner as the market and most shops close down by 1600.

Le La-Oso Nite Club, a large bar 150 meters up from the Salelologa ferry, is open Wed.-Sat. 1000-midnight. On Friday and Saturday from 2000 the vicinity is serenaded by Le La-Oso Band (S$4 cover): the name means "sunrise."

Other Practicalities

The ANZ Bank (tel. 51-213) is next to the market, and the Pacific Commercial Bank (tel. 51-208) is farther up the same way, near the T-junction with the circuminsular road. (A second Pacific Commercial Bank branch is at Vaisala near Asau, two km from the Vaisala Hotel.)

RESORTS AROUND THE ISLAND

Eastern Savai'i

The **Safua Hotel** (Private Mail Bag, Salelologa; tel. 51-271, fax 51-272), in a garden setting at

Samoan boy, Savai'i

Lalomalava, six km north of the wharf, was the first hotel on Savai'i. The 12 rustic Samoan *fales* with private facilities and fan are S$77/88/99 single/double/triple. Rooms here are twice as expensive if booked through a travel agent overseas and one shouldn't expect luxury. Mammoth meals cost S$12/12/27 for breakfast/lunch/dinner if paid directly. Campers may pitch their own tents in the garden at S$10 pp on the understanding that they'll take dinner. The owner/hostess Moelagi Jackson and her family eat with guests at a long table, and Sunday lunch is a special treat. Moelagi, one of the very few female *failauga* in Samoa, is an expert on tapa making, and she usually keeps a few high-quality pieces on hand to sell. Island tours by minibus are arranged, or just ask to be shown around the family plantation. The Safua is not on the beach but an informal bar faces a shady garden, and there's a large library. You'll enjoy sitting in the lounge chatting with the other guests. Budget.

The **Savaiian Hotel** (Roger and Ama Gidlow, Box 5082, Salelologa; tel. 51-206, fax 51-291), behind the Mobil service station just south of the Safua at Lalomalava, has less Samoan atmosphere but more creature comforts. Built in 1992, it's on a rocky shore but is spacious and clean. The six a/c duplex units with cooking facilities, fridge, and private bath (hot water) are S$95/115/135 single/double/triple. Four thatched *fales* at the back of the yard are S$35 single, or

S$25 pp for two, three, or four. These have a toilet, fan, and four beds but no cooking facilities. The hotel band plays soft Samoan pop music in the restaurant until midnight on Friday and Saturday nights. Free transfers to the airport or wharf are offered. Budget to inexpensive.

If you want to be at the beach, pick the **Siufaga Beach Resort** (Box 8002, Tuasivi; tel. 53-518, fax 53-535), also known as the Caffarelli Hotel, just a km north of the new hospital at Tuasivi and about six km north of Lalomalava. Created by an Italian doctor and his Samoan family, the resort has a large green lawn that faces lovely Faga Beach, one of the top swimming/snorkeling locales in Samoa. It's in something of a rain shadow so it's drier than Salelologa. The six attractive *fales* with private bath, kitchenette, and local Samoan decor go for S$108/122/135 single/double/triple, and campers are also welcome to pitch their tents in the shade of a big banyan tree for S$27. There's a good grocery store opposite the post office, a 10-minute walk south of the resort, but no cooking facilities for campers. Dr. Peter Caffarelli is an interesting character who enjoys chatting with guests on his veranda. The Puapua bus (S$1) will bring you here from Salelologa wharf, otherwise a taxi from the wharf will run S$15. Inexpensive.

Northeastern Savai'i

Way overpriced is **Le Lagoto Beach Fales** (Box 34, Fagamalo; tel. 58-189), near Fagamalo Post Office at Savai'i's northernmost tip. The four individual *fales* facing the beach are S$267 single or double, S$297 triple. Each fan-cooled unit has a tiny kitchenette, fridge, and private bath (hot water), and there's a large store opposite where you can buy groceries and drinks. In Samoan, "lagoto" means sunset and you can often enjoy good ones sitting outside your unit. Expensive.

Tanu Beach Fales (Taito Muese Tanu, c/o Fagamalo Post Office; tel. 54-050) sits on a nice beach at Manase village, a couple of km west of Fagamalo and 45 km northwest of Salelologa. There are 16 open Samoan *fales* and one three-bedroom wooden house at S$50 pp including breakfast and dinner. Camping with your own tent will shave S$10-15 off the price. Drinking water, bananas, and nippy showers are free, and their store sells beer and cold drinks. The

SALELOLOGA

0 ————— 500 yds
0 ————— 500 m

To Lalomalava

To Satuiatua

SAVAI'I CAR RENTALS

PACIFIC COMMERCIAL BANK

Nu'upulu Island

WEST END CO.

ANZ BANK
BUS STATION
MARKET

SAVAI'I ISLAND

TAFFY'S PARADISE INN

RITA'S ACCOMMODATION

LE LA-OSO NITE CLUB

SAVAI'I OCEAN VIEW HOTEL

FERRY TERMINAL

SALELOLOGA WHARF

© DAVID STANLEY

meals are served at a long common table and are variable. Evening entertainment features amplified music. The managers arrange half day tours covering most sites between here and the Taga blowholes at S$40 pp if six people go. It makes a good base for visiting Mt. Matavanu and is a safe, convenient place to stop and unwind on your way around the island. Many backpackers stay here (and most readers said they liked it). Budget.

Stevenson's at Manase (Box 210, Apia; tel. 58-219, fax 54-100), right next to Tanu Beach Fales, is more upmarket with 18 small a/c rooms in a long prefabricated block at S$172 single or double, plus five a/c villas with fridge and TV at S$300, plus tax. These prices are sharply reduced when things are slow. Get a room away from the noisy generator. Stevenson's also caters to backpackers with six beach *fales* at S$30 pp, but there are no cooking facilities and meals in the hotel restaurant are expensive but good. The beach is also nice, but on nighttime strolls watch out for soft sand around a small spring. Outrigger canoes are S$11 a day. They organize full-day circle-island tours and half-day excursions, otherwise rental cars are S$120 a day. Transfers from Maota Airport or Salelologa Wharf are S$60 pp return. Stevenson's is often almost empty due to the unpopular food prices, so check that they're still operating. Budget to inexpensive.

Southwestern Savai'i

You can sleep in one of five *fales* at dark **Ananoa Beach** near Faaala in Palauli for S$10 pp, otherwise it's S$5 per car to use the beach. There's surfing here.

Savai'i's original backpackers camp is **Satuiatua Beach Resort** (Box 5623, Salailua; tel. 56-026) at Satuiatua, 55 km west of Salelologa wharf. For S$50 pp you get a mattress in an open Samoan beach *fale* with electric lighting, plus breakfast and dinner. The meals are huge with the emphasis on Samoan cuisine. Their small store across the road sells cold beer at normal prices (when available). The white beach is protected by a long lava ledge, making it safe for children, and you can snorkel. One of Samoa's best left-handers is nearby, and during the surfing season Satuiatua can get crowded. Tiny biting sand flies can be a problem. The whole complex is nestled in a row of huge *pulu*

(banyan) trees. If you've got a couple of hours to spare, ask the staff to guide you to a lava tube up in the bush behind the resort. Otherwise hike west along the coast. A pickup truck is available for tours to Falealupo at S$25 pp (minimum of three). Guests must present themselves at church on Sunday morning. The Fagafau bus, which meets all ferries from Upolu, will bring you directly here for S$2.50. Budget.

In winter many surfers stay with the Methodist pastor at Salailua.

At Faiaai village, six km northwest of Satuiatua, you'll find a few *fales* by the highway where you can stay for S$15 pp, plus another S$15 for meals. There's a lovely beach at the bottom of the cliff below the village and you might be able to camp there for a similar price. For information about this place, call 56-023.

Western Savai'i

Right in the center of Falealupo-tai village, **Utusou Beach Fales** offers three *fales* with stone floors at S$30 pp a night including meals. The beach is lovely.

Tanumatiu Beach Fales, 800 meters southwest of Falealupo-tai, is on an even more spectacular beach with more privacy. The six *fales* with mats on the floors are also S$30 pp with meals, or S$5 per car if you're just picnicking. It's run by the Gisa Seumanutafa family; they can supply buckets of water from their home a few hundred meters away.

The only regular hotel on northwestern Savai'i is the **Vaisala Hotel** (Box 570, Apia; tel. 58-016, fax 58-017), four km west of Asau on the north coast. The 40 rooms in a cluster of European-style buildings overlooking a nice beach go for S$89/95/110 single/double/triple (sometimes they offer specials). Ask for a room with a balcony overlooking the beach. Although the accommodations are good, with private bath, coffee-making facilities, and fridge (but no cooking), meals in the restaurant are pricey at S$13.20 for breakfast and S$27.50 for dinner. You can rent the hotel outrigger canoe at S$35 a day. An Aussie named Keith Martin works out of the hotel as a surf guide and he has a boat to take you on "surfaris" to the offshore waves. The Vaisala makes a convenient base for exploring the northwest coast by rental car. Transfers from Asau Airport (six km) are S$7 pp each way. Budget.

GETTING THERE

By Air

For those who turn deep green at the thought of an hour-and-a-half ferry ride, **Polynesian Airlines** (tel. 21-261) operates flights to Savai'i from Fagali'i Airport (FGI), five km east of Apia. There are three 10-minute flights a day to Maota airstrip, a few km west of Salelologa, costing S$34/60 one-way/roundtrip. Polynesian also has a daily flight to Asau airstrip at S$55/100 one-way/roundtrip. Only five kilograms of checked baggage are allowed on this eight-passenger Islander aircraft, but overweight luggage is just 40 cents a kilo (make sure it goes with you). If you fly you'll have to pay a taxi fare upon arrival at Maota, costing S$7 to Salelologa, S$15 to Lalomalava, or S$20 to Faga. If flying into Asau, arrange to be picked up by the Vaisala Hotel's car.

The Polynesian Airlines agent is Savai'i Tours and Travel (tel. 51-206) opposite the Pacific Commercial Bank in Salelologa. The Polynesian Airlines agent at Asau is T & M Vaai & Sons Ltd.

Samoa Air has flights from Maota direct to Pago Pago four times a week at S$145/244 one-way/roundtrip. These should be booked before leaving Apia.

By Boat

The **Samoa Shipping Corporation** (tel. 51-477) operates the car ferry MV *Lady Samoa II* between the wharfs at Mulifanua (Upolu) and Salelologa (Savai'i), departing each wharf two or three times daily. The ferry leaves Mulifanua Mon.-Sat. at 0800, 1200, and 1600, and Sunday at 1200 and 1600. Departure times from Salelologa are Mon.-Sat. at 0600, 1000, and 1400, Sunday at 1000 and 1400. Passenger fares are S$6 pp each way (children under 11 S$3); bicycles and motorcycles are S$5, cars S$30. Reservations are recommended for vehicles (and sometimes even foot passengers have to fight to get a ticket). To ensure that you'll get on the boat, buy a ticket as soon as your bus arrives at the dock and queue up when you see the others doing so—this may be the only time you'll ever see Samoans in a hurry. The trip takes an hour and a half. On the way across, you get a good view of Apolima Island's single village cradled in the island's classic volcanic crater, and flying fish and dolphins are often spotted.

In early 1999, the 220-passenger ferry *Lady Naomi* was brought into service between Apia and Salelologa, leaving Apia for Savai'i Tuesday at 0800 and returning in the afternoon (this introductory schedule should be checked well ahead). The 2.5 hour trip costs S$10.

GETTING AROUND

Travel around Savai'i is easy thanks to the broad paved highway that encircles the island, and bus service from the wharf is good. Yet all public transportation on Savai'i is a bit irregular, so don't plan tight itineraries or count on being able to get back to Upolu to catch an international flight the same day. If a storm came up and the ferries were canceled, you'd be as stranded as anyone else.

By Bus

Bus service on Savai'i focuses on the wharf at Salelologa, with departures to almost any point on the island immediately after a ferry comes in. Over a dozen buses will be revving up as the ferry arrives from Upolu, and they fill up fast, so quickly jump on the bus of your choice. They'll be marked Pu'apu'a or Tuasivi for the east coast, Letui, Paia, Sasina, or Safotu for the north coast, Gataivai or Sili for the south coast, or Asau or Fagafau for the west coast. Fares from Salelologa average 50 *sene* to Lalomalava or Palauli, S$1 to Faga, S$2 to Sasina or Taga, S$2.50 to Satuiatua, and S$5 to Falealupo or Asau.

The buses pull out as soon as they're full, and you'll see as many as five buses racing along the same way, one right after another, then none until another ferry comes in. Buses that leave the wharf fully loaded won't stop to pick up additional passengers along the way, which can make it hard to carry on from places halfway around the island. If a ferry service is canceled, so will be the buses. Going back toward the ferry is much more inconvenient but early morning departures from villages in the northwest corner of Savai'i are a way of life. The last bus leaving Asau for the wharf via the west coast departs at 0600 and some buses leave Asau at 0300 and 0500!

Some of the Asau buses follow the north coast while others go via the south coast. The Tufutafoe bus generally uses the south road, while the Neiafu bus runs along the north coast (ask to be sure). Therefore, to go right around the island by bus, you could take the Tufutafoe bus from Salelologa to Falealupo, then after a couple of days at the beach *fales* there, try to get the Neiafu bus along the north coast as far as Manase where you could also stop. Getting back to the wharf from Manase is no problem. If you don't manage to catch the north coast bus in the very early morning, you could try hitching from Asau to Manase or go on the Forestry truck around 1300 weekdays (see below). Keep in mind that the Asau buses may not stop to pick up passengers in the middle of their runs (Manase or Satuiatua), so the only way to be sure of reaching Falealupotai without a tremendous struggle is to go directly there from the wharf and visit the midway points on the way back to Salelologa. The Tuasivi bus runs up and down the east coast fairly frequently throughout the day.

Hitchhiking

Hitchhiking is an option on Savai'i as most vehicles will stop, and the completion of paving right around the island has seen an increase in traffic. It's always good to offer the equivalent of the bus fare, although most drivers will refuse payment from *palagi*. Traffic diminishes greatly after 1400.

One useful thing to know about is the flatback truck jammed with plantation laborers, which leaves the Forestry Office near Asau Post Office for Safotu weekdays at 1300. The driver is usually willing to give travelers a lift, in which case a pack of cigarettes would be welcome.

Others

Taxis are expensive on Savai'i, so be sure to settle the price before setting out. A full-day trip right around Savai'i by taxi will cost S$300 (or S$200 after bargaining) for the whole car.

Rental vehicles are scarce on Savai'i, and some of the car rental agencies in Apia won't allow you to bring their vehicles over on the ferry (be sure to ask, otherwise the insurance won't be valid). It would be risky to do so anyway as you'd be fully responsible for getting the vehicle back to Apia in case of trouble.

West End Co. (tel. 51-415, fax 51-603), opposite the ANZ Bank in Salelologa, has Suzuki jeeps at S$100 a day, plus S$10 for insurance (S$250 deductible). Motor scooters are S$50 a day. This company is unreliable and some of their vehicles are in bad shape.

Savai'i Car Rental (tel. 51-206, fax 51-291), opposite the Pacific Commercial Bank in Salelologa, is more reputable but slightly more expensive at S$120 for a Samurai jeep or S$132 for a Sidekick, insurance included (S$1,000 deductible). It's run by Savai'i Tours and Travel and you should call ahead from Apia to reserve. Neither of the Salelologa car rental companies will pick up at the wharf but their offices are only a 10-minute walk away.

Victor's Rentals (Box 1016, Asau; tel. 58-066, fax 58-114), at T & M Vaai & Sons Ltd. in Asau, rents Samurai vehicles at S$80 and up. It's just three km east of the Vaisala Hotel but they charge S$20 for delivery (if required). To deliver to Asau Airport (3.5 km) is S$15.

While driving through villages on Savai'i go very slowly as the local kids often use passing cars as moving targets and the rental agency will hold you responsible if a stone goes through the windshield. By going slowly your chances of seeing trouble ahead increase and you can defuse the situation by reducing your speed to dead slow.

Beware of traffic cops around Tuasivi and Salelologa who will pull you over in the hope of receiving a bribe if you don't use your turn signal, fail to stop at a crosswalk, or commit any of the other minor infractions that 90% of Samoan motorists do with impunity all the time. Gas stations are found at Salelologa, Vaisala, Asau, Manase, and Lalomalava.

The easiest and safest way to get around is on an organized sightseeing tour conducted by retired geologist Warren Jopling from the Safua Hotel. Warren has achieved a measure of notoriety from descriptions in the Australian guidebooks, which, depending on his mood, he finds complimentary or an annoyance. He does informative trips north across the lava fields to Mt. Matavanu and "short people's cave," and southwest to the Pulemelei stone pyramid and Taga blowholes, but only if four or five people sign up. The cost is around S$67 pp for a half day, S$112 a full day (including lunch and custom fees). If only two people sign up, the full day tour is S$125 pp.

AMERICAN SAMOA

the death of Captain de Langle, second in command of the La Pérouse expedition, and navigator Lamanon at Aasu, Tutuila, on 11 December 1787

INTRODUCTION

American, or Eastern, Samoa, 4,000 km southwest of Hawaii, is the only U.S. territory south of the equator. Elbow-shaped Pago Pago Harbor (pronounced "Pahngo Pahngo"), made famous in Somerset Maugham's *Rain*, is one of the finest in the South Pacific, a natural hurricane shelter for shipping. It was this feature that attracted American attention in the late 19th century, as Germany built a vast commercial empire based around the coconut plantations of neighboring Upolu.

Until 1951 American Samoa was run as a naval base, but with advances in U.S. military technology it became obsolete, and control was turned over to civilian colonial administrators who created the welfare state of today. To replace lost income from the base closure, U.S. companies were encouraged to build tuna canneries in the territory. Today traffic constantly winds along Tutuila's narrow south coast high-

way, and American-style cops prowl in big black-and-white cruisers. Shopping centers and department stores have spread from the head of Pago Pago Harbor out into suburbia beyond the airport.

American Samoa is a fascinating demonstration of the impact of American materialism on a communal island society. Although the Samoans have eagerly accepted the conveniences of modern life, the *fa'a Samoa*, or Samoan way, remains an important part of their lives. Thus far the Samoans have obtained many advantages from the U.S. connection, without the loss of lands and influx of aliens that have overwhelmed the Hawaiians. While this part of Samoa will always be American, the Samoans are determined to prevent it from going the way of Hawaii.

Don't believe all the negative things you hear about American Samoa, especially from people who have never been there. You'll find it a friendly, relaxing place to visit with spellbinding scenery, easygoing people, inexpensive food and transportation, and a wide variety of things to see and do. The territory gets few bona fide tourists other than yachties, and once the locals know you're a short-term visitor who has only come to see their islands, you'll usually get a very positive reaction. About the only times the Samoans are a nuisance are if they've been drinking or if they think you're being too active on Sunday. One of the least known—and most spectacular—parks in the U.S. national park system is here. If you can spare the cash, it's well worth the trip from Apia.

The Land

American Samoa is composed of seven main islands. Tutuila, Aunu'u, and the Manu'a Group (Ofu, Olosega, Ta'u) are high volcanic islands; Rose and Swains are small coral atolls. Tutuila is about midway between the far larger island of Upolu and the smaller Manu'a Group.

Tutuila is by far the largest island, with a steep north coast cut by long ridges and open bays. The entire eastern half of Tutuila is crowded with rugged jungle-clad mountains, continuing west as a high broken plateau pitted with verdant craters of extinct volcanoes. The only substantial flat area is in the wide southern plain between Leone and the airport. Fjordlike Pago Pago Harbor, which almost bisects Tutuila, is a submerged crater, the south wall of which collapsed millions of years ago. Despite the natural beauty, recent studies have shown that the harbor is dying biologically as a result of pollutants dumped by

the two tuna canneries and local villagers, and the culminating effect of oil and ammunition spills by the U.S. Navy decades ago. The marinelife of inner Pago Pago harbor is poisonously contaminated by heavy metals and unsafe for human consumption.

Climate

Although the climate is hot and humid year-round, it's hotter and rainier Nov.-April (the hurricane season). The frequency of hurricanes has increased dramatically in recent years. The old rule of thumb was one every 7-10 years, but during the five-year period up to 1991, three major storms hit Tutuila. Many believe this is related to rising ocean temperatures caused by the greenhouse effect—and things could get worse in the future. Most hurricanes move into the area from the north but they can also come from east or west.

Temperatures are usually steady, but the stronger winds from May to October ventilate the islands. The prevailing tradewinds are from the east or southeast, with west or northwest winds and long periods of calm during the wetter season.

As warm easterlies are forced up and over Tutuila's Rainmaker Mountain, clouds form that drop their moisture on the harbor just to the west. Apia receives only half the annual rainfall of Pago Pago. From December to March the rain can continue for days, while the rest of the year it often comes in heavy downpours. The exact amount of rain in any given month varies greatly from year to year, and much of it falls at night.

AMERICAN SAMOA AT A GLANCE

ISLAND	POPULATION (1990)	AREA (SQUARE KM)	HIGHEST POINT (METERS)
Tutuila	44,643	137	652
Aunuu	400	2	88
Ofu	353	7	494
Olosega	225	5	639
Ta'u	1,136	46	965
Rose	nil	1	5
Swains	16	3	5
AMERICAN SAMOA (total)	46,773	201	

PAGO PAGO'S CLIMATE

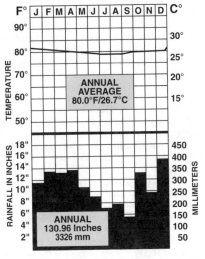

Actually, the weather can change from bright sunshine to heavy rain within five or 10 minutes at any time of year.

You can hear a recorded weather report with tide times by calling 699-9333. Dial 633-4949 and you'll be told the date, time, and temperature.

Fauna

Some 61 species of birds are found in American Samoa, including forest birds such as the *lupe* (Pacific pigeon), *manutagi* (purple-capped fruit dove), *ve'a* (banded rail), and *'iao* (wattled honeyeater), and seabirds like the *fua'o* (red-footed booby) and *tava'e* (white-tailed tropicbird). The rarest of the territory's birds is the *manuma* (many-colored fruit dove), with only about 50 birds left in the wild. The only food the *manuma* has ever been observed to eat is the fruit of the *aoa* (banyan) tree, and the bird is now facing extinction largely due to the disappearance of the *aoa,* many of which have been cut down by humans or blown over by hurricanes.

Hurricanes have also been blamed for an 85% drop in populations of the two species of *pe'a* (flying fox fruit bat) between 1987 and 1992. The white-throated flying fox is often seen soaring above the ridgetops around sunset as the bats leave their roosts to feed at night. The Samoan flying fox is more active during the morning and late afternoon. These native bats eat fruit and pollen, and are an essential link in the pollination of plants of the rainforest. Introduced bulbuls and mynahs are now common on Tutuila, but in the Manu'a Group there are only native birds. In an attempt to protect Samoa's endangered wildlife, a ban on hunting birds and bats was enacted in 1992.

Over 1,000 species of tropical fish dwell along American Samoa's coasts (twice the number found around Hawaii). Only 120 female hawksbill and green turtles still nest here, and there's a US$10,000 fine for killing a sea turtle. Humpback whales visit American Samoa Aug.-Oct. to bear their young in these warm waters before returning to Antarctica, where they pass the southern summer. Sperm whales also call occasionally.

Two land snakes exist, neither poisonous. The blind potted soil snake, which looks rather like a plump earthworm, was introduced to Tutuila accidentally. The two-meter-long Pacific boa of Ta'u is found on islands from Indonesia to Samoa. Both are extremely rare and it's highly unlikely you'll ever see one.

History

The Polynesians emerged in Samoa some 3,000 years ago. By 600 B.C. they'd established a settlement on Tutuila at Tula. This nucleus (or a similar one in the Manu'a Group) may have been the jumping-off point for colonizing Eastern Polynesia (Tahiti and the Marquesas) about A.D. 300. The Samoans maintained regular contact by canoe with the other island groups of Western Polynesia, Tonga, and Fiji. Both Samoas belong to a single cultural area: the chiefs of Tutuila were subordinate to those of Upolu.

The first European in Samoa was the Dutchman Jacob Roggeveen, who visited the Manu'a Group in 1722. In 1786 Antoine de Bougainville, who was French, christened Samoa the "Navigator Islands" for the islanders in canoes he observed chasing schools of tuna far offshore. Another Frenchman, La Pérouse, called in 1787 and had a bloody encounter with the islanders. The Samoans nicknamed these early visitors *papalagi,* or "sky bursters," shortened today to *palagi* and applied to all whites.

Protestant missionary John Williams arrived in 1830 with eight Tahitians and influenza. His son,

John Williams, Jr., became one of the first European traders. Nearly 40 years later, American businessmen chose Pago Pago Harbor as an ideal coaling station for their new steamship service from San Francisco to Australia. In 1872 the U.S. Navy sent a ship to negotiate a treaty with local chiefs. Though never ratified by the U.S. Senate, this agreement kept the other powers out of Tutuila. By the treaty of 7 November 1899, Germany and the U.S. partitioned Samoa between themselves, with British interests recognized in Tonga. In 1900 the U.S. annexed Tutuila and Aunu'u, adding the Manu'a Group in 1904. This act was not formally ratified by the U.S. Congress until 1929.

From 1900 to 1951 American Samoa was under the Navy Dept.; since then it has been the responsibility of the Department of the Interior. Thousands of U.S. Marines were trained on Tutuila during WW II, and concrete pillboxes built at that time still punctuate much of the island's coastline. The only action experienced, however, was a few shells lobbed from a Japanese sub on 11 January 1942, which ironically damaged the store of one of Tutuila's few Japanese residents, Frank Shimasaki.

The Americanization of Samoa

Outside the war years, little happened to alter the centuries-old lifestyle of the Samoans until the early 1960s, when a United Nations mission visiting the U.S.-administered Trust Territory of the Pacific Islands in Micronesia, north of the equator, leveled criticism at Washington for its "benign neglect." In 1961, with neighboring Western Samoa on the verge of independence and U.S. "colonialism" in Samoa becoming an issue, President Kennedy appointed Governor H. Rex Lee, a Mormon, to dispense a giant infusion of federal funds. A massive public works program financed construction of roads, schools, housing, port facilities, electrification, a new hospital, a tuna cannery, a modern hotel, and an international airport. Lee's most publicized innovation was educational television, introduced in 1964; by the mid-'70s, however, the emphasis of the broadcasts had shifted to the usual commercial programming.

This excessive government spending has created an artificial American standard of living. The Samoans became so dependent that three times they voted down proposals to increase home rule for fear it would mean fewer subsidies from Uncle Sam. Only in 1976, after a short tenure by unpopular Gov. Earl B. Ruth, did they finally agree in a referendum to elect their own governor. Even today, American Samoans receive over US$5 million a year in food stamps, and lobbying for more money from Washington is the favorite pastime of local politicians.

In 1997 neighboring Western Samoa renamed itself Samoa, as it had been known at the United Nations since 1976. Although both Governor Sunia and Congressman Faleomavaega commented that the country's name was a matter for the "western" Samoans to decide, a few rabble-rousing "American" Samoan politicians recognized a low-risk opportunity to wave their personal flags by professing to be upset at the inference that "American" Samoans weren't 100% pure Samoans. The local legislature passed a bill requiring that Samoan passports include the word "Western" to be recognized for entry into American Samoa. Some of these same "American" Samoan legislators look down on their western cousins, calling them *sulu'ie* for the traditional kilts they often wear instead of trousers, and immigration officials in Pago Pago often confiscate the passports of "real" Samoans upon arrival to ensure that they'll return home. Of course, without "western" Samoans to do the dirty work, much of American Samoa's economy would soon grind to a halt, and the bill eventually died without becoming law.

Government

While Samoa received independence from New Zealand in 1962, American Samoa remains an "unincorporated" territory of the United States, meaning the U.S. Constitution and certain other laws don't apply. The Samoans have no desire to be brought under the jurisdiction of the U.S. Constitution, as this would mean an end to their system of chiefs and family-held lands, and would open the territory to uncontrolled migration and business competition from the U.S. mainland. Neither are they interested in independence so long as Washington is holding the purse strings and a majority of their people reside in the U.S. itself.

The territory is also defined as "unorganized," because it doesn't have a constitution sancioned by the U.S. Congress. In 1966 federal officials authorized a Samoan constitution that included a bill of rights and gave legislative authority to the Fono, a body composed of 20 representatives (two-year term) elected by the public at large and 18 senators (four-year term) chosen by the customary Samoan *matai* (chiefs). American Samoa's own colony, Swains Island, has a nonvoting representative. None of this has yet been made U.S. law by Congress.

The powers of the Fono increased during the 1970s; it now exercises considerable control over budget appropriations and executive appointments, though the Secretary of the Interior in Washington retains the right to cancel any law passed by the Fono, remove elected officials, and even cancel self-government itself without reference to the Samoans. The Secretary of the Interior appoints the Chief Justice of the High Court.

Every four years since 1977, American Samoans have elected their own governor and lieutenant governor. The governor can veto legislation passed by the Fono. Local political parties don't exist, although candidates often identify themselves with the U.S. Democratic or Republican parties.

Since 1981 the territory has been represented in Washington by a nonvoting congressman elected every two years. Representative Eni F.H. Faleomavaega, a Democrat, was elected in 1988 (and reelected in 1990, 1992, 1994, and 1996). In 1995 Faleomavaega displayed great personal courage and commitment by sailing to Moruroa Atoll aboard the Greenpeace ship *Rainbow Warrior* to protest French nuclear testing in the Pacific. He was among those protesters detained by the French military and deported to Tahiti, where he was promptly released.

Local government is conducted by three district governors, 15 county chiefs, and 55 *pulenu'u* (village mayors), all under the Secretary of Samoan Affairs, a leading *matai* himself.

Economy

Government, the largest employer, accounts for about a third of the workforce, followed by the tuna canneries with another third. The Government of American Samoa receives an annual US$72 million in subsidies and grants from Washington, half of its income. In fact, the territory gets more money in U.S. aid than the entire budget of independent Samoa, although American Samoa has one-third the population. This, and diverging living standards, ensure that the two Samoas will never be reunited. Residents of the territory pay exactly the same level of income tax as stateside taxpayers and all such revenue is retained by the Government of American Samoa. Yet despite U.S. largess, the local government faces multimillion-dollar budgetary deficits every year, due largely to debts resulting from overstaffing and the provision of free health and education services. Three-quarters of the local budget is spent on paying the salaries of the 4,000 government employees. American Samoans receive a total of US$18 million a year in federal social security payments.

American Samoa's primary industry is tuna processing by the Samoa Packing Co., user of the "Chicken of the Sea" label, and StarKist Samoa, a subsidiary of H.J. Heinz. The first cannery opened in 1954, and American Samoa today is the world's fourth-largest tuna processor and the most important commercial fishing port under the U.S. flag (Dutch Harbor, Alaska, is a distant second). Canned fish, canned pet food (from the blood meat), and fish meal (from the skin, guts, and bones) now account for the bulk of the territory's industrial output. Wastes from the canneries are barged out and dumped into the ocean.

Canneries thrive in this tiny U.S. territory because they allow Asian fishing companies to avoid U.S. import tariffs of up to 35% on processed fish. Goods have duty- and quota-free entry to the U.S. if 30% of their value is added in the territory. Federal law prohibits foreign commercial fishing boats from offloading tuna at U.S. ports; however, American Samoa is exempted. Thus the greater part of the South Pacific tuna catch is landed here, supplying the U.S. with about half its canned tuna, worth US$300 million a year. Even with this trade, imports into American Samoa are double exports (manufactured goods, food, and fuel are the biggest imports).

Both canneries pay virtually nothing in taxes to the local government and employ 4,000 cheap nonunion workers from western Samoa who put in two shifts. American Samoans themselves aren't at all interested in cleaning fish for

US$3.10 an hour and instead work in business or government. Though they make millions on their tuna operations, the canneries have threatened to relocate if the minimum wage is raised or if the workers became unionized (cannery workers have several times voted against becoming members of the International Brotherhood of Teamsters). American Samoa and the Northern Mariana Islands are the only U.S. jurisdictions where federal minimum wage legislation doesn't apply.

The trend now is away from rust-eaten Korean and Taiwanese longline tuna boats, toward large California purse seiners worth a couple of million dollars apiece. StarKist has 35 purse seiners under contract, Samoa Packing about 10. A total of 82 Korean and 36 Taiwanese longline boats also work out of Pago Pago. Most of the fish are taken in Papua New Guinea and Federated States of Micronesia waters (the Samoa canneries don't can fish caught by setting nets around dolphins). In aggregate, the canneries contribute about US$25 million a year to the local economy in wages, and spend another US$40 million on support services, fuel, and provisioning.

The Marine Railway near the canneries can dry-dock vessels up to 3,500 tons. In recent years harbor facilities have been upgraded through government investment as part of a scheme to make Pago Pago a transshipment center for surrounding countries, although not much has come of these plans.

The local government has recently established an industrial park at Tafuna near the airport where companies can lease land on which to build factories. Here manufacturers can exploit the territory's low minimum wages and duty- and quota-free tariff relationship with the United States, and with the local tuna canneries facing increasing competition from Mexican canneries under the North American Free Trade Agreement (NAFTA), this may be the way of the future for American Samoa's economy. The first such company, Bao California Textile Corporation, brought in 300 Chinese "trainers" to work with a few hundred western Samoans producing cheap shirts to be sold by U.S. retailers. However, in late 1998 BCTC announced it was closing its plant, which had become less competitive due to global free trade.

Tourism development has been hampered by an unstable air connection to Honolulu, a reputation for unsuitable accommodations, environment degradation, and the incompetence of the local tourism authorities. Of the 39,802 arrivals in 1997, only about 10% were actual tourists. The rest came on business, to visit relatives, for employment, or in transit. Most were from the other Samoa, with U.S. citizens a distant second. The government-owned Rainmaker Hotel has only made a profit during two years of its three decades of operations and repeated attempts to sell the hotel have failed. It's now hoped that the creation of National Park of American Samoa will stimulate tourism.

The People

Between 1980 and 1998 the population of American Samoa almost doubled, from 32,297 to 61,600, an average increase of 3.7% a year. This is the fastest growth rate in the South Pacific, and at 308 persons per square kilometer American Samoa is the second most densely populated South Pacific entity (after Tuvalu). All of this growth was on Tutuila; the population of the Manu'a Group declined slightly. The population of the harbor area is growing 8.2% a year.

American Samoans are U.S. "nationals," not citizens, the main difference being that nationals can't vote in U.S. presidential elections nor be drafted. American Samoans have free entry to the U.S., and some 65,000 of them now live in California and Washington State, and another 20,000 are in Hawaii, most in the lower income bracket. Nearly 70% of high school graduates leave within a year of graduation, many of them to voluntarily join the Armed Forces. About 1,175 students attend the American Samoa Community College at Mapusaga, a two-year institution established in 1970.

The people of the two Samoan groups are homogeneous in blood, speech, and traditions, and as fast as American Samoans leave for the States, people from the other Samoa migrate from west to east. Much intermarriage has occurred, and about 20,000 western Samoans now live in American Samoa. Some 1,750 Tongans and 900 Caucasians are also present, and only 41% of residents aged 15 years and over were actually born in the territory.

Although the young have largely forgotten their own culture in their haste to embrace that of the U.S., the *fa'a Samoa* is tenaciously defended by those who choose to remain in their home villages. For a complete description of the *fa'a Samoa*, see the Samoa **Introduction.** Under treaties signed with the Samoan chiefs in 1900 and 1904, the U.S. government undertook to retain the *matai* system and protect Samoan land and rights. To its credit, it has done just that. In addition, the innate strength and flexibility of "the Samoan way" has permitted its survival in the face of German, New Zealand, and American colonialism.

On Tutuila the people live in 60 villages along the coast. After a hurricane in 1966, the U.S. government provided funds to rebuild the thatched Samoan *fales* in plywood and tin, resulting in the hot, stuffy dwellings one sees today. The most farsighted act of the former naval administration was to forbid the sale of Samoan land to outsiders. Except for a small area owned by the government and the two percent freehold land alienated before 1900, 90% of all land in the territory is communally owned by Samoan extended families *(aiga),* who even bury relatives in the yards in front of their homes to reinforce their titles. The family *matai* assigns use of communal land to different members of the *aiga.* If American citizens were allowed to buy land, the Samoans would undoubtedly be exploited as they have little knowledge of property values. Non-Samoans can lease Samoan land for up to 55 years, however.

American Samoa's largest churches are the Congregational Christian Church (20,680 adherents), the Catholic Church (8,500 adherents), the Church of Jesus Christ of Latter-day Saints (4,950 adherents), the Methodist Church (3,900 adherents), the Assemblies of God (2,700 adherents), and the Seventh-Day Adventists (1,700 adherents).

Away from Pago Pago Harbor, if there's a village behind a beach, you're expected to ask permission before swimming. Never swim anywhere near a church on Sunday, and be aware that most Samoans don't wear bathing suits— they swim in shorts and T-shirts. Foreigners in swimsuits on a village beach could give offense, hence the necessity of asking permission first.

During *sa* every afternoon around 1830 villagers pause in whatever they're doing for a brief prayer. If you hear a village bell around this time, stop walking, running, or riding to avoid raising the Samoans' ire. Some remote villages also have a 2200 curfew.

weaving fine mats in a Samoan fale

ON THE ROAD

Highlights

American Samoa's throbbing heart is Fagatogo Market, where buses unload passengers from both ends of Tutuila. Mt. Alava, the canneries, Rainmaker Mountain, and Pago Pago Harbor are all visible from the market. Mt. Alava itself may be the island's second best sight, accessible on foot from the Fagasa road. A colorful island tour is easily arranged by boarding a bus to Tula or Leone. Those with more time, perseverance, and funds can catch a flight to the twin islands of Ofu and Olosega with their spectacular beaches and cliffs. A week is ample time to see Tutuila, and with two weeks you could do all of the above, if you can manage to get on the flight.

National Park

In 1988 the U.S. Congress authorized the creation the National Park of American Samoa, comprising 32 square km of tropical rainforest, coastal cliffs, and coral reef on Tutuila, Ofu, and Ta'u, and in 1993 nine villages signed 50-year leases involving annual fees of US$370,000 in total (this is the only U.S. national park in which the federal government leases the land).

On Tutuila the park stretches from Fagasa Bay to Afono Bay, encompassing everything north of the knifelike ridge. Countless seabirds nest on Pola Island. The largest unit is on Ta'u with Mt. Lata and the entire southeast corner of the island, including coastal, lowland, montane, and cloud forest communities. Ta'u's soaring cliffs and Laufuti Falls are spectacular. On Ofu the lovely southeastern beach and coral reef are included. Two endangered species of *pe'a* (flying fox), pollinators of the rainforest, are protected in the park.

This splendid national park, which ranks with Yellowstone and the Grand Canyon in majesty, seems destined to become American Samoa's biggest tourist attraction if an appropriate infrastructure for visitors can be put in place. Current information is available from the park visitor center (tel. 633-7082, fax 633-7085) in Suite 114 of the Pago Plaza at Pago Pago.

Public Holidays and Festivals

All standard U.S. public holidays are observed in American Samoa: New Year's Day (1 January), Martin Luther King Day (third Monday in January), Presidents' Day (third Monday in February), Flag Day (17 April), Good Friday (March/April), Memorial Day (last Monday in May), Independence Day (4 July), Labor Day (first Monday in September), Veteran's Day (11 November), Thanksgiving (fourth Thursday in November), and Christmas Day (25 December).

During Samoa Days in early April, schoolchildren perform traditional dances. American Samoa's **Flag Day,** 17 April, commemorates the first flying of the Stars and Stripes in 1900. This enthusiastic two-day celebration features *fautasi* (longboat) racing plus song and dance competitions in Fagatogo. Tourism Week in early July sees barbecues, canoe races, cultural demonstrations, fireworks, music, a parade, and the crowning of Miss American Samoa at Utulei.

dancers, Flag Day

Beach. (An invitation has been extended to the President of the United States to visit American Samoa for the centenary celebrations on 17 April 2000, possibly on his way to the Sydney Olympics.) Manu'a Cession Day is 16 July.

The second Sunday in October is White Sunday, when children dress in snow-white clothes and walk to church in procession, singing as they go. The children take the seats of honor and lead the service. After church there are family feasts, and gifts are given to the kids. Although European explorers didn't find Samoa until 230 years after Christopher got to America, Columbus or "Discoverer's" Day (second Monday in October) is also a public holiday. In fact, it's one of the biggest holidays of the year because it happens to coincide with White Sunday.

The **Moso'oi Tourism Festival** in mid-October is the occasion for sporting events, *fautasi* races, cultural performances, food and flower shows, a beauty pageant, and musical competitions. Most events are held at the Lee Auditorium.

Another important event is the rising of the palolo (coral worms) in late October or early November. When the moon and tide are just right and the palolo emerge to propagate, Samoans are waiting with nets and lanterns to scoop up this cherished delicacy, the caviar of the Pacific (See the special topic **The Rising of the Palolo**.)

Visas and Officialdom

No visa is required for a stay of 30 days. An onward ticket is required of U.S. citizens and foreign nationals alike. Everyone except Americans require a passport for entry. Americans can enter by showing a certified birth certificate, though a passport will be necessary to visit the other Samoa. Due to previous abuse of subsidized medical facilities, "alien" women more than six months pregnant are refused entry to American Samoa. Entry requirements are set by the Government of American Samoa—the U.S. Immigration and Naturalization Service does not exercise jurisdiction here.

Visa extensions are difficult to obtain (US$25 a month up to 90 days total) and work permits almost impossible unless you have a special skill somebody needs, in which case your sponsor will have to post a bond. For more information write: Chief Immigration Officer, Box 7, Pago Pago, American Samoa 96799 (tel. 633-4203).

Their office is in the Executive Office Building in Utulei. If you're proceeding to Hawaii from Pago Pago and need a U.S. visa, be sure to pick it up at the U.S. Embassy in Apia or elsewhere as there's no visa-issuing office here.

Those interested in employment in American Samoa should send a resume to: Director of Manpower Resources, American Samoa Government, Pago Pago, American Samoa 96799.

Before departing Hawaii for American Samoa, cruising yachts must obtain a U.S. Customs clearance. Pago Pago is the only port of entry for cruising yachts and few try to fight their way back to Ofu and Ta'u against the wind. At Pago Pago, US$25 clearance fees are charged, plus an additional US$25 departure fee. On both occasions you must take your boat to the customs dock, where the waves bang it against the rough concrete. Tutuila is infested with the giant African snail. Customs officials in neighboring countries know this and carefully inspect baggage and shipping originating in Pago Pago.

Money

U.S. dollars are used, and to avoid big problems and exorbitant commissions when changing money, non-U.S. residents should bring traveler's checks expressed in American currency. Samoan currency is exchangeable in American Samoa but at a poor rate. If you lose your traveler's checks or credit cards, you can report American Express cards and checks at the Amerika Samoa Bank and Visa at the Bank of Hawaii.

North American tourism has introduced tipping to the upmarket restaurants of the territory. The local saying goes, "it's not only accepted, it's expected." There's no bargaining in markets or shops.

Post and Telecommunications

Because U.S. postal rates apply, American Samoa is a cheap place for airmailing parcels to the U.S. (sea mail takes about 30 days to reach Oakland, California, by container). The mail service is reported to be erratic, so mark all mail to or from Pago Pago "priority post." The U.S. postal code is 96799, and regular U.S. postage stamps are used.

Long-distance telephone calls to the U.S. are unexpectedly more expensive than from Apia. A three-minute call costs US$5.70 to New Zealand or Australia, US$6 to the U.S., US$8 to Britain or Canada. Evenings and weekends you'll be eligible for a discount amounting to a few pennies on overtime charges to the U.S. but not elsewhere. Collect calls can be made to the U.S. only. More expensive but also available is AT&T's "USADirect" service at tel. 633-2771 (www.att.com/traveler).

Local telephone calls from public telephones anywhere in American Samoa cost only 10 cents each and the phones do work—get back into the habit of using them. Yes, it's only 10 cents to call the Manu'a Group from Tutuila. Local calls from private residences are free.

Local directory assistance is tel. 411. For the international operator, dial 0. American Samoa's telephone code is 684.

Media

The privately owned *Samoa News* (Box 909, Pago Pago 96799; tel. 633-5599, fax 633-4864, e-mail: samoanews@samoatelco.com), published weekdays, has been around since the 1960s. Special deals on accommodations and airfares are sometimes advertised in the *News,* and you get local insights.

Channel 2 at government-operated KVZK-TV (tel. 633-4191) broadcasts PBS, CNN, and a couple of hours of local programming 0600-2400 daily (local programs are on in the evening). Catch CNN Headline News weekdays at 0800 and 1000, and KVZK local news weekdays at 1730. Commercial channel 4 has ABC/CBS/NBC programs 1500-2400 weekdays, 1200-2400 weekends. You can see the ABC world news weekdays at 1700, and the NBC nightly news weekdays at 1800. The tapes are broadcast with Hawaiian advertising. In 1995 satellite-generated cable television was introduced to the territory by two private companies, and although these cost about US$360 a year, dozens of channels are accessible 24 hours a day.

Privately operated Radio Samoa WVUV (tel. 688-7397, fax 688-1545) broadcasts 24 hours a day over 648 kHz AM. The music is a mix of Samoan, country, and adult contemporary, but there's no news.

KSBS-FM (Box 793, Pago Pago 96799; tel. 633-7000, fax 622-7839, www.samoanet.com/ksbsfm), at 92.1 MHz, broadcasts daily 0600-midnight, and you can pick it up everywhere on Tutuila. Throughout the day they play mostly island music and oldies, while in the evening there is also some top 40s for youthful listeners. KSBS re broadcasts AP network news on the hour with live news in the morning.

Information Offices

The **American Samoa Office of Tourism** (Box 1147, Pago Pago, AS 96799, U.S.A.; tel. 633-1091, fax 633-1094, www.samoanet.com/americansamoa, e-mail: samoa@samoatelco.com), run by the Department of Commerce, occasionally mails out brochures upon request. The main purpose of the office is to provide jobs for the people employed there.

In the U.S. you can put your questions to American Samoa's congressman in Washington, the Hon. Eni F.H. Faleomavaega (tel. 1-202/225-8577, fax 1-202/225-8757, www.house.gov/faleomavaega).

TRANSPORTATION

Getting There

Hawaiian Airlines (tel. 699-1875, fax 699-1282) links Pago Pago to Honolulu twice a week, with connections in Honolulu to/from Los Angeles, Las Vegas, Portland, San Francisco, and Seattle. Pago Pago-Honolulu costs US$728 roundtrip; Pago Pago-Los Angeles is US$1,028 roundtrip. Thirty-day advance purchase return fares are US$200 lower, but you must be physically there to buy such a ticket. One-way fares from Pago Pago are US$420 to Honolulu or US$600 to Los Angeles. Don't forget to reconfirm your onward flight if you don't want to get bumped. Since Hawaiian got rid of their ancient DC-8 and began using a wide-body, 230-seat DC-10 on this route, the service has improved.

Privately owned **Samoa Air** (Box 280, Pago Pago 96799; tel. 699-9106, fax 699-9751, e-mail: samoaair@samoatelco.com) has flights to Apia (US$69/93 one-way/roundtrip) four times a day or more, and to Maota on Savai'i (US$81/120) four times a week. Add US$8 tax to these fares. Most Samoa Air flights to Apia land at Fagali'i Airstrip and only those connecting with Air New Zealand go to Faleolo International Airport. When booking always check carefully which airport you'll be using.

Polynesian Airlines (tel. 699-9126) also has flights to Pago Pago from Apia six times a day, one landing at Faleolo International Airport and the other five at Fagali'i Airstrip. Polynesian charges fares one or two dollars lower than Samoa Air, and due to currency differences, tickets for the Pago Pago-Apia flight are much cheaper when purchased in Apia than in American Samoa or elsewhere. Most of the Apia flights on both airlines are on 19-seater Twin Otter aircraft. Beware of baggage handling irregularities on the flights of both companies, as damaged, delayed, or lost luggage is routine here—carry anything irreplaceable in your hand luggage.

Polynesian Airlines has connections in Apia to/from Australia and New Zealand on their own aircraft, to/from Honolulu and Los Angeles on Air New Zealand, and to/from Fiji on Air Pacific. Polynesian's 45-day Polypass (US$999) is valid for travel between the Samoas, Tonga, Australia, and New Zealand. For US$150 extra you can begin in Honolulu and for US$400 extra it's good from Los Angeles.

For those interested in a quick prearranged side trip from independent Samoa, **Oceania Tours** (tel. 685/24-443, fax 685/22-255), near the Kitano Tusitala Hotel in Apia, offers overnight fly/drive packages to Pago Pago. Beginning at US$159/250 single/double plus various taxes, these include return airfare, one night at the Apiolefaga Inn, and a car for 24 hours. They can also organize guided day-trips from Apia.

To/From Vava'u

Samoa Air's nonstop flight to Vava'u, Tonga (US$178/325 one-way/roundtrip), operates twice a week (currently on Tuesday and Friday) using a twin-engined, nine-seater Beechcraft King Air 100 plane. This is a useful connection, allowing you to visit Pago Pago, Vava'u, and Ha'apai for about the same price it might cost to fly straight from Apia to Nuku'alofa. The trouble is, such a routing is very difficult to arrange.

Since 98% of Samoa Air's customers are Tongans or Samoans, they couldn't be bothered going after international business, thus their fares aren't computerized in universal booking systems, and it's almost impossible to buy one of their tickets outside of Samoa or Tonga. This is a real problem since you need a ticket to leave American Samoa or Tonga before you'll be allowed entry, yet the Pago Pago-Vava'u ticket is very hard to obtain.

To order tickets directly from Samoa Air, you must call their office in Pago Pago to determine the exact price including the cost of shipping the tickets to you, then mail them an international money order expressed in U.S. dollars for that amount (credit cards are not accepted). Flight bookings can be made at the same time you check the ticket price, and you can always change them later.

Rather than get tied up in a clumsy, unreliable procedure such as this, you're better off having a Pago Pago, Apia, or Nuku'alofa travel agency handle your arrangements. Three well established companies to try are Royal Samoa Travel (Box 3483, Pago Pago, AS 96799, U.S.A.; tel. 684/633-5884, fax 684/633-1311), Oceania Travel (Box 9339, Apia, Samoa; tel. 685/24-443, fax 685/22-255), and Teta Tours (Box 215, Nuku'alofa, Tonga; tel. 676/21-688, fax 676/23-238, e-mail: tetatour@kalianet.to).

Hopefully by the time you read this, Samoa Air will have gotten their act together and you'll be able to purchase their tickets at any travel agency worldwide, but don't count on it.

Local Flights

Samoa Air (tel. 699-9106) has two flights a day from Pago Pago to Ofu and Ta'u, leaving Pago Pago at 0600 and 1500 (US$44/86 one-way/roundtrip). The interisland flight *between* Ofu and Ta'u is US$22 and it's only guaranteed on Wednesday. Special fares are sometimes advertised in the local newspapers. The nine seats on these flights are often fully booked a week ahead, so inquire early and try making a telephoned reservation well in advance, if you're sure you want to go. Carefully reconfirm your Samoa Air flights every step of the way as this is a rather eccentric airline. The baggage limit on flights to Manu'a is 20 kilograms.

By Ship

The Samoa Shipping Corporation's ferry *Queen Salamasina* leaves Pago Pago bound for Apia Thursday at 1600 (eight hours, US$30/50 one-way/roundtrip). On major public holidays the ship makes two weekly trips, departing Pago Pago at 1600 on Wednesday and Friday. Safety regulations limit the number of passengers aboard to 206, and when that number of tickets have been sold, the ship is "full." Thus it's wise to book before noon a day ahead (take your passport). If you have to buy your ticket at the wharf, you'll be the last person allowed aboard and you won't find a proper place to sleep. The booking agent is **Polynesia Shipping** (Box 1478, Pago Pago 96799; tel. 633-1211), across from Sadie's Restaurant. Make sure your name is added to the passenger list or you won't be allowed on board. As your departure date approaches, keep in close touch with the agent as the schedule is subject to frequent change.

Boat fares are lower in the other Samoa, thus it's cheaper to buy only a one-way ticket to Apia and purchase your return portion there, although the Samoan ticket-to-leave requirement makes it difficult to take advantage of this savings. Coming from Apia, get a roundtrip ticket if you intend to return. Go aboard early to get a wooden bunk. The action of the southeast trade winds makes this a smoother trip westbound toward Apia than vice versa (but it can be rough anytime). Even veteran backpackers consider this a rough trip.

Immigration formalities at both ends are chaotic because everyone pushes to be the first person off. Non-Samoans arriving on Tutuila by boat can expect to be closely scrutinized by American Samoan immigration, so if there's anything at all "irregular" about your status, be sure to come by plane. Persons holding passports from places other than Western Europe, Canada, the U.S., Japan, Australia, and New Zealand are singled out and could well be refused entry. One American reader sent us this:

I just wanted to make a quick sidetrip to American Samoa on the Queen Salamasina *and planned to return to Apia with the same ship. In Pago Pago I was searched and questioned for hours by the harbor authorities, police, FBI, CIA, and God knows who else. Nobody would believe that anyone would do this trip for "fun" and return the same day. Usually all tourists fly in, so I*

guess for them I was the "perfect" smuggler, or something. If anybody else decides to do anything like this, they should have a good story ready.

We don't know of any scheduled passenger boats from Pago Pago to Tonga, the Cook Islands, or Fiji. The main season for hitching rides to Tonga or Fiji on private yachts is mid-April to October. Somebody at the Utulei Yacht Club may be able to advise.

The Port Administration, **Water Transportation Department** (tel. 633-5532), across the street from the Samoa News Building, runs a landing craft-type supply vessel, the *Manu'a Tele III,* to the Manu'a Group, an eight-hour trip. The boat leaves every two weeks on "pay week" when government employees get their checks, usually on a Wednesday, and it's US$20 each way to Ofu or Ta'u (or US$10 between these two islands).

Airport
Pago Pago International Airport (PPG) is built over the lagoon at Tafuna, 11 km southwest of Fagatogo. Transport to town is 75 cents by public bus or US$10-15 by taxi (agree on the price before and be sure you have exact change—the drivers *never* do). Public buses stop fairly frequently in front of the terminal (except on Sunday or after dark). Most of the car rental booths in the terminal open only for flights from Hawaii, although Avis stays open all day.

There's no tourist information desk or bank at the airport. The shops in front of the airline offices at the airport sell handicrafts, cheap ice cream cones, and snacks. The duty-free shop in the departure lounge is generally more expensive than these and is often closed. The restaurant (tel. 699-6070) around the corner behind the check-in counters serves filling American-style meals at reasonable prices. Watch your tickets and baggage tags carefully when you check in here, as the agents will happily book you through to wherever or strand you. The US$3 airport tax and US$5 "entry declaration fee" are included in the ticket price.

TUTUILA

The main island of American Samoa, Tutuila, is shaped like a Chinese dragon, 32 km long, anywhere from one to 10 km wide. Alone it accounts for 68% of American Samoa's surface area and over 95% of its population. Surprisingly, this is one of the most varied and beautiful islands in the South Pacific. Its long mountainous spine twists from east to west with wild coastlines and cliffs on the north side, gentler landscapes and plains on the south. There are lots of good beaches scattered around, but for a variety of reasons, finding a good place to swim takes some doing. When it's calm the snorkeling is fine off the empty golden beaches all along the north coast, and the reef-break surfing along the south coast is especially good Dec.-March.

Fagatogo, the largest town, looks out onto elbowlike Pago Pago Harbor, while government is centered at Utulei, just east of Fagatogo. Despite the oil slicks and continual flood of pollution from canneries, shipping, yachts, and residents, this harbor is dramatically scenic with many fine hikes in the surrounding hills. Among the seemingly incompatible elements thrown together here are slow-moving Samoan villagers, immigrant cannery workers, taciturn Asian fishermen, carefree yachties, and colorful American expatriates—only tourists are missing. It's an unusual, unpretentious place to poke around for a few days.

SIGHTS AND RECREATION

Utulei

At **Blunt's Point,** overlooking the mouth of Pago Pago Harbor, are two huge six-inch naval guns emplaced in 1941. To reach them from Utulei, start walking southeast on the main road past the oil tanks and keep watching on the right for a small pump house with two large metal pipes coming out of the wall. This pump is across the highway from a small beach, almost opposite two houses on the bay side of the road. The overgrown track up the hill begins behind the pump house. If arriving by bus from the west, get out as soon as you see the oil tanks and walk back. The lower gun is directly above a large green water tank, while the second is about 200 meters farther up the ridge. Concrete stair-

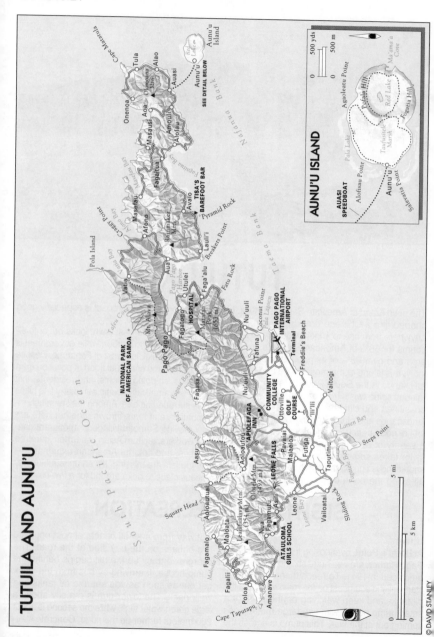

TUTUILA AND AUNU'U

South Pacific Ocean

Cape Matatula

Tula
Aiao
Alao
Olomauu Mtn.
Auasi
Aunu'u
SEE DETAIL BELOW
Aunu'u Island
Red Lake

Onenoa
Aoa
Amouli
Alofau
Masausi
Amaua

Fagaitua
TISA'S BAREFOOT BAR
Masefau
Afono
Avaio
Laulu'i
Matmu Mtn.
Pyramid Rock
Breakers Point

Craggy Point
Masa Bay
Nuuuli Bay
Vaitogi Bay
Pola Island
Vatia

Pago Pago
Mt. Alava
Fagasa
NATIONAL PARK OF AMERICAN SAMOA

Telefoi Cove
Fagaloa Bay
Aua
Utulei
Faga'alu
HOSPITAL
Fagatogo
Matafao Peak (653 m)
Fatu Rock
Coconut Point
Nu'uuli
Pala Lagoon
Breakers Point

Nafanua Bank
Taema Bank

Tafuna
PAGO PAGO INTERNATIONAL AIRPORT
Terminal
Freddie's Beach

Aasu
COMMUNITY COLLEGE
GOLF COURSE
Ottoville
Nu'uuli
'Ili'ili
Vaitogi

APIOLEFAGA INN
Aoloaufou
Malaeloa
Pavaiai
Futiga
Larsen Bay
Steps Point

Square Head
Aoloautuai
Olotele Mtn. (491 m)
LEONE FALLS
Asili
Leone
Taputimu
Taputimu
Vailoatai
Sliding Rock

Fagamalo
Malota
Leafulaalava Mtn. (354 m)
Nua
Fagamutu
ATAULOMA GIRLS SCHOOL

Fagalii
Poloa
Amanave
Cape Taputapu

Maloata Bay
Maumu Bay

© DAVID STANLEY

0   5 mi
0   5 km

AUNU'U ISLAND

Aqaoleatu Point
Mata'afa Cove
Faimu Hill
Red Lake
Pola Lake
Taufusitele Marsh
Faatia Hill
Alofisau Point
Aunu'u
Sailele Point
Sailevaata Point

AUASI SPEEDBOAT

0   500 yds
0   500 m

one of the guns set up during WW II to defend the entrance to Pago Pago Harbor

ways lead to both guns but they're completely covered by vegetation, so be prepared.

After visiting the guns, walk back toward town as far as the Yacht Club where you see three long *fautasi* longboats, then turn left to the US$10-million **Executive Office Building** erected in 1991 at Utulei. It's well worth going in to catch a glimpse of the territory's formidable bureaucracy. Behind this building is the new **Feleti Barstow Library** (1998), and beyond it a paved road winds up to the former **cable-car terminal** on Solo Hill. Here a monument recalls a 1980 air disaster in which a U.S. Navy plane hit the cables and crashed into the Rainmaker Hotel, killing the six servicemen aboard and two tourists at the hotel. The hotel manager refused to allow the memorial to be erected on the hotel grounds.

The cableway, one of the longest single-span aerial tramways in the world, was built in 1965 to transport TV technicians to the transmitters atop Mt. Alava (491 meters). The car would sway for a kilometer and a half over Pago Pago Harbor, with mountains such as rugged Rainmaker (524 meters) in full view, making this the most spectacular aerial ride in the Pacific. In 1992 Hurricane Val put the cableway out of service, but in early 1998 it was announced that a US$3 million federal grant would allow the cableway to be repaired in time for American Samoa's centenary in the year 2000. If so, the facility will allow easy access to the National Park facilities on Mt. Alava. Whatever happens, it's worth visiting the Utulei terminal for the excellent view of Rain-maker Mountain from the viewpoint.

Also in Utulei is the **Lee Auditorium** (1962) and American Samoa's **television studios,** which may be visited weekdays around 1030. In 1964 American Samoa became the first Pacific country to receive television, and although the original educational use has disappeared, KVZK-TV continues to broadcast commercially over two channels. Channel 2 is semi-educational, while Channel 4 is strictly commercial television. Channel 5 was blown off the air by Hurricane Val in 1992 and its equipment cannibalized to keep the other two channels going.

Fagatogo

The **Governor's Mansion,** on a hilltop just west of the Rainmaker Hotel, was built in 1903 during the naval administration as the Commandant's Residence, becoming Government House in 1951. A large sign requests the public not to enter the grounds. The **Jean P. Haydon Museum** (tel. 633-4347; open weekdays 1000-1500, admission free), farther west, was erected in 1917 as a naval commissary and served as the island's post office 1950-1971. The museum features exhibits on natural history, tapa making, and tattooing, plus a collection of war clubs, kava bowls, model canoes, and old photos.

Facing the Malae-O-Le-Talu field, where local chiefs ceded the island to the U.S. in 1900, is the **Fono Building** (1973), in which the territory's legislature convenes for 45-day sessions twice a year. The **police station,** across the field from the Fono, was originally the barracks of the Fitafita Guard, the former Samoan militia. Next to the police station is the **old jail** (1911), now the archives office.

Farther west just before the market is the old **courthouse** (1904), built in the U.S. Deep-South style. The **Fagatogo Public Market** is busiest early Saturday morning, when screaming red-faced evangelists backed up by ear-splitting gospel music harangue vendors selling tropical fruits and vegetables. Just inside the **Department of Marine and Wildlife Resources** office facing the bus station next to the market is a very good display of fish and birdlife of Samoa. Ask at the Education Office here for a copy of the booklet *American Samoa: Natural History and Conservation Topics.*

West of here is the former guesthouse where Somerset Maugham stayed in 1916, now **Sadie's Restaurant.** Today Maugham's tale of hooker Sadie Thompson and the repressed missionary, set here, is discussed over upscale seafood.

Pago Pago

Continue west to a sign reading National Park Visitor Center 1/4 Mile, where a road runs up the hill into Happy Valley. On this side road you pass six WW II ammunition bunkers on the left before reaching a dirt road, also on the left, which leads to a large **concrete bunker** used during WW II as a naval communications headquarters. Many of these military structures are now inhabited, and you'll need to ask permission before approaching the bunker, which is in a backyard.

The **National Park Visitor Center** (weekdays 0800-1600, Saturday 0800-1200, admission free), in Room 114 at Pago Shopping Plaza, contains a small collection of Samoan artifacts, seashells, coral, maps of American Samoa, and photos of the park. You can ask to see a brief video and the friendly staff will answer questions.

At the west end of the harbor is Pago Pago village, this area's namesake, and around on the north side of the harbor is the **Marine Railway,** which provides maintenance and repair facilities to the fishing fleet. The tuna canneries are nearby. To visit the **Samoa Packing Plant** (formerly owned by Van Camp) call the personnel office beforehand at tel. 644-5273 and make an appointment. You could also try asking at the

gate. They'll want to know who you are, where you work, why you wish to visit, etc., and only persons wearing shoes and long pants are allowed inside the plant. **StarKist** (H.J. Heinz) is less amenable to visitors.

High on the reef just east of the canneries are eight Taiwanese and Korean fishing boats thrown up by Hurricane Val in 1992.

The North Coast

The easiest way to escape the congested Pago Pago harbor area is to jump on a bus to **Vatia** on Tutuila's north coast. Three buses (US$1.50) shuttle back and forth via Aua and Afono all day, so getting there is easy. Vatia is a picturesque village with a nice beach, and the scenery around here is superb with jungle-covered peaks surrounding the village on all sides. Look across to unforgettable Pola Island (also known as the "Cockscomb") with its sheer 100-meter cliffs and wheeling seabirds. Vatia is in the center of the Tutuila section of National Park of American Samoa, and if you're interested in some organized hiking or boating while at Vatia, call local resident Roy West (tel. 644-1416) who offers boat trips at US$25 pp and who can arrange hiking guides at the same rate.

The East End

Two more six-inch WW II guns are on the hillside near **Breakers Point.** Walk up past Mr. Paleafei's house, the large two-story dwelling at the high point in the road. The hill directly opposite the guns bears a small lighthouse with a view, while by the water at the bottom of the hill on the bay side is a concrete ammunition bunker now used for dynamite storage.

Eastern Tutuila is easily accessible on the frequent Tula buses that wind along the southeast coast through the day. At **Alao** and **Tula** are wide sandy beaches, but beware of the undertow. Unfortunately empty milk cartons and other trash from the nearby elementary school litter the area. From Tula (the end of the bus route), the road continues around to the north side of Tutuila as far as Onenoa.

Aunu'u Island

There's a single village on Aunu'u Island off the southeast end of Tutuila, but no cars. Motorboats shuttle across to Aunu'u constantly from the small boat harbor at Auasi, taking passengers at US$2 pp each way or US$10 one-way for a charter trip. Go over first thing in the morning and you shouldn't have any trouble getting back. Don't come on a Sunday though, as the locals don't appreciate *palagi* picnickers that day.

Aunu'u's eel-infested **Red Lake** in the sprawling crater is difficult to approach. Cliffs along the south coast and thick bushes make hiking around the island heavy going. Aunu'u's notorious stretch of red **quicksand** at Pala Lake is fairly close to the village, but you may have to wade through a swamp to get to it. The **taro swamps** just behind the village are easier to see, and a walk around to the new elementary school reveals an appealing slice of island life. At **Ma'ama'a Cove** on the east side of the island waves rush into "the teacup" with much splashing. It's picturesque, but don't swim here.

Ottoville

At Ottoville on the Tafuna plain is **Holy Family Catholic Cathedral** (1994) containing a wonderful picture of the Holy Family on a Samoan beach painted by Duffy Sheridan in 1991. Samoan carver Sven Ortquist did the 14 deep-relief Stations of the Cross and other woodcarvings in the cathedral and designed the stained glass windows.

Near the cathedral and adjacent to the Fatuoaiga Catholic Church Center is a small **historical park** with restored *tia seu lupe* (pigeon-catching mound) that in many ways resembles the later *marae* of Eastern Polynesia. Similar (if usually smaller) *tia* dot ridgelines and jungles in many parts of Tutuila. The park is well laid out and sits next to the only swatch of lowland rainforest still extant on Tutuila. It's accessible on the Tafuna bus and well worth a visit, especially around twilight if you're a birder.

Around Leone

The Leone bus will drop you at **Leala Sliding Rock**, between Vailoatai and Taputimu, where the local kids take a running slide down the large, flat rocks covered by slimy algae. It's dangerous to imitate unless you know exactly how. From here you can hike east along the lovely coast toward Fagatele Point, but only in dry weather at low tide as the rocks become extremely slippery and dangerous when it rains.

There are several clear tidal pools here where you can swim at low tide and even a blowhole. Fagatele Bay, a drowned volcanic crater now a designated National Marine Sanctuary, cannot be reached from this side due to high cliffs.

From Sliding Rock it's a pleasant two km walk (or another bus) northwest to Leone village. Just before you reach the intersection with the main south coast road, ask someone to direct you to the former **Fagalele Boys School,** on the coast behind a row of large banyan trees. Built in the mid-19th century, this is the oldest European-style building on the island, unfortunately destroyed by Hurricane Val in 1992.

Leone was the ancient capital of Tutuila, and when Samoa's first missionary, John Williams, visited Tutuila on 18 October 1832, it was here that he landed. A monument to Williams is in front of **Zion Church** (1900) at Leone and the church itself is worth entering for its finely carved wooden ceiling. Until steamships were invented, Leone was the preferred anchorage of sailing ships unwilling to risk entering Pago Pago Harbor, and much of the early contact between Samoans and Europeans took place here. Two km up the road beginning beside the nearby Catholic church is **Leone Falls** (closed Sunday), where there's freshwater swimming.

Both Fagalele and Zion were built by the London Missionary Society, and a couple of kilometers west of Leone is the former **Atauloma Girls School** (1900), a third relic of LMS activity. Today the school building is owned by the territory and used as government housing for *palagi*—Samoans refuse to live there out of fear that it's haunted. When the sea is calm you can snorkel on the reef in front of Atauloma Girls School, and since there isn't a church is this village, it's usually okay to swim there even on Sunday. There's also surfing off the beaches at Atauloma and nearby Fagamutu.

Cape Taputapu

There's beautiful scenery along the road west of Leone. Get off the bus just beyond Amanave where the road swings north to Poloa. At low tide you can hike along the south coast from Amanave to Cape Taputapu in about 30 minutes, passing several lovely isolated beaches and rocky offshore islets. At high tide look for the slippery, muddy trail that cuts behind sev-

coastline at Cape Taputapu National Natural Landmark, Tutuila

eral of the more difficult stretches. There's a lovely white-sand beach at uninhabited Loa Cove halfway to the cape. The cape itself is magnificent, and it's exciting to stand on the rocky westernmost headland and watch the ocean rise and fall before you as it crashes into the shore.

The Northwest Coast

Buses run fairly frequently between Pavaiai and Aoloaufou, high in the center of the island. It's a short walk up a paved road from Aoloaufou to the radio towers on **Mt. Olotele** (493 meters) for the view.

From beyond Aoloaufou, a muddy, slippery trail leads down to Aasu village on **Massacre Bay,** about an hour each way. Only one family still lives here and in front of one of the houses is a monument erected in 1883 and surmounted by a cross. This memorializes 11 French sailors from the ships *Astrolabe* and *Boussole* of the ill-fated La Pérouse expedition, who were killed here in an encounter with the Samoans on 11 December 1787. The French had come ashore to fill their casks with water, but as they were returning to their ships the two longboats became stranded on the reef due to a miscalculation of the tide, and the Samoans attacked. A Chinese member of the expedition and the 39 Samoans who also died are not mentioned on the monument. A year later La Pérouse and all of his ships were lost when a storm drove them onto a reef in Solomon Islands. Ask someone at Aasu to indicate the way to the waterfalls (and re-

member that this whole area is private property).

Another trail from Aoloaufou goes down to **Aoloautuai;** the trailhead is behind a house on the left near the northwest end of the road. Aoloautuai is a deserted village site on a lovely bay where you could camp for a few days if you took enough food. It may also be possible to hike from Aoloaufou west to **Fagamalo,** putting yourself back on Tutuila's road network. The first half of the way follows the ridge, and one should set out early and not hesitate to turn back if the final descent to Fagamalo looks impassable. This route is seldom used and you'd be on your own if anything went wrong.

Hiking

One of Tutuila's easiest and most rewarding hikes is through **National Park of American Samoa** to the TV towers on **Mt. Alava** (491 meters). The hourly Fagasa bus (50 cents) from Fagatogo Market runs up to the trailhead at the pass, but ask someone at the bus station where you should be waiting as the vehicle bears no destination sign. Don't worry if you have to sit there a while, as it's fun to observe the colorful locals coming and going, and on the way back to town it's easy to walk down through the village.

The TV towers on the summit are a two-hour walk northeast along a five-km jeep track from the Fagasa road (no chance of getting lost). A spectacular view of Pago Pago Harbor and Rainmaker Mountain is obtained from Mt. Alava, and if you're patient you may see an occasional flying fox glide silently by, even at midday. An over-grown trail down to Vatia on the north coast be-gins at the circular observation pavilion on the very top of the hill. Follow the ridge about 30 minutes east until you see power lines, which you follow down to Vatia. This trail is steep and should only be attempted in dry weather. Good boots and a some hiking experience are essen-tial. Hopefully, the park authorities will upgrade this trail to make it accessible to everyone.

Mt. Matafao (653 meters), Tutuila's highest peak, can be climbed in half a day via a trail that begins directly opposite the beginning of the Mt. Alava track on the pass just mentioned. Climb the white metal ladder up onto the ridge south of the road; the trail is fairly obvious on top. It'll take about three hours up through a beautiful rainforest—stay on the ridge all the way. No special gear is required for this climb and you could even go alone, but avoid rainy weather when it gets slippery. In clear weather the view is one of the finest in the South Pacific.

SPORTS AND RECREATION

Scuba Diving

Scuba diving is organized by the **Tutuila Dive Shop** (Box 5137, Pago Pago 96799; tel./fax 699-2842), under the big banyan tree in the cen-ter of Vaitogi village. It's run by John and Pisita Harrison: John has been diving Tutuila since 1986, Pisita runs the store and also dives. They charge US$65 for a two-tank dive including gear and a refreshment, and they rent tanks at US$7 a day, plus US$4 for a fill. A PADI open-water certification course is US$300.

Chuck Brugman's **Dive Samoa** (Box 3927, Pago Pago 96799; tel. 699-4980) operates out of Safety Systems (tel. 633-1701) in Faga'alu. You can also contact him through the Yacht Club. Chuck runs scuba trips at US$25 pp (min-imum of two) for one tank, US$45 pp for two tanks, night dives US$35 (all gear is extra). Snorkelers can go along for US$10 pp, and sightseeing boat rides are US$10 pp (minimum of four persons). Most of Chuck's clients are local divers, and there's almost always a trip on Saturday. Unfortunately fish populations have been decimated by Samoans spearfishing with the help of scuba gear, and large areas of flat coral have been pulverized by fishermen stand-ing on them or breaking off pieces to extract marinelife. On the up side, the currents aren't bad if the sea is flat.

Snorkeling

Snorkeling in the polluted waters off Utulei and Faga'alu is not recommended. The closest points outside the harbor are the open reefs opposite Aveina Bros. Market at Matu'u, or at Lauli'i. These can be treacherous when the southeast tradewinds are blowing and there's a rather heavy break. If the water is quiet, get into one of the *avas*—the channels going out—and enjoy undersea caves and canyons. Just beware of sneak bumper waves and strong currents in the channels: you might have to come back in over the reef and the break varies considerably. Nei-ther spot is outstanding, however, and you might see more trash than fish.

Better snorkeling locales are found at the east and west ends of Tutuila, but beware of strong currents and undertow. The north coast is best of all, as it's well protected from most pollution and the prevailing winds. However, better snorkel-ing by far is available at Ofu in the Manu'a Group. Shark attacks are extremely rare around Ameri-can Samoa—coral cuts and undertow or cur-rents are much more of a hazard.

Windsurfing

The windsurfing in Pago Pago Harbor is good year-round, although there's more wind June-October. The main drawback is the harbor's pollution. If you'd like some specific informa-tion, contact Bill Hyman at the Island Business Center (tel. 633-7457), behind the courthouse in Fagatogo.

Fishing

Captain Timothy D. Jones Sr. (Box 1413, Pago Pago 96799; tel. 633-2190) has a fishing boat called the *Miss Mihi,* which he charters at US$200 a half day (0630-1230) or US$300 a whole day. Up to four people can go for that price. If the fish are biting, Tim won't insist on returning to port or charge you extra, even if you only booked half a day. To motor out to the banks (50 km each way) where fish are guar-anteed costs US$25 pp an hour (minimum of three people).

Golf and Tennis

Visitors are welcome at the 18-hole **'Ili'ili Golf Course** (tel. 699-2995 or 699-1762; open daily), maintained by the Department of Parks and Recreation at 'Ili'ili. You'll enjoy good views of the mountains and sea from the fairways, and inexpensive food and drink are available at the adjacent Country Club (tel. 688-2440). Greens fees for the 9/18 holes are US$3/5 weekdays, US$4/7 weekends and holidays, or US$30 a month. Cart hire is US$7/14, plus US$10 for clubs (bring your own balls and tees). It's not necessary to book starting times, but clubs and carts should be reserved as they're in limited supply. The public tennis courts at Pago Pago and Tafuna are free.

PRACTICALITIES

ACCOMMODATIONS

Budget

Whether you love or hate Tutuila may well depend on the type of accommodations you get. Several good medium-priced places to stay do exist, but you should still expect to pay more than you would for similar accommodations elsewhere in the South Pacific. Knowing this in advance, it won't come as quite as much of a shock, and many other things such as food, drinks, groceries, toiletries, clothes, transportation, admissions, and telephone calls are relatively cheap, so it sort of averages out.

There aren't any regular budget accommodations in the harbor area, and camping is not allowed in public parks. However, some local residents welcome guests at US$35 pp a week and up, and Pago Pago village at the head of the harbor is a good place to start looking. For example, Mrs. Fetu Vaiuli (Box 792, Pago Pago 96799; tel. 633-1340) rents rooms to travelers by the week or month. It's the sixth house on the left past the huge derelict church up Fagasa Road from Pago Pago village.

Mr. Elmer "Sama" Nakiso (Box 152, Pago Pago 96799; tel. 633-4803) in Fagatogo village also rents rooms on a long-term basis (about US$150 a month). To find his house turn left at Herb and Sia's Motel and follow the road around to the end.

The people in small corner grocery stores around the island may know of similar places, if they understand what you really want. These are private homes, so you ought to look upon it as a sort of cultural exchange and approach people with sensitivity. Your first question should not be the price. You'll probably end up staying with a lot of "real" Samoans working at the canneries, and as neighbors they're quite interesting. For further advice, call Louie the Fish (tel. 633-4888), a Samoan bone carver and fisherman who often knows of places to stay (and also takes visitors out fishing and scuba diving). If he's not there, ask for Sasa and say you got their names out of this book.

The **Office of Tourism** (Box 1147, Pago Pago 96799; tel. 633-1091), near the Yacht Club in Utulei, has a little-used *Fale, Fala ma Ti* (house, mat, and tea) program of rather costly accommodations with Samoan families, starting at US$20-45 pp a day without food. This is a nice way to meet people while finding a place to stay, but unfortunately it's very disorganized. Many of the families on the list have moved, changed their prices, or simply forgotten they were listed at all. Reconfirm everything by phone before going anywhere. Be prepared for huge complementary meals with lots of meat and breadfruit, friendly people, no privacy, free rides around town, outdoor showers called "watertaps," and remote locations. The Samoans are warm, hospitable people and if they like you, you'll immediately become part of the family.

About the closest you'll come to backpackers' accommodations on Tutuila is offered by **Roy West** (Box 3412, Pago Pago 96799; tel. 644-1416), who lives in Vatia village on the north coast. He arranges places to stay with his extended Samoan family in the village at US$10 pp, and also has a secluded cabin at Amalau Bay, off the road to Vatia, which he rents at US$10 pp. Several beach *fales* are also here at US$5 pp, but you'd need a mosquito net. (The Amalau valley is a prime bird- and bat-watching area.) In addition, Roy has a plantation shack and accommodation in tent sites at Tafeu Bay, west of Vatia, accessible by trail in three hours or by boat in 10 minutes, plus 20 minutes on foot. Roy is probably your best bet for low-budget accommodations on Tutuila, so call him up as soon as you arrive. If you get his answering machine and don't have a number to leave, just say you're on your way and catch a bus over to Vatia (Roy says this system works fine). Other residents of Vatia also offer accommodations, if you don't manage to connect with Roy.

Another good choice for backpackers is **Tisa's Barefoot Bar** (Box 3576, Pago Pago 96799; tel. 622-7447), at Alega Beach on the southeast coast between Lauli'i and Avaio villages. Tisa has two small *fales* right on the beach at US$25 for the entire *fale* (up to four people) with pillows, mosquito nets, and mats provided. If there are only one or two of you, they'll throw in breakfast. Running water is available, and Tisa's is in a secluded location away from the village. The bus service is cheaper and more frequent than to/from Vatia, but call ahead to check availability and prices.

Inexpensive

Herb and Sia's Motel (Box 430, Pago Pago 96799; tel. 633-5413), in the heart of Fagatogo, has gone downhill in recent years, although the prices haven't followed. The rooms, six with shared bath and three with private bath, all cost US$40/45 single/double. There's no hot water or cooking facilities, the air-conditioning and fridges may be out of order, and to be frank, the whole place is a dump. Avoid rooms five and six, which are without outside windows, and lock your door securely when you go out to the toilet. Be prepared for the sound of midnight "action" in adjacent rooms—women traveling alone shouldn't stay here.

Duke and Evalani's flashy **Motu O Fiafiaga Motel** (Box 1554, Pago Pago 96799; tel. 633-7777, fax 633-4767) is a big step up from Herb and Sia's for only a few dollars more. The 12 a/c rooms with TV and shared bath are US$60 single or double if you stay only one night, US$50 for two or more nights, breakfast included. This well-maintained two-story building overlooks a noisy highway, so ask for one of the five rooms on the back side if traffic bothers you, and while you're at it, try to get one in the end of the building away from the cabaret. House guests have

access to an exercise room and sauna. The adjacent restaurant/bar under the same friendly management serves excellent and inexpensive American and Mexican food.

The top accommodation value in this category is without doubt **Barry's Bed & Breakfast** (Box 5572, Pago Pago 96799; tel. 688-2488, fax 633-9111), in a quiet residential area near the waterfalls at Leone. The four rooms in Barry's comfortable and solidly built two-story house go for US$35/40/50 single/double/triple including a large breakfast. There are full cooking facilities, hot water showers, a washing machine, TV, and a large tropical garden at your disposal. You can even borrow Barry's set of golf clubs. Local telephone calls are free. Barry Willis, a fifth generation part-Samoan, will make you feel right at home. Although it may at first appear out of the way, it's actually a bit closer to the airport than Fagatogo. Barry's makes a great base for seeing western Tutuila and is easily accessible on public transport with buses every 10 minutes throughout the day. Just be sure to catch the last bus back from town at 1700 and plan on spending Sunday around Leone. The bus rides back and forth from Fagatogo will be a memorable part of your visit.

Moderate

Tutuila's only big hotel is the 182-room **Rainmaker Hotel** (Box 996, Pago Pago 96799; tel. 633-4241, fax 633-5959), erected in the mid-'60s by Pan American Airways but now government-owned. The oval neo-Samoan architecture echoes Rainmaker Mountain across the bay. Rates start at US$60 single or double standard, US$72 beachfront, US$85 deluxe (with TV). More expensive *fales* and suites are also available. Third persons pay US$15, but children under 12 are free. Unfortunately it's rather run-down, so if the first room they give you is in bad condition, go back and ask for another. Request an upstairs room facing the beach. The Rainmaker features the usual bars, restaurants, gift shops, swimming pool, car rental offices, and landscaped grounds. The location is convenient and it should be your choice if you like Holiday Inn or TraveLodge type of places.

Pago Airport Inn (Box 783, Pago Pago 96799; tel. 699-6333, fax 699-6336) is a large two-story concrete building in the middle of Tafu-

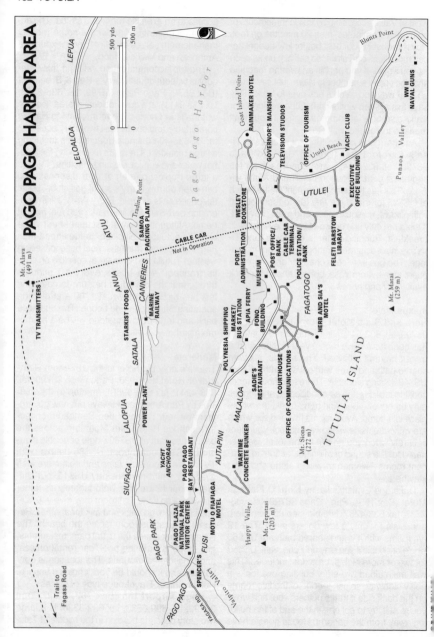

PAGO PAGO HARBOR AREA

na village, two km from the airport (US$4 by taxi). The 20 a/c rooms with bath, fridge, and TV are US$65/75/85 single/double/triple (or US$350/400/450 a week). Food can be a problem as there are no cooking facilities in the rooms and no restaurant is nearby. It's not a convenient place to stay unless you're in transit for one night and don't wish to go into town.

Chande Lutu-Drabble operates **Ta'alolo Lodge** (Box 1266, Pago Pago 96799; tel. 688-7311 or 688-7294, fax 688-7178), an upscale bed and breakfast a few minutes walk from the 'Ili'ili Golf Course. The five clean rooms in this renovated two-story house vary in price from US$75 single or double for a fan-cooled room with shared bath, US$115 for an a/c upstairs room with shared bath, or US$135 for the a/c master bedroom with private bath. Continental breakfast is included in the rates and other meals can be ordered in advance at $8-22 each, plus US$3 for dessert. Permission to use the lodge kitchen to cook for yourself may be granted. A swimming pool, summer house, and outdoor bar are at your disposal, and Chande is quite knowledgeable about Samoan culture and can help with your arrangements. Ta'alolo Lodge also caters to business travelers and would be a good choice if you were the fussy type.

Your final choice is the 20-room **'Apiolefaga Inn** (Box 336, Pago Pago 96799; tel. 699-9124, fax 699-4892), in Mesepa village back behind the Community College west of the airport. The seven standard a/c rooms are US$50/60 single/double, while the 10 larger deluxe rooms are US$60/70. The three recently renovated "VIP" rooms are US$80 single or double. Extra persons pay US$15 in all cases, but children under 12 are free. Not all of the standard rooms have a TV and fridge (ask), but the cheaper units are usually full anyway. A bar and pool are on the premises.

FOOD

Fast Food

An excellent selection of inexpensive eateries awaits you, although fried, high-sodium, and high-cholesterol foods are the norm at these. Most places provide the standard "bottomless" cup of coffee dear to American hearts. **Teo's Kitchen** (tel. 633-2250; open Saturday until

1600), beside Fagatogo Market, offers filling US$2 lunch specials, and it's always full of locals watching TV.

Da Maks Island Style Restaurant (tel. 633-5838; open weekdays 0700-1630), harborside behind the market, is more expensive with breakfast and "ono" lunch specials from US$5 a plate. You'll like Mel and Gretchen's mix of Samoan, Chinese, and Hawaiian foods, and the terrace just above the water is also nice.

Alamoana Fast Food (tel. 633-1854; weekdays 0700-1700, Saturday 0700-1500), next to the Record Store behind the Office of Communications, serves a hearty US$2 lunch. You point to what you want in a warmer at the counter.

Pinoy's Fast Foods, near the Samoa News Building between the Rainmaker and town, serves tasty Filipino dishes beginning at 0800 daily except Sunday and continuing until the food runs out. The portions are huge and prices excellent. Longshoremen and sailors are the clientele.

Krystal's Burger (tel. 688-2335), with four locations around Tutuila, puts McDonald's to shame with their tasty hot dogs, hamburgers, Mexican food, combo plates, and ice cream. They're open from 1000 until well after midnight (on Sunday from 1430). Look for them opposite the bus station in Fagatogo, and at Nu'uuli, Leone, and the airport.

Better Restaurants

The dining room at the **Rainmaker Hotel** (tel. 633-4241) offers a Samoan buffet lunch Friday 1130-1330 (US$9). Also try breakfast (0630-1100) or fish and chips (US$5.75) in the surprisingly good hotel coffee shop (open daily until 1800).

Vegetarians will have no trouble ordering at **Signore Paisano's Pizzeria** (tel. 633-2837; closed Sunday) in the Samoa News Building. Owner Jimmy Stevens, an animated New Jersey Italian, is kept hopping feeding homesick crews off the big purse seiners based nearby. Paisano's bakes some of the best pizza west of Santa Monica, plus huge submarine sandwiches jampacked with corned beef, pastrami, and Italian sausage. Real mozzarella cheese is used.

Tutuila's top place to eat is **Sadie's Restaurant** (tel. 633-5981; closed Sunday), just west of the market. Despite the Maugham theme, Sadie's is as unpretentious as everything else on

Fagatogo's Hotel Sadie Thompson as it looked prior to WW II; today an upscale restaurant occupies the premises.

Tutuila and the American expats you see enjoying themselves at the tables are putting on no act. Dinner will set you back a lot farther than lunch, but the tuna dishes are said to be worth it.

The upmarket menu at the **Pago Bay Restaurant** (tel. 633-4197) in Pago Pago goes from hamburgers to Chinese food, with fresh seafood and U.S.-quality steak somewhere in between. Their fish and chips are worth asking for (here too, lunch is much less expensive than dinner).

Evie's Cantina (tel. 633-7777; lunch 1100-1400, dinner 1800-2200), at the Motu O Fiafiaga Motel in Pago Pago, dishes out some of the tastiest Mexican food in the South Pacific, plus karaoke nightly and a feature film with Sunday dinner. Need we say more?

Nu'uuli

The **Golden Conda Restaurant** (tel. 633-7749), on the main road a bit east of the hospital turnoff at Faga'alu, serves Chinese dishes weekdays 0800-1600/1700-2200, weekends 1700-2200 only.

Similar is **Sunny's Chinese Restaurant** (tel. 699-5238; Mon.-Sat. 0900-2200, Sunday 1100-1400/1700-2200), east of Transpac in Nu'uuli.

Rubbles Tavern (tel. 699-4403; Mon.-Sat. 1100 to midnight), in the Nu'uuli Shopping Center next to Transpac, is an a/c American-style diner with a smart bar. Steaks, fish, and pasta dishes are on the medium-priced menu.

A & A Pizza Drive-Thru (tel. 699-9428), at Malaeimi, a bit east of the Community College on the main road, is the favorite pizza place outside the bay area.

ENTERTAINMENT

The **Wallace Theaters** (tel. 699-9334), aka Nu'uuli Place Cinemas, in Nu'uuli, screens recent Hollywood films in two halls. All shows before 1800 weekdays and before 1300 weekends cost US$3.50 admission.

Bingo is now played (nightly except Sunday from 2000) in the former bowling alley across from Spencer's in Pago Pago.

Evalani's Cabaret Lounge (tel. 633-4776), at the Motu O Fiafiaga Motel in Pago Pago, has a spacious dance floor (dancing 2100 to closing), karaoke videos, and a nice local crowd. Co-owner Duke Wellington plays Tutuila's only grand piano during happy hours (1800-2100). The purse seiner guys tend to stand at the bar and cause trouble among themselves under the watchful eye of the mountainous bouncer.

Happy hours at the **Pago Bay Restaurant** (tel. 633-4197) in Pago Pago are a yachtie institution with free *pupu* (snacks) and US$2 drinks, weekdays 1700-1900. **Sadie's Restaurant** (tel. 633-5981) has happy hours weekdays 1630-1830 with the beer reduced from US$3 to US$2 (great with sashimi).

The Sadie Thompson Lounge off the main dining room at the **Rainmaker Hotel** has a consistently good happy hour band weekdays 1630-

1830 (a favorite hangout of local politicians). Come early or you won't find a table. Shorts and bare feet are not permitted in the lounge after 1600; in fact, all of the places mentioned above except the bingo hall have strict dress codes in the evening. The drinking age in American Samoa is 21.

A good drinking place out beyond the airport is **Players Sports Club** (tel. 699-4317), on Ottoville Rd., Tafuna. The **Country Club** (tel. 688-2440), next to 'Ili'ili Golf Course, is farther west.

On Alega Beach between Lauli'i and Avaio villages is **Tisa's Barefoot Bar** (tel. 622-7447), subject of a number of magazine articles about a certain fertility tattoo on the proprietress. Tisa's is open on Sunday and you can swim here—a good place to go that day. Call to find out if they'll be serving the traditional Sunday *umu* lunch. "Tisa's jungle hop," a three-hour guided hike through the bush behind the bar, is US$10 pp including a snack.

Cultural Show for Visitors

A Polynesian variety show accompanies the Friday night Fia Fia buffet in the dining room at the Rainmaker Hotel (tel. 633-4241). Dinner is from 1830 and the show starts at 2000 (US$15 pp, reservations recommended). The food is excellent (prime rib, great salads), and you'll witness Maori war dances, Hawaiian hulas, and even a tropical version of "My Way!" The only other chance to see Samoan dancing is when a cruise ship arrives or leaves (which happens about four times a year), or on a local holiday.

SHOPPING

American Samoa is a poor place to shop for handicrafts and many of the items sold at the airport shops and elsewhere are imported from Tonga. About the easiest places to pick up souvenirs are the shops facing the airline offices at the airport (not the duty free shop in the departure lounge).

Clothing is a good buy here, and those long *puletasi* dresses make unique souvenirs. **Forsgren's** (tel. 633-5431) in Fagatogo has nice Samoan T-shirts and cut-rate clothes at some of the best prices in town. It's always crowded with nonresident Samoans who make the long pilgrimage from Apia just to shop here. **TK's Clothing** (tel. 633-2173), near Forsgren's, is another place to shop for cheap tropical garb and *lavalava*. **Tedi of Samoa** (tel. 633-4200) sells Samoan fashions and Reebok shoes in their Hawaiian-style store across from the courthouse in Fagatogo. While other local stores sell Chinese products, Tedi has mostly American-made clothing and sportswear but fewer bargains. **Spencer's** (tel. 633-4631) in Pago Pago also carries inexpensive clothing and shoes.

The **Transpac Corporation** (tel. 699-9589), in the Nu'uuli Shopping Center and below Sadie's Restaurant, has a good selection of imported goods. **The Record Store** (tel. 699-1283) sells cassette tapes of Samoan pop at two locations: Nu'uuli and Fagatogo. **Tropik-Traders** (tel. 699-5077), near Transpac in Nu'uuli, is the place to pick up magazines, compact discs, and gifts. Downtown closing time is inconveniently early at 1630 weekdays and 1200 on Saturday. You can buy tents at the hardware store across the street from Laufou Shopping Center in Nu'uuli.

In general, American Samoa is a cheap place to shop for consumer items because importers pay only three percent duty and there's no sales tax. Neighboring Samoa has a 10% sales tax and double-digit duties.

SERVICES AND INFORMATION

Money

The only place on the island that will change foreign currency is the Bank of Hawaii (tel. 633-4226, fax 633-2918; weekdays 0900-1500), beside the post office in Fagatogo and at Pava'ia'i out toward Leone. Brace yourself for a US$7.50 commission (no commission on U.S.-dollar traveler's checks). An ATM stands outside the Bank of Hawaii.

The locally owned Amerika Samoa Bank (tel. 633-1151) has branches next to the police station in Fagatogo and at Tafuna, both open Mon.-Fri. 0830-1500, Saturday 0900-1200. They won't touch foreign currencies, but will cash U.S.-dollar American Express traveler's checks without commission (as will most other businesses in the territory). The Amerika Samoa Bank charges 1% commission on Visa traveler's checks (and other types are not accepted), so go to the Bank of Hawaii in you have anything other than American Express.

American Express itself is not represented in American Samoa.

Post and Telecommunications

The main post office (Monday and Friday 0900-1630, Tues.-Thurs. 0900-1500, Saturday 0900-1300) is in Fagatogo with a contract station at Leone. There is no residential mail delivery but around 5,000 post office boxes are in use at the main post office. Mail addressed to General Delivery, Pago Pago, American Samoa, U.S.A. 96799, can be picked up at the main office Mon.-Fri. 0930-1100 and 1300-1500, Saturday 1030-1130 (mail is held 30 days). If you're a yachtie, ask the clerk to also check under the name of your boat.

Place long-distance telephone calls at the Office of Communications (tel. 633-1126; open 24 hours), diagonally across from the Fono Building in Fagatogo. Go at odd hours as this office is jammed around mid-afternoon. You can receive faxes addressed to fax 633-9111 here at a cost of US$3 for the first page, US$1 additional pages.

Laundromats and Toilets

Malia's Laundromat (tel. 633-5980; open daily until midnight), up the street opposite Fagatogo Market, charges 75 cents to wash or dry. You'll save 25 cents on the washing by going to Mary's Laundromat (closed Sunday), opposite Herb and Sia's Motel in Fagatogo, and there are many other laundromats around the island (ask the locals where they are).

The nameless laundromat next to The Tool Shop (tel. 633-7025), opposite the fisheries dock in Malaloa, has public showers (US$1) as well as washing machines.

Public toilets are next to the Jean P. Haydon Museum and near Da Maks Restaurant at the market.

Yachting Facilities

Harbormaster permitting, anchor your vessel as far away from the noise and smell of the canneries and power plant as you can. When all is calm, the stench can be almost unbearable and you feel this really is the armpit of the Pacific. There's bad holding in the harbor because the soft oozy bottom is covered with plastic bags. Lock your dinghy when you go ashore.

The Pago Pago Yacht Club (tel. 633-2465; Mon.-Thurs. 1130-2000, Fri.-Sun. 1130-2100) at Utulei is a friendly place worth frequenting in the late afternoon if you're looking to hitch a ride to Apia, Fiji, Wallis, Vava'u, or wherever. They can call any yachts in the vicinity over VHF channel 16. Check their notice board, or borrow a book from their exchange. Friday 1600-1800 the whole yachting community converges here for happy hour-priced drinks and free *pupu* (snacks). That's also the time when local club members break out their longboats *(fautasi)* for a row around the harbor. The weekday luncheon menu is also good and visitors are always most welcome (ignore the Members Only sign on the door).

Pago Pago is a good place for cruising yachts to provision—ask about case discounts. For example, Tom Ho Ching Inc. (tel. 633-2430; open daily 0530-2300), in Faga'alu, has good case lot prices on a variety of U.S. products. An even better place is Cost-U-Less (tel. 699-5975; Mon.-Fri. 0800-2000, Saturday 0800-1900, Sunday 1000-1800), a warehouse-style bulk store in Tafuna on the road from 'Ili'ili to the airport. Manager Jim Lutgen swears he won't be undersold. It's also easy to order yacht supplies from the U.S. mainland, and they're imported duty-free.

Tom French of Safety Systems (tel. 633-1701) opposite Matafao Elementary School at Faga'alu can repair life rafts and fire prevention systems for yachts. They also fill air tanks for scuba divers.

Information Offices

The rather muddled Office of Tourism (weekdays 0730-1600; tel. 633-1091), in the back of an old wooden building by the shore between the Rainmaker Hotel and the Yacht Club, can supply the usual brochures and answer simple questions. (This office has moved half a dozen times in as many years, so don't be surprised if they've moved again.)

The Department of Commerce (tel. 633-5155), in the Executive Office Building in Utulei, sells the *American Samoa Statistical Digest* (US$7.50).

The Wesley Bookshop (Box 4105, Pago Pago 96799; tel. 633-2201) at Fagatogo carries books by Samoan novelist Albert Wendt, which are hard to find in Apia.

There's good reading at the Feleti Barstow Library (tel. 633-1182; weekdays 0730-1200 and 1300-1530), behind the Executive Office Building in Utulei. The Community College between Utulei and Leone also has a library (tel. 699-1151, weekdays 0730-1600).

Hawaiian Airlines (tel. 699-1875), Polynesian Airlines (tel. 699-9126), and Samoa Air (tel. 699-9106) all have their offices at the airport. Samoa Air represents Air New Zealand. If possible, reconfirm your flight out as soon as you arrive. The travel agencies directly above the post office in Fagatogo sell air tickets for the same price as the airlines, and they are usually less crowded and more helpful.

Health

The 140-bed LBJ Tropical Medical Center (tel. 633-1222, fax 633-1869) in Faga'alu has doctors on call 24 hours a day in the Outpatients Department (US$2 fee). A dental checkup is also US$2 (appointment required). Inpatient rates at the hospital are US$60 a day. Prescription drugs are US$3 per item, but no malaria pills are available.

Several private medical clinics are at Nu'uli, including Anesi Medical Clinic (tel. 699-1276; open weekdays 1630-2030), 50 meters east of Laufou Shopping Center, and F & P Clinic (tel. 699-5118; weekdays 1600-2100), in a corner of Laufou Shopping Center.

Dr. Isara T. Tago's private Family Dental Practice (tel. 699-9812), near Krystal's Burger at Nu'uli, is open weekdays 0800-1600.

The Drug Store (tel. 633-4630) has branches in Laufou Shopping Center at Nu'uuli and on the road to the hospital.

GETTING AROUND

For an American territory, bus services on Tutuila are extremely good. Family-owned *aiga* buses offer unscheduled service from Fagatogo to all of the outlying villages. You can flag them down anywhere along their routes, and you bang on the roof when you want to get off. Not all the buses are marked with a destination, however; also, there's no service after 1600 on Saturday, and very little on Sunday or after dark any day. Bus service begins at 0400 to get workers to the first shift at the canneries—useful if you have to catch an early flight. No standing is allowed, so the rides are usually a lot of fun. Most buses play blaring music.

Bus fares are very reasonable. You pay as you leave and it's smart to carry small change: ask someone how much the fare should be before you get on and just pay the exact amount. A trip anywhere in the congested zone from the canneries to the hospital is 25 cents. Westbound to the airport intersection is 50 cents, US$1 to Leone and Amanave, US$1.25 to Fagamalo; eastbound it's 50 cents to Lauli'i, 75 cents to Avaio or Fagasa, US$1 to Aoloaufou or Tula. Service from Fagatogo to Leone is fairly frequent, and you can change buses at Leone for points west. Change at Pavaiai for Aoloaufou.

downtown Fagatogo, Tutuila

The bus across the island to Vatia leaves from in front of Da Mak Restaurant at Fagatogo market about once an hour (US$1.50).

Taxis are expensive and it's important to agree on the price before getting into a meterless taxi anywhere on Tutuila. Expect to pay at least US$1 a mile. You'll find taxi stands at the market and airport (tel. 699-1179), otherwise call **Pago Cab Service** (tel. 633-5545) or **Samoa Cab Service** (tel. 633-5870), both next to the market, or **Island Taxi** (tel. 633-5645), near the Office of Communications.

Car Rentals

Bus service to the north coast villages of Fagamalo, Fagasa, Masefau, Aoa, and Onenoa is infrequent, so to reach them easily you'll need to rent a car. The main car rental companies have counters at the airport. If no one is present, use the nearby public telephones to call around, checking current prices and requesting a car delivery to the airport.

The most professional car rental company on Tutuila is **Avis** (tel. 699-4409 at the main office at Pavaiai, tel. 699-2746 at the airport, fax 699-4305). They charge US$45 a day, plus US$8 insurance (US$500 deductible), for their cheapest car.

Royal Samoa Car Rental (tel. 633-4545 at the Rainmaker Hotel) only staffs their airport counter for Hawaiian Airlines flights. They charge US$45 daily for a non-a/c car, plus US$5 for third-party liability insurance (US$500 deductible).

Oceania Rental Cars (tel. 633-1172, fax 633-1173), next to Royal Samoa at the Rainmaker, charges US$67 including insurance.

Pavitts U-Drive (tel. 699-1456 during business hours, tel. 699-2628 after hours) usually has a representative at the airport during the day and also for all Hawaiian Airlines flights. Pavitts charges US$50 a day but it's not possible to buy collision insurance coverage on their cars.

Collins Rental Agency (tel. 633-2652, fax 633-2654), above the post office in Fagatogo, rents cars at US$40 a day including insurance.

All rates include unlimited mileage and all vehicles must have public liability insurance. Most of the agencies only rent to persons over the age of 25 and your home driver's license is honored here for 30 days. Lock your car and don't leave valuables in sight. One of the biggest problems with driving on Tutuila is the lack of places to pull over and get out. Most villages have open *fales* facing the beach, so you'll often feel like an intruder.

Driving is on the right and the speed limit is 48 kph (30 mph) unless otherwise posted. You must stop if you see a yellow school bus loading or unloading, unless the driver signals you to proceed. Transporting open alcoholic beverage containers is illegal. On the other hand, seat belts and child restraints are not mandatory, you may drive a car barefoot or while listening to music with headsets, and it's okay to transport passengers in the back of an open pickup truck (verify these points with the rental agency—the rules may have changed). Motorcyclists must wear helmets.

Local Tours

Roy West of **North Shore Tours** (Box 3412, Pago Pago 96799; tel. 644-1416) offers a wide range of hiking, mountain climbing, birdwatching, snorkeling, and boat trips at very reasonable prices. Roy's ecotours cost US$25-35 pp for a full day, plus US$5 for lunch (if required). If you want to hike along Tutuila's rugged north coast, climb Rainmaker Mountain, or get dropped off at an inaccessible bay for a few days of real Robinson Crusoe living, Roy is the guy to call. He also has a good knowledge of Samoan plans. His base is at Vatia, so many of the trips leave from there.

Royal Samoa Travel (tel. 633-2017), next to the Fale Fono at Fagatogo, offers three-hour sightseeing tours of either the east or west sides of Tutuila at US$30 pp (two-person minimum).

THE MANU'A GROUP

The three small islands of the Manu'a Group, 100 km east of Tutuila, offer spellbinding scenery in a quiet village environment. Ta'u is the territory's most traditional island, but the beaches are far better and more numerous on Ofu and Olosega. All three islands feature stimulating hiking possibilities and an opportunity for the adventurer to escape the rat race on Tutuila. The biggest hassle is canine: a real or pretend-ed stone will keep the dogs at bay.

Although a couple of small guesthouses are available, few tourists make it to Manu'a. Regular air service from Tutuila has now made these islands more accessible, but book early as local commuters fill the flights. Remember that telephone calls from Tutuila to the Manu'a Group cost only 10 cents each, so don't hesitate to call ahead to check on accommodations.

OFU AND OLOSEGA

Ofu and Olosega appear to be the remaining northern portions of a massive volcano whose southern side disintegrated into the sea. Some of the best snorkeling is around the concrete bridge that links these soaring volcanic islands; just be aware of currents. The strong current between Ofu and Nuutele islands makes snorkeling off Alaufau or Ofu villages risky, though the small-boat harbor just north of Alaufau is better protected than the one on Ta'u. The airstrip is by a long white beach on the south side of Ofu, about an hour's walk from Olosega village, and it's still possible to have to yourself this quintessential Polynesian paradise of swaying palms, magnif-icent reef, and mountains rising out of the sea. The beach and reef between Papaloloa Point and the bridge are now part of National Park of American Samoa. Bring your own snorkeling gear as none is available locally.

To climb to the television tower atop Ofu's **Tumu Mountain** (494 meters), take the five-km jeep track up the hill from near the wharf at Alaufau village and continue up to the ridge top, then over the mountain to a spectacular lookout on Leolo Ridge (458 meters) above the airstrip. Notice how the vegetation changes as you rise.

For Olosega's **Piumafua Mountain,** follow

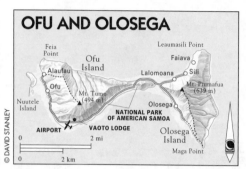

OFU AND OLOSEGA

the shoreline south almost to Maga Point, then cut back up along the ridge to the 639-meter summit. The cloud forest atop the steep hill *after* you think you've hit the peak is like the Old Forest in *The Lord of the Rings.* No goblins—only mosquitoes—but be very careful not to get turned around, as the trees cut off the view, though the forests on Ofu and Olosega are open and easy to cross after the trails give out. There is no trail along Olosega's forbidding east coast.

Accommodations and Food
Most visitors stay at **Vaoto Lodge** (Box 1809, Pago Pago 96799; tel. 655-1120 or 699-9628), near the beach beside the airstrip on Ofu. The 10 fan-cooled rooms with private bath are US$35/40/50 single/double/triple. Cooking facilities are not available but hosts Tito, Marty, and Marge Malae prepare good local meals at US$15 for all three. They'll make you feel like one of the family; ask Tito to tell you a ghost story. Inexpensive.

Don and Ilaisa's Motel (Box 932, Pago Pago 96799; tel. 655-1212) in Olosega village has five rooms at US$25/35 single/double. Some rooms have private bath, some shared, and all guests have access to a common kitchen and fridge. Not only is the price a little lower than at Vaoto Lodge but you'll get more of a feeling for outer island life. There's a small store in the village where you can get basic supplies. Often the whole building is rented out to contract workers for extended periods, so be sure to call ahead to check availability.

Prior to your arrival, try calling Faufano Autele (tel. 655-1123), who can sometimes arrange budget accommodations on Ofu. Ta'auau Peau (tel. 655-1110) in Ofu village rents rooms and provides meals at the same rate as Vaoto Lodge.

Rather than camp along Ofu's beautiful south coast beach, which is now part of the national park, keep east toward the bridge, then just before you reach the bridge cut down to the deserted beach on the north side of the island. You'll be less likely to have visitors here than you would by the road, but bring all the food and water you'll need.

TA'U

Ta'u is a rectangular island 10 km long and five km wide. It's only 11 km southeast of Olosega, with a submarine volcano between the two. Eons ago the south side of Ta'u collapsed, leaving dramatic 500-meter-high cliffs that rise directly from the southern sea. Five smaller craters dot the steep northern slopes of Lata Mountain (995 meters), the highest peak in American Samoa.

The entire southeast corner of Ta'u is included in National Park of American Samoa, the largest of the park's three units. Craters punctuate the island's wild, thickly forested interior, known for its steep slopes and gullies. Terrain and bush can change suddenly from easy hiking to difficult, and most of the upland area is inaccessible.

From Ta'u the Tui Manu'a ruled the entire group. In 1925, as a young woman of 24, Margaret Mead researched her book, *Coming of Age in Samoa,* at Luma village on Ta'u. The present inhabitants of Ta'u live in villages in the northeast and northwest corners of the island. Small-boat harbors are at Luma and Faleasao, with the most sheltered anchorage for yachts at Faleasao. The reef pass is very narrow, and Luma harbor is used mostly by local fishing boats (not recommended for yachts). The airstrip is at Fitiuta in the northeast corner of the island.

Sights
At Luma village, see the tomb of the Tui Manu'a and other chiefly burials near the **Sacred Water,**

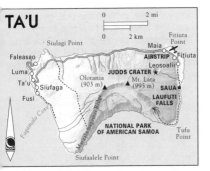

TA'U

0   2 mi

0   2 km

Siulagi Point

Faleasao

Luma

Ta'u

Fusi

Siufaga

Fitiuta Point

Maia

AIRSTRIP   Fitiuta

Leosoalii

JUDDS CRATER ★

Olotania   Mt. Lata

(903 m)   (995 m)   SAUA

LAUFUTI FALLS

NATIONAL PARK OF AMERICAN SAMOA   Tufu Point

Siufaalele Point

or "royal pool" (dry). Also of interest is the **cave of Ma'ava,** the legendary giant. There's a nice beach at **Fagamalo Cove,** halfway down the west coast south of Fusi.

From Fitiuta it's possible to hike south along the coast into American Samoa's extraordinary national park. Legend tells how the god Tanga-loa created humans at Saua, a couple of km south of Fitiuata, and from here they colonized Polynesia. Everything south of here is included in the national park. The track continues south to Tufu Point, around which are views of waves crashing into Ta'u's rocky, volcanic southern coast, where sheer volcanic cliffs soar in two or three steps to cloud-covered Mt. Lata. It's pos-

sible to follow the shoreline a couple of km west to 450-meter-high **Laufuti Falls,** although fallen trees and huge rocks block the way in places. Beyond Laufuti, one must bushwhack.

Accommodations and Food

The most convenient place to stay is **Fitiuta Lodge** (Box 1858, Pago Pago 96799; tel. 677-3501 or 677-3411), in Fitiuta village a short walk from the airstrip. The eight rooms with shared bath are US$25/45 single/double and cooking facilities are provided. Inexpensive.

The **Ta'u Motel** (Box 637, Pago Pago 96799; tel. 677-3467 or 677-3504) is near the small-boat harbor in Luma village, on the opposite side of the island from the airstrip. It has nine clean rooms with bath and fridge at US$25/40 single/double, and you can cook your own food. Discounts are possible for long stays and often the entire motel is booked out by local contractors for extended periods, so call ahead (ask for Niumata Mailo). He can pick you up at the airport at between US$10-20 for the trip (not pp), depending on whether he has to go anyway. Inexpensive.

No restaurants are to be found on Ta'u, only small village stores. If your baggage isn't overweight, bring some food with you on the plane from Tutuila. There's no bakery on Ta'u so it's a good idea to bring bread from Pago Pago.

CORAL ATOLLS

Rose Atoll

Discovered by French navigator Louis de Freycinet in 1819, Rose Atoll was visited by the U.S. Exploring Expedition under Commodore Charles Wilkes in 1839. In 1921 the U.S. claimed this uninhabited atoll, 125 km east of Ta'u. A reef of pink coral surrounds the square, three-by-three-km atoll with a pass into the lagoon. Of the atoll's two small islands, Rose is covered with coconut and other trees, while Sand is devoid of vegetation.

Large numbers of red-footed boobies and frigate birds nest near the top of Rose's large *buka* trees, while black noddies and white terns use the middle and lower branches. Green and hawksbill turtles lay eggs on the beach. To protect the turtles and seabirds, in 1974 Rose Atoll was included in the **Pacific Islands National Wildlife Refuges,**

administered by the U.S. Fish and Wildlife Service (Box 50167, Honolulu, HI 96850, U.S.A.; tel. 1-808/541-1201, fax 1-808/1216, www.fws.gov). Special permission is required to land.

Swains Island

Swains Island, 340 km northwest of Tutuila, is a circular coral atoll about two km across and 13 km around the fringing reef. There's a large lagoon in the center not connected to the sea. Swains is far closer to Tokelau than to the rest of Samoa. In fact, its customary owners were the Tokelauans of Fakaofo, who knew it as Olohega. In 1856 a New England whaling captain, Eli Jennings, arrived to set up a coconut plantation with the help of Polynesian labor; his descendants still run it as a private estate today. At present about a dozen people live on Swains.

Olohega was included in the Union Group (Tokelau), which Britain incorporated into the Gilbert and Ellice Islands Colony in 1916. In 1925, when Britain transferred Tokelau to N.Z. administration, the U.S. took advantage of the opportunity to annex Swains to American Samoa. Finally, in 1980 the U.S. government forced the Tokelauans to sign a treaty recognizing American sovereignty over Swains as a condition for the withdrawal of U.S. "claims" to the entire Tokelau Group and recognition of Tokelau's 200-nautical-mile fisheries zone.

Since the frigate bird doesn't have the oily waterproofing of other seabirds, it can't dive for its own food. Instead, it spooks other species into disgorging their catch in midair.

TONGA

an 18th-century Tongan chief

members of Captain Cook's 1777 expedition watching a night dance by women at Ha'apai

INTRODUCTION

The ancient Kingdom of Tonga, oldest and last remaining Polynesian monarchy, is the only Pacific nation never brought under foreign rule. Though sprinkled over 700,000 square km of ocean from Niuafo'ou, between Fiji and Samoa, to the Minerva Reef 290 km southwest of Ata, the total land area of the kingdom is only 691 square km.

Tonga is divided into four main parts: the Tongatapu Group in the south, with the capital, Nuku'alofa; the Ha'apai Group, a far-flung archipelago of low coral islands and soaring volcanoes in the center; the Vava'u Group, with its immense landlocked harbor; and in the north, the isolated, volcanic Niuas. The four groups are pleasingly diverse, each with interesting aspects to enjoy: no other Pacific country is made up of components as scenically varied as these.

More than 100 km of open sea separate Tongatapu and Ha'apai, then it's another 100 between Ha'apai and Vava'u, then *another* 300 km north to remote Niuafo'ou and Niuatoputapu. In all, Tonga comprises 170 islands, 42 of them inhabited. Even though they're some of the most densely populated in the Pacific, the Tongan islands are set quite apart from the 20th century. Due to the position just west of the international date line, the Tonga Visitors Bureau uses the marketing slogan "where time begins," but they could just as well use "where time stands still."

The Land

Tonga sits on the eastern edge of the Indo-Australian Plate, which is forced up as the Pacific Plate pushes under it at the Tonga Trench. This long oceanic valley running 2,000 km from Tonga to New Zealand is one of the lowest segments of the ocean floor, in places over 10 km deep. Tonga is on the circum-Pacific Ring of Fire, which extends from New Zealand to Samoa, then jogs over to Vanuatu and the Solomons. Where Tongatapu (a raised atoll), Lifuka (a low coral island), and Vava'u (another uplifted atoll) are today, towering volcanoes once belched fire and brimstone. When they sank, coral polyps gradually built up the islands.

Study the map of Tonga and you'll distinguish four great atolls in a line 350 km long. The two

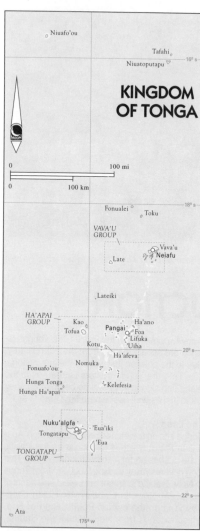

KINGDOM OF TONGA

facing in. Tonga is moving east-southeast at the rate of 20 millimeters a year and the crack in the earth's crust that originally built Tonga has shifted northwest. Thus, the active volcanoes of today are in a line 50 km west of Ha'apai-Vava'u: Fonuafo'ou, Tofua, Lateiki, Late, Fonualei, and Niuafo'ou have all erupted during the last 200 years.

Climate

The name Tonga means south; it's refreshingly cooler and less humid here than on islands closer to the equator (such as sultry Samoa). December-April is the hot, rainy season, with especially high humidity Jan.-March. June-Aug. can be cool enough to make a sweater occasionally necessary.

Tonga gets an average of two tropical hurricanes a year, usually between November and April, although they can occur as late as May. Rainfall, temperatures, and the probability of hurricanes increase the farther north you go. The southeast tradewinds prevail from May to November, and easterlies the rest of the year; in Tonga, west and northwest winds herald bad weather. In February and March north winds bring heat waves and heavy rains.

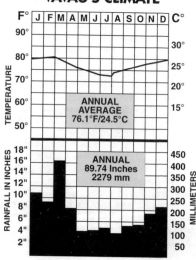

VAVAU'S CLIMATE

central atolls (Ha'apai) are now largely submerged, with Lifuka and Nomuka the largest remaining islands of each. As Ha'apai sank under the weight of new volcanoes such as Kao and Tofua, the outermost groups, Vava'u and Tongatapu, tilted toward the center, creating cliffs on their outer edges and half-submerged islands

TONGA AT A GLANCE

ISLAND	POPULATION	AREA (SQUARE KM)	HIGHEST POINT (METERS)
'Eua	4,924	87	312
Tongatapu	66,577	259	82
Ha'apai Group	8,148	109	1,046
Vava'u Group	15,779	119	519
Niuas*	2,018	72	506
TONGA	97,446	646**	

* Niuafo'ou, Niuatoputapu, Tafahi
** inhabited islands only

For local weather information dial 23-401 in Nuku'alofa during business hours.

HISTORY AND GOVERNMENT

Prehistory

According to myth, the demigod Maui acquired a fishhook from Samoa that he used to yank the Tonga Islands out of the sea. He then stamped on the islands to make them flat and suitable for gardening. The historic Polynesians reached Tonga from Fiji over 3,000 years ago. These early arrivers made incised *lapita* pottery, though the art was lost around A.D. 200. Tangaloa, the creator god, descended from the sky and had a son, Aho'eitu, by a beautiful Tongan maiden named Va'epopua. This child became the first hereditary king, or Tu'i Tonga, perhaps around A.D. 950, initiating the "classical era" in Tongan history, which continued until about 1600. Many of the great monuments of Tongatapu were built during this period, which gradually ended after European contact. The Tu'i Tonga were absolute monarchs and the only Tongan males who were not tattooed or circumcised; there was an elaborate etiquette to be observed in all contacts with their subjects.

Fierce Tongan warriors traveled throughout Western Polynesia in large double-hulled canoes *(kalia)*, each capable of carrying up to 200 people. In the 13th century the domain of the Tu'i Tonga extended all the way from Rotuma in the west through part of the Lau Group, Wallis and Futuna, Samoa, and Tokelau, to Niue in the east. The eventual collapse of this empire led to unrest and a series of Tu'i Tonga assassinations, so in 1470 the 24th Tu'i Tonga delegated much of his political power to a brother, the *hau* or temporal ruler, while retaining the spiritual authority. Later the power of the *hau* was divided between the Tu'i Ha'atakalaua and Tu'i Kanokupolu, resulting in three distinct lines.

European Contact

Although the Dutchmen Schouten and Le Maire sighted the Niuas in 1616, another Dutchman, Abel Tasman, was the first European to visit Tongatapu and Ha'apai. Arriving on 19 January 1643, as Tongans approached his ship in narrow canoes, Tasman fired a gun—terrifying the chief. A trumpet, violin, and flute were then played in succession to this chief's further astonishment. Tasman received sorely needed food and water to carry on with his journey. At one point he escaped disaster by charging full-tilt over the Nanuku Reef, which was luckily covered with sufficient water to be traversed.

When Captain Cook visited Tonga in 1773, 1774, and 1777, he and his men were received with lavish friendliness—pyramids of food were offered them, and dances and boxing matches in which little girls and women took part were staged in their honor. (The skillful Tongan pugilists made short work of Cook's crew in a competition.) Some say the islanders intended to roast and eat Cook and his men as part of the feast, but Cook's profuse thanks at his reception prompted them to change their minds. Cook presented the Tu'i Tonga with a male Galapagos tortoise, which was left to wander blind in the royal garden right up until 1966, when it died at

a Tongan chief conversing with European explorers aboard ship

the ripe old age of over 200. Ever since Cook's visit, Tonga has been known as "The Friendly Islands." Cook never visited Vava'u, which was only "discovered" in 1781 by the Spaniard Antonio Mourelle.

The Formation of a Nation

European contact led to a decline in population as warring chiefs turned newly acquired muskets and cannons on each other. The new armaments also allowed Tongan warriors to conquer the Lau Group of Fiji about this time. Members of the London Missionary Society arrived in 1797, in the middle of these civil wars, but were unable to attract a following, and by 1804 all had left.

A British Wesleyan (Methodist) missionary, Rev. William Lawry, arrived in 1822. He and his associates built the first school in Tonga in 1829, and in 1831 printed the first book, the Bible of course. Their most noteworthy convert (in 1831) was Taufa'ahau, chief of Ha'apai, who defeated two rival dynasties with the missionaries' help and in 1845 became King George Tupou I, ruler of a united Tonga. In 1862 he freed the Tongan people from forced labor on the estates of the chiefs while making hereditary nobles of the chiefs. Tupou I decreed that each of his subjects be allotted a *tax'api* consisting of a town lot and 3.34 hectares of farmland for only T$3.20 annual rental. At the same time, the king established constitutional government, with a Privy Council of his choice and representation for both nobles and commoners in a Legislative Assembly.

This system, institutionalized in the Tongan Constitution of 4 November 1875, remains in force today. A year later Germany concluded a Treaty of Friendship, which recognized Tongan independence and the sovereignty of the king. Similar treaties were signed with England (1879) and the U.S. (1888). The king's closest adviser in all of this was a Wesleyan missionary, Rev. Shirley Baker, who served as premier during the 1880s. Tupou I died in 1893 at 97 years of age, the creator of a unified Christian Tonga and one of the most remarkable men of the 19th century. The pervasive influence of the missionaries, who dominated Tonga from the early 19th century onward, can still be experienced any Sunday.

The Twentieth Century

Tonga (along with Japan, Thailand, Nepal, and a few Middle Eastern states) is one of the few countries in the world that has never been colonized by a European power. Germany had strong influence in Tonga during the late 19th century and wanted to include it in its colonial empire but bowed out to the British in exchange for a free hand in Samoa. In 1900 Tupou I's grandson, King George Tupou II (ruled 1893-1918), signed a new Treaty of Friendship with Britain, which gave the latter control of Tonga's foreign affairs as a means of forestalling encroachments by other colonial powers. The British protection remained in effect until 1970, but the rule of the royal family continued unbroken.

Magnificent, much-loved Queen Salote Tupou III ruled Tonga from 1918 until her death in 1965. Her achievements included the reunification of part of the Wesleyan church and the development of public health and education services. In 1953, she won the hearts of millions by riding through London in an open coach, despite torrential rain, at Queen Elizabeth's coronation. In fact, she was only observing the Tongan custom of showing respect for royalty by appearing before them unprotected in bad weather.

Although just short of his mother's two-meter height, H.R.H. King Taufa'ahau Tupou IV, the present monarch, looks every bit the Polynesian king he is. As crown prince during WW II, he studied at the University of Sydney, becoming the first Tongan to earn a university degree. He served as prime minister from 1949 until his coronation in 1967. Tupou IV initiated a cautious modernization program, opening Tonga to the world by having the airport upgraded for jet aircraft and approving the construction of the first large hotels. On 4 June 1970 he reestablished Tonga's full sovereignty, which allowed Tonga to receive aid money from other countries.

For almost three decades Tupou IV has steered Tonga on a conservative course. Unlike Samoa, which has had diplomatic relations with mainland China for decades, Tonga recognized the Taiwan-based Republic of China until November 1998, when it abruptly switched recognition to Beijing in a move believed to be related to the satellite communications business. The Taiwanese Embassy is the largest diplomatic mission in Nuku'alofa by far, and in 1995 Taiwan paid for the 4,000-seat Queen Salote Memorial Hall on Taufa'ahau Road, counterpart of the Beijing-funded Government Building in Apia, and a flashy new Taiwanese Embassy had only opened in Nuku'alofa in 1997. Yet way back in 1976 Tonga became the first South Pacific country to establish diplomatic relations with the USSR, leading to an absurd panic over alleged Soviet expansionism in the Pacific. This worked to Tonga's advantage as overdue aid money from Australia, New Zealand, and the U.S. came pouring in.

Government

Tonga is a constitutional monarchy in which the king rules absolutely. He appoints the 12 members of the Cabinet, including the governors of Ha'apai and Vava'u, who retain their posts for life. They sit in the 30-seat Legislative Assembly or Parliament, along with nine members who represent the 33 Nobles of the Realm, and another nine elected every three years to represent Tonga's 100,000 commoners. The king appoints one of the nobles as speaker of parliament (the king also decides who will hold the 33 noble titles). The king can dissolve parliament, dismiss ministers, veto legislation, suspend habeas corpus, and proclaim martial law at will.

The king's younger brother, Prince Fatafehi Tu'ipelehake, served as prime minister for 26 years until his retirement in 1991. Until May 1998, the king's eldest son and heir, Crown Prince Tupouto'a, was minister of foreign affairs and defense. He resigned on his 50th birthday to devote himself to business activities and the king appointed his youngest son, Prince 'Ulukalala Lavaka Ata, to replace him. It's rumored that the crown prince may soon be appointed prime minister.

Their Majesties, King Taufa'ahau Tupou and Queen Halaevalu Mata'aho, king and queen of Tonga

DOUG HANKIN

There are no municipal councils; Nuku'alofa is administered directly by the central government. Though appointed by the king, the judiciary is independent, with the highest court of appeal consisting of three judges from other Commonwealth countries. Tonga faces no external threat but the country still maintains a 200-person defense force, with facilities behind the royal palace, at the airport, and near Queen Salote Wharf (the only other South Pacific countries with armies are Fiji and Papua New Guinea). Much of the press and radio are government-owned, and formal criticism of the king is prohibited.

Yet as educational levels increase and Tongan commoners become economically independent, the power of the privileged few is being called into question. There have been allegations of corruption, and church leaders have backed increased democracy. The 1990 elections gave candidates advocating an increase in the number of people's representatives five of the nine commoner seats, and in August 1992 four of them banded together to form the Tonga Pro-democracy Movement (TPDM). Constitutional reform was discussed at a landmark November 1992 convention, which foreigners and overseas Tongans with foreign passports were prevented by the government from attending.

In subsequent elections the pro-democracy members have been reelected with those from Tongatapu and Ha'apai winning by large margins. Tongatapu representative 'Akilisi Pohiva is the best known spokesman for the TPDM, but unfortunately several attempts to create a viable people's party have degenerated into factional squabbles. In late 1998, the TPDM was reorganized as the Tonga Human Rights and Democracy Movement, in a move intended to put constitutional reform squarely on the national agenda. The old guard has attempted to intimidate the elected members through legal action, and journalists have been imprisoned for reporting events. No one questions the continued existence of the monarchy, and King Tupou IV is dearly loved by most of his subjects, but the intermediate noble class is declining in both economic and political influence.

In a way, Tonga's current political problems are a direct result of the absence of colonization, because a European system of representative government was not instituted in Tonga as part of a normal decolonization process, as happened in virtually every other island state. The world has changed beyond recognition since 1875, yet Tonga's missionary-inspired constitution remains the law of the land. This cannot last forever and the future of the monarchy may well depend on its ability to adapt to the times and accept a fully elected parliament. Interestingly Crown Prince Tupouto'a is a computer-savvy mover and shaker who may leapfrog Tonga from the 19th into 21st century as soon as he becomes king.

ECONOMY

Agriculture and Land

In Tonga's feudal system, all land is property of the crown but administered by nobles who allot it to the common people. The king and nobles retain 27% of the land for their own use, while the government owns another 18%. Although Tongan commoners still have a right to the 3.34-hectare *tax'api* granted them by King George Tupou I, there's no longer enough land to go around. This system has not been altered substantially since 1862, and a 1976 parliamentary law intended to redistribute unused land was vetoed by the king. Frustrations with the system are relieved by migration to New Zealand, Australia, and the United States. If those avenues were to close, Tonga would face serious unrest. Foreigners cannot purchase land, and even leasing requires Cabinet approval.

Only half the population is involved in the cash economy; the rest live from subsistence agriculture, fishing, and collecting. The production of food, housing, and handicrafts used by the producer is higher than the value of all goods sold for cash, a situation rarely reflected in official statistics. The staples are yams, taro, manioc, and sweet potato. Crops are rotated, and up to two-thirds of a garden is left fallow at any time. In many localities, humans are outnumbered by domestic pigs, which range freely across the islands.

The biggest cash crop is pumpkins (squash), and since its introduction in 1987, this vegetable has become Tonga's biggest export by far, shipped mostly to Japan by air and worth T$11 million a year. Over 13,000 tonnes of Tongan pumpkins supply about half Japan's requirements for November and December, a "niche market" producers in other parts of the world can't cover for climatic reasons. Some 700 small farmers grow pumpkins July-Dec., and overproduction has led to soil degradation, groundwater pollution, deforestation, and an increase in pests. Much of the income has gone into cars, and throughout the day there's now bumper-to-bumper traffic on Nuku'alofa's Taufa'ahau Road as nouveau riche Tongans drive up and down to show off. Tonga's growing dependence on this monoculture carries with it the risk of economic collapse should the Japanese market evaporate due to competition from producers in Vanuatu and New Caledonia, a fall in yields caused by depleted soils, plant disease, or any other cause. In 1998 the harvest was 50% lower than usual due to drought. Vanilla is seen as an alternative, and the production, though still small, fetches top prices on world markets.

Trade and Development

Tonga's main exports in order of importance are pumpkins, vanilla, tuna, leather goods, clothing, coconut oil, and taro. Although it had a favorable trade balance prior to 1960, Tonga now imports seven times as much as it exports, with food imports alone exceeding all exports. Australia and New Zealand profit most from the trade imbalance, selling food, machinery, fuels, and manufactured goods to Tonga. Japan, Australia, the European Union, New Zealand, the United Nations Development Program, and the Utah-based Church of Latter-day Saints are Tonga's largest aid donors, and total aid compensates for a third of the trade deficit.

In 1980 the government created a Small Industries Center (SIC) in the eastern section of Nuku'alofa for companies producing consumer goods for export to Australia and New Zealand under the regional free-trade agreement, SPARTECA, which was designed to correct the imbalance. In recent years the value of SPARTECA had declined due to "globalization," a worldwide liberalization of trade, and Tongan exports of knitwear, leather jackets, and footballs have been pushed off Australasian markets by competitors in Asia. Today companies in the SIC produce mostly for a tariff-sheltered local market. Traditional agricultural exports to New Zealand such as bananas were wiped out by transnational producers and strict quarantine requirements. The replanting of Tonga's aging coconut plantations has been inadequate and copra exports have dwindled to almost nothing in recent years. The Tonga Commodities Board coconut products plant outside Nuku'alofa closed in 1996. Commercial fishing is on the increase with longline vessels supplying tuna to the Pago Pago canneries and quality fish like red snapper to restaurants in Honolulu and Tokyo by air freight.

Tonga has thus far avoided the financial crises that have gripped Samoa in recent years, but both countries are still very much part of the third world. The T$50 million a year remitted by Tongans living abroad, the country's largest single source of income, is crucial to maintaining the balance of payments, covering over half Tonga's import bill. In future years these amounts could decline as emigrants lose touch with relatives and friends back home. Meanwhile rural areas are neglected as government facilities and light industry gravitate toward Nuku'alofa. A quarter of all Tongans now live in the capital, and hundreds more commute daily from outlying villages. Shantytowns have sprung up in the suburbs of Nuku'alofa, and there's a growing gap between the haves and have-nots. In 1986 the income tax was slashed from 40% to a flat 10% and company taxes were greatly reduced; the lost revenue was made up by a five percent sales tax, an unprecedented shift in taxation from rich to poor. Labor unions are banned.

The royal family itself has used its unquestioned political clout to assemble extensive business interests. Crown Prince Tupouto'a is a major shareholder in Royal Beer Company, MBf Bank Ltd., and Sea Star Fishing Co., plus electricity generation, an insurance company, computer technology, and real estate developments, while Princess Pilolevu Tuita is involved in the airport duty free trade and satellite communications. According to New Zealand journalist Michael Field, the crown prince and princess have squabbled recently over control of Tonga's lucrative satellite slots, and Tonga's abrupt diplomatic switch from Taiwan to China in November 1998 was a result of lobbying by Princess P.

Communications

In 1989 Tonga scored a coup by claiming six satellite orbital slots, which it registered with the International Telecommunications Union over the objections of most large satellite communications companies. One condition was that the slots had to actually be used within 10 years, so a company called Tongasat was formed with Princess Pilolevu as 60% shareholder. Thanks to American telecommunications experts who arranged the leasing of Tonga's valuable slots, Tongasat managed to get two satellites into orbit launched from Kazakhstan and several more have been sub-let to Asian companies (Beijing is the latest target market). Tongasat and the government have split income from this arrangement: *Forbes Magazine* reports that Princess P herself has pocketed a cool US$25 million.

A lot of complicated maneuvering has gone on behind the scenes. In 1995 the scheme's Malaysian financiers filed suit when the U.S. partner declared bankruptcy after being paid US$38 million by the Malaysians. The transnational Intelsat has claimed that the scheme violates international agreements that declare that geostationary arcs are common property and not meant to be claimed by countries with the intention of leasing them to third parties. In 1993 an Indonesian company muscled into one of Tonga's slots and in 1995 they started radio-jamming Tonga's other satellites to warn the Tongans to back off. To remain a commercial satellite superpower, Tonga has had to take on the big boys.

A similar scheme involves the marketing of Tonga's internet code ".to" for use in registering desirable domain names already occupied under the ".com" ending. In its first year, Tonic (www.tonic.to), a join venture between Crown Prince Tupouto'a and a couple of California computer bugs, sold 7,000 domain names at US$50 each. This is a lot cheaper than the US$1,000 a name being charged for Tuvalu's catchier ".tv" ending! (Despite all the high tech dabbling, Tonga's domestic telephone network is unchanged since the early 1950s.)

Sale of Passports

In recent years Tonga has peddled its nationality directly by selling Tongan passports to Hong Kong Chinese and others in need of an alternative nationality. In 1983 Tonga began selling "Tongan Protected Persons" passports to all comers at US$10,000 a shot. As the bearers still required a visa to enter Tonga, many countries, including Australia and New Zealand, refused to recognize them. Thus in 1984 legislation was passed allowing ordinary Tongan passports and naturalization certificates to be issued to anyone willing to pay US$20,000—among the takers were Imelda Marcos and her children. This was questioned by commoner members of the Tongan parliament, who pointed out that the five-year residency requirement was being ignored, so in 1988 the previous legislation was repealed, but the sales strangely continued.

In 1989 Mr. 'Akilisi Pohiva, the leading people's representative in parliament, filed suit against the ministers of finance and police and the government, claiming that the sale of passports to foreigners was unlawful. It took Pohiva a year to formulate his case, then another year to get a court date, and in February 1991, just as the Supreme Court was about to act, the government called an emergency session of parliament to alter the constitution to legalize things. When it became obvious that the government intended to use its large majority of appointed members to ram through the amendment, the three people's representatives from Tongatapu walked out. On 7 March 1991, 2,500 people marched through Nuku'alofa to the Royal Palace to present petitions protesting the constitutional changes, the largest popular demonstration of its kind in Tongan history.

In all, some 450 ordinary passports and another 2,570 "special" passports were sold between 1983 and 1991. The passport scheme has brought in an estimated US$25 million, and the sales may be continuing (although the government periodically denies this). Many countries, including Australia, New Zealand, and Fiji, do not recognize these mail-order passports, and even genuine Tongans traveling on bona fide Tongan passports occasionally face unexpected immigration hassles abroad as a result of this scam. The number of Chinese-operated hotels and restaurants in Nuku'alofa indicates where many of the buyers ended up.

Tourism

Earnings from tourism are higher than all exports combined, and a larger proportion of the tourist dollar remains in Tonga than is the case elsewhere in the Pacific because of the high proportion of small, locally owned guesthouses and motels. Tonga is off the beaten track and is seldom overrun by tourists (Fiji gets 14 times as many visitors). About 26,000 tourists a year visit Tonga, coming from New Zealand, the U.S., Australia, Germany, and Fiji, in that order. Nearly half are overseas Tongans visiting friends and relatives.

Vava'u is being developed as Tonga's main international tourist center, and the European Union has provided funds to upgrade Vava'u's airport to allow direct flights from Fiji. One of the South Pacific's most important yacht charter operations has been based at Vava'u for years, and since 1995 whalewatching has been developed. Scuba diving, kayaking, fishing, and cultural tourism are all on the upswing at Vava'u.

THE PEOPLE

For visitors, Tonga is its culture and people. The Tongans are exceptionally warm, relaxed, impassive toward delays, etc., and with the world's lowest death rate, it seems Tongans even pass away slowly. They have a lot of fun and tease each other and sympathetic visitors constantly. The very happy, contented lifestyle is summed up in expressions like *mo'ui fiemalie* (a contented life), *mo'ui nonga* (a peaceful life), *nofo fiefia* (living happily), and *nofo fakalata* (making others feel at home). It's also said that if a Tongan loses his identity, he will slowly become cold and die.

Tonga is typical of developing countries, with its large families and young population. Tongans reside in small villages near their bush gardens, and except in the Europeanized areas, isolated houses along the roads are rare. Most Tongans live in tin-roofed wooden or cement block houses with electricity and running water, and only 12% still live in traditional thatched *fales.* With 150 people per square kilometer, Tonga is one of the most densely populated countries in the Pacific (twice as dense as the Cooks, three times as dense as Fiji). Yet despite a high birth rate, emigration has kept population figures stable since the 1970s. Around 3,000 Tongans a year leave the country, many for good, and some 24,000 now live in New Zealand, 11,000 in the U.S., and 4,500 in Australia.

In Tonga women have traditionally enjoyed a higher social status than in some other parts of Polynesia due to the *fahu* system, which gives Tongan women certain authority over male family members. The eldest sister is the family matriarch, exercising considerable control over younger brothers, nephews, and nieces. Public life in Tonga, however, is almost completely dominated by men due to sexist succession and land ownership laws, as well as cultural norms.

The missionaries increased the importance of the family unit. Each family member has a role, with the older persons commanding the most respect. Children may reside with an aunt or uncle just as easily as with their parents and

ta'ovala-clad women at a wedding

are taught obedience from an early age, which is why they are so much better behaved than Samoan children. The most important occasions in Tongan life are first and twenty-first birthdays, marriages, and funerals. Tonga has the lowest infant mortality rate and one of the highest levels of school enrollment in the South Pacific, and 99.6% of Tongans are literate.

Acculturation is proceeding fast in Nuku'alofa, where many families now have a VCR, and the dozens of video rental outlets do roaring business. There are few controls on videos, and Tongans can see everything from horror to soft pornography on their screens. The videos have effectively done away with *faka'apa'apa,* or respect between brother and sister, an old taboo that would never have allowed them to sit in the same room and watch a sex scene. (This also explains some of the physical attention lone foreign women receive from Tongan men at discos.)

Tongans have a long traditional history, and many can name up to 39 generations by heart. There is little social mobility: a commoner can never become a noble, though a noble or a member of the royal family can be stripped of his title. Commoners have been appointed Cabinet ministers through education and ability, however, and may be elevated to the rank of *matapule* (talking chief), a spokesperson for the king or a noble. Ordinary Tongans must use a special

CEMETERIES

Tongan cemeteries are unique. Usually set in a grove of frangipani trees, the graves are strange, sandy mounds marked with flags and banners, surrounded by inverted beer bottles, artificial flowers, seashells, and black volcanic rocks. Recent innovations are the miniature houses and concrete tombs, painted in the national colors red and white or decorated with art. Prior to emancipation in 1862 the graves of commoners were unmarked, and when popular cemeteries began to materialize, the Tongans adopted a scaled-down *langi* form that had been used for centuries by nobility. To honor the dead, valuable gifts such as tapa cloth, fine mats, quilts, and family heirlooms are placed on the graves, and these are *tapu*. Family members, great mats tied about their waists, spend several weeks after the funeral sitting next to the burial, leaving the area at night for fear of ghosts. They continue to visit with declining frequency for about a year, but after that the grave is abandoned as it's believed that the spirit of the deceased remains and can cause sickness among the living and even another death. On public holidays such as All Saint's Day and Christmas people return to the cemeteries to clean up the family plots.

Beer bottles are recycled into grave markers in cemeteries such as this one at Makave, Vava'u.

dialect quite different from everyday Tongan when speaking to a noble or member of the royal family. An equivalent English example for "eating heartily" might go as follows: commoners *gorge,* the nobles *feed,* and the king *dines.*

To a Tongan, great physical size is the measure of beauty—Tongan women begin increasing prodigiously in beauty from age 15 onward.

Traditional Dress

The *ta'ovala* is the distinctive Tongan traditional skirt. The custom may have originated when Tongan mariners used canoe sails to cloak their nakedness. Made of a finely woven pandanus-leaf mat, the *ta'ovala* is worn around the waist. The men secure it with a coconut-fiber cord, while the women wear a *kiekie* waistband. The sight of a group of Tongan women on the road, each with a huge pandanus mat tied around herself, is truly striking. Worn especially on formal occasions, these mats are often prized heirlooms. Tongans dress in black and wear huge *ta'ovalas* when mourning. The king and queen wear European dress to a European function but dress in their plaited *ta'ovala,* tied around the waist over the *vala* (skirt or kilt), and wear sandals or go barefoot to a Tongan ceremony or entertainment.

Religion

The bold red cross in the upper left corner of the royal red Tongan flag symbolize the facts of life in this country. The Tongan Constitution (drafted by Methodist missionary Shirley Baker) declares the Sabbath day forever sacred: it's unlawful to work, hold sporting events, or trade on Sunday. Contracts signed that day are void. Most tours are also canceled, though picnic trips do run to the small islands off Nuku'alofa. All shops and most restaurants are closed on Sunday. The Sabbath is so strong that even the Seventh-Day Adventists here observe Sunday as the Lord's Day (not Saturday). They claim this is permissible because of the "bend" in the international date line, but it would be intolerable to have two Sundays in Tonga!

Tongans are great churchgoers—a third of all Tongans and most of the noble class are members of the mainstream Free Wesleyan Church. Three other branches of Methodism also have large followings in Tonga: the Free

Church of Tonga (9,250 members), the Church of Tonga (6,250 members), and the Tokaikolo Christian Fellowship (2,600 members). In addition, there are 14,200 Mormons, 13,500 Roman Catholics, and 5,000 Seventh-Day Adventists. Smaller groups include the Anglicans, Assemblies of God, and Baha'is. In all, 16 official churches are active in the country, and missionaries from new groups are arriving all the time. Between 1966 and 1992 affiliation in the new religious groups increased from 9.7% to 29.5% of Tongans as all four Methodist churches declined.

Attend the service at Centenary Church (Free Wesleyan) in Nuku'alofa Sunday at 1000 to hear the magnificent church choir and perhaps catch a glimpse of the royal family. Gentlemen are expected to wear coats and ties (although tourists are usually admitted without). After church, the rest of the day is spent relaxing, strolling, and visiting friends—what Tongans like to do anyway, so it wasn't hard for the missionaries to convince them to set aside a whole day for it.

The Mormons

Mormons account for around 15% of the population of Tonga, the highest such ratio in the world. The Church of Latter-day Saints has become the largest private employer in the kingdom, spending more on construction than even the government, and the American church sends far more financial aid to its Tongan flock than the U.S. government provides to Tonga as a whole. Mormon missionary efforts in Tonga are aimed at making this the first country on earth with a Mormon majority.

Assembly line Mormon churches (with their inevitable basketball courts) are popping up in villages all over Tonga as the children of Israel convert in droves to be eligible for the free buildings, schools, sporting facilities, and children's lunches. Many Tongans become "school Mormons," joining as their children approach high school age and dropping out as they complete college in Hawaii. Unlike Cook Islanders and American Samoans, Tongans don't have the free right of entry to a larger country, so church help in gaining a toehold in Honolulu or Salt Lake City is highly valued.

Mormonism still has a lower profile in Nuku'alofa, however, as the king, a Wesleyan, is reputed to be uncomfortable with the new fast-faith religion. A building behind the International Dateline Hotel was a Mormon church until it was judged too close to the palace for comfort. The present Nuku'alofa Tonga Temple, the largest building in Tonga, is beside Mormon-operated Liahona High School near Houma on the opposite side of the island. Recently the king has been refusing to renew any Mormon land leases. Yet the Church of Jesus Christ of Latter-day Saints is a bastion of conservatism and a strong supporter of the political status quo (which is rather ironic in view of American posturing on democracy and human rights in other parts of the world).

CONDUCT AND CUSTOMS

The key to getting things done in Tonga is knowing how to find the right person. Tongans hate to say no to requests, and if you ask people to do things which really aren't their responsibility, they may give the impression of agreeing to do them, but in fact nothing will happen. Tongans in official positions may seem sluggish and could keep you waiting while they finish chatting with friends over the phone. Just keep smiling and be patient: they'll notice that and will usually go out of their way to be helpful once they get around to you. Impatiently demanding service will have the opposite effect (it's illegal to anger or threaten a civil servant in Tonga). One reader's comment: "Although definitely not as open and outgoing as Fijians, I appreciated the Tongans' uncomplicated and straightforward way of dealing with foreigners. I didn't pick up any of Apia's strange vibes here."

Both men and women appearing in public topless are punished with a T$20 fine. Of course, this doesn't apply to men at the beach. Like Victorian English, Tongans often go swimming fully dressed—most of them don't even have bathing suits. For a Tongan woman to appear in a halter top and miniskirt is almost unthinkable, and female travelers too will feel more accepted in skirts or long pants than in shorts. A woman in a bathing suit on a beach anywhere other than in front of a resort will attract unwelcome attention, and it would be prudent to keep a T-shirt on at all times and to cover your legs with a *lavalava* while out of the water. It's also considered bad form to kiss or even hold hands in public. (Despite all the strident public morality, in private Tongans are often sexually permissive, and it's commonplace for married men to have affairs.)

In Tonga the possession of dope is a serious offense, and the word soon gets around. Customs watches for yachts with drugs aboard. If you're busted, they'll toss you in a tiny flea-ridden cell and throw away the key. Make no mistake—they mean business.

Be careful too with your gear in Tonga, as there have been reports of thefts—don't tempt people by leaving valuables unattended. Even hotel rooms are unsafe. It's said that a Tongan will never buy anything if he thinks he can borrow or steal it. Thus, *everything* left unattended will be pilfered, especially if it's out where anyone could have taken it. This also applies to food and drink left in the communal fridge at a hotel or guest house that also has Tongan guests. It's safe to invite one or two Tongans to your home or room, but with three or more things will disappear. Items left on the beach while you're in swimming will have vanished by the time you come out of the water. Armed robbery, on the other hand, is almost unheard of.

Dogs can be a nuisance in Tonga, chasing cyclists and barking through the night. They can be especially aggressive as you approach a private residence, but pretending to pick up a stone will usually be enough to scare them away. (Looking at it the other way, you'll see some of the most wretched, abused dogs in the world in Tonga, and it's not surprising that they bite.)

ON THE ROAD

HIGHLIGHTS

Tonga stands out for its living Polynesian culture, which can be traced from the Ha'amonga trilithon on northeastern Tongatapu through the ancient *langi* or royal tombs of Mu'a to the gingerbread Royal Palace in downtown Nuku'alofa. Traditional arts and crafts are nurtured and preserved at the Tonga National Center just south of town. The country's most charming town, however, is Neiafu, which faces Vava'u's magnificent Port of Refuge Harbor. In fact, along with Levuka in Fiji and Gizo in the Solomons, Neiafu is one of the three most picturesque towns in the South Pacific.

Tonga's foremost natural feature is probably its coastal cliffs, especially the striking limestone formations at Keleti Beach Resort on Tongatapu, the east coast of 'Eua Island, and the north coast of Vava'u. Lovers of wildlife will not wish to miss the flying foxes of Kolovai on Tongatapu. Humpback whales come to Ha'apai and Vava'u to mate and calve July-Oct., and there are whale-watching cruises from Neiafu at this time. You're even allowed to snorkel with the whales, if conditions allow.

SPORTS AND RECREATION

Although Tonga's preeminent hiking areas are on 'Eua and its only golf course is on Tongatapu, it is Vava'u that has the most to offer water sports enthusiasts. Vava'u is a famous sailing locale with one of the South Pacific's largest yacht charter operations. It's also perfect for ocean kayaking with lots of lovely protected waterways; a kayak touring company operates in this area. Deep-sea anglers too will find Tonga's top charter fishing boats based here. There's also undeveloped potential for windsurfing at Vava'u, but the mecca for regular reef-break surfers is Ha'atafu Beach on Tongatapu. In Samoa the surfing waves tend to be far offshore (boat required), while in Tonga you can often swim out from shore. It's no place for beginners, however.

Southern swells arrive May-Sept., northern swells from Dec.-February.

Scuba divers are well catered for by professional dive shops in Nuku'alofa, Lifuka, and Neiafu, with many outstanding diving possibilities. Snorkelers have even more options, beginning with the island resorts off Nuku'alofa, all of which operate day-trips by boat. The finest snorkeling off Tongatapu itself is reputed to be at Ha'atafu Beach. At Ha'apai there's excellent snorkeling at the Captain Cook Beach Resort on Uoleva Island. At Vava'u, visitors can get in some excellent snorkeling by taking a day excursion from Neiafu by boat.

MUSIC AND DANCE

Music

Tongan church music is renowned and the singing of choir and congregation is often backed by a Salvation Army-style brass band. Traditionally a *lali* (slit drum) is beaten just before the service to call the faithful to prayer. The Tongans transformed the hymns taught by early missionaries, singing in minor instead of major. They also created hymns of their own, called *hiva usu,* which are closer to traditional chants than the imported hymns. The *hiva usu* are now most commonly sung at services of the Free Church of Tonga and the Church of Tonga, the most conservative of Tonga's four branches of Methodism.

Harmonious Polynesian singing can also be heard at kava-drinking sessions *(faikava),* when groups of men sing popular Tongan songs to entertain themselves. Tonga's traditional string bands (guitar, violin, banjo, bass, and ukulele) have been upstaged by modern electric pop bands, though the former may still be heard at hotels, private parties, or even *faikava.* Public festivities and parades are animated by college brass bands. The traditional *fangufangu* (bamboo nose flute) would probably have died out had not the 'Atenisi Institute in Nuku'alofa begun to teach its use. The *'utete* (jew's harp) is a child's toy formed from a coconut leaf held horizontally across the mouth by a palm leaf midrib, which is twanged. Other Tongan instruments include the *nafa* (skin drum), *kele'a* (conch shell), and the *tutua* (tapa-beating mallet). The *mimiha* (panpipes) seen by Captain Cook are no longer used.

Dance

Traditional Tongan dances are stories sung by the singers and acted out by the dancers. As in Samoa (and unlike Tahiti and Rarotonga), the words are represented by movements of the hands and feet, not the hips. The graceful movements of the female dancers contrast with those of the males, who dance with great vigor. A *punake* is a combination poet, composer, and choreographer who writes the songs then trains and leads the dancers.

The *lakalaka* is a standing dance that begins slowly but builds to a rhythmic finish. The male and female dancers stand on opposite sides of the stage, backed by a choir, and everyone sings a song especially composed for the occasion. A major *lakalaka* can involve hundreds of people and last half an hour. The *ma'ulu'ulu* is a sitting dance usually performed by groups of women accompanied by *nafa* on formal occasions. Standing girls perform the *ula*. Unlike these, the *kailao,* or war dance, has no accompanying song. The stamping feet, shouts of the leader, and insistent rhythm of the drums combine to make this dance popular among visitors. Very different is the dignified *tau'olunga,* in which a girl dances alone, knees held closely together, at weddings or village functions.

Your best chance to see real Tongan dancing is a fund-raising event (watch how the Tongans contribute, then give your share), on national holidays or during visits by VIPs. The Tonga National Center in Nuku'alofa presents two Tongan dance shows a week, as do some of the hotels and resorts. For a listing of compact discs of traditional Tongan music turn to Resources at the end of this volume.

PUBLIC HOLIDAYS AND FESTIVALS

Public holidays include New Year's Day, Good Friday, Easter Monday (March/April), ANZAC Day (25 April), Crown Prince's Birthday (4 May), Emancipation Day (4 June), King's Birthday (4 July), Constitution Day (4 November), King Tupou I Day (4 December), and Christmas Days (25 and 26 December).

The **Vava'u Festival** during the first week of May features all sorts of sporting, cultural, and social events to mark Crown Prince Tupouto'a's birthday on 4 May. The **Ha'apai Festival** coincides with Emancipation Day in early June. Nuku'alofa's **Heilala Festival,** with brass band and dancing contests, parades, and sporting competitions, occupies the week coinciding with the king's birthday, the first week in July. The Miss Galaxy beauty contest for *fakaleitis* (men dressed as women) is great fun and always sold-out. On the night of 4 July and again on New Year's Eve, Tongans standing along the beach light palm-leaf torches, illuminating the entire coast in rite called *tupakapakanava.*

Agricultural shows are held throughout Tonga during September and October, with the king in attendance at each. The ferry *Olovaha* makes special trips at these times, so ask and book early. Red Cross Week in May is marked by several fund-raising activities, including a grand ball. During the National Music Association Festival in late June and early July you can hear string bands, brass bands, electric bands, and singers. A military parade in Nuku'alofa marks the closing of parliament in late October. The Tonga Visitors Bureau should know what's happening.

ARTS AND CRAFTS

Most of the traditional handicrafts are made by women: woven baskets, mats, and tapa cloth. The weaving is mostly of tan, brown, black, and white pandanus leaves. The large sturdy baskets have pandanus wrapped around coconut-leaf midribs. A big one-meter-high laundry basket makes an excellent container to fill with other smaller purchases for shipment home. (Remember, however, that the post office will not accept articles more than a meter long or weighing over 10 kilograms by airmail or 20 kilograms by surface mail, though this does vary according to destination.) The soft, fine white mats from the Niuas, often decorated with colored wool, are outstanding but seldom sold.

Tonga's tapa cloth originates mostly on Tongatapu, where the paper mulberry tree *(Brous-*

sonetia papyrifera) grows best. When the tree is about four meters high the bark is stripped and beaten into pieces up to 20 meters long, then hand-painted with natural brown and tan dyes. The cloth itself is called tapa but the painted product is known as *ngatu*. Big pieces of *ngatu* make excellent wall hangings or ceiling covers. In the villages, listen for the rhythmic pounding of tapa cloth mallets. The women are always happy to let you watch the process, and you may be able to buy something directly from them. Small-

Miniature wooden statues of this kind were the only graven images made in Tonga. In 1830 the missionary John Williams witnessed the desecration of five of these at Ha'apai by hanging.

er pieces made for sale to tourists are often sloppily painted in a hurried fashion, and serving trays, fans, and purses made from tapa are often in poor taste.

Unfortunately too, Tongan woodcarving is now oriented toward producing imitation Hawaiian or Maori "tikis" for sale to tourists. Some shops will tell you the figures represent traditional Tongan gods, which is nonsense. Buy them if you wish, but know that they're not traditionally Tongan. The beautiful war clubs one sees in museums are rarely made today, perhaps out of fear they might be used! Tongan kava bowls are also vastly inferior to those made in Samoa and Fiji.

Many handicraft shops in Tonga sell items made from turtle shell, whale bone, ivory, black coral, seeds, and other materials that are prohibited entry into the U.S., New Zealand, and many other countries, so be careful. Triton shells, conch shells, giant helmet shells, giant clam shells, winged oyster pearl shells, trochus shells, green snail shells, and other sea shells may also be banned. It's one of the negative aspects of tourism that such a catalog of endangered species should be so widely sold.

ACCOMMODATIONS AND FOOD

All of the middle and upmarket hotels add five percent sales tax to their rates, plus a further five percent room tax, which covers the salaries of the staff at the Tonga Visitors Bureau—money well spent, right? This 10% tax usually won't be included in the amount you're quoted when you ask the price of a room and will be added when the time arrives to pay. We also do not include tax in the Tonga accommodation prices listed in this book.

Inexpensive accommodations are readily available, but upmarket places are less common, and even in the select few, the service is often lacking. Many of the larger upscale hotels are over a quarter of a century old and it shows. Tonga has nothing to compare with the luxury hotels of Bora Bora or the designer resorts of Fiji where one can easily spend a thousand dollars a day, but who needs them? Just be aware that some of the shoestring and budget lodgings listed herein are extremely basic. This has advantages and disadvantages, but for the adventurous it's mostly advantageous. And although sometimes a bit more expensive than Samoa, Tonga has some beautifully situated places to stay, for example, at the Popao Village Eco Resort at Vava'u one can experience Tongan life as it was decades ago.

Two organized campgrounds are just outside Nuku'alofa and some of the budget beach resorts will also allow you to pitch your own tent on their grounds. Camping was recently banned in Ha'apai, so if you were thinking of unrolling the tent, don't stop there. Unlike in Fiji and Samoa (but as in the Cook Islands), you'll rarely be invited to spend the night in a local home. It's not forbidden to stay with the locals (as it is on Rarotonga), it's just that the Tongans prefer to keep a certain distance between themselves and *palangi* tourists. On the plus side, you won't be expected to conform to as many complex social mores here as you would in Samoa, and people tend to leave you alone.

Self-catering accommodations are harder to find than in Cook Islands or Fiji, and only a few of the guesthouses in Nuku'alofa have cooking facilities. At Ha'apai most accommodations do allow cooking, but grudgingly, and they levy a T$2 pp charge for gas and electricity. Several places at Vava'u allow you to cook. Neiafu and Nuku'alofa have good public markets. Some stores sell horrendous fatty New Zealand mutton flaps called *sipi*, which unfortunately constitute the diet of many Tongans. Canned corned beef and salty luncheon meat are also popular. Restaurant meals are inexpensive, and Tonga is an ice cream lover's paradise with huge, inexpensive cones easy to find in Nuku'alofa. *Ota* is raw fish marinated in lime juice and coconut cream.

Of Tonga's gargantuan feasts, the most spectacular are those marking such important events as King Tupou IV's coronation or Queen Elizabeth's visit, which feature a whole roasted suckling pig for *each* of the thousands of guests. Literally tons of food are piled on long platters *(polas)* for these occasions, including taro, yams, cassava, breadfruit, sweet potato, fish, lobster, octopus, chicken, pork, corned beef, cooked taro leaves, and fruit. Cooking is done in an underground oven *(umu)*, and coconut cream is added to everything. Less earthshaking feasts

are put on for visitors to Tongatapu and Vava'u. Try to attend at least one.

The tap water is chlorinated and it won't bother you if you have a strong stomach, otherwise boil it or drink something else. Several readers have reported that the water made them sick. Unfortunately beer is expensive in Tonga because it only comes in little 330-ml bottles, not the big 750-ml bottles used in most other Pacific countries.

SERVICES AND INFORMATION

Visas and Officialdom

Visitors in possession of a passport and onward ticket do not require a visa for a stay of one month. Extensions of up to six months are possible at T$25 each (although the actual length of the extension is entirely up to the officers).

Government authorization is required to do any sort of scientific research in Tonga, including archaeological excavations and sociological studies. The application fee of T$1,000 is refundable if your project is approved. Clearly, officialdom wants to control just who is poking around. Recently one researcher on alcoholism had his application rejected. No drinking problems in Tonga, was the reply!

Ports of entry for cruising yachts are Niuafo'ou, Niuatoputapu, Vava'u, Lifuka, and Nuku'alofa. Yachts arriving from the east should call at Vava'u before Nuku'alofa (and Samoa before Tonga), as the prevailing winds make it much easier to sail from Vava'u to Nuku'alofa than vice versa and there are fewer hazardous reefs between Nuku'alofa and Fiji than between Vava'u and Fiji. Customs and immigration are closed on weekends, and even on weekdays once can expect long waits at Vava'u before the officials come aboard to clear you in.

Money

The Tongan *pa'anga* (divided into 100 *seniti*) is worth about the same as the Australian dollar (around US$1 = T$1.65), although the actual value fluctuates slightly. From 1976 to 1991 the *pa'anga* was actually tied to the Australian dollar, but it's now based on a basket of the Australian, New Zealand, and U.S. dollars. There are notes of one, two, five, 10, 20, and 50 *pa'anga,* and coins of one, two, five, 10, 20, and 50 *seniti*. Try to keep a supply of small coins in your pocket if you don't want petty expenditures to be rounded up to your disadvantage. Tongan banknotes are difficult to exchange outside Tonga, so get rid of them before you leave.

The Bank of Tonga is 40% government-owned, with the Bank of Hawaii and the Westpac Bank of Australia each holding another 30%. Change money at the bank branches in Nuku'alofa, Ononua ('Eua), Pangai (Lifuka), and Neiafu (Vava'u). The banks are very crowded on Friday (pay day) but a few branches in Nuku'alofa and Neiafu are open Saturday mornings. Foreign banknotes are changed at a rate about four percent lower than traveler's checks. The banks will give cash advances on credit cards for a T$6 commission. Cash advances through hotels cost about 10% commission and many businesses add 4.5% to all charges paid by credit card. Thus it's probably better to carry the bulk of your travel funds in traveler's checks. There's no American Express representative in Tonga.

Tipping and bargaining are not customary here, although monetary gifts *(fakapale)* are often given to performers at cultural events (Tongans stick small bills onto the well-oiled arms and shoulders of the dancers during the performance). A five percent sales tax is added to all goods and services. It's often hard to tell if this tax is included in sticker price. Many stores include it, but some (such as Morris Hedstrom Supermarket) add it on at the cash register. At hotels and restaurants, you really never know and the only way to be sure is to ask first.

Post and Telecommunications

The government-owned Tonga Telecommunications Commission (Box 46, Nuku'alofa; tel. 24-255, fax 24-800) runs the domestic telephone service within Tonga, while the British company Cable & Wireless (Private Mailbag 4, Nuku'alofa; tel. 23-499, fax 22-970, www.candw.to) operates the international service. Guess which one is more efficient.

As in Samoa, the local telephone system is hasn't changed much since it was installed in the 1950s, and there are no public card or coin telephones for domestic calls. To place a local call, you must use your hotel phone or go to a central telephone office and have the clerk dial

the number for you. When your party answers, the clerk will direct you to a booth and what you pay will depend on how long you spoke. This procedure must be repeated for each individual call you wish to make. Everyone in the office will hear everything you say as you'll have to shout to be heard at the other end. The upside is that it's cheap: long-distance interisland calls within Tonga are only T$1 for three minutes. Urgent telegrams within Tonga cost 10 cents a word.

In 1995 card telephones were introduced on Tongatapu, but only for international calls. You cannot use these phones to call another island or even the number across the street. International telephone cards are available in denominations of T$5, T$10, and T$20. Not only do they make calling easier and more private but they're also cheaper since three-minute minimums don't apply with the cards. As with all direct-dial telephones in Tonga, the international access code is 00.

Three-minute calls cost T$5 to Australia or New Zealand, or T$9.50 to Canada, the U.S., or Europe. Person-to-person calls are T$2.50 extra. Collect calls are possible to Australia, New Zealand, the U.S., and the U.K. (but not to Canada or Germany). Internationally, faxing is a good inexpensive alternative to telephoning.

The telephone exchanges where you can make phone calls are listed in the travel sections of this chapter. Calls placed from hotel rooms are much more expensive. Directory assistance is 919, the interisland operator 910, the international operator 913. The Telecom "New Zealand Direct" number is tel. 080-0646. Tonga's telephone code is 676.

Cable and Wireless operates Tonga's kalianet.to e-mail service, named for the double-hulled Tongan war canoe called the *kalia*. If any of the e-mail addresses in this book don't work, try substituting candw.to for kalianet.to or vice versa, and consult the e-mail directory at www.candw.to. Nuku'alofa's cybercafe is listed in the Nuku'alofa section.

Business Hours and Time

Normal business hours are weekdays 0800-1300/1400-1700, Saturday 0800-1200. Government working hours are weekdays 0830-1230 and 1330-1630. Banking hours are weekdays 0900-1530. Post offices are open weekdays 0830-1600. Almost everything is closed on Sunday.

Due to its position just west of the international date line, Tonga is the first country in the world to usher in each new day. In fact, the date line seems to have so confused the local roosters that they crow constantly just to be safe. A tremendous bash is planned for New Year's Eve, 1999, as hundreds of world celebrities usher in the new millennium in an extravaganza to be televised around the world. All Tongan hotel rooms for that period were fully booked years in advance. Tonga shares its day with Fiji, New Zealand, and Australia, but is one day ahead of Samoa, Niue, Tahiti, and Hawaii. The time is the same as in Samoa, but one hour behind Hawaii and one ahead of Fiji and New Zealand.

Tonga's sacred Sunday adds to the fun of the date line confusion. Commercial flights (and most other transport) are banned in the kingdom that day. Don't get worried if you suddenly realize that it's Sunday on a flight to Tonga from Honolulu or Samoa—you'll land on Monday. Just keep repeating: "If it's Sunday for the Samoans, it's Monday for the monarch."

Friday is a much bigger party night than Saturday because most Tongans get paid on Friday, so there's money to spend and the fun doesn't all have to stop at midnight. Only holy rolling is allowed on Sunday, but some bars, discos, and cinemas reopen a few minutes after midnight on Monday morning and try to make up for the time lost on the sabbath.

Electricity
The electric voltage is 240 volts, 50 cycles, with a three-pronged plug used, as in Australia and New Zealand.

Media
The government-owned *Tonga Chronicle* (Box 197, Nuku'alofa; tel. 23-302, fax 23-336, e-mail: chroni@kalianet.to) comes out every Thursday and you can usually pick up a copy at the Friendly Islands Bookshop in Nuku'alofa. The English edition is less extensive than the one in Tongan.

Taimi 'o Tonga (Times of Tonga, Box 880, Nuku'alofa; tel./fax 23-177, www.tongatimes.com, e-mail: times@kalianet.to), is a privately operated Tongan-language weekly paper with a circulation of 6,100. (In September 1996 Mr. 'Akilisi Pohiva, the leading pro-democracy member of parliament, and the editor and sub-editor of the *Times* were arrested for "contempt of parliament" after the paper published the text of an impeachment motion against the minister of justice. The three were tried by parliament and the minister himself was one of those voting for a guilty verdict, and they were sentenced to 30 days in jail. After the three had spent 26 days behind bars, the chief justice of the Supreme Court ruled that they had been detained illegally and ordered their release. When parliament later voted by a narrow margin to hold an impeachment hearing against the minister of justice, the king dissolved parliament. Subsequently the sub-editor was rearrested for publishing a letter critical of the government in the *Times*.)

Also watch for the monthly newsletter *Kele'a* (Box 1567, Nuku'alofa), published by 'Akilisi Pohiva, leader of the democratic reform movement in parliament. The newsletter's attempts to expose corruption among the old guard have made it the object of libel suits involving awards of thousands of *pa'anga* in damages.

The worldwide subscription rate to the bimonthly national news magazine *Matangi Tonga* (Box 427, Nuku'alofa; tel. 25-779, fax 24-749, e-mail: vapress@kalianet.to) is US$25 (airmail)—a practical way to keep in touch. The same company publishes a free tourist newspaper called *'Eva.*

Radio
The government-run Tonga Broadcasting Commission (Box 36, Nuku'alofa; tel. 23-555, fax 24-

The Tonga Chronicle

40 seniti

Where Time Begins

Nuku'alofa, TONGA

417) transmits in Tongan and English over 1017 kHz AM Mon.-Sat. 0600-2400 and Sunday 1600-2300. FM 97 at 97.2 MHz broadcasts in English only Mon.-Sat. 0630-2300 and Sunday 1600-2300. On both stations you can hear the BBC news at 0700 and Radio Australia news at 0800, followed by a weather report. The FM station presents the news in brief at 1100 and 1700, and major news bulletins at 0900, 1300, and 1900, while the AM station has the Radio Australia news at 2000. An hour of classical music is broadcast over the AM station Sunday at 1630. The TBC transmitter at Vava'u was destroyed during a hurricane and you can only receive the AM station there very weakly. The AM is much stronger at Ha'apai and you should be able to receive both stations clearly on Tongatapu and 'Eua.

A private commercial station called The New Millennium Radio A3V (tel. 25-891, e-mail: vearw@alaska.net) at FM 89.1 MHz broadcasts no news but plays the best selection of pop music you'll hear anywhere in the South Pacific. It's part of the empire of the Vea brothers, Ron, Phil, and Sam, who also own Loni's Cinema and the adjacent video rental shop in Nuku'alofa. Ron has lived in Alaska since 1970 and tapes a show there, while Sam actually runs the station and Phil takes his turn as DJ.

Vavau's local station, FM1, is a private commercial operator broadcasting over 89.3 MHz 24 hours a day.

Information Offices

The Tonga Visitors Bureau (Box 37, Nuku'alofa; tel. 21-733, fax 23-507, www.vacations.tvb.gov.to, e-mail: tvb@kalianet.to) has information offices in Nuku'alofa, Lifuka, and Neiafu. Drop in or write for a supply of free brochures. These offices are good places to ask about events and much useful data is posted on their information boards.

TRANSPORTATION

Getting There

Tonga's government-owned flag carrier, **Royal Tongan Airlines** (Private Mail Bag 9, Nuku'alofa; tel. 23-414, fax 24-056, e-mail: rtamktng@kalianet.to), has flights to Tongatapu from Sydney via Auckland twice a week, from Nadi three times a week, and from Auckland four times a week.

Weekly flights operate between Apia and Tongatapu (T$303 one-way or T$320 for a one-month excursion return), between Niue and Tongatapu (T$228/357 one-way/roundtrip), and between Nadi and Vava'u (T$265/399 one-way/roundtrip). Royal Tongan also controls seats on one of Air New Zealand's flights to Honolulu with connections to Los Angeles under a code sharing arrangement. In the U.S., call 1-800/486-6426 for information about Royal Tongan, and check their useful internet website (www.candw.to/rta), which explains some of their air passes and provides schedules.

Samoa's **Polynesian Airlines** (tel. 21-566) arrives from Apia, Auckland, and Sydney twice a week. The Fijian airline, **Air Pacific** (tel. 23-423), has service to Tongatapu from Nadi three times a week. Around Christmas all flights are fully booked six months in advance by Tongans returning home.

Air New Zealand (tel. 23-828) has direct weekly flights from Apia, Honolulu, and Los Angeles with connections from London. Their flights between Tonga and Auckland operate three times a week. This Coral Route connection is discussed under **Getting There** in the main Introduction.

Samoa Air (tel. 70-644) has services twice a week from Pago Pago to Vava'u (US$235/424 one-way/roundtrip), a useful backdoor route. Their Tonga agents are S.F. Paea & Sons in Neiafu and Teta Tours in Nuku'alofa.

Getting Around by Air

In 1991 **Royal Tongan Airlines** (tel. 23-414) replaced Friendly Islands Airways as Tonga's national carrier. Royal Tongan has Twin Otter flights from Tongatapu to 'Eua (T$19), Ha'apai (T$67), Vava'u (T$129), Niuatoputapu (T$227), and Niuafo'ou (T$279), but never on Sunday. The flights to 'Eua and Ha'apai operate daily, to Vava'u twice a day, to the Niuas every other week. Book a northbound Friday or Saturday flight from Nuku'alofa to escape a depressing Sunday in the capital. Ask about special packages from Nuku'alofa to Vava'u including airfare, transfers, accommodations, breakfast, and some meals. A 30-day "Kingdom Pass" allowing flights from Tongatapu to 'Eua, Ha'apai, and Vava'u is available at T$250 (a 20% savings over regular fares), but it must be purchased beforehand in Europe or North America. The baggage allowance is only 10 kilos, but if your Royal Tongan domestic flights were booked from abroad as part of an international ticket the baggage allowance is 20 kilos. Overweight baggage is 45 cents a kilogram.

In "emergencies" Royal Tongan bumps passengers with confirmed reservations if VIPs need their seats. This doesn't happen often, but be forewarned and check in early (never less than 30 minutes prior to the flight). Always reconfirm your onward flights a few days in advance. "No shows" are liable for a penalty of 50% of the ticket price if they fail to use confirmed space, but Royal Tongan reserves the right to cancel any flight without compensation. Flights to Vava'u are heavily booked. In fact, the staff is friendly and cooperative, which makes the occasional hiccup easier to take.

Getting Around by Ship

The government-owned **Shipping Corporation of Polynesia** (Box 453, Nuku'alofa; tel. 21-699, fax 22-617), at Queen Salote Wharf, Nuku'alofa, offers reliable boat service among the Tonga Islands. Their large car ferry, the MV *Olovaha,* departs Nuku'alofa every Tuesday at 1730, arriving at Pangai (T$28 deck) very early Wednesday morning and Vava'u (T$42 deck) on Wednesday afternoon. It leaves Vava'u again Thursday afternoon, calling at Pangai in the middle of the night and arriving back in Nuku'alofa Friday afternoon. In Ha'apai the ship calls at both Ha'afeva and Pangai. It's usually punctual.

Deck travel is sometimes very crowded but when the ship isn't too full you can stretch out on the plastic benches or the floor in a clean, protected room. No meals are included. Cabins cost four times the deck fare, as you must book an entire twin room (T$120 double to Ha'apai, T$170 double to Vava'u). There are only four such cabins, and they can be just as noisy as deck, though more comfortable. The Shipping Corporation runs a boat from Vava'u to Niuatoputapu (T$50) and Niuafo'ou (T$60) about once a month.

The private **Uata Shipping Lines** ('Uliti Uata, Box 100, Nuku'alofa; tel. 23-855, fax 23-860), also known as the Walter Shipping Lines, has four red-and-white ships, the MV *Loto Ha'angana,* the MV *Tautahi,* the MV *'Ikale,* and the MV *Pulupaki.* The 32-meter *Loto Ha'angana,*

an old Japanese ferry, is larger and faster than the *Olovaha,* but it does toss a bit more. The *Loto Ha'angana* or *Tautahi* leaves Nuku'alofa Monday at 1700, reaching Pangai in the middle of the night and Vava'u Tuesday afternoon. It departs Vava'u for Ha'apai and Nuku'alofa Wednesday at 1400, stopping at Pangai late that night and reaching Nuku'alofa Thursday morning. No cabins are available. Take food, water, and anti-seasickness pills. The *Loto Ha'angana* has lots of long padded benches on which you can stretch out and try to get some sleep if it's not too crowded (as is usually the case between Ha'apai and Vava'u). The loud music broadcast over the ship's public address system all night is a disadvantage.

Other small ships serving Ha'apai irregularly include the wooden *Langi Fo'ou,* which leaves Nuku'alofa's Faua Jetty for Nomuka Wednesday mornings, an eight-hour trip.

Several boats shuttle back and forth between Nuku'alofa and 'Eua (2.5 hours, T$6). The blue-and-white *Alai Moana* departs Faua Jetty daily except Sunday at 1300, leaving 'Eua for the return around 0600 in the morning. You pay onboard. It's a safe metal ferry with rows of plastic seats. The 24-meter MV *Pulupaki,* smallest of the Uata Shipping Lines ferries, and the 220-passenger *'Ikale,* also travel between Nuku'alofa and 'Eua. One or the other is supposed to leave Faua Jetty Mon.-Fri. at 1230, returning in the early morning, but the trip is canceled in choppy weather. However you go, be prepared for an extremely rough four-hour eastbound trip and a smoother, faster westbound voyage.

Note that all of the above information is only an indication of what might or should happen in ideal weather—the reality is often quite different. Make careful inquiries upon arrival and be prepared for a few delays. It's all part of the fun. (For information on yacht charters, turn to the **Vava'u** section.)

Airport

Fua'amotu International Airport (TBU) is 21 km southeast of Nuku'alofa. The new terminal building was constructed with Japanese aid money in 1991. The airport is closed on Sunday.

The airport bus (T$6 pp) operates four times a day. If there are two or more of you, the T$12 taxi fare to town is just as good or better. Be sure to check the fare before getting into the taxi, and don't let the driver steer you to some hotel you never intended to stay at just so he can collect a commission. Often they will tell you the hotel you requested is closed only in order to trick you into going where *they* want. Hope that your flight doesn't arrive in Tonga late at night as the taxis demand as much as T$30 then. Avis and E.M. Jones Travel have car rental offices at the airport.

Airport-bound, the International Dateline and Pacific Royale hotels have buses directly to the terminal costing T$6 pp, but they're only worth taking if you're alone. If you're on the lowest of budgets you could also take the infrequent Fua'amotu bus (70 cents) right to the airport access road, or any Mu'a bus to the crossroads at Malapo, then hitch the last six km. An Austrian reader sent us this comment:

I was put off by the dudes at the airport. Those people are worse than the most vicious hostel runners at European railway stations during the summer peak season. I had hardly left the terminal and had people all over me. It helps if you know exactly what you want and where (and how) to go.

The Tonga Visitors Bureau counter and the MBf Bank exchange office are to the right as you come out of arrivals. The MBf Bank at the airport changes traveler's checks at a rate similar to the banks in town, less their standard T$3 commission. The snack bar at the airport is reasonable and offers a good selection, and across the parking lot is a small farmers market with coconuts, pineapples, bananas, peanuts, etc. The duty-free shop in the departure lounge is also reasonably priced. The departure tax on international flights is T$20 (passengers in transit for under 24 hours and children under 12 are exempt).

TONGATAPU

Tongatapu's 259 square km are just over a third of the kingdom's surface area, yet two-thirds of Tonga's population lives here. Of coral origin, Tongatapu is flat with a slight tilt—from 18.2-meter cliffs south of the airport to partly submerged islands and reefs to the north. Some 20,000 years ago Tongatapu was blanketed with volcanic ash from the explosion of Tofua Island, creating the rich soil that today supports intensive agriculture.

Tongatapu, or "Sacred Tonga," is the heartland of Tongan culture, history, and political power. Here Captain James Cook conferred with Tu'i Tonga, and the island is still the seat of Tongan royalty. The Tonga National Center outside the capital, Nuku'alofa, showcases Tongan culture, and compelling megalith monuments and royal tombs testify to Tongatapu's historical weight. Vying for visitor attention are noisy colonies of sacred flying foxes, an admirable bird park, breathtaking beaches, remarkable coastlines, tapping tapa mallets, and evocative archaeological remains. And unlike Samoa, no "custom fees" are collected from visitors out to see the island's sights. Cook was enthralled by Tongatapu, and you will be too.

NUKU'ALOFA

Nuku'alofa (population 22,000) is just north of the azure Fanga'uta Lagoon, now sterile after sewage from adjacent Vaiola Hospital eliminated the fish and other marinelife. It's a dusty, ramshackle little place. Tourism, industry, commerce, and government are all concentrated in the town, which retains its slow-paced South Seas atmosphere. You'll find a good selection of places to stay, eat, and drink, reasonable entertainment (except on Sunday), a well-developed transportation network, and many reminders of Tonga's Victorian past and present. The name means "Abode of Love." A few days poking around here are certainly well spent, but this should not be the beginning and end of your Tongan trip as the other islands have even more to offer.

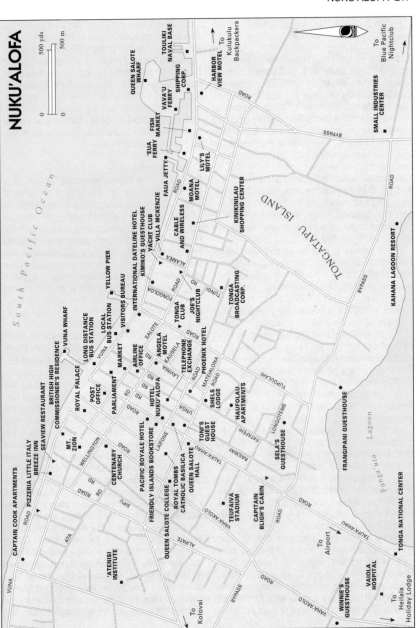

NUKU'ALOFA

SIGHTS

Begin your visit at **Vuna Wharf,** the main port of entry to Tonga from 1906 until construction of Queen Salote Wharf in 1967. The **Treasury Building** (1928), opposite the wharf, was once Nuku'alofa's main post office. Nearby on Railway Road (named for a former line that once carried copra to the wharf and still Nuku'alofa's only one-way street) is the **House of Parliament,** a small wooden building prefabricated in New Zealand and reassembled here in 1894. The 30 members of parliament deliberate May-Oct. (no visitors). Walk through the park across the street from the parliament building, passing the **Tongan War Memorial,** and turn left on Taufa'ahau Road to the century-old **prime minister's office,** with its central tower.

Continue west across the soccer field beside the Bank of Tonga to the Victorian **Royal Palace,** closed to the public but easily viewed from outside the grounds. This gingerbread palace was also prefabricated in New Zealand for reassembly here in 1867. The second-story veranda was added in 1882. The gables and scalloped eaves of this white frame building are crowned by a red roof and surrounded by Norfolk pines. (The king and queen no longer live here but in the Fua'amotu Palace south of the airport. The stately villa of the crown prince is at Pea, on the airport road, and across the street from it is the residence of another prince with a pair of white Bengali tigers guarding the gate.)

Many old colonial-style residences line Vuna Road west of the palace, including the **British High Commissioner's residence,** with a flagpole surrounded by cannon from the privateer *Port-au-Prince,* sacked at Ha'apai in 1806. South of the residence is **Mt. Zion,** site of an 18th-century Tongan fortress and, in 1830, the first missionary chapel. This hill is now crowned by several communications towers.

Centenary Church (1952), south of Mt. Zion, is the principle house of worship of the Free Wesleyan Church, the largest of Tonga's three Methodist denominations. Some 2,000 persons can be seated here, and most Sunday mornings the king and queen are among them for the 1000 service. The church's president lives in the impressive mansion (1871) on the west side of the church, a former residence of 19th-century missionary and Tongan premier Rev. Shirley Baker.

East on the south side of Laifone Road are the **Royal Tombs,** where Tongan royalty has been buried since 1893. Across Laifone Road from the Royal Tombs is another important Free Wesleyan church, which was only completed in 1985. The striking **Basilica of St. Anthony of Padua** (1980), back on Taufa'ahau Road, is worth visiting for its soaring interior.

Cultural Center

Don't miss the **Tonga National Center** (Box 2598, Nuku'alofa; tel. 23-022), a complex of Polynesian-style buildings beside the Fanga'uta Lagoon opposite Vaiola Hospital; the complex was built in 1988 using Japanese aid money. Here you'll see handicraft demonstrations (tapa and canoe making, woodcarving, basket making, mat weaving), contemporary art, and historical displays. The Center's impressive Exhibition Hall contains historic photos of Tonga and Samoa, a collection of war clubs and other carvings, and model canoes. The hall is open weekdays 0900-1600, admission T$2.

Weekdays at 1230 the Center prepares a barbecue lunch and traditional fashion show (T$12), and at 1400 the excellent two-hour guided cultural tour begins, featuring a kava ceremony, the telling of ancient legends and myths, and traditional Tongan dancing in the 450-seat amphitheater (T$8). The handicraft workshops will be operating at this time, and craft items may be purchased directly from the artisans. Some of the activities are curtailed or canceled when not enough visitors are on hand, so you might check that there really will be a performance in the amphitheater that day. Tuesday and Thursday are the usually the best days to come; otherwise just visit the museum and craft shop and come back for the evening performance another day.

Not to be missed is the dinner show put on every Tuesday and Thursday at 1900 (T$20). The package includes a visit to the exhibition hall, string band entertainment, kava drinking, an all-you-can-eat buffet dinner of authentic Tongan cuisine, and some very good traditional dancing (take small banknotes to give to the dancers). A small additional charge is collected for minibus hotel transfers. Advance reservations are required if you want to take lunch or dinner. Reserve the evening shows before 1630 at either the Tonga Visitors Bureau or directly by phone. Admission for children under 12 is half price to all of the above events.

Sports and Recreation

Since 1984 Bob and Sioa Holcomb of **Coralhead Diving Ltd.** (Box 211, Nuku'alofa; tel. 22-176) have offered scuba diving using the dive boat *African Queen*. A two-tank boat dive will cost T$95 pp, plus 5% tax. Lunch at Pangaimotu Island is T$10 extra. They depart Mon.-Sat. at 1000. Coralhead also does one-week PADI certification courses (T$400 pp), an excellent opportunity to learn diving. They will rent or repair equipment and fill tanks, and they specialize in underwater photography and night dives. Drop into their office on the back street behind Davina's Restaurant near Faua Jetty for information.

Tonga's newest scuba operation, the **Deep Blue Dive Center** (Box 913, Nuku'alofa; tel. 25-392, fax 29-647, e-mail: deepblue@kalianet.to), on Wellington Rd. near Fakalato Chinese Restaurant, is under German management. In 1999 they bought out another local scuba operator and while much of Coralhead's trade comes from government and business contracts, Deep Blue caters almost exclusively to the tourist market. A full-day package, including two dives and lunch, is T$105/120 without/with equipment. Reductions are available for five or 10 dives, and snorkelers can go along for T$35. Their open-water certification course is T$400. Their 15-meter dive boat *Deep Blue* is always accompanied by a speedboat for fast pickups and deliveries.

One of the favorite local dive sites is **Hakaumama'o Reef**, 14 km north of Nuku'alofa, a deep wall populated by large numbers of brilliant parrot fish. **Malinoa Island** to the southeast features a great variety of marinelife on the surrounding reef, plus a lighthouse and some old graves on the island itself. Both of the above are marine reserves, and taking fish, clams, or coral is prohibited (T$200 fine). Black coral can be seen at **Kings Reef** just off Nuku'alofa. Visibility ranges from 15 meters within the Tongatapu Lagoon to 50 meters on the barrier reefs. A wetsuit is recommended during the cooler months, April-August.

The nine-hole **Tonga Golf Club** (no phone; closed Sunday) is opposite the indoor stadium at Alele near Veitongo on the road to the airport. Greens fees are only T$5 but club hire is not available. Saturday 1130-2100, the club bar is worth a stop. The Heilala Classic Golf Tournament is at the beginning of July. The club is easily accessible on the Folaha, Malapo, Vaini, or Veitongo buses.

Friday or Saturday at 1500 (April-June) catch a game of rugby at the Teufaiva Stadium. During the soccer season (May-July) you can watch the teams compete at the Pangai Soccer Field on the waterfront next to the Bank of Tonga Saturday at 1500. Joggers meet in front of the Bank of Tonga every Monday at 1700 for a recreational run. It's a good way to meet local expats.

ACCOMMODATIONS

The accommodations listings below are arranged beginning with those closest to Queen Salote Wharf and Faua Jetty, then southwest through town. The only places with satisfactory communal cooking facilities are Kulukulu Backpackers, Toni's Guest House, Sela's Guest House, Breeze Inn, Angela Motel, Liubeck Motel, Winnies Guesthouse, Heilala Holiday Lodge, Friendly Islander Hotel, and Captain Cook Apartments, although not all rooms at these have access. Unless otherwise stated, add 10% tax to all accommodation rates quoted below.

Shoestring

The **Kulukulu Backpackers and Tentsite** (Box 1682, Nuku'alofa; tel. 22-412, fax 24-113), next door to the Friendly Islander Hotel, is three km east of town. The road next to Flemming Engineering leads directly back to the shady campsite where you'll pay T$6 pp to pitch your own tent. There's also an unusual domed dormitory with rooms of three and four beds at T$9 pp. Otherwise take one of the four beds on the second floor of the wooden building opposite the waterfront at T$12 pp. Communal cooking and fridge facilities are provided in both dorms and picnic tables are available for campers. Bring groceries as no stores are nearby. The Octopusy Bar adjacent to the campground has another bizarre dome that conveys whispers from one side of the room to the other. This eccentric place is the creation of a Danish woman named Brida Hou—a memorable place to stay. Although a little far from town, it's quite convenient to Queen Salote Wharf and Faua Jetty (take the Va'epopua bus from opposite the Tonga Visitors Bureau).

Kimiko's Guest House (Box 1323, Nuku'alofa; tel. 22-170), next to the Chinese Embassy on Vuna Rd., has nine bare but clean rooms with shared bath at T$10 pp (discounts for long stays). Empty beds in the double rooms are filled up as new guests arrive—singles must share or pay for both beds. There are no cooking facilities in this old wooden house (where the author stayed on his first visit to Tonga in 1978) but their agreeable Chinese restaurant is one of the few places open on Sunday. The fresh sea breeze is another plus (though no fans are in the rooms).

Angela Guest House (Box 1617, Nuku'alofa; tel. 22-896), above Angela Restaurant on Taufa'ahau Rd. and opposite the Pacific Royale Hotel, has five rooms with shared bath at T$10 pp. There are no cooking facilities. Angela Motel, included in our budget category and under the same Chinese management, is better value unless you're alone and just want a cheap single.

The Chinese-operated **Phoenix Hotel** (Box 2410, Nuku'alofa; tel. 23-270, fax 21-834) on Fatafehi Rd. has rooms with bath at T$20 single or double downstairs or T$25 upstairs. Noise from the adjacent nightclub rocks the whole complex nightly except Sunday, and this place is only of interest to lowlife swingers.

Toni's Guest House (Toni, Kesi, and Vili, Box 3084, Nuku'alofa; tel. 21-049, fax 22-970), on Mateialona Rd. near Queen Salote Memorial Hall, has eight clean rooms with shared bath at T$10 pp (bring mosquito coils). It's a good place to meet other travelers as guests swap stories around the kava bowl every evening. There's a pleasant lounge, but Toni's biggest advantage are the cooking facilities, which are the best you'll find in the shoestring range. Kesi's full day minibus tour is a bargain at T$15 pp (T$20 for nonguests), otherwise the Mu'a and Hihifo buses stop right across the street from the guesthouse if you'd rather go on your own. Toni's rents bicycles to guests only (T$5-10 a day), and snorkeling gear is free. Some travelers

find Toni's English reserve and Kesi's forthright enthusiasm a bit odd, but you'll enjoy being with them if you accept them as they are. Toni charges T$6 pp for airport transfers. Don't believe airport taxi drivers who tell you this place is closed or full: they only want to take you elsewhere in order to collect a commission—insist on being driven straight to Toni's.

Though a bit out of the way, **Sela's Guest House** (Box 24, Nuku'alofa; tel. 21-430, fax 22-755), south of town, has been a favorite of overseas volunteers working in Tonga since the mid-1970s. There are nine clean rooms with shared facilities at T$15/24 single/double, plus a T$8 eight-bed dormitory. The six rooms with private bath and hot shower are T$30/36 double/triple. Discounts are available for long stays. Cooking facilities for guests are provided, or you can order a full breakfast for T$4.50 and a large dinner for T$10. Sela serves the best home-cooked meals you'll receive at any guesthouse in Nuku'alofa (which perhaps accounts for the many repeat visitors). If noise bothers you, however, ask for a room away from the VCR and dining room. On the positive side, you can sit and watch videos or CNN to your heart's content. It's a good family-style place to relax and local meet people, and it's seldom full. The Halaleva bus from opposite the Tonga Visitors Bureau will bring you to within a block and a half of the guesthouse (ask).

Budget

The **Harbor View Motel** (Box 83, Nuku'alofa; tel. 25-488, fax 25-490), next to the Fakafanua Center opposite Queen Salote Wharf, has 12 clean rooms with private bath in a modern three-story building. Prices range from budget rooms downstairs with shared bath at T$35/50 single/double, to standard a/c rooms on the middle floor with private bath at T$60 single or double, and deluxe rooms on the top floor with fridge at S$120 single or double. No cooking facilities are available but a buffet breakfast is included. It's a good medium-priced choice near the interisland ferries and some colorful eating and drinking places.

Lily's Motel (Private Bag 38, Nuku'alofa; tel. 24-226, fax 24-389), opposite Faua Jetty, has six rooms with bath behind their large Chinese restaurant at T$30/35 single/double. Friday nights a live band plays until 0400.

The **Moana Motel** (Box 169, Nuku'alofa; tel. 21-440), opposite Faua Jetty, has three bungalows with private facilities at T$14/28 single/double. Although the location is great if you're planning to catch a ferry, the Moana is poorly managed and you may have difficulty finding anyone to check you in. For this reason (and their noisy bar) there are seldom any guests.

The five-room **Fasi-moe-Afi Guest House** (Box 1392, Nuku'alofa; tel. 22-289, fax 23-313), next to the Visitors Bureau on Vuna Rd., is T$15 pp, including a good breakfast. The lighting in the rooms could be better—ask for one on the outside. The adjacent cafe/pizzeria is great for cappuccino and a sandwich on the terrace. The Fasi-moe-Afi is something of a hangout for Italian backpackers, and a live band plays in the back yard until well after midnight on Thursday and Friday nights.

The **Breeze Inn** (Box 2739, Nuku'alofa; tel. 23-947, fax 22-970), next to the Seaview Restaurant west of the palace on Vuna Rd., has seven spacious rooms with private bath (hot water) at T$30/40 single/double. Communal cooking facilities are available. This place is run by a very helpful Japanese woman who keeps everything spotlessly clean, so make it your choice if you're the fussy type.

Two-story **Angela Motel** (Box 1617, Nuku'alofa; tel. 23-930, fax 22-149), on Wellington Rd. in the center of town, has eight small, clean rooms with private bath at T$20/30/45 single/double/triple. The Taiwanese managers provide guests with a common kitchen and fridge. It's convenient enough for a couple of nights.

Shels Lodge (Box 1752, Nuku'alofa; tel. 25-037), on Fatafehi Rd. a block south of the Phoenix, offers 34 fan-cooled rooms with bath at T$20/30 single/double. The rooms are arrayed around the interior courtyard of an unfinished two-story building and construction seems to have halted abruptly. The communal cooking facilities are extremely basic, consisting of only a stove and fridge (bring your own pots and plates). Until they fix up the kitchen and do a bit more work on the building, this place should not be your choice. Most of the guests are Chinese transients waiting for visas to somewhere else.

The **Liubeck International Motel** (Box 1282, Nuku'alofa; tel. 25-948, fax 25-678), on Unga Rd., is a small two-room bungalow with shared bath, lounge, kitchen, and fridge at T$30/40 single/double per room. Discounts are available for long stays. The Liubeck is rocked on Friday and Saturday nights by a heavy disco beat from the Phoenix Disco two blocks away.

Frangipani Guest House (Box 1416, Nuku'alofa; tel. 22-036), on Alaivahamamgo Rd. southeast of town, has one single room at the back of the house for T$25 and a double facing the Fanga'uta Lagoon at T$45. Both have private bath but cooking facilities are not available. You'd have to pretty foolish to stay here as the owner's vicious dogs are certain to get you eventually.

Winnies Guesthouse (Box 3049, Nuku'alofa; tel./fax 25-215), on Vaka'akolo Rd. near Vaiola hospital, two km south of the center, tries to recapture the atmosphere of an old South Seas guesthouse. The four rooms with shared bath are T$25 pp including a fruit and toast breakfast, and good communal cooking facilities are available. It's comfortable, with a plush sitting room where videos are shown nightly, and Winnie Santos and her son Mark are very helpful. The Vaiola bus stops at their door.

A variety of accommodations are available at **Heilala Holiday Lodge** (Box 1698, Nuku'alofa; tel. 29-910, fax 29-410), in a pleasant rural setting at Tofoa, three km south of town (off the road to the airport). The four fan-cooled rooms upstairs in the main two-story house are T$24/28 single/double, and there's also a larger family room at T$32 for up to three. Bathrooms are shared (hot water and *very* clean) and communal cooking facilities are provided. Out back in the garden are two thatched *fales* with bath costing T$45 single or double. The six new a/c deluxe bungalows with fridge and TV are T$60. In addition, Heilala offers Tonga's number one **camping facilities** across the street at T$6 pp. There's a rain shelter, picnic tables, and adjacent toilets/showers, and you can make tea from the lemongrass growing in the garden or feed on the papayas and bananas. If you don't have a tent, they'll rent you one at T$2 a night. When enough guests are present, an *umu* lunch is prepared at the campground at T$8 pp. A portable swimming pool and restaurant are on the premises. The whole place runs efficiently under the firm hand of a German woman named Waltraud Quick (or Maria as the Tongans call her) and her more laid back son Sven. They arrange six-hour island tours with German-speaking guides at T$35 pp (minimum of four); one day they cover the west side of the island, another day the east side. Two weeks free luggage storage if offered against a T$20 deposit that can be applied to future accommodation charges (after two weeks the deposit is nonrefundable). Many of the guests are German or Swiss, which surprisingly seems to put off the Germans as much as it does some of the other nationalities. Airport transfers are usually free (T$3 pp for campers)—ask for Sven at the airport. Heilala is easily accessible to town by bus or taxi, and bicycles are available at T$5 a day.

Inexpensive

The 31-room **Friendly Islander Hotel** (Box 142, Nuku'alofa; tel. 23-810, fax 24-199), on Vuna Rd. 500 meters beyond the Shell oil storage tanks three km east of town, has long been a favorite medium-priced place to stay. The 12 older fan-cooled apartments with cooking facilities and balcony in a two-story building near the main road are T$50/60 single/double for a one-bedroom or T$60/70 for a two-bedroom. The eight smaller bungalows without cooking facilities across the lane are T$65/75, while the six larger a/c units (also without cooking facilities) are T$85 for the first person, then T$10 for each additional person. All units have a fridge. In the hotel's rear garden is the Culture Bar, dedicated to the concept of "eco-tourism," with a small botanical garden, a woodcarvers workshop currently run by master carver Steven Fehoko, a kava drinking hall, and a regular bar. Campers are allowed to pitch their own tents in this garden and a cultural show with *umu* cooking is organized for groups. A restaurant, swimming pool, and the 'Ofa Atu Night Club round out the facilities. The Friendly Islander is run by Papiloa Foliaki, a former elected member of parliament and current head of the local transvestite association—an interesting person to meet! The hotel is easily accessible on the Va'epopua bus from opposite the Tonga Visitors Bureau.

Captain Cook Vacation Apartments (Phillip Vea, Box 1959, Nuku'alofa; tel. 23-615, fax 25-600), on Vuna Rd. facing the lagoon a kilometer west of the Royal Palace, offers four two-bedroom apartments accommodating up to four persons at T$55/65/75/85 single/double/triple/quad. Each apartment has a kitchen, living room, and private bath. It's an excellent choice for two couples traveling together, but book ahead.

The German-owned **Hotel Nuku'alofa** (Uthana Sanft Taumoepeau, Box 32, Nuku'alofa; tel. 24-244, fax 23-154), above the MBf Bank on Taufa'ahua Rd., has 14 spacious a/c rooms with private bath and fridge at T$60/75/90 single/double/triple. There's a restaurant and bar.

The Italian-operated **Kahana Lagoon Resort** (Box 3097, Nuku'alofa; tel./fax 24-967) is on the Fanga'uta Lagoon about five km southeast of town. The seven spacious, attractively decorated *fales* units with private bath vary in price from T$65/80 single/double to T$100 or T$140 double, depending on size and location. The swimming pool could use a cleaning and there's no beach, but canoes are available for use on the lagoon. Cooking facilities are not provided, but the resort has a large restaurant/bar. The whole resort is cooled by gentle breezes across the lagoon, but it has a bit of an abandoned feel. It's easily accessible on the Halalevu bus from town, but. . . .

Moderate

Anne and Milton McKenzie's **Villa McKenzie** (Box 1892, Nuku'alofa; tel./fax 24-998), on Vuna Rd. near the Yacht Club, offers four comfortable rooms with bath in a colonial-style house at T$85/115 single/double including tax and full breakfast. There's a spacious lounge, but no cooking facilities for guests (dinner is T$15 pp extra). Although expensive for what is offered, it's a good alternative to the Dateline and Pacific Royale, with a lot more South Seas atmosphere.

The three-story, government-owned **International Dateline Hotel** (Box 39, Nuku'alofa; tel. 23-411, fax 23-410) on Vuna Rd. was originally built in 1967 to accommodate guests at the coronation of King Taufa'ahau Tupou IV. The 76 a/c rooms with private bath and fridge begin at T$81/94/105 single/double/triple in the old wing along Vuna Road. The rooms in the adjacent new wing on Tupoulahi Rd. are better at T$109/120/130. Renovations and extensions are planned for the millennium celebrations. The Dateline has a pleasant resort feeling and the location is excellent. Their reasonably priced restaurant is one of the few open to the public on

Sunday, and Polynesian dance shows are staged here Wednesday and Saturday nights at 2030. If you pay T$18 for the buffet (Wednesday) or the set three-course menu (Saturday), there's no cover charge. Otherwise T$5 is collected at the door. Despite the flip-flop-shod waiters, persons dressed in shorts, T-shirts, or sandals are not admitted to the dining room. A cold beer by the Dateline's pool is the perfect way to top off an afternoon and nonguests are allowed to swim upon payment of a T$2 fee (remember this if you're stuck in town on Sunday). Excursions to the islands just off Nuku'alofa can be booked at the hotel's tours and information desk, and transportation to the wharf is included.

The more commercial **Pacific Royale Hotel** (Box 74, Nuku'alofa; tel. 23-344, fax 23-833) on Taufa'ahau Rd. is owned by the Ramanlal brothers, sons of a Fiji Indian father and Tongan mother. The 15 standard rooms are T$70/85/95 single/double/triple, the 45 superior rooms T$99/115/125. All 60 rooms have private bath, fridge, and noisy air-conditioners, but they're dimly lit and rather overpriced. Back from the flashy reception area, just past the restaurant, is a tiny garden and swimming pool. Although the service is good here, the Dateline is a more memorable place to stay.

Long Stays

The information board at the Tonga Visitors Bureau lists furnished houses for rent at T$300-500 a month. You could also talk to Jimmy Matthews at the **House Rental Agency** (Box 134, Nuku'alofa; tel. 22-011, fax 22-970; weekdays 0930-1200) in the Tungi Arcade, who will try to place you at two-story Holiday Apartments, in an industrial area near Vaiola Hospital at Havelulotu, two km south of town. A one-bedroom there will be T$50/70 single/double a night, a two-bedroom T$65/90 (reductions for long stays), including cooking facilities, gas, electricity, and telephone (local calls free), and a swimming pool is on the premises. Occasionally Jimmy also organizes cheaper flats at under T$400 a month without phone or hot water, over T$400 a month with hot water. In these you must supply your own linen, cutlery, and crockery.

A more local place to stay is Dr. Mumui Tatola's **Olo Resort** (Box 2834, Nuku'alofa; tel. 29-945), beside the Fanga'uta Lagoon, four km south of town on the airport road. The eight smaller *fales* with private bath and cooking facilities are T$150 a month, while two larger houses are T$500 a month. Beds and cooking utensils are provided, but you have to pay for your own gas, water, and electricity, and supply your own sheets. The units are in a garden setting, some near the road, others pleasantly located on a slope overlooking the lagoon. Inquire at Olota'ane Store, which is accessible on the Vaiola bus.

Haufolau Apartments (tel. 21-151), on Fatafehi Rd., charges T$250 double or T$300 quad per month for each of the three two-bedroom self-catering apartments fully furnished with fridge and utensils. You must pay your own gas, electricity, and water, which might total another T$50 a month. Of course, at those prices it's almost always full.

FOOD

Budget

'Ahopanilolo's Training Restaurant (tel. 25-091), down the street beside St. Mary's Catholic Cathedral opposite Queen Salote Wharf, serves a "pot luck" lunch at T$3-6 on Tuesday, Wednesday, and Friday 1200-1400. It's only open during the school year, March-Nov., but is always fun.

John's Place Takeaway (tel. 21-246), on Taufa'ahau Rd. in the center of town and opposite Vaiola Hospital (close to the Tonga National Center), dishes out hamburgers, grilled chicken and chips, and cassava and curry. It's okay for a quick snack, but with a little effort you'll do better elsewhere for the same money. They're open until midnight, but closed Sunday. **Angela Restaurant** (tel. 23-341; closed Sunday), next door to John's Taufa'ahau Rd. location, is similar but better.

Akiko's Restaurant (tel. 25-339; open Mon.-Fri. 1130-1400 and 1830-2000), in the basement of the Catholic basilica on Taufa'ahau Rd., has long been a budget standby. The lunch special is good, and there's a more extensive menu at dinner (but no alcohol).

Captain Bligh's Cabin (tel. 23-841), on Taufa'ahau Rd. next to Asco Motors south of the center, has a nice terrace where you can enjoy lunch specials at around T$4. Beer is sold.

Chinese

One of the best value Chinese places is **Kimiko Restaurant** (tel. 22-170) on Vuna Rd. facing the waterfront: try the wonton soup (T$2). Kimiko's is one of the few places open on Sunday.

The **Tong Hua Restaurant** (tel. 24-343) on Salote Rd. serves a substantial fried chicken lunch 1100-1400 for T$2.50.

The attractive **Fakalato Chinese Restaurant** (tel. 24-044, closed Sunday), above a super-market on Wellington Rd., serves medium-priced Cantonese dishes of the type familiar to North Americans, so there will be no difficulty ordering. (While you're there, check out the Italian ice cream place nearby on the corner of Taufa'a-hau Road.)

Italian

The **Italian Garden Restaurant** (tel. 23-313), at the Fasi-moe-Afi Guest House near the Tonga Visitors Bureau on Vuna Rd., serves pizzas big enough for two or three people. The appealing garden atmosphere compensates for the slow service, so long as you're not in a hurry. It's one of the few places in Nuku'alofa that's open for dinner on Sunday (1800-2300).

Pizzeria Little Italy (tel. 21-563; Mon.- Sat. 1200-1400/1830-2300), west on the waterfront beyond the Seaview Restaurant, serves some of the tastiest pizza and pasta in Tonga.

Upscale Restaurants

Several seafood restaurants are opposite the fish market at Faua Jetty, including **Davina's Restaurant** (tel. 23-385; closed Sunday), the **Waterfront Grill** (tel. 24-692), and **Lily's Chinese Restaurant** (tel. 24-226). Davina's has an elegant indoor dining room with a piano. The **Billfish Bar and Restaurant** (tel. 24-084, closed Sunday), opposite Queen Salote Wharf, has Italian dishes.

Nuku'alofa's finest place to eat is the **Seaview Restaurant** (tel. 23-709; weekdays 1800-2200, closed Saturday and Sunday), in a colonial-style house on Vuna Rd. west of the palace. The German chefs, Lothar and Martina, ensure that the food and atmosphere are excellent. Red snapper is around T$20, lobster or steak T$25, and tropical fruit appears in some dishes. They're open for dinner 1800-2200 (reservations recom-mended), and if you've got anything to celebrate or just want to treat yourself right, this shoul(be your choice.

Groceries

Talamahu Market (closed Sunday) has all the fruit and vegetables you'd expect, and mos prices are posted (beware of overcharging i they're not). Unexpectedly, you're not allowed tc eat in the market, as the police may advise yov if you do.

The large **Morris Hedstrom Supermarke** (tel. 23-355), opposite the market on Salote Rd. opens weekdays 0800-1800, Saturday 0800-1900.

Nuku'alofa's largest supermarket is the **Kinikinilau Shopping Center** (tel. 24-044; Mon.-Thurs. 0730-1800, Friday 0730-2100, Saturday 0730-1300) on Salote Rd. toward Faua Jetty. The adjacent bottle shop is called the Supa-Kava Market.

The **Tonga Cooperative Federation Store** (tel. 23-777), on Taufa'ahau Rd. opposite Tung Arcade, is often cheaper than the others.

If you'll be spending a Sunday in Nuku'alofa, buy a few snacks on Saturday to tide you over as the whole town will be dead.

ENTERTAINMENT

Nuku'alofa's only movie house is **Loni's Cinema** (tel. 23-621), also known as Finau Theater Twin. Films begin Mon-Sat. at 2000, with additional showings at 1300, 1500, 2200, and midnight on certain days. The Sunday midnight showing gets around Tonga's notorious blue laws, but all films are heavily censored. Expect the movie to start 20 minutes late if they think they can sell a few more tickets (admission T$3).

Friday is the big night at Nuku'alofa's discos because on Saturday they must be firmly shut by midnight. Amusingly, many of them reopen a few seconds after at midnight on Sunday, and there's dancing until sunrise Monday morning. Such are the wonderful ways of the Lord! At most of the places mentioned below, men must wear long pants and a shirt with a collar if they want to be admitted. These rules are for the convenience of doormen trying to keep out troublemakers, but there may be no exceptions. A $100 silk Gucci T-shirt won't do if it doesn't have a collar.

The trendiest disco is currently Italian-operated **Ambassador Night Club** (tel. 23-338), just beyond the Tonga National Center south of town. The location is nice next to Fanga'uta Lagoon and you can even get a table right beside the water. It's open Mon.-Sat. from 2000 (no cover Monday, Tuesday, Wednesday, and sometimes Saturday)—take a taxi to get there.

Also very popular is the **Blue Pacific International Night Club** (tel. 25-994), at Maufanga on the Bypass Rd. four km southeast of town (take a taxi). They're open Thursday, Friday, and Saturday nights, playing rock music and reggae. When you tire of dancing inside, you can sit out on the terrace and chat. It's safe, and large crowds turn out for the various beauty pageants, including one for cross dressers.

The downmarket disco at the **Phoenix Hotel** (tel. 23-270) has live music from 2000 Mon.-Saturday. Occasional fistfights break out here among the local Tongans.

Joe's Tropicana Top Club (tel. 21-544), on Salote Rd., offers rock music by Pacific Comets and the Barbarians. Watch your drinks when you get up to dance. Right next door is the even rougher **Jungle Niteclub.** These places are okay for single males but not recommended for women or couples.

Bars

Friday nights Wanda's Bar at the **Pacific Royale Hotel** has a happy hour from 1800 to closing with T$2 Royal beer and T$1.50 wine.

The **Yacht Club** (tel. 21-840) on Vuna Rd. is a good place for a beer, but sandals and shorts are not acceptable dress. Despite the name, this club is not involved in any yachting activities but foreign visitors are welcome. It's one of few bars open on Sunday (1100-2300)!

Drink with the local elite at the **Tonga Club** (tel. 22-710). You're supposed to be a member, but you'll be welcome if you look all right. They're open daily until 2300 (on Sunday enter through the side door).

The quaint, old **Nuku'alofa Club** (tel. 21-160), on Salote Rd. near the Royal Palace, has been a hangout for local male expats since 1914, and they're a bit selective about who they let in: poorly dressed men and females of all descriptions are most unwelcome. Before you'll be served, the bartender will have to find someone to sign

ROYAL BEER COMPANY LTD, NUKU'ALOFA, THE KINGDOM OF TONGA.

you in, and you'll probably be asked where you're staying (don't say the Pacific Royale unless it's true as the manager is a regular here). Watch the reaction if you mention a backpacker hostel.

The **Utulea Club** on Unga Rd., a block and a half up from the market, is a local kava drinking bar (T$1.50 a bowl).

Cultural Shows for Visitors

Traditional Tongan dancing can be witnessed at Fafa Island Resort on Monday nights, at the Tonga National Center on Tuesday and Thursday nights, at the International Dateline Hotel on Wednesday and Saturday nights, and at the Good SamariTAN Inn on Friday nights. Package tours with dinner and transfers are available to all of the above.

Intellectual Activities

The privately run **'Atenisi Institute** (Box 90, Nuku'alofa; tel. 25-034 or 24-819, fax 24-819, http://kalianet.candw.to/atenisi), in the western part of the city, began as an evening high school in 1963 but now offers university-level courses right up to Ph.Ds. It has an international reputation for its classical school of thought—a bastion of critical mindedness and creative thinking in the devout/happy-go-lucky South Pacific! If you're an "expert" on anything, Professor Futa Helu or Director 'Okusitino Mahina may invite you to lecture the students. Write in advance or make an appointment soon after you arrive. There's no pay, but someone might end up buying you lunch. During the school year (Feb.-Oct.) there's a free public lecture at the Institute every Monday at

2000. It's a good opportunity to meet a few of the students over coffee, but you might call ahead or visit beforehand to check the subject and to make sure there really will be a lecture that week. The traditional graduation ceremonies in November are not to be missed if you happen to be there at the time. (The Institute receives no government or church funding, and is in urgent need of overseas assistance. Unfortunately, the Tongan Government has attempted to cripple this unique institution it doesn't control by insisting that all foreign funding proposals go through official channels, then deliberately holding up the paperwork until the application deadlines have passed.)

SHOPPING

Handicraft prices in Tonga have increased sharply in recent years but you can still find bargains if you shop around. Baskets, mats, and occasionally tapa are reasonable buys, and there's no hard sell anywhere, so you can browse at leisure. A good place to begin is **Langafonua,** the Tongan Women's Association Handicraft Center (tel. 21-014) on Taufa'ahau Rd. in the center of town. Also try the **Friendly Islands Marketing Cooperative Handicraft Shop** (Box 523, Nuku'alofa; tel. 23-155), otherwise known as "FIMCO" or "Kalia Handicrafts," opposite the Tungi Arcade. A fishing goods shore behind FIMCO sells snorkeling gear.

Also check upstairs at **Talamahu Market,** where you can buy directly from the craftspeople, but avoid buying anything at the market on a cruise-ship day when prices are jacked up. Tapa is best purchased directly from the producers—just listen for the sound of the beating while you're touring the island. In the market tapa sells for T$10 a "lane" or line.

The handicraft shop at the **Tonga National Center** is more expensive, and their woodcarvings are mostly nontraditional masks and tikis. The whalebone carvings sold here are prohibited entry into most countries under endangered species legislation, as is the black coral jewelry. It's a shame the center sells this type of tacky tourist art.

Ginette at **Tapa Craft** (no phone; weekdays 1200-1600), next to the Baha'i Temple on Lavina Rd., makes small tapa souvenirs and dolls which are excellent souvenirs. She also sells used paperbacks at T$1 apiece, and trades two of your books for one of hers. (If you love cats, drop in to visit Ginette's large family.)

The **Philatelic Bureau** (Box 164, Nuku'alofa; tel. 22-238), above the post office, sells beautiful stamps and first-day covers from Tonga and Niuafo'ou.

Bring with you all the film you'll need as it's rather expensive in Tonga.

SERVICES AND INFORMATION

Money

The Bank of Tonga (tel. 23-933; Mon.-Fri. 0900-1530, Saturday 0830-1130), on Taufa'ahau Rd., and the ANZ Bank (tel. 24-332; Mon.-Fri. 0900-1600, Saturday 0830-1130), diagonally opposite the police station, change traveler's checks without commission (except Saturday when a 50-cent charge applies). The Malaysian-owned MBf Bank (tel. 24-600), below Hotel Nuku'alofa, charges T$2 commission all the time. Outside banking hours the Dateline Hotel will change money for about two percent less than the banks. You must show your passport to change money.

The Bank of Tonga gives cash advances on MasterCard and Visa for T$6 commission, and they'll store valuables for you in their vault at T$5 per sealed envelope. American Express is not represented here.

Post and Telecommunications

Postage in Tonga is inexpensive compared to other countries, but if you plan on making any heavy purchases it's a good idea to drop in at the post office (tel. 21-700) beforehand to check on the rules and rates. It should be possible to mail parcels up to 20 kilograms by surface mail, although this does vary according to the destination country. Poste restante mail is held "one year," or until they get tired of seeing the letter, at which time it's sent back. If you're expecting a parcel, ask them to check that too. The DHL Worldwide Express agent (tel. 23-617) is next to Loni's Cinema on Wellington Road.

To make a domestic long-distance telephone call to 'Eua, Ha'apai, Vava'u, or anywhere else in Tonga you must go to the Telecom Telephone Exchange on Unga Rd. (open 24 hours daily).

The Cable and Wireless office (tel. 23-499) in Salote Rd. is open for international telephone calls, faxes, and telegrams Mon.-Fri. 0600-2400, Saturday 0700-2400, Sunday 1600-2400. You can receive faxes sent to fax 676/22-970 here at 50 cents a page.

Card telephones for international calls only are outside the main post office, at the Cable and Wireless office on Salote Rd., at the airport, and at a few other locations around Nuku'alofa. The post office sells the cards.

Internet Access

The Kalia Cafe (tel./fax 25-733, http://invited.to/ kalia-cafe, e-mail: kaliacafe@invited.to; open weekdays 0800-1800), on the top floor of the Tonga Cooperative Federation Building on Taufa'ahau Rd. opposite Tungi Arcade, offers casual walk-in internet access at T$16 an hour, broken down into four 15-minute blocks. They're helpful in setting up a "free" e-mail address—the world at your fingertips. Breakfast is served 0800-1000, coffee anytime.

Visas and Officialdom

You can get an extension of stay for T$25 from the Immigration Office (tel. 23-222; Monday, Tuesday, and Thursday 0900-1200 and 1400-1600, Wednesday and Friday 0900-1200) at the central police station on Salote Road.

The countries with diplomatic representatives in Nuku'alofa are France (tel. 21-831), on Taufa'ahau Rd., Germany (tel. 23-477), on Taufa'ahau Rd. between the Pacific Royale Hotel and Air Pacific, Korea (tel. 24-044), on Salote Rd., New Zealand (tel. 23-122), on Salote Rd. opposite the post office, Sweden (tel. 22-855), on Salote Rd. opposite the Reserve Bank of Tonga, China (tel. 21-766), on Vuna Rd., and the United Kingdom (tel. 24-285), on Vuna Rd. west of the Royal Palace. The European Union (tel. 23-820) has an office on Taufa'ahau Rd. near Asco Motors. The Australian High Commission (tel. 23-244; weekdays 0900-1100), on Salote Rd. behind the International Dateline Hotel, also rep-

resents Canadians. The U.S. is not represented in Tonga and U.S. citizens in need of assistance must contact the embassy in Suva, Fiji (tel. 679/314-466, fax 679/300-081).

Cleaning and Cutting

Savoy Dry Cleaners (tel. 23-314; Mon.-Fri. 0800-1800, Saturday 0800-1400), on Fatafehi Rd. south of the center, washes and dries laundry at T$1.20 a kilo. Unfortunately there have been reports of items going missing here.

Baby Blue Beauty Salon (tel. 22-349), next to the Baha'i Temple on Lavina Rd., is an upscale hairdresser charging T$7/10 for men's/women's haircuts.

Yachting Facilities

Cruising yachts can tie up to the seawall in the small boat harbor beside Queen Salote Wharf three km east of Nuku'alofa, though the channel is only two and a half meters deep in the center. Customs is on the wharf, but immigration is at the police station in town. Keep valuables carefully stowed, as there have been many thefts from boats here.

Tonga Visitors Bureau

The Tonga Visitors Bureau (open Mon.-Fri. 0830-1630, Saturday 0830-1230; tel. 21-733) on Vuna Rd. is usually helpful (if disorganized) and has lots of free brochures. Peruse their notice boards for all the latest tourist news. They will also help you make your accommodation or tour bookings.

Maps

Get good maps from the Lands and Survey Department (tel. 23-611) in the back yard of the Ministry Block.

Navigational charts (T$14 each) of Tonga, Samoa, and New Zealand are available at the Hydrographic Office (tel. 24-696; weekdays 0800-1600) at Touliki Naval Base, just east of Queen Salote Wharf. The hassle here is that you must first go the base to select your charts and get an invoice, then you must visit military headquarters near Centenary Church in town to pay, then return to the base with the stamped invoice to pick up the charts. The Dateline Bookshop (Box 1291, Nuku'alofa; tel. 24-049), opposite Loni's Cinema on Wellington Rd., sells some of the same nautical charts at T$16 each without all the running around.

Bookstores and Libraries

The **Friendly Islands Bookshop** (tel. 23-787, fax 23-631, e-mail: fibs@kalianet.to), below Tungi Arcade, is great for browsing. Ask for books by local authors 'Epeli Hau'ofa, Pesi Fonua, Konai Helu Thaman, and Tupou Posesi Fanua. They also carry Tongan music cassettes and compact discs, and topographical maps of Tonga. For a mail-order list of books on Tonga write: Friendly Islands Bookshop, Box 124, Nuku'alofa. Manager David May and his staff have built this bookshop into one of the best in the South Pacific.

Family Christian Bookshop (Box 167, Nuku'alofa; tel. 22-562), opposite the Tonga Development Bank on Fatafehi Rd., has place mats and posters bearing marvelous photos of Tongan lifestyle and culture.

The 'Utue'a Public Library (Box 1, Nuku'alofa; tel. 21-831; open weekdays 1500-2100, Saturday 1000-1500), below the Catholic basilica on Taufa'ahau Rd., charges T$5 annual membership. There's also a good library in the University of the South Pacific, Tonga Campus (tel. 29-055) near the Golf Club at Ha'ateiho, out on the road to the airport. Ask to see their collection of antique Tongan war clubs.

Travel Offices

The Air New Zealand office (tel. 23-828) is in the Tungi Arcade. The Air Pacific agent is E.M. Jones Ltd. (tel. 23-423) on Taufa'ahau Road. The Royal Tongan Airlines office (tel. 23-414) is in the Royco Building on Fatafehi Road. Polynesian Airlines (tel. 21-566) is at the corner of Fatafehi and Salote Roads.

If you need a travel agent, Vital Travel (Box 838, Nuku'alofa; tel. 23-617) next to Loni's Cinema on Wellington Rd. is recommended.

Health

Medical and dental consultations are available at Vaiola Hospital (tel. 23-200), just outside town on the way to the airport.

Unless you have unlimited time and are on the barest of budgets, it's better to attend the German Clinic (Dr. Heinz Betz, tel. 22-736, after hours tel. 24-625), adjacent to the International Pharmacy on Wellington Rd., a block east of the cinema. Clinic hours are weekdays 0930-1230/1500-1900, but make an appointment. Next door is Dr. Lee Saafi's Town Clinic (tel. 24-784 or 23-695).

A recommended dentist is Dr. Sione Ui Kilisimasi (tel. 24-780), beside Fasi Pharmacy Clinic on Salote Rd. near the Australian High Commission.

TRANSPORTATION

For information on air and sea services from Tongatapu to the other Tongan islands, see **Transportation** in the chapter introduction.

Ferries to 'Eua leave from Faua Jetty, but all ships to Ha'apai and Vava'u depart the adjoining Queen Salote Wharf. The office of **Uata Shipping** (tel. 23-855) is upstairs in the building at the corner of Taufa'ahau and Wellington Roads. The **Shipping Corporation of Polynesia** office (tel. 21-699) is at the entrance to Queen Salote Wharf.

By Bus

A local bus station opposite the Tonga Visitors Bureau has buses to Halaleva, Ma'ufanga, Va'epopua, and Vaiola. The Halalevu bus goes south to Fanga'uta Lagoon, then east to Queen Salote Wharf. The Va'epopua bus travels east to Queen Salote Wharf and the Friendly Islander Hotel. The Vaiola bus goes south to the hospital.

Opposite the Ministry Block farther west on the waterfront is another station with long-distance buses marked Fahefa or Ha'akame to the Houma blowholes, marked Hihifo or Masilamea to the Kolovai flying foxes and Ha'atafu Beach, marked Veitongo, Folaha, or Vaini to the golf course or Tongan Wildlife Center, marked Malapo, Lapaha, or Mu'a to the Lapaha archaeological area, and marked Niutoua to the Ha'amonga trilithon. Fares are 50 cents to the blowholes, 60 cents to the Lapaha tombs, 70 cents to Ha'atafu Beach, and T$1 to the Ha'amonga trilithon. Visitors often use these buses.

The bus to the airport (70 cents) from opposite the Ministry Block might be labeled Halaliku or Fua'amotu. Some (but not all) of the larger Liahona buses also pass the airport, as does the large green-and-yellow Malolelei Transport bus. It's unusual for a tourist to take one of these buses to the airport as the entire tourism establishment assumes you'll want to take a special airport bus or a taxi.

The last bus back to Nuku'alofa from Kolovai and Ha'amonga is at 1500. The buses stop running around 1700 and don't run at all on Sunday. They're inexpensive and relatively efficient, and a great way to observe Tongan life.

Taxis

Throughout Tonga, registered taxis have a "T" on their license plate. Meterless taxis at the market are T$1 for a trip in town, T$2 and up for a longer trip in the vicinity, T$12 to the airport. Always ask the price beforehand. Taxis must purchase a special police permit to work on Sunday, so you won't see many around that day, and if you want one then, arrange it with a driver on Saturday and expect to pay a higher fare. Also, only telephone for a taxi at the exact moment you need it. If you call and ask them to come in 30 minutes they'll probably forget and not come at all. City Taxi (tel. 24-666) has a stand near Teta Tours.

Some taxi drivers double as tour guides, and an island tour with them will run T$6-80 for up to four people (check the price beforehand). There have been reports of thefts in taxis, involving drivers who removed objects from handbags left in the car while visitors got out to take photos, etc., so be forewarned.

Car Rentals

Foreign and international driver's licenses are not accepted in Tonga, so before renting a car you must first visit the Traffic Department at the Central Police Station (tel. 23-222) on Salote Rd. (weekdays 0830-1230 and 1330-1630) to purchase a Tongan driver's license (T$10). You must queue up several times—once to get the form, another time to pay, then again to get a stamp—so allow at least an hour. This is strictly a revenue generating operation and no practical test is required.

The speed limit is 40 kph in town and 65 kph on the open road. Speed limits are strictly enforced on Tongatapu by police with hand-held radar, and on-the-spot T$50 fines are routine. Avoid hitting a pig, as heavy compensation will have to be paid. Also beware of getting hit from behind when you stop. Never drive a car in Tonga unless you're sure the insurance is valid, otherwise you'll have big problems in case of an accident. Driving is on the left.

Avis (Box 74, Nuku'alofa; tel. 23-344, fax 23-833), at the Pacific Royale Hotel, rents cars with unlimited mileage beginning at T$60 a day. The T$8 daily collision insurance only covers damages above the first T$1,000, which you'll be responsible for in any case, and tax is 5% extra. Weekend rates are available.

E.M. Jones Travel (tel. 23-423), Taufa'ahau and Wellington Roads, rents cars at T$50 a day including insurance.

Sisifa Rental Cars (tel./fax 24-823), formerly known as Makalita Rental Cars, at Kiwi Tonga Garage on Salote Rd. behind the Chinese Embassy, has cars at T$55 a day all inclusive (T$750 deductible insurance). Their weekend special price of T$100 gets you a car from Friday at 1600 until Monday at 0900.

Budget Rent a Car (Box 51, Nuku'alofa; tel. 23-510, fax 24-059) is on Taufa'ahau Rd. south of town next to Asco Motors.

By Bicycle

Rather than going to all the trouble and expense of renting a car, see Tongatapu by bicycle. From Nuku'alofa you can easily reach all the main sights in two days, visiting the east and west sides of the island on alternate days. The main roads are excellent without too much traffic, and steep hills don't exist. The open landscape invites you to look around at leisure and there are lots of small villages. Abundant road signs make it very easy to find your own way, but don't trust the indicated distances. Cycling can be tiring and dusty, but the friendly islanders are quick to smile and wave at a pedaling visitor. And if you happen to see a long dark limousine with a police escort coming your way, pull over and let them pass: you're about to see the king and queen!

Quality 15-speed mountain bikes are for rent at **Niko Bicycle Rental** on the waterfront opposite the Dateline Hotel. They charge T$8/18 for one/three days. Many guesthouses also rent bicycles. A bicycle tour is a good way to liven up a dull Tongan Sunday, provided you've reserved your bike by Saturday morning.

Local Tours

The easy way to see Tongatapu is on a bus tour with **Teta Tours** (Box 215, Nuku'alofa; tel. 21-688, fax 23-238, e-mail: tetatour@kalianet.to), at Railway and Wellington Roads. Three-hour sightseeing tours to western and eastern Tongatapu are T$15 pp each, and they also book day cruises to Fafa Island Resort at T$35 including lunch. If you're interested, check well ahead, as they need a certain number of people to run a tour and don't go every day. The friendly, helpful staff can also book hotel rooms anywhere around Tonga.

Kingdom Tours (tel. 25-200, fax 23-447), in the Tungi Arcade next to Air New Zealand, also offers a variety of tours and cruises at slightly higher prices. The Tonga Visitors Bureau can also help arrange sightseeing tours. Few of the road tours operate on Sunday and it's more common to do a boat trip to one of the islands off Nuku'alofa that day (see **Getting There** in the Offshore Islands section that follows).

The 12-meter motor catamaran *Hakula* (Stuart and Francis Bollam, Box 1969, Nuku'alofa; fax 23-759), based at Faua Jetty, does day charters out to uninhabited islands like Malinoa and Nuku off northern Tongatapu at T$250 for up to seven people (bring your own lunch). They also offer extended charters to the idyllic atolls of the Ha'apai Group at T$500 a day for the boat, comfortable sleeping arrangements for up to six included. Catering on the overnight trips is T$25 pp for three meals. They'll do fun fishing along the way, but game fishing is not their specialty. Stuart and Francis are friendly, down-to-earth hosts who will do their best to make your trip a success without adding a lot of unnecessary frills.

Pacific Island Seaplanes (Box 1675, Nuku'alofa; tel. 25-177, fax 25-165, e-mail: pacisair@kalianet.to) uses a six-seater Canadian Beaver seaplane based on the Fanga'uta Lagoon next to the Tonga National Center for flightseeing trips all around Tonga. A scenic flight around Tongatapu costs T$85 pp (minimum of four), but their most unique offering takes you to the volcanic island of Tofua in the Ha'apai Group (T$250 pp, minimum of four). You land on a freshwater crater lake and hike across the active, smoking volcano. For an extra T$50 pp, this trip can be extended with flightseeing down the eastern Ha'apai chain.

moray eel

AROUND TONGATAPU

WESTERN TONGATAPU

Take the Hihifo bus (70 cents) or ride a bicycle to Kolovai to see the **Flying Fox Sanctuary,** where countless thousands of the animals *(Pteropus tonganus)* hang in casuarina trees for about a kilometer along the road. Flying foxes are actually bats (the only mammals that can fly) with foxlike heads and wingspans of up to a meter across. Nocturnal creatures, they cruise after dark in search of food and hang upside down during the day. Legend says the bats were a gift from a Samoan maiden to an ancient Tongan navigator. Considered sacred, they may only be hunted by members of the royal family.

Just beyond Kolovai is the turnoff for the **Good SamariTAN Inn,** 1.5 km off the main road. Farther west, behind the primary school at **Kanokupolu,** is the *langi,* or stone-lined burial mound of the Tu'i Kanokupolu, an ancestor of the present royal family. The stones to built this tomb were quarried at nearby **Ha'atafu Beach,** and a few partially cut slabs are still anchored to the bedrock at the water's edge, just where the access road meets the beach. The marinelife at Ha'atafu is good because it's a designated "reef reserve" and there's a T$200 fine for fishing. Ha'atafu is a *palangi* beach, which means there's no hassle about swimming on Sunday, but if you come for a picnic or a swim don't leave any rubbish or you'll also be liable for the fine. There's

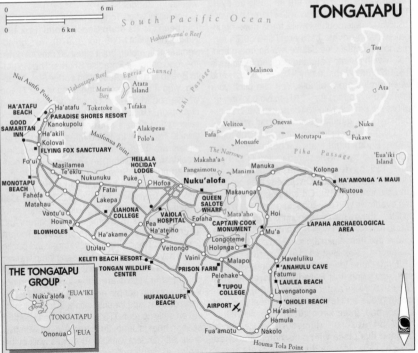

TONGATAPU

© DAVID STANLEY

excellent snorkeling, especially at high tide—see dozens of species of fish. Just watch out for an east to west current. Some of the best reef-break surfing in Tonga is here, also at high tide, but even then it's challenging due to the shallow water, and a protective wetsuit is almost essential equipment. On the plus side, the waves are only 100 meters offshore. The Paradise Shores Resort at Ha'atafu Beach serves reasonably priced food and drink to nonguests.

Hihifo buses from Ha'atafu head straight back to town, but there's no bus from Fo'ui to Fahefa. If you want to go on to the blowholes discussed below, you'll find it a pleasant five-km walk (or hitch).

Accommodations

The **Good SamariTAN Inn** (Box 214, Nuku'alofa; tel. 41-022, fax 41-095) on Kolovai Beach, 18 km west of Nuku'alofa, is not such a great choice. Although prices have crept up here in recent years, the rooms are as basic as ever. The nine older bungalows with shared bath are T$35/50 single/double, while three newer bungalows with private bath are T$45/60/75 single/double/triple. One deluxe two-bedroom bungalow with private bath and cooking facilities is T$50/70/85. All prices include breakfast, and weekly rates are available. You can pitch your tent on the grounds for T$10 pp. No cooking facilities are provided, so you must use the Inn's expensive and variable restaurant/bar which sits on a large concrete terrace overlooking the rocky shore. Friday night there's a buffet dinner accompanied by Polynesian dancing (T$20 pp, plus T$5 pp for return bus transfers from Nuku'alofa, if required). On Sunday they prepare an *umu* lunch (T$15). On cruise-ship days the Inn overflows with day-tripping passengers (fortunately, they're not that frequent). Take the Hihifo bus to Kolovai, then walk one and a half km to the Inn. A taxi from Nuku'alofa will cost T$12, from the airport T$20. Budget to inexpensive.

If you came to Tonga for the sand, tan, and salt, you'll find it at **Paradise Shores Resort** (Box 976, Nuku'alofa; tel./fax 41-158), in a coconut grove on Ha'atafu Beach, near the end of the road, three km north of Kolovai. In July 1997 an Arizonan named Dave Bergeron opened this place with nine simple thatched *fales* at T$35 single or double. There are also a few set tents and a long thatched dormitory *fale* all T$10 pp. Camping with your own gear is T$1(per tent. Dave's guests share common toilets showers, and cooking facilities (outside alco holic drinks are not allowed on the premises) The resort bar is reasonable, and the restau rant serves steaks or pan fried fish at around T$13. Less expensive sandwiches are also avail able and you get a great ocean view from the restaurant terrace. The large Elvis photo ove the bar explains Dave's hairdo (ask him to de an impersonation, if you get him going). Par adise Shores experiences water shortages, bu it's on a better beach than the Good Samari TAN with great snorkeling. It's a nice relaxec place to stay—a mecca for surfers and back packers. There's even a jacuzzi and satellite TV! Bicycles are for rent. This resort is just a five-minute stroll from the Hihifo bus stop. It offer fills up on Saturday night, so check to see if any rooms are available before heading out for the weekend. Budget.

For many years Tonga's premier surfing resort has been the **Ha'atafu Beach Motel** (Box 490, Nuku'alofa; tel. 41-088, fax 22-970). No sign advertises this motel, but it's just 20 meters down the road opposite Paradise Shores. The Ha'atafu Beach is run by Australian surfer Steve Burling, who first came to Tongatapu in 1977, and whose son Michael is Tonga's national surfing champion. Unlike his neighbor, Steve doesn't cater to day-trippers who only drop in for lunch or drinks. The eight thatched *fales* with shared facilities are T$90/130 single/double including breakfast, buffet dinner, and nonmotorized sporting equipment. Shared rooms are T$70 pp. These prices only apply if you book directly; through a travel agent it's about 20% more. Call ahead if you don't have a booking, as they only take 15 guests at a time and are often full. There's a 10% discount if you stay a month (many do). The dining room, lounge, and public toilets have electricity, but kerosene lamp lighting is used in the *fales*. The meals are ample and excellent, and videos are shown every evening. When enough people are interested, Steve organizes boat trips for snorkeling, fishing, or surfing on outlying reefs (T$10 pp). The peak surfing season here is June, July, and August with five great left-handers within a 10-minute walk of the motel, as southern swells generated around

New Zealand crash into the Ha'atafu coast. From January to March you have a choice of four right-handers and one left nearby, but at this time it's usually better to take a boat around to the reefs on the northwest side of Tongatapu, which catch waves rolling down from Hawaii. Steve knows all the better waves and his motel is *the* place for serious surfers (you must bring your own board). Inexpensive.

SOUTHERN TONGATAPU

Surf forced through naturally formed air vents creates spectacular **blowholes** on the rocky, terraced southwest coast near Houma, 15 km from Nuku'alofa. From the end of the road, walk along the path to the right. Waves batter the coral cliffs and spout water up to 30 meters in the air through eroded tunnels. These impressive blowholes number in the hundreds—come at high tide on a windy day! Bus service from Nuku'alofa to Houma is fairly frequent and continues west to Fahefa.

Just east of Utulau a dirt road branches off the paved highway (and bus route) between Houma and Nuku'alofa via Pea and runs along the south coast. Three km along this dirt road is **Keleti Beach Resort,** with more blowholes and several small but strikingly beautiful beaches and pools protected from the open sea by unusual coral terraces. Keleti is down a road to the right, distinguishable from other similar roads

by the electricity lines. As previously mentioned, there's no bus service east of the Utulau-Pea road, so you're better off coming by bicycle.

The **Tongan Wildlife Center** (tel./fax 29-449), also known as the Veitongo Bird Park, is near the coast, a short distance east of Keleti on the south coast road. If you want to come by bus you'll have to walk about two and a half km south from the main highway at Veitongo (a taxi from the corner will only be T$2). The Center is unique in Tonga for its small bird park and botanical garden. Examples of most native Tongan land birds are kept in aviaries brimming with vegetation— take the time to wait for them to appear. The small botanical garden displays all of the common Polynesian food plants, and at the entrance is an informative photo display on Tongan birds and reptiles. The Center is open Mon.-Sat. 0900-1600, Sunday and holidays 0900-1800. It's run by a nonprofit organization working to save endangered species of Tongan birds, so your T$3 admission fee goes to a good cause.

Also on the south coast is **Hufangalupe** ("Pigeon's Doorway"), a huge natural coral bridge with a sandy cove flanked by towering cliffs, six km east of the bird park and four km from Vaini, the closest bus stop. Make your way down the inside of the fault from the back to see the bridge and sea before you. As you return to the main south coast road, watch for a path on the left at the bottom of a slight dip, which leads down to a lovely white beach (beware of theft while you're swimming).

The Houma Blowholes are an impressive sight at high tide as the waves crash into the coral terraces, sending surf soaring skyward.

The cornerstones of Lapaha's Paepae 'o Tele'a, burial place of the 28th Tu'i Tonga, are massive L-shaped blocks of limestone.

Accommodations

Secluded **Keleti Beach Resort** (Box 3116, Nuku'alofa; tel./fax 24-654), on the south coast 10 km from Nuku'alofa, has four individual *fales* with private bath and cold showers at T$30/40 single/double. Four duplex *fales* with shared facilities are T$30/40 single/double, and families can rent an entire duplex unit for T$60 and comfortably accommodate two adults and two children. Weekly rates with full board are available. No cooking facilities are provided, but meals prepared by an Italian chef are served Western style in a restaurant overlooking the sea. The accommodations are better than those at the other three beach resorts on Tongatapu, and if you don't mind paying T$25-40 pp a day for meals, Keleti is an excellent choice. The coast here is strikingly beautiful with several small beaches, blowholes, and coral terraces—in fact, this is Keleti's main attraction. Several golden sandy beaches are at your disposal, and one can snorkel among the brightly colored tropical fish in the large tidal pools at the foot of the resort, just be aware of the currents. Otherwise just sit on the rocks watching the waves crash onto the reef. The Tongan Wildlife Center is only a short walk away. This is the least crowded of the Tongatapu beach resorts, and in the off season (Dec.-April) you could have the place to yourself. It's isolated here, so be aware of theft. You should also know that the Italian owners tend to ignore their guests unless they speak Italian and the place is often empty. To get there

from Nuku'alofa take the Folaha, Malapo, Vaini, or Veitongo buses to the turnoff, then a taxi three km down to the resort for T$2. A taxi straight from Nuku'alofa or the airport shouldn't be over T$10. Budget.

EASTERN TONGATAPU

Tupou College (tel. 32-240) at Tuloa is three km off the airport road. No bus service reaches the college, but you can take a Malapo, Lapaha, or Mu'a bus to Malapo, then walk south on the road beside the Mormon church. Tupou College is the oldest secondary school in the South Pacific, established by the Free Wesleyan Church in 1866, and it's believed that the first royal capital of Tonga was near here. The college has a small museum of dusty local relics, crafts, and artifacts. There are no fixed hours, but someone will let you in if you ask at the school office.

The main reason to come is the **Tuloa Rainforest Reserve,** the last six hectares of natural forest remaining on Tongatapu. Most of the forest was cut down during the building of Fua'amotu Airport in 1940, and this remaining fragment is just 900 meters southeast of the college administration building. Take the road south beside a deep pit behind the library, and turn left onto a dirt road after 300 meters, then right to an old information shelter. Although the reserve is not as well cared for as might be desired, many of the trees are still labeled, and colorful butterflies fluter across the trails. More importantly, Tuloa shelters a large colony of flying foxes, and it's much more intriguing to observe them here in their natural habitat than along the main road at Kolovai.

NORTHEASTERN TONGATAPU

Across the lagoon from Nuku'alofa, just southwest of Mu'a is a monument marking the spot where in 1777 Captain Cook landed from his ship the *Endeavor* and rested under a banyan tree (which has since disappeared). He then continued into Lapaha, the capital of Tonga at the time, to visit Pau, the Tu'i Tonga. Retrace Cook's footsteps into this richest archaeological area in western Polynesia.

For over 600 years beginning around A.D. 1200, **Lapaha** (Mu'a) was the seat of the Tu'i Tonga dynasty. Nothing remains of the royal residence today, but some 28 *langi* (burial mounds of ancient royalty) have been located in or near Mu'a. Due to local objections, none have yet been excavated. Several of these great rec-

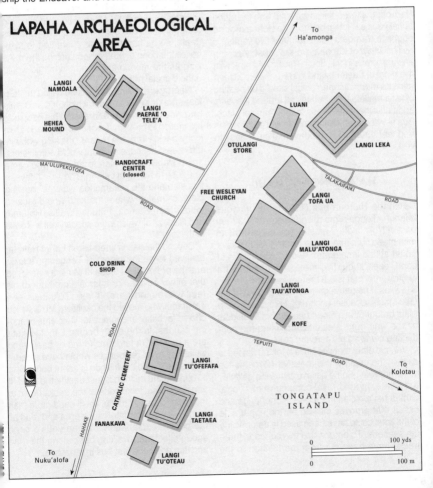

LAPAHA ARCHAEOLOGICAL AREA

To Ha'amonga

LANGI NAMOALA

LANGI PAEPAE 'O TELE'A

HEHEA MOUND

LUANI

LANGI LEKA

OTULANGI STORE

MA'ULUPEKOTOFA

HANDICRAFT CENTER (closed)

ROAD

TALAKAIFAIKI

ROAD

FREE WESLEYAN CHURCH

LANGI TOFA UA

LANGI MALU'ATONGA

COLD DRINK SHOP

ROAD

LANGI TAU'ATONGA

KOFE

TEPUITI

ROAD

To Kolotau

CATHOLIC CEMETERY

LANGI TU'OFEFAFA

TONGATAPU ISLAND

FANAKAVA

LANGI TAETAEA

HAHAKE

To Nuku'alofa

LANGI TU'OTEAU

0   100 yds

0   100 m

tangular platforms with recessed tiers of coraline limestone are clearly visible from the main road, including the *langi* of the last Tu'i Tonga (1865), a Catholic, which has a cross on top.

The finest of the terraced tombs, rather hidden down a side road, is the **Paepae 'o Tele'a,** built during the early 17th century for the 29th Tu'i Tonga. Notice in particular the gigantic L-shaped monoliths at the corners, the slanting upper surfaces, and the feet that extend underground. In its context, this mighty monument has all the power and emotional impact of a classical Greek temple. Adjacent to the Paepae 'o Tele'a is the **Namoala,** a three-tiered pyramid with the stone burial vault still intact on top. The **Hehea mound** opposite Namoala bears another two vaults.

The *langi* of Lapaha are the most imposing ancient tombs in the South Pacific and rank with the *moai* of Easter Island and Huahine's Maeva ruins as major archaeological sites. The beating of tapa mallets from houses all around the *langi* adds an otherworldliness to this magical place. Bus service from Nuku'alofa to Mu'a (20 km) is frequent throughout the day, making it easy to visit.

HA'AMONGA 'A MAUI

Catch the Niutoua bus (T$1) to this famous trilithon, Tonga's most engaging relic, 32 km east of Nuku'alofa. The structure consists of an arch made from three huge rectangular blocks of nonstratified limestone. Two upright pillars of coral, each about five meters high, support a central lintel that is 5.8 meters long and weighs 816 kilos. The name means "The Burden of the God Maui" because, according to myth, the hero Maui brought the trilithon here on his shoulders all the way from Wallis Island using the connecting stone as his carrying pole.

Various other theories have been advanced to explain the origin of this massive 12-metric-ton stone archway. Some believe it was the gateway to Heketa, the old royal compound of Tonga. Others have called it Tonga's Stonehenge and assert that grooves incised on the upper side of the lintel could have been used in determining the seasons. To emphasize this concept, three tracks have been cut from the trilithon to the

coast, the better to observe sunrise on the equinox, as well as the summer and winter solstices. This would have been useful to determine the planting and harvesting periods for yams or the sailing seasons. Most scholars believe, however, that the grooves were cut long after the trilithon was built and discount their utility as an astronomical calendar.

Since few archaeological excavations of ancient monuments have been conducted in Tonga, it's not known for sure when or why the Ha'amonga 'a Maui was built. Local tradition attributes it to the 11th Tu'i Tonga, Tu'itatui, who reigned around A.D. 1200. Evidently this king feared that his two sons would quarrel after his death, so he had the trilithon erected to symbolize the bond of brotherhood uniting them. As long as the monument stood, its magic would uphold social harmony.

Nearby is a 2.7-meter-tall slab called the **'Esi Makafaakinanga** against which, it's said, this king would lean while addressing his people, a precaution to prevent anyone from spearing him in the back. His name means "the king who hits the knees" because Tu'itatui would administer a sharp slap with his staff to anyone who came too close to his regal person. The area between this slab and the Ha'amonga was the meeting place or *mala'e* where the king would receive tribute from Samoa, Futuna, Wallis, Rotuma, and Niue, all of which were subservient to Tonga at that time.

Beyond the slab is three-tiered **Langi Heketa,** believed to be the oldest of Tongatapu's *langi* and the prototype of those at Mu'a. It's believed that either Tu'itatui or a female member of his family is buried here. It was Tu'itatui's son Tal'atama who moved the capital to Mu'a, which offered far better anchorage for their large seagoing canoes. In the bush behind Langi Heketa are a number of large platforms or *paepae* on which the royal residences would have stood.

Bus service to the trilithon is about hourly until 1700, and the trilithon is just beside the road. If you have time, follow one of the tracks down to the rocky coast. Actually, you'll need more than an hour to visit this interesting area and read all the posted explanations. When you've seen enough, just start walking back along the road and flag down the first bus that passes.

POLYNESIAN STONEHENGE

JOHN PENISTON

Ha'amonga means "a burden as carried by two men." This archway of coral rock near the village of Niutoua is thought to have been the entrance gate to the royal compound of the old Tongan capital. The two upright stones are calculated to weigh 30-40 tons apiece, and the cross piece is almost six meters long. The structure was built around A.D. 1200 by King Tu'itatui, a ruler who felt dissention within his family, since each of the upright columns represents a son, while the massive lintel mortised into supports represents the bond between the sons. Nearby is a 2.7-meter tall slab against which, it's said, this king would lean while addressing his people, a precaution to prevent anyone from spearing him in the back. It's been suggested that the trilithon was also a seasonal calendar, a sort of Polynesian Stonehenge. The structure has notches on the lintel that correspond to the sun's rising on the longest and shortest days of the year.

THE EAST COAST

It's a three-km walk southeast from the bus stop at Mu'a Police Station to Haveluliku village (no bus service). Ask someone here to point out the *makatolo,* huge stones that the demigod Maui reputedly threw across from 'Eua Island at an errant chicken. **'Anahulu Cave** is on the coast near the village. You'll need a flashlight to explore the stalactite cave. The large freshwater pool inside is swimmable and the intrepid could swim back into another hidden cavern, but don't leave your possessions in too obvious a spot, as there have been thefts here. You may be charged T$2 pp admission. Upon request the dive shops in Nuku'alofa will organize scuba diving in the cave.

At low tide only, you can walk south from the cave to **Laulea Beach.** The beach continues unbroken for several km to **'Oholei Beach** where Tongan feasts were once staged in the Hina Cave. There's a fine view across to 'Eua Island.

Sporadic bus service runs from Lavengatonga village near 'Oholei back to town.

OFFSHORE ISLANDS

Some of the many small islands off Tongatapu's north coast bear small tourist resorts that are favorite day-trip destinations for tourists staying in Nuku'alofa, especially on Sunday. Pangaimotu Island and Makaha'a Island tend to cater to budget or independent travelers, while Fafa Island is more upmarket, and Atata Island is set up for packaged tourists from New Zealand. Scuba diving is possible upon prior arrangement, but these are mostly picnic places where you go to get some sun and have a day at the beach.

Accommodations
Pangaimotu Island Resort (Box 740, Nuku'alofa; tel. 22-588, fax 23-759), also known as "Tongan Beachcomber Island Village," is the closest island resort to Nuku'alofa. It's owned by the

royal family and the name means "royal island." The four simple *fales* are T$45/60 single/double, while the six-bed dorm is T$20 pp and camping is T$15 pp. No cooking facilities are provided, and meals at their restaurant are medium priced: fish and chips lunch T$8, dinner T$15. The tap water is saline. The reef around the island is good, and there's even a half-sunken ship, the *Marner,* sticking up out of the water for snorkelers to explore. If you're a yachtie you'll want to know that Pangaimotu has excellent anchorage (all the other offshore islands are surrounded by treacherous reefs). Boat transfers are T$10 pp return. It's a day-trip island and somewhat of a local hangout. On Sunday many local expats come over to booze, and while it's not officially banned to bring over your own lunch, you'll be more comfortable having your picnic well away from the resort and other tourists. Budget.

Sun Island Resort (Private Bag 44, Nuku'alofa; tel. 23-335, fax 22-915), on Makaha'a Island just beyond Pangaimotu, is smaller, quieter, and less expensive than the other resorts. It's owned by Princess Pilolevu, but locally managed and a bit rundown with poor service—a do-your-own-thing type of place. There are just three *fales:* one double right on the beach at T$60 single or double, another double a bit back from the beach at T$45, and a triple a bit away from the beach at T$60 for up to three. Overnight campers pay T$10 pp. No cooking facilities are provided, but the restaurant/bar charges just T$5/7.50/10 for breakfast/lunch/dinner—less than at the other places. A range of water sports is available. Though the beach isn't as good as at Pangaimotu, the nearby reef features huge coral formations alive with baby fish (T$5 extra charge for boat shuttles to the reef). Their boat leaves Faua Jetty weekdays at 1000, weekends at 1000, 1100, and 1200 (T$10 roundtrip). Budget.

Fafa Island Resort (Box 1444, Nuku'alofa; tel. 22-800, fax 23-592), quite a distance farther out than Pangaimotu, is very professionally managed by Rainer Urtel. The eight standard *fales* with private bath (T$75/85/100 single/double/triple) are rustic but adequate, while the eight superior beachside *fales* (T$150 single or double, T$190 triple) are larger and more luxurious with open shower, sun deck, and garden. The marvelous meals in their pleasant thatched restaurant/bar are T$50/60 pp for two/three (no cooking facilities for guests). A full range of nonmotorized sporting activities is offered in the sapphire blue lagoon surrounding this delightful palm-covered, seven-hectare island. Snorkeling gear is loaned free but windsurfing and Hobie cat riding are T$20 an hour. The initial 30-minute boat ride is T$16 pp roundtrip, but once you're staying they'll ferry you into town and back as often as you like at no extra cost. Their shuttle boat leaves the island at 0900 and 1630, leaves Faua Jetty at 1100 and 1730, so you can easily spend the day in town. Fafa can be a little quiet at times, and would not be a good choice if you were out for aggressive motorized watersports, sightseeing, or socializing. Inexpensive to moderate.

The New Zealander-oriented **Royal Sunset Island Resort** (Box 960, Nuku'alofa; tel./fax 21-254), on Atata Island 11 km northwest of town, is the most remote of the small island hotels off Tongatapu. The entire island is owned by the king's third son, Prince Lavaka, and most of Royal Sunset's local employees are from the 233-person Tongan village on the island. The 26 units with private bath, fridge, kitchenette, and overhead fan are T$110/120/160/185 single/double/triple/quad for an eastern unit or T$116/135/180/205 on the western side. If you book through a travel agent abroad you could pay considerably more. Their three-meal plan is T$64 pp, and opinions about the food vary. Drinks at the bar are on the expensive side, so take along a couple of bottles of duty-free booze if somebody booked you in here. There's a swimming pool, and free activities for guests include tennis, Hobie cat sailing, paddleboarding, windsurfing, rowboating, and snorkeling. Scuba diving is T$70 for two tanks with equipment rental available at an additional charge. The resort is right on a broad white-sand beach, and the snorkeling along Egeria Channel is great. Deep-sea fishing is T$60 an hour (minimum of four hours) and up to six people can go for that price. The resort has a three-cabin yacht, the *Impetuous,* available for overnight charters at T$750 a day, plus T$45 pp for food. Island transfers from Nuku'alofa on their large catamaran *Manutahi II* are T$34 pp roundtrip. Royal Sunset is the place to go if you want lots of sporting activities and organized entertainment. Moderate.

Getting There

While the cost of scuba diving in Tonga is high, the various day-trips to offshore islands are cheap and a leisurely boat trip to one of the island resorts described above is recommended. The Pangaimotu Island boat leaves daily at 1000 and 1100, with extra trips at 1200 and 1300 on Sunday (T$10 for transfers only). Children under 12 pay half price. Sun Island charges T$10 for roundtrip transfers Mon.-Sat. at 1000, Sunday at 1000, 1100, and 1200. Fafa Island also does excellent day-trips daily at 1100 (T$30 including a good lunch). On Monday, Fafa Island Resort offers a romantic dinner cruise with a Polynesian floor show departing Nuku'alofa at 1730 (T$40). Royal Sunset's day-trip departs Sunday at 1000 (T$30 including a barbecue lunch). All these leave from Faua Jetty near Nuku'alofa's fish market, and bookings can be made at Teta Tours or at the International Dateline Hotel tour desk (no booking required for the Pangaimotu and Sun Island shuttles). Provided the weather cooperates, they're an excellent way to pass Nuku'alofa's pious Sunday, and you'll have a better chance of meeting interesting people if you go that day.

early 19th-century Tongan houses

'EUA ISLAND

A rough 40-km boat ride from Nuku'alofa, 'Eua is a good place to go for the weekend. Since tourist facilities are undeveloped you won't feel as oppressed as you might on a Nuku'alofa Sunday, and you'll have to entertain yourself here anyway. Bony bareback horses can be hired, but all spots on the island are within walking distance.

'Eua's hills are a contrast to flat Tongatapu. The thickly forested spine down the east side of 'Eua drops to perpendicular cliffs, while the west half is largely taken up by plantations and villages. At 87 square km, it's Tonga's third-largest island.

Facilities on 'Eua are extremely basic; this is a chance to get off the beaten tourist track and see real Tongan life. It's a rather scrubby, depressing place, indicative of why so many Tongans live in Auckland. Three full days are enough to get the feel of the island.

SIGHTS

Matalanga 'a Maui

Legend tells how the demigod Maui thrust his digging stick into 'Eua and pulled it back and forth in anger at his mother, threatening thereby to upset the island. To visit the great pothole that remains from this momentous event, head south of the sawmill and Ha'atua Mormon Church, take the second bush road on the left, and walk inland about 10 minutes. You'll need keen intuition or a guide to locate the pit hidden in the middle of a plantation on the right, although the lower level of the trees growing in it is an indicator. Holding onto vines, you can get right down into Matalanga 'a Maui itself for an eerie view of jungle-clad walls towering around you.

Southern 'Eua

Most of the families in Pangai and farther south were relocated from Niuafo'ou Island after a devastating volcanic eruption there in 1946. The road south from the wharf terminates after 10 km at **Ha'aluma Beach.** The deserted beach is a weathered reef with sandy pools to swim in, but it's only safe as long as you hug the shore. There are some small blowholes and a view of Kalau Island.

Just before the descent to the beach, take the road to the left and keep straight one hour almost to the south tip of the island. Here a track veers left through high grass and starts going north up the east coast past a gate. The first cliff you come to across the field from the track is **Lakufa'anga,** where Tongans once called turtles from the sea. So many have been slaughtered that none appear anymore. Look down on the grassy ledges below the cliffs and you'll spot the nesting places of seabirds.

Legend tells how Li'angahuo 'a Maui on 'Eua was formed when the demigod Maui hurled his spear across the island.

Continue north on the track a short distance, watching on the left for a huge depression partly visible through the trees. This is **Li'angahuo 'a Maui,** a tremendous natural stone bridge by the sea, which you can pass right over without realizing if you're not paying attention. Work your way around the side of the pothole for a clear view of the bridge. The story goes that after creating Matalanga, Maui threw his digging stick across 'Eua. It pierced the cliffs at this point and dove into the sea to carve out the Tonga Deep. After this impressive sight, continue up the coast a short distance to see more cliffs, which explain why the east side of 'Eua is uninhabited.

Northern 'Eua

Tufuvai village, two km south of 'Ononua wharf, is attractive but the undertow is deadly on an outgoing tide. Both this and **Ufilei Beach,** just two km north of the wharf across Tonga's only river bridge, are fine for a sunset stroll.

Tonga's most spectacular scenic viewpoint is just northeast of Houma village at **Anokula,** where in 1983 the king built himself a palace of which only the concrete foundations now remain. The soaring cliffs drop 120 meters straight into the coastal strip, creating an unsurpassed panorama of power and beauty.

After this visual blast look for a trail north up the coast to another access road that leads down to **Kahana Spring,** which supplies 'Eua with Tonga's purest water. Just beyond the spring is a second magnificent viewpoint over the east coast, directly above **Fungatave Beach.**

The Interior

Tonga's finest tropical forest is on the slopes just above Futu. Take the road inland a little south of Haukinima Motel toward the Forestry Experimental Farm. Continue east along the main road about 30 minutes till you reach the nursery. **Hafu Pool** is near the office, down a trail that continues straight ahead from the road on the right, but it's hardly worth the effort.

The forest, on the other hand, is well worth exploring for the many exotic species planted by the Ministry of Agriculture and Forestry (pine, red cedar, tree ferns) and the abundant birdlife, especially Pacific pigeons, crimson-crowned fruit doves, white-collared kingfishers, blue-crowned lorikeets, and red-breasted musk parrots. Now

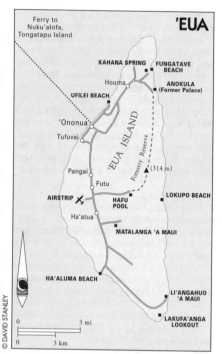

Ferry to
Nuku'alofa,
Tongatapu Island

'EUA

KAHANA SPRING   FUNGATAVE BEACH

Houma   ANOKULA (Former Palace)

UFILEI BEACH

'Ononua
Tufuvai

'EUA ISLAND

Forestry Reserve

Pangai   (314 m)

Futu

AIRSTRIP   HAFU POOL   LOKUPO BEACH

Ha'atua

MATALANGA 'A MAUI

HA'ALUMA BEACH

LI'ANGAHUO 'A MAUI

LAKUFA'ANGA LOOKOUT

0   3 mi

0   3 km

© DAVID STANLEY

both forests and birds of 'Eua are threatened by villagers who burn the trees for land on which to plant their sweet potatoes and yams. After a few years the soil is depleted and the farmers move on, while the loss of trees lowers 'Eua's water table, threatening the island with drought.

The road on the left at the nursery leads through the forest reserve to Topuva'e 'a Maui (312 m), the highest point on the island, where there's the simple grave of a New Zealand soldier who died here during WW II. A track leads down to Lokupo Beach from just north of the grave.

PRACTICALITIES

Accommodations

The two guesthouses on 'Eua are about 200 meters apart on or near the main road down the middle of the island, a five-minute walk north of the airstrip (T$2-3 by taxi from the wharf). Your best bet is **Setaita Guest House** (Setaita Archibald, tel. 50-124), 400 meters north of the airport and three km south of the wharf. The three rooms in this two-story building are T$25/27 single/double. Camping in the yard is T$5. You can pay a small fee for gas and cook for yourself or order meals from the family. Bicycle rental is T$10 a day. Budget.

The **Haukinima Motel** (Sione Manukia, tel. 50-088) nearby has eight rooms with shared bath are T$17/22 single/double. Grubby communal cooking facilities are provided (watch your food!) and simple but filling Tongan meals are served. Royal Tongan beer is available at the bar on the premises, which is where the problem lies. Unless you're stone deaf, don't expect to get any sleep until they close (ask Sione what time that might be). Shoestring.

Some of those who camped on the beach on the inhabited west side of the island have become victims of theft, and if you're interested in camping wild, a much better plan would be to trek around to the southeast side beyond Li'angahuo 'a Maui. Carry all the food and water you'll need.

Entertainment

The optimum time to come to 'Eua is late August or early September during the 'Eua Agricultural Show. The show grounds are right by the hospital at Futu.

If the nightlife at the Haukinima Motel doesn't satisfy you, there's **Maxi Disco Hall** across the street. A live band plays Friday and Saturday at 2000 and quite possibly a couple of other nights too. The hall is run by Taina, who named it after her cat, Maxi. On dance nights the place is packed.

Services

What facilities 'Eua offers are near 'Ononua wharf, including the Bank of Tonga (tel. 50-145), post office (tel. 50-066), Telecom center (tel. 50-115), Friendly Islands Bookshop (tel. 50-167), and TCFS Supermarket (tel. 50-120). Kaufana Airport and both guesthouses are in the center of the island, three km south. Here too are the Forestry Division (tel. 50-116), with a good map on the wall, and Niu'eiki Hospital (tel. 50-111), a bit back toward 'Ononua. A public bus shuttles back and forth between 'Ononua and Ha'atua every half hour or so on weekdays.

Getting There

Royal Tongan Airlines (tel. 50-188) has daily flights Mon.-Sat. between Nuku'alofa and 'Eua (T$19 one-way, T$36 roundtrip).

To charter an aircraft between 'Eua and Nuku'alofa from **Pacific Island Seaplanes** (tel. 25-177) would cost T$360 for four persons (maximum 64 kilos of luggage total). They'll only fly to 'Eua when the wind is from the east or northeast.

The two boats shuttling between Nuku'alofa and 'Eua are described under **Getting Around by Ship** in the chapter introduction. In general the boats leave 'Eua Mon.-Sat. at 0630, departing Nuku'alofa's Faua Jetty for the return at 1300 the same days. Both charge T$6 each way. Due to the action of the southeast trades the four-hour boat trip is far less rough westbound than eastbound, so if you're a terrible sailor you might want to fly over from Nuku'alofa and catch the boat back. In fact, so many people have figured that one out that the airline folks have made their roundtrip tickets slightly cheaper!

The harbor at 'Eua is less secure than the one at Nuku'alofa, so if strong winds are blowing or a hurricane warning has been issued for anywhere within a thousand km, that day's ferry trip will be canceled and the boat will remain tied up at Faua Jetty in Nuku'alofa. Of course, this happens more frequently during the southern summer (Dec.-April), but one should always be prepared to spend a day or two longer on 'Eua than planned or be prepared to fly back. The Saturday trip from Nuku'alofa is the most likely to be canceled in bad weather, so it's safer to go over on Friday and not count on being able to come back on Monday. When the boat is canceled, Royal Tongan schedules additional flights.

ATA AND MINERVA

Ata Island, 136 km southwest of 'Eua, has been uninhabited since the 1860s, when King George Tupou I ordered the 200 villagers to move to 'Eua, where he could better protect them against the depredations of Peruvian slavers. Ata is an extinct volcano, and one of its twin peaks reaches 382 meters. The lack of a harbor and remote location have made resettlement unlikely. Ata is the main breeding place in Tonga of the wedge-tailed shearwater, red-footed booby, Kermadec petrel, masked booby, blue-grey noddy, and red-tailed tropicbird.

Tonga ends at the two Minerva reefs, far to the south of Fiji's Lau Group and 290 km southwest of Ata. Minerva's only visitors are yachties who call occasionally between Vava'u and New Zealand, or New Zealand and Fiji. A deep pass on the northwest side of North Minerva's circular reef gives access to a protected lagoon five km wide with good anchorage on the north and east sides. At low tide you can walk across the reef's flat surface, but at high tide the only things visible between you and the breakers are old shipwrecks, a few coral boulders thrown up by storms, and a flagpole without a flag to the south. This recalls an attempt by right-wing American millionaires to seize Minerva Reef in the early 1970s for the creation of a taxless utopian state. In 1972 the king arrived in person to declare Tongan sovereignty. It's an eerie place, the outer edge of paradise.

an early 19th-century view of Nomuka

THE HA'APAI GROUP

This great group of 51 low coral islands and two volcanoes between Nuku'alofa and Vava'u is a beachcomber's paradise. Perfect white powdery beaches run right around the mostly uninhabited islands, but treacherous shoals keep cruising yachts away. There are two clusters: Nomuka is the largest of the seldom-visited southern islands, while Lifuka is at the center of a string of islands to the north. Some 8,000 people live on 16 of the islands. Ha'apai is mostly for beach people; if you're not a beach lover you'll soon get bored. Snorkelers and scuba divers have 150 km of untouched barrier reef, vast banks of soft and hard coral, and 1,600 species of tropical fish to keep them busy. Humpback whales (July-Oct.), spinner dolphins, and sea turtles add to the fun.

The first European to visit Ha'apai was Abel Tasman who called at Nomuka in 1643. Captain Cook made prolonged stops on the same island in 1774 and 1777; on a visit to Lifuka in 1777 he coined the term "Friendly Islands," unaware of a plot by the Tongans to murder him. Later, off Tofua on 28 April 1789, Fletcher Christian and his mutineers lowered Captain William Bligh and 18 loyal members of his crew into a whaleboat, beginning one of the longest voyages in an open boat in maritime history, from Tongan waters to Timor in the Dutch East Indies (6,500 km)—a fantastic accomplishment of endurance and seamanship. Bligh's group suffered its only casualty of the trip, John Norton, quartermaster of the *Bounty,* when they landed on the southwest side of Tofua just after the mutiny and clashed with Tongans.

Tofua

Tofua (56 square km) is a flat-topped volcanic island about 505 meters high with a steep and rocky shoreline all the way around the island. The 10 abandoned houses and three churches at Hokula near the north coast, and Manaka, a tiny settlement on the east coast, are used by villagers from Kotu Island, who come to harvest Tofua's potent kava. It takes about an hour to climb up to Tofua's rim from Hokula. The large steep-sided, four-km-wide caldera in the interior is occupied by a freshwater crater lake 30 meters above sea level and 250 meters deep. Tofua is still active: steam and gases issue from a volcanic cone on the north side of the lake, and a hot pool is on the east side. Passing ships can see flames at night.

Larry Simon and John Way of **Pacific Island Seaplanes** (tel. 25-177, fax 25-165) run charter flights to Tofua from Nuku'alofa. The Beaver seaplane makes a photo pass over Kao and lands on Tofua's crater lake. Passengers then hike across the caldera for an hour to a smoking crater, and later there's time for a swim in the lake. From Nuku'alofa this memorable excursion costs T$250 pp (four-person minimum), and for an extra T$50 pp the trip can be extended to Ha'apai. In Pangai ask Jürgen at the Sandy Beach Resort.

Kao

This extinct 1,046-meter-high volcano, four km north of Tofua, is the tallest in Tonga; on a clear day the classic triangular cone is visible from Lifuka, 56 km east. There's no anchorage, but it's possible to land on the south side of the uninhabited island in good weather. The lower slopes are well wooded, becoming barren higher up. Kao can be climbed in a long day.

Fonuafo'ou

One of the world's outstanding natural phenomena, this geographical freak 72 km northwest of Tongatapu was first observed in 1865 by the crew of HMS *Falcon*. Jack-in-the-box Fonuafo'ou (New Land) alternates between shoal and island. Sometimes this temperamental volcanic mound stands 100 meters high and three km long; other times the sea washes the exposed part away and it's completely under water. If you walk on it you're ankle deep in hot, black scoria (shaggy lava), an extremely desolate, blackened surface. At last report Fonuafo'ou was submerged again for the fifth time in the past 120 years.

Ha'afeva

Ha'afeva, 42 km southwest of Pangai, is sometimes visited in the night by the ferry *Olovaka* plying between Lifuka and Nuku'alofa. Around 310 people live on this 181-hectare island but there's little reason for anyone else to get off here.

Nomuka

Although the main island the southern Ha'apai group, Nomuka has only 551 inhabitants and the number has fallen steadily in recent years. In the 18th century Nomuka was far from being the backwater it is today, and Tasman, Cook, and Bligh all called here to take on water from one of Nomuka's springs. A large brackish lake called Ano'ava sits in the middle of this triangular, seven-square-km coral island, each of the three sides of which is four km long.

LIFUKA AND VICINITY

Most visitors to Ha'apai spend their time on Lifuka (11 square km) and its adjacent islands. There are convenient facilities in Pangai, a sleepy big village (3,000 inhabitants) strung along Holopeka Road parallel to the beach. There's even electric lighting! Although Lifuka is Tonga's fourth most populous island, it's only a 10-minute walk out of this "metropolis;" then you're all alone among the coconut palms or strolling along an endless deserted beach. The most convenient and enjoyable way to explore Lifuka and Foa is by rented bicycle.

It was near the north end of Lifuka that Captain Cook was so well received in 1777 that he called

these the Friendly Islands. On the same spot in 1806, the crew of the British privateer *Port-au-Prince* received a different welcome when Tongan warriors stormed aboard and murdered most of the crew. The captain's clerk, William Mariner, age 15, was spared and taken under the protection of Chief Finau 'Ulukalala II. Mariner remained in Tonga four years, participating in 'Ulukalala's conquest of Tongatapu using cannon taken from the ship. Eventually a passing ship carried him back to England where he spent the rest of his life as a stockbroker, accidentally drowning in the Thames in 1853. In 1816 Mariner published *An Account of the Natives of the Ton-*

gan Islands in the South Pacific Ocean, the classic narration of pre-Christian Tonga.

Sights

On Holopeka Road at the south end of town is the **King's Palace,** with many fine old trees bordering the compound. The king comes every September for the agricultural fair, which is held in the field across the street.

Just north of the palace and inland a block on Faifekau Road is the Free Wesleyan Church, where a **miraculous cross** appeared in 1975. The spot is now outlined in cement on the grass outside the church. Palasi Road, the next street north, runs right across the island to the long, lonely **beach** of high golden sands extending down the east side of Lifuka, only a 10-minute walk from town. Unfortunately the locals have adversely affected the beauty of this beach by mining it for sand.

Just north of Pangai is the grave and monument of Wesleyan missionary **Reverend Shirley**

Baker (1836-1903), an adviser to King George Tupou I, who helped frame the Emancipation Edict of 1862 and the 1875 constitution. In 1880 Baker resigned his ministry and governed Tonga in the name of the elderly king. To increase his power he persuaded King George to break with Wesleyan headquarters in Australia and establish the independent Free Wesleyan Church. Baker's persecution of Tongan Wesleyans still loyal to the Australian church and his dictatorial rule prompted the British High Commissioner in Fiji to send a warship to collect him in 1890. Baker was later allowed to retire to Ha'apai and his children erected this monument after his death.

Sports and Recreation

One of the main reasons to visit Ha'apai is the diving, and **Watersports Ha'apai** (Box 65, Pangai; tel./fax 60-097) based at the Niu'akalo Beach Hotel can show you some pretty incredible things with the help of a snorkel or tank. It's run by a German named Roland Schwara who charges

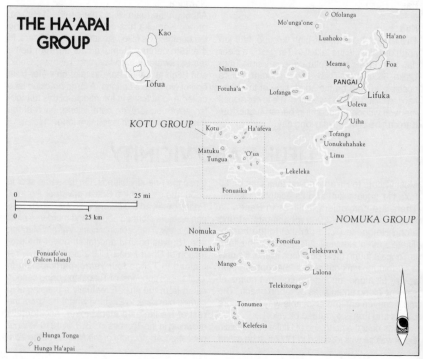

THE HA'APAI GROUP

Ofolanga
Mo'unga'one
Kao
Luahoko
Ha'ano
Meama
Foa
Niniva
PANGAI
Tofua
Fotuha'a
Lofanga
Lifuka
Uoleva
KOTU GROUP
Kotu
Ha'afeva
'Uiha
Tofanga
Uonukuhahake
Matuku
'O'ua
Limu
Tungua
Lekeleka
Fonuaika
NOMUKA GROUP
0   25 mi
0   25 km
Nomuka
Fonoifua
Fonuafo'ou
Nomukaiki
Telekivava'u
(Falcon Island)
Mango
Lalona
Telekitonga
Tonumea
Kelefesia
Hunga Tonga
Hunga Ha'apai

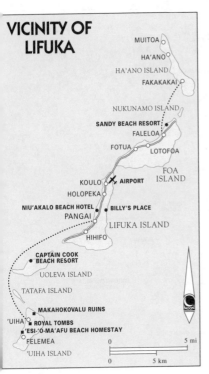

VICINITY OF LIFUKA

MUITOA
HA'ANO
HA'ANO ISLAND
FAKAKAKAI
NUKUNAMO ISLAND
SANDY BEACH RESORT
FALELOA
FOTUA
LOTOFOA
FOA ISLAND
KOULO ✈ AIRPORT
HOLOPEKA
NIU'AKALO BEACH HOTEL • **BILLY'S PLACE**
PANGAI
LIFUKA ISLAND
HIHIFO
CAPTAIN COOK BEACH RESORT
UOLEVA ISLAND
TATAFA ISLAND
MAKAHOKOVALU RUINS
'UIHA ■ **ROYAL TOMBS**
'ESI-'O-MA'AFU BEACH HOMESTAY
FELEMEA
'UIHA ISLAND

0   5 mi
0   5 km

tional charge for cooking gas is levied to use the communal kitchen. Of course, they'd rather do the cooking for you at T$4-6 for breakfast and T$8-12 for dinner, but you must order in advance. Their food is good and the portions are gargantuan (as you'd expect in Tonga), but at those prices it gets expensive. If you really do want to cook for yourself, check out the kitchen as soon as you arrive and ask about extra charges for gas and electricity if you use it. Expect to have to share the facilities with the managers, who will be cooking for other guests. In addition to the places listed below, the **Government Rest House** (tel. 60-100), behind the Tonga Visitors Bureau, sometimes accepts tourists at T$10 pp.

Fifita's Guest House (Fifita Vi, tel. 60-213), near the center of the village, offers eight comfortable rooms in a two-story building at T$15/22 single/double. You can cook your own food for a daily T$2 fee (or Fifita will happily do it for you). Bicycle rentals are T$5 and boat trips to Uoleva

T$50/80 for one/two tanks, plus T$15 for gear. His scuba resort course is T$75 (no certificate), and he'll happily take you snorkeling at T$16/25 a half/full day including a mask and snorkel. A guided day-trip in a sea kayak is T$48 including lunch (kayak rentals without lunch or guide are T$25 a day). If a group of six can be found, Roland will run a speedboat trip to the volcano on Tofua, costing T$150 pp for the boat, plus T$60 pp a day for guides and meals. Overnight trips almost anywhere in Ha'apai are possible. If countless colorful fish swimming above unbroken coral in crystal clear water is your idea of paradise, you'll find it here (plus a shark or two).

ACCOMMODATIONS

Pangai

All of the guesthouses in Pangai itself allow guests to cook their own food, but a small additional

This distinctive monument just outside Pangai marks the grave of Rev. Shirley Baker, adviser to King George Tupou I and prime minister of Tonga.

PANGAI

Island can be arranged at T$40 for up to four persons. Airport transfers are free upon request. Shoestring.

Evaloni Guest House (Mrs. Sitali Hu'akau, Box 56, Pangai; tel. 60-029), back behind the Visitors Bureau in Pangai, has eight basic rooms for T$18/25/30 single/double/triple. Meals are available at T$5 for breakfast or lunch, T$12 for dinner. It costs T$2 pp a day to use the cooking facilities. They're seldom full. Budget.

The friendly, nine-room **Fonongava'inga Guest House** (Mrs. Langilangi Vi, Box 14, Pangai; tel. 60-038) nearby has five small rooms in the main building at T$10/15 single/double and four larger rooms in the new wing at T$15/22/30 single/double/triple. The bathroom facilities are communal in all cases but only the new rooms have access to hot water. You can cook your own food in the owners' house next door at T$2 pp a week, or order excellent meals at T$3 for breakfast or lunch, T$8 for dinner. The atmosphere here is pleasant, with a large living room and front porch available to travelers. Bicycles are for hire at T$7. Langilangi is very kind and helpful. Shoestring.

In the southern section of Pangai is **Lindsay Guest House** (tel. 60-107), Pangai's newest place to stay, with six shared-bath rooms at

T$15/25 single/double. Meals are served or you can cook, and a small grocery store and bakery are on the premises. Bicycles are T$5 a day. Budget.

By the beach at the south end of Hihifo village is the **Vaimoana Holiday House** (Mrs. Selai Taufetofua, Box 13, Pangai; tel. 60-105) with four rooms and cooking facilities. It's often full or closed.

North of Town

The quiet **Niu'akalo Beach Hotel** (Box 18, Pangai; tel. 60-028), north of town between Pangai and Holopeka, offers 12 neat little rooms on landscaped grounds facing a long, sandy beach only good for swimming at high tide. A small room with shared bath in a four-room standard unit is T$16.50/22 single/double, while rooms with private bath in the duplex deluxe units are T$27.50/32 single/double, or T$60 for a complete unit (up to six persons). Each cluster has a common living room shared by all guests, but there's only cold water. The biggest drawback is the price of the meals in the restaurant/bar, and no cooking facilities are available for guests. Friday at 1900 there's a beach barbecue or a full Tongan feast, depending on how many guests are present. Rental snorkels, boats, and bicycles (T$10) are available. Your charming hosts, Mrs. Seletute Falevai, her husband, son, and two daughters, are very helpful. Shoestring to budget.

Billy's Place (Box 66, Pangai; tel./fax 60-058), also known as Evaloni Beach Fales, is run by Viliami Hu'akau and his American wife Sandy with a bit of help from Milika. Unlike the places in Pangai that are serenaded all night by barking dogs and rocked by legions of church bells at the crack of dawn, Billy's is in a coconut plantation on a long, deserted beach, 1.5 km north of town. It's on the breezy ocean side of the island, across narrow Lifuka from the Niu'akalo Beach Hotel. Watch for flying foxes headed north in the morning, south in the evening. Billy's five *fales* with lockable doors are T$35/55 single/double, a free breakfast, bicycle, and snorkeling gear included. Guests and nonguests alike can order surprisingly good burritos, fish, pizza, and pasta to be consumed on their pleasant patio (lunch is no problem, but order dinner in advance). One Swiss reader said she liked the cozy atmosphere and thought it was loads of fun. Airport transfers are free. Budget.

Telefoni Sunset Beachhouse (tel. 60-044) is farther north, beside the lagoon between the wharf and the airport. The three rooms in this family dwelling are T$15/28 single/double and all guests share the bathroom, kitchen, and lounge. Bicycles rent for T$10. Budget.

The **Mele Tonga Guest House** (tel. 60-042) is on a reasonable beach at Holopeka about 500 meters south of the airstrip. At T$15/20 single/double with breakfast, there are two double rooms and a single in the main house, plus another double in an adjacent *fale,* and a communal kitchen in a separate building. For T$7 you can rent a bicycle. It's run by a local schoolteacher named Letty, and if she's not around when you arrive, ask at the small store beyond the church next to the guesthouse. Shoestring.

OTHER PRACTICALITIES

Food and Entertainment

Pangai has several adequate stores opposite the Bank of Tonga and a small market on the north side of town. **Meloise Restaurant** is also near the Bank of Tonga. Ask around for dances in church halls on Friday and Saturday nights. You can drink kava all evening at several saloons around Pangai for a flat fee.

Services and Information

The Bank of Tonga (tel. 60-933) changes traveler's checks weekdays 0930-1230 and 1330-1530. The **Telecom telephone exchange** (tel. 60-255), where you can place long-distance calls, is on the small street behind the Visitors Bureau. If you want to fax anyone on Lifuka, or receive a fax yourself, direct those messages to fax 60-200 (the clerk will call whoever is named on the fax and ask them to come and pick it up). Yachties should report their arrival at the post office even if they've already checked in at Vava'u.

The Tonga Visitors Bureau (Mele Likiliki, tel./fax 60-733) has an office on Holopeka Rd. in the center of Pangai that can provide brochures and good local advice.

Niu'ui Hospital (tel. 60-201) is two kilometers south of the wharf.

Getting There

Royal Tongan Airlines (tel. 60-566), next to the post office, flies from Tongatapu to Ha'apai (T$67) daily except Sunday, and from Ha'apai to Vava'u (T$67) twice a week. Pilolevu Airport (HPA) is at Koulo, five km north of Pangai. Most of the places to stay offer free transfers, otherwise a taxi will be around T$3 for the car.

A unique way to arrive is on Pacific Island Seaplanes' Beaver aircraft. A direct flight from Nuku'alofa will cost T$240 pp (minimum of four), but a more exciting route would be via Tofua Island with a landing on the freshwater crater lake (T$300 pp, 4.5 hours). Only 16 kilos pp of luggage may be brought on this flight, but it's an option well worth considering if you were planning to fly to Ha'apai anyway. The seaplane can land in Pangai harbor or directly off the Sandy Beach Resort (to arrange such a trip *from* Ha'apai, contact Jürgen at the Sandy Beach Resort).

Ferries between Nuku'alofa and Vava'u call regularly at Pangai, northbound very early Tuesday and Wednesday mornings, southbound in the middle of the night on Wednesday and Thursday. The *Loto Ha'angana* or *Tautahi* runs a day before the *Olovaha* in both directions. The *Olovaha* office (tel. 60-699) is inside the red container on Taufa'ahau Wharf. The office of the *Loto Ha'angana* and *Tautahi* (tel. 60-855) is in the adjacent cream-colored container (open only on ship days). Deck fares from Pangai are T$28 to Nuku'alofa and T$21 to Vava'u. Ships tie up to Taufa'ahau Wharf near the center of Pangai; turn right as you disembark. There's a large passenger shelter on the wharf where you can wait until dawn if you happen to arrive in the middle of the night (as is usually the case). When there are strong westerly winds, the ships may not risk landing at Pangai.

ISLANDS AROUND LIFUKA

Foa

A causeway links Lifuka and Foa (population 1,439). Weekdays from early morning until around 1600, and also on Saturday morning, buses leaves intermittently from Pangai for **Faleloa,** Foa's northernmost village. Continue 20 minutes on foot to Foa's northern tip to look

a quiet waterfront scene at Pangai

across to **Nukunamo Island,** owned by the king. The beach is beautiful here and the snorkeling is fine at slack tide.

Outboard motorboats bring villagers from **Ha'ano Island** to the wharf at Faleloa, and you can go back with them most afternoons for about T$1 one-way.

The **Sandy Beach Resort** (Box 61, Pangai; tel./fax 60-600) opened in 1995 near the north end of Foa Island, one and a half km from Faleloa. The 12 well-constructed beachfront bungalows with ceiling fan, fridge, 24-hour electricity, porch, and private bath cost T$140 single or double (third persons T$27). Cooking facilities are not provided for guests and children are not accepted. Like the accommodations, the fancy food in the restaurant is geared to a more upscale clientele than the backpacker places on Lifuka (T$45 for breakfast and dinner). The swimming and snorkeling are fine, even at low tide, and snorkeling gear, bicycles, and an outrigger canoe are loaned free. Dolphins swim offshore. Paid activities include bareback horse riding, boat trips, amphibian excursions, and ocean kayaking. German instructor Monika Rahimi handles scuba diving. All facilities (including the restaurant) are for resort guests only. The Sandy Beach is run by a German couple named Jürgen and Sigi Stavenow, former managers of the Seaview Restaurant in Nuku'alofa, and before you leave you'll know all there is to know about them. The weekly Tongan cultural show is good too. Airport transfers are free. Moderate.

Uoleva

From the south end of Lifuka, three and a half km from town, you can wade across the reef at low tide to sparsely populated Uoleva Island, which has super snorkeling off its southwest end. Check tide times at the Visitors Bureau in Pangai and don't set out if the tide is about to come in as it takes at least 30 minutes to cross. Rubber booties or reef shoes will be required to protect your feet. Sunday is a good day to go as you won't meet any copra cutters.

The **Captain Cook Beach Resort** (Soni Kaifoto, Box 49, Pangai; tel. 60-014), on the northwest side of Uoleva, offers a real South Seas experience. The four rooms in two basic duplex units cost T$15/20 single/double, plus T$10 pp for breakfast and dinner. If you were thinking of camping here, check beforehand that it will be allowed. You should also carry some food with you as nothing can be purchased on the island although water is supplied. The long white beach is fabulous and you'll share this sizable, coconut-covered island with only your fellow guests, the occasional local who comes to work his/her garden, and free-ranging cows, goats, and pigs. It's restful, just don't expect luxuries like electricity and running water. Enjoy the sunsets off their beach, the stars in the sky, and the utter tranquility. One male reader wrote: "I fell in love with this place the minute I arrived." Unfortunately some female readers have had a different experience, and the Captain Cook can only be recommended to couples and men alone. Shoestring.

At low tide Uoleva can be reached on foot from Lifuka, but it would take several hours to walk/wade from Pangai to the Captain Cook Resort and it might be very dangerous to try to do so laden with a backpack when a current was running (carry a pole for balance). A much better idea is to come/go by boat and transfers from Pangai cost about T$8 pp each way. Try contacting the owner, Soni Kaifoto, at his home on Haufolau Rd. in Pangai, or if you're staying at Fifita Guest House, ask Fifita as Soni is her uncle. Otherwise the people in the shop on the Pangai waterfront can help you organize transfers for the same price.

'Uiha

'Uiha Island (population 756), south of Lifuka, is more slow moving than Pangai, but there are things to see, an agreeable place to stay, and fairly regular access by boat. The burial ground of the Tongan royal family was on 'Uiha until the move to Nuku'alofa. Also to be seen in front of the church in the middle of 'Uiha village is a cannon from the Peruvian slave ship *Margarita,* which was sacked off 'Uiha in 1863. A second cannon inside the church serves as a baptismal font. Also visit the Makahokovalu, an ancient monument composed of eight connecting stones at the north end of 'Uiha Island. Uninhabited Tatafa Island between 'Uiha and Uoleva can be reached from near here on foot at low tide. The beach and snorkeling are good and a colony of flying foxes can be seen.

The only place to stay is **'Esi-'O-Ma'afu Beach Homestay** (tel. 60-605), run by Hesekaia and Kaloni 'Aholelei. It's on the beach at Felemea village, a 15-minute walk south of the boat landing at 'Uiha village. The three Tongan *fales* with shared bath are T$12/18 single/double. Breakfast is T$4, dinner T$6 (or T$8 if lobster), or you can cook for yourself. An outrigger canoe can be borrowed. One reader's comments: "Wonderful family . . . we really participated in village life . . . our best experience in the South Pacific." Shoestring.

'Uiha is fairly easy to get to on small boats departing the beach at Pangai, but at best the service is only once a day, so you'll have to spend the night. The regular trip is about T$10 pp each way. The people at Tu'ifua Vaikona's store (tel. 60-605) on the Pangai waterfront can take you over to 'Uiha Island for a few hours sightseeing and bring you back at around T$80 for the boat—worth considering if you can get a small group together.

THE VAVA'U GROUP

Vava'u is Tonga's most scenic region. It's an uplifted limestone cluster that tilts to cliffs in the north and submerges in a myriad of small islands to the south. A labyrinth of waterways winds between plateaus thrust up by subterranean muscle-flexing. In Vava'u one superb scenic vista succeeds another, all so varied you're continually consulting your map to discover just what you're seeing. Only Port Vila (Vanuatu) is comparable.

The Vava'u Group measures about 21 km east to west and 25 km north to south, and of the 34 elevated, thickly forested islands, 21 are inhabited. At 90 square km, the main island of Vava'u is Tonga's second largest. Ships approach Vava'u up fjordlike Ava Pulepulekai channel, which leads 11 km to picturesque, landlocked Port of Refuge Harbor, one of the finest in the South Pacific. The appealing main town of Neiafu, 275 km north of Nuku'alofa, looks out onto Puerto del Refugio, christened by Captain Francisco Antonio Mourelle, whose Spanish vessel chanced upon Vava'u in 1781 while en route from Manila to Mexico, making Vava'u one of the last South Pacific islands to be contacted by Europeans.

The many protected anchorages make Vava'u a favorite of cruising yachties, and it's also a prime place to launch an ocean kayak. Waters on the west side of the archipelago are generally deeper and better protected than those on the east. Beaches can be hard to find on the main island but there are many on the islets to the south. Vava'u is an economic backwater with industry limited to a giant-clam breeding project at Falevai on Kapa Island, and pearl-clam farming near Utulei in Port of Refuge Harbor and at three other locations. Three-quarters of Tonga's vanilla is produced here on plantations covering over 500 hectares, and Vava'u vanilla is among the best in the world.

Tourism is growing with direct flights from Fiji and Pago Pago, and one of the South Pacific's two most important yacht charter operations is based here (the other is on Raiatea in Tahiti-Polynesia). Places to stay abound, both in town and on the outer islands, the entertainment is varied, and watersports such as kayaking, sailing, scuba diving, and fishing are well developed. July-Oct., this is the South Pacific's main whalewatching venue. May-Oct. is the prime time for yachting, and if you arrive in the off season, Nov.-April, you could have the place almost to yourself. Vava'u is one Pacific island group you can't afford to miss.

NEIAFU

Neiafu is Tonga's second "city" but it's still a sleepy little town of 6,000 inhabitants. It's a great place to explore on foot, visiting the market or local attractions, shopping for handicrafts or groceries, dropping into a cafe or bar to hear yachties chatter, visiting travel offices to organize excursions, or hiking out into the unspoiled countryside all around. Neiafu is a much more colorful, attractive, appealing, and restful town than Nuku'alofa. The longer you stay, the more you'll like it, and the better you'll become attuned to the relaxed pace of life. You get the impression that this is a place where everyone knows one another, and where things can be arranged on short notice. The only drawback is that no swimmable beaches exist near town.

Be aware that virtually all shops, restaurants, and bars in Neiafu are closed on Sunday (except those at the Paradise Hotel). The only people you're likely to meet on the street on Sunday are those coming or going to church. Sunday nights a church service consisting mostly of hymns accompanied by rock music is broadcast across Neiafu on loudspeakers. This really is an unusual place.

Sights

One of the overgrown burials in the **cemetery** between the Bank of Tonga and Mormon church is of the ancient *langi* type, and it's believed that a daughter of the 35th Tu'i Tonga is buried here. Also resting in this cemetery is the Rev. Francis Wilson, who established the first seminary in Tonga and died here in 1846. The nameless

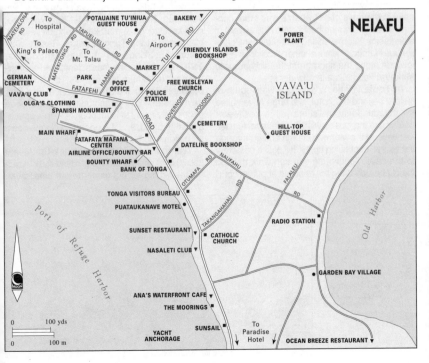

tombstone right next to Wilson's is that of early Methodist missionary David Cargill, who rendered the Tongan and Fijian languages into writing.

The old fig tree in front of Neiafu's red-and-white colonial-style **post office** is a local meeting place. Notice the Spanish monument across the street. The **Vava'u Club** up the hill is the former German Club, founded by trader Hermann Karl Guttenbeil in 1875. The old German cemetery is just a bit farther up the hill, past the club and on the left.

For a splendid view of Port of Refuge and much of the archipelago, climb **Mt. Talau** (131 meters), the flat-top hill that dominates Neiafu to the west. Take the road between the police station and the market and follow it west for 25 minutes high above the shoreline. Where the road begins to descend and you reach an isolated house on the left, look for a trail up the hill on the right just beyond. Turn right at the top of the hill. This is an easy trip from town.

East of town is Neiafu's old harbor, which was used in the days of sail when it was more convenient to land on the beach. With the advent of steamships, interest shifted to the deeper Port of Refuge Harbor. There's another excellent walk at low tide along the shore from the old harbor to **Makave;** you pass a freshwater spring.

At **Toula** village, a half-hour walk south of Neiafu beyond the hotel, is a large cave called Ve'emumuni near the shore with a freshwater pool where the locals swim. To get there, turn left just beyond the Mormon church and go through the village, continuing up the hill past a cemetery to the cave. At low tide you can walk back to the old harbor along the beach in about an hour.

Sports and Recreation

Beluga Diving (Sybil and Huib Kuilboer, tel. 70-327), on the wharf below the Paradise Hotel, offers two-tank boat dives at T$80/95 without/with equipment. They also fill tanks at T$6, and their open-water certification course is T$350.

Dolphin Pacific Diving (Box 131, Neiafu; tel. 70-160, fax 70-292, VHF channel 71), based at the Tongan Beach Resort at 'Utungake, has a five-day PADI open-water scuba certification course, as well as diving.

Scuba divers frequent the wreck of the 123-meter-long *Clan McWilliam,* a copra steamer that burned and sank in Port of Refuge Harbor in 1927. Huge fish and clams hang around the wreck 20 meters down, marked by a buoy just out past the yacht anchorage. Many other good dive sites are only 30 minutes by speedboat from Neiafu. Most diving is drift diving and there aren't many spots where dive boats can anchor, so it's important to note the current.

The **Friendly Islands Kayak Company** (Private Bag, Neiafu; tel./fax 70-173, www.fikco.com/kayaktonga, e-mail: kayaktonga@kalianet.to), based at the Tongan Beach Resort, runs guided kayaking trips of six to eight days at T$100 a day including meals, tents, and snorkeling gear (minimum two nights). The Canadian operators, Doug and Sharon Spence, also offer day-trips at T$50 pp including lunch. These prices only apply to local bookings on a space-available basis, and the operation closes down for holidays in March and April.

Year-round Jim McMahon's **Hook-Up Vava'u** (tel. 70-541) offers sportfishing "island style," which means fishing for big game from a small boat.

early 19th-century Tongan canoes on a reef

Jim takes clients out in a five-meter, twin-engined fiberglass boat, equipped with professional fishing gear, swivel seats, radio, etc. It's T$95/130 a half day (five hours) for one/two anglers, T$160/200 a full day, and you're welcome to bring along a non-fishing child or spouse and still pay the one-angler rate. Jim also charters his four-passenger boat for sightseeing, snorkeling, and scuba diving. Reserve through the Paradise Hotel reception.

Two larger powerboats offering game fishing at Vava'u are Henk and Sandra Gros's eight-meter *Target One* (tel./fax 70-647), and Pat and Keith McKee's 10-meter *Kiwi Magic* (Box 153, Neiafu; tel./fax 70-441). Fishing from *Target One* costs T$150 pp a day (minimum of three). The McKee's, who are based at the Vava'u Guest House, charge T$300/600 for a half/full day (up to four anglers). While more expensive than Jim's boat, these two are faster and have better electronic and fishing gear (as well as toilets!). They also offer some shelter in case the weather turns bad.

Delray Charters (Box 104, Neiafu; tel./fax 70-380), at the Tongan Beach Resort, offers deep-sea game fishing. New Zealander John Going and his 14-meter cruiser *Delray* are based here June-Oct. only. Marlin, mahimahi, spearfish, and tuna are caught along the dropoffs below 200-meter cliffs on the northwest side of the island.

See rugby Saturday afternoons (April-June) on the Fangatongo Rugby Ground, just off the road to Mt. Talau.

ACCOMMODATIONS

Shoestring

The **Potauaine Tu'iniua Guest House** (Box 65, Neiafu; tel. 70-479), also known as "Port Wine Guest House," a block west of the market, has four rooms with shared bath at T$10/18 single/double. This comfortable wooden house with a large lounge and communal cooking facilities and fridge is very central, and well worth checking out if you're looking for the least expensive accommodations.

Budget

The friendly **Hamana Lake Guest House** (Box 152, Neiafu; tel. 70-507), just west of the King's Palace, has a panoramic location on the hillside overlooking Port of Refuge. The six smallish

rooms are T$20/30 single/double with shared bath (T$25/35 with a view), tax included. There's a communal kitchen.

The clean and attractive **Hill-Top Guest House** (tel. 70-209, fax 70-522) offers even more spectacular views of Neiafu and the harbor. The 10 rooms vary in price from T$13/23 single/double for a small, stuffy room with no view, to T$20/27 or T$28/35 for a large, airy room with a view, and T$45/55 for a four-person apartment with kitchen and private bath. They sometimes have water problems but there's a swimming pool. The excellent communal cooking facilities allow you to save a lot of money on restaurant meals. Standard precautions against theft should be taken here; for example, don't leave money and valuables in the room when you go out, and make sure nothing is within reach of an open window at night. If you wish, the manager provides safe-deposit boxes. If you leave food or beer in their common fridge, conceal it in a plastic bag or expect it to disappear. Noisy parties can also be a problem if the wrong crowd is present and some of the long-term residents dampen the atmosphere. The Hill-Top offers scooter rentals at T$20 a day. This guesthouse has had a succession of German managers who eventually moved on to better things or were denied visa extensions by the authorities, and at last report the place was being run by an Italian named Franco Sabatini who had previously operated a restaurant on Niue. It's impossible to say who will be in charge when you get there, but you'll probably find him/her to be an interesting character.

The **Puataukanave Motel** (Box 24, Neiafu; tel. 70-644, fax 70-080), below S.F. Paea & Sons opposite the Tonga Visitors Bureau, has six fan-cooled rooms with private bath and balconies overlooking the bay at T$25/35 single/double. There are no cooking facilities for guests, and it's directly above a noisy disco open Thursday, Friday, and Saturday nights, so only stay there if you'll be spending a lot of time drinking, dancing, or watching satellite TV in the lounge.

On the old harbor is the 13-room **Garden Bay Village** (Box 102, Neiafu; tel. 70-025, fax 70-200). The four duplex units (eight rooms) in the front row are T$20/35 single/double with private bath, while the two-room Princess Fale is T$48 for up to six persons (it's called that because one of the king's daughters once stayed there on a visit to Vava'u). Camping may be possible here. Continental breakfast is included, and if you ask, they'll allow you to use the restaurant kitchen to cook your own food when things aren't too busy. Two units with kitchen and fridge at the back of the property are rented out at T$250 a month for an entire unit, great if you get one. Manager Marlene Moa arranges island tours. Loud music blares from the Garden Bay's nightclub on Wednesday, Friday, and Saturday nights (free admission for hotel guests).

Mikio Filitonga's **Vava'u Guest House** (Box 148, Neiafu; tel. 70-300, fax 70-441), right across the street from the Paradise Hotel, has a laid-back atmosphere. The five basic rooms with shared bath in an old stone building are T$9/14 single/double, while the five spacious bungalows with private bath, fan, and a table and chairs are T$20/25/30 single/double/triple. Unfortunately no cooking facilities are provided. The bountiful family-style dinners (T$11) served in the restaurant are quite good, although the service is extremely slow. Nonguests are welcome to eat here, and when there's sufficient demand Mikio stages a Sunday barbecue at 1700 (T$10 pp)—reserve directly by Friday.

Inexpensive

The **Paradise Hotel** (Box 11, Neiafu; tel. 70-211, fax 70-184), on a hill overlooking Port of Refuge Harbor near Neiafu, was purchased in 1981 by Kentucky millionaire Carter Johnson, who has done his best to keep the place up through the lean years of few tourists (the hotel is presently for sale at US$2.3 million). The 43 rooms with private bath start at T$47/52/62 single/double/triple for a fan-cooled budget room and go up to T$100/110/122 single/double/triple for a deluxe a/c harbor-view room—good value. The economy a/c rooms have older furnishings and cold showers only, but they're clean with lots of towels and satisfactory beds. It's certainly Tonga's finest large hotel, and unlike some resorts in this category, the Paradise doesn't mind nonguests wandering in to use the restaurant, bar, and even the swimming pool (T$2 fee), and the atmosphere is friendly, relaxed, and welcoming. The bar at the Paradise is a good place to meet yachties and other visitors (try the ice cream), but skip the overpriced, poorly served meals in the restaurant. There's disco dancing to live music on Friday and Saturday nights; things pick up after 2200. Video films (T$2) are shown nightly at 2030; if you're a hotel guest ask to see the movie list and request a favorite. A book exchange is available at the reception. Not only does the hotel have a large pool. but there's good ocean swimming off their wharf. Fiberglass kayaks are for rent at T$10/20 a half/full day (pay and pick up the paddles at the bar). Airport transfers are free for guests.

Marcella Resort (tel./fax 70-687), on a hill directly behind the Three Stars Petroleum storage tanks at Toula, a 45-minute walk south of Neiafu, opened in 1996. The six duplex units with bath (but no cooking facilities) are T$40/60/70 single/double/triple. Although there's a reasonable view of Port of Refuge from the restaurant terrace, no beach is here and the resort has little going for it (except perhaps as a base camp for anglers).

Long Stays

Olga Moa at **Olga's Clothing** (Box 84, Neiafu; tel. 70-064), just up from the post office, has a few apartments for rent by the month. The flat below her clothing factory is T$250 a month, but it's dark and gets a lot of noise from the adjacent fish freezer. Another house up on the hill has two three-bedroom apartments, T$500 for the one upstairs, T$350 for the one downstairs. Add T$100 to these rates if you require linen.

FOOD

Tavake Refreshments (tel. 70-651), facing the main wharf behind Olga's Clothing, serves a good T$2 fish lunch weekdays until 1500.

The **Bounty Bar** (tel./fax 70-493; closed weekends), across from the banks in the center of town, serves breakfast, lunch, and dinner on weekdays. The menu includes five kinds of burgers, fried rice, and sandwiches. It's a real yachtie hangout and you get a great view of everything (including sunsets) from the back porch, though it's often hard to find a table. Live entertainment is often offered on Friday nights during the high May-Oct. season.

Ana's Waterfront Cafe (tel. 70-664; closed Sunday), directly below The Moorings, serves breakfast and lunch, and is a good place to come at happy hour (weekdays 1700-1800). The waerside location facing a dingy dock makes it another yachtie hangout. It's in a sort of cave, or *ana* in Tongan—there's no person called Ana here (The Moorings owns the place).

Francesco and Sonia Donati's **Sunset Restaurant** (tel. 70-397; closed Sunday), opposite the prominent Catholic church in Neiafu, serves Pisa-style Italian dishes and pizza on their harborfront terrace. Yachties can tie their dinghies to the Sunset's dock.

Neiafu's top place to eat may be the **Ocean Breeze Restaurant** (tel. 70-582, VHF channel 74), on the old harbor southeast of Neiafu. Yachties anchored off Makave in the old harbor often use the Ocean Breeze's stone jetty to come for dinner. They specialize in seafood such as lobster, but also have steak, lamb, and chicken. You'll like the large portions, wine list, outstanding service, and excellent views. It's open daily 1800-2100 with reservations required on Sunday. One reader called it "an immaculate oasis of civilization." (Whenever at least three people want to go, English restaurateur John Dale runs day tours to outlying islands in his fiberglass speedboat. Ask to be shown the flying foxes.)

Groceries

Sailoame Market at Neiafu is crowded with people selling bananas, cabbage, carrots, Chinese lettuce, coconuts, green beans, lettuce, manioc, onions, papaya, tomatoes, taro, yams, zucchini, and oranges. Everything is about T$1 a bunch, and you're only assured a fair selection of fresh vegetables if you arrive early. You can also have lunch here for about T$2. The largest market is on Saturday and, if you come early enough, you'll hear street evangelists preach to the crowd outside as a policeman directs traffic.

Neiafu's two largest supermarkets, the **Tonga Cooperative Federation** (tel. 70-224), beside the MBf Bank, and the **Fatafata Mafana Center** (tel. 70-500), across the street, close weekdays at 1600, Saturday 1200, so shop early. Buy fish directly from locals at the harbor (no fish poisoning problems here).

ENTERTAINMENT

The **Neiafu Club** (tel. 70-566), near the Paradise Hotel, has a nice mix of tourists and locals. Once you sign the guest book, the bartender will remember your name next time you come in. It opens around 1500 daily (including Sunday) with happy hour starting at 1800.

The **Vava'u Club,** up the hill from the post office, has a great view but is more of a men's drinking place. They have two enormous pool tables where snooker and other such games are played; the bartender keeps sets of balls for eight-ball (hi-lo) and 15-ball pool. Beware of "mosquitoes" who will want you to buy them drinks. These characters are not allowed in the Neiafu Club.

From 2000 on Thursday, Friday, and Saturday nights a live dance band plays at the flashy **Puataukanave Disco** (tel. 70-644), below S.F. Paea & Sons opposite the Tonga Visitors Bureau (cover charge T$2/3 for women/men). A slightly older crowd frequents the nightclub at the **Garden Bay Village** (tel. 70-025) which cranks up on Wednesday, Friday, and Saturday nights.

For real earthy interplay, visit the **Nasaleti Club,** opposite the Catholic church. Here you can drink watery *kavatonga* all evening for a T$2.50 flat fee (open Mon.-Sat. 1930-2400).

Cultural Shows for Visitors

Several "feasts" are organized weekly for both land-based and water-bound visitors. For a set fee of around T$20 (half price for children under 10) you get a buffet-style meal of island foods such as roast suckling pig, octopus, fish, clams, lobster, crayfish, and taro, all baked in an *umu* (earth oven). Cooked papaya with coconut cream in the middle is served in half-coconut shells, and lots of watermelon is eaten while sitting on mats on the ground. Have a swim as soon as you arrive, then enjoy a drink (extra charge) to the strains of guitar music. Traditional dancing is performed later, and handicrafts are available for sale.

All of the feasts take place on outlying beaches; clients of The Moorings and Sunsail and other yachties are the biggest customers. Free minibus transfers are provided for visitors staying in Neiafu. Mr. 'Aisea Sikaleti of **Lisa Beach** and Matoto Latavao at **Ano Beach** always stage an island feast on Saturday afternoon, and sometimes also on Wednesday if demand warrants. John and Neti Tongia prepare a "gigantic roast" with traditional dancing and a kava ceremony at **Rove Hinakauea Beach** adjacent to Ano

Beach on Thursdays—good reports.

Book your spot for the feasts at the Paradise Hotel (tel. 70-211), the Bounty Bar (tel. 70-493), The Moorings, or Teta Tours. Often the feasts are canceled if not enough people sign up. Ask other visitors for their recommendations, as conditions do vary.

Events

The consummate time to be in Vava'u is the first week of May for the **Vava'u Festival** marking the crown prince's birthday on 4 May. There will be a display of handicrafts, sporting events, a game fishing tournament, a yacht regatta, boat parades, the Vava'u Marathon, island nights, concerts, dances, feasts, art exhibitions, church choir meetings, traditional Tongan games, a baby show, and a grand ball with the crowning of Miss Vava'u. Hotel rooms should be booked ahead at this time, as they should during the **Agricultural Show** in September when the king will be present.

Sunday morning the singing at the Free Wesleyan Church on Tui Rd. opposite the market is almost worth the plane fare to Vava'u.

Shopping

Handicrafts can be purchased at the **Langafonua Shop** (tel. 70-356), next to the Tonga Visitors Bureau, at the **FIMCO Handicraft Shop** (tel. 70-614), across the street, and at the **Vava'u Handicraft Shop**, in front of the post office.

Fa Sea Jewelry, opposite the yacht charter offices, also has crafts, some of them made from endangered species.

With enough lead time **Olga's Clothing** (tel. 70-064), between the post office and the Vava'u Club, makes clothes to order.

SERVICES AND INFORMATION

Money

The Bank of Tonga (tel. 70-068), near the Tonga Visitors Bureau, changes traveler's checks without commission, while the MBf Bank deducts T$2 commission. On the positive side, the MBf is open Saturday 0900-1130, when the Bank of Tonga is not. The ANZ Bank is next to the Fatafata Mafana Center. When the banks are closed the Paradise Hotel changes money for a small commission, but only for hotel guests.

Navigators and Explorers of the Pacific
Captain William Bligh
90s
The Bounty
TONGA

Post and Telecommunications

Vava'u poste restante holds mail for two months. You can place local and long-distance telephone calls at the Telecom Telephone Exchange (tel. 70-255; open 24 hours) behind the post office. If you wish to receive a fax at Vava'u, you can have it sent here via fax 70-200 (T$1 a page to receive). Yachts, restaurants, and the police generally use VHF channel 16 to communicate.

Visas

Officially, extensions of stay up to six months are available for T$25 at the immigration office in the police station near the market. In practice, however, it's entirely up to the officers how long you'll get, and your attitude could have a lot to do with it.

Tonga Visitors Bureau

The Tonga Visitors Bureau (tel. 70-115, fax 70-630; closed Saturday afternoon and Sunday) in Neiafu has the usual brochures and can answer questions. Take the time to peruse their information boards to find out what's on around Vava'u. Teta Tours and the Paradise Hotel also have notice boards well worth checking. The Bounty Bar has a VHF radio that can be used to contact yachts at Vava'u.

The **Friendly Islands Bookshop** (tel. 70-153), diagonally opposite the Bank of Tonga and just up from the market, has postcards and a few good books about the islands.

Maps

The Dateline Bookshop (tel. 70-213), a bit up the side street from the Bank of Tonga, sells marine charts at T$18 each and carries foreign newspapers.

The Moorings (tel. 70-016) produces a 32-page *Cruising Guide,* which comes with a chart indicating their 42 designated anchorages.

around Vava'u. The Friendly Islands Bookshop may sell a reproduction of their chart.

Other Information

The Vava'u Public Library, in front of the post office, is open weekdays 1330-1700.

Teta Tours (tel. 70-488), next to the Bounty Bar, is a travel agency booking most activities and accommodations around Vava'u. They're usually very helpful.

Health

Ngu Hospital (tel. 70-201), on the northwest side of town, opened in 1981. You'll get better attention for T$25 at Dr. Alfredo Carafa's Italian Clinic (tel. 70-607; weekdays 0900-1400), behind the Bank of Tonga.

TRANSPORTATION

By Air

Royal Tongan Airlines (tel. 70-253) flies to Vava'u twice a week from Ha'apai (T$67) and fortnightly from Niuafo'ou (T$170) and Niuatoputapu (T$114). Service from Nuku'alofa (T$129) is twice daily except Sunday. The flights are often heavily booked, and cancellations occur without warning, so reconfirm early. Royal Tongan operates direct weekly flights between Vava'u and Nadi, Fiji (T$265/399 one-way/roundtrip).

Samoa Air (tel. 70-644, e-mail: tfpel-vv@kalianet.to), at S.F. Paea & Sons opposite the Tonga Visitors Bureau, sells tickets for the twice-weekly flight from Vava'u to Pago Pago (T$235/424 one-way/roundtrip). In past this flight has been on Wednesday and Saturday.

Lupepau'u Airport (VAV) is nine km north of Neiafu. The Paradise Hotel bus is T$4 pp (free for hotel guests) and a taxi is T$8 for the car (T$12 to the Tongan Beach Resort). Local buses (40 cents) run to/from Leimatu'a village, two km south of the airport, sporadically on weekdays and Saturday mornings; otherwise, it's easy to hitch from the airport into town (offer the driver a couple of pa'anga). There's no bank at the airport.

By Ship

Ships tie up to the wharf. The **Uata Shipping Lines** ferries *Loto Ha'angana* or *Tautahi* leave Neiafu for Ha'apai (T$21) and Nuku'alofa (T$42) Wednesday at 1400, whereas the **Shipping Corporation of Polynesia** ferry *Olovaha* leaves Thursday at 1600. Departures to the Niuas are about once a month. The office of the Shipping Corporation (tel. 70-128) is in the red container on the main wharf. The Uata Shipping office (tel. 70-490) is in the nearby white kiosk. See **Transportation** in the chapter introduction for more information.

By Yacht

To crew on a cruising yacht, put up notices at the Paradise Hotel, the Bounty Bar, and Ana's Waterfront Cafe, and ask around the bar at the Neiafu Club and at the hotel. The yachting season is March-October. Until September try for a watery ride to Fiji; later most boats will be thinking of a run south to New Zealand.

Getting Around

Getting around Vava'u by public transport isn't really practical, although passenger trucks and minibuses departing Neiafu market do cover most of the roads on an unscheduled basis. Leimatu'a is fairly well serviced, as is Tu'anekivale. If you want to go to Holonga, you must take a bus as far as Mataika or Ha'alaufuli, then walk. Hitching is easy, but offer to pay if it looks like a passenger truck. They'll seldom ask more than T$1. Taxis charge about T$1.50 for the first kilometer, 50 cents each additional km. Waiting time is T$2.25 an hour. Check the price beforehand.

You can rent a car from **Teta Tours** (tel. 70-488), next to the Bounty Bar, at T$30/60 a half/full day. **Liviela Taxi** (tel. 70-240), opposite the Fatafata Mafana Center, charges T$70 a day. The adjacent **Vava'u Law Office** (tel. 70-549) asks T$50-60 a day. Before you taking a car, you'll have to obtain a Tongan driver's license (T$8) at the police station around the corner (bring your home driver's license). Insurance is not available and serious problems can arise in the event of an accident, so take care (ask how much extra they'll charge to supply a driver with the car). The speed limit is 40 kph in town or 60 kph on the open road.

Hill-Top Guest House (tel. 70-209 or 70-522) rents scooters at T$15/20/120 a half day/full day/week for a one-seater, or T$20/25/150 for a two-seater (Tongan license required).

THE WHALES OF TONGA

In June or July over a hundred humpback whales arrive in Tonga from their summer feeding areas in Antarctica. They spend the austral winter in Tonga, mating and bearing their young, before heading south again in October or November. This annual migration is necessary because there's little food for whales in Tongan waters but the calves require warm seas to survive as they're poorly insulated at birth. During the first few months of their lives the baby whales grow at a rate of 45 kilograms a day. They're solely dependent on their mother's milk for sustenance, and by the end of the season a nursing female may have lost 25% of her body weight. As soon as the offspring are ready in spring, the animals return to their summer home thousands of kilometers south to fatten up on a tiny plankton called krill. Pregnancy lasts 12 months, just long enough for the mother to put on adequate weight in Antarctica to have a child in Tonga.

While in Tonga the humpbacks engage in elaborate courtship displays and mating rituals that can last for hours. The males sing complex songs that have been studied and found to contain syllables and rhyming phrases. During the displays the humpbacks often breach, and to see a 14.5-meter male rise from the sea, five-meter flippers flapping at its side, only to crash back on its side, is truly spectacular. A female chaperoning its calf is another favorite sight. Southern hemisphere humpbacks have a characteristic white belly, quite different from the black bellies of northern hemisphere humpbacks, and individuals are recognizable by their patterns.

Humpbacks prefer shallow waters close to shore, and are often curious about humans, characteristics that have worked to their disadvantage in past. From a population of around 100,000 in the 19th century, southern hemisphere humpback whales presently number only about 3,000, a drop of 97%. Subsistence shore whaling was only prohibited in Tonga in 1979 and the 10 whales previously taken each season did have an impact. However it was the collapse of the Soviet Union in 1991 that contributed more to the whales' survival since it put an end to illegal whaling from Soviet ships. Japanese whale boats continue the dirty business even today in defiance of world opinion.

Though Vava'u is a lot hillier than Tongatapu, a bicycle is still a good way to get around, and these can be rented from David Lavakeiaho (tel. 70-274), who lives between Chanel College and the Neiafu Club almost opposite the Paradise Hotel.

Local Tours

Minibus tours of Vava'u are offered by **Soane's Scenic Tours** (tel. 70-211) at T$35 pp without lunch (minimum of three persons). Book through the reception at the Paradise Hotel or Teta Tours.

Yacht Charters

Vava'u is one of the Pacific's top cruising grounds with more than 50 "world class" anchorages. Florida-based **The Moorings** (Box 119, Neiafu; tel. 70-016, fax 70-428, VHF channel 72, www.moorings.com, e-mail: moorings. tonga@kalianet.to) has a variety of charter yachts based here, beginning at US$370 a day for a two-couple Moorings 365 and increasing to US$680 daily for a 10-person Moorings 510. Add US$32 pp daily for provisioning, US$25 daily insurance, and tax. If you're new to sailing (they check you out) it's another US$100 a day for a skipper. Additional crew might include a cook (US$80 daily) and a guide (US$60 daily). These charges soon add up—a party of four can expect to spend around US$4,000 a week to rent an uncrewed bareboat Beneteau yacht, meals included.

A 20% discount and security insurance waiver are possible if you book in person through the Vava'u office instead of booking ahead, although of course, there'd be no guarantee they'd have a acht available for you if you followed that route. More information on The Moorings is provided under **Getting There** in the main introduction.

Sunsail (Private Bag, Neiafu; tel./fax 70-646), own by the water on the east side of The Moorings, has five charter yachts based here in the off season (Jan.-March), a dozen in the full season (April-Dec.). It's a bit cheaper than The Moorings because their prices are based on New Zealand dollars (from NZ$360/460 daily off/full season, plus tax). For more information contact Sunsail (Box 33729, Takapuna, Auckland, New Zealand; tel. 64-9/307-7077, fax 64-9/307-7177, www.sunsail.co.nz, e-mail: res.v@sunsail.co.nz). One-day trips around Vava'u by yacht are covered under Day Cruises, below.

Sailing Safaris (Box 153, Neiafu; tel./fax 70-650) is an independent yacht charter company based at Toula village. Some of their yachts are smaller than those offered by The Moorings and Sunsail, allowing couples to experience bareboat chartering without the high costs related to larger charter yachts. Prices range from T$225 a day for a 7.5-meter sloop accommodating two people to T$600 for an eight-person, 11-meter catamaran (plus T$115 for a skipper, if required). The minimum bareboat charter is three days. Aside from bareboat and skippered chartering, they also do day excursions at T$55 pp and whalewatching.

Day Cruises

A much more economical way to enjoy some sailing is to go out on Verne Kirk's 13-meter trimaran *Orion*. Verne offers a cruise to Swallows Cave and other sites daily 1000-1630 at T$35 pp (T$95 minimum). Verne is to be found near the swimming pool at the Paradise Hotel most afternoons at 1700. Similar is the 15-meter ketch *Melinda* owned by Christy Butterfield (tel. 70-861).

If the *Orion* and *Melinda* have sailed away by the time you get there, ask around for something similar. Small local operators like these know their waters and will take you on the South Seas adventure of your dreams.

Whalewatching

Each winter from July to October, over a hundred humpback whales come to Vava'u to bear their young before returning to the colder Antarctic waters for the southern summer. They generally stay on the western side of the group, in the lee of the prevailing tradewinds. Lots of tour and fishing boats around Vava'u do whalewatching trips, and you'll easily see eight whales on a good day.

Whale Watch Vava'u (tel./fax 70-493) is the main operator with a specially designed boat including a proper viewing platform and a hydrophone that allows the mating songs of the males to be broadcast over speakers on board. Whale Watch offers full-day trips during the season, departing the Bounty Bar wharf at 0930 (T$65 pp, minimum of six). Lunch is T$10 extra. Under ideal conditions it's sometimes possible to swim with the whales, and snorkeling gear is provided. These trips can be booked at the Bounty Bar.

Whalewatching on the 10-meter fishing boat *Kiwi Magic* is T$55 pp with a minimum rate of T$120. Ask for Pat or Keith McKee (tel./fax 70-441) at the Vava'u Guest House.

AROUND VAVA'U

SOUTH OF NEIAFU

The road south from Neiafu crosses two cause-ways before reaching **Nga'unoho** village (10 km), which has a lovely, clean beach. You can also swim at the Tongan Beach Resort at 'Utungake, and at Lisa and Ano Beaches south of Pangaimotu, although the snorkeling at all four is only fair. By bicycle, you'll find this is the hilliest part of Vava'u.

Accommodations

The **Tongan Beach Resort** (Box 104, Neiafu; tel./fax 70-380, VHF channel 71) is at 'Utungake village, about nine km from Neiafu. The beach here is fairly good and the 12 duplex bungalows (T$108/120/144 single/double/triple, tax included) are comfortable, although the six triples are nicer than the six doubles. The two overwater bungalows are T$220 double. There's a three day minimum stay, and children 12 and under are half price. Rooms booked from abroad must be paid in full prior to arrival and will be more expensive. Scuba diving, game fishing, kayaking and yacht charters are offered. One drawback is the cost of eating in their fancy thatched restaurant—it'll take some effort not to run up a daily food bill equal to the cost of your room (T$60 pp meal package available). Drinks at the bar are also expensive, so bring something along to put in your fridge (day-trippers from Neiafu are welcome to use the resort beach if they buy a few drinks). Actually, this resort suffers from its isolation without achieving the exotic effect of an outer island hideaway (it faces the main shipping channel and is surrounded by a small Tongan village). Return airport transfers will be T$33 pp if arranged by the hotel, but you can get a taxi from Neiafu at T$7 for the car. Moderate.

WILL MARINER'S STORY

Will Mariner was a well-schooled 13-year-old Londoner who embarked on the English privateer *Port-au-Prince*. In 1806 this ship stopped at Lifuka, Ha'apai, for repairs. They had been given a friendly reception, but suddenly the vessel was attacked on all sides by war canoes and all but one of the ship's crew was killed. The youth Mariner was taken prisoner. Since the chief of the Ha'apai, Finau 'Ulukalala II, took a liking to him, his life was spared and he became the chief's adopted son and a chief himself. Mariner spent four years in Tonga, wholeheartedly adapting himself to the 19th century Tongan way of life. He was at last given the chance to depart on a passing brig. Back in England, Mariner wrote an account of his life in Tonga, in collaboration with an English doctor. When this was published in 1816 it enjoyed great success. Four cannon from the *Port-au-Prince* can still be seen in front of the British High Commissioner's residence in Nuku'alofa.

The **Matamoana Tourist Court** (Toimoana and Kafoatu Taufaeteau, tel. 70-068, fax 70-832), right next to the Tongan Beach Resort, has four self-catering units with fan and fridge in two duplex blocks at T$42/48/53 single/double/triple—excellent value compared to the resort. It faces a beach only slightly worse than that of the resort itself. Budget.

The Tongia family operates **Rove Hinakauea Guesthouse** (VHF channel 16), on a lovely stretch of sand adjacent to Ano Beach at the south end of Pangaimotu Island. The four simple concrete bungalows with bath are T$20/35 single/double, and a T$6 pp dorm may also be available. The meals served here are expensive, but you may be able to do your own cooking (bring food). One the other hand, the T$20 feasts here on Thursday and Saturday evenings are good value. Ask about this place at the Tonga Visitors Bureau in Neiafu. A taxi from Neiafu will be around T$6.

WEST OF NEIAFU

From the Seventh-Day Adventist church on Tui Road in Neiafu a new highway leads west across the Vaipua Inlet causeway to western Vava'u. Beyond the causeway is a long steep incline at the top of which is a hill on the left called **Sia Ko Kafoa.** The track up the hill is on the left near the point where the road begins to descend again. Sia Ko Kafoa is an ancient burial mound built by the legendary chiefs Kafoa and Talau. It's an eerie, evocative spot with a good view of much of the island.

Keep straight (or left) at Tefisi and follow the rough track along the north side of **Lake Ano,** the still, fresh waters of which are easily accessible at one point. At Longomapu turn right and climb a long hill to **Toafa Church Farm** (Box 313, Neiafu; tel. 70-269) at the west end of the island, where there's a splendid view of the cliffs of Hunga and many small islands trailing southward. If you have binoculars, you may see whales off Hunga July-October. A two-bedroom house with cooking facilities is sometimes for rent at the farm, but call ahead to make sure it's available and bring all of your own food. The Longomapu truck will drop you at the access road.

NORTHEAST OF NEIAFU

At **Feletoa** village, ask to see the burial place of Finau 'Ulukalala II behind the house opposite the primary school. The large rectangular *langi* is surrounded by big stone slabs. It was Finau's father, Finau 'Ulukalala I, who had ordered the sacking of the British privateer *Port-au-Prince* at Ha'apai and who later adopted Will Mariner into his family. With the help of cannon from the ship and military advice from the survivors, 'Ulukalala II conquered Vava'u in 1808, and in 1810 he allowed Mariner to return to England. The dynasty came to an end when 'Ulukalala III's young son was deposed by King George Tupou I. Two centuries ago Feletoa was the center of power on Vava'u, and a Polynesian fortress was built here in 1808, but little remains today.

For a splendid view of the north coast, travel due north from Neiafu to Holonga. About two km beyond the village, turn left when the trail begins to descend to the beach, then right some 500 meters farther along. With a little luck you'll come out on **'Utula'aina Point,** a sheer cliff a couple of hundred meters above the sea. The quiet beach here is fine for relaxing but the water is too shallow for swimming. You could spend a whole day exploring this area.

OFFSHORE ISLANDS

The classic day tour at Vava'u encompasses Mariner's Cave, Swallows Cave, and Nuku Island. **Mariner's Cave** is a hollow in Nuapapu Island, southwest of Neiafu. You can approach it through an underwater tunnel in the island's stone face. The story goes that a young noble, fearing a despotic king might kill his sweetheart, hid her in this secret cave, coming back each night with food and water. Finally the young man and his friends built an oceangoing canoe and spirited the girl away to safety in Fiji. The cave gets its name from William Mariner, who told the story to the world.

To find it, go west along the cliff about 300 meters from the northeast tip of Nuapapu, watching for a patch of dark, deep water. White calcium deposits speckle the rocks to the right of the

THE VAVA'U GROUP

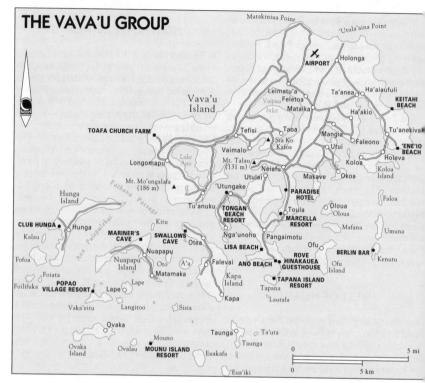

underwater opening; a single coconut tree standing high above also marks the place. Snorkeling gear is recommended for entry, though a strong swimmer could go in without. The opening is about one meter below sea level at low tide, and you have to swim about four meters underwater to get through (it's comparable to diving under a yacht). The water is illuminated by sunlight, but come up slowly to avoid banging your head on a ledge. Swimming into Mariner's Cave is a bit like doing a bungee jump: it's certainly not for everyone and claustrophobic souls should give it a miss.

Swallows Cave on Kapa Island is far more obvious, and a small boat can motor right inside. Inside Swallows Cave is a rock that rings like a bell when struck, and in front of the entrance to another cave next to Swallows is a huge round coral that looks like an underwater elephant. There are also sea snakes here and an exciting

vertical drop-off. All these caves face west, so the best conditions for photography are in the afternoon. Day-trips to these spots usually include a picnic on **Nuku Island** where the snorkeling is good. One of the customary owners of Nuku may show up to collect a T$1 pp fee, one of the few places in Tonga where this happens.

Boat trips to the caves cost T$20-35 pp, depending on where you book, how many people are going, and whether lunch is included. **Soki Island Tours** (Sione Katalau) is a good company to go with, and all the guesthouse owners know about it. There's also Orion Charters and a few others. Soki Island Tours usually includes snorkeling on the Mala Island reef and along the dropoff at A'a Island in the Mariner's Cave trip (T$25 pp). Soki departs from the Bounty Wharf daily except Sunday at 1000, so long as four people book.

Vili Helu at the Island Gas Station (tel. 70-491), just below the ANZ Bank on the road to the wharf, runs all day boat trips at T$20 per head for our or more people, T$25 per head for three bring your own lunch).

If you enjoyed the Mariner's Cave tour and are staying longer, consider going on the eastern islands tour (T$25) with **Lekeleka Tours** (Siaosi Maeakafa, tel. 70-101). Siaosi takes you from Neiafu's Old Harbor to Umuna Island (interesting cave), Kenutu Island (sea cliffs with huge breakers), and Ofu Island (nice beach). It's also possible to spend a few days at Siaosi's house in Ofu village.

The two tourist cafes, the Bounty Bar and Ana's Waterfront Cafe, are all good sources of information about all tours and activities around Vava'u, and can quickly put you in touch. The guesthouse managers too are very knowledgeable about such things, and Teta Tours can make the bookings. These trips are among the least expensive all-day boat excursions in the South Pacific.

Accommodations

A number of small resorts and restaurants exist on small islands south of Neiafu, and the easiest way to obtain current information on these is to check the information boards at the Bounty Bar, Tonga Visitors Bureau, Teta Tours, and the Paradise Hotel.

Tapana Island Resort (tel. 70-115), on a small island with seven beaches off Ano Beach, has three beach *fales* at T$10/12 single/double, plus camping space at T$3.50 pp. Meals are served at reasonable prices. It's run by a Tongan woman named Salote and her family, and information about this place is available at Teta Tours or at the Bounty Bar. Shoestring.

In 1994 a German named Joanna and her Tongan husband Moses set up a rustic restaurant and hideaway resort called the **Berlin Bar** on Kenutu Island, off the east side of Vava'u. There's good snorkeling in the turquoise green sea off their beach and scenic limestone cliffs just across the island. They cater mostly to yachties who come for a fried fish dinner, a German curry wurst, or the homemade bread, but you can also sleep in a thatched treehouse with balcony, toilet, and shower at T$100 pp, or rent one of their "doll house" *fales* at T$80 pp, both including all meals (minimum stay two nights). Joanna claims this is the easternmost bar in the world, where

the first sundowners are consumed every evening (and they make good ones). The shuttle boat leaves Neiafu's old harbor daily at 1000 May-Oct. (T$20 pp), provided someone has reserved. On Sunday there's a day-trip. Bookings can be made from the Bounty Bar over VHF channel 16. (In January 1998 Hurricane Ron damaged the Berlin Bar and lease, health, and theft problems have arisen, so check to be sure that they're open.) Inexpensive.

Pete and Hapi Appleton manage **Club Hunga** (tel./fax 70-611), on the western island of Hunga. They have a two-bedroom house with kitchen for up to four people at T$150, and another three-room house with no cooking facilities at T$50/70 single/double. Transfers to the island are T$29 pp. When there are sufficient guests, a Sunday barbecue is arranged at T$25 pp, otherwise rather pricey meals can be ordered in their restaurant. It's on a nice little beach with good snorkeling, and the accommodations are constructed from local materials. Inexpensive to expensive.

Whale Watch Vava'u operates **Mounu Island Resort** (Allan and Lyn Bowe, tel. 70-576, fax 70-493, VHF channel 77), on a tiny island southeast of Vaka'eitu, with three *fales* are T$125 single or double (minimum stay three nights, children under 12 not accommodated). The three-meal plan is T$60 pp, return airport transfers T$30 pp. Whalewatching trips cost T$55 per head. Information is available at the Bounty Bar. Moderate.

Hans and Mele Schmeisser operate a small resort on otherwise uninhabited Vaka'eitu Island, near the southwest end of the Vava'u Group. **Popao Village Eco Resort** (tel. 70-308, fax 70-522) tries to recapture the lifestyle of an old Tongan village of thatched *fales* decorated with tapa wall hangings. The complex is set in natural surroundings on a low hill with grand views. The upper village has four deluxe *fales* with double beds, private bath, and wooden floors at T$50 double, and two traditional *fales* each with two single beds, shared bath, and gravel/mat floors at T$38. In the lower village are three standard *fales* at T$22/28 single/double. Discounts are available for those who stay 14 nights or more. There's no camping, electricity, generator, or traffic noise. Bucket showers are provided in a central bathhouse—you really experience everyday Tongan life as it was several decades ago. Breakfast, afternoon coffee and cake, and dinner are T$17 pp (T$7 extra for lunch, if required), and only fresh local foods are served. Guests are welcome to help with the cooking, which is done in the traditional way over an open fire or in a lava-stone *umu*. Fresh bread and rolls are baked in a firewood stone oven. Yachties anchored offshore can also eat in the Lighthouse Cafe if they announce their arrival over VHF channel 16 (and bring a flashlight). The snorkeling off the north end of Vaka'eitu is fantastic and small outrigger canoes are provided free. Fishing trips are organized using traditional methods such as the long spear and round throwing net *(kupenga)*. You can also try octopus fishing. Popao organizes yacht charters for whalewatching or visits to remote villages at T$29 pp (minimum for four), and boat trips to the southernmost Vava'u islands not visited by the tour boats from Neiafu are possible. Boat transfers from Neiafu to Popao cost T$29 pp each way (T$17 if you stay over a week). Popao is highly recommended as a totally unique Tongan experience, provided you don't mind roughing it a bit. Budget.

OTHER ISLANDS OF VAVA'U

Late Island (17 square km), 52 km west of the main Vava'u Group, is visible from the west side of Vava'u on a clear day. This 519-meter-high dormant volcano last erupted in 1854. In the late 1860s King George Tupou I evacuated the Late people to Hunga Island over worries about the residents being kidnapped for use as slave labor in the mines of Peru. Recently this densely forested, uninhabited island has itself become a resettlement area for the endangered Tongan megapode bird, or *malau,* which is threatened due to human activities on its native Niuafo'ou.

Fonualei (four square km) lies 70 km northwest of Vava'u, 19 km beyond smaller Toku Island. This dormant volcano 195 meters high last erupted in 1846, spewing ash across Vava'u. It's presently uninhabited and the Spaniard Mourelle called it Amargura or "bitterness" in 1781 out of disappointment for not finding food and water there.

THE NIUAS

The isolated volcanic islands of Niuatoputapu, Tafahi, and Niuafo'ou sit midway between Vava'u and Samoa, and often share the devastating hurricanes common to the latter. Two owe their names to their ubiquitous coconut trees *(niu)*. Surprisingly, these were the first Tongan Islands to be seen by Europeans (by Schouten and Le Maire in 1616). The number of visitors to the Niuas today is negligible, but the islands have a lot to offer and are well worth including in your trip, if you can afford the extra airfare (and if the air service is operating).

NIUATOPUTAPU

Niuatoputapu Island, 300 km north of Vava'u, is a triangular island of 18 square km with a long central ridge 150 meters high. You can climb this ridge from Vaipoa village in the north and explore the many bush trails, which lead to small garden patches on top. A plain surrounds the ridge like the rim of a hat, and lovely white sandy beaches fringe the island, with a sheltered lagoon on the north side and pounding surf on the south. Much of the island is taken up by gardens producing copra and exquisite limes, but some fast-disappearing native forest remains in the south.

Niuatoputapu is a traditional island, where horse-drawn carts are still widely used and fine pandanus mats are made. All 1,300 inhabitants live in the three villages along the north coast. Hihifo, the administrative center, is about three km north of the airstrip. The wharf at Falehau offers good anchorage for yachties, good swimming for everyone.

The finest beaches are on **Hunganga Island,** accessible by wading at low tide. The channel between Hihifo and Hunganga is strikingly beautiful, with clean white sands set against curving

NIUATOPUTAPU

© DAVID STANLEY

The top time to come is mid- to late Augus' when the king arrives for the annual Agricultura Show.

Getting There
Royal Tongan Airlines has fortnightly flight. to Niuatoputapu (NTT) from Nuku'alofa (T$227 and Vava'u (T$114). Unfortunately there are n scheduled interisland flights between the Niua and you must return to Vava'u to reach the other

The supply ship from Nuku'alofa and Vava't arrives about every month. Niuatoputapu is a port of entry and clearance for cruising yachts most of which call on their way from Samoa to Vava'u between June and September.

TAFAHI ISLAND

Fertile, cone-shaped Tafahi Island, 3.4 square km in size and nine km north of the Niuatoputapu wharf, produces some of the highest quality kava and vanilla in the South Pacific. Some 500 people live on the island and the only access is by small boat at high tide from Niuatoputapu. There are 154 concrete steps from the landing to clusters of houses on Tafahi's north slope.

The climb to the summit (555 meters) of extinct Tafahi volcano takes only three hours—get fresh water from bamboo stalks on top. On a clear day Samoa is visible from up there! You can also walk around the island in half a day, using the beach as your trail.

palms, the majestic cone of Tafahi Island looming in the distance. The waterways south of the village are not only scenic but also idyllic swimming areas. Within Hihifo itself is **Niutoua Spring**, a long freshwater pool in a crevice—perfect for an afternoon swim. Countless pigs forage on the beach at Hihifo.

Practicalities
The only place to stay is **Kalolaine's Guest House** (tel. 85-021) in Hihifo, with five rooms at T$18/22 single/double (shared facilities). Meals can be ordered here. Shoestring.

The Produce Board maintains an adequate general store at Hihifo, and traveler's checks can be cashed at the post office. There's a bakery near the Mormon church at Vaipoa.

NIUAFO'OU

Niuafo'ou is Tonga's northernmost island, 574 km from Nuku'alofa and equidistant from Savai'i (Samoa), Taveuni (Fiji), and Vava'u. Despite the airstrip that opened in 1983, Niuafo'ou remains one of the most remote islands in the world. The supply ship calls about once a month, but there's no wharf on the island. Landings take place at Futu on the west side of the island.

For many years Niuafo'ou received its mail in kerosene tins wrapped in oilcloth thrown overboard from a passing freighter to waiting swimmers or canoeists, giving Tin Can Island its other name. In bad weather, rockets were used to shoot the mail from ship to shore. Early trader Walter George Quensell doubled as postmaster and brought fame to Niuafo'ou by stamping the mail with colorful postmarks. Special Niuafo'ou postage stamps, first issued in 1983, are prized by collectors.

The Land
Niuafo'ou (50 square km) is a collapsed volcanic cone once 1,300 meters high. Today the north rim of the caldera reaches 210 meters. The cen-

ter of the island is occupied by a crater lake, **Vai Lahi,** nearly five km wide and 84 meters deep, lying 21 meters above sea level. From this lake rise small islands with crater lakes of their own—lakes within islands within a lake within an island. Grayish *lapila* fish live in these sulfurous waters.

Presently Niuafo'ou is dormant, but the southern and western sides of the island are covered by bare black **lava fields** from the many eruptions earlier this century. Lava flows emanating from fissures on the outer slopes of the caldera destroyed the villages of 'Ahau in 1853 and Futu in 1929. After Angaha disappeared under lava in 1946, the government evacuated the 1,300 inhabitants to 'Eua Island, where many live today. In 1958 some 200 refugees returned to Niuafo'ou, and by 1976 there were 678 people on the island once more (in 1996 735 people were present). Signs of the 1946 eruption are apparent in the vicinity of the airstrip.

Apart from the lava fields, the island is well forested. Incubator or megapode birds *(malau* in Tongan) lay eggs one-fifth the size of a grown bird in burrows two meters deep in the warm sands of the hot springs by the lake. Natural heating from magma close to the surface incubates the eggs, and after 50 days the megapode chicks emerge fully feathered and ready to fend for themselves. Unfortunately those *malau* eggs that aren't collected by the islanders for food are dug up by free-ranging pigs and the birds are facing extinction. Many tracks lead to the lake from all directions.

Facilities

Most government offices on Niuafo'ou are at Esia, but the Telecom office and Civil Aviation offices are at Sapa'ata. There are no official accommodations on Niuafo'ou, though some of the locals will accept paying guests. The Royal Tongan Airlines agent on Niuafo'ou should be able to arrange accommodation, and the airline office in Vava'u will radio ahead to let them know you're coming.

Getting There

Niuafo'ou (NFO) is theoretically accessible twice on a month on the **Royal Tongan Airlines** flights from Nuku'alofa (T$279) and Vava'u (T$170). In practice the plane has a 50-50 chance of landing, as Niuafo'ou's airstrip is placed in such a way that dangerously strong winds whip across it. When that happens, the plane has to fly all the way back to Vava'u, and the people on the island see their long-awaited cargo go back where it came from for another two weeks. No scheduled flights go to Niuatoputapu.

NIUAFO'OU

AIRSTRIP

Angaha — Alele'uta
Esia — Sapa'ata
— Fata'ulua
— Mata'aho

Site of Futu
Motu Molemole

Motu Lahi

Motu Si'i

Vai Lahi

Mu'a

Sulphur Lagoon

Site of 'Ahau
Tongamama'o
Petani

Lava Field

Lava Field

0   1 mi
0   1 km

KINGDOM OF TONGA
6s
NIUAFO'OU MEGAPODE
NIUAFO'OU
TIN CAN ISLAND

NIVE

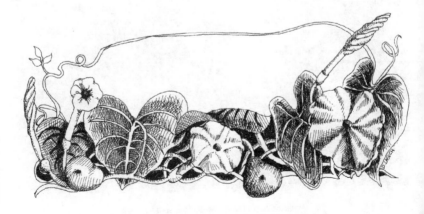

Matapa Chasm is a former bathing spot for royalty.

NIUE

INTRODUCTION

A single 259-square-km island, Niue is one of the world's smallest self-governing states (in free association with New Zealand). It stands alone 560 km southeast of Samoa, 386 km east of Vava'u, and 2,400 km northeast of New Zealand. The name comes from *niu* (coconut tree) and *e* (behold). This little-known island boasts some of the finest coastal limestone crevices and chasms in the South Pacific, all open to visitors and freely accessible. Each is unique—you'll need at least a week to do them justice.

Niue is for the explorer who likes to get out and make discoveries on his or her own, for the skin diver in search of clean clear water brimming with coral, fish, and sea snakes, and for those who want to relax in a peaceful, uncommercialized environment among charming, friendly people, without sacrificing creature comforts. Niue is perhaps the most unspoiled main island in the Pacific—it's an island of adventure.

The Land

Niue is an elevated atoll shaped like a two-tiered wedding cake with two terraces rising from the sea. It's one of the largest coral islands in the world (though 692-square-km Rennell Island in the Solomons is much bigger). The lower terrace rises sharply, creating the 20-meter coastal cliffs that virtually surround the island. Inland, the second terrace rises abruptly from this coastal belt to a central plateau some 60 meters above the ocean. A fringing reef borders much of the coast, but in places the ocean breakers smash directly into the cliffs. Faulting during the island's uplifting has created the chasms and crevices that are Niue's greatest attractions. Water dripping from their ceilings has added a touch of the surreal in the form of stalactites and stalagmites.

Climate

December-March are the hurricane months, with average temperatures of 27° C. The southeast trades blow April-Nov. and temperatures average 24° C. The 2,047 mm of annual rainfall is fairly well distributed throughout the year, with a slight peak during the hot southern summer. There is good anchorage at Alofi, except during strong westerly winds.

Flora and Fauna

The waters off Niue are clear as can be, with countless species of colorful fish. There are also many varieties of sea snakes—though poisonous, their mouths are too tiny to bite, and divers handle them with impunity. On most dives underwater sightseers also spot white-tip reef sharks, but they aren't dangerous and add to the thrill.

Butterflies are everywhere, as are orchids, hibiscus, frangipani, and bougainvillea. One-fifth of the island's surface is covered by undisturbed primary forest, much of the rest by secondary growth. A profusion of huge "crow's nest" *(nidum)* and other ferns, rhododendron, and poinsettia grow wild, and there are ancient ebony trees. The birdlife is rich; white long-tailed terns, weka, swamp hens, and parakeets abound.

History

Niue was colonized by Samoans in the 9th or 10th century A.D., then Tongans invaded in the 16th century, and the present Niuean language is related to both. Captain Cook made three landings in 1774, but he got a hostile reception from warriors with red-painted teeth! Cook called it Savage Island (as opposed to the Friendly Islands, Tonga), a name still heard from time to time. In 1830 the redoubtable missionary John Williams was also thrown back by force. A Samoa-trained Niuean named Peniamina managed to convert some of the islanders to Christianity in 1846, but it was a series of Samoan pastors, beginning in 1849, who really implanted the faith on the island. This paved the way for the first resident English missionary, George Lawes, who arrived in 1861.

Much of the early hostility to foreigners was motivated by a very real fear of European diseases. The islanders' reputation for ferocity had always kept the whalers away, but then in the 1860s came the Peruvians and Bully Hayes, who were able to entice Niuean men to leave their island voluntarily to mine phosphate for years at a time on distant Malden Island. Mataio Tuitonga was made king in 1876 and his successor, Fataaiki, appealed to Britain for protection. Finally, in 1900, Niue was taken over by the U.K. and a year later transferred to New Zealand.

Government

In 1959 the appointed Island Council was replaced by an elected Legislative Assembly (Fono Ekepule). Niue became internally self-governing in free association with New Zealand on 19 October 1974. The Assembly has 20 elected members, 14 from village constituencies and six from a single island-wide constituency. The premier is elected by the Assembly from its own ranks by a show of hands. The premier in turn chooses three cabinet ministers from among the Assembly members. The Assembly meets in the impressive Fale Fono (tel. 4200) in Alofi. Local government is provided by the 14 village councils elected every three years.

Niue's first elected premier, Hon. Sir Robert R. Rex, served continuously as government leader from 1974 until his death in 1992. Now Sir Robert's son, Robert Rex Jr., is an elected member of the legislature. Other local politicians of note include Mr. Young Viviani, a former secretary-general of the Pacific Community; Mr. Frank Lui, Sir Robert's successor as prime minister; and noted photographer Michael Jackson.

Government ministers brook no criticism. When the editor of the local newspaper became overly annoying to the powers that be, her expatriate

AUCKLAND INSTITUTE AND MUSEUM

Togia, the last king of Niue, addressing a gathering in 1903

husband suddenly had visa problems. In early 1995 an Australian Catholic priest with years of service on Niue was subjected to deportation proceedings after he dared comment publicly on nepotism in the allocation of government scholarships. In a small community like Niue's one has to take care not to step on the wrong toes.

Economy

Niue is totally dependent on official aid from New Zealand, which supplies three-quarters of the local budget. Overseas aid totals about NZ$6 million a year, or NZ$3,158 per capita, the highest such level in the South Pacific. Most of the money is used to support the infrastructure, which maintains an artificial, consumer-oriented standard of living. Many government services are provided free to residents. In 1996, under the threat of a reduction in this aid, the government downsized the public service from 750 to 320, and many of the redundant workers and their families have since moved off island.

Imports are 20 times higher than exports, an imbalance of trade only exceeded in the French colonies. In the past hand-sewn footballs sent to N.Z. were the biggest export, but transportation difficulties have halted this and virtually all other exports. Tourism, the sale of postage stamps to philatelists, and limited royalties from overseas fishing companies help balance the island's cash flow. In 1996 a quarantine station opened on Niue for around 600 alpacas, which spend a year here en route from Peru to Australia.

Of the 2,041 "tourists" who visited Niue in 1997, two-thirds were overseas Niueans visiting relatives and three-quarters of the remainder arrived on cheap packaged holidays from New Zealand. Niue received three American tourists in 1993, one in 1994, and none at all in 1995. In fact, because Niue isn't on any main air routes and is an expensive side trip, so few tourists come that many of the facilities listed in this chapter are actually retirement projects for people who made their money elsewhere. In 1996 the New Zealand government spent NZ$10 million extending the airport runway and building a new resort in the hope of promoting tourism to Niue. Yet apart from official visitors, both of the larger government-owned hotels stand empty most of the time and just two Tongan aircraft touch down on the shiny new airstrip each week.

In 1993 Niue set up a "financial center" similar to those of Vanuatu and Cook Islands to support overseas firms trying to avoid taxation in their actual places of business. Although this scam brings in NZ$400,000 in licensing fees each year from the 200 companies involved, the Audit Office of New Zealand is unhappy about being refused access to the records and official aid has been cut back. In 1996 Niue was earning US$50,000 a month by leasing its international telephone circuits to route overseas sex calls to "phone girls" in New Zealand, but in 1997 Niue's prime minister canceled the arrangement after complaints from local residents who were being accidentally connected to phone-sex clients in the U.S., Britain, and Japan.

Niue has also profited from the sale of its internet ending .nu, which has been marketed worldwide by local entrepreneur Stafford Guest via http://something.really.nu. At just US$25, top level .nu domain names are among the cheapest on the web and thousands have been sold.

Although attempts have been made to stimulate agriculture, the economy is continually undermined by emigration of working-age Niueans to New Zealand (to which Niueans have unhindered entry). In the past, small quantities of passion fruit, lime juice, canned coconut cream, and honey have been exported. The coconut cream factory closed in 1989 after a hurricane wiped out the island's coconut plantations; in 1990 Hurricane Ofa destroyed the lime and passion fruit crops. Periodic droughts have also taken a heavy toll. Taro, yams, cassava, sweet potatoes, papaya, and bananas are actively cultivated in bush gardens for personal consumption by the grower. Some Niue taro is sold in Auckland. Local farmers also grow vanilla, and some pigs, poultry, and beef cattle are kept. Saturday is bush day when people go inland to clear, plant, and weed their gardens.

The People

Niueans are related to Tongans and Samoans rather than to Tahitians. The population is about 1,900 and falling (down from 4,000 at self-government in 1974). Another 14,400 Niueans reside in New Zealand (all Niueans are N.Z. citizens), and every year more people leave "the Rock" (Niue) to seek employment and opportunity abroad. Many of the landowners have left—

you'll never see as many empty houses and near-ghost towns as you see here. The villages on the east coast give an idea of how Europe must have looked in the Middle Ages after a plague, as direct flights to Auckland have drained the population. Remittances from Niueans in New Zealand are important sources of income.

The inhabitants live in small villages scattered along the coast, with a slight concentration near the administrative center, Alofi. After disastrous hurricanes in 1959 and 1960, the New Zealand government replaced the traditional lime-plastered, thatched-roofed houses of the people with tin-roofed "hurricane-resistant" concrete-block dwellings. Niue has the lowest population density of any Pacific country (excluding Papua New Guinea). At 15 per thousand, Niue's birth rate is the lowest in the Pacific, and the life expectancy is the lowest in Polynesia at 60 for men and 65 for women.

All land is held by families. Three-quarters belong to the Ekalesia Niue, founded by the London Missionary Society. Other churches such as the Catholics and Mormons have only a few hundred members. There are no longer any chiefs, and lineage means little. Since the 1950s education has been free and compulsory until the age of 14 and literacy is almost 100%. Two Polynesian dialects are spoken: Motu in the north and Tafiti in the south. Everyone on the island knows one another.

A major event for a teenage boy is his hair-cutting ceremony, when the long tail of hair he has kept since childhood is removed. Guests invited to the concurrent feast each contribute hundreds of dollars to a fund that goes to the boy after celebration expenses are paid. For girls there's a similar ear-piercing ceremony. These gatherings are usually held on a Saturday in private homes; you may be allowed to observe if you know someone.

Public Holidays and Festivals

Public holidays include New Year's Day, Commission Day (2 January), Waitangi Day (6 February), Good Friday, Easter Monday (March/April), ANZAC Day (25 April), White Sunday (second Sunday in May), Queen Elizabeth's Birthday (a Monday in early June), Constitution Days (19 and 20 October), Peniamina Day (fourth Monday in October), and Christmas Days (25 and 26 December).

Prayer Week and Takai Week are both held during the first week of January. The main event of the year is the Constitution Celebrations, which last three days around 19 October. There are traditional dancing and singing, parades, sports, and a display of produce and handicrafts at the high school grounds two km inland from Alofi. A highlight is the exciting outrigger canoe race off Alofi wharf. Peniamina Day falls on the Monday during the Constitution Celebrations.

SIGHTS AND RECREATION

Exploring Niue

Virtually all of Niue's scenic attractions are within earshot of the sea, but while sites on the west coast are easily accessible in a few minutes from the road, those on the east coast are only reached over slippery rough trails requiring hikes of up to 40 minutes. Some of these trails, such as those through the fantastic petrified coral forests at Vaikona and Tongo, are not well marked. Sturdy shoes are required to go almost anywhere off the road on Niue.

If you're a good walker, you could visit the sites south of Alofi on foot in less than a day. Those to the north can be covered by a combination of walking, hitching, and good luck, but to

get to the places on the northeast and southeast coasts and return to Alofi the same day, you'll need your own transport. Alternatively, camp in one of the east coast villages and visit the area more at your leisure. Take your own food with you, as little is available in the villages. The Huvalu Forest Camp near Hakupu village described below is ideal for hikers interested in spending time in this unspoiled area.

Photographers should note that conditions on the east coast are best in the morning, on the west coast in the afternoon. Vaikona and Tongo are definitely not afternoon trips, as the declining light in the forest makes the trails hard to discern. Also, limestone makes for slow walking.

Near Alofi

The **Huanaki Museum and Cultural Center** (tel. 4011, open weekdays 0800-1500, free) is next to the hospital near the junction of the airport and coastal roads in Alofi. According to popular tradition, Captain Cook landed at **Opaahi Reef** opposite the Mormon church in Alofi. It's a scenic spot, well worth the short detour.

Two kings of Niue, Mataio Tuitonga (reigned 1876-87) and Fataaiki (reigned 1888-96), are buried at the **royal tombs** in front of the LMS Church opposite Alofi's post office. Nearby, adjoining the war memorial, are two stone backrests used by these kings. The last king of Niue, Togia (died 1917), ceded his kingdom to Britain on 21 April 1900, just four days after the Americans annexed Eastern Samoa. He's buried in front of the church at Tuapa.

It's fascinating to walk on the reef southwest of Alofi wharf at low tide. Crevices, cliffs, and coral

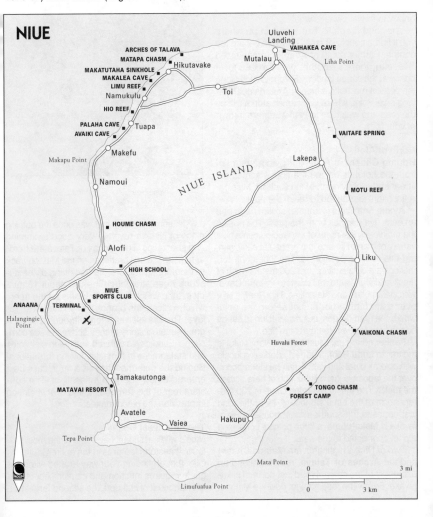

NIUE

abound, and there are natural pools on the reef where you can swim safely. Beware of waves heralding the incoming tide, however.

South of Alofi

A couple of small government-run food processing plants and experimental farms are in the area around the airport. Passion fruit, limes, and papaya are grown here, and honey is produced. It's interesting to poke around a bit and the people you meet will probably be only too happy to explain what's what.

The road drops to **Tamakautonga,** where you'll find a couple of small beaches behind the church. Farther south at **Avatele** (pronounced Avasele), there's another poor excuse for a beach at the canoe landing. Return to Alofi along the coastal road with a stop at **Anaana** near Halangingie Point, where you can sit atop a cliff by the road and watch as tons of water are thrown at your feet.

North of Alofi

Houme Chasm at Alofi North, about four km from the hotel, is behind the house across the street and slightly north of the Catholic Mission. A flashlight is required to reach the pool.

Avaiki Sea Cave is another six km north and an easy five minutes from the road. The pool in the main cave just north of the landing contains a variety of marinelife and is a great place to swim, but this is often prohibited. The limestone formations are outstanding. Just 200 meters north of the Avaiki sign is the trail down to **Palaha Cave,** with stalagmites and stalactites. **Hio Reef,** a little over a km farther north, just before the point where the road divides, is a nice secluded sandy beach best for swimming at high tide.

Farther north again, just beyond Namukulu, is the trail to **Limu Reef,** a perfect snorkeling locale with colorful coral and fish. A natural stone bridge over the lagoon is just a little north of here across the rocks. The trail to **Makalea Cave** is 200 meters north of the Limu signboard. Near the road just opposite the southernmost house in Hikutavake is **Makatutaha,** a large pothole containing a pool connected to the sea.

Two of Niue's highlights are **Matapa Chasm** and the **Arches of Talava,** reached along an extension of the coastal road just north of Hikutavake. Follow the road straight down to Matapa,

Avaiki Sea Cave is just the place for a refreshing swim.

a wide, sunken chasm that was once the bathing place of Niuean royalty—very good swimming and snorkeling. The Arches of Talava are harder to find. The trail branches off the Matapa track to the right just before the beginning of the descent. Keep straight on the trail about 15 minutes, then watch for yellow marks on the trees, which indicate the branch trail on the left to Talava. The site itself is entered through a cave. A great series of stone arches above the sea complement side caves with red and green stalactites and stalagmites in fantastic flowing formations. Behind the outermost arch is a large cave best entered at low tide with a flashlight. The constant roar of the surf adds to the overwhelming impression the place makes.

The Southeast Coast

Niue's wild east coast has some of the most fantastic limestone features in the entire South Pacific, though finding your way around without a guide requires intuition and caution. About four km northeast of Hakupu, the second-largest village on the island, is the unmarked trail to **Tongo Chasm.** After a 20-minute walk you reach a wasteland of coral pinnacles much like the interior of Nauru Island. The path leads down to a wide chasm with coconut trees growing on the sandy bottom. Climb down the ladder to the sand, and swim in the pools at each end of the chasm. The green of the coconut trees combined with the golden sand contrasts sharply with the rocky wasteland, creating an almost North African effect—until you hear the ocean crashing into the cliffs just meters away: one of the scenic wonders of the Pacific.

From the Tongo trailhead, travel northeast another four km through the **Huvalu Forest,** with its many species of banyan, Tahitian chestnut, and *kafika* trees, to the Vaikona trailhead. The trail to **Vaikona Chasm** is partially marked with red paint, but careful attention is required, as there is a good chance of getting lost. This trip is for experienced hikers only, unless you come with a guide. As you approach the coast through pandanus brush covering the jagged limestone, you pass a sudden opening straight down into the chasm. Wind your way around the back of the opening and drop into a deep cave, grasping the stout orange rope provided for the purpose. You enter the chasm over huge rocks from the cave. There are two crystal clear pools to swim in, one at each end of Vaikona; tiny freshwater crayfish and black carp live here.

It would take a major expedition to explore all this chasm has to offer. Resembling a ruined Gothic cathedral, the walls soar 30 meters to a canopy of vegetation, and huge blocks of the collapsed roof litter the floor. The stalagmites and stalactites of the entrance cave are like images on a broken medieval portal; by plunging into the cool, clear water of the pools, one has communion with the bowels of the earth. The crashing of the breakers into the coast nearby is like the expurgation of sin—a spectacular visual experience. This awe-inspiring chasm is outstanding even for Niue. Hopefully Vaikona, Tongo, and the Huvalu Forest will someday be set aside as a national park.

The Northeast Coast
The trail to **Motu Reef** is about a kilometer south of Lakepa. There's a wide wooden stairway down to the reef from the cave where canoes are stored. It's a 25-minute walk along an easy-to-follow trail from the trailhead to **Vaitafe Spring,** a couple of km north of Lakepa. Fresh water from a crevice at the foot of a sheer cliff bubbles into a pool where you can swim, but the area is accessible only at low tide. You can reef walk here.

At the north end of the island, opposite the church in **Mutalau** village, is a monument commemorating the arrival of the first Christian missionaries; the first Niuean convert, Peniamina (1846); and Paulo (1849), the first Samoan teacher. A jeep track across from the monument leads down to Uluvehi Landing, an easy five-minute walk. This was the main landing on the island in the early days; the islanders' sleek outrigger canoes are still stored in caves in the cliffs. To reach **Vaihakea Cave,** look for an overgrown trail just 100 meters inland from the streetlight at Uluvehi on the east side of the track. Once you get on the trail, it's only a five-minute walk to this fantastic submerged cave full of fish and coral, but you must climb down a sharp limestone cliff near the trail end. There's excellent swimming and snorkeling at low tide.

The sites mentioned above are only the *highlights* of Niue; there are many other caves for the avid spelunker to explore.

SPORTS AND RECREATION

Kevin Fawcett of **Niue Dive** (Box 140, Alofi; tel. 4311 or 3483, fax 4028, www.dive.nu, e-mail: niuedive@dive.nu), behind the hospital, offers scuba diving at NZ\$50/175/350/475 for one/three/six/eight-dive packages with a mix of shore and inflatable boat dives. Gear rental (if required) is NZ\$15 per dive. Kevin is a professional and his equipment is first class. A certification card is required, otherwise a PADI openwater course will be NZ\$500 pp (minimum of two). Featured are dives through caves to drop-offs and Niue's small, timid sea snakes. If you're very lucky, you may be able to dive with dolphins or migrating whales (June-Nov.). Due to the absence of rivers, the water is unbelievably clear—worth every penny. Niue Dive also arranges snorkeling, whalewatching or coastal sightseeing trips at NZ\$30 pp.

Game fishing is available on an eight-meter *alia* catamaran operated by Paul Pasisi's **Horizon Charter** (tel. 4067). More of the same is offered by **Wahoo Fishing Charters** (Box 112, Alofi; tel./fax 4345, e-mail: wahoo@sin.net.nu) which has a six-meter aluminum tri-hull fishing boat available at NZ$220/360 for four/eight hours (up to four anglers). Fish caught belong to the boat. Wahoo's Graham Marsh has been fishing Niue's waters since 1983. The main season for wahoo is July-Nov.; marlin, sailfish, tuna, and mahi mahi are taken from Nov.-April. Fishing on Sunday is taboo.

Visitors are welcome at the nine-hole **golf course** (tel. 4292) near the airport. An annual tournament is in November.

Sporting events such as soccer (March-June), rugby (June-Aug.), and netball (June-Aug.) take place on the high school grounds. Cricket (Dec.-Feb.) and softball matches are usually held in the villages on alternating Saturdays. The locals will know what is happening.

PRACTICALITIES

ACCOMMODATIONS

Budget

The **Waimanu Guest House** (Asu and Mine Pulu, tel. 4366, fax 4225), next to the public works depot at Amanau southwest of Alofi, has two singles at NZ$40, two doubles with shared bath at NZ$55, one double with private bath at NZ$66, and two self-catering suites at NZ$80. A communal kitchen is available to all. It's good value for scuba divers or anglers.

Peleni's Guest House (Fita and Toke Talagi, Box 11, Alofi; tel. 4135, fax 4322, e-mail: peleni@mail.gov.nu) is in a former family house near the Handicraft Center in central Alofi. The three very homey bedrooms with shared bath and cooking facilities are NZ$35/40 single/dou-

ble. A three-bed family room costs NZ$50. Prepared meals are available at reasonable cost and everything is clean and well maintained. It's handy to great swimming spots at Utuko and the wharf. They rent cars to guests only at NZ$25 a day. Airport transfers are free.

Kololi's Guest House (Box 177, Alofi; tel. 4171), near the Commercial Center in central Alofi, charges NZ$35 single or double for the three standard rooms and NZ$50 for the family room upstairs. Your hosts Neil and Opo Morrisey provide convenient communal cooking and laundry facilities in this stylishly designed guesthouse.

Right above the Avaiki Caves a bit north of Makefu is the **Anaiki Motel** (Moka and Ataloma Mitihepi, Box 183, Alofi; tel. 4321, fax 4320) with five units in a long block at NZ$50 single or dou-

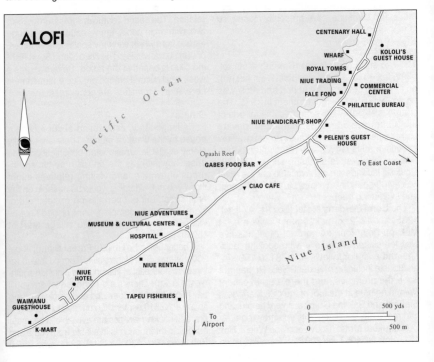

ble, NZ$65 triple, tropical breakfast included. A hot plate is provided for heating up simple meals. It's a nice place from which to see the sunset and watch the local fishermen launching their canoes on the evening tide. Your kind hosts will be happy to show you around the village.

Esther's Village Motel (Lilly and Esther Pavihi, Box 107, Alofi; tel. 3708) in Avatele has three double units with private bath and full kitchens at NZ$48/52 single/double, and one four-bed family unit at NZ$62 triple (children under 12 are free). The large veranda is a great place for an evening meal while watching the sunset. A village store and beach are nearby—families will like it here. There's a small shop on the premises, but the distance from Alofi (seven km) is a drawback.

Damiana's Holiday Motel (Box 95, Alofi; tel. 4286), also at Avatele, is very similar to Esther's with two duplex units with good cooking facilities and private bath, NZ$55/65/75 single/double/triple (children under 12 free). Their tropical garden is really lovely. A recent report indicates that Esther's and Damiana's are presently closed, so check.

Moderate

The two-story **Niue Hotel** (Box 80, Alofi; tel. 4092, fax 4310, e-mail: niuehotel@sin.net.nu), on the coast between the airport and Alofi, was originally built by the government in 1975. The charge is NZ$109/125 single/double for one of the 32 fan-cooled rooms with fridge, private bath, transfers, and breakfast. An ocean-view executive suite is NZ$135/160 single/double, while a family suite sleeping six is NZ$175. Cooking facilities are not available but the hotel has a 100-seat dining room, plus bar, gift shop, and swimming pool.

The **Coral Gardens Motel** (Box 91, Alofi; tel. 4235, fax 4222, e-mail: sguest@cas.nu), at Makapu Point four km north of Alofi, has five wooden clifftop bungalows with cooking facilities and excellent views at NZ$120/150 single/double including breakfast. Sails Restaurant is on the premises, and there's an excellent swimming hole at the foot of the cliff. Managers Stafford and Salome Guest are very helpful and can make any arrangements you may require.

Namukulu Motel (Robyn and Joe Wright, Box 171, Alofi; tel. 4052, fax 3001), at Namukulu nine km north of Alofi, offers three self-catering bungalows with fridge and TV at NZ$105/130/155/180 single/double/triple/quad. There's a swimming pool and three of Niue's finest reef swimming pools are nearby. Ten-speed bicycles are loaned free. Airport pickups are complimentary.

Expensive

The upscale **Matavai Resort** (Box 133, Alofi; tel. 4360, fax 4361, e-mail: matavai@mail.gov.nu), perched on a cliff at the south end of Tamakautonga village, was built in 1996 with NZ$2.4 in New Zealand aid money and the government retains 51% ownership. Radio Sunshine general manager Hima Douglas and K-Mart owner Russell Kars are partners. The 24 rooms with fridge and TV in two-story blocks begin at NZ$150/170 single/double, continental breakfast included (no cooking facilities). Specials may be available when business is slow. The dramatic location has made the managers reluctant to accept children under 12 who might be endangered, and parents or guardians may be required to sign a release. The resort features a restaurant, bar, two swimming pools, tennis courts, and a huge terrace from which you may spot dolphins, turtles, or humpback whales. The Niue Island Sport Fishing Club is based at the resort. Several nights a week local cultural groups provide entertainment here. Airport transfers are complimentary.

Others

For a longer stay, ask around about renting a house by the week or month. There are usually plenty available. Unexpected complications can arise, however, as the house may have hundreds of owners, and visiting relatives might throw you out! Camping would be possible on the east coast, but get permission or keep out of sight. For indoor camping, unfurnished houses without hot water in Hakupu village start at NZ$50 a week.

A better bet is the **Huvalu Forest Camp,** about 200 meters south of the trail to Tongo Chasm (or three km northeast of Hakupu and eight km southwest of Liku). There's a bunkhouse where you'll pay NZ$15 pp for a dorm bed and ample camping space at NZ$10 per tent. Communal toilets, showers, and cooking facilities are available in separate buildings. Information is available from Afele and Pati Paea (Box 130, Alofi; tel. 4244) who live at

Namoui between Alofi and Makefu. The Forest Camp makes a great base for exploring the most beautiful part of the island, so long as you're prepared to rough it a bit. It's beautiful in the moonlight: wonderfully silent except for the sounds of the forest (and occasional mosquito). Ask for Robert Jackson at the bakery in Hakupu who rents mountain bikes at NZ$5/30 a day/week.

OTHER PRACTICALITIES

Food and Entertainment
The dining room at the **Niue Hotel** (tel. 4092) serves lunch 1200-1300 sharp (open daily). Check to see if they're still serving endangered species like the *unga* (coconut crab), fruit bat, and native pigeon to tourists. Thursday or Sunday at 1900 (check to find out which day) the hotel has a tropical smorgasbord, sometimes followed by disco dancing to recorded music. The hotel bar picks up in the afternoon as people get off work, but they close early if nobody's around, even on Friday night.

Light snacks are served at **Mitaki's Cafe** (tel. 4084) south of Alofi, at the **Huanaki Snack Bar** (tel. 4071) at the Cultural Center, and at the **Tavana Cafe** (tel. 4334) in the Commercial Center in Alofi. The **Ciao Cafe** (tel. 4316) near the Mormon Church offers cappuccino, pizza, lasagna, spaghetti, and gelato. Up on the road toward the airport is **Tapeu Fisheries** (tel. 4106) with super seafood. **Island Style Restaurant** (tel. 3707) is at Talamaitonga near Avatele.

Gabes Food Bar (tel. 4379) in Alofi lays on an "island night buffet" featuring Polynesian vegetables and seafoods at NZ$15 pp. Included is a cultural show and live music—ask about this as dates vary.

Sails Restaurant (tel. 4235), at the Coral Gardens Motel north of town, serves good food at prices lower than those asked at the Niue Hotel. Their patio is a great place for a drink around sunset, and a live band plays on Friday night (closed Sunday and Monday). Ask about their weekly barbecue.

The **Niue Sports Club** (tel. 4292), better known as the Top Club, at the nine-hole golf course near the airport, is nominally private, but visitors are welcome and bar prices low. Village dances take place on Friday and Saturday

THE COCONUT CRAB

The coconut crab *(Birgus latro)* is a nocturnal creature that lives in burrows it excavates in the ground. The life cycle of the crab begins in November or December when an adult deposits millions of eggs in the sea. These eggs hatch into larvae that drift until they manage to attach themselves to a reef, where they remain until they've grown sufficiently to emerge from the water and become island dwellers. The crabs can live over 50 years, and a mature adult will weigh more than two kilograms. The coconut crab uses its enormous, powerful claws to force open coconuts, which are its preferred food although it also eats vegetation and any scraps it can find. Unfortunately, coconut crabs are themselves considered a delicacy by humans and have become an endangered species almost everywhere due to overhunting.

LOUISE FOOTE

nights. The **Pacific Way Bar,** near the Niue Hotel southwest of Alofi, has the local Fia Fia beer on tap.

Liquor is sold by the Treasury Department near the post office. On paydays the Department's hours are restricted; alcoholism is a problem here and drunks can suddenly turn aggressive, so be careful what you say in such situations. Consuming alcohol in the street is prohibited. The tap water is safe to drink on Niue.

Shopping
Imported goods are fairly expensive. The largest supermarkets are Niue Trading (tel. 4080), Rex's Store (tel. 4027), and Jessop's (tel. 4306), all in Alofi. Check their snack bars. They close at 1600

weekdays and don't open at all weekends, so if you arrive on the Friday flight from Auckland, head straight there to do your weekend grocery shopping. Otherwise bring along some instant noodles and canned foods to avoid being dependent on the rather expensive restaurants all weekend (but don't bring fresh fruits or vegetables, which could cause quarantine complications). There's only a market once a week, held early Friday morning beside Rex's Store. Buy a bottle of Niue honey, if you can.

A **Commercial Center** in Alofi houses the bank, telephone center, butcher shop, gift shop, stationery store, art gallery, and several handicraft shops. The **Philatelic Bureau** (Box 73, Alofi; tel. 4371, fax 4386) in this center sells beautiful stamps, which make excellent souvenirs.

The people produce very fine, firmly woven baskets of pandanus wound over a coconut-fiber core—among the sturdiest in Polynesia. Fine pandanus and coconut leaf bud hats are also made. Visit the **Niue Handicraft Shop** (tel. 4144) in Alofi and **Hinapoto Handicrafts** (tel. 4340) at the Cultural Center. Coral and valuable shells cannot be exported from Niue.

Services

The administration buildings in Alofi contain the post office and Treasury Department. Change money at the Westpac Bank branch (tel. 4221, weekdays 0900-1500). New Zealand currency is used. Many hotels and restaurants accept credit cards, but ask first.

Telecom Niue (tel. 4000, open 24 hours) next to the satellite dish in Alofi handles overseas calls and wires. You can send a fax to anyone on the island at fax 4010 and they'll be called and asked to pick it up here. Niue's telephone code is 683.

Doctors and dentists are available at Lord Liverpool Hospital (tel. 4100; weekdays 0730-1500).

Yachting Facilities

Yachts anchor in about 15 meters (good holding) in an open roadstead off Alofi and are well protected except for winds from the west. The **Niue Island Yacht Club** (Box 129, Alofi; e-mail: yachtclub@sin.net.nu) provides 18 secure moorings in Alofi Bay which can be used for a NZ$5-a-day charge. Water, toilets, and showers are available at the wharf, but it's necessary to have a bri-

dle arrangement on the dingy to allow it to be lifted out of the water using an electronic winch. Yachts must call "Niue Radio" on VHF channels 10 or 16 for clearance before coming ashore, and Customs and Immigration (tel. 4122, fax 4150) are closed on weekends (exceptions are occasionally made). The NZ$20 pp departure tax also applies to yachties. An annual yacht race is held around the end of August if enough boats are in the bay. Niue makes an excellent stop for yachts sailing between Rarotonga/Aitutaki and Vava'u.

Information

The Tourism Office (Box 42, Alofi; tel. 4224, fax 4225, www.niueisland.com, e-mail: niuetourism@mail.gov.nu) in Alofi's Commercial Center can answer most questions about the island and books activities. Every Wednesday night they organize a *fia fia* at Hakupu village at NZ$35 pp for transportation, a village tour, island food, and entertainment. It's well worth going.

The public library (tel. 4019, weekdays 0800-1600) has a good Pacific section. The USP Extension Center (Box 31, Niue; tel. 4049, fax 4315) at Niue High School sells a few books on Niue.

An excellent map of Niue can be purchased at the gift shop or South Seas Traders in the Commercial Center. The DHL Courier agent Geoff Harding (tel. 4295) stocks posters and historical books about the island.

The *Niue Star* (Box 84, Alofi; tel. 4207) is an independent weekly newspaper published in English and Niuean on Fridays (circulation around 600). An airmailed subscription to Stafford Guest's informative monthly *Niue Economic Review* (Box 91, Alofi; tel. 4235) is NZ$60 a year. *The Niue News* (Box 3056, Auckland, New Zealand) serves the overseas Niuean community.

The Broadcasting Corporation of Niue (Box 68, Alofi; tel. 4026) provides television service 1800-2300 daily and Radio Sunshine broadcasts over 594 kHz AM and 91 MHz FM 0600-2130, but both are off the air on Sunday. Most TV programs are supplied by Television New Zealand.

Getting There

Royal Tongan Airlines flies a Boeing 737 to Niue from Auckland once a week, returning to New Zealand via Tonga. Royal Tongan also has a second weekly flight to Niue from Nuku'alofa using a propeller-driven, 40-seat Hawker-Sidley 748, connecting with flights to/from Auckland n Tonga. These services are only viable due to subsidies from the Niue government which has designated Royal Tongan as Niue's national carrier. Rumor has it that Polynesian Airlines may take over from Royal Tongan and recommence service to Apia and Rarotonga, and that might lead to service to/from Tonga being canceled, so check. Also ask about direct flights from Niue to Vava'u.

Meanwhile it's T$217/434 one-way/roundtrip from Nuku'alofa, with a 28-day excursion fare of T$340 available year-round. From Auckland the 90-day excursion fare is NZ$1,185/1,381 low/high season (the high season is June-Oct. and December). Avoid Christmas when the flights will be packed full of islanders returning home. Flying from Auckland or Nuku'alofa to Niue you arrive a day earlier because you cross the international date line, so check your flight dates carefully (Niue and Samoa share the same day).

Go International Travel (Box 9144, Auckland, New Zealand; tel. 64-9/914-4700, fax 64-9/307-3235), **Go Pacific Holidays** (tel. 64-9/379-5520, fax 64-9/377-0111), and **ASPAC Vacations Ltd.** (Box 4330, Auckland, New Zealand; tel. 64-9/623-0259, fax 64-9/623-0257, e-mail: southpacific@aspac-vacations.co.nz) offer well-planned package tours to Niue from Auckland. These trips start at NZ$959, which is less than a regular roundtrip ticket, and yet airfare, seven nights double-occupancy lodging, and transfers are included! In Australia contact **Hideaway Holidays** (Val Gavriloff, 994 Victoria Rd., West Ryde, NSW 2114; tel. 61-2/9807-4222, fax 61-2/9808-2260, www.hideawayholidays.com.au).

Reconfirm your flight reservations well ahead at **Peleni's Travel Agency** (tel. 4317, fax 4322) in Alofi, the Royal Tongan Airlines agent. The same office should have information about the monthly Cook Islands National Line supply ship *Ngamaru III* to Rarotonga (cabin passage is NZ$100 a day). Ask at Niue Trading Store (tel. 4080) in Alofi about occasional boats to Tonga (NZ$50 one-way). Large ships must anchor offshore; their cargo is transferred by lighters.

Getting Around

There's no bus service on Niue but taxi services are available from Cedric's (tel. 4245) and Mitaki's (tel. 4084). Hitching is easy along the west coast, but you could get stranded on the east. Don't underestimate the size of the island: it's a long, long way to walk. The road around the island is 64 km and the pavement doesn't extend beyond the west coast.

Four car rental companies operate on Niue. **Budget Rent-a-Car** (Box 81, Alofi; tel. 4307, fax 4308), also known as Ama's Rentals, is at Helen's Niue Tours next to the Niue Hotel. **Niue Rentals** (Box 146, Alofi; tel. 4216, fax 4065, e-mail: niuerentals@sin.net.nu), between the Niue Hotel and the hospital, may give you a 15% discount if you show this book. **Alofi Rentals** (Wally and Mary Saunders, Box 204, Alofi; tel. 4017, e-mail: alofirentals@sin.net.nu) is next to the Niue Adventures shop or about 50 meters from the Mormon church. **Paradise Rentals** (tel. 4364) is next to the Commercial Center. Rates are competitive, around NZ$65/80 for a five/nine-seater

Dugout canoes and outboards are pulled up on the beach at Avatele.

van, NZ$30-50 for a car, NZ$25 for a motor-bike, NZ$20 for a scooter, and NZ$5 for bicycles. On a weekly basis you usually get one day free. Car rentals include kilometers and insurance but you're still responsible for the first NZ$1,000 in "excess" damages in case of an accident. Before heading around the island on a scooter make sure the tank is full and ask the renter if you can make it on one tank. All rental vehicles are in short supply, so don't wait until the last minute. A Niue driver's license (NZ$5) must be obtained at the police station opposite the Commercial Center (no test required if you have any other license). Driving is on the left and speed limits are 40 kph in the villages or 60 kph on the open road. The penalty for being caught inebriated at a roadside breath analyzer test is NZ$1,500.

Helen's Niue Tours (Helen Sipeli, Box 81, Alofi; tel. 4054, fax 4167) next to the Niue Hotel offers a variety of trips, including tours to Vaikona Chasm, a breakfast bush walk, a "behind the hedges" tour, a circle-island tour, and a Huvalu Forest and Tongo tour. Ask about the Saturday afternoon *fia fia* feast tour with *umu* food and Niuean dancing.

Tali Magatogia of **Tali's Tours** (tel. 3505) can take you to hard-to-reach attractions such as Tongo Chasm, Vaikona Chasm, Ulupaka Cave, and Anatoloa Cave. Ulupaka (near Lakepa) is over a km long and coated with dirty black fungus. At NZ$20 pp including transportation, sandwiches, and lamps, Tali's cave tours are highly recommended unless you're claustrophobic, just be prepared to get a little dirty. Misa Kulatea (tel. 4101) also offers three-hour forest walks at NZ$25 pp (don't allow him to capture any endangered coconut crabs for your amusement).

Airport

Hanan International Airport (IUE) is three km southeast of Alofi. Some accommodations offer free airport transfers while others charge NZ$5 each way. Otherwise it's fairly easy to hitch a ride into town. Though you'll need a passport and onward ticket, no visa is required for a stay of up to 30 days. There's no bank or duty-free shop. The airport departure tax is NZ$20.

RESOURCES
INFORMATION OFFICES

REGIONAL

Tourism Council of the South Pacific, Box 13119, Suva, Fiji Islands (tel. 679/304-177, fax 679/301-995, www.tcsp.com; e-mail: spice@is.com.fj)

Tourism Council of the South Pacific, Box 7440, Tahoe City, CA 96145, U.S.A. (tel. 1-530/583-0152, fax 1-530/583-0154, e-mail: HPascal@compuserve.com)

Tourism Council of the South Pacific, 375 Upper Richmond Road West, East Sheen, London SW14 7NX, United Kingdom (tel. 44-181/392-1838, fax 44-181/392-1313)

Tourism Council of the South Pacific, Petersburger Strasse 94, D-10247 Berlin, Germany (tel. 49-304/225-6027, fax 49-304/225-6287, e-mail: tcsp.de@interface-tourism.com)

Tourism Council of the South Pacific, 13 rue d'Alembert, F-38000 Grenoble, France (tel. 33-4/7670-0617, fax 33-4/7670-0918)

Tourism Council of the South Pacific, Dirkenstrasse 40, D-10178 Berlin, Germany (tel. 49-302/381-7628, fax 49-302/381-7641, e-mail: 100762.3614@compuserve.com)

Pacific Asia Travel Association, One Montgomery St., Telesis Tower, Suite 1000, San Francisco, CA 94104-4539, U.S.A. (tel. 1-415/986-4646, fax 1-415/986-3458, www.pata.org, e-mail: patahq@pata.org)

Pata Pacific Division, Box 645, Kings Cross, NSW 2001, Australia (tel. 61-2/9332-3599, fax 61-2/9331-6592, e-mail: pata@world.net)

SAMOA

Samoa Visitors Bureau, Box 2272, Apia, Samoa (tel. 685/26-500, fax 685/20-886, www.samoa.co.nz, e-mail: samoa@samoa.net)

Samoa Visitors Bureau, 1800 112th Ave. N.E., Suite 220E, Bellevue, WA 98004-2939, U.S.A. (tel. 1-425/688-8513, fax 1-425/688-8514, e-mail: SDSI@compuserve.com)

Samoa Visitors Bureau, Box 361, Minto Mall, Minto, NSW 2566, Australia (tel. 61-2/9824-5050, fax 61-2/9824-5678, e-mail: samoa@ozemail.com.au)

Samoa Visitors Bureau, Level 1, Samoa House, 283 Karangahape Rd., Box 68-423, Newton, Auckland, New Zealand (tel. 64-9/379-6138, fax 64-9/379-8154, e-mail: samoa@samoa.co.nz)

AMERICAN SAMOA

Office of Tourism, Box 1147, Pago Pago, American Samoa 96799, U.S.A. (tel. 684/633-1091, fax 684/633-1094, www.samoanet.com/americansamoa, e-mail: samoa@samoatelco.com)

KINGDOM OF TONGA

Tonga Visitors Bureau, Box 37, Nuku'alofa, Kingdom of Tonga (tel. 676/21-733, fax 676/23-507, www.vacations.tvb.gov.to, e-mail: tvb@kalianet.to)

Tonga Visitors Bureau, Box 18, Neiafu, Vava'u, Kingdom of Tonga (tel. 676/70-115, fax 676/70-630, e-mail: tvbvv@kalianet.to)

Tonga Visitors Bureau, 4605 Driftwood Court, El Sobrante, CA 94803-1805, U.S.A. (tel. 1-510/223-1381, fax 1-510/758-6227, e-mail: tonga@value.net)

Tongan Consulate, 360 Post St., Suite 604, San Francisco, CA 94108, U.S.A. (tel. 1-415/781-0365, fax 1-415/781-3964, e-mail: tania@sfconsulate.gov.to)

Tonga Visitors Bureau, 642 King St., Newtown, Sydney, NSW 2042, Australia (tel. 61-2/9519-9700, fax 61-2/9519-9419)

Tonga Visitors Bureau, Box 24-054, Royal Oak, Auckland 1003, New Zealand (tel. 64-9/634-1519, fax 64-9/636-8973)

Tongan High Commission, 36 Molyneux St London W1H 6AB, United Kingdom (tel. 44 71/724-5828, fax 44-171/723-9074)

NIUE

Niue Tourism Office, Box 42, Alofi, Niue (tel 683/4224, fax 683/4225, www.niueisland.com e-mail: niuetourism@mail.gov.nu)

Niue Tourism Office, Box 68-541, Newton, Auck land, New Zealand (tel. 64-9/366-0716, fax 64-9/308-9720, e-mail: niuetourism@clear net.nz)

BIBLIOGRAPHY

GUIDEBOOKS

Cruising Guide to The Kingdom of Tonga. The Moorings, 1997. Something of a misnomer since only Vava'u is covered, this handy booklet combines anchorage descriptions with photocopied charts.

Hammick, Anne. *Ocean Cruising on a Budget.* Camden, ME: International Marine Publishing, 1991. Hammick shows how to sail your own yacht safely and enjoyably over the seas while cutting costs. Study it beforehand if you're thinking of working as crew on a yacht. Also from International Marine is Beth A. Leonard's *The Voyager's Handbook: The Essential Guide to Blue Water Cruising.*

Health Information For International Travel. "The Yellow Book" is an excellent reference published annually by the Centers for Disease Control, U.S. Public Health Service. Available from the Superintendent of Documents, Box 371954, Pittsburgh, PA 15250-7954, U.S.A. (tel. 1-202/512-1800, fax 1-202/512-2250, www.cdc.gov/travel/index.htm)

Hinz, Earl R. *Landfalls of Paradise: Cruising Guide to the Pacific Islands.* Honolulu: University of Hawaii Press, 1999. With 97 maps and 144 illustrations, this is the only cruising guide to Oceania's 75 ports of entry and many lesser harbors and anchorages.

Parkinson, Susan, Peggy Stacy, and Adrian Mattinson. *Taste of the Pacific.* Honolulu: University of Hawaii Press, 1995. Over 200 recipes of South Pacific dishes.

Ryan, Paddy. *The Snorkeler's Guide to the Coral Reef.* Honolulu: University of Hawaii Press, 1994. An introduction to the wonders of the Indo-Pacific reefs.

Schroeder, Dirk. *Staying Healthy in Asia, Africa, and Latin America.* Chico, CA: Moon Publications. Order a copy of this book produced by Volunteers in Asia if you'd like to acquire a degree of expertise in tropical medicine.

Seward, Robert. *Radio Happy Isles: Media and Politics at Play in the Pacific.* Honolulu: University of Hawaii Press, 1998. An insightful and unexpected look at radio stations all across the Pacific.

Stanley, David. *South Pacific Handbook.* Chico, CA: Moon Publications, 1999. Covers the whole South Pacific from Easter Island to the Solomons in the manner of the book you're reading. There's also a *Tahiti Handbook* covering Tahiti-Polynesia, Easter Island, and the Cooks, and a *Fiji Handbook.*

DESCRIPTION AND TRAVEL

Bell, Gavin. *In Search of Tusitala.* London: Picador, 1994. A young Scottish journalist's experiences in the Marquesas, Tahiti, Hawaii, Kiribati, and Samoa in the footsteps of Robert Louis Stevenson.

Gravelle, Kim. *Romancing the Islands.* Suva: Graphics Pacific, 1995. In these 42 stories ex-American Fiji resident Kim Gravelle shares a quarter century of adventures in the region. A delightfully sympathetic look at the islands and its characters. Copies can be ordered from the author at Box 12975, Suva, Fiji Islands (US$25 postpaid).

Ledyard, Patricia. *Friendly Isles, a Tale of Tonga.* Nuku'alofa: Vava'u Press, 1984. A new edition of Ledyard's 1956 classic; Ledyard also wrote *Utulei, My Tongan Home* (1974) about her many years at Vava'u.

Lewis, David. *We, the Navigators.* Honolulu: University of Hawaii Press, 1994. A 2nd edition of the 1972 classic on the ancient art of landfinding in the Pacific. Lewis' 1964 journey from Tahiti to New Zealand was the first in modern times on which only traditional navigational means were used.

Phelan, Nancy. *Pieces of Heaven*. St. Lucia, Australia: University of Queensland Press, 1995. After four decades away, a former aid worker returns to the Cook Islands, Samoa, and Kiribati, and the Pacific of the 1950s and 1990s combine in a fascinating portrait of the region.

Stevenson, Robert Louis. *In the South Seas*. New York: Scribner's, 1901. The author's account of his travels through the Marquesas, Tuamotus, and Gilberts by yacht in the years 1888-90.

Takai, Moeaki, et al. *The Fire Has Jumped*. Suva: Institute of Pacific Studies, 1986. Fifteen eyewitness accounts of the eruption and evacuation of Niuafo'ou, Tonga.

Theroux, Paul. *The Happy Isles of Oceania*. London, Hamish Hamilton, 1992. The author of classic accounts of railway journeys sets out with kayak and tent to tour the Pacific.

Velt, Kik. *Stars Over Tonga*. Nuku'alofa, 1990. Astronomy mixed with astute observations on Tongan culture.

GEOGRAPHY

Crocombe, Ron. *The South Pacific: An Introduction*. Suva: Institute of Pacific Studies, 1989. A collection of lecture notes covering a wide range of topics from one of the region's leading academics.

Oliver, Douglas L. *The Pacific Islands*. Honolulu: University of Hawaii Press, 1989. A 3rd edition of the classic 1961 study of the history and anthropology of the entire Pacific area.

Ridgell, Reilly. *Pacific Nations and Territories*. A high school geography text that provides an overview of the region and also focuses on the individual islands. *Pacific Neighbors* is an elementary school version of the same book, written in collaboration with Betty Dunford. Both are published by Bess Press, 3565 Harding Ave., Honolulu, HI 96816, U.S.A. (tel. 1-800/910-2377 or 1-808/734-7159, fax 1-808/732-3627, www.besspress.com).

NATURAL SCIENCE

Cox, Paul Alan. *Nafanua: Saving the Samoa Rainforest*. Available from the Seacology Foundation (www.seacology.org). The heart wrenching story of how a Utah Mormon saved the rainforests of Falealupo, Savai'i, from destruction.

Lebot, Vincent, Lamont Lindstrom, and Mark Marlin. *Kava—the Pacific Drug*. Yale University Press, 1993. A thorough examination of kava and its many uses.

MacLeod, Roy M., and Philip F. Rehbock. *Darwin's Laboratory*. Honolulu: University of Hawaii Press, 1994. Evolutionary theory and natural history in the Pacific.

Mitchell, Andrew W. *A Fragile Paradise: Man and Nature in the Pacific*. London: Fontana 1990. Published in the U.S. by the University of Texas Press under the title *The Fragile South Pacific: An Ecological Odyssey*.

Muse, Corey, and Shirley Muse. *Birds and Birdlore of Samoa*. Seattle: University of Washington Press, 1983. Descriptions and illustrations of the 72 bird species inhabiting or visiting Samoa, 31 of which are found nowhere else.

Randall, John E., Gerald Robert Allen, and Roger C. Steene. *Fishes of the Great Barrier Reef and Coral Sea*. Honolulu: University of Hawaii Press, 1997. An identification guide for amateur diver and specialist alike.

Veron, J.E.N. *Corals of Australia and the Indo-Pacific*. Honolulu: University of Hawaii Press, 1993. An authoritative, illustrated work.

Watling, Dick. *Birds of Fiji, Tonga, and Samoa*. Wellington, Millwood Press, 1982.

Whistler, W. Arthur. *Flowers of the Pacific Island Seashore*. Honolulu: University of Hawaii Press, 1993. A guide to the littoral plants of Hawaii, Tahiti, Samoa, Tonga, Cook Islands, Fiji, and Micronesia.

Whistler, W. Arthur. *Samoan Herbal Medicine: O La'au ma Vai Fono o Samoa*. Honolulu: University of Hawaii Press, 1996. This book discusses traditional and contemporary herbal medicinal practices in Samoa. A 1993 book deals with *Tongan Herbal Medicine*.

Whistler, W. Arthur. *Wayside Plants of the Islands*. Honolulu: University of Hawaii Press, 1995. A guide to the lowland flora of the Pacific islands.

HISTORY

Beaglehole, J.C. *The Life of Captain Cook*. Stanford, 1974. A well-written account of Cook's achievements in the context of the era in which Cook lived. Beaglehole also edited Cook's three volumes of journals.

Bellwood, Peter. *The Polynesians: Prehistory of an Island People*. London: Thames and Hudson, 1987. A succinct account of the archaeology of Polynesian expansion.

Blanton, Casey, ed. *Picturing Paradise: Colonial Photography of Samoa, 1875 to 1925*. Daytona Beach, FL: Southeast Museum of Photography, 1995. The essays included in this catalog contain much information on the history of culture contact in the islands.

Bott, Elizabeth. *Tongan Society at the Time of Captain Cook's Visits*. Wellington: 1982. Discussions with Her Majesty Queen Salote Tupou.

Crocombe, Ron. *The Pacific Islands and the USA*. Suva: Institute of Pacific Studies, 1995. A comprehensive study of almost every aspect of the relationship from the 18th century to the present day. Crocombe's account of the self-serving manipulations practiced by a succession of U.S. officials over the years should chasten any Americans still unwilling to come to terms with their country as just another imperialistic colonial power.

Daws, Gavin. *A Dream of Islands: Voyages of Self-Discovery in the South Seas*. Honolulu: Mutual Publishing. Includes biographies of John Williams and Robert Louis Stevenson, among others.

Denoon, Donald, et al. *The Cambridge History of the Pacific Islanders*. Australia: Cambridge University Press, 1997. A team of scholars examines the history of the inhabitants of Oceania from first colonization to the nuclear era. While acknowledging the great diversity of Pacific peoples, cultures, and experiences, the book looks for common patterns and related themes, presenting them in an insightful and innovative way.

Fanua, Tupou Posesi. *Malo Tupou: An Oral History*. Honolulu: University of Hawaii Press, 1997. As told to Lois Webster. An 81-year-old woman recounts her memories of adolescence in Tonga.

Field, Michael J. *Mau: Samoa's Struggle for Freedom*. Auckland: Pasifika Press, 1991. A wealth of fascinating detail about Samoa's nonviolent freedom movement, admirably told by a leading New Zealand journalist.

Gray, Captain J.A.C. *Amerika Samoa and its Naval Administration*. Annapolis: 1960.

Hekau, Maihetoe, et al. *Niue: A History of the Island*. Suva: Institute of Pacific Studies, 1982. A dozen residents of Niue reveal history, politics, and knowledge of the island.

Herda, Phyllis, Jennifer Terrell, and Neil Gunson, eds. *Tongan Culture and History*. Canberra: Australian National University, 1990. This collection of papers covers a wide range of interesting topics.

Hiery, Hermann Josep. *The Neglected War: The German South Pacific and the Influence of World War I*. Honolulu: University of Hawaii Press, 1995. A reexamination of the German period in Samoa.

Hough, Richard. *Captain James Cook*. W.W. Norton, 1997. A readable new biography of Captain Cook that asserts that Cook's abrupt manner on his third journey may have been due to an intestinal infection that affected his judgment and indirectly led to his death at the hands of Hawaiian islanders.

Latukefu, Sione. *Church and State in Tonga.* Canberra: 1974. The Wesleyan Methodist missionaries and political development, 1822-1875.

Martin, John. *Tonga Islands: William Mariner's Account.* Nuku'alofa: Vava'u Press, 1981. Mariner, a survivor of the 1806 *Port au Prince* massacre at Ha'apai, became the adopted son of the warrior king Finau 'Ulukalala II and stayed in Tonga four years before returning to England. *The Tonga Book* by Paul W. Dale (Minerva Press) also deals with the William Mariner story.

Meleisea, Malama. *The Making of Modern Samoa.* Suva: Institute of Pacific Studies, 1987. The struggle between Samoan and western ideas of government and law are the theme of this view of history from a Samoan perspective.

Meleisea, Malama, and Penny Schoeffel Meleisea, eds. *Lagaga: A Short History of Western Samoa.* Suva: Institute of Pacific Studies, 1987. Thirteen Samoan writers explore various themes in Samoan history.

Rutherford, Noel. *Shirley Baker and the King of Tonga.* Honolulu: University of Hawaii Press, 1996. A fascinating account of an East London minister who did much to shape the Tonga of today.

Smith, Percy S., and Pulekula. *Niue: The Island and its People.* Suva: Institute of Pacific Studies, 1983. A reprint of articles originally published in the *Journal of the Polynesian Society* in 1902-3.

Stevenson, Robert Louis. *A Footnote to History: Eight Years of Trouble in Samoa.* Honolulu: University of Hawaii Press, 1996. An eyewitness account of colonial manipulation told in the lively Stevenson way.

Tarburton, Shirley. *History Makers of Samoa.* Desktop Publishing, Apia, 1996. Brief biographies of 145 key individuals who influence the way Samoa is today.

Thomson, Basil. *Savage Island, account of sojourn in Niue and Tonga.* London: 1902 Reprinted in 1984.

Turner, George. *Samoa: A Hundred Years Ago and Long Before.* Suva: Institute of Pacifi Studies, 1984. A reprint of the 1884 classic written by a member of the London Missionar Society.

PACIFIC ISSUES

Culture and Democracy in the South Pacific Suva: Institute of Pacific Studies, 1992. A major book presenting essays and poetry about freedom by 16 Pacific writers.

Emberson-Bain, 'Atu, ed. *Sustainable Development or Malignant Growth? Perspectives o Pacific Island Women.* Suva: Marama Publications, 1994. Contains valuable background information of the regional environment.

Ernst, Manfred. *Winds of Change.* Suva: Pacific Conference of Churches, 1994. A timely examination of rapidly growing religious groups in the Pacific islands and unequaled source of information on contemporary religion in the South Pacific.

Faleomavaega, Eni F.H., *Navigating the Future. A Samoan Perspective on U.S.-Pacific Relations.* Suva: Institute of Pacific Studies, 1995. American Samoa's congressman in Washington lays out the issues of the day.

Hau'ofa, Epeli, et al. *A New Oceania: Rediscovering Our Sea of Islands.* Suva: University of the South Pacific, 1993. A collection of papers by 20 academics on the theme of islands and ocean as part of an undivided whole (in contrast to the usual perception of tiny islands lost in a boundless sea).

alal, Patricia Imrana. *Law for Pacific Women: A Legal Rights Handbook.* This 700-page book is essential reading for anyone planning an extended stay in Cook Islands, Fiji, Samoa, Solomon Islands, Tuvalu, or Vanuatu. Order from the Fiji Women's Rights Movement, Box 14194, Suva (tel. 679/313-156, fax 679/313-466).

New Politics in the South Pacific. Suva: Institute of Pacific Studies, 1994. A collection of 21 essays by Pacific writers about sovereignty, free association, the role of non-government organizations, women's rights, local government, culture, and similar subjects.

SOCIAL SCIENCE

Calkins, Fay. *My Samoan Chief.* Honolulu: University of Hawaii Press, 1971. The life of a young American woman in her Samoan husband's native land. A delightful account of cross-cultural contact.

Fairbairn-Dunlop, Peggy. *Tamaitai Samoa: Their Stories.* Suva: Institute of Pacific Studies, 1996. Autobiographies of Samoan women in various walks of life.

Foerstel, Lenora, and Angela Gilliam, eds. *Confronting the Margaret Mead Legacy: Scholarship, Empire, and the South Pacific.* Philadelphia: Temple University Press, 1992. Mead's impact on western anthropology and her views of colonialism, imperialism, and business interests in the South Pacific.

Freeman, Derek. *Margaret Mead and Samoa: The Making and Unmaking of an Anthropological Myth.* Cambridge, Mass.: Harvard University Press, 1983. An Australian academic refutes Margaret Mead's theory of Samoan promiscuity and lack of aggression.

Krämer, Dr. Augustin. *The Samoa Islands.* Auckland: Pasifika Press, 1994. A definitive, two-volume ethnological work translated from the German original of 1903. Volume two was published by the University of Hawaii Press in 1995.

Mead, Margaret. *Letters from the Field.* Edited by Ruth Nanda. New York: Harper & Row, 1977. Describes Mead's experiences in American Samoa, Manus, the Sepik, and Bali. See also Mead's 1928 classic *Coming of Age in Samoa,* researched at Ta'u in the Manu'a Group.

Morton, Helen. *Becoming Tongan: An Ethnography of Childhood.* Honolulu: University of Hawaii Press, 1996. Child-rearing practices in Tonga.

Oliver, Douglas L. *Native Cultures of the Pacific Islands.* Honolulu: University of Hawaii Press, 1989. Intended primarily for college-level courses on precontact anthropology, history, economy, and politics of the entire region.

Orans, Martin. *Not Even Wrong: Margaret Mead, Derek Freeman, and the Samoans.* Novato, CA: Chandler & Sharp, 1996. By carefully examining Mead's field materials, Orans found that her findings regarding Samoan female sexuality had been influenced by ideology and were thus "not even wrong."

Pollock, Nancy J. *These Roots Remain.* Honolulu: University of Hawaii Press, 1992. Food habits of the central and western Pacific since European contact.

Tupouniua, Penisimani. *A Polynesian Village: The Process of Change.* Suva: Institute of Pacific Studies, 1977. Socio-political, economic, religious, and educational change in Hoi, a village on Tongatapu.

LITERATURE

Bermann, Richard A. *Home from the Sea.* Honolulu: Mutual Publishing. A reprint of the 1939 narrative of Robert Louis Stevenson's final years in Samoa.

Figiel, Sia. *The Girl in the Moon Circle.* Suva: Institute of Pacific Studies, 1996. A collection of short stories in which Samoan life and events are seen through the eyes of a 10-year-old girl.

Figiel, Sia. *Where We Once Belonged.* Auckland: Pasifika Press, 1996. The acclaimed first novel by a female storyteller that recounts the experience of growing up in a Samoan village. Sex, violence, and the struggle for a personal identity in an island setting. Available in North America through the University of Hawaii Press.

Fisk, Samantha J. *Where in the World is Tonga?* KIN Publications, 558 East Double St., Carson, CA 90745, U.S.A. (tel./fax 1-310/549-0920, e-mail: DPouesi@aol.com). Samantha's first visit to Tonga was at age two and since then she has returned from the States every couple of years. Now her photo album, diary, and personal mementos have been combined in a well designed children's book that really conveys the warmth of Tonga.

Hau'ofa, Epeli. *Tales of the Tikongs.* Auckland: Longman Paul Ltd., 1983. Reprinted by Beake House (Fiji) in 1993 and the University of Hawaii Press in 1994. An amusingly ironic view of Tongan life: "Our people work so hard on Sunday it takes a six-day rest to recover." The development aid business, exotic religious sects, self-perpetuating bureaucracy, and similar themes provide a milieu for the tales of the Tikongs: in Tiko nothing is as it seems. The University of Hawaii Press has also reprinted Hau'ofa's *Kisses in the Nederends,* a satire of life in a small Pacific community.

Malifa, Fata Sano. *Alms for Oblivion.* New York: Vantage Press, 1993. A rather pessimistic novel about hypocrisy and corruption in Samoan society by the founder of the *Samoa Observer.* As the protagonist Niko develops from nonconformist Bohemian to successful businessman and finally terminal alcoholic, the petty avarice of church, chiefs, and politicians is revealed in hyperbolic detail.

Maugham, W. Somerset. *The Trembling of a Leaf.* Honolulu: Mutual Publishing. The responses of a varied mix of white males—colonial administrator, trader, sea captain, bank manager, and missionary—to the peoples and environment of the South Pacific. Maugh-am is a masterful storyteller, and his journey t Samoa and Tahiti in 1916-1917 supplied hir with poignant material, including the stor "Rain."

Pouesi, Daniel, and Michael Igoe. *The Ston Maiden and Other Samoan Fables.* KIN Publications, 558 East Double St., Carson, CA 90745, U.S.A. (tel./fax 1-310/549-0920, e mail: DPouesi@aol.com). A collection of 18 fables used to illustrate Samoan proverbs.

Pouesi, Namulauulu Paul V. *Folksongs o Samoa.* KIN Publications, 558 East Double St., Carson, CA 90745, U.S.A. (tel./fax 1 310/549-0920, e-mail: DPouesi@aol.com). A music book for children.

Steubel, C., and Brother Herman. *Tala O Le Vavau: The Myths, Legends, and Customs of Old Samoa.* Auckland: Pasifika Press, 1987 Distributed in North America by the University of Hawaii Press.

Velt, Kik. *Reminiscences of the Mirthful Islands* Nuku'alofa: Tau'olunga komipiuta, 1998. A satire of life in the principality of Hiki & Haha Fuiva Tava wanted so much to escape from her village and to experience the glamorous lifestyle of the palangi.

Wendt, Albert. *Flying Fox in a Freedom Tree.* Auckland: Longman Paul Ltd., 1974. A collection of short stories in which the men cannot show fear or emotion, while the women appear only as sex objects.

Wendt, Albert. *Leaves of the Banyan Tree.* Honolulu: University of Hawaii Press, 1994. A reprint of the 1980 Wendt classic. Wendt was the first South Pacific novelist of international stature and his semi-autobiographical writings are full of interest.

Wendt, Albert, ed. *Nuanua: Pacific Writing in English Since 1980.* Honolulu, University of Hawaii Press, 1995. This worthwhile anthology of contemporary Pacific literature illustrates the reluctance of many indigenous writers to divulge the underlying power structures of island societies. The selections by Alistair

Campbell are among the few with any deeper psychological content, and most of the rest are rather superficial descriptions of reality with little exploration of the motives and relationships below the surface. One feels Wendt's writers would have been more comfortable expressing themselves in their native tongues to an audience of their peers.

Wendt, Albert. *Pouliuli.* Auckland: Longman Paul Ltd., 1977. This is probably Wendt's finest novel, masterfully depicting the complex values and manipulative nature of Samoan society. No other book explains more about Samoa today.

Wendt, Albert. *Sons for the Return Home.* Auckland: Longman Paul Ltd., 1973. The story of a Samoan youth brought up amid discrimination in New Zealand, yet unable to readjust to the cultural values of his own country. The University of Hawaii Press distributes reprints of Wendt's early works, plus his 1995 novels *Ola* and *Black Rainbow.*

THE ARTS

Arbeit, Wendy. *Tapa in Tonga.* Honolulu: University of Hawaii Press, 1995. A 32-page booklet explaining the manufacture and decoration of bark cloth.

Kaeppler, Adrienne L. *Poetry in Motion: Studies of Tongan Dance.* Suva: Institute of Pacific Arts, 1993.

Kaeppler, Adrienne, C. Kaufmann, and Douglas Newton. *Oceanic Art.* Abrahams, 1997. The first major survey of the arts of Polynesia, Melanesia, and Micronesia in over three decades, this admirable volume brings the reader up to date on recent scholarship in the field. Of the 900 illustrations, over a third are new.

Linkels, Ad. *Sounds of Change in Tonga.* Published in 1998 by Mundo Étnico, Sibeliusstraat 707, 5011 JR Tilburg, The Netherlands, this book is a complete survey of Tongan music

and dance with notes of the culture. Linkels has also produced a booklet on Samoan music entitled *Fa'a-Samoa: The Samoan Way.*

Moyle, Richard. *Tongan Music.* Auckland: Auckland University Press, 1987. A look at one of the South Pacific's best-preserved musical systems, in which song and dance are living parts of the culture.

St. Cartmail, Keith. *The Art of Tonga.* Honolulu: University of Hawaii Press, 1997. The first book solely devoted to this powerfully fresh art style.

Thomas, Nicholas. *Oceanic Art.* London: Thames and Hudson, 1995. Almost 200 illustrations grace the pages of this readable survey.

LANGUAGE

Allardice, R.W. *A Simplified Dictionary of Modern Samoan.* Auckland: Pasifika Press, 1985.

Churchward, C. Maxwell. *Tongan Grammar.* Nuku'alofa: Vava'u Press, 1985. For specialists only. Churchward has also produced a *Tongan-English Dictionary.*

Hunkin, Galumalemana Afeleti L. *Gagana Samoa: A Samoan Language Coursebook.* Auckland: Pasifika Press, 1988. An accompanying cassette is available. In North America order through the University of Hawaii Press.

Lynch, John. *Pacific Languages: An Introduction.* Honolulu: University of Hawaii Press, 1998. The grammatical features of the Oceanic, Papuan, and Australian languages.

Milner, G.B. *Samoan Dictionary.* Honolulu: University of Hawaii Press, 1993. Samoan-English and English-Samoan.

Schultz, Dr. E. *Samoan Proverbial Expressions.* Suva: Institute of Pacific Studies, 1980. Grouped according to subject, with English translations and explanations.

Shumway, Eric B. *Intensive Course in Tongan.* A 130-lesson course available for US$25 from the Institute for Polynesian Studies, Brigham Young University, Box 1979, Laie, HI 96762, U.S.A. (tel. 1-808/293-3665). The accompanying set of 23 cassette tapes is US$80.

Simanu-Klutz, Fata. *Samoan Word Book.* Honolulu: University of Hawaii Press, 1998. Samoan vocabulary through illustrations, accompanied by a cassette.

Tu'inukuafe, Edgar. *A Simplified Dictionary of Modern Tongan.* Honolulu: University of Hawaii Press, 1992.

REFERENCE BOOKS

Connell, John, et al. *Encyclopedia of the Pacific Islands.* Canberra: Australian National University, 1999. Published to mark the 50th anniversary of the Pacific Community, this important book combines the writings of 200 acknowledged experts on the physical environment, peoples, history, politics, economics, society, and culture of the South Pacific.

Craig, Robert D. *Dictionary of Polynesian Mythology.* Westport, CT: Greenwood Press, 1989. Aside from hundreds of alphabetical entries listing the legends, stories, gods, goddesses, and heroes of the Polynesians, this book charts the evolution of 30 Polynesian languages.

Craig, Robert D. *Historical Dictionary of Polynesia.* Metuchen, NJ: Scarecrow Press, 1994. This handy volume contains alphabetical listings of individuals (past and present), places, and organizations, plus historical chronologies and bibliographies by island group.

Douglas, Ngaire and Norman Douglas, eds. *Pacific Islands Yearbook.* Suva: Fiji Times Ltd. Despite the title, a new edition of this authoritative sourcebook has come out about every four years since 1932. Although a rather dry read, it's still the one indispensable reference work for students of the Pacific islands.

Fry, Gerald W., and Rufino Mauricio. *Pacific Basin and Oceania.* Oxford: Clio Press, 1987. A selective, indexed Pacific bibliography which actually describes the contents of the books, instead of merely listing them.

Holmes, Lowell D. *Samoan Islands Bibliography.* Wichita, Kansas: 1984.

Jackson, Miles M., ed. *Pacific Island Studies: A Survey of the Literature.* Westport: Greenwood Press, 1986. In addition to comprehensive listings, there are extensive essays that put the most important works in perspective.

Motteler, Lee S. *Pacific Island Names.* Honolulu: Bishop Museum Press, 1986. A comprehensive gazetteer listing officially accepted island names, cross-referenced to all known variant names and spellings.

Selected Pacific Economies: A Statistical Summary. Nouméa: Pacific Community. Trade patterns, price indices, aid flows, tourism, and population and social characteristics are covered in this useful publication issued every couple of years.

Silveira de Braganza, Ronald, and Charlotte Oakes, eds. *The Hill Collection of Pacific Voyages.* San Diego: University Library, 1974. A descriptive catalog of antique books about the Pacific.

BOOKSELLERS AND PUBLISHERS

Many of the titles listed above are out of print and not available in regular bookstores or from www.amazon.com. Major research libraries should have a few, otherwise write to the specialized antiquarian booksellers or regional publishers listed below for their printed lists of hard-to-find books on the Pacific. Sources of detailed topographical maps or navigational charts are provided in the following section.

Antipodean Books, Box 189, Cold Spring, NY 10516, U.S.A. (tel. 1-914/424-3867, fax 1-914/424-3617, www.antipodean.com, e-mail:

antipbooks@highlands.com). They have a complete catalog of out-of-print and rare items.

Bibliophile, 24A Glenmore Rd., Paddington, Sydney, NSW 2021, Australia (tel. 61-2/9331-1411, fax 61-2/9361-3371, www.ozemail.com.au/~susant, e-mail: susant@anzaab.com.au). An antiquarian bookstore specializing in books about Oceania. View their extensive catalog on line.

Bishop Museum Press, 1525 Bernice St., Honolulu, HI 96817-0916, U.S.A. (tel. 1-808/848-4135, fax 1-808/848-4132, www.bishop.hawaii.org/bishop/press). They have an indexed list of books on the Pacific; a separate list of "The Occasional Papers" lists specialized works.

Book Bin, 228 S.W. 3rd St., Corvallis, OR 97333, U.S.A. (tel. 1-541/752-0045, fax 1-541/754-4115, e-mail: pacific@bookbin.com). Their indexed mail-order catalog, *Hawaii and Pacific Islands,* lists thousands of rare books, plus current research, art books, and atlases, and they also carry all the titles of the Institute of Pacific Studies in Suva. If there's a particular book about the Pacific you can't find anywhere, this is a place to try.

Books of Yesteryear, Box 257, Newport, NSW 2106, Australia (tel./fax 61-2/9918-0545, e-mail: patbooks@ozemail.com.au). Another source of old, fine, and rare books on the Pacific.

Books Pasifika, Box 68-446, Newtown, Auckland 1, New Zealand (tel. 64-9/303-2349, fax 64-9/377-9528, www.ak.planet.gen.nz/pasifika, e-mail: books@pasifika.co.nz). Besides being a major publisher, Pasifika Press is New Zealand's leading source of mail order books on Samoa and Tonga, including those of the Institute of Pacific Studies.

Bushbooks, Box 1370, Gosford, NSW 2250, Australia (tel. 61-2/4323-3274, fax 61-2/9212-2468, e-mail: bushbook@ozemail.com.au). An Australian source of the publications of the Institute of Pacific Studies in Suva.

Cellar Book Shop, 18090 Wyoming Ave., Detroit, MI 48221, U.S.A. (tel./fax 1-313/861-1776, http://members.aol.com/cellarbook, e-mail: cellarbook@aol.com). Their catalog, *The 'Nesias' & Down Under: Some Recent Books,* includes a wide range of books on the Pacific.

Cruising Guide Publications, Box 1017, Dunedin, FL 34697-1017, U.S.A. (tel. 1-800/330-9542 or 1-813/733-5322, fax 1-813/734-8179, e-mail: cgp@earthlink.net). The cruising guide to Vava'u published by The Moorings is in this catalog.

Empire Books, Colin Hinchcliffe, 12 Queens Staith Mews, York, YO1 6HH, United Kingdom (tel. 44-1904/610679, fax 44-1904/641664, e-mail: colin@empires.demon.co.uk). An excellent source of antiquarian or out-of-print books, maps, and engravings.

Friendly Islands Bookshop Catalog, Box 124, Nukualofa, Tonga (tel. 676/23-787, fax 676-23-631, e-mail: fibs@kalianet.to). Your best source of books in Tongan and about Tonga.

Institute of Pacific Studies, University of the South Pacific, Box 1168, Suva, Fiji Islands (tel. 679/313-900, fax 679/301-594, e-mail: ips@usp.ac.fj). Their catalog, *Books from the Pacific Islands,* lists numerous books about the islands written by the Pacific islanders themselves. Some are rather dry academic publications of interest only to specialists, so order carefully. USP centers all across the region sell many of these books over the counter. For internet access to the catalog, see the University Book Centre listing below.

International Marine Publishing Co., Box 548, Blacklick, OH 43004, U.S.A. (tel. 1-800/262-4729, fax 1-614/759-3641, www.pbg.mcgrawhill.com/im). Their catalog, *Boating Books,* includes all the books you'll ever need to teach yourself how to sail. They also have books on sea kayaking.

Jean-Louis Boglio, Box 72, Currumbin, Queensland 4223, Australia (tel. 61-7/5534-9349, fax 61-7/5534-9949, www.ozemail.com.au/~boglio). An excellent source of books on Oceania.

Michael Graves-Johnston, Bookseller, Box 532, London SW9 0DR, United Kingdom (tel. 44-171/274-2069, fax 44-171/738-3747). Sells antiquarian books only.

Mutual Publishing Company, 1215 Center St., Suite 210, Honolulu, HI 96816, U.S.A. (tel. 1-808/732-1709, fax 1-808/734-4094, www.pete. com/mutual, e-mail: mutual@lava.net). The classics of expatriate Pacific literature, available in cheap paperback editions.

Pan Pacifica, 4662 Sierra Dr., Honolulu, HI 96816, U.S.A. (fax 1-808/739-2326, www.Pan-Pacifica.com, e-mail: panpac@lava.net). A source of recent official publications and research-level documents from museums and universities. Their primary clients are large research libraries.

Peter Moore, Box 66, Cambridge, CB1 3PD, United Kingdom (tel. 44-1223/411177, fax 44-1223/240559). The European distributor of books from the Institute of Pacific Studies of the University of the South Pacific, Fiji. Moore's catalog also lists antiquarian and secondhand books.

Serendipity Books, Box 340, Nedlands, WA 6009, Australia (tel. 61-8/9382-2246, fax 61-8/9388-2728, www.merriweb.com.au/serendip). The largest stocks of antiquarian, secondhand, and out-of-print books on the Pacific in Western Australia. Free catalogs are issued regularly.

South Pacific Regional Environment Program, Box 240, Apia, Samoa (tel. 685/21-929, fax 685/20-231, www.sprep.org.ws). They have a list of specialized technical publications on environmental concerns.

University Book Centre, University of the South Pacific, Box 1168, Suva, Fiji Islands (tel. 679/313-900, fax 679/303-265, www.usp.ac. fj/~bookcentre). An excellent source of books written and produced in the South Pacific itself. Check out their site.

University of Hawaii Press, 2840 Kolowalu St., Honolulu, HI 96822-1888, U.S.A. (tel. 1-888/847-7377 or 1-808/956-8255, fax 1-808/988-6052, www2.hawaii.edu/uhpress). Their annual *Hawaii and the Pacific* catalog is well worth requesting if you're trying to build a Pacific library.

MAP PUBLISHERS

Defense Mapping Agency, Nautical Charts and Publications, Public Sale: Region 8, Oceania. NOAA Distribution Division N/ACC3, National Ocean Service, Riverdale, MD 20737-1199, U.S.A. (tel. 1-800/638-8972 or 1-301/436-8301, fax 1-301/436-6829, www.noaa.gov). A complete index and order form for nautical charts of the Pacific.

International Maps. Hema Maps Pty. Ltd., Box 2660, Logan City, Queensland 4114, Australia (tel. 61-7/3290-0322, fax 61-7/3290-0478, www.hemamaps.com.au). Maps of the Pacific, Fiji, Solomon Islands, Vanuatu, and Samoa.

Pacific Islands, Catalog of topographic and other published maps. Information Services, U.S. Geological Survey, Box 25286, Denver Federal Center, Denver, CO 80225-9916, U.S.A. (tel. 1-303/202-4700, fax 1-303/202-4693). A description and order form for the two color maps of American Samoa available from the USGS.

Reference Map of Oceania. Honolulu: University of Hawaii Press, 1995. A most useful double-sided map of the Pacific by James A. Bier, who also produced the worthwhile *Islands of Samoa* map (1990).

PERIODICALS

Asia & Pacific Viewpoint. Department of Geography, Victoria University of Wellington, Box 600, Wellington, New Zealand (tel. 64-4/472-1000, fax 64-4/495-5127, www.blackwell-publishers.co.uk). Three times a year; annual subscription US$42. A scholarly journal concerned with the systematic, regional, and theoretical aspects of economic growth and social change in the developed and developing countries.

Ben Davison's In Depth. Box 1658, Sausalito, CA 94966, U.S.A. (www.undercurrent.org). A monthly consumer protection-oriented newsletter for serious scuba divers. Unlike virtually every other diving publication, *In Depth* accepts no advertising or free trips, which allows Ben to tell it as it is.

Center for South Pacific Studies Newsletter. Centre for South Pacific Studies, University of New South Wales, Kensington, NSW 2052, Australia (tel. 61-2/9385-3386, fax 61-2/9313-6337, www.arts.unsw.edu.au/Centres/SouthPacific/homepage.html, e-mail: J.Lodewijks@unsw.EDU.AU). A useful publication that catalogs scholarly conferences, events, activities, news, employment opportunities, courses, scholarships, and publications across the region.

Commodores' Bulletin. Seven Seas Cruising Assn., 1525 South Andrews Ave., Suite 217, Fort Lauderdale, FL 33316, U.S.A. (tel. 1-954/463/2431, fax 1-954/463-7183, www.ssca.org, e-mail: SSCA1@ibm.net; US$53 a year worldwide by airmail). This monthly bulletin is chock-full of useful information for anyone wishing to tour the Pacific by sailing boat. All Pacific yachties and friends should be Seven Seas members!

The Contemporary Pacific. University of Hawaii Press, 2840 Kolowalu St., Honolulu, HI 96822, U.S.A. (tel. 1-808/956-8833, fax 1-808/988-6052, www2.hawaii.edu/uhpress, e-mail: uhpjourn@hawaii.edu, published twice a year, US$35 a year). Publishes a good mix of articles of interest to both scholars and general readers; the country-by-country "Political Review" in each number is a concise summary of events during the preceding year. The "Dialogue" section offers informed comment on the more controversial issues in the region, while recent publications on the islands are examined through book reviews. Those interested in current topics in Pacific island affairs should check recent volumes for background information.

Environment Newsletter. The quarterly newsletter of the South Pacific Regional Environment Program, Box 240, Apia, Samoa (tel. 685/21-929, fax 685/20-231, www.sprep.org.ws). Back issues can be viewed on their website.

Europe-Pacific Solidarity Bulletin. Published monthly by the European Center for Studies Information and Education on Pacific Issues, Box 151, 3700 AD Zeist, The Netherlands (tel. 31-30/692-7827, fax 31-30/692-5614, www.antenna.nl/ecsiep, e-mail: ecsiep@antenna.nl).

German Pacific Society Bulletin. Dr. Freidrich Steinbauer, Feichtmayr Strasse 25, D-80992 München, Germany (tel. 49-89/151158, fax 49-89/151833). At DM 90 a year, Society membership is a good way for German speakers to keep in touch. News bulletins in English and German are published four to six times a year, and study tours to various Pacific destinations are organized annually.

Islands Business. Box 12718, Suva, Fiji Islands (tel. 679/303-108, fax 679/301-423, e-mail: subs@ibi.com.fj; annual airmailed subscription A$35 to Australia, NZ$55 to New Zealand, US$45 to North America, US$55 to Europe). A monthly newsmagazine with in-depth coverage of political and economic trends in the Pacific. It's more opinionated than *Pacific Islands Monthly* and even has a gossip section which is an essential weather vane for anyone doing business in the region. In the December 1995 issue "Whispers" accurately forecast the devaluation of the Fiji dollar two years later. Travel and aviation news gets some prominence, and subscribers also receive the informative quarterly magazine *South Pacific Tourism.*

Journal of Pacific History. Division of Pacific and Asian History, RSPAS, Australian National University, Canberra, ACT 0200, Australia (tel. 61-2/6249-3140, fax 61-2/6249-5525, http://coombs.anu.edu.au/Depts/RSPAS/PAH/index.html or http://sunsite.anu.edu.au/spin/RSRC/HISTORY/jphsite.htm). Since 1966 this publication has provided reliable scholarly information on the Pacific. Outstanding.

Journal of Pacific Studies. School of Social and Economic Development, University of the

South Pacific, Box 1168, Suva, Fiji Islands (tel. 679/314-900, fax 679/301-487). Focuses on regional developments from a social sciences perspective.

Journal of the Polynesian Society. Department of Maori Studies, University of Auckland, Private Bag 92019, Auckland, New Zealand (tel. 64-9/373-7999, extension 7463, fax 64-9/373-7409, www2.waikato.ac.nz/ling/PS/journal.html). Established in 1892, this quarterly journal contains a wealth of material on Pacific cultures past and present written by scholars of Pacific anthropology, archaeology, language, and history.

Matangi Tonga. Vava'u Press, Box 427, Nuku'alofa, Tonga (tel. 25-779, fax 24-749, e-mail: vapress@kalianet.to, US$25 a year airmail). Tonga's bimonthly national news magazine.

Pacific Affairs. University of British Columbia, Suite 164, 1855 West Mall, Vancouver, B.C. V6T 1Z2, Canada (tel. 604/822-6508, fax 604/822-9452, www.interchange.ubc.ca/pacifaff, quarterly). Each issue contains four new articles and 50 book reviews, although most are oriented toward Asia.

Pacific Arts. Pacific Arts Association, c/o Dr. Michael Gunn, PAA Secretary/Treasurer, c/o A.A.O.A., The Metropolitan Museum of Art, 1000 5th Ave., New York, NY 10028-0198, U.S.A. (tel. 1-212/650-2209, fax 1-212/396-5039). For US$40 PAA membership, one will receive their annual magazine "devoted to the study of all the arts of Oceania" and intermittent newsletter.

The Pacific Islander. KIN Publications, 558 E. Double St., Carson, CA 90745, U.S.A. (tel. 1-310/549-0920, fax 1-310/830-0711, e-mail: DPouesi@aol.com; US$22 for six issues). Daniel Pouesi's lively tabloid newspaper serving the Samoan and Tongan communities on the U.S. west coast.

Pacific Islands Monthly. Box 1167, Suva, Fiji Islands (tel. 679/304-111, fax 679/303-809, www.pim.com.fj, e-mail: fijitimes@is.com.fj; annual subscription A$40 to Australia, A$45 to New Zealand, US$40 to North America, and A$60 to Europe). Founded in Sydney by R.W. Robson in 1930, *PIM* is the granddaddy of regional magazines. In June 1989 the magazine's editorial office moved from Sydney to Suva and it's now part of the same operation that puts out *The Fiji Times.* Sadly, star columnists Roman Grynberg and David North recently left the magazine.

Pacific Magazine. Box 25488, Honolulu, HI 96825, U.S.A. (tel. 1-808/377-5335, fax 1-808/373-3953, www.pacificmagazine.com; every other month; US$15 a year surface mail, US$27 airmail to the U.S., US$39 airmail elsewhere). This business-oriented newsmagazine, published in Hawaii since 1976, will keep you up-to-date on what's happening in the South Pacific and Micronesia. The format is built around pithy little news bites on people and events rather than the longer background articles one finds in the other regional magazines.

Pacific News Bulletin. Pacific Concerns Resource Center, 83 Amy St., Toorak, Private Mail Bag, Suva, Fiji Islands (fax 679/304-755, e-mail: pcrc@is.com.fj; A$15 a year in Australia, A$30 a year elsewhere). A 16-page monthly newsletter with up-to-date information on nuclear, independence, environmental, and political questions.

Pacific Studies. Box 1979, BYU-HC, Laie, HI 96762-1294, U.S.A. (tel. 1-808/293-3665, fax 1-808/293-3664, websider.byuh.edu/departments/ips, e-mail: robertsd@byuh.edu, quarterly, US$30 a year). Funded by the Polynesian Cultural Center and published by Hawaii's Brigham Young University.

Pacifica. Quarterly journal of the Pacific Islands Study Circle (John Ray, 24 Woodvale Ave., London SE25 4AE, United Kingdom, http://dspace.dial.pipex.com/jray/pisc.html, e-mail: jray@dial.pipex.com). This philatelic journal is exclusively concerned with stamps and the postal history of the islands.

Pacifica Review. The Institute for Peace Research, La Trobe University, Bundoora, Victoria 3083, Australia (tel. 61-3/9479-2676, fax 61-3/9479-1997; twice a year, A$25/35 local/overseas). A journal focusing on peace, security, and global change in the Asia Pacific region.

South Sea Digest. Box 4245, Sydney, NSW 2001, Australia (tel. 61-2/9288-1708, fax 61-2/9288-3322, A$150 a year in Australia, A$175 overseas). A private newsletter on political and economic matters, published every other week. It's a good way of keeping abreast of developments in commerce and industry.

Surf Report. Box 1028, Dana Point, CA 92629, U.S.A. (tel. 1-949/496-5922, fax 1-949/496-7849, www.surfermag.com; US$35 a year). Each month this newsletter provides a detailed analysis of surfing conditions at a different destination. Back issues on specific countries are available, including a 14-issue "South Pacific Collection" at US$50. This is your best source of surfing information by far, and the same people also put out the glossy *Surfer Magazine* (US$25 a year).

Tok Blong Pasifik. South Pacific Peoples Foundation of Canada, 1921 Fernwood Rd., Victoria, BC V8T 2Y6, Canada (tel. 250/381-4131, fax 250/388-5258, www.sppf.org, e-mail: sppf@sppf.org; C$25 a year in Canada, US$25 elsewhere). This lively quarterly of news and views focuses on regional environmental, development, human rights, and disarmament issues.

Washington Pacific Report. Fred Radewagen, Box 26142, Alexandria, VA 22313, U.S.A. (tel. 1-703/519-7757, fax 1-703/548-0633, e-mail: piwowpr@erols.com; published twice a month, US$164 a year domestic, US$189 outside U.S. postal zones). An insider's newletter highlighting U.S. interests in the insular Pacific.

WorldViews. 1515 Webster St., No. 305, Oakland, CA 94612-3355, U.S.A. (tel. 1-510/451-1742, fax 1-510/835-9631, www.igc.org/worldviews, e-mail: worldviews@igc.org, subscription US$25 to the U.S. and Canada, US$45 overseas). A quarterly review of books, articles, audiovisual materials, and organizations involved with development issues in the third world.

DISCOGRAPHY

Music lovers will be pleased to hear that authentic Pacific music is becoming more readily available on compact disc. In compiling this selection we've tried to list non-commercial recordings that are faithful to the traditional music of the islands as it exists today. Island music based on Western pop has been avoided. Most of the CDs below can be ordered through specialized music shops; otherwise write directly to the publishers.

Fanshawe, David, ed. *Exotic Voices and Rhythms of the South Seas* (EUCD/MC 1254). Cook Islands drum dancing, a Fijian *tralala meke,* a Samoan *fiafia,* a Vanuatu string band, and Solomon Islands panpipes selected from the 1,200 hours of tapes in the Fanshawe Pacific Collection. Order from ARC Music Inc., Box 2453, Clearwater, FL 33757-2453, U.S.A. (tel. 1-727/447-3755,

fax 1-727/447-3820, www.arcmusic.co.uk, e-mail: arcamerica@ ij.net), or Fanshawe One World Music (Box 574, Marlborough, Wilts, SN8 2SP, United Kingdom (tel. 44-1672/520211, fax 44-1672/ 521151, www.fanshawe.com, e-mail: fanshaweuk@cwcom.net).

Fanshawe, David, ed. *Spirit of Polynesia* (CD-SDL 403). Saydisc Records, Chipping Manor, The Chipping, Wotton-U-Edge, Glos. GL12 7AD, United Kingdom (tel. 44-1453/845-036, fax 44-1453/521-056, www.qualiton.com, e-mail: Saydisc@aol.com). An anthology of the music of 12 Pacific countries recorded between 1978 and 1988.

Linkels, Ad, and Lucia Linkels, eds. *Afo 'o e 'ofa* (PAN 2088CD). Tongan string band music recorded in 1986 and 1990. This and the other PAN Records compact discs listed below form part of the series "Anthology of Pacific Music" and extensive booklets explaining the music come with the records. Music stores can order PAN compact discs through Arhoolie, 10341 San Pablo Ave., El Cerrito, CA 94530, U.S.A. (tel. 1-510/525-7471, fax 1-510/525-1204).

Linkels, Ad, and Lucia Linkels, eds. *Fa'a-Samoa* (PAN 2066CD). PAN Records, Box 155, 2300 AD Leiden, The Netherlands (tel. 31-71/521-9479, fax 31-71/522-6869, e-mail: paradox@dataweb.nl). This 29-track recording made in 1982 contains everything from the blowing of a conch shell to traditional dance music, string bands, drumming, brass bands, church choirs, and even unexpected village sounds, such as the calling of the pigs.

Linkels, Ad, and Lucia Linkels, eds. *Fiafia* (PAN 150CD). The traditional dances of 11 Pacific countries recorded during six field trips between 1979 and 1992. Some songs and rhythms are provided in two versions: the original version and a new one, or two different original versions.

Linkels, Ad, and Lucia Linkels, eds. *Faikava: The Tongan Kava Circle* (PAN 2022CD). Kava drinking songs by nine different ensembles recorded in 1986 and 1990.

Linkels, Ad, and Lucia Linkels, eds. *Hula, Haka, Hoko!* (PAN 162CD). A selection of traditional Polynesian dance music recorded on Easter Island, Cook Islands, Tuvalu, Rotuma, Tonga, and Samoa between 1982 and 1996.

Linkels, Ad, and Lucia Linkels, eds. *Ifi Palasa: Tongan Brass* (PAN 2044CD). On this CD recorded in 1982, 1986, and 1990, brass bands mix with Polynesian conch shell blasts and traditional nose flutes.

Linkels, Ad, and Lucia Linkels, eds. *Ko E Temipale Tapu* (PAN 7007CD). Selections of polyphonic Tongan church music recorded in 1986 and 1990.

Linkels, Ad, and Lucia Linkels, eds. *Malie! Beautiful!* (PAN 2011CD). An outstanding survey of Tongan dance music recorded during important celebrations and competitions in 1982, 1986, and 1990.

Linkels, Ad, and Lucia Linkels, eds. *Tonga: Sounds of Change* (PAN 2098CD). Current musical styles on Tonga and their links to tradition.

Music of Polynesia, Volume IV (VICG 5274). In the series "World Sounds" produced by Victor Entertainment, Inc., Tokyo, Japan, and distributed in the U.S. by JVC Music, Inc., 3800 Barham Blvd., Ste. 305, Los Angeles, CA 90068, U.S.A. (tel. 1-213/878-0101, fax 1-213/878-0202). The music of Samoa and Tonga.

THE INTERNET

USEFUL INTERNET SITES

American Samoa
www.samoanet.com/americansamoa
The Office of Tourism site offers most of the travel information you'd expect, although some of it is out of date or incomplete. The weather report is worth a look and there are lots of links.

Cable & Wireless Kalianet
www.candw.to
The e-mail directory posted here by Tonga's internet provider is the place to check if one of the Tonga addresses in this book doesn't work. The /local.htm section contains the home pages of many tourism businesses, while the /tonga.htm section features banking, real estate, tourism, and the 'Atenisi Institute's site.

Friendly Islands Kayak Company
www.fikco.com/kayaktonga
This nicely designed site is a model of what a commercial tourist site should be. It's mostly about their own tours, but you do get a taste of Tonga.

Niue, Rock of Polynesia
www.niueisland.com
Lots of detailed tourist information is provided on flights, sights, diving, fishing, caving, events, hotels, and car rentals, plus contact addresses. A complete Royal Tongan Airlines timetable is posted, but the aggressive cookies are nuisance.

Olsen Currency Converter
www.oanda.com
Quick quotes on most international currencies.

Our Kingdom of Tonga
www.tongatapu.net.to
The book reviews and legends of Tonga have earned this site a place here, but it's a little chaotic and the frames don't help.

Pacific Islands Internet Resources
www2.hawaii.edu/~ogden/piir/index.html
Michael R. Ogden's vast catalog of South Pacific links.

Pacific Islands Monthly
www.pim.com.fj
A salutary source of news and commentary with about eight feature articles summarized monthly.

Pacific Islands Report
http://pidp.ewc.hawaii.edu/pireport
A joint project of several educational institutions in Hawaii, it's your best source of recent political and economic news from the islands. Around 15 stories are posted every weekday and you can browse through recent issues.

Samoa Chat
www.samoa.as
The indefatigable Joseph Matua does it again with four funny chat rooms and loads of useful links. Look here if you want to know whose birthday it is, need a Samoan recipe for dinner, would like to peruse somebody's scrapbook, or were considering establishing a website with an American Samoa address.

Samoanet, Internet Gateway to Samoa
www.samoanet.com
Posted by American Samoa's internet provider, you can access an extensive government directory and some tourist information here. Samoanet leads you to the CIA country reports, Bank of Hawaii economic surveys, and a weather report for American Samoa.

Samoan Sensation
www.samoa.co.uk
Here's another fun site offering a wealth of information about Samoa, chat pages, and intriguing links hidden in the text.

Talofa
www.house.gov/faleomavaega
The personal site of American Samoa's non-voting congressman in Washington is useful for political news related to the territory. This is real information, not brochure fare.

The Pacific Forum
www.pacificforum.com/kavabowl/index.html
The Kava Bowl features a variety of chat rooms or forums where people from all across the Pacific add their often frivolous comments.

The Tonga Chronicle
www.netstorage.com/kami/tonga/news
The weekly news summaries here are excellent and it's easy to delve into the archives. Just remember that this paper is government owned.

Tonga On Line
www.tongaonline.com
Although fraught with royalist and religious overtones, Tonga On Line assembles an impressive body of information. Their Tongan phrasebook might be worth printing out, and a link is provided to the Tongan History Association, which is difficult to access directly. The Millennium site www.tonga2000.net is run by the same people, who must have some kind of government contract.

Tonga Times
www.tongatimes.com
The small frames make it hard to read the undated articles, letters, editorials, and news reports here. Since the *Times* is privately run and more likely to provide juicy details the official sites might choose to ignore, one can only hope tongatimes.com gets better.

Welcome to Samoa
www.samoa.co.nz
The quality of the Samoa Visitors Bureau's online brochure is variable, to say the least. An older version of the same site at www.interwebinc.com/samoa sometimes provides more information but is chaotic.

Welcome to Tonga
www.vacations.tvb.gov.to
Here you have only brochure information from the Tonga Visitors Bureau, but it's still worth checking for Royal Tongan Airlines schedules, unreliable hotel information, and snippets about Tongan culture.

WEBSITE DIRECTORY

General
Air New Zealand: www.airnz.co.nz
Air Pacific, Nadi:
www.bulafiji.com/airlines/airpac/htm
Air Pacific, Nadi:
www.fijiislands.org/airlines/airpac.htm
Air Promotion Systems, Los Angeles:
www.pacificislands.com
Centers for Disease Control and Prevention:
www.cdc.gov/travel/index.html
City Seahorse, Dallas, Texas:
www.SeaHorseTales.com
CocoNET Wireless:
www.uq.oz.au/jrn/coco/index.htm
Hawaiian Airlines: www.hawaiianair.com
Hideaway Holidays, Australia:
www.hideawayholidays.com.au
Kavabowl:
www.pacificforum.com/kavabowl/index.html
Moon Travel Handbooks: www.moon.com
Pacific Asia Travel Association: www.pata.org
Pacific Media Watch:
www.pactok.net.au/docs/pmw
Polynesian Airlines:
www.polynesianairlines.co.nz
Polynesian Voyaging Society:
http://leahi.kcc.hawaii.edu/org/pvs
Royal Tongan Airlines, Nuku'alofa:
http://kalianet.candw.to/rta
Royal Tongan Airlines, Nuku'alofa:
www.candw.to/rta
Sea for Yourself: www.snorkeltours.com
Tourism Council of the South Pacific:
www.tcsp.com
United Nations Development Program:
www.undp.org.fj
Weather Reports: www.accuweather.com

Samoa
Aggie Grey's, Apia:
www.samoa.net/local/aggies.html
Books Pasifika:
www.ak.planet.gen.nz/pasifika
Chamber of Commerce, Samoa:
www.samoa.net/coc

Coconuts Beach Club, Upolu:
www.coconutsbeachclubsamoa.com
Computer Services Limited, Apia:
www.samoa.net
Dept. of Trade, Commerce & Industry:
www.samoa.net/invest
Eco-Tour Samoa Ltd., Upolu:
www.ecotoursamoa.com
Government of Samoa:
www.interwebinc.com/samoa
Hotel Insel Fehmarn, Apia:
www.samoa.net/local/insel.html
Paradise Cove: www.vpp.net/teenhelp/pc.html
Pasefika Inn, Apia:
www.samoa.net/local/pinn.html
Pasefika Publications:
www.samoa.net/local/pp.html
Regional Environmental Program, Apia:
www.sprep.org.ws
Sails Restaurant, Apia:
www.samoa.net/local/sails.html
Samoa Internet Service Provider:
www.samoa.net
Samoa Realty & Investments, Apia:
www.samoa.net/samoareality
Samoa Sensation: www.samoa.co.uk
Samoa Visitors Bureau, Apia:
www.samoa.co.nz
Samoa Visitors Bureau, Apia:
www.interwebinc.com/samoa
Seacology Foundation, Utah:
www.seacology.org
Seipepa Samoan Travel Home, Apia:
www.d90.se/seipepa
Sinalei Reef Resort, Upolu:
www.samoa.net/local/sinalei.html
Waterways Travel, U.S.A.:
www.waterwaystravel.com

American Samoa

Asnic Domain Registry: www.nic.as
Congressman Faleomavaega, Washington:
www.house.gov/faleomavaega
Fagatele Bay Sanctuary:
http://wave.nos.noaa.gov/nmsp/FBNMS
Joseph Matua's Samoa Mall:
www.samoamall.as
KSBS-FM, Pago Pago:
www.samoanet.com/ksbsfm
National Park of American Samoa:
www.nps.gov/npsa/index.htm

Office of Tourism, Pago Pago:
www.samoanet.com/americansamoa
Pagopago, Inc.: www.pagopago.com
http://planet-samoa.com
Samoa News, Pago Pago: www.iPacific.com
Telecommunications Authority:
www.samoatelco.com

Tonga

'Atenisi Institute:
http://kalianet.candw.to/atenisi
ANZ Bank, Nuku'alofa: www.candw.to/banks
Cable & Wireless, Nuku'alofa: www.candw.to
Fafa Island Resort, Nuku'alofa:
http://kalianet.candw.to/fa
Friendly Islander, Nuku'alofa:
http://kalianet.candw.to/papiloa
Friendly Islands Kayak Company:
www.fikco.com/kayaktonga
Friendly Islands Kayak Company:
www.islandnet.com/kayaktonga
Heilala Holiday Lodge, Nuku'alofa:
http://kalianet.candw.to/quick
Hotel Nuku'alofa, Nuku'alofa:
http://kalianet.candw.to/sanft
Kalia Cafe, Nuku'alofa:
http://invited.to/kaliacafe
Kiwi Magic, Vava'u:
http://kalianet.candw.to/kiwifish
Matangi Tonga:
www.netstorage.com/kami/tonga/matangi
Moore Electronics, Nuku'alofa:
www.tongatapu.net.to
Millennium Site: www.tonga2000.net
Paradise Adventures:
www.paradiseadventures.com.au/
tonga.htm
Paradise Hotel, Neiafu:
http://kalianet.candw.to/paradise
Paradise Shores Resort:
http://kalianet.candw.to/parashor
Royal Beer Co., Nuku'alofa: www.royalbeer.to
Royal Sunset Island Resort:
http://kalianet.candw.to/royalsun
Sailing Safaris, Vava'u:
www.tongaonline.com/sailingsafaris
Sunsail Yacht Charters, Auckland:
www.sunsail.co.nz
Teta Tours, Nuku'alofa:
http://kalianet.candw.to/tetatour
The Moorings, Florida: www.moorings.com

Times of Tonga, Nuku'alofa:
www.tongatimes.com
Tonga Chronicle, Nuku'alofa:
www.netstorage.com/kami/tonga/news
Tonga Game Fish Association:
http://kalianet.candw.to/TIGFA
Tonga On Line: www.tongaonline.com
Tonga Study Circle:
http://members.aol.com/TongaJan/ttcmsc.ht
ml
Tonga Visitors Bureau, Nuku'alofa:
www.vacations.tvb.gov.to
Tongan Beach Resort, Vava'u:
www.thetongan.com
Tongan Wildlife Center:
http://kalianet.candw.to/birdpark
Tonic Domain Name Registry, Nuku'alofa:
www.tonic.to

Niue
.Nu Domain Name Registry:
www.nunames.nu
Niue Dive, Alofi: www.dive.nu
Niue Telecom: www.niuenet.comNiue
Tourism Office, Alofi: www.niueisland.com
Niue Tourism Office, Alofi: www.visit.nu
This is Something Really .Nu!:
http://something.really.nu

E-MAIL DIRECTORY

Samoa
Aggie Grey's Hotel, Apia:
aggiegreys@samoa.net
Apia Rentals, Apia: apiarentals@samoa.net
Coconuts Beach Club, Upolu:
cbcsamoa@aol.com
Coconuts Beach Club, Upolu:
cbc@samoa.net
Eco-Tour Samoa Ltd., Upolu:
enquiries@ecotoursamoa.com
Funway Rentals, Apia:
funwayrentals@samoa.net
Island Hopper Vacations, Apia:
islandhopper@samoa.net
Jane's Tours, Apia: damonjay@samoa.net
Kitano Tusitala Hotel, Apia:
kitano@samoa.net
Magik 98 FM, Apia: magic98fm@samoa.net
Pacific Internet Services, Apia:
cafe@samoa.net
Pacific Quest Divers, Upolu:
pqdivers@samoa.net
Polynesian Airlines:
enquiries@polynesianairlines.co.nz
Rainforest Ecolodge, Upolu:
ecotour@samoa.net
Safua Hotel, Savai'i: tuisafua@samoa.net
Salani Surf Resort, Upolu:
salanisurf@samoa.net
Samoa Marine, Apia: pmeredith@samoa.net
Samoa Visitors Bureau, Apia:
samoa@samoa.net
Samoa Visitors Bureau, Australia:
samoa@ozemail.com.au
Samoa Visitors Bureau, New Zealand:
samoa@samoa.co.nz
Samoa Visitors Bureau, U.S.A.:
SDSI@compuserve.com
Samoan Outrigger Hotel, Apia:
outrigger@samoa.net
Seipepa Samoan Travel Home, Apia:
seipepa@samoa.net
Sinalei Reef Resort, Upolu:
sinalei@samoa.net

American Samoa
KSBS-FM, Pago Pago:
ksbsfm@samoanet.com
National Park:
NPSA_Administration@ccmail.itd.nps.gov
Office of Tourism, Pago Pago:
samoa@samoatelco.com
Samoa Air, Pago Pago:
samoaair@samoatelco.com
Samoa News, Pago Pago:
samoanews@samoatelco.com
Ta'alolo Lodge, Ili'ili: taalolo@samoatelco.com
Tutuila Dive Shop, Vaitogi:
tutuiladiveshop@samoatelco.com

Tonga
Beluga Diving, Neiafu: beluga@kalianet.to
Deep Blue Diving, Nuku'alofa:
deepblue@kalianet.to
Fafa Island Resort, Nuku'alofa:
fafa@kalianet.to
Friendly Islander Hotel, Nuku'alofa:
papiloa@kalianet.to
Friendly Islands Bookshop, Nuku'alofa:
fibs@kalianet.to

Friendly Islands Kayak Company, Vava'u: kayaktonga@kalianet.to

German Clinic and Pharmacy, Nuku'alofa: medical@kalianet.to

Heilala Holiday Lodge, Nuku'alofa: quick@kalianet.to

Hook-Up Vava'u, Neiafu: hookup@kalianet.to

Hotel Nuku'alofa, Nuku'alofa: sanft@kalianet.to

International Dateline Hotel, Nuku'alofa: idh@kalianet.to

Kalia Cafe, Nuku'alofa: kaliacafe@invited.to

Kiwi Magic, Neiafu: kiwifish@kalianet.to

Langafonua, Nuku'alofa: lgafonua@kalianet.to

Matangi Tonga Magazine: vapress@kalianet.to

Moore Electronics, Nuku'alofa: moore@tongatapu.net.to

Mounu Island Resort, Vava'u: mounu@kalianet.to

New Millennium Radio A3V: vearw@alaska.net

Pacific Island Seaplanes, Nuku'alofa: pacisair@kalianet.to

Pacific Royale Hotel, Nuku'alofa: royale@kalianet.to

Paradise Hotel, Neiafu: paradise@kalianet.to

Paradise Shores Resort, Tongatapu: paradise_shores@kalianet.to

Polynesian Airlines, Nuku'alofa: polyair@kalianet.to

Popao Village Eco Resort, Vava'u: Popao@hotmail.com

Royal Sunset Island Resort, Nuku'alofa: royalsun@kalianet.to

Royal Tongan Airlines, Nuku'alofa: rtamktng@kalianet.to

Sailing Safaris, Neiafu: sailingsafaris@kalianet.to

Samoa Air, Neiafu: tfpel-vv@kalianet.to

Sandy Beach Resort, Foa: sandybch@tongatapu.net.to

Sisifa Rental Cars, Nuku'alofa: kiwitonga@kalianet.to

Sunsail, Auckland: res.v@sunsail.co.nz

Target One, Neiafu: fishtarget@kalianet.to

Teta Tours, Nuku'alofa: tetatour@kalianet.to

The Moorings, Neiafu: moorings.tonga@kalianet.to

Times of Tonga, Nuku'alofa: times@kalianet.to

Tonga Chronicle, Nuku'alofa: chroni@kalianet.to

Tonga Telecommunications Commission: ttc@kalianet.to

Tonga Visitors Bureau, Lifuka: tvbhp@kalianet.to

Tonga Visitors Bureau, Neiafu: tvbvv@kalianet.to

Tonga Visitors Bureau, Nuku'alofa: tvb@kalianet.to

Tonga Visitors Bureau, U.S.A.: tonga@value.net

Tongan Beach Resort, Neiafu: tonganbeach@kalianet.to

Tongan Consulate, San Francisco: tania@sfconsulate.gov.to

Tongan Wildlife Center, Tongatapu: birdpark@kalianet.to

Winnies Guesthouse, Nuku'alofa: winnies@kalianet.to

Niue

Alofi Rentals, Alofi: alofirentals@sin.net.nu

Coral Gardens Motel, Niue: sguest@cas.nu

Matavai Resort, Niue: matavai@mail.gov.nu

Niue Dive, Alofi: niuedive@dive.nu

Niue Hotel, Alofi: niuehotel@sin.net.nu

Niue Island Yacht Club, Niue: yachtclub@sin.net.nu

Niue Rentals, Alofi: niuerentals@sin.net.nu

Niue Tourism Office, Auckland: niuetourism@clear.net.nz

Niue Tourism Office, Niue: niuetourism@mail.gov.nu

Peleni's Guest House, Alofi: peleni@mail.gov.nu

Wahoo Fishing Charters, Alofi: wahoo@sin.net.nu

GLOSSARY

aa **lava**—*see* pahoehoe

AIDS—Acquired Immune Deficiency Syndrome

aiga—the Samoan extended family

aitu—spirit or ghost in Samoan

alia—a catamaran fishing boat in Samoa

ali'i—Samoan high chief or chiefs

ANZUS Treaty—a mutual-defense pact signed in 1951 between Australia, New Zealand, and the U.S.

archipelago—a group of islands

atoll—a low-lying, ring-shaped coral reef enclosing a lagoon

bareboat charter—chartering a yacht without crew or provisions

bark cloth—see *tapa*

barrier reef—a coral reef separated from the adjacent shore by a lagoon

bêche-de-mer—sea cucumber; an edible sea slug

blackbirder—A 19th-century European recruiter of island labor

breadfruit—a large, round fruit with starchy flesh grown on an *uru* tree *(Artocarpus altilis)*

BYO—Bring Your Own (an Australian term used to refer to restaurants that allow you to bring your own alcoholic beverages)

caldera—a wide crater formed through the collapse or explosion of a volcano

cassava—manioc; the starchy edible root of the tapioca plant

chain—an archaic unit of length equivalent to 20 meters

ciguatera—a form of fish poisoning caused by microscopic algae

coir—coconut husk sennit used to make rope, etc.

confirmation—A confirmed reservation exists when a supplier acknowledges, either orally or in writing, that a booking has been accepted.

copra—dried coconut meat used in the manufacture of coconut oil, cosmetics, soap, and margarine

coral—a hard, calcareous substance of various shapes, composed of the skeletons of tiny marine animals called polyps

coral bank—a coral formation over 150 meters long

coral head—a coral formation a few meters across

coral patch—a coral formation up to 150 meters long

custom owner—traditional tribal or customary owner based on usage

cyclone—Also known as a hurricane (in the Caribbean) or typhoon (in Japan). A tropical storm that rotates around a center of low atmospheric pressure; it becomes a cyclone when its winds reach force 12 or 64 knots. At sea the air will be filled with foam and driving spray, the water surface completely white with 14-meter-high waves. In the Northern Hemisphere, cyclones spin counterclockwise, while south of the equator they move clockwise. The winds of cyclonic storms are deflected toward a low-pressure area at the center, although the "eye" of the cyclone may be calm.

deck—Australian English for a terrace or porch

desiccated coconut—the shredded meat of dehydrated fresh coconut

direct flight—a through flight with one or more stops but no change of aircraft, as opposed to a nonstop flight

dugong—a large plant-eating marine mammal; called a manatee in the Caribbean

EEZ—Exclusive Economic Zone; a 200-nautical-mile offshore belt of an island nation or seacoast state that controls the mineral exploitation and fishing rights

endemic—native to a particular area and existing only there

ESCAP—Economic and Social Commission for Asia and the Pacific

expatriate—a person residing in a country other than his/her own; in the South Pacific such persons are also called "Europeans" if their skin is white, or simply "expats."

fa'afafine—the Samoan term for men who act and dress like women; called *fakaleiti* in Tonga

fa'a Samoa—the Samoan way

AD—fish aggregation device

afa—a "spinach" of cooked taro leaves

aka Tonga—the Tongan way

ale—thatched Samoan or Tongan house

autasi—a Samoan longboat or rowing canoe

autau—the highest formal representative of the Samoan people

ia fia—an island-style party in Samoan

ilaria—parasitic worms transmitted by biting insects to the blood or tissues of mammals. The obstruction of the lymphatic glands by the worms can cause an enlargement of the legs or other parts, a disease known as elephantiasis.

issure—a narrow crack or chasm of some length and depth

FIT—foreign independent travel; a custom-designed, prepaid tour composed of many individualized arrangements

fono—a Samoan council

fringing reef—a reef along the shore of an island

GPS—Global Positioning System, the space age successor of the sextant

guano—manure of seabirds, used as a fertilizer

guyot—a submerged atoll, the coral of which couldn't keep up with rising water levels

Havaiki—legendary homeland of the Polynesians

HIV—Human Immunodeficiency Virus, the cause of AIDS

hurricane—*see* cyclone

jug—a cross between a ceramic kettle and a pitcher used to heat water for tea or coffee in Australian-style hotels

kava—a Polynesian word for the drink known in the Samoan language as 'ava and in English slang as "grog." This traditional beverage is made by squeezing a mixture of the grated root of the pepper shrub *(Piper methysticum)* and cold water through a strainer of hibiscus-bark fiber.

knot—about three kilometers per hour

kumala—sweet potato *(Ipomoea batatas)*

lagoon—an expanse of water bounded by a reef

langi—a megalithic tomb for early Tonga kings, in the form of a stepped limestone pyramid

lapita pottery—pottery made by the ancient Polynesians from 1600 to 500 B.C.

lavalava—a Samoan saronglike wraparound skirt or loincloth; *sarong* in Indonesian

lava tube—a conduit formed as molten rock continues to flow below a cooled surface during the growth of a lava field. When the eruption ends, a tunnel is left with a flat floor where the last lava hardened.

LDS—Latter-day Saints; the Mormons

leeward—downwind; the shore (or side) sheltered from the wind; as opposed to windward

lei—a garland, often of fresh flowers, but sometimes of paper, shells, etc., hung about the neck of a person being welcomed or feted

LMS—London Missionary Society; a Protestant group that spread Christianity from Tahiti (1797) across the Pacific

lotu—religious service or prayer

mahimahi—dorado, Pacific dolphinfish (no relation to the mammal)

malae—a Samoan village green

mana—authority, prestige, virtue, "face," psychic power, a positive force

mangrove—a tropical shrub with branches that send down roots forming dense thickets along tidal shores

manioc—cassava, tapioca, a starchy root crop

matai—the Samoan holder of a chiefly title

matrilineal—a system of tracing descent through the mother's familial line

Melanesia—the high island groups of the western Pacific (Fiji, New Caledonia, Vanuatu, Solomon Islands, Papua New Guinea); from *melas* (black)

Micronesia—chains of high and low islands mostly north of the Equator (Carolines, Gilberts, Marianas, Marshalls); from *micro* (small)

monoï—perfumed coconut oil

motu—a flat reef islet

NAUI—National Association of Underwater Instructors

ngatu—see *tapa*

NGO—Nongovernment organization

NFIP—Nuclear-Free and Independent Pacific movement

nu'u—village in Samoan

oka—raw fish in Samoan; *ota* in Tongan, *sashimi* in Japanese

Oro—the Polynesian god of war

overbooking—the practice of confirming more seats, cabins, or rooms than are actually available to ensure against no-shows

Pacific rim—the continental landmasses and large countries around the fringe of the Pacific

PADI—Professional Association of Dive Instructors

pahoehoe lava—A smooth lava formation with wavy, ropelike ripples created when very hot, fluid lava continues to flow beneath a cooling surface. *Aa* lava, on the other hand, is slow-moving, thick, and turbulent, creating a rough, chunky surface.

palagi—a Samoan word used to refer to Europeans; also *papalagi*, and in Tongan *palangi*

palolo—in Samoan, a reef worm *(Eunice viridis)*

palusami—a Samoan specialty of coconut cream wrapped in taro leaves and baked

pandanus—screw pine with slender stem and prop roots. The sword-shaped leaves are used for plaiting mats and hats.

parasailing—a sport in which participants are carried aloft by a parachute pulled behind a speedboat

pass—a channel through a barrier reef, usually with an outward flow of water; called an *ava* in Samoan

passage—an inside passage between an island and a barrier reef

patrilineal—a system of tracing descent through the fathers familial line

pawpaw—papaya; *esi* in Samoan

pe'a—tattoo, flying fox (Samoan)

pelagic—relating to the open sea, away from land

poe—a sticky pudding made from bananas, papaya, pumpkin, or taro mixed with starch, baked in an oven, and served with coconut milk

Polynesia—divided into Western Polynesia (Tonga and Samoa) and Eastern Polynesia (Tahiti-Polynesia, Cook Islands, Hawaii, Easter Island, and New Zealand); from *poly* (many)

popao—Tongan outrigger canoe; *paopao* in Samoan

pulenu'u—a Samoan village mayor

puletasi—a long Samoan female dress

punt—a flat-bottomed boat

pupus—bar snacks in Samoa

Quonset hut—a prefabricated, semicircular metal shelter popular during WW II; also called a Nissan hut

rain shadow—the dry side of a mountain, sheltered from the windward side

reef—a coral ridge near the ocean surface

sa—a Samoan vespers

sailing—the fine art of getting wet and becoming ill while slowly going nowhere at great expense

scuba—self-contained underwater breathing apparatus

SDA—Seventh-Day Adventist

self-contained—a room with private facilities (a toilet and shower not shared with other guests); the brochure term "en-suite" means the same thing; as opposed to a "self-catering" unit with cooking facilities

sennit—braided coconut-fiber rope

shareboat charter—a yacht tour for individuals or couples who join a small group on a fixed itinerary

shifting cultivation—a method of farming involving the rotation of fields instead of crops

shoal—a shallow sandbar or mud bank

shoulder season—a travel period between high/peak and low/off-peak seasons

siapo—see tapa

siva—a graceful, individualized Samoan dance

SPARTECA—South Pacific Regional Trade and Economic Cooperation Agreement; an agreement that allows certain manufactured goods from Pacific countries duty-free entry to Australia and New Zealand

SPREP—South Pacific Regional Environment Program

subduction—the action of one tectonic plate wedging under another

subsidence—geological sinking or settling

symbiosis—a mutually advantageous relationship between unlike organisms

tabu—also *tapu;* taboo, sacred, set apart, forbidden, a negative force

talofa—a common Samoan greeting; hello

Tamaha—daughter of the *Tu'i Tonga Fefine* (queen of Tonga)

anoa—a special wide wooden bowl in which kava is mixed; used in ceremonies in Tonga and Samoa

ta'ovala—a mat worn in Tonga by both sexes over a kilt or skirt

tapa—a cloth made from the pounded bark of the paper mulberry tree *(Broussonetia papyrifera).* It's soaked and beaten with a mallet to flatten and intertwine the fibers, then painted with geometric designs; called *siapo* in Samoan, *ngatu* in Tongan.

tapu—see tabu

taro—a starchy elephant-eared tuber *(Colocasia esculenta),* a staple food of the Pacific islanders

taupou—a chief's virgin daughter who officiates at a kava ceremony

tautau—an untitled Samoan; see also *matai*

timeshare—part ownership of a residential unit with the right to occupy the premises for a certain period each year in exchange for payment of an annual maintenance fee

TNC—transnational corporation (also referred to as a multinational corporation)

trade wind—a steady wind blowing toward the equator from either northeast or southeast

trench—the section at the bottom of the ocean where one tectonic plate wedges under another

tridacna clam—eaten everywhere in the Pacific, its size varies between 10 centimeters and one meter

tropical storm—a cyclonic storm with winds of 35 to 64 knots

tsunami—a fast-moving wave caused by an undersea earthquake

tu'i (Polynesian)—king, ruler

tulafale—a Samoan talking chief or orator; *malapule* in Tongan

umu—an underground, earthen oven. After A.D. 500, the Polynesians had lost the art of making pottery, so they were compelled to bake their food, rather than boil it.

vigia—a mark on a nautical chart indicating a dangerous rock or shoal

volcanic bomb—lumps of lava blown out of a volcano, which take a bomblike shape as they cool in the air

VSO—Volunteer Service Overseas, the British equivalent of the Peace Corps

windward—the point or side from which the wind blows, as opposed to leeward

yam—the starchy, tuberous root of a climbing plant

zories—rubber shower sandals, thongs, flip-flops

CAPSULE SAMOAN VOCABULARY

Although you can get by with English in both Samoas, knowing a few words of the Samoan language will make things more enjoyable. Written Samoan has only 14 letters. Always pronounce *g* as "ng," and *t* may be pronounced "k." Every letter is pronounced, with the vowels sounding as they do in Spanish. An apostrophe indicates a glottal stop between syllables.

afakasi—half-caste
afio mai—a Samoan greeting
afu—waterfall
'ai—eat
aiga—extended family
aitu—ghost, spirit
alia—catamaran fishing boat
ali'i—high chief
alofa—love
alu—go
alu i fea?—where are you going?
'ata—laugh

fa'afafine—transvestite
fa'afetai—thank you
fa'afetai tele—thank you very much
fa'amafu—home-brewed beer
fa'amolemole—please
fa'apefea mai oe?—how are you?
fa'a Samoa—the Samoan way
fa'a se'e—surfing
fafine—woman
fa'i—banana
faia—sacred
faife'au—an ordained church minister
failauga—orator
fai se miti lelei—have a nice dream
fale—house
faleoloa—store
fautasi—a Samoan longboat
fia fia—happy; a Samoan feast
fono—council
fou—new

i—to, toward
i'a—fish
ietoga—fine mat
inu—drink

ioe—yes

lafo—a ceremonial exchange of gifts
lali—a large wooden drum
lavalava—traditional men's skirt
le—the
leai—no
leaga—bad
lelei—good
lelei tele—very good
le tau—the cost, price
lotu—religion

maamusa—girlfriend
malae—meeting ground
malaga—journey
malo—hi
malo lava—response to *malo*
manogi—smell
manuia!—cheers!
manuia le po—good night
matafaga—beach
matai—head of an *aiga*
mau—opposition
mea alofa—gift
moe—sleep
motu—small island
musu—to be sullen

niu—coconut
nofo—sit
nu'u—village

oi fea—where is
ou te alofa ia te oe—I love you
ou te toe sau—I shall return

paepae—the stone foundation of a *fale*
palagi—a non-Samoan; also *papalagi*
paopao—canoe
pe fia?—how much?
pisupo—canned corned beef
poo fea a alu iai?—where are you going?
pule—authority, power
pulenu'u—village mayor
puletasi—traditional women's dress
pupu—blowhole

ṭa—taboo, sacred
ṭau—come
ṭavali—walk
ṣene—a cent
ṣiapo—tapa cloth
ṣili—best
ṣiva—dance
ṣoifua—good luck
ṣua—an important ceremonial presentation

ṭaamu—giant taro
ṭaavale—car
ṭai—sea, toward the coast
ṭala—dollar
ṭalofa—hello
ṭalofa lava—hello to you
ṭama—a boy
ṭamaloa—a man

tamo'e—run
tanoa—kava bowl
taulealea—untitled man
taupou—ceremonial virgin
tautau—untitled people, commoners
tele—much
tofa—goodbye
tofa soifua—fare thee well
tuai—old
tulafale—talking chief, orator

uku—head lice
ula—lei (flower necklace)
uma—finished
umu—earth oven
uta—inland

va'a—boat

CAPSULE TONGAN VOCABULARY

Although Tongans generally have a much better knowledge of English than do Samoans, a few words of Tongan will enrich your stay. Listen for the many glottal stops (marked below by apostrophes), which sound something like co'n (for cotton) in American English. In Tongan, "ng" is pronounced as in longing, not as in longer, making it Tong-a, rather than Tong-ga. The vowels sound as they do in Spanish or Italian.

afe to'ohema—turn left
afe to'omata'u—turn right
aha—no
alu—go (singular)
'alu e—goodbye (to person going)
'alu hangatonu—go straight
amo—yes

baro—maybe
bimi—later

fakaleiti—transvestite
fakamolemole—please (polite form)
fale—house
fe'unga—that's enough
fefe hake?—how are you?
fefine—woman

ha'u—come (singular)

hena—there (by you)
heni—here (beside me)

'i fe?—where?
ika—fish
'ikai—no
'ikai ha taha—none, nothing
'io—yes

kataki—please (common form)
kaukau—bath
kaume'a—friend
koau—I
ko e ha?—what?
ko e me'a 'e fiha?—how many?
ko fe 'a e fale malolo?—where is the toilet?
kohai ia?—who is it?
ko koe—you
ko moutolu—you (plural)
kovi—bad

lahi—big, much

ma'ama'a—cheap
makona—full (of food)
malo—thank you
malo 'aupito—thank you very much
malo e lelei—hello
malohi—strong

malo pe—no thank you (at meals)
mamafa—expensive
mohe—sleep
mou nofo a e—goodbye (to several staying)
mou o a e—goodbye (to several going)

niu mata—drinking nut
niu motu'u—mature coconut
nofo a e—goodbye (to person staying)

o—go (plural)
'ofa—love
'oku fiha?—how much?
'oku mau—we
'oku nau—they
'oku ou fieinua—I'm thirsty
'oku ou fiekaia—I'm hungry
omai—come (plural)

palangi—foreigner

sai—good
sai pe—just fine
si'i—small

ta'ahine—girl

talitali fiefia—welcome
tamasi'i—boy
tangata—man
tulou—excuse me
tu'u—stop

NUMBERS

taha—1
ua—2
tolu—3
fa—4
nima—5
ono—6
fitu—7
valu—8
hiva—9
tahanoa—10
tahataha—11
uanoa—20
uanima—25
teau—100
tahaafe—1,000
tahamano—10,000

INDEX

Italicized page numbers indicate information in captions, charts, illustrations, maps, or special topics.

DIVING

FESTIVALS

MUSEUMS

PLEASE HELP US

Well, you've heard what *we* have to say, now we want to hear what *you* have to say! How did the book work for you? Your experiences were unique, so please share them. Let us know which businesses deserve a better listing, what we should warn people about, and where we're spot on. It's only with the help of readers like yourself that we can make *Tonga-Samoa Handbook* a complete guide for *everyone.* The address is:

David Stanley
c/o Moon Publications Inc.
5855 Beaudry St.
Emeryville, CA 94608, U.S.A.
e-mail: travel@moon.com

ABOUT THE AUTHOR

THREE DECADES AGO, *David Stanley's right thumb carried him out of Toronto, Canada, onto a journey that has so far wound through 171 countries, including a three-year trip from Tokyo to Kabul. His travel guidebooks to the South Pacific, Micronesia, Alaska, Eastern Europe, and Cuba opened those areas to budget travelers for the first time.*

During the late 1960s, David got involved in Mexican culture by spending a year in several small towns near Guanajuato. Later he studied at the universities of Barcelona and Florence, before settling down to get an honors degree (with distinction) in Spanish literature from the University of Guelph, Canada.

In 1978 Stanley linked up with future publisher Bill Dalton, and together they wrote the first edition of South Pacific Handbook. *Since then, Stanley has gone on to write additional definitive guides for Moon Publications, including* Fiji Islands Handbook *and* Tahiti-Polynesia Handbook, *and early editions of* Alaska-Yukon Handbook *and* Micronesia Handbook. *He wrote the first three editions of Lonely Planet's* Eastern Europe on a Shoestring *as well as their guide to Cuba. His books have informed a generation of budget travelers.*

Stanley makes frequent research trips to the areas covered in his guides, jammed between journeys to the 73 countries and territories worldwide he still hasn't visited. In travel writing and internet surfing, David Stanley has found a perfect outlet for his restless wanderlust.

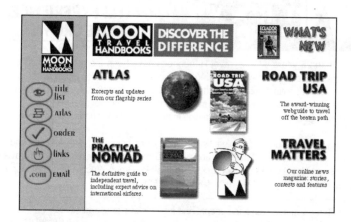

LOSE YOURSELF IN THE EXPERIENCE, NOT THE CROWD

For more than 25 years, Moon Travel Handbooks have been the guidebooks of choice for adventurous travelers. Our award-winning Handbook series provides focused, comprehensive coverage of distinct destinations all over the world. Each Handbook is like an entire bookcase of cultural insight and introductory information in one portable volume. Our goal at Moon is to give travelers all the background and practical information they'll need for an extraordinary travel experience.

The following pages include a complete list of Handbooks, covering North America and Hawaii, Mexico, Latin America and the Caribbean, and Asia and the Pacific.To purchase Moon Travel Handbooks, check your local bookstore or order c/o Publishers Group West, Attn: Order Department, 1700 Fourth St., Berkeley, CA 94710, or fax to (510) 528-3444.

"An in-depth dunk into the land, the people and their history, arts, and politics."
—*Student Travels*

"I consider these books to be superior to Lonely Planet. When Moon produces a book it is more humorous, incisive, and off-beat."
—*Toronto Sun*

"Outdoor enthusiasts gravitate to the well-written Moon Travel Handbooks. In addition to politically correct historic and cultural features, the series focuses on flora, fauna and outdoor recreation. Maps and meticulous directions also are a trademark of Moon guides."
—*Houston Chronicle*

"Moon [Travel Handbooks] . . . bring a healthy respect to the places they investigate. Best of all, they provide a host of odd nuggets that give a place texture and prod the wary traveler from the beaten path. The finest are written with such care and insight they deserve listing as literature."
—*American Geographical Society*

"Moon Travel Handbooks offer in-depth historical essays and useful maps, enhanced by a sense of humor and a neat, compact format."
—*Swing*

"Perfect for the more adventurous, these are long on history, sightseeing and nitty-gritty information and very price-specific."
—*Columbus Dispatch*

"Moon guides manage to be comprehensive and countercultural at the same time . . . Handbooks are packed with maps, photographs, drawings, and sidebars that constitute a college-level introduction to each country's history, culture, people, and crafts."
—*National Geographic Traveler*

"Few travel guides do a better job helping travelers create their own itineraries than the Moon Travel Handbook series. The authors have a knack for homing in on the essentials."
—**Colorado Springs** *Gazette Telegraph*

MEXICO

"These books will delight the armchair traveler, aid the undecided person in selecting a destination, and guide the seasoned road warrior looking for lesser-known hideaways."
—*Mexican Meanderings* Newsletter

"From tourist traps to off-the-beaten track hideaways, these guides offer consistent, accurate details without pretension."
—*Foreign Service Journal*

Archaeological Mexico	**$19.95**
Andrew Coe	420 pages, 27 maps
Baja Handbook	**$16.95**
Joe Cummings	540 pages, 46 maps
Cabo Handbook	**$14.95**
Joe Cummings	270 pages, 17 maps
Cancún Handbook	**$14.95**
Chicki Mallan	240 pages, 25 maps
Colonial Mexico	**$18.95**
Chicki Mallan	400 pages, 38 maps
Mexico Handbook	**$21.95**
Joe Cummings and Chicki Mallan	1,200 pages, 201 maps
Northern Mexico Handbook	**$17.95**
Joe Cummings	610 pages, 69 maps
Pacific Mexico Handbook	**$17.95**
Bruce Whipperman	580 pages, 68 maps
Puerto Vallarta Handbook	**$14.95**
Bruce Whipperman	330 pages, 36 maps
Yucatán Handbook	**$16.95**
Chicki Mallan	400 pages, 52 maps

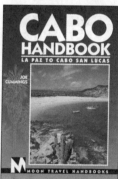

"Beyond question, the most comprehensive Mexican resources available for those who prefer deep travel to shallow tourism. But don't worry, the fiesta-fun stuff's all here too."
—*New York Daily News*

LATIN AMERICA AND THE CARIBBEAN

"Solidly packed with practical information and full of significant cultural asides that will enlighten you on the whys and wherefores of things you might easily see but not easily grasp."

—*Boston Globe*

Belize Handbook	**$15.95**
Chicki Mallan and Patti Lange	390 pages, 45 maps
Caribbean Vacations	**$18.95**
Karl Luntta	910 pages, 64 maps
Costa Rica Handbook	**$19.95**
Christopher P. Baker	780 pages, 73 maps
Cuba Handbook	**$19.95**
Christopher P. Baker	740 pages, 70 maps
Dominican Republic Handbook	**$15.95**
Gaylord Dold	420 pages, 24 maps
Ecuador Handbook	**$16.95**
Julian Smith	450 pages, 43 maps
Honduras Handbook	**$15.95**
Chris Humphrey	330 pages, 40 maps
Jamaica Handbook	**$15.95**
Karl Luntta	330 pages, 17 maps
Virgin Islands Handbook	**$13.95**
Karl Luntta	220 pages, 19 maps

NORTH AMERICA AND HAWAII

"These domestic guides convey the same sense of exoticism that their foreign counterparts do, making home-country travel seem like far-flung adventure."

—*Sierra Magazine*

Alaska-Yukon Handbook	**$17.95**
Deke Castleman and Don Pitcher	530 pages, 92 maps
Alberta and the Northwest Territories Handbook	**$18.95**
Andrew Hempstead	520 pages, 79 maps
Arizona Handbook	**$18.95**
Bill Weir	600 pages, 36 maps
Atlantic Canada Handbook	**$18.95**
Mark Morris	490 pages, 60 maps
Big Island of Hawaii Handbook	**$15.95**
J.D. Bisignani	390 pages, 25 maps
Boston Handbook	**$13.95**
Jeff Perk	200 pages, 20 maps
British Columbia Handbook	**$16.95**
Jane King and Andrew Hempstead	430 pages, 69 maps

Canadian Rockies Handbook	**$14.95**
Andrew Hempstead	220 pages, 22 maps
Colorado Handbook	**$17.95**
Stephen Metzger	480 pages, 46 maps
Georgia Handbook	**$17.95**
Kap Stann	380 pages, 44 maps
Grand Canyon Handbook	**$14.95**
Bill Weir	220 pages, 10 maps
Hawaii Handbook	**$19.95**
J.D. Bisignani	1,030 pages, 88 maps
Honolulu-Waikiki Handbook	**$14.95**
J.D. Bisignani	360 pages, 20 maps
Idaho Handbook	**$18.95**
Don Root	610 pages, 42 maps
Kauai Handbook	**$15.95**
J.D. Bisignani	320 pages, 23 maps
Los Angeles Handbook	**$16.95**
Kim Weir	370 pages, 15 maps
Maine Handbook	**$18.95**
Kathleen M. Brandes	660 pages, 27 maps
Massachusetts Handbook	**$18.95**
Jeff Perk	600 pages, 23 maps
Maui Handbook	**$15.95**
J.D. Bisignani	450 pages, 37 maps
Michigan Handbook	**$15.95**
Tina Lassen	360 pages, 32 maps
Montana Handbook	**$17.95**
Judy Jewell and W.C. McRae	490 pages, 52 maps
Nevada Handbook	**$18.95**
Deke Castleman	530 pages, 40 maps
New Hampshire Handbook	**$18.95**
Steve Lantos	500 pages, 18 maps
New Mexico Handbook	**$15.95**
Stephen Metzger	360 pages, 47 maps
New York Handbook	**$19.95**
Christiane Bird	780 pages, 95 maps
New York City Handbook	**$13.95**
Christiane Bird	300 pages, 20 maps
North Carolina Handbook	**$14.95**
Rob Hirtz and Jenny Daughtry Hirtz	320 pages, 27 maps
Northern California Handbook	**$19.95**
Kim Weir	800 pages, 50 maps
Ohio Handbook	**$15.95**
David K. Wright	340 pages, 18 maps
Oregon Handbook	**$17.95**
Stuart Warren and Ted Long Ishikawa	590 pages, 34 maps

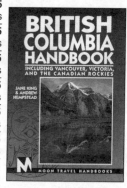

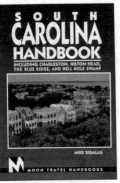

Pennsylvania Handbook	**$18.95**
Joanne Miller	448 pages, 40 maps
Road Trip USA	**$24.00**
Jamie Jensen	940 pages, 175 maps
Road Trip USA Getaways: Chicago	**$9.95**
	60 pages, 1 map
Road Trip USA Getaways: Seattle	**$9.95**
	60 pages, 1 map
Santa Fe-Taos Handbook	**$13.95**
Stephen Metzger	160 pages, 13 maps
South Carolina Handbook	**$16.95**
Mike Sigalas	400 pages, 20 maps
Southern California Handbook	**$19.95**
Kim Weir	720 pages, 26 maps
Tennessee Handbook	**$17.95**
Jeff Bradley	530 pages, 42 maps
Texas Handbook	**$18.95**
Joe Cummings	690 pages, 70 maps
Utah Handbook	**$17.95**
Bill Weir and W.C. McRae	490 pages, 40 maps
Virginia Handbook	**$15.95**
Julian Smith	410 pages, 37 maps
Washington Handbook	**$19.95**
Don Pitcher	840 pages, 111 maps
Wisconsin Handbook	**$18.95**
Thomas Huhti	590 pages, 69 maps
Wyoming Handbook	**$17.95**
Don Pitcher	610 pages, 80 maps

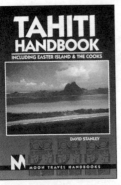

ASIA AND THE PACIFIC

"Scores of maps, detailed practical info down to business hours of small-town libraries. You can't beat the Asian titles for sheer heft. (The) series is sort of an American Lonely Planet, with better writing but fewer titles. (The) individual voice of researchers comes through."

—Travel & Leisure

Australia Handbook	**$21.95**
Marael Johnson, Andrew Hempstead, and Nadina Purdon	940 pages, 141 maps
Bali Handbook	**$19.95**
Bill Dalton	750 pages, 54 maps
Fiji Islands Handbook	**$14.95**
David Stanley	350 pages, 42 maps
Hong Kong Handbook	**$16.95**
Kerry Moran	378 pages, 49 maps

Indonesia Handbook	$25.00
Bill Dalton	1,380 pages, 249 maps
Micronesia Handbook	**$16.95**
Neil M. Levy	340 pages, 70 maps
Nepal Handbook	**$18.95**
Kerry Moran	490 pages, 51 maps
New Zealand Handbook	**$19.95**
Jane King	620 pages, 81 maps
Outback Australia Handbook	**$18.95**
Marael Johnson	450 pages, 57 maps
Philippines Handbook	**$17.95**
Peter Harper and Laurie Fullerton	670 pages, 116 maps
Singapore Handbook	**$15.95**
Carl Parkes	350 pages, 29 maps
South Korea Handbook	**$19.95**
Robert Nilsen	820 pages, 141 maps
South Pacific Handbook	**$24.00**
David Stanley	920 pages, 147 maps
Southeast Asia Handbook	**$21.95**
Carl Parkes	1,080 pages, 204 maps
Tahiti Handbook	**$15.95**
David Stanley	450 pages, 51 maps
Thailand Handbook	**$19.95**
Carl Parkes	860 pages, 142 maps
Vietnam, Cambodia & Laos Handbook	**$18.95**
Michael Buckley	760 pages, 116 maps

OTHER GREAT TITLES FROM MOON

"For hardy wanderers, few guides come more highly
recommended than the Handbooks. They include good
maps, steer clear of fluff and flackery, and offer plenty of
money-saving tips. They also give you the kind of
information that visitors to strange lands—on any budget—
need to survive."

—*US News & World Report*

Moon Handbook	**$10.00**
Carl Koppeschaar	150 pages, 8 maps
The Practical Nomad: How to Travel Around the World	**$17.95**
Edward Hasbrouck	580 pages
Staying Healthy in Asia, Africa, and Latin America	**$11.95**
Dirk Schroeder	230 pages, 4 maps

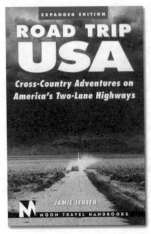

WHERE TO BUY MOON TRAVEL HANDBOOKS

BOOKSTORES AND LIBRARIES: Moon Travel Handbooks are distributed worldwide. Please contact our sales manager at info@moon.com for a list of wholesalers and distributors in your area.

TRAVELERS: We would like to have Moon Travel Handbooks available throughout the world. Please ask your bookstore to contact us for ordering information. If your bookstore will not order our guides for you, please contact us for a free catalog.

Moon Travel Handbooks
C/o Publishers Group West
Attn: Order Department
1700 Fourth Street
Berkeley, CA 94710
fax: (510) 528-3444

IMPORTANT ORDERING INFORMATION

PRICES: All prices are subject to change. We always ship the most current edition. We will let you know if there is a price increase on the book you order.

SHIPPING AND HANDLING OPTIONS: Domestic UPS or USPS priority mail (allow 10 working days for delivery): $6.00 for the first item, $1.00 for each additional item.

UPS 2nd Day Air or Printed Airmail requires a special quote.

International Surface Bookrate 8-12 weeks delivery: $5.00 for the first item, $1.00 for each additional item. Note: We cannot guarantee international surface bookrate shipping. We recommend sending international orders via air mail, which requires a special quote.

FOREIGN ORDERS: Orders that originate outside the U.S.A. must be paid for with an international money order, a check in U.S. currency drawn on a major U.S. bank based in the U.S.A., or Visa, MasterCard, or American Express.

INTERNET ORDERS: Visit our site at: www.moon.com

ORDER FORM

Prices are subject to change without notice. Please check our Web site
at **www.moon.com** for current prices and editions.
(See important ordering information on preceding page.)

Name: _____ Date: _____

Street: _____

City: _____ Daytime Phone: _____

State or Country: _____ Zip Code: _____

QUANTITY	TITLE	PRICE

Taxable Total_____

Sales Tax in CA and NY_____

Shipping & Handling_____

TOTAL_____

Ship: ☐ UPS (no P.O. Boxes)   ☐ Priority mail   ☐ International surface mail

Ship to: ☐ address above   ☐ other _____

_____

Make checks payable to: **PUBLISHERS GROUP WEST**, Attn: Order Department, 1700 Fourth St.,
Berkeley, CA 94710, or fax to (510) 528-3444. We accept Visa, MasterCard, or American Express.
   To Order: Fax in your Visa, MasterCard, or American Express number, or send a written order
with your Visa, MasterCard, or American Express number and expiration date clearly written.

Card Number: ☐ **Visa**   ☐ **MasterCard**   ☐ **American Express**

☐ ☐ ☐ ☐   ☐ ☐ ☐ ☐   ☐ ☐ ☐ ☐   ☐ ☐ ☐ ☐

Exact Name on Card: _____

Expiration date:_____

Signature: _____

Daytime Phone: _____

U.S.~METRIC CONVERSION

1 inch = 2.54 centimeters (cm)
1 foot = .304 meters (m)
1 yard = 0.914 meters
1 mile = 1.6093 kilometers (km)
1 km = .6214 miles
1 fathom = 1.8288 m
1 chain = 20.1168 m
1 furlong = 201.168 m
1 acre = .4047 hectares
1 sq km = 100 hectares
1 sq mile = 2.59 square km
1 ounce = 28.35 grams
1 pound = .4536 kilograms
1 short ton = .90718 metric ton
1 short ton = 2000 pounds
1 long ton = 1.016 metric tons
1 long ton = 2240 pounds
1 metric ton = 1000 kilograms
1 quart = .94635 liters
1 US gallon = 3.7854 liters
1 Imperial gallon = 4.5459 liters
1 nautical mile = 1.852 km

To compute celsius temperatures, subtract 32 from Fahrenheit and divide by 1.8. To go the other way, multiply celsius by 1.8 and add 32.

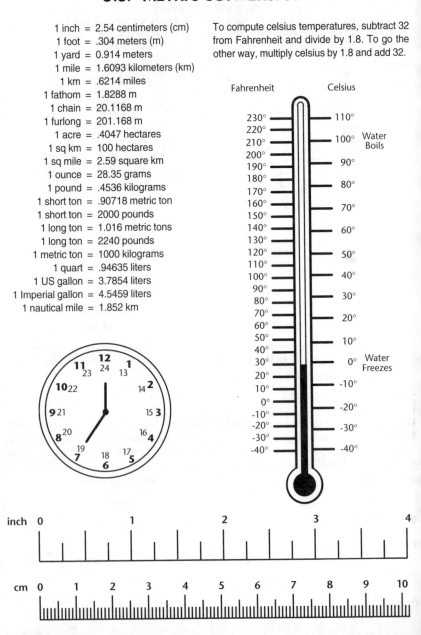